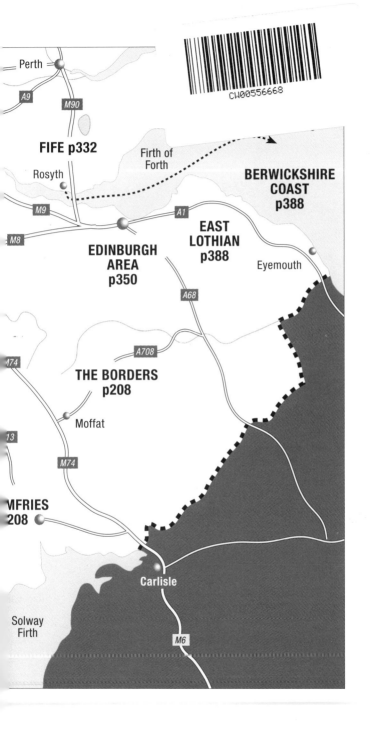

Perth

A9 *M90*

FIFE p332

Firth of Forth

Rosyth

BERWICKSHIRE COAST p388

M9

A1

M8

EAST LOTHIAN p388

EDINBURGH AREA p350

Eyemouth

A68

A708

174

THE BORDERS p208

Moffat

13

M74

MFRIES 208

Carlisle

Solway Firth

M6

LOWLAND OUTCROPS
Rock and Ice Climbs

With contributions from John Craven,
Andrew Fraser, Bruce Kerr, Dave MacLeod,
Grahame Nicoll, Adrian Plumb,
Tom Prentice, Stephen Reid, Mark Robson
George Szuca, Michael Tweedley
& John Watson

Edited by Tom Prentice
Series Editor: Brian Davison

SCOTTISH MOUNTAINEERING CLUB
CLIMBERS' GUIDE

Published in Great Britain by The Scottish Mountaineering Trust,
2004

ISBN 0 907521 84 3

*Front Cover: Dave MacLeod on the bold and desperate Achemine, E9 6c,
Dumbarton Rock – Scotland's first traditional E9 (photo Cubby Images)*

A catalogue record for this book is available from the British Library

Route descriptions of climbs in this guide, together with their grades
and any references to in situ or natural protection are made in good
faith, based on past or first ascent descriptions, checked and
substantiated where possible by the authors.
However, climbs lose holds and are altered by rockfall, rock becomes
dirty and loose and in situ protection deteriorates. Even minor
alterations can have a dramatic effect on a climb's grade or
seriousness. Therefore, it is essential that climbers judge the
condition of any route for themselves, before they start climbing.
The authors, editors, friends and assistants involved in the
publication of this guide, the Scottish Mountaineering Club, the
Scottish Mountaineering Trust and Scottish Mountaineering Trust
(Publications) Ltd, can therefore accept no liability whatever for
damage to property, nor for personal injury or death, arising
directly or indirectly from the use of this publication.

This guidebook is compiled from the most recent information and
experience provided by members of the Scottish Mountaineering
Club and other contributors. The book is published by the Scottish
Mountaineering Trust, which is a charitable trust.
Revenue from the sale of books published by the Trust is used for the
continuation of its publishing programme and for charitable
purposes associated with Scottish mountains and mountaineering.

Diagrams & Maps: Mary Benstead, Ken Crocket, Andrew Fraser
Bruce Kerr, John Mackenzie, Grahame Nicoll
Design concept: Curious Oranj, Glasgow
Production: Scottish Mountaineering Trust (Publications) Ltd
Typesetting: Ken Crocket, Tom Prentice
Diagram & map graphics: Tom Prentice
Colour separations: Core Image, East Kilbride
Print: St Edmundsbury Press, Bury St Edmunds
& Core Image
Binding: Hunter & Foulis, Haddington

Distributed by Cordee, 3a DeMonfort Street, Leicester. LE1 7HD
(t) 0116 254 3579, (f) 0116 247 1176, (e) sales@cordee.co.uk

For details of other SMC guidebooks see inside rear endpaper

Contents

Ayrshire by Tom Prentice

Galloway Hills by Stephen Reid

The Borders & Dumfries by Stephen Reid

Galloway Sea-cliffs
by Andrew Fraser & Dave MacLeod (Garheugh Port bouldering)

Introduction & Acknowledgements

In the west, the rise and rise of bouldering has led to a phenomenal increase in standard at Dumbarton Rock and the development of venues throughout the Trossachs. Elsewhere in the west, a number of sports climbs have been added to the mica schist crags of Loch Lomond and the Trossachs, while Auchinstarry Quarry has suffered another purge, but seems to have 'bounced' back again. On the Rosneath peninsula opposite Helensburgh, slate has entered the game in a big way with nearly 200 new routes – all the work of a single climber.

The mountain and sea-cliffs of Galloway and the Solway Coast have also seen a staggering number of new crags and new routes. The boulderers have been active here too, adding to the attractions of Garheugh Port, The Thirlstane, Sandyhills Bay and Clifton. The winter climbers have been poking about too. While the previous edition hardly warranted the title Rock and Ice Climbs, this edition has too many winter routes for this to be ignored.

The principle change in the Stirling Area has been the steady addition of new routes to Thorntons Quarry and Fourth Quarry in Cambusbarron. The names of these quarries have only come to light recently and are used here for the first time in preference to Cambusbarron Closed and Cambusbarron Open or West. The bouldering at Wolfcrag Quarry is also documented for the first time.

While the west and south-west have seen substantial changes, the east has been relatively quiet. Ratho Quarry is at last open again and routes have started to be re-climbed. Unfortunately the deadline for this guide and on-going diffi-culties at the Adventure Centre conspired against us including fully revised descriptions. Developments at Craigy Hill north of Haddington and on the faces surrounding the sports routes at North Berwick Law are the work of just a few climbers – a reminder that new routes come in all grades. Climbing now takes place at Salisbury Crags South Quarry and access may be given to other areas in the future. The Berwickshire Coast continues in much the same pace Some new routes have been added, while some of the existing routes have started to revert to their natural state.

At more than 460 pages, this is a bumper guide. No doubt the next edition will be even bigger.

Tom Prentice
Autumn 2004

Thanks to: John Biggar, Reuben Brown, Alasdair Gillies, Ian Magill, Alastair Matthewson, Calum Mayland, the late George Macadam, Robin McAllister, Dave McGimpsey, Neil Morrison, Alan Pert, Dave Redpath, Mike Reed, Alastair Robertson, scottishclimbs.com, Ian Taylor, Matthew Thompson, Steve Wright, Martin Whitaker, Allan & Raymond Wallace and authors of previous editions

The Trossachs, Glasgow Area & Ayrshire: 1891 - 1993

Ken Crocket, Roger Everett, Gary Latter & Tom Prentice

"A precipice 20 feet high does not sound very serious, but there may be more fun and real climbing in getting up or down such a place than there is in ascending the 4,406 feet of Ben Nevis... A quarry face is by no means bad fun, if one can either find a place free from onlookers, or can turn a deaf ear to their somewhat personal remarks about the sundry coppers missing from the shilling..."

This comment about outcrop climbing was by Gilbert Thomson, one of the founder members of the Scottish Mountaineering Club. It was published in January 1892, by which time various rock athletes from that club – themselves young at some point in their lives – had scurried up quite a few crags. On Saturday, December 12 1891, the day following that Club's Third Annual Dinner, a team of hard men paid a visit to The Whangie. This was the third visit to that crag, the party on this day consisting of: Horace Walker, President of the Alpine Club: Professors Ramsay and Veitch; Messrs Maylard, Munro, Naismith, W.A.Ramsay, and Thomson. Despite snow on the moor and ice-filled cracks, some time was "very enjoyably spent in various pieces of fancy climbing".

The following July, Maylard, Naismith and Thomson attacked The Whangie with two 40-foot ropes; joining them together and climbing the isolated pinnacle now known as The Gendarme by techniques dubiously modern. Crag climbing had arrived in Southern Scotland.

Other crags were being visited at this time; Craigton, Pillar Crag, Salisbury Crags glowering over Auld Reekie, and Loudoun Hill in Ayrshire. Ben An in The Trossachs came under siege in May 1896, by that crag-rat Thomson, H.C.Boyd and his brother the Rev Arnold Boyd. The lower rocks appeared too steep and difficult, the party tackling instead two vegetatious gullies.

Thomson and his friends thus recorded the first route on Ben An with Left-Hand Gully, Very Difficult. The other gully, on which they failed that day, was climbed two years later by Naismith, Douglas and Maclay, on New Year's Day, 1898. On January 22 1898, Harold Raeburn and J.S.Napier visited the crag and recorded the Oblique Crack, a Very Difficult on the Upper Tier.

Loudoun Hill meanwhile had been visited by Naismith as long ago as 1895, when he had attempted to solo a route up the Central Wall. Returning alone by cycle in April 1896, he managed to reverse his line, finding great difficulty climbing in the rain wearing cycling shoes. His route, more of a scramble, starts under The Edge and traverses up and right.

The rocks at Dumbarton Castle were known of by those pioneers, but footwear then was inadequate for the technical gems waiting to be found on the boulders. Outcrops in any case were regarded by most as a convenient means of obtaining fitness with amusement at the same time, an attitude which persisted for over 70 years. This early, casual approach to the crags has inevitably led to a dearth of recorded history. With a few exceptions, most of the routes climbed before the 1970s have no sure claimant. Only since the early 1970s has a section of climbers attached more importance to the outcrops, recording routes in minutiae, leading or soloing routes and problems previously top-roped, freeing aid routes.

The initial phase of exploration by the SMC died out during the first three decades of the twentieth century. Only with John 'Jock' Nimlin in 1930 can we put a date on the renaissance. In that year W.White led the Ash Wall on Ben An, graded then as an 'Amiable Severe'. Nimlin that same year recorded several other excellent routes, including the Birch Wall, The Last 80, and The Rent, the latter Severe or Very Severe, depending on one's jamming abilities.

With mass unemployment in the 1930s great numbers of young people took to walking, the cheapest sport available. For some, climbing naturally followed, with many new clubs being formed. Jock Nimlin from Glasgow was the force behind the Ptarmigan Club, while Andy Sanders formed the Creagh Dhu. The Lomond M.C. also came into being at this time.

With the end of the Second World War The Whangie especially took a beating, the talents of the Creagh Dhu and the Glencoe M.C. being prominent. Hamish MacInnes left a visiting card with several peg routes; to be freed many years later. Craigmore was also visited by the Creagh Dhu – this area was where they first explored the outdoors after all – but not being accustomed to digging for their routes they soon left that future crag in peace, though not without in all probability first climbing the prominent Craigmore Corner.

Loudoun Hill saw further activity in the 1930s. In an article in SMCJ Vol. XX (1935), Douglas Scott describes climbs which later became known as Pulpit Arete, Left Crack, Foxglove Chimney, Jackdaw Chimney and Dusk Route. Hamish Hamilton climbed The Edge on a top-rope during this period. However, the most significant advances here came in the 1960s when the late John Jackson and friends climbed many of the most obvious lines. These routes were recorded in a small private guide, which was preserved by John Jackson's father. This records a remarkable series of ascents, which included Slings (climbed with some aid), and Lunge.

Probably as rock boots began to find their way over the channel, Dumbarton Rock began development. The leading light was the late Neil MacNiven, killed in the Alps in 1963 at the age of 21. His brilliance at the 'Rock' led to ascents of such routes as Stonefall Crack, Stonefall Crack Direct, and the aid route Chemin de Fer. MacNiven also climbed about half of the boulder problems, including Pas Encore, Route Royale (with Brian Shields), Suckers Slab, B.N.I. and Nemesis.

Brian Shields, Michael Connolly and others climbed the remainder of the Dumbarton routes in the early 1960s, Shields being responsible for recording them. Climbs put up by Shields included: Longbow (with Jimmy Houston, using 7 pegs and 8 wedges), Windjammer Crack, and Monsoon Gully, the latter seeing a failed attempt on a direct finish by MacNiven and Shields. Many of the boulder problems fell to Shields, including Short Notice, Skint Knuckles (one sling), and Switch Direct (in Vibrams). Shields was also responsible, with Connolly, for the big aid route Requiem, the finish up the headwall requiring expansion bolts. The other aid route from Shields was The Big Zipper, with A.Baillie.

This wave of activity passed, though the comparative trough was to be short-lived, as a new group of climbers was spawned at the 'Rock'. The 'Dumbarton Boys', whose core included 'Big' Ian Nicolson, Rab Carrington, John Jackson, 'Wee' Ian Fulton and others, found newer and harder boulder problems, some of which took weeks to work out. All this was at the end of the 1960s and into the 1970s. Shields had two more routes to record however, with the aid route Cyclops, and Desperado.

At the beginning of the 1970s a visiting gritstone climber, Steve Belk, began to investigate the 'Rock'. This led to Bobtail, the first free ascent of Longbow, and the top-rope ascent of Grey Wall. On January 3 1971, Belk and Ken Crocket climbed Requiem, with Belk making a superb lead on tied-off blade pegs at the top of the wall, where the wide crack fades. No signs of any bolts were found on this ascent, supposedly the third.

Craigmore began to have its concealing cover of turf removed in secret, the diggers being expatriate Welshman John Kerry and Gordon Jeffrey. The latter had climbed on Craigmore in the late 1960s. 'Lord' John Mackenzie was also living in Glasgow at this time, his enthusiastic explorations finding many lines on Craigton, Pillar Crag and Dunglas, the latter with Colin Garthwaite. Craigmore was such a well-kept secret that it was not included in the first outcrop guide to be published for this area – Ken Crocket's *Western Outcrops* (Nevisport, 1975).

Auchinstarry Quarry was rediscovered in 1975 by Ken Johnstone, and was included in a second volume of the Glasgow Outcrops. Johnstone recorded the first routes here with Trundle and Mascarade. Kerry soon homed in on this old quarry, finding such popular routes as Spirogyra and Red Lead. Willie Todd climbed the thin arete of Nijinski, employing a runner on the neighbouring Promontory Direct, having first top-roped the route. In 1982 Dave Cuthbertson cleaned the arete by abseil then made the first lead with no side runner.

Back at Dumbarton, Andy Kelso recorded Ciamar a Tha Sibh and a short aid route, later freed by Willie Todd to give Snowhite. Two fine aretes succumbed, Nick Colton's Fever Pitch and Todd's Gaucho. Johnstone was also busy here, with ascents of Slainte, Drizzle, Rough Sea, and the fine crack of Antigrav, using two aid points and later freed by Todd.

The boulder problems at Dumbarton, the 'black Fontainebleu', were gradually being expanded in 1978, with Mark Worsley on Supinator, Greenwell on Gorilla, and Todd on Good Nicks. Auchinstarry saw further developments from Rob Kerr with Power Play and two years on, both top-roped routes on the Trundle Slab were soloed to give Walk on the Wild Side and Midas Touch.

1983 saw much activity at Auchinstarry, with Jerry Handren producing Dream Machine, Blade Runner, and Death is the Hunter. Ben Masterton boldly climbed the late lamented Balance of Power while Gary Latter made a two-day ascent of Carouselambra. Duncan McCallum solved 'the last great problem' in the quarry with his ascent of the blank-looking wall of Surface Tension.

On the boulder front at Dumbarton, Latter added Mestizo, Toto and Physical Graffiti. The old peg problem Pongo was freed. But the big guns were aimed at the aid routes of the face. Cuthbertson worked hard in the spring of 1980, recording Woops, an alternative, fingery start to The Big Zipper. The same climber also succeeded in freeing Chemin de Fer, over the course of several evenings. Cuthbertson returned in 1981, freeing the uncompromising corner of Cyclops, taking successive falls on to a preplaced peg runner.

Two years later Latter climbed the excellent Rock of Ages, and made the first lead of Grey Wall. Latter went on to free the two aid bolts on The Big Zipper, taking six day's work spread throughout the summer. The last great problem on Dumbarton Rock was the great crack of Requiem. This fell at last to Cuthbertson after a heroic struggle encompassing six weeks of humid climbing in the summer of 1983. At the time of climbing, it was Scotland's hardest pitch.

Publication of the 1986 guide led to renewed activity at Auchinstarry Quarry. Meanwhile, Simon Yates and Davy Gardner visited Creagan Tom Dubh, the obvious wall on the hillside above the east bank of Loch Lomond. Also active on the loch shores in 1986 was John Christie, who discovered the slate quarry at Ross Point. Around this time Craig Macadam climbed the impressive Craig's Wall right of Layback Crack at Craigmore.

1990 was a year of controversy. After two bolt routes were placed on Dumbarton Rock, the owners, Historic Scotland, took action and had the bolts and other in situ protection removed. For a while threatening noises were made about enforcing the ban on climbing at the Rock. Glasgow's sport climbers started looking for alternative venues. The overhang at Dumbuck was bolted to give three routes, the best of which is Awaken (F8a), and then in 1992, attention turned to Dunglas. The small steep wall on the west face between Deviant and Wall of Horrors had already received two new routes – The Beef Monster (E5) from Bruce Kerr and Steel Finger (E3) from Graham Dudley. Three bolts routes were added to the collection, of which the best is Airhead (F7a).

With a new guidebook nearing completion, the crags of Glen Afton came under renewed scrutiny, resulting in a number of fine routes including Stone Circle (E1) from McAllister. In 1992 McAllister took a deep breath and added Sweet Liberty (E3) and Delirium (E4), two of the hardest routes to be climbed in Ayrshire.

In late 1992 and early 1993 tragedy struck the local Glasgow climbers, when Kilsyth District Council were advised by their insurers to instigate an attempt to stabilise Auchinstarry Quarry. Several of the better and more solid climbs were totally destroyed, but by way of consolation, a number of new worthwhile climbs were created from the rubble.

The Trossachs, Loch Lomond, Gare Loch & Glasgow Area: 1993 - 2004

Dave MacLeod

During the mid 1990s, developments centred very much on the glaring gaps on the

Dumbarton boulders. In 1994, a fit Andy Gallagher had the pick of the lines, climbing Mugsy Traverse (Font 7b) and the ultra classic Consolidated Traverse (Font 7b+), an honorary stamina route despite never reaching more than a foot above the ground. Despite Andy's frequent presence among the boulders, the steely strong Malcolm Smith made numerous successful raids, stealing the often tried lines of The Shield and B.N.I. direct start (both Font 7b+). Around this time it became increasingly clear that bolted sport climbs could co-exist quite happily with the trad lines (with sensible bolting). More and more bolt lines appeared and became instantly popular. An unwitting John Dunne grabbed the first ascent of Benny's Route (F7c) with an onsight before Benny Mclaughlan could climb it himself. Andy Gallagher and Cameron Phair worked together to provide several classics such as Omerta (F7c) and Dum Dum Boys (F7c+).

The potential up at the nearby Dumbuck overhangs was also slowly realised with Flesh for Fantasy (F7c+) from Cameron Phair and, after a protracted struggle, Andy Gallagher's piece de resistance; Voodoo Magic (F8b). Several other ambitious projects received attention at the time from the likes of Andy, Mark 'Face' McGowan and Malcolm Smith, several of which remain unfinished to date such as the awesome blank walls on either side of Requiem, thought to be in the mid F9s!

In 1996, 17 year old Dave MacLeod fresh from an apprenticeship on the Dumbarton boulders began repeating many of Andy Gallagher's classic lines at the rock such as Dum Dum boys, Consolidated and the bold Trick of the Vale (E6 6c). In the following few years, Dave went on to repeat all the existing problems at the rock and add many new ones such as In Bloom (Font 7c) and Dressed for Success (Font 7b+). Malcolm Smith beat the locals once again to the most coveted project around and made a one-day ascent of the sit start to the crack of Pongo (Font 8a). Another strong Edinburgh raider, Dave Redpath was also working away on several projects and came away with the Shield Sit Start (Font 7c) and Second Sights (F7c+) at Dumbuck. Andy Gallagher continued to enthusiastically equip new lines such as Persistence of Vision (F7a+) which has become the most climbed sport route in this guide.

Andy also revisited the neglected Craigton to produce the desperate grit-like arete; Far From the Maddening Crowd (Font 7c). Elsewhere, Dunglas saw a new routing revival in 1998 from MacLeod and 'Baggy' Mike Conner who added several serious routes (using top rope practice) to the lower prominent black overhangs on its north face. MacLeod's E5 5c, Don't Wake Up Now saw repeat solo ascents from Conner and Niall McNair, who flashed the route without warming up (in order "not to give himself time to think about what he was doing"). MacLeod also made a lead of Craig's Wall at Craigmore (E7 6c), thinking it was a first lead. Apparently the route was soloed in 1989 by A. Ford, an inspired ascent which must have rated among the hardest in Scotland at the time. This gnarly little route has seen no further ascents since 1997.

Sport climbing was growing in popularity in Scotland from the early '90s onwards. Beyond 1994, the early venues such as Glen Ogle and the Angus Quarries reached a plateau and a hardcore of new routing protagonists began to explore more remote and interesting areas. At the forefront of this exploration were Perthshire climbers Colin Miln, Isla Watson, Janet Horrocks and George Ridge. It was clear that the highlands, from Loch Lomondside northwards held a huge resource of relatively short, very steep and compact mica schist crags. These crags although not being particularly attractive to the trad climber, made superb sport climbing venues. Development first extended into the Lowland Outcrops area in late 1997 when the Stronachlachar crags were discovered. The first route here, My Own Private Scotland (F6c+) by Miln, reflected the quietude and abundance of untouched rock, not normally associated with traditional European sport venues.

Several pleasant routes on High Crag at Stronachlachar followed from Miln and Watson. Around this time Ridge bolted the giant boulder hidden in trees below High Crag, later dubbed the G-Spot. The routes were left untouched until the team returned in 2000 to climb the technical groove of Venga boys (F6c+) and the balancy Hideous Kinky (F7a).

The sport developments also spread to the collection of steep buttresses overlooking Loch Lomond just north of Inversnaid. This relatively remote area is characterised by a wild feel and beautiful scenery. The initial bolted projects on the barrel shaped buttresses were left behind (the projects remain unclimbed to date) in favour of larger faces to the north. Wild Swans Crag yielded some excellent little routes from Miln and Watson such as Wild Swans (F6c) and Dark Skies (F6b+).

The jewel in the crown of the Inversnaid developments was Crystal Crag. This unusual steep wall with a quartzy patina yielded several crimpy routes such as the long and excellent Fear and Self Loathing from Miln (F7b) and the viciously blind Far From the Malham Crowds from Watson (F7a). The potential of the sport crags hereabouts has not nearly been realised and will no doubt feature in the new route books for some time to come.

Throughout the '90s, Auchinstarry continued to buzz with popularity. The routes damaged by the council's stabilisation work became sound and clean once more. Even the E5s such as Surface Tension saw ascents and amusing failures into the pond which apparently still harbours a mythical Pike ("with teeth like screws"). Nick Tarmey balanced up Death is the Hunter without its side runner (at E5 6c) and later boldly soloed Nijinski after much practice. Dave MacLeod, with Stewart Paterson filled in some gaps in the trundle slab area with The Javelin (E2), Glasgow No More (VS) and the enticing borehole above Foxy Woxy; Shiny Happy People (E3) part of which may have been climbed before prior to council clensing.

2000 saw a serious revival at Dumbarton with many new lines being enthusiastically unearthed such as Gorilla Hanging start (Font 7a) by Darren Stevenson, Gorilla Warfare and Silvers Route Sit start (6b) by 'Geordie' Mike Rudden. Visiting Sheffield climber Ben Pritchard also made an impression repeating In Bloom and adding Hap Slappy (Font 7c). The ever present Dave MacLeod grabbed the glaring sit start to Mestizo (Font 7a+) and went on (after John 'Spider' Mackenzie) to repeat Requiem (E8 6b) placing all the gear on lead. Dave was also active at Dumbuck cleaning up an old project of Andy Gallagher's to give the short but nasty So Be It (F8a+). Voodoo Magic had seen one repeat from visiting Frenchman Olivier Froideval but had lain neglected since it lost several important holds. Dave MacLeod returned to reinstate the climb with another ascent and no change in grade. Also in 2000, Bowling crag was unearthed again by 'Irish' John Watson, leading and naming all the main lines and added bolt lower-offs. The crag had been used intermittently for years but was never taken seriously.

In 2001 Mike Rudden cleaned up the forgotten line of bolts taking Dumbuck's most striking feature; the central scoop to give the delightfully named Dirty Sanchez (F7c+). MacLeod revisited the Dunglas overhangs, breaching the upper wall for the first time with the dangerous Drink Up For Tomorrow We Die! (E7 6b). Dumbarton locals Iain 'Bevvy' Beveridge and the powerful Martin Casey added the obvious wall problem at Bowling, The Thin White Line (Font 7a). This line was later mistakenly claimed by MacLeod in 2002 who also added the desperate The Fold (Font 7a+). Back on the Dumbarton boulders, new classics continued to be found such as Silverback and Hoop (both Font 7c) by MacLeod.

The sport developments at Stronachlachar were complemented in January 2001 when a series of visits from Edinburgh climber Dave Redpath resulted in a string of fine boulder problems. The best of these were the slopey traverse of Virgin Suicides (Font 7a+) and the somewhat highball Pimp With a Limp (Font 7a+).

The main development of 2001 however was MacLeod's eventual success on Achemine E9 6c in early October. This ascent was the result of an epic struggle involving 11 long falls from the smooth headwall (F8b climbing) before cooler autumn conditions arrived. The route was Scotland's first E9 and is still among the hardest traditional leads in the UK.

2002 was a quiet year apart from MacLeod's ascent of the big linkup of the Gorilla arete; King Kong (Font 8a). Bouldering at Craigmore took another resurgence with the addition of the classic sit start to The Wizard (Font 7b) from Paul Savage. 2003 kicked off with the hardest line on the Dumby boulders to date; Sabotage, at a huge grade of Font 8a+, again from MacLeod. This attracted the curiosity of Malcolm Smith who bagged a second ascent across two days. Pongo Sit

Start also had a third ascent from a strong new-comer and Dumby regular Joe Newman (MacLeod had made the second ascent in 2000). Martin Casey unearthed a substantial new line on the Shield wall to give Totality (Font 7b+). The main face also received renewed attention with MacLeod adding Calm Before the Storm (E6 6c) and the very bold arete of Blackout (E6 6a), with Stephen Richardson making the second ascent the following day. MacLeod's main contribution though was the superb new line traced through the sufferance wall; Tolerance at a sustained and deceptive F8b. Stephen Richardson also made an impressive repeat of MacLeod's razor thin Dumb & Dumber (E7 6c), but not before taking a scary tumble from beyond the crux. Richardson was also responsible for a string of repeats of the 'bold boulders' such as the first repeat of MacLeod's Nadjilation (E6 6b) and Shadow (E3 6b).

The collection of fine compact boulders above Loch Katrine, on the lower slopes of Ben Venue received a whirlwind development during 2003. The boulders had (as is so often the case) been used casually in the past by Jon Read among others Read had produced a small topo on his website which prompted John Watson to take an interest. John, along with 'Kelso' Tim Morrozo and Bob Ewan repeated Read's existing problems such as Lecturing the Masses (5c) and began climbing the large number of remaining unclaimed lines. Many of these, including Watson's Sebastopol (Font 6a+) and TNT (Font 6b) featured immaculate rock which gave the place great appeal among an exploding number of new bouldering venues. Dave MacLeod made productive couple of visits, coming away with Lock, Stock (Font 7c) and the dynamic Paralysis by Analysis (Font 7a+). The rush for new lines slowed down by late summer with Watson's Fight Club (Font 6c) and Stephen Richardson's technical Big Up Orra Glesga Peeps (Font 7a+). This venue is probably the most significant new crag to be added to the Lowland Outcrops guide in this edition; its instant popularity is sure to continue.

With rumours of a new edition of the guide and another bout of stabilisation by the council, Auchinstarry became a new routing target once more, yielding several re-ascents of altered old lines and excellent new finds such as Return of the King (E3 5c) and Danger U.S.R. (HVS) from Raymond and Allan Wallace. MacLeod and Stephen Richardson investigated the remains of Think of England with the intention to climb the adjacent blank arete. The right arete of the pillar turned out to be more amenable, producing Think of Scotland (E6 6b). The nasty looking landing was tested by Richardson immediately prior to his solo ascent.

Spurred on by the imminent publication of a new guide, MacLeod returned to Dumbuck to work a project of Dave Redpath's. A sunny break in an otherwise wet autumn resulted in Devastation Generation (8c), the hardest route in this guide and Scotland's first 8c.

The most prominent development since the last guide has been the explosion in popularity of bouldering. This has opened up a previously untapped resource of new lines, providing great enjoyment and a fresh lease of life to many traditional areas. On the other hand, a few of the traditional routes have suffered as a result of neglect such as those at Craigmore. Hopefully this trend will be offset at Craigmore given the re-introduction of traditional leading grades. Future new routing in the Glasgow area will increasingly become limited to the highest grades although many unclimbed lines still exist on Dunglas and the dolerite quarries (often involving loose rock). Dumbarton Rock has several 'last great lines' waiting to be done such as the roof under High Flyer, the cave traverse into Sabotage and the walls on either side of Requiem among others. The net result of the diversification of climbing styles, continued new route development and advancing grades at the top level is a richer and more varied climbing resource for central Scotland's locals and visitors alike.

South-West: 1906 - 1998

Roger Everett, Andrew Fraser, Craig Macadam, Tom Prentice & Stephen Reid
Investigating the development of climbing in the south-west does not yield any dramatic results nor any complete heritage. The early history is one of possibilities

rather than events: the few articles from the turn of the century, though they mention all the crags in the Galloway Hills, describe no real climbing. Indeed, in the SMC Journal of 1906, which gives the first comprehensive round-up of walking and climbing in this area, the Climbs section points the prospective climber to the steepest and most continuous crags but, perhaps in character, records no routes.

Rock climbing in the south-west was given an obtuse start with the ascent of The Witch Rock at Portpatrick by E.C.M.Heath in 1899. Thereafter there were no developments until 1932 when E.C.Thomson and company discovered Benbeoch, and soloed the easiest line in the centre of the crag. The general tone of the early articles is apologetic and pleading, perhaps because the south-west has always been something of an unknown quantity. The pleas having been largely unheeded, this tone is still apparent in 1958 when A.G.Waldie wrote of the first climbing in the district: "The disconsolate climber, enervated by the balmy climate of Galloway and preserving his nails on its lush vegetation, might well consider selling his rope to the Solway boatmen".

Waldie nevertheless goes on to give a series of reasons, in the shape of sea cliffs and outcrops, as well as the crags of the Galloway Hills, that might persuade the climber to hold on to his rope. Recording the first routes in the Galloway Hills, Waldie tells of climbing on most of the major crags including the Cooran Buttress on the Dungeon of Buchan, Craig an Eilte, and the Clints of Dromore. The hardest route of the era being G.Fraser's 1959 Central Route (VS 5a) on Craigdews. From this time on, local knowledge has it that climbing continued, though without any recording of routes or any direct contact between those taking part. The lack of a tradition or the relative youth of the climbers is perhaps the reason for this.

Waldie notes a further area of development, what is now known as the Dumfries Outcrops. Again, the inquisitive climber can only discover the number of routes that were climbed, as opposed to locating any one of them. Sixteen climbs are mentioned at Clifton, from Easy to Very Severe. This means progress has to be gauged in numbers and grades: there are now 48 routes on this cliff, up to E4. This increase in activity started in 1976, when Craig and George Macadam were pointed to the cliff. Technical standards began to move and the following year the first Extremes were climbed. Jugular Vein was the first to fall, then Wall Street was exposed from behind a tenuous line of ivy on the first ascent. Finally, the Toddamundo arete was soloed, after a quick brushing. 1978 saw the first 5c in The Arete, now 5b, and in 1979, the first 6a climbs, Fingerlust, and Lemur.

However, unknown to the local climbers, and predating the first climbs at Clifton, the serious Vomit (VS) had been climbed at the Mull of Galloway by Lakes climbers W.Renshaw and R.Kenyon. Nore significantly, the larger sea-cliffs south of Kirkcudbright were being developed. Bill Cheverst had started climbing at Meikle Ross in 1972. His first route, Limehouse Blues, climbed in April of that year, is not the most obvious when an entire cliff is available. Limehouse Blues, however, was climbed in the days before precleaning was common-place as it is now, and this route stays naturally clean. This was the same with K.9, Cheverst's other major climb. These routes were the first advance in standards for 20 years.

Cheverst, significantly, wrote the first article on climbing in the south-west since A.G.Waldie. This was published in Rocksport, and brought the attention of a number of other climbers to this area. After a two-year lull, John Kerry was brought south from Glasgow by the Rocksport article. He gardened and climbed a series of major routes in the period from March 1975 to September 1977, which were recorded in the Glasgow Outcrops, Volumes 1 and 2. Initially, Kerry's attention was focused on the eye-catching crack- lines, which are a feature of these cliffs. Salty Dog (HVS 4c) was climbed in March 1975, the same day as Kerry led the twin bulges of Mellow Yellow, in Little Zawn. However, excellent as these routes are, Kerry's real interest was in the longer layback grooves of the main cliff. Galloway Corner, climbed in early 1975 by Andy Hunter, though favoured at the time, is not of the same quality as Side Track, which, by climbing direct to the first stance, avoids a 15m walk and gives the route a more sustained interest and difficulty. The first pitch of Side Track is part of a natural groove line, 60m high. Kerry returned in May 1977 and completed this route, Back Track, E1 5a the boldest in the area at that time.

Craig Macadam was alerted to these sea-cliffs through the *Glasgow Outcrops* guide. However, as an inexperienced climber, these more intimidating cliffs proved more of a test than the local outcrops. Kerry's technical high-point, Bloody Crack (E1 5b), climbed in January 1976. However, excellent routes were found by a thorough examination of the cracks and spaces on Limehouse Blues Cliff, with the hardest and best of these, the wall of Finesse, climbed in October 1978, only just inside the Extreme category. It was only surpassed in 1979 by Macadam's first E3 at the Ross – Fil d'Or.

Late in 1979, the discovery of Burrow Head turned attention away from the locally established crags. The steeper smoother greywacke has meant that the routes are more strenuous and more sustained than those of the Ross. Conquistador, climbed in January 1980, was the first E2 on the sea-cliffs. However, the pace of development, while constant, was never quickened by the threat of competition and seven months later, Naked Fun, another sustained E2, was climbed.

The period from 1975 to 1980 was one of great activity, with the discovery of four new crags and the consequent surfeit of unclimbed rock. The same could has not be said forbeen true of the years from 1981 to 1985. There are were a number of reasons for this. A lack of information deterred potential first ascentionists from further afield; and, as most of the major lines had been climbed, there was not the same scope for the few that knew of the latest developments.

These years did see major new additions on all the main crags, and a small increase in the number of active climbers. Two years behind Clifton, Macadam climbed the first E3s at Meikle Ross in 1981. Burrow Head was visited in 1981 by Ian Duckworth and Macadam, then Stirling based. The result was Mirror, Mirror, E3 5c, by a direct start – a bold on-sight lead by Duckworth.

A border raid by Pete Whillance and Jim Fotheringham was the only activity of 1982. Of their three routes, The Highwayman had been climbed by G.Little in 1968, exemplifying the recording problems in this area. Of the other routes, Saddle Tramp, E2 5c, makes excellent use of the terraced buttress it climbs.

Nothing of any importance was climbed in 1983, but 1984 more than compensated for this. After a four year gap, the first new routes were put up on Clifton. Derek Austin climbed through the curving overhang of Moonshine to make Beyond the Terminator, and Macadam, after one fall, completed Toddamundo by forcing the headwall above the initial arete, the first E4 in the south-west.

Meikle Ross was closely scrutinised, and a number of possibilities were spotted. Austin climbed the deceptive crack of Corridor of Power, E3 5c. This climb is unusual as it is formed by the edge of the bedding planes, the first climb to do this, but surely not the last. Catalysed by this activity, Macadam returned to the Ross and forced Sunshine Superman up the smooth wall right of Mellow Yellow.

Following publication of the new guide, Tom Prentice turned his attention to the sea-cliffs of the south-west and in particular the Rhinns of Galloway. Portobello was found in 1986 and Laggantalluch Head with Simon Richardson in 1987. That same year a small group of Glasgow climbers spent a leisurely time climbing some 20 of the most obvious lines at both areas including The Man From Del Monte (E3), Thunderbolt (HVS), Laggantalluch Corner (HVS), Ape Escape (E2) and Freewheeling (E2).

Satisfied with their achievements at Portobello and Laggantalluch, the Glasgow climbers passed the crags to irrepressible south-west activist Andrew Fraser and members of the Ayr-based Kyle Club. The results were dramatic: 34 new routes at Portobello between 1989 and 1992 and 27 at Laggantalluch between 1991 and 1992. Among the best are St Elmo's Fire (E3) and The Cruel Seaside (E2) at Portobello and Davy Jones's Locker (E1) and Heart of Darkness (HVS) at Laggantalluch.

Inland, the potential at Dungeon of Buchan in the Galloway Hills had been known for some time, but it was left to a group of Lake District climbers, inspired by Stephen Reid, to take up where Pete Whillance and Jim Fotheringham had left off in 1982. During the spring and summer of 1991 they utilised mountain bikes to make eight visits to the area, cleaning and recording 15 routes. Of these, Heir Apparent (HVS) and Colonel's Corner (HVS) on the 100m main buttress are worth particular mention, as is Parcel of Rogues (E3) on the immaculate granite of the smaller Dungeon Buttress.

Fired up by their new routes on the sea-cliffs, Kyle Club members, most notably Robin McAllister, Dave McGimpsey, Mike Reed and, of course, Andrew Fraser, refused to let lichen grow between their toes. In 1992 Money Head was found, resulting in 14 routes and the same year the excellent Crammag Head, the granite headland just south of Laggantalluch, offered up 24 enjoyable outings, the best of which are Molotov Cocktail (E1) and Yosemite Sam (HVS). Meanwhile, Graham Dudley had visited Laggantalluch Head and swiped the obvious and much-eyed crack-line in the overhanging prow, to give Quick Seal (E3). The technical high points were McAllister and Reed's Waster (E5) and Sweaty Trembler (E5) both climbed at Portobello in 1993. The lightning development at the strangely named Kiln o' the Fuffock illustrated the possibility that would crags with excellent routes awaited discovery in hidden inlets along the coast.

Between sea-cliff sojourns, members of the Kyle team were poking round the accessible inland crags climbing the odd route at Clints of Dromore and Craigencallie. This latter crag already had three routes, climbed, but not recorded, by Graham Little in 1977, and a few more had been added in the early 1980s. The hardest of their new routes was Across The Barricades (E4) by Fraser in 1992 and Delta of Venus (E4) by Donald Gibson in 1993.

South-West: 1994 - 2004

Andrew Fraser

The years 1994 to 2003 will perhaps be seen as a coming of age of Galloway climbing. The 1994 guide contained some 450 routes in the South-West, whereas this guide contains over 770. While 200 of the new climbs are on the sea-cliffs, the 120 new routes in the Galloway hills have nearly trebled the climbing in that area.

During the 1994-1997 period, the Ayrshire based team of Andrew Fraser, Robin McAllister, Dave McGimpsey and Mike Reed had the area largely to themselves, with the bulk of the new development being on the Stranraer peninsula of the Rhinns. This period also saw a leap in standards, largely motivated by McAllister. 1994 saw a number of good fillers at existing crags including Violently Happy (E3 5c) at Crammag Head, and Holy Grail (HVS 5a) at Laggantalluch from McAllister, as well as a number of extremes at Craigencallie including the Empty Quarter (E2 5b) from Fraser.

1995 saw more significant developments. McAllister had spotted Finnarts Point from the Irish ferry, and started development in February when the overhanging main cliff was uncooperatively covered in verglas. Elsewhere, McAllister climbed two big sea-cliff lines. First was Beers, Smears and Queers (E4 6a), at Crammag. Next was Spectacular Bid, the 'last great problem' on the Meikle Ross's Main Cliff. Previously inspected and named by Craig Macadam some 10 years earlier, this weighed in at E6 6b. Unbeknown to the locals, this was not the hardest route in the South-West. This honour went to Martin Dale's Haste Ye Back (E6 6b/c) at Larbrax. Lancashire climbers, Glen Brookes and Dale had secretly developed these excellent slabs.

Developments on Mullwharchar, in the wilds of the Galloway hills, were more unusual. Brigadoon (E1), by Fraser and McAllister, climbed the monolithic main corner of the crag, first attempted by Graham Little in the '70s. News leaked to Pete Brown, a Californian living in Irvine. As his swansong before returning to the States, Pete back-rope soloed four routes on Mullwharchar including Phoebus Mask (E3 5c) and Yucatan (HVS 5a), as well as Heretic (E3 5c) on Craigencallie. Although Phoebus Mask had already been gardened by McAllister, the other routes were climbed on sight, adding significantly to their difficulties.

By contrast, 1996 was a quiet year in Galloway. The big routes were at Finnarts Point with the outrageous Edge of the Abyss (E4 6a) from McAllister and the intimidating Lloyd Quinan is a Weatherman (E3 5c) from McGimpsey. The year also saw the development of the immaculate Orange Wall at Kiln O' the Fuffock, as well as some bold solos. The solos included Total Immersion (E4 6a, McAllister and Reed), the more terminal Waster (E5 6b, McAllister), as well as a number of solo first ascents at Portobello by Matthew Thomson.

The big freeze of January 1997 allowed some of the prize multi-pitch ice routes in the Galloway hills to be captured, notably the Spout of the Clints (V 5) by Stephen Reid and Chris Bonington, and Smear Test (IV 4) by Reid and Doug Scott.

The year was also to prove the swansong of the Ayrshire climbers, with McAllister, McGimpsey, Reed and Stewart Mearns all departing the area. Before leaving, they amassed a number of hard and fine new routes. From McAllister there were Zero Tolerance (E5 6b), involving numerous long falls onto RPs, the technical Read the Small Print (E5 6b) and Toxygene (E5 6b), all at Laggantalluch; Full Speed Ahead (E3 6a) at Finnarts; the bold Screamadelicca (E5 6b) at Portobello; and the worrying Unscathed (E5 6a) at the Mull of Galloway. From McGimpsey were the classic Sam I Am (E4 6a) at Laggantalluch, Release the Pressure (E3 6a) and the theatrical Smarty-Pants (E1 5b) at the Mull of Galloway and Camp Boss, Won't Cook (E3 5c) at Finnarts. Other significant routes were Last Night at the Prawns (E3 5c) at Finnarts from Fraser and Paranoid Android (E5 6b) at Portobello from Reed.

The rediscovery of the Mull of Galloway was also a significant event of 1997. While parts of it are appallingly loose, the 4-km E1 sea traverse (involving two swims and multiple abseils) provided Stuart Lampard and McGimsey with a true sea-cliff classic.

Prior gardening is a necessary evil on the harder greywacke climbs, and this, together with the occasional use of a shunt, inevitably provides some prior knowledge of routes. In this context, it is worthwhile to record Mike Reed's role in making the on-sight second ascent of many of the harder routes.

Galloway Sea-cliffs: 1998 - 2004

With the departure of the Ayrshire team's main performers, the period between 1998 to 2003 has been noted for a change of direction, away from the hard 'last great problems', back to a more exploratory phase. This has produced a breadth of new middle grade routes in a range of venues.

McAllister's final contribution to Galloway was the fine Ceud Mille a Failte (E4 6a) at Larbrax, a leftover project from the Lancashire team. While the following year saw two fine extremes at Larbrax from Fraser (now teamed up with Ian Magill), the last great problem was clearly the unclimbed right-hand slab. This thin and bold undertaking was climbed in 2000 by Julian Lines to give Elegance (E6/7 6c), Galloway's hardest route to date.

That the old order was finally changing was also evident from the activities of Martin Whitaker, Pat Cocks, Iain Weir and friends in 1999 and 2000. These Sheffield-based climbers rampaged across the south-west sea-cliffs, visiting most of the existing cliffs and recording some 70 new routes. High-spots were probably Born to Boogie (E1 5a) on the Red Slab at Meikle Ross; the development of the crags south of Crammag Head; and some 36 routes on the Carrickcorie crags of the Mull of Galloway, including the memorable An Arm and a Leg (E1 5b) and the fine Anemone Action (VS 4c). While many of these routes are in the easier grades, the sheer number of new routes is testimony to the amount of new rock left in the area.

Much of 2001 was dominated by crag closures occasioned by the foot and mouth outbreak. Fraser, Magill and Alasdair Gillies, followed the crag opening timetable with a series of routes at Garheugh, Portobello and Larbrax including Jack the Kipper (E2 5c) and Trapdoor Fandango (E2 5c). When Garheugh Port had been developed in the mid-'80s, extensive bouldering had been done by Carlisle and Dumfries based climbers, but not recorded. This left Dave Redpath and friends to fully develop and document the extensive bouldering.

2002 to 2004 were quiet years, although contrasting climbs on the Rhinns from Fraser, Gillies and Magill perhaps provide an indicator of future trends. Portobello Belle (E3 5c), and Axis of Weasels (HVS) at Crammag, showed that the developed cliffs could still reveal gems. By contrast, Fortress Slab (HVS), and the development of the unexpected Fish Kettle were new crags, which had remained undiscovered on isolated stretches of coast.

Galloway Hills 1998 - 2004
Andrew Fraser & Stephen Reid

The period from 1998 to date has seen significant development of the Galloway hills. As in 1990/1991, Lakes-based climber, Stephen Reid was to be the main protagonist, albeit ably assisted by John Biggar and 'the secret weapon' of Chris King. First however, it was Colin Hossack, who in 1998 discovered the pleasant and easily accessible Corwar, hidden in the Galloway forests. Combinations of Hossack, Reid and Andean veteran John Biggar scrubbed the crag clean to give a number of excellent routes including the Peach (HVS), Plum Line (E2 5b) and Corwar Wall (HVS 5a).

Craig an Eilte on Cairnsmore of Fleet was also reassessed, providing a further nine routes, the best of which are probably Y Geifr (HVS 5a) from Reid and Biggar in 2000 and In the Hall of the Mountain King (VS) from Reid and King in 2002. 2000 saw the start of development of the previously unapproachable Craigdews, ten minutes from the A712. Reid negotiated a lifting of the goat park access restrictions, unaware that Fraser and Magill were surreptitiously developing the crag with Goats of Delirium (HVS 5a) and Amazing Technicolour Dreamgoat (E1 5b).

2001 started cold, with Hell Freezes Over (IV,5), a winter ascent of the plum but rarely in condition Cooran Buttress on Dungeon Hill by Fraser and Magill. At the other end of the year, when most sensible people were again dreaming of snow, Reid, Biggar and King completely overhauled Clints of Dromore with 17 new routes including the fine Make my Day (E1 5a) on the overlooked Black and White Walls.

2002 proved to be a golden year in the hills, with the Reid/King team in full flow. The Dungeon Hill saw a renaissance, with 15 new routes, including Horns of a Dilemma (HVS) from Fraser and Magill; Castles in the Air (HVS) from Reid and Mike Cundy; Sprauchlers Groove (VS) from John and Linda Biggar; and Aughty Star (E1 or E2 if you brave the skin-rasping off-width finish), Snakes and Ladders (E1) and the verglassed Bickerdike's Buttress (VS), all from Reid and King. To the remote Tauchers Reid and King also added the finger-searing Dragonslayer (E3) and Smaug (E2), while Loch Grannoch crag was also blitzed in a day by the same team. 2003 saw the rediscovery of Craiglee by Reid and Biggar, while King and Reid beat the 2004 guidebook deadline with Thin It Is (E2), Craigdew's last great problem.

Until this guide, winter climbing in the Galloway hills has been an unknown commodity, restrained by the short winter season, and a lack of appreciation that the copious vegetation was ideal for ice smears and a Southern Highlands style of technical mixed/turf climbing. In January 2003 Craignaw saw continuing development, including The Sleigh Team (III,4) from Fraser and Magill, Hidden Chimney (IV,5) from Reid and Alan Hinkes, and Silver Sliver (IV,3) from Hinkes and Steve Prior. Hinkes's performance was understandably hindered by having to take mobile calls from Kathmandu whilst engaged in the climbing! Elsewhere, the notable routes were Flowers of the Forest (III,4) on Craig an Eilte, and the four pitch ice of The Lang Scots Miles (IV,-4) on The Merrick, both from Fraser and Magill.

The Borders & Dumfries: 1998 - 2004

Pickings at these outcrops have been thin since the last guide. At Clifton, Reid and others added ten routes between Severe and E1. In the grassy Lowther hills, Ian Scobie, John Smith and Alastair Carruthers developed the unexpected Craighoar crag. Fatlips Crag near Hawick received several additions, the most impressive of these being the serious Crest of a Knave (E3 5c) from Mark Lyons. A number of worthwhile II/III icefalls have also been recorded in the Moffat Hills, providing good alternatives when the Grey Mare's Tail is unfrozen.

Away from the mainstream however, were the bouldering activities of Paul

Savage. In terms of technical difficulty, his problems at Thirlstane, Sandyhills and Clifton dwarf anything else in this area. At the time of writing, My Evil Twin (Font 8a/8a+) at Sandyhills, and Chinese Democracy (Font 8a) at Thirlstane, are reckoned to be the hardest and third hardest problems in Scotland.

In spite of these developments, Galloway remains a backwater, probably the least frequented climbing area in Britain. There are too many distractions, such as long approaches across floating bogs, uncooperative bird life, tide or sea conditions or unfamiliarity with the subtleties of greywacke. Ultimately however, it is this element of uncertainty and adventure which is the area's main attraction. Given that tremendous opportunities still remain for exploratory climbing on the sea-cliffs, it is likely that future developments will continue to expand the number of venues. Who knows what that next walk down the coast or into the hills will reveal?

Stirling Area: 1970 - 1993

Craig Macadam & Roger Everett

Though the rambling cliffs of the Ochils have been scrambled upon in the dim and distant past, the first real climbing in the area took place in the mid-1970s when Bob Conway and friends from the naval base at Rosyth climbed a series of routes on The Wallace Monument cliffs. However, during a cleaning session a large block ended up on the road below the cliff resulting in a ban which continues to this day.

The steep and sheltered walls of Wolfcrag Quarry made it a fine training ground in the pre-climbing wall days. The first routes and boulder problems were done by Dave Powers who lived in Bridge of Allan, while Neil Morrison belayed and seconded Powers on what are now The Arete and a line approximating to that of Kalahari. Morrison also introduced Pete Billsborough and Allan Pettit to the crag and they adopted it as their own. In order to maximise the training potential, lines of holds were later chipped all over the quarry wall, much to the horror of Morrison, who had spent the summer of 1979 working and eventually cracking the then desperate low level traverse.

Ian Duckworth led Leonardo and Ian's Wa' before Tony Kay took over as the main activist with ascents of Up on the Catwalk, Experiments in Incest and (after some jiggery pokery) Tribal Look. In the late 1980s, Craig Macadam soloed Waterfront and The Outsider (one of the quarry's few all natural routes) and Ron Cowel led Lock-it and Thirty Frames a Second.

In the early 1980s more cliffs were discovered and Cowels in particular deserves credit for the discovery of North Third, Limekilns in Fife and Thorntons Quarry at Cambusbarron. At North Third, Cowels was responsible for cleaning and climbing most of the routes to give a fine series of crack climbs, including the superb diagonal crack of Red Shift, later freed by Gary Latter.

Thorntons Quarry, Cambusbarron received its first route in 1983 when Kay and Cowels climbed Big Country Dreams, with one rest point. This very fine climb soon attracted other climbers to the quarry. In early 1984 Murray Hamilton free-climbed Big Country Dreams and went on to add Formica Crack, and Murray's Corner, while Rab Anderson added Fuel for Thought. An intense May Day weekend's activity led to Oink Oink (which subsequently fell down, leaving the smooth chimney of what is now Pig Route), Quantum Grunt (since made harder by the unnatural disappearance of a small tree used by the first ascentionists at the start) and the intriguing Both Ends Burning from Duncan McCallum, Graham Pedley and Kenny Spence.

Craig Macadam led Visions of Monaco and Purr-Blind Doomster, the latter being straightened out by McCallum before being led without the in situ protection by Spence. The last big climb of the summer was Gary Latter's route Power of Endurance. As well as the routes, Graham Livingstone added a number of worthwhile boulder problems, of which Spanking the Monkey was both bold and impressive for its time.

Of the less important cliffs Dollar Quarry was developed by Jamie Main in 1981.

It gave some worthwhile climbs (particularly Applause from The Gallery and Energy Transfer), but has since fallen into neglect due partly to the dirty and often dangerous top outs.

McCallum was busy again in Thorntons Quarry in 1985, sticking his neck out on The Crowd, while Rab Anderson added Economy Drive. The following year Anderson added three routes including the aptly-named Thug of War. The most significant development around this time was the landscaping of Fourth Quarry to create a sheltered, sunny and fast drying crag with a pleasant outlook - quite unlike most of the other central belt quarries.

Some of the best routes here were the mid grade classics established on the fine Easy Contract buttress. Although the tally of routes in the quarry had by now increased dramatically from only one (Easy Contract) listed in the 1986 Guidebook to just under twenty, scope clearly remained for more – especially if work on the scale required to construct Chisel (a blatant rock sculpture) was applied to more of the thin crack lines.

Stirling Area: 1993 - 2004

Mark Robson

While the number of routes in the two Cambusbarron quarries doubled during this period, there was a decline at many of the other crags in the Stirling area, such as North Third (despite being home to such excellent routes as Red Shift) and Dollar Quarry.

The exception was at Wolfcrag Quarry, Bridge of Allan. Although only a handful of new routes were added to Wolfcrag (by Gordon Lennox and Craig Adam in the mid '90s), the quarry saw a huge growth in popularity for bouldering. Thanks to John Craven, this publication incorporates the first attempt at documenting some of the many superb boulder problems and low level traverses to be found there.

At Fourth Quarry and Thorntons Quarry, Cambusbarron, developments continued to gather pace. In Fourth Quarry the omission of several routes from the previous guidebook led to some confusion and multiple first ascent claims to Cross in Oz; Cross Town Traffic; Pipistrelle; and Ramplin' – all the handiwork of brothers Raymond and Allan Wallace in 1993. Of these, the converging cracks of Cross in Oz and Cross Town Traffic proved particularly popular. Another focus for conflicting activity was the Easy Contract buttress where a number of minor variations to both Easy Contract and Not Easy Contract were claimed. In 1995 this buttress also saw the addition of the rather good Bo's Girdle by Craig Adam and Gordon Lennox.

By 1996 exploration away from the main walls had begun in earnest and Mark Worsley and T.Wood found The Rock of Crack and Confessions of a Speed Freak high on the west wall. Earlier that year the same pair had cleaned and climbed Bird's Nest Crack – a line attempted three years earlier by Allan Wallace, but unfinished due to loose rock. In April of the following year, Gordon Lennox made the first ascent of Production Line without recourse to the in situ pegs for protection.

In 1999, Mark Somerville appeared on the scene and, as well as duplicating the Wallace brothers' 1993 efforts, claimed a number of lines including the bold Arse on Stumps and Looney Tunes. In 2000 he returned to give the quarry its first sport route, Scales of Injustice. The following year saw the addition of Public Spirited Individual, a fine line by R.Welch, A.Marr and Michael Tweedley which followed a heavily cleaned crack system. At this time routes were put up in the previously untouched area to the left of Scaresville (Thank God for Friends and Buttons, courtesy of Alan Pert and partners), while Scaresville itself had a new variation start added by Pert and S.Burge. This replaced the earlier variation start which had lost its crucial flake.

After a break of almost a decade, Allan Wallace renewed his interest in Fourth Quarry in 2002, climbing The Cutter and Toddle. Dubious rock featured on both and the latter, bravely(?!) tackled cracks to the right of the tottering pillar which had repulsed demolition attempts by local youths involving a moped and a length of fencing. A year later, Gareth Hughs and partners narrowly escaped accident on this part of the crag when two huge blocks parted company from the top of Doobie Brothers just to the left.

Finally, 2004 saw one of the best new additions in the quarry, Le Bal des Oiseaux Fantomes, climbed by the Wallace brothers. They cracked the problem without using the gear placement manufactured two years earlier during a failed attempt by others.

In Thorntons, as had been the case in Fourth Quarry, a number of lines received multiple claims. However this time the confusion was not so widespread and related largely to easier lines on the buttress now home to Bo's Groove and Bo's Arete; first climbed in 1996 by Craig Adam and Gordon Lennox. A direct version of the arete was soloed by Adam on the same day. More significantly, 1996 also saw Lennox and Adam lay claim to the area's first E7, Anabolic Steroids, although the grade later settled at E6 following the appearance of two good holds at the crux after blocks fell out of the crack during repeats by Steve Richardson and Niall McNair. A couple of months later Lennox returned, this time with D.Parr, to take up the challenge of the large corner of Contortionism.

Activity was limited over the next five years or so. Dave MacLeod made a couple of forays into Thorntons adding The Bustup and In Hiding (which soon reverted to such) and Lennox produced Auto Giro (1998), based around the arete of Adulterer's Repentance. On the west wall, the obvious open groove of Moving Shadows escaped attention until 2001 when Michael Tweedley and Lee Byrnes laid it to rest (with a peg for protection). This year also saw the first bolts placed in Thorntons Quarry when the same pair created Tarzan. This only climbed as far as the large ledge and a bolted lower-off. The bolts were later removed and the line climbed to the top by Adam (2003), who offered Cheetah as an alternative name.

The very dry summer of 2003 also saw Raymond and Allan Wallace succeed on the often damp crack of Dr Dre's Orgazmatron which had been cleaned by various parties over the years (as far back as 1986 judging by the Malteser packet found stuffed in the crack). However, the real breakthrough occurred in 2004 when Gordon Lennox cracked Nandrolone bringing the area its first E8. Dave MacLeod repeated the route not long afterwards, placing all the gear on the lead and confirming both the grade and solid three star status.

2004 also saw the addition of the first sport route in the quarry when Simon Munro controversially bolted up the crack and arete of Sexed Up, as well as adding a new problem, Jerkin' the Gherkin, to the Spanking the Monkey block. Finally, armed with a bouldering mat and eternal enthusiasm, the Wallace brothers added a series of micro routes to the short walls at the east side of the quarry as well as returning with a rope to claim Gun Fury.

Whilst details have not yet surfaced, there are rumours of exploration now taking place in the neighbouring and massive Murrayshall Quarry and it remains to be seen whether this will provide the next set of challenges for climbers in the area, or whether Fourth and Thorntons quarries are still not quite worked out.

Fife, Edinburgh Area, East Lothian & Berwickshire Coast: 1890 - 1993

Jerry Handren & Grahame Nicoll

Most of the early activity in the Edinburgh area centred around the cliffs of Holyrood Park. Indeed until the late 1940s this area was the scene of a series of developments which marked it as one of the main forcing grounds in Scotland. Harold Raeburn was the first to explore the possibilities. The 1896 SMC Journal includes an article and map by him detailing some 20 climbs on the Salisbury Crags. Around 1900 he made ascents of Fallen Column climb and the vicious central crack on the Dassies, while on Salisbury Crags he found a fine route up the buttress to the right of the Cat Nick. W.Inglis Clark, in the SMCJ of 1900, used photo-diagrams for perhaps the first time for a Scottish outcrop, and included a photograph of an early ascent of Raeburn's Cracked Slabs Route.

These routes, together with Collier's Climb up the left-hand buttress of the Cat Nick, paved the way for the epic ascent of Great Buttress (originally 'Eastern Buttress of the Great Quarry') in 1902. Climbed by Morrison, Newbigging and the Swiss guide Briquet, this route caused quite a stir at the time, not so much for the difficulty of the climbing as for the steep, exposed and loose nature of the rock.

The 1914-18 war left a long shadow over Scottish climbing and it was not until the 1930s that activity began to pick up again. Around this time Jimmy Hewit, Alan Horne and Archie Hendry added a series of routes to the area around the South Quarry on Salisbury Crags. Hewit's Groove, Horne's Slab and Archie's Slab all gave climbing at VS/HVS standard at a time when few cliffs in Scotland could offer any routes harder than Severe. Apart from the usual problems of dubious rock and no protection these climbers now had to contend with a ban on climbing which had come into operation after the Great War, and which has undoubtedly contributed to the general lack of awareness of the historical significance of the climbing here. In 1939 Hewit wrote a guide to the crags, unfortunately never published, but which formed the basis of the comprehensive guide of the late '40s by J.G.Parish, C.G.M.Slesser and D.H.Haworth, and also of a selective E.U.M.C. guide of around 1950.

As the 1940s approached a strong group of climbers from Edinburgh University appeared on the scene. The main activist was D.H.Haworth. Despite being a relatively obscure character nowadays he made an important contribution to Scottish climbing, with a string of classic routes throughout the mountain areas. He made many first ascents in Holyrood Park, the finest of which was undoubtedly Steeplejack's Staircase, the original route in the Great Quarry at Salisbury Crags. As with many other hard routes of the day it was top-roped prior to its ascent; nevertheless it was probably the hardest route in the country at the time, and went unrepeated for nearly 15 years before Jimmy Marshall and Robin Smith made the second and third ascents. Both found the route very near their limit at the time.

In the early 1950s Geoff Dutton discovered the pleasant crags on the southern flank of Traprain Law and with the Edinburgh J.M.C.S. climbed a few of the easier lines. In 1955, Robin Smith, the Marshall brothers and the 'Currie Boys' began to take an interest and soon the cliff was covered with a network of pleasant routes on good rock. Smith led Burp and Chute and Jimmy Marshall led Wobble, and Piglet by its left-hand variation. As well as these harder routes many of the classic easier routes such as Great Corner, Left Edge and M.S. Route were first climbed during this period. The same group also explored the cliffs of Dalmahoy Hill, but unlike Traprain the routes here were rather loose and vegetated and the cliff was quickly forgotten.

After this brief period of activity things remained quiet until new faces began to emerge in the early 1960s. Dave Bathgate, Bugs McKeith, Brian Robertson and Ian MacEacheran formed the nucleus of a group of climbers that later became The Squirrels. In 1962 they discovered and developed The Hawcraig, a steep sea-cliff on the Fife coast. MacEacheran climbed Gaucho, Cranium Crack and The Beast, while Bathgate made ascents of Squirrel Slab, Diptera and, with McKeith, the High Girdle. Neil MacNiven climbed Pain Pillar, still the classic route of the cliff, and Jim Brumfitt climbed Guano, which was probably the hardest of those earlier routes.

During the mid '60s climbers began to explore the more extensive sea-cliffs of the Fast Castle area. Ian Campbell had described some scrambling traverses by the Fast Castle in 1935, but the first real development was a series of routes on Fast Castle Head itself, climbed by a group of Newcastle climbers led by Gordon Davidson. That same year (1965) Dave Bathgate climbed the impressive sea stack of The Souter by its landward face, and a year later returned with the rest of the Squirrels to climb some interesting routes in the very secluded bay to the east of the Brander. John Cleare visited the area while researching for his book Sea-Cliff Climbing in Britain and added a route up the seaward face of The Souter. Despite all this activity the climbing on this stretch of coast did not become popular with the majority of local climbers, and the area was not included in Graham Tiso's guide to *Creag Dubh and the Eastern Outcrops*, published in 1967.

After the publication of this guide only a few minor routes were added to the traditional crags, though 'Lord' John Mackenzie's free ascent of Beatle Crack at Traprain was a fair achievement. It soon became obvious that Traprain and Hawcraig had little more to offer as far as new routes were concerned and development remained at a standstill, until attention turned to the many dolerite quarries dotted around the region.

In 1972 local climbers from Rosyth began to develop Rosyth Quarry, just over the Forth road bridge. Ravelrig Quarry was a better find. This was developed during 1973 by members of the M.E.S.L. Mountaineering Club, with Chris Masterton in particular being responsible for many of the routes. Routes such as Headline, Beeline and Demo route were found to give good climbing on solid rock, and the cliff quickly became popular. Pete Myles and Alistair Borthwick climbed Plumbline using a few nuts for aid, and Masterton later made a free ascent to establish one of the best routes in the area. Unfortunately in 1979 the local landowner blew up the Plumbline wall, totally destroying Plumbline and its neighbouring routes.

Around the same time members of The Jacobite M.C. began to add routes at Rosyth Quarry. Willie Jeffrey was the main activist with routes such as Waullie, Iconoclast and Inspiration, which all gave quite hard climbing. The Jacobites also made the first inroads into Ratho Quarry, perhaps the biggest and most imposing of the local quarries. Willie Jeffrey again made some good ascents including Shear Fear. This and Murray Hamilton's free ascent of Rained In at Ravelrig at about the same time were the first routes in the area to improve on the standard set by Haworth in 1946.

In 1975 members of the Edinburgh J.M.C.S. re-discovered the cliff on Dalmahoy Hill. After an extended gardening session they completed around 20 routes, most of which gave good climbing on rough rock. The only evidence of the passing of the Currie Boys some 20 years previously was a couple of rusty pitons on what is now called Resurrection.

Despite all this activity the quarries had so far only yielded rather scrappy and uninteresting routes (apart from the better climbs at Ravelrig). Climbers lost interest and once again development stood still. During the next five years, while the rest of Scotland was being shaken by an explosion of new routes and rising standards, the Edinburgh cliffs remained quiet. Combinations of Rab Anderson, Dave Brown and Murray Hamilton climbed Grinding, Wheelchair Route and Snowflake Crack at Ravelrig, and Murray Hamilton and Dave Cuthbertson added a few eliminate lines at Hawcraig, but otherwise little was achieved.

In 1980 the quiet was rudely shattered when Pete Hunter made a superb series of ascents at Ratho Quarry. Doomed Oasis covered some impressive ground but Diverticulitis and Pettifer's Wall were really fine routes, giving the hardest and best climbing in the area at the time. The following year he returned to add Sahara, Ouroborus Eliminate and Pete's Wall. In March and April 1981, unknown to locals, a group of Northumberland based climbers added a fine series of routes to the Brander area of Fast Castle. Kevin Howett, in particular, made some fine ascents with routes such as Blue Moves, Sea Sprite and the suicidally loose Lucky Day. Though these events passed more or less unnoticed, local climbers began to re-assess the area and soon came to realise that there was plenty of scope for good new routes.

Limekilns, two limestone blocks hidden in the woods on the Fife side of the Firth of Forth, was a unique find by Stirling area climber Ron Cowals. The first route here was Humbug by Martin Bennett in 1981, then Tony Kay, Neil Morrison and Derek Claxton swooped in to exploit the potential. Morrison led Cruel Summer, New Gold Dream, Colours Fly and The Struggler whilst Tony Kay added most of the eliminate lines on the Humbug face and the fine arete of Methods of Dance. Cowels eventually got in on the act with Marley's Ghost but by now all eyes had turned to the two superb cracks splitting the overhanging north face of the Sentinel. These held out until early 1984 when Kenny Spence led Velvet Glove and John McKenzie led Iron Fist. The year 1984 also saw the addition of first route to the Gellet Block, Allan Pettit's Elgin's Crack.

In March 1982 the short walls surrounding The Souter saw a sudden burst of activity. Kenny Spence was the first to spot the potential, but it was John (Spider) McKenzie who grabbed the best routes with his ascents of Fast Bleeder and Walnut. Rab Anderson, Bob Duncan, Jim Melrose, Jerry Handren and Alan Taylor got involved and in the space of a few weekends about 20 routes had been climbed. Though many of these routes are quite short they give good steep climbing in an unusual setting, and perhaps deserve to become more popular.

That summer Gordon Bisset climbed the excellent Golden Brown at Ravelrig and on the same crag Pete Hunter freed the old bolt route to give The Prowler. At Ratho Rab Anderson led Slow Strain and in the East Bay Kenny Spence climbed a very fine and unusual route which he later named Gruel Brittania. By now it was obvious that there really was a great deal to be done and a gold rush mentality began to develop. In August Spence, Hamilton, Anderson and Handren added another batch of routes to The Souter area. The best of these was Souterrain by Spence, though Hamilton climbed a serious route up the wall to the right of Walnut to give The Porker's Wall – the first E4 in the area. A point worth mentioning is that the routes at Fast Castle and Ratho required mammoth gardening sessions to reveal solid rock before ascents were possible. The lessons learned in the process were put to good use in the development of other areas in the future.

Spence scoured the countryside for new rock and came up with Benarty Hill. That September he climbed Cubism to give the crag its first route and at the same time cleaned off several other lines. During the winter months Salisbury Crags are often to be found bone dry and basking in the sun. That winter the temptation of so much rock so close at hand proved too much, and after a series of night-time gardening sessions Jerry Handren added three routes to the area around Steeplejack's Staircase. This effort proved worthwhile and, despite the attentions of the Park Police, these routes have since become very popular.

1983 was a bumper year. Again it was Kenny Spence who led the field. In early April he led Wally 1 at Ratho and with Rab Anderson began to snatch up the remaining lines. Anderson led Welcome to the Cruise, Ane Ledge and Rebel without Claws, but it was Spence who took the best lines with his ascents of Wallies 2 and 3, Artho, and the superb This Septic Heil – the hardest route in the quarry. The only climbers to intrude on this monopoly were Jim Melrose with Time's Last Gift, Jerry Handren with the Lone Groover and Gerry Rooney with Beanpud. Pete Hunter's routes at last got the popularity they deserved and almost all the new routes saw several repeat ascents. Thus in the space of a few months Ratho had become one of the best and most popular crags in the area.

Spence returned to Benarty Hill to climb the lines which he had cleaned the previous year. Dolly Parton followed a horrific wide crack, not dissimilar in appearance to the great lady's cleavage. The two other routes – Ram and A Fist Job were both led by John McKenzie.

That summer, Spence tackled the tremendous north side of The Souter, a line which had been looked at by several other notables. The resulting route – Squid Vicious – turned out to be one of the best in the area, giving a very strenuous and serious climb. Towards the end of the summer the pace of development began to slow down a little. During work for the guide Bruce Kerr led two old top-rope problems at Ravelrig to give Men at Work and Overkill. Jerry Handren climbed Prime Cut to give Queensferry Quarry its first route and in October added three more routes at Salisbury Crags to give Transatlantic Trip, Blackdance and After the Axe.

During the autumn yet another new crag was developed. This time it was Rab Anderson and Duncan McCallum who cleaned and climbed the first routes at Lennie Quarry. Though only six miles from the centre of Edinburgh, an evil pool at the base of the main wall had discouraged many would-be explorers. Nevertheless routes such as Dive in Movie, Think Sink and Dunker's Delight gave good climbing in an exciting position.

By 1984 activity seemed to have slowed down as climbers began to explore other areas, particularly the newly developing Stirling outcrops. Perhaps the most notable event was the draining of Lennie Quarry, which immediately became very popular. New routes soon followed with Duncan McCallum leading Staying Alive and Chris Dale The Creature from the Black Lagoon. Later in the year Rab Anderson led White Tide and Murray Hamilton led Hard Contract, a very fine climb which had stopped several strong attempts and been the scene of at least one spectacular failure. In early 1985 Lennie received another batch of new routes, but the most important event was undoubtedly John McKenzie's superb lead of Staying Alive without using the two bolts that McCallum had placed for protection.

The summer of 1985 was very poor and few routes were added. At Lennie Quarry Murray Hamilton added Tar McCallum, a hard layback problem, while at Ratho Quarry the wall left of Godzilla finally received an ascent by Duncan McCallum, resulting in The Blob. The bouldering areas saw a large proportion of the climbing activity in the east in 1985, the indefatigable Ken Spence being responsible for yet another significant addition with the cleaning of the Lennie bouldering wall.

The same year saw considerable activity at the Gellet Block at Limekilns, with the number of routes increasing to over 20, many being the work of D.Baker, A.Borthwick, A.McCord, D.Moffat and M.Russell. Of the harder routes, the generally acknowledged classic would seem to be Duncan McCallum's Ivy League, Murray Hamilton being responsible for The Charleston to the left.

The 1986 edition of the guide did not contain any routes at Roslin Glen, where developments had taken place in secret. Kenny Spence and Gerry Rooney started their explorations in June 1985, but it was not until January 1987 (40 routes later) that the area was publicised in *Mountain* magazine. John 'Spider' McKenzie and Rab Anderson had been let into the secret, but it was Spence who had picked the plums – Hanging Rock, The Wrinklies, Plunging Neckline, Piano Player and Duncrankin are all his work. However, two of the best routes, Beyond Traprain and Gaping Gap, were later found to have been climbed (but not recorded) by Pete Hunter in 1980. This was around the same time that he put up Diverticulitis and Pettifer's Wall at Ratho. Beyond Traprain, at E4 6b, was an outstanding achievement for 1980. It is also worth mentioning that Willie Jeffrey had put up the first recorded route (Centre Line) four years earlier, and it seems likely that there were other unrecorded ascents even earlier.

Rosyth Quarry received little more than a passing mention in the 1986 guide. However, the quarry has some good routes and remained popular despite the lack of information. A few additions have been made over the years, but 1986 saw the best and certainly the hardest with Ian Cropley's free ascent of Matinee Cracks.

Undoubtedly the most significant events in the late 1980s in this area was the loss of several crags. Lennie Quarry, which had become very popular since being drained, began to get filled in, and over the following four years the routes diminished in height until only the top few moves were available as boulder problems.

In September 1987 Tarmac applied for planning permission to start quarrying at Ravelrig and Dalmahoy. Permission was granted, and Ravelrig was soon filled in with waste. The cliffs at Dalmahoy survive, but in a markedly inferior environment. Sadly, as a result of extensive cleaning, litter and offensive graffiti the landowner took steps to restrict access to Limekilns in the same year – a prime example of a minority of mindless climbers spoiling it for everyone. A high fence was erected round the blocks, the holds were liberally smeared with grease and estate staff began to patrol the area. The only good news was that Traprain Law was bought by East Lothian District Council, thereby securing its future as a climbing venue.

The expected popularity of Roslin Glen, after its divulgence in Mountain, failed to materialise. The climbing is an acquired taste, not to everyone's liking. However, a few enthusiasts (notably Rick Campbell and Owen Hayward) continued development through 1988, raising standards in the process. The high point was Hayward's lead of Röslin Roulette, after extensive top-rope practice. This ethic has become the norm on Roslin's friable and poorly protected sandstone.

In the spring of 1988, Rab Anderson started the development of North Berwick Law quarry (although it was Spence who had first noted its potential). The first route followed a line of old bolts of unknown origin, then a further six routes were added on the steep main wall, mostly with bolts for protection. These bolts seem to have been cordially accepted, and the crag has become very popular. More recently, a couple of eliminate routes have been added, and more bolts added at the top to aid lowering off. In contrast to the bolted lines at North Berwick, in 1989 two very bold new routes were established. After a long cleaning session, Bruce Kerr led the friable Twilight Hour on the Cockleshell Fin at the Fast Castle sea-cliffs, and Rick Campbell soloed the short but very hard Hezbollah at Roslin, after top-rope practice.

In April 1990, the Chimpanzee Fin at The Souter (Fast Castle) was discovered, and by August seven fine little routs had been completed, all the work of Malcolm Smith, Paul Thorburn, Rick Campbell and Ian Dawson. On another sea-cliff, The Hawkcraig at Aberdour, Psylocibie was squeezed into the gap between Gaucho and Rebel's Groove. This is typical of several poor eliminates that continue to be claimed at both Aberdour and Traprain Law, but many of these have almost certainly been climbed previously and thought unworthy of recording.

New route activity increased in 1991, perhaps due to the rumour that a new guide was about to be produced! Jamie Andrew, unemployed at the time, was particularly productive. Having climbed most of the existing routes at Holyrood Park, he started adding routes of his own, and together with Al Matthewson he filled in many of the gaps at Roslin Glen. Most of these were the easier lines which had been overlooked by previous parties. Down at Fast Castle, the wide space at the right-hand end of The Brander was filled by Matthewson's Bouma Sequence and Up-helly-aa, and Andrew's Ancient Mariner – three fine but not too well protected routes that deserve to become popular.

The bad news in 1991 came when Whimpey Asphalt applied for planning permission to in-fill Ratho Quarry. The MCofS and many individuals submitted objections, and for once the outcome was favourable: Wimpey withdrew their application in April 1992. Another notable event at Ratho took place soon afterwards, when Jamie Andrew managed to re-climb Sahara, an excellent route that had remained unclimbed since the loss of a crucial flake. This is now the toughest route in the quarry.

Meanwhile, at Roslin, the stick men Paul Thorburn and Rick Campbell were working on a string of exceedingly difficult new routes, which culminated in Thorburn's ascent of Walk on By, probably the hardest route in this area. Mention must also be made of the first ascent of the impressive Lover's Leap Cliff by Jamie Andrew. More good routes were also being done at The Brander, particularly Drop the Pilot by George McIntyre and Voyage of the Mad Manxman by Bruce Kerr. McIntyre also completed the first route at Midden Crag, just north of Fast Castle.

In comparison, 1993 was a quiet year for new routes, although access issues were once again to the fore. The Deep Sea World at North Queensferry Quarry opened for business, effectively halting climbing there, and Ratho was once again under threat, this time from the M8 extension. On a brighter note, discussions regarding access to Salisbury Crags were underway.

Fife, Edinburgh Area, East Lothian & Berwickshire Coast: 1993 - 2004

Tom Prentice

The biggest development during this decade was the development of the Adventure Centre at Ratho Quarry. Threats to in-fill and from the M8 extension had threatened the quarry's future, but its purchase and subsequent development into the largest climbing wall venue in the world, appeared to secure its future.

Unfortunately, things have not turned out as planned. Not long after opening The Adventure Centre went into receivership and at the time of publication of this guide the future for Ratho remained uncertain. The loss of this fantastic climbing wall and the traditional routes in the quarry outside would be a disaster. One can only hope that should the centre close to climbers we will fight any such proposals to the bitter end and be victorious.

The Adventure Centre development did not leave the quarry walls unscathed and the first half dozen climbs on the West Wall, including The Blob, Godzilla, Sahara and Doomed Oasis were incorporated into the indoor arena and significantly altered. In the rest of the quarry there were surprisingly few changes, although lack of climbers over five years made its mark on some routes. Ratho has a sunny aspect and dries quickly, so hopefully the routes outside will become popular again.

Elsewhere in the Edinburgh area restrictions were relaxed at Salisbury Crags' South Quarry and it is hoped that access will increase in the future. The cliffs are a fabulous and undeveloped resource for local climbers

At The Hawkcraig on the Fife coast, many of the gaps and eliminates referred to in the previous history have now been documented. This is such a popular cliff that it is unlikely that some have not been climbed before. Further west at Rosyth Quarry a few new routes have filled the gaps, while at Limekilns, small numbers of climbers have made low profile forays back to the blocks where the grease had begun to disappear. But the access situation remained volatile and unresolved.

The Berwickshire coast saw sporadic development through the late 1990s. In spring 1996 Mark Robson, Tracy Ward, Brian Ottewell and Janet Vince added a number of routes on the previously unclimbed faces of the Second Sight Fin and the Doll Fin. The following year Bruce Kerr spearheaded the development of the small walls in the vicinity of Dowlaw Dean. In 2001 attention turned to the cliffs round Cove, with four routes added by T.Pitcairn and A.Smith.

As usual, just as the guide was going to print, Robson noticed mention of an unclimbed sea-stack while checking the page proofs of the Cove section. A quick call to Simon Richardson in Aberdeen and the stack – Hollow Rock – was swiftly despatched. Further investigation that same day led the team further south to Burnmouth and the altogether more impressive and unclimbed Breeches Rock near the Maiden's Stone. Undoubtedly the coast still holds considerable scope for unclimbed rock and exploration.

The biggest change in this section of the guide was the addition of more than 70 new routes to crags in the East Lothian area. The sea-cliff at Dunbar received passing mention in the previous guide but now has four sport routes. The rock is sandy and soft and makes for slightly disappointing climbing. The bolts have a covering of anti-corrosive paint, but how long they will last is anyone's guess. No more than a decade, judging by the bolts on Celebration Day and the abandoned projects nearby.

Apart from re-bolting and re-equipping at North Berwick Law and the addition of a couple new sport routes, most of the new route activity at this crag has been traditional. Through 1996 and for the next few years Adrian Plumb, Mike Balharry and others added a range of middle to lower grade routes to the small walls beyond the Main Face. Of these, Neck It or Deck It (HVS 4c) and Mr Slappy (VS 4c) on the unprotected Westy Slab are worth a particular mention. The rock is not above suspicion in places and the top-outs require care, but North Berwick Law now has something for everyone.

In 1997 Plumb turned his attention to the massive quarry on the north side of Traprain Law. The result was a handful of traditional multi-pitch outings of a serious nature in impressive surroundings; some of the longest routes in the area. By 2002 he had moved on to the small, roadside Yellow Craigs and Craigy Hill further north, climbing mostly with his son Oisin. Craigy Hill offers a range of routes in the lower grades and faces south-east – a worthwhile addition to the area.

Although the additions in this section have not been as extensive as elsewhere in this guide it is clear that new rock and routes can be found by anyone with an interest, or prepared to look at established areas from a different perspective.

Environment

With ever larger numbers of walkers and climbers going to the Scottish hills, countryside and coasts, it is important that all who do so recognise their responsibilities to those who live and work in these environments, to our fellow climbers and to the environment in which we find our pleasure and recreation.

The Scottish Mountaineering Club and Scottish Mountaineering Trust, who jointly produce this and other guidebooks, wish to point out that it is in everybody's interests that good relations are maintained between visitors and landowners.

Access

The Land Reform (Scotland) Act 2003 established a statutory right of responsible access over all land and inland water in Scotland for the purpose of recreation and passage, subject to certain exclusions. The Scottish Outdoor Access Code provides detailed guidance on the responsible use of these rights.

- Take responsibility for your actions;
- Respect people's privacy and peace of mind;
- Help land managers and others work safely and effectively;
- Look after your environment;
- Keep your dog under proper control;
- Take care if you are organising an event or running a business.

The stag stalking season is from 1st July to 20th October, although many estates don't start at the beginning of the season. Hinds continue to be culled until 15th February. The grouse shooting season is from 12th August until 10th December, although the end of the season is less used. It is also important to avoid disturbance to sheep, particularly during lambing from March to May.

The Mountaineering Council of Scotland (see below) and Scottish Natural Heritage operate a Hillphones service giving daily recorded information of the location of stalking on some estates in the popular hillwalking areas.

Footpath Erosion

The number of walkers and climbers on the hills is leading to increased footpath erosion. Part of the revenue from the sale of this and other Scottish Mountaineering Club books is granted by the Scottish Mountaineering Trust as financial assistance towards the repair and maintenance of hill paths in Scotland.

As a general rule, if a path exists then try to stay on it. If the path is wet and muddy avoid walking along its edges as this only extends the erosion sideways. Do not take short-cuts at the corners of zigzag paths. The worst effects of erosion are likely to be caused during or soon after prolonged wet weather when the ground is soft and waterlogged. At such times a route on stony or rocky hillside is likely to cause less erosion than one on bare soil or grass. Always try to follow a path or track through cultivated land and forest, and avoid causing damage to fences, dykes and gates by climbing over them carelessly.

Bird Life

When climbing, don't cause direct disturbance to nesting birds, particularly the rarer species, which are often found on crags (eg, golden eagle, white tailed (sea) eagle, peregrine falcon, razorbill, guillemot, puffin, fulmar, kittiwake, cormorant, shag, buzzard, kestrel, raven). Usually this is between 1st February and the end of July, but on coasts it may be later.

Intentional disturbance of nesting birds is a criminal offence and if convicted, you face a fine of up to £5000 and confiscation of climbing equipment. **It is the individual's responsibility to find out from the MCofS (see below) about voluntary restrictions at any particular location and to obtain advice as to whether their presence might disturb any nesting birds.**

Vegetation

When cleaning routes in summer take care what you remove; some of the flora may be rare. Many crags are designated Sites of Special Scientific Interest (SSSI). This doesn't mean climbing is not allowed, but it may mean there are restrictions on activity. When winter climbing, minimise damage to underlying vegetation by only climbing when it is fully frozen. Crag and Winter Climbing Codes are available from the MCofS (see below).

Litter and Pollution

Do not leave litter of any sort anywhere, take it down from the hill or crag in your rucksack. Do not cause pollution, and bury human waste carefully out of sight, far away from any habitation or water supply. Avoid burying rubbish as this may also pollute the environment.

Bicycles

Although the use of bicycles can greatly assist access to remote hills and crags, they can cause severe erosion and damage when used 'off road' on soft footpaths and open hillsides. Bicycles should only be used on hard tracks such as vehicular or forest tracks.

Cairns

The proliferation of navigation cairns detracts from the feeling of wildness, and may be confusing rather than helpful as regards route-finding. The indiscriminate building of cairns on the hills is discouraged.

Car Use

Do not drive along private roads without permission, and when parking, avoid blocking access to private roads and land or causing any hazard to other road users.

Bothies

The Mountain Bothies Association has about 100 buildings on various estates throughout Scotland which it maintains as bothies. The MBA owns none of these buildings, they belong to estates which generously allow their use as open bothies. Bothies are there for use by small groups (less than six) for a few days. If you wish to stay longer permission should be sought from the owners. The increased number of hill users have put a greater strain on the bothies and their surrounding environment. It is therefore more important than ever that the simple voluntary bothy code be adhered to, This and more information can be found on the MBA website <www.mountainbothies.org.uk>:

- If you carry it in, carry it out.
- Have respect for the bothy, its owners and users,
- Leave the bothy clean and dry.
- Guard against fire.
- Bury human waste carefully, far away from the bothy and the water supply.
- Avoid burying rubbish.

Mountaineering Council of Scotland

The MCofS is the representative body for climbers and walkers in Scotland. One of its primary concerns is the continued free access to the hills and crags. Information about bird restrictions, stalking and general access issues can be obtained from the MCofS. Should any climber or walker encounter problems regarding access they should contact the MCofS, whose current address is: The Old Granary, West Mill Street, Perth PH1 5QP, tel (01738 638 227), fax (01738 442 095), email <info@mountaineering-scotland.org.uk>, website <www.mountaineering-scotland.org.uk>.

Safety

Participation

"Climbing and mountaineering are activities with a danger of personal injury or death. Participants in these activities should be aware of and accept these risks and be responsible for their own actions and involvement."
UIAA participation statement.

Liabilities

You should not hold landowners liable for an accident (even if a 'no win, no fee' solicitor tempts you), even if it happens while climbing over a fence or dyke. The same is true of bolted sport climbs, or routes with any protection in place. It is up to you to assess the reliability of bolts, pegs, slings or old nuts on the understanding that they may, over time, become corroded and degraded and fail.

Sea-cliff and Mountain Rescue

Contact the police, either by phone (999) or in person. Give concise information about the location and injuries of the victim and any assistance available at the accident site. It is often better to stay with the victim, but in a party of two, one may have to leave to summon help. Leave the casualty warm and comfortable in a sheltered, well marked place.

Equipment and Planning

Good equipment, clothing, forward planning and navigation skills in the mountains, can all help reduce the chance of an accident. While mobile phones and GPS can help in communications and locating your position, consider that the former do not work in many places in South-west Scotland and both rely on batteries and electronics which can fail or be easily damaged. Consequently, they can never be a substitute for good navigation, first aid or general mountain skills.

Rock Climbing

Two-thirds of accidents are the result of a lengthy fall, either due to holds breaking or rockfall. About one-third are the result of planning errors – being too ambitious (trying a route that's too hard) or simply failing to judge how long a route will take and becoming benighted. When climbing on sea-cliffs remember that incoming tides may cut off your retreat even if the cliff base itself is not tidal.

Snow and Ice Climbing

These accidents are twice as likely as for rock climbing, but the fatality rate is almost half. A substantial number are related to navigation errors when getting down from routes. Benightment and numerous other incidents are often the result of poor planning. The greatest number of accidents are falls while climbing.

Avalanches

Climbers venturing on to the hills in winter should be familiar with the principles of snow structure and avalanche prediction. To minimise the risk of exposure to avalanche it is sensible to avoid icefalls and gullies during periods of thaw and immediately following a heavy snowfall. The buttress climbs can provide alternatives in these conditions.

All gullies and most slopes between 30 and 60 degrees should be considered suspect. The greater the amount of fresh snow, the higher the risk. Fresh snow can include wind-blown deposits, so that stormy weather can maintain an avalanche risk for prolonged spells. Past and present weather conditions are very important. Climbers preparing for winter climbing should familiarise themselves with basic avalanche theory. In the field, much can be learned by digging a pit and examining the snow profile, looking especially for different layers of snow with different degrees of bonding. Slab avalanches, for example, will be caused when a weakly cohesive layer of snow collapses underfoot. Such a weak layer may be hidden under a firmer layer, hence its great potential as a killer.

If avalanched, try and either jump free, or anchor yourself for as long as possible, depending on circumstances. If swept down protect your access to oxygen by 'swimming' to stay on the surface, by closing your mouth, and by preserving a space in front of your face if buried. Wet snow avalanches harden rapidly on settling, so try and break free if possible at this point. If trapped try to stay calm, which will reduce oxygen demand. If you witness an avalanche accident it is vital to start a search immediately, given it is safe to do so. Victims will often be alive at first, but their chances of survival lessen rapidly if buried. Unless severely injured, some 80% may live if found immediately, but only 10% after a three-hour delay. Mark the burial sight if known, listen for any sound, look for any visual clue and search until help arrives if possible. A working knowledge of first aid may save a life, as many victims stop breathing.

Maps

Symbols are used on SMC maps to indicate different categories of summit. Tops are not marked on the maps in this guide: Munro – black triangle; Corbett – black circle; Graham – black diamond; Other – crossed circle. Place names and map references have in general been taken from OS 1:50000 Landranger maps. The following maps cover areas in this guide:

Sheet 56	Loch Lomond
Sheet 57	Stirling & The Trossachs
Sheet 58	Perth & Alloa
Sheet 59	St Andrews
Sheet 63	Firth of Clyde
Sheet 64	Glasgow
Sheet 65	Falkirk & Linlithgow
Sheet 66	Edinburgh
Sheet 67	Duns, Dunbar & North Berwick
Sheet 70	Ayr
Sheet 71	Lanark
Sheet 72	Upper Clyde Valley
Sheet 74	Kelso & Coldstream
Sheet 76	Girvan
Sheet 77	Dalmellington & New Galloway
Sheet 78	Nithsdale
Sheet 82	Stranraer
Sheet 83	Newton Stewart & Kircudbright
Sheet 84	Dumfries

Books

The following SMC publications, *The Munros, The Corbetts, Southern Highlands, Scottish Uplands, Scottish Hill and Mountain Names, Scottish Hill Tracks* and *A Chance in a Million? – Scottish Avalanches* are useful for hill walking routes and general mountain interest in this area. For more information and to order SMC and SMT publications, visit the SMC website <www.smc.org.uk>. See also the publications list at the end of this guide.

Technical

Summer Grades

Traditional Routes – The grading system ranges from Easy, Moderate, Difficult, Very Difficult, Severe, Hard Severe, Very Severe (VS), Hard Very Severe (HVS) to Extremely Severe. The Extremely Severe grade has been subdivided into E1, E2, E3, E4, E5, E6 and E7 and so on.

Technical grades are given for routes of VS and above where known. The normal range for technical grades expected on routes of the given overall grade are as follows: VS – 4b, 4c, 5a; HVS – 4c, 5a, 5b; E1 – 5a, 5b, 5c; E2 – 5b, 5c, 6a; E3 –

5c, 6a; E4 – 5c, 6a, 6b; E5 – 6a, 6b. Routes with a technical grade at the lower end of the range will be sustained or poorly protected, while those with grades at the upper end, are likely to have a shorter and generally well protected crux. Grading information is in some cases scanty or even lacking, particularly in some of the older or more obscure routes. These routes are marked with a dagger symbol (†) or have been graded Scottish VS.

Winter Grades

Climbs have been graded using the two-tier system. The technical grades, which are shown by the Arabic numbers, apply to the hardest move or crux sequence of a route, while the Roman numeral gives an indication of the overall difficulty of the climb. The combination of the two grades makes the system work in a similar way to how the E grades and the numerical grades are used in summer.

In this way a V,4 is normally a serious ice route and V,5 would be a classic ice route with adequate protection, V,6 would be a classic mixed route and V,7 would indicate a technically difficult but well protected mixed route. Each route has the same overall difficulty (Grade V) but with differing degrees of seriousness and technical difficulty. Both parts of the grading system are open-ended.

Grade I – Uncomplicated, average-angled snow climbs normally having no pitches. They may, however, have cornice difficulties or long run-outs.

Grade II – Gullies which contain either individual or minor pitches, or high-angled snow with difficult cornice exits. The easiest buttresses under winter conditions.

Grade III – Gullies which contain ice in quantity. There will normally be at least one substantial pitch and possibly several lesser ones. Sustained buttress climbs, but only technical in short sections.

Grade IV – Steeper and more technical with vertical sections found on ice climbs. Mixed routes will require a good repertoire of techniques.

Grade V – Climbs which are difficult, sustained and serious. If on ice, long sustained ice pitches are to be expected; mixed routes will require a degree of rock climbing ability and the use of axe torquing and hooking and similar winter techniques.

Grade VI – Thin and tenuous ice routes or those with long vertical sections. Mixed routes will include all that has gone before but more of it.

Grade VII – Usually mixed routes which are very sustained or technically extreme. Also sustained routes on thin or vertical ice.

Grade VIII – Very hard and sustained mixed routes.

Equipment and Style

Scotland has a tradition of bold climbs with leader-placed protection. Rock routes are graded assuming any pegs that are mentioned are in place and stable. If pegs are essential on new rock routes, they should be kept to a minimum and left in place. A number of the hardest rock climbs will have been cleaned or otherwise inspected prior to the first ascent. Although every attempt is made to grade them for an on-sight lead, this should be borne in mind.

In winter pegs are still necessary on some routes to make them acceptably safe. More often than not these are the harder climbs. In winter conditions the Scottish ethic is for ground-up leads. Pre-placing gear, making a summer ascent or abseil inspection is not considered good style. Though it is accepted that pre-inspection does sometimes happen, the ideal ascent is on-sight in a single push with no aid or weighting of the protection. The defining characteristic of Scottish winter climbing is the weather – the humidity tends to produce hoar frost or rime on the rock, which makes progress more complex than movement over pure rock and ice. Some of the cliffs are too low to form rime; winter conditions should then be defined as easier to climb with axes and crampons than without (generally this means snow on all the holds).

After consultation the Mountaineering Council of Scotland issued a policy statement on the use of bolts in Scotland. The policy is endorsed by the SMC.

"The MCofS acknowledge that there is a place for bolts in the future development of Scottish climbing. However, to ensure that the highly regarded ethos of, and future development of, traditional climbing (involving the use of leader-placed and second-removed protection) is not threatened, it is felt that the use of bolts should be limited to the production of sport climbs. There should be no retrospective bolting of established climbs for protection or belays, and there should be no minimalist bolting.

"The production of sport climbs with bolts is acceptable on natural rock only when all the following conditions have been satisfied: (1) On low-lying cliffs, provided that such development is not against the wishes of the landowner. Bolts are inappropriate on mountain cliffs and sea-cliffs; (2) Where natural protection is absent or is inadequate for the repeated falls that such routes necessitate; (3) Where the rock is steep and provides climbs of a high order of difficulty, at the forefront of developments of the day; (4) Where there is no historical or local anti-bolt ethic.

"Concerning quarried rock, it is felt that any future development should be constrained only by points (2) and (4) above. Finally, it is felt that bolts should be located to ensure minimum visual impact and should be placed according to current best practices. It is intended that these principles are not seen as simply restrictive rules, but as a guide to promote the positive development of Scottish climbing, where sports climbing, rather than becoming a substitute for traditional climbing, grows alongside it." The use of bolts on winter climbs is considered unacceptable.

Left and Right

The terms refer to a climber facing the direction being described, ie, facing the cliff for a route description, facing downhill in descent for mountain cliffs. For many crags, however, the descent is planned before the route is started, and here the direction is facing up (but the direction is specified, often by the compass point). Routes are described from left to right unless indicated otherwise.

Pitch Lengths

Pitch lengths are often rounded to the nearest 5m, although pitches below 20m are sometimes rounded to the nearest 2m. The descriptions assume the use of 50m ropes.

Diagrams

Numbered routes will be found on diagrams close to the relevant text. The numbers of the climbs in the text correspond to the numbers on the diagrams.

Recommended Routes

* Good climbing, but lacking line, character, situation or balance.
** A good route but lacking one or more of the features that would make it a climb of quality.
*** An outstanding route of the highest quality, combining superb climbing with line, character, situation and balance.
**** One of the best climbs of its class.

In winter, quality will vary with conditions so stars, like grades, are applied for the conditions when the route is commonly climbed.

First Ascensionists

The year of the first ascent is given in the text. The full date and first ascensionists are listed by area in chronological order at the back of the guide. If climbed originally using aid, this is listed, usually with the first free ascent. When a route has not had a free ascent the aid point(s) are mentioned in the route description. If a rest point was used on the first ascent it is listed in the First Ascents list. Details of variations are given under the parent route. An ascent in winter conditions is indicated by a W at the start of an entry.

The number and quality of indoor climbing walls in the Lowland area has improved dramatically since the last edition of this guide and indeed, now boasts a world class facility. Brief details of these facilities are listed below. The entry fee quoted is an adult fee in autumn 2004 (some of the walls have student/child and off-peak discounts).

TROSSACHS
McLaren Leisure Centre, Callander
This modern but small top-roping and bouldering facility is situated in the new leisure centre on the southern approach to Callander, just off the A81. Given the limited space the bouldering is reasonable, with good features and a steep cave, but the routes are short. Entry fee: £3. Tel: 01877 330000. Opening hours: Mon & Sat 09.00-21.00, Tues-Fri 07.30-22.00, Sun 08.30-21.00.

GLASGOW
Glasgow Climbing Centre
A very popular and extensive climbing centre in a converted church in Ibrox on Glasgow's south side. It lies at 534 Paisley Road West and is easily approached by bus, underground (to Ibrox) or road (leave the M8 motorway at junction 23). Parking is usually possible near the entrance. The wall has excellent leading, top-roping, dry tooling and bouldering facilities with new routes and problems set regularly. There are several walls to choose from including a very steep lead wall and various leading and top-roping walls. There are 6 separate bouldering walls of varying types, campus boards etc. The wall is very busy during evenings, but there is enough climbing space to accommodate everyone. Entry Fee: £6. Tel: 0141 427 9550. Opening hours: 12.00-22.00 Mon-Fri, 10.00-20.00 weekends. <www.glasgowclimbingcentre.co.uk>.

Kelvin Hall
This small bouldering wall is located in Kelvin Hall International Sports Arena on Argyle Street (opposite the Museum and Art Galleries). Car parking is available on the west side of the centre (beside the river). The once popular old panels have been replaced with modern flat, vertical and overhanging panels with bolt-on holds. Reasonable bouldering but rather limited and very warm. Entry fee: £3.05. Tel: 0141 357 2525. Opening hours: 09.00-22.30 (except Wednesday open at 10.00-22.30 and Sat 09.00-18.30).

FIFE
Carnegie Leisure Centre, Dunfermline
An excellent bouldering facility with many good problems on varied angles. The centre lies on Pilmuir Street (a section of the A823) just north of the town centre. There is a small car park at the centre. Entry fee: £3.20. Tel: 01383 314200. Opening hours: 07.00-22.00. <www.fifeleisure.com>.

EDINBURGH
Adventure Centre, Ratho
With 2.4km^2 of climbing wall, this superb facility was the largest indoor wall in the world when it opened. There are a number of 30m leading pitches, other leading pitches and some impressive features, along with top-roping, bouldering and natural rock. It can be cold in winter. The centre lies near Ratho on the outskirts of Edinburgh, just off the B7030. If approaching from the west, leave the M8 at junction 2 to the Newbridge roundabout. The same roundabout can be reached from the east via the A8 and from the north via the M9. The centre is well signposted. Entry fee: £8. Tel: 0131 333 6333. Opening hours: 10.30-22.30 (09.30-20.00 weekends). <www.adventurescotland.com>.

Alien Rock 1

A dedicated climbing centre in a converted church located by Newhaven harbour. There is good quality leading and top-roping, with a good range of angles and grades and a small bouldering room. It can become rather crowded in winter evenings. It is situated on the seafront in Leith (8 Pier Place). There is parking on the street outside the centre. Entry fee: £6. Tel: 0131 552 7211. Opening hours: 12.00-23.00 (10.00-21.00 weekends). <www.alienrock.co.uk>.

Alien Rock 2

A superb bouldering wall with an extensive and varied range of angles and problems. It is located on West Bowling Green Street in Leith, in a small industrial estate, off Ferry Road. Turn off Ferry Road onto Newhaven Road, left onto Graham Street and right onto West Bowling Green Street. Entry Fee: £5.50. Tel: 0131 555 3650. Opening hours: 16.00-22.00 (12.00-19.00 weekends). <www.alienrock.co.uk>.

Heriot Watt University

A rather dated top-roping and bouldering from the 1970s, complete with holds built into the brick wall. Situated in the Centre for Sport & Exercise on Heriot Watt University's Riccarton campus. If approaching from Edinburgh city centre, take the A71. Heriot Watt University is well signposted from here. Entry fee: £1.90. Tel: 0131 451 3000. Opening hours: 09.00-21.15 (climbing may not always be possible if there are other events in the sports hall; call reception to check before a visit).

Other useful contacts

This guide covers some of the most popular tourist destinations in Scotland with an abundance of hotels, b&bs, hostals and campsites. The best starting point for booking accommodation is VisitScotland, which can supply accommodation brochures for all areas (0845 225 5121), <www.visitscotland.com>. The following may also be useful:

Independent Hostels (01479 831331) <www.hostel-scotland.co.uk>

SYHA Hostels (01786 891400 & 0870 1553255) <www.syha.org.uk>

Climbers' Huts The MCofS (0738 638227) has a list of huts available to individual MCofS members and members of clubs which are affiliated to the BMC or MCofS. See their website <www.mountaineering-scotland.org.uk>.

Weather Forecasts

Radio Scotland: As well as the regular forecasts, there is a specific Outdoor Activities forecast every evening. The time varies from year to year but in autumn 2004 it was at 6.58pm (7.58pm on Sunday).

TV: The BBC Reporting Scotland forecast at 6.50 to 6.55pm is the only good daily one.

Web: There are a wide variety of forecasts on the internet, including: <www.onlineweather.co.uk>, <www.bbc.co.uk/weather> and <metcheck.com>

Telephone forecasts are expensive but handy:
Weathercall (0906 81819): +24 East Central, +23 Edinburgh, South Fife, Lothian, Borders, +22 Glasgow & Strathclyde, +21 South-west.

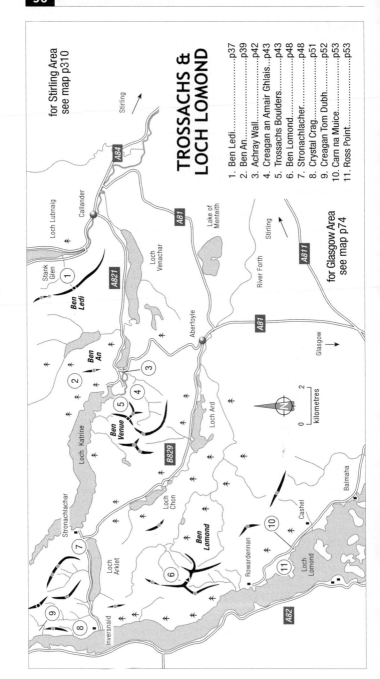

for Stirling Area
see map p310

TROSSACHS &
LOCH LOMOND

for Glasgow Area
see map p74

THE TROSSACHS, LOCH LOMOND & GARE LOCH

This chapter describes the climbing from Ben Ledi, round lochs Achray, Katrine and Arklet, to the crags near the east shore of Loch Lomond, then south to the newly developed quarries at Rosneath on the west side of the Gare Loch opposite Helensburgh. With the exception of the southern slate quarries of Cashel, Ross Point, Clynder and Rosneath, all of the climbing is on mica schist.

Ben Ledi, Loch Archray & Loch Katrine

These crags are easily accessed from Aberfoyle to the south and Callander to the east. The boulders and pinnacles in Stank Glen on Ben Ledi have seen renewed interest, although climbers have been visiting Ben An since the late 1800s. Micro-routing/soloing/bouldering is not a purely modern phenomenon.

BEN LEDI

(NN 566 105)   Alt 450m   Map p36

The pinnacles and boulders on the Stank Glen flank of Ben Ledi offer excellent highball problems with a fine outlook and good landings. Many more routes and problems have been done than are recorded here.

Approach: From the car park at NN 586 092, follow the lochside road, then the waymarked path up Ben Ledi. The boulders and pinnacles are visible up and left near the head of the glen. Directly below a white post in the glen (No Waymarking On Open Hill), a path leads from a low boulder to a stile in a fence. 50 mins.

COTTAGE (NO 1) BOULDER

Three boulders make up this large mass of rock, directly ahead after crossing the stile. Various scrambly routes have been recorded.

JUGULAR (NO 2) BOULDER

Uphill from Cottage Boulder and identified by a steep diamond shaped, brown streaked wall facing Stank Glen. Routes are described right, then left, from the shallow corner of Cop Out on the diamond wall's left side.

Cop Out   5m   Font 6a   (2004)
Climb the shallow corner until you can bridge across to jugs.

**Snake Master   5m   Font 6c ** **   (2004)
As for Cop Out but don't bridge. Climb the hanging arete in its entirety.

Sunshine Wall   6m   Font 6a+ *   (2004)
The centre of the diamond wall on crimps, to gain the crack and a worrying pinch.

Poo da Pants   6m   Font 6b   (2004)
The overhanging right arete of the wall to flakes at the top, then right into groove.

Watkins Overhang   10m   Severe   (1970s)
The stepped groove right of Poo da Pants and left of the undercut finger-crack.

Sunset Wall   10m   Very Difficult   (1970s)
The overhang right of the finger crack, then left up the wall.

The following lie left of Cop Out.

Count Jugular   5m   Font 6b *   (2004)
Sit start as for Cop Out, then climb the arete on improving holds.

Killar Weed   4m   Font 6c ** (2004)
Sit start to the left of Count Jugular. Crank up to good holds then heel-hook. Move up to crimps then gain hanging boss. Use this and go to other crimp and final hold which is a kind of crack.

Killa Cam   4m   Font 4+ (1970s)
Sit start on obvious jugs left of Killar Weed and climb crack. Only the sit start is new.

Troopa   10m   Font 7a * (2004)
Start on the wee arete groove to the left of Killa Cam. Traverse right along slopey, juggy lip to finish up Count Jugular. The lip and wall offer an easy ascent (1970s).

Super Troopa   20m   Font 7b *** (2004)
As for Troopa but continue traversing across Sunshine Wall and up Poo da Pants. Kind of route graded.

CORTEGE (NO 3) BOULDER

The next large boulder uphill has an obvious thin crack in its uphill (south) facing wall. Routes are described anti-clockwise from the crack; Cortege Crack.

Cortege Crack   4m   Font 6a **
The obvious thin crack, with a long reach to finish.

Lunar   5m   Font 6a+ * (2004)
The wall right of the crack on juggy layaways. Where they end and the wall blanks out, stretch to high crimp.

Cortege   4m   Font 6b * (2003)
Just right of a small tombstone-shaped rock near the arete separating the south wall and the overhanging south-east wall. Sit start near the left arete on poor slopers. Up to an inverted-V hold, then crank high to better holds.

Rudeboy   7m   Font 7b *** (2004)
Follow Cortege to inverted-V hold and finish from slopey boss to dyno rightwards as for Cortege Noir.

Heads High   4m   Font 6b (2004)
In the middle of wall to the right of Cortege. Sit start on small undercut, then direct following vague crack to rattly holds. Move right to good hold and top.

Like a pimp   4m   Font 6b * (2004)
Start sit to right of Heads High down at undercut and move up to quartz and sharp crimp. Use these to gain inverted-V hold and improving holds.

Cortege Noir   5m   Font 7a *** (2003)
Sit start from right arete, gaining a sidepull and undercut to reach for poor crimp sloper, then dyno up and right to regain arete.

Sloping Crack   6m   Severe (1970s)
The right to left crack on the left side of the wall facing Stank Glen.

Mantelshelf   6m   Severe (1970s)
The right side of the Stank Glen wall. Gain the ledge at 2m and up the wall above.

WEE BOULDER

The boulder facing Cortege Crack has an overhanging arete.

**Thug Anthem   5m   Font 6c ** ** *(2004)*
Sit start using quartz pinch and boss on the arete. Up to crimp, traverse left on slopers to quartz jug and battle it out to top.

CORPSE (NO 4) BOULDER

This solitary boulder lies 70m north-west (right, facing uphill) from the stile and has an easily identified heather ledge at half height. Routes are described anti-clockwise from the Stank Glen (north) face, which has an obvious groove and an impressive right arete. Named after Lochan nan Corp (Little Loch of the Corpses) on the col.

Burnie's Climb   6m   Very Difficult * *(1970s)*
The obvious right to left groove.

**Pass of the Corpse   6m   Font 4+ ** **
The impressive arete to the right is highball and climbed on both sides.

Zombie   4m   Font 5+ *(2004)*
Climb the north-west facing wall to slopey quartz then jug. Either side can be climbed at Font 4/5 (**Piker**, 1970s). The right arete is also Font 4/5.

Weeping Wall   3m   Font 6a *
The left side of the uphill (south) wall is green and black streaked. From pockets gain a pinch and crank to a thin break up and left.

**28 Days Later   20m   Font 7a ** ** *(2004)*
Traverse from Pass the Corpse rightwards round the boulder. The crux is the low lying lip and turning the wall onto the corpse wall.

BEN AN

(NN 505 082)   Alt 300m   South-East facing   Map p36   Diagram p40

The crags lie on the south side of the hill, with a fine outlook to Ben Venue and over the eastern end of Loch Katrine. However, the aspect of many of the walls means that sunshine can't be guaranteed for an evening's sport. The rock is quite solid, though mossy and quite polished in places, so care should be taken in damp conditions.

Approach: Start from the car park at NN 508 070, about 100m before the Trossachs Hotel. Opposite the car park follow the signposted path uphill and into the forest. After 15 to 20 minutes a grassy area with boulders is reached, from where the crags can be viewed. Where the main path steepens, a small path leads off left to the base of the Lower Tier.

LOWER TIER

A steep buttress with an impressive corner is encountered first. Left of this is a rocky gully then a long undercut wall which ends at an ash tree. The first seven routes are described right to left.

Preamble   13m   Severe
Starting just right of the lowest point of the crag, climb a small overhang. Finish as for The Edge, or more easily by moving right.

The Edge   13m   VS 4c *
Good airy climbing up the right arete of the corner. Swing strenuously over the bulge and move up and left to overlook the corner. Finish up the crack and edge.

Tricky Vicky   12m   E4 6a * *(1985)*
Technical unprotected climbing up the right wall of the corner.

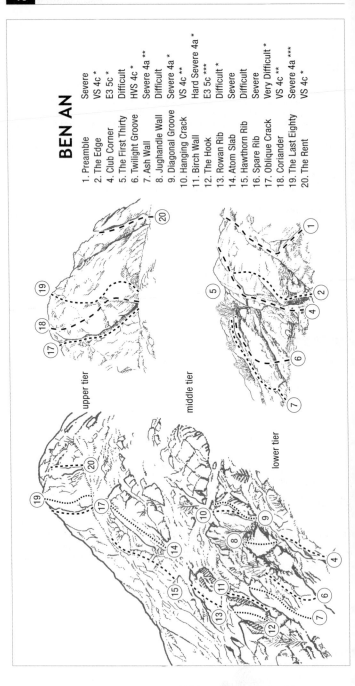

BEN AN

1. Preamble — Severe
2. The Edge — VS 4c *
4. Club Corner — E3 5c *
5. The First Thirty — Difficult
6. Twilight Groove — HVS 4c *
7. Ash Wall — Severe 4a **
8. Jughandle Wall — Difficult
9. Diagonal Groove — Severe 4a *
10. Hanging Crack — VS 4c **
11. Birch Wall — Hard Severe 4a *
12. The Hook — E3 5c ***
13. Rowan Rib — Difficult *
14. Atom Slab — Severe
15. Hawthorn Rib — Difficult
16. Spare Rib — Severe
17. Oblique Crack — Very Difficult *
18. Coriander — VS 4c **
19. The Last Eighty — Severe 4a ***
20. The Rent — VS 4c *

upper tier

middle tier

lower tier

4 Club Corner   12m   E3 5c *
The steep corner gives a strenuous bridging problem with little protection. Faith and friction lead to the thank God hold and a finish up The Edge.

5 The First Thirty   10m   Difficult
Left of the obvious corner is a wall forming the right side of the gully. Good but polished holds lead to the top.

6 Twilight Groove   20m   HVS 4c *
A short corner is the main feature on the long undercut wall left of the gully. The corner is awkward to enter, protection difficult to arrange and contact with the rock surprisingly tenuous. May raise a few goose pimples.

The wall to the right has been top-roped; **Blind Faith**, 6a. Start right of Twilight Groove, and trend right on thin holds.

7 Ash Wall   30m   Severe 4a **   (1930)
This takes a well worn line behind the ash tree, about 12m left of the rocky gully splitting the first tier. Gain the top of the polished flake and step left into the groove. Climb this to a slab which is followed for about 15m until it is possible to reach a rib on the left edge. Follow the rib to finish just right of a prominent tree.

The next three routes take lines on the left wall of the gully splitting the Lower Tier.

8 Jughandle Wall   13m   Difficult
Opposite the top of The First Thirty is a slabby wall. Take the line of least resistance via an outrageous jug.

9 Diagonal Groove   10m   Severe 4a *
Higher up the gully is an impressive crack. Climb to below the crack, then follow the ramp rightwards to a balancy move round the corner.

0 Hanging Crack   10m   VS 4c **
Despite its brevity, the crack is shockingly steep with a high fall potential. Start as for Diagonal Groove, but gain the niche then layback boldly up the crack.

The next two routes lie above and slightly left of the finish of Ash Wall. They can also be gained by a left traverse from the gully splitting the Lower Tier.

1 Birch Wall   13m   Hard Severe 4a *   (1937)
Behind the tree is an obvious polished corner. Smear into the corner and wobble upwards on gradually improving holds.

2 The Hook   10m   E3 5c ***
Forceful climbing with poor protection up the right side of the steep wall left of Birch Wall. Move up to a vertical pocket and continue with difficulty above. Often top-roped, rarely led.

The centre of the wall left of The Hook has been top-roped – **Crunchy** (5c).

3 Rowan Rib   10m   Difficult *
Directly above the finish to Birch Wall is a polished bulge with a metal spike. Pull over awkwardly to a hidden jug and continue more easily to belay at a large boulder.

CENTRAL TIER

This is characterised by indefinite rock ribs on the left, divided by vegetated gullies.

14 Atom Slab   5m   Severe
Above and right of Rowan Rib is a minute crag with assorted problems and a polished top wall.

15 Hawthorn Rib   40m   Difficult
Across the scrub left of the top of Rowan Rib is an indefinite rib line. This is the cleanest rock on the central tier and the way followed by most parties heading for the upper tier.

To the left of Hawthorn Rib are two vegetated gullies, **Right-Hand Gully** and **Left-Hand Gully**, both Very Difficult. They were first ascended in 1898 and 1896, but are rarely climbed now.

UPPER TIER

Directly below the summit, this tier contains some good routes in a superb position and is easily recognised by a quartz banded face, flanked on the right by striking crack-lines and on the left by the deep slanting chimney of The Oblique Crack.

Left of the deep chimney are a number of gullies, probably best left for enthusiastic botanists; **McLay's Chimney** (Very Difficult) and **Right-Hand Gully Continuation** (Severe).

16 Spare Rib   25m   Severe
Left of the deep chimney is a rib. Climb this up and left to an edge, then finish more directly.

17 Oblique Crack   20m   Very Difficult *   *(1898)*
Follow the left-slanting chimney – very character building.

18 Coriander   25m   VS 4c **   *(1970)*
Right of the chimney is an impressive open face covered in quartz. This route climbs grooves on the left edge. Climb the overhanging crack right of the start of The Oblique Crack, or from the start of the chimney reach out right to a large quartz hold and swing on to the edge. Either way, climb the slab above and follow poorly protected grooves always to the left of The Last Eighty.

19 The Last Eighty   25m   Severe 4a ***   *(1930)*
Enjoyable climbing on interesting and ever steepening rock. Start below a small overhang, just left of the lowest part of the buttress. Pull over the bulge on good holds and continue fairly directly on well marked rock, to finish up a steep corner at the top. The first roof can be avoided by traversing in from the right.

20 The Rent   25m   VS 4c *   *(1934)*
To the right of the quartz face is a vertical crack which gives a more elegant and delicate climb than expected.

Ben An provides a final party piece with the **Record Slab**, the apex of which actually forms the summit. From a standing start with toes touching the lowest part of the slab, timed ascents can be made to both feet on the summit.

ACHRAY WALL

(NN 504 066)   Alt 100m   East facing   Map p36
About half a dozen routes have been done on this small, steep and often wet crag, but only these two are recorded. There are a couple of boulder problems too.

Approach: Park in a small lay-by opposite the crag on the banks of Loch Achray, about 280m north-east of the Loch Achray Hotel.

The Bow   25m   HVS 5a   *(1983)*
Start at the open groove at the lowest part of the crag, facing the road. Climb the groove to a niche, move up the slabby ramp to the left, then go right to the top. A bit dirty at the top.

**The Arrow   20m   E2 5c ** **   *(1983)*
Climb the vague hanging groove to the right of The Bow, past a protection peg. Steep and strenuous, but with big holds.

High Roller   Font 5   *(2003)*
The boulder with the memorial, left of the face. Climb near the left corner avoiding the obvious step and the memorial. Reach for the slopey top from the two handed hold and mantel to finish.

Descendance   Font 5+   *(2003)*
From behind High Roller and the sapling. Stand start on the little pinnacle of rock at knee-height. Traverse along the shelf using the slopers at the big curve then reach for the better holds to the right. Finish down the step like holds to end with two hands on the lowest sloper before stepping down.

CREAGAN AN AMAIR GHLAIS

(NN 488 063)   Alt 200m   North-East facing   Map p36

This impressive looking crag lies on the east flank of Ben Venue, overlooking the south-east end of Loch Katrine. The crag gets a fair amount of drainage and is slow to dry.

Approach: From the car park behind the Loch Achray Hotel (NN 502 064) follow the Bealach nam Bo path. On leaving the forest, cross the stile and head south, steeply up the slope to the crags.

Root Beer   10m   E1 5b   *(1992)*
The lower wall is steep and lichenous, and may be recognised by its light green colouration. This route follows a discontinuous crack at the right-hand end of the wall, with some loose holds. Start in an alcove at the right-hand end and climb steeply above to an obvious crack. Finish with a hard move at the top on sloping holds.

Sarsaparilla   15m   E2 5b   *(1991)*
This takes the most direct line up the clean slabby middle wall, which lies some 200m up the slope behind a terrace with trees. Start in a small niche on the grassy ledge, just left of the lowest rocks. An awkward move onto a ramp leads slightly left to the main slabby wall (poor peg runner possible), then climb direct to the steep upper wall and finish using shallow cracks leading to a grassy terrace and tree.

TROSSACHS BOULDERS

(NN 484 072)   East facing   Map p36

Situated above the south-east basin of Loch Katrine on the path to the Bealach nam Bo, these popular boulders have some of the best mica schist in the Southern Highlands, granitic and rough in texture, with good landings and a fine outlook. They are best in spring, before the bracken gets too high and the midges become rife.

Approach: From the car park behind the Loch Achray Hotel (NN 502 064) follow the Bealach nam Bo path alongside the south bank of the Achray Water to the Loch Katrine dam. After the dam, continue on the path for a few hundred metres, past the sluices and a holly tree in the burn. You soon come to the Fight Club Boulder. It is another 15 mins to the furthest boulder – the Bosporus Boulder.

FIGHT CLUB BOULDER

This squat boulder sits by the left of the burn's gravel fan and has a patio of stones to start from. The obvious roof is:

Fight Club   6b (Font 6c) ★★★   *(2003)*
Scotland's alternative to Brad Pit! Sit start from the obvious hand ledge and crank up and right on slopers to snatch right and mantel.

The short blunt roof to the right is an open project.

Cross the stream and then another two burns after the Fight Club Boulder and you come across the two obvious sentinel boulders which provide the hub of the bouldering here, as well as a fine place to picnic.

JAWA BOULDER

The top boulder has a slabby wall facing the fence. Problems are described left to right, anti-clockwise.

Left Arete   5a
The left arete, off the wee boulder.

Mind-Trick   6a *
Fierce crimps and difficult toe shunt just right of the arete might gain the top.

Jawa   6b (Font 6c) ★★★
The wonderfully frustrating central wall off the only good handholds – flexibility required. Can be dynoed, but that's just as hard!

Right Arete   4c
The right arete, pulling off from start of the last problem.

The Traverse   6b (Font 6b) ★★★
From Left Arete, traverse right to finish up the right arete. Fingery and tenuous for the feet, but much easier in cool conditions.

Descent Ledges   3a

Left Arete, North Face   5a *

Steve's Problem   6c
The left central wall of the Dark Side via a long reach to small crimps.

Big Up Orra Glasgae Peeps   6c (Font7a+) ★★★   *(2003)*
The right central wall, off a desperate mantel and one-finger undercut.

Ninja Midge   6b (Font 6c) ★★
A sit-start at the Nose and a low-level traverse left to finish up the left arete.

The Nose   6b (Font 6c+) ★★
The sit-down to the overhanging nose. From the mantel holds, swing right onto the Nose and climb it direct. An aggressive approach required.

TOURIST BOULDER

Just below the Jawa boulder, it has an overhanging south face. Problems are described from the left descent niche, anti-clockwise:

Scooped Niche   3a
The scooped niche on the left is also the descent.

**The Tourist   6a (Font 6b)   ** **
From the central slopers, struggle over onto the slab.

Paralysis by Analysis   6c (Font 7a+) * (2003)
The overhang from a sit -start. Take a press sidepull and pinch (right foot on nubbin), then launch desperately for the edge and finish up The Tourist.

**Lecturing the Masses   5c ** **
Jump for the right arete's pointy sloper, then hand-traverse left to finish up the niche. Shouldery and fun.

Tourist Trap   6b   (Font 7a) * **
Sit-down under the right arete and find a way out! If you gain the pointy sloper, the best finish is along Lecturing the Masses. Devious.

HB   6a ** (Font 6b)
Follow the right arete from the low jug on the right. Which hand do you use? Remarkably similar to a Dumbarton problem.

North Wall   4b *
The slabby north wall is best started from the right and up and left.

Quartz Crack   4b
Best finished right and up Scooped Niche.

ART SCHOOL BOULDER

Well hidden! At the second burn crossing, 100m before the Jawa Boulder, follow a burn up over the fence and into the trees. A huge boulder leans over the burn.

Watercolour Challenge   6a (Font 6a+) * *** (2003)
The technical central wall looking upstream. Gain the pockets and a good finger-ledge, then use slopers and good footwork to stretch for the finishing jug.

Spider   5a
The nose and arete left of Watercolour Challenge.

Greensleeves   5a
The central slab at its blankest part.

The Art School   6a (Font 6b) * ***
The blunt arete facing downstream. Pull up to slopers and finish thrillingly!

Pawprint   5a
The oddly marked scooped groove left of the arete and right of the quartz band.

The Quartz Band   4c *
The obvious feature facing downstream.

THE HYDROPONICUM

This boulder leans over a burn just before the sentinel boulders. It has a magnificently steep central problem:

Hydroponicum   5c (Font 5+) * ***
Harder if you miss the tricks. Start sitting in the fern garden and pull up on good

holds to finish directly up the groove and over onto the slab via a good hold. Do it ten times for the training.

Ikebana 6c (Font 7b) * (2003)
From the start of the above, gain undercut to left and slap up for a sidepull, then desperately reach left for the 'eye' pocket. From this, snatch up right for a diagonal edge which allows the good railing to be gained and a scruffy finish out left.

BEALACH BOULDER

Follow the path up past the two central boulders, past a boggy boulder with a heather bonnet, and climb up to the obvious bealach boulder field. There are many boulders here, but they suffer from cluster and many are dirty and have poor landings. The Bealach Boulder is the obvious low boulder with cleaned holds, facing downhill. The rock is oddly water worn in places.

Early Redemption Penalty 6b (Font 7a) *
Start sitting down just right of the water pool, cross-handed, right hand in slot, and slap left, then right into sidepull. Reach far left for the lip and rock over via a sharp pocket and slot.

The Knob 6b (Font 6c+) **
Sit-down as above and pull directly up via slopers and the obvious knob to rock over the lip onto the slab.

The Dog-House 6a (Font 6b+)
The right-hand arete above the flat block. From a sit-down at the lowest cleaned hold, traverse right, then crank up left to a poor crimp, slap the arete and finish via a mantel or rocking out right.

SEBASTOPOL BOULDER

In the wee glen below the bealach, follow the stream downhill. There is a large, beautifully textured boulder below the crags. This is the Sebastopol Boulder. It has a slabby left wall and a roofed right arete with grooves.

Slab Direct 5a
Pull on at the far left and climb the slab direct.

Bob's Bitch 5c (Font 6a) *
From the stand-up start to Navigator, rock over left and finish up slabs.

Navigator 5c (Font 5+) **
The left-hand groove in the nose – contortionism required.

Rise Up and be Strong 6b (Font 6c) ** (2003)
The sit-down to Navigator. From sidepulls, Egyptian like crazy to gain the corner holds on the nose, then slap desperately right to finish up Sebastopol.

Sebastopol 6a (Font 6a) *** (2003)
Right of the nose, pull onto the rough slopers, stand on the flat hold and gain the right-hand groove. Technical and good for you.

Lock, Stock and Barrel 7a (Font 7c) *** (2003)
Feels very independent of the last problem! Sit under the roof and use the flat hold to gain a right–hand sloper. Now heel-hook and slap desperately up left to the good slopers and cruise up Sebastopol.

Back Slab 4c

TNT BOULDER

This small boulder, further downhill from Sebastopol, has an obvious central crack and an 'exploded' belly. It provides some quality problems for its size.

Dynamite Traverse   5c (Font 5+) *
Sit-down on the right and follow the lip all the way left to rock over on the left arete. Good fun.

The Wall   4a
The wall by the left arete.

TNT   4b *
The obvious crack, 4c from the sit-down.

The next two problems depend on which bicep is stronger. You choose!

Nitro Left-hand.   6a (Font 6b) **
From the two left-hand undercuts in the exploded wall, pull on and bicep to the crimp, left-handed, and rock over the top.

Nitro Right-Hand   6a (Font 6b) **
From two and three of the three undercuts, reach up with your right hand...

BOSPORUS BOULDER

The furthest away boulder, seen perched high on the nose overlooking the 'Bosporus' of Loch Katrine. It has an undercut flying roof looking north over the water.

Big-nose   6c (Font 7a)
Slap and pull desperately up the rounded nose from the flying jug.

Why did Constantinople Get the Works?   6a (Font 6b) **
Start well back in the cave, traverse out on the jammed boulders then toe-hook and reach the flying jug on the nose. Cut loose, gain crimps and rock up to the handrail to finish left.

It's Nobody's Business but the Turks.   6b (Font 6c+) ***   (2003)
Traverse. A sit-start from a rounded boss on the right. Throw up a good heel-hook and crank left along the lip, using heels and toes creatively to lock-off up to the handrail. Finish up this as for the last problem.

THE JOHN GILL EXPERIENCE

These are the walls below the Bosphorous Boulder, which face over the shoreline. They have various highball problems and projects. The obvious hanging slab from a platform, **The John Gill Experience**, is a committing **5c** **. The obvious crack round the corner from this has yet to be climbed. There are many other possibilities on the crags and boulders in the area – these have not been documented and are left for the explorative and civic-minded boulderer.

On the A821 over the Duke's Pass between Aberfoyle and The Trossachs there are a number of small buttresses on the left, a short distance after a house and about 3km north of Aberfoyle. Three routes have been done on consecutive buttresses on the hillside Creag a' Mhadaidh (NN 514 035): **Midged Off** (15m Hard Severe 4a), on the Lower Wall, **Midget** (5m Hard Severe 4a), on the Continuation Wall and **Midge Bite**, (5m VS 4b) on the Top Wall.

A couple of routes have been done in the 25m Aberfoyle Quarry (NN 514 016) about 400m north of the town. They are loose and not recommended by the first ascentionists. **John's New Bike** (HVS 4b), takes the right-slanting diagonal crack and groove bounding the large black overhung slab. **Jackson's Hole** (E1 4c), climbs the obvious grey slab starting 3m left of the arete. Approach by walking west for 5mins from the David Marshall Lodge car park (NN 519 015).

Loch Chron & Loch Arklet

Since the last edition, considerable development has taken place in the vicinity of Stronachlachar. This section includes the winter routes on Ben Lomond.

BEN LOMOND

(NN 367 029)   800m   North facing   Map p36

The north corrie has a number of winter routes at I and II, some of which were climbed in summer in days of old.

Approach: Start from NN 433 037 on the B829 at the east end of Loch Chon, west of Aberfoyle. Follow the track to Comer Farm at the north end of Gleann Dubh and ascend to the corrie.

The following route takes the central largest area of steep cliff, finishing on the north-east spur.

Zigzag   145m   III/IV   *(1992)*
1. 30m Follow an icy ramp to a line of grooves and a large ledge, belaying under an overhang near a detached flake.
2. 35m Go left over the overhang into a broad easy scoop, then follow the groove diagonally leftwards to an overhanging corner. Climb this using the right wall to a ledge on the left. Traverse 8m right to belay on a ledge to the right of a roof.
3. 35m Climb the small steep arete directly above the belay, then follow a groove to a broken ledge beneath the very steep upper wall. Make a hard move diagonally left over the bulge to reach holds leading across the slabby wall to the base of a hanging corner.
4. 45m Continue up the corner. At its top, move diagonally right to easier ground.

STRONACHLACHAR

Map p36

A collection of small crags and boulders lie on the steep wooded slopes of Garradh, above the tiny hamlet of Stronachlachar near Loch Arklet. The area offers short sport routes on good rock and worthwhile bouldering in a spectacular setting with views along Loch Katrine and Loch Arklet. The crags are a real suntrap and can be climbed on all year round. There is potential for further bouldering development which would make this a superb venue.

Approach: Turn right at the T-junction just before Stronachlachar and park immediately beside the cottage (NN 397 099). The crags can be seen in the woods above the cottage.
   From the T-junction, two adjacent buttresses can be seen near the top of the wooded area. The right-hand one has no routes, the left-hand one is Chasm Buttress. The G-Spot lies hidden in trees directly below Chasm Buttress. High Crag lies well up and left of the wooded crags.

THE BOULDERS

(NN 393 100)   Alt 200m   South facing

Several large boulders litter the hillside directly above the cottage at the base of the woods. An obvious long boulder can be seen at the edge of the trees. The problems are described starting with this boulder.

Mike's Problem   6b (Font 7a+) *(2003)*
The long boulder has a shallow cave in the centre. Left of this is an obvious ear-shaped flake on the wall. Climb this and the blank looking wall above. Highball.

Nameless   6b (Font 6b) *(2001)*
Start at the left end of the shallow cave, move up to a juggy handrail and follow this rightwards past the sloper of Pimp.

Pimp With a Limp   6b (Font 6c) ** *(2001)*
Sit-start near the right end of the cave at a large pocket. Climb the steep wall direct to a large sloper. A big lock gains better holds.

Toy Soldiers   6a (Font 6b) *** *(2001)*
Sit-start just left of a massive flake at the right end of the boulder. Move up to a good flat hold and lunge for a high crimp. A flat top-out.

Virgin Suicides   6b (Font 7a+) *** *(2001)*
Behind and slightly right of the long boulder, hidden in trees is the Virgin Block, characterised by a long, low slopey lip facing downhill. This problem traverses the lip slopers from a sit start at a square hold at the extreme right end.

Hook, Line and Sinker   6a (Font 6c) * *(1999)*
This problem lies on the open slope on the approach to the long boulder (the boulder is crowned by a small sapling). The uphill face of this block has an excellent slopey traverse taking the handrail in its entirety. Usually green in winter.

The Boomer   5b (Font 5) *** *(1999)*
This superb dyno problem lies on one of two boulders down and right of the long boulder, by a fence. Leap from the obvious finger flake to a high apex jug.

Periscope   6b (Font 6b) * *(2003)*
The short sloping lip traverse and rock over on the same block as The Boomer has a long reach to finish.

HIGH CRAG

(NN 388 102)   Alt 300m   South facing

Approach: Walk directly up the steep bracken slope on the left-hand (east) border of the woods. The crag lies above and left of the top of the woods.

Raksasha   6m   F7a *(1997)*
The extended boulder problem at the left-hand end.

High and Mighty   6m   F7b+ *(2004)*
Another tough bouldery line on tiny crimps.

Lady of the Loch   10m   F6b * *(1998)*
The line of small hidden pockets.

My Own Private Scotland   10m   F6c+ *(1997)*
The sustained central line has a crux at the top.

Highland Cling   10m   F6b * *(1997)*
The rightmost line of bolts on the face.

THE CHASM

(NN 390 102) Alt 250m South facing

The left-hand of two adjacent steep walls seen from the road has one route at present and potential for several more lines at all grades. The rock is a little sandy in places. Named after the huge chasm at the base formed by a fallen boulder.

Approach: As for High Crag until level with the buttress, then contour across to it.

Unnamed   15m   F7b+
This climbs the grossly leaning wall near the left end. A very deceptive move gains the ledge below the roof. Above it, pumpy climbing leads to a sting in the tail.

THE G-SPOT

(NN 390 101) Alt 250m South facing

This hidden little wall is actually a giant boulder of good rock. A nice alternative to the steep and thuggy climbing normally associated with mica schist sport climbing, offering technical, off-vertical climbing. It is somewhat difficult to find.

Approach: Up the left side of the woods, as for High Crag. When approximately 30m below Chasm Buttress (which can be seen poking out of the trees, traverse into the woods and continue a short way until the huge boulder is found.

Rhumba al Sol   12m   F6a   *(2000)*
The left-hand arete has good climbing but is a little mossy due to the adjacent tree.

**Hideous Kinky   12m   F7a ** **   *(2001)*
Climb the blank scoop then teeter up the thin wall to the easy finishing niche.

**Venga Boys   12m   F6c+ ** **   *(2000)*
Climb the right to left diagonal groove with technical moves to pass the initial roof. Good climbing.

El Mundo Fanatico   12m   F7a+   *(2000)*
Follow Venga Boys to the top of the groove, then step right to a technical finish up the headwall above.

**Live-in Skin   12m   F7c ** **   *(2004)*
Start up Venga Boys but pull rightwards through the initial groove on crimps to a thin diagonal crack. Step right and climb the thin technical wall (crux).

Inversnaid Area

Various outcrops lie on the east bank of Loch Lomond and are accessed from the B829 at Inversnaid. The area is wild and quiet with spectacular views over Loch Lomond. The crags are steep and west facing and are often dry and sunny during the autumn and winter months, when the bracken is down and they are more easily approached. Save for Creagan Tom Dubh, most of the buttresses have been developed as sport crags. Crags One to Four lie northwards in a line about 1.5km north of Inversnaid, clearly visible from the west bank of Loch Lomond, but more difficult to spot through the trees in summer from the approach. Further north, on the west side of Maol an Fhithich, can be found Creagan Tom Dubh.

Approach: Start from the car park by the Inversnaid Hotel (NN 337 089) and walk north along the West Highland Way for a few minutes to a boat shed. Just beyond this, follow a good path uphill into the woods past a picnic bench. 100m after a small wooden bridge, break right and ascend northwards to a small plateau and sheep paths running below the line of crags. The wave-like profile of Crag Two is obvious once spotted.

CRAG ONE

(NN 334 102) Alt 100m West facing

Hobble 10m F7a+ *(1997)*
A bouldery route near the right-hand end of the crag.

Project 12m
A good looking line on the steep pocketed wall 5m left of Hobble.

The next two buttresses running northwards have several bolted projects which have been abandoned. Crag Two is a stunning wave-like feature which will yield several hard routes. Crag Three lies just beyond and has stepped roofs and slabs.

WILD SWANS BUTTRESS

(NN 334 103) Alt 100m West facing

This is the best of this group of crags with a pleasant outlook towards the loch. It lies just beyond and at a slightly lower level than the first three crags.

The Ridge 10m F6c *(1998)*
Traverse leftwards to the arete (crux), then move up to easier climbing.

Dark Skies 10m F6b+ *(1997)*
A fingery start leads to a faint groove and better holds above.

Wild Swans 10m F6b+ * *(1997)*
The central line on the pocketed wall with immaculate rock.

Moonlight Sonata 10m F6b * *(1998)*
Start at the right end of the wall. Trend left to join the final section of Wild Swans.

Wild Goats 10m F7b *(2004)*
Start up Moonlight Sonata. From a finger pocket immediately above its third bolt, climb the smooth wall above on tiny crimps, trending slightly right to a flat hold. Finish into the scoop above.

CRYSTAL CRAG

(NN 336 109) Alt 200m West facing Map p36

This crag lies further to the north and is best visited on its own. There are several good longer routes which gives sustained fingery climbing on unusual quartz edges. Again, the crag is best visited in the autumn and spring and stays remarkably dry.

Approach: Follow the West Highland Way as for the previous crags but continue northwards along the path, passing Rob Roy's Cave. Shortly after crossing a bridge, you have to squeeze between two large boulders on the path. At this point, climb steeply through the woods to reach the crag. The approach takes around 45 mins but is worth it for the climbing, views and relative absence of midges.

Been Caught Stealin' 15m F7c * *(2004)*
Interesting fingery climbing directly up the smooth wall at its left end, to join Fear and Self Loathing at the end of its crux. A long sling is useful on the third bolt.

Fear and Self Loathing 15m F7b ** *(1998)*
An excellent outing. Break left from the lower section of Age of Aquarius and make a fingery traverse leftwrads to gain the upper wall and, eventually, better holds.

Age of Aquarius 15m F7a+ ** *(1998)*
Another superb, sustained route. Technical moves on sharp holds lead to a ramp. Trend leftwards up this until it is possible to break out onto the finishing wall.

Purgatory   15m   F7b *   *(1999)*
Start up Age of Aquarius but climb directly over the roof above (crux). Move left above the roof to the Age of Aquarius lower-off.

Roadkill Recipies   10m   F7a *   *(1998)*
Start by a small tree. Climb up and right through an overhang. Technically the warm-up route of the crag but pretty tough all the same!

Ruby Slippers   10m   F7a   *(2000)*
Pleasant climbing up the lower wall leads to a blind crux below the overhang.

Rebel Without Applause   10m   F7b   *(1998)*
Gain the ramp, then move up to a quartz boss. Use this to gain the tricky headwall via a very blind crimpy sequence. Desperate to on-sight!

Far From the Malham Crowds   10m   F7a **   *(1999)*
Thin and technical climbing near the right edge of the wall. Desperate to on-sight.

One route has been recorded on the crag at Rob Roy's Cave (NN 334 100) above the West Highland Way. **Tree Creeper** (35m, E2 5b) climbs the obvious slab left of a holly bush, then goes left at an overlap and right to the top.

CREAGAN TOM DUBH

(NN 337 136)   Alt 200m   West facing   Map p36

This crag lies below Maol an Fhithich, about 1km south of the houses at Doune (NN 333 144) on the east shore of the northern end of Loch Lomond. The lower tier is the conspicuous wall, well seen from the A82 on Loch Lomond's west shore.

Approach: Via West Highland Way; south from the Inverarnan Hotel (NN 318 185), or north from the Inversnaid Hotel (NN 337 089). 1hr 30mins.

LOWER TIER

Sequestrator   30m   E3 5b **   *(1989)*
Start 3m right of the central arete. Climb up and left to a small ledge on the crest, where good holds lead up and right to the final wall, crux. Excellent but serious.

Mahabharata   25m   E2 5b   *(1989)*
Start 10m right of Sequestrator below a faint crack in the lower part of the wall. Climb past the crack, peg runner on the left, and make a difficult move onto a horizontal break, crux. Bigger holds lead to the top. Protection is sparse and fiddly.

UPPER TIER

Athena   30m   E1 5b   *(1986)*
Climb the main corner-groove past two roofs. Steeper and harder than it looks.

Perfect Strangers   15m   E1 5a   *(1986)*
To the left of the previous route is a narrow slab giving unprotected climbing.

Crazy Cow   20m   E1 5b   *(1986)*
The slab about 20m left of Athena. Pull over the roof at the right end of the slab and climb a short wall to a scoopy ledge. Traverse left a short distance and climb the wall above to another ledge. Step right and finish straight up.

South Loch Lomond

The following crags are lie on the south-east shore of Loch Lomond and are all reached from the minor road leading north from Balmaha to Rowardennan.

CARN NA MUICE

(NS 385 951)   South-west facing   Map p36

Despite appearances and a pleasant location on the east bank of Loch Lomond, this is a disappointing crag. The exposure of quality rock is limited and most routes deteriorate in quality and increase in vegetation after steep starts.

Approach: About 5.5km north of Balmaha on the minor road to Rowardennan, the road passes Sallochy on the right and starts to rise up a hill, at which point a road into the forest leads off right (NN 389 951). Park here and descend the hill to follow the West Highland Way, then the loch-side to the crag.

A large fallen block marks the left side of the crag, in the centre is a prominent ridge and to the right a small steep wall topped by a roof, with a slab right of that.

Bite The Dust   45m   E4 6a   *(1991)*
Start below a thin quartz seam in the blank slab at the far right end. Ascend to a quartz pocket and a small crack, move left onto a quartz vein, then go up to the overlap. Move right to a diagonal crack, go up to a small face, then continue up and left to another face.

The Bat Flake   45m   VS 4c   *(1987)*
Climbs a steep pocketed rib behind the large block and right of a smooth slab.

The Drag   45m   VS 4c   *(1990)*
Climb the layback flake right of The Bat Flake.

Sunset Ridge   40m   Severe 4a   *(1987)*
The central ridge. Start up and right of the wide crack, and traverse left to the tree. The crack is HVS 5a from the ground.

Brimbles   40m   Very Difficult   *(1991)*
From a small chimney right of Sunset Ridge, climb up then right to a small ledge. Follow a clean line until level with trees, then move left to belay. Go left and up alongside the ridge. A direct start takes the clean slab to the right.

Twilight Slab   40m   VS 4c   *(1987)*
A prominent downward- pointing flake can be seen on the small steep wall right of Sunset Ridge. Climb up to this, traverse right below the small roof and follow mossy slabs to the steep crack in the final wall.

Sallochy Slab   40m   Very Difficult   *(1987)*
Right of the wall is a line of clean slanting slabs. Climb these to the top without a lot of protection. Not a bad route.

ROSS POINT

(NS 374 955)   North-west facing   Map p36

This impressive wall of slate lies in a large cleft on the east shore of Loch Lomond close to Glasgow University Research Station. The crag is probably natural, but the slate waste at the east end indicates quarring at some time in the past.

Approach: The crag is on the second headland south-west of the Sallochy Bay car park (NS 380 958), 6.5km north-west of Balmaha (poor Forestry Commission car park sign). Follow the West Highland Way west along the loch side to the boat house below the research station. A path behind the boat house leads onto a good track which is followed almost to the top of the second hill (about 630m from the boat house). Turn left into the wood, passing a conifered hill until the east end of the wall is met – about 240m. Scramble through the cleft to its western end. 15mins. The climbing is pleasant but limited and the midges can be unbearable.

MAIN WALL

The routes lie on the wall opposite the massive cracked boulder.

**Crystal Junction   10m   E4 6a ** *(1986)*
Climb the overhanging arete facing the cracked boulder, past three peg runners (which may not always be in place).

One Way Trip   15m   E4 6a *(1987)*
Start up Crystal Junction, traverse right and finish up Slug Death.

Slug Death   10m   E2 5b *(1987)*
Climb the right-hand corner past two peg runners.

To the right of the corner is an impressive long wall with an old bolt route and chipped holds. About halfway along is a ledge about 2m off the ground with a crack at its left and right ends.

Legover   4m   E2 5c *(1991)*
Mantelshelf onto the ledge and continue up the left-hand crack.

Pullover   4m   E2 5b *(1991)*
The right-hand crack.

THE BLOCK

Opposite the Main Wall is a massive boulder with an obvious forked crack.

Diagonal Chimney   8m   Severe 4a
The scary chimney on the right-hand side of the boulder.

Son of Cog   8m   E4 5c *(1991)*
The right arete of the boulder, facing Crystal Junction, gives unprotected climbing with the crux at the top.

Forked Lightning   8m   VS 4b *(1989)*
The left fork of the crack gives a pleasant route. The right fork is Severe.

Clynder & Rosneath Quarries

The following route descriptions were received late in the guide's production and are published here unchecked. All of the routes were rope soloed or soloed on the first ascent. Visitors should approach the given grades with caution, bearing in mind the fact that many routes are sparsely protected, or completely unprotected, and are relatively serious as a consequence.

HOLE IN THE FOREST QUARRY

(NS 245 838)   North facing

This is the most northerly of the three quarries above Clynder. Protection is generally a bit better than Rosneath.

Approach: From Clynder post office head north and take the first road on the left, Aonach Mhor Road. Head uphill, crossing the back road. At the next junction take the left fork, past a house, to an old iron gate. Cross a small stream and follow the track uphill into the forest. Follow the path leftwards (uphill) to the crag (15 mins).

Lilliputian Banquet   11m   VS 5a *(2003)*
The obvious groove-crackline right of the tree at the left side of the crag. Gain a

good hold from the quartzite footledge and follow the crack-line to a dirty niche just left of the tree, thread. Move right onto the slab, or continue to lower-off.

Mesmerised Potato   11m   E1 5c   *(2003)*
Start at the black wall at the left side of the quarry. Climb directly up wall to the thread and pull straight over the slabby bulge just right of the small tree. Good holds higher lead right lead to the tree lower-off. Well protected on the top section.

Pocket Battleship   12m   E1 5c *   *(2003)*
Follow Mesmerised Potato to the thread, then move up and left to a dirty niche just right of a small tree. Move right to two good pockets and a thread, then right again to a bigger pocket and finish directly.

Plod   16m   HVS 5a **   *(2003)*
This mid-height girdle is the best protected line on the crag. Follow Pocket Battleship to the thread then traverse right on good holds past Narcoman to the niche, thread. Move right again to the crack of Barbizon and finish up this. Lots of medium Friends.

Fly Agaric   13m   HVS 5b   *(2003)*
Just right of the previous routes is an obvious quartz ledge at about 3m. From its left side make a committing move up and left and follow a line of good but spaced holds to a thread. Hand-traverse right to a small niche, then move up and left using a left slanting crack, to a good pocket. Finish straight up taking care with the holds.

Narcoman   13m   E1 5b **   *(2003)*
Start as for Fly Agaric. Make the first moves but, instead of going left, continue straight up the wall on good holds to gain the horizontal fault-ledge, just right of a small sapling. Move right past a small niche and up to two good holds. Pull into the crack above, and finish slightly right. Poorly protected low down.

Absolu Lulu   12m   E3 6a   *(2003)*
Gain the quartz ledge of Fly Agaric in the middle. Using the big hold for the right-hand, face right and make a committing move up left to a small slot just right of the good holds on Narcoman. At the horizontal fault use jugs to gain the next horizontal break, then move right along it past a small niche. Up and right to Narcoman, then back left to finish as for Fly Agaric.

The following three routes start at the right-hand edge of the quartz ledge.

Hounds of Hell   15m   E3 5c *   *(2003)*
A sustained and poorly protected lower section. Attain a standing position on the ledge, then move right slightly to gain good holds for the right hand. Move left to under the niche, then left and up to good holds in the horizontal crack on Narcoman. Move right into the niche, thread, and exit it straight up onto the top wall and good holds. Finish left onto the good big hold on Narcoman.

Saucer Full of Secrets   15m   E4 6b   *(2003)*
The lower crux section is unprotected. Attain a standing position on the ledge, then move slightly left and climb the wall above on spaced holds moving left. Move right once the horizontal ledge is gained and follow this to the good holds on Narcoman. Traverse right to the niche and exit it right. Climb the wall just left of the Barbizon crack, up and left to good holds. Move left then back right to finish.

Barbizon the Bamboozler   15m   E2 5c *   *(2003)*
Follows the obvious crack in the top right-hand section of the crag. Attain a standing position on the quartz ledge, then move up to good holds on the right. Move right then straight up on the obvious line of holds (some loose) to gain the crack. Follow the crack to finish on big holds. Necky start.

Loosifer   16m   E3 5b *(2003)*

More than its fair share of loose holds and poorly protected. Gain the quartz ledge and traverse hard right onto a flat quartz foothold. Move up and right to better holds leading right. Move up to gain a big ledge on the left and follow a line of flaky holds to a small niche. Climb up and left onto the wall and use a big loose hold to finish just right of the tree.

Variation: **Rosemary's Baby   E1 6a** *(2003)*

Start a few feet to the right and gain the flat foothold direct. Ascend to a line of holds leading to the right traverse.

Once in a Lifetime   21m   E5 6a *(2004)*

Unprotected. Start as for Rosemary's Baby and traverse right on good big holds to the right side of the quartz ledges. Move up then slightly down and right to a good hold. Follow a crack up and horizontally right to a good small spike for the right hand, loosish. Move up and left using sidepulls in the small niche above to a longish reach to a good small jug, crux. Up and slightly right to the top of the crag.

The following route is a high girdle of the crag.

**Damien Trotter   18m   E2 5b/c ** *(2003)*

Climb Pocket Battleship to the big pocket below the lower-off. Move right to Narcoman, do the crux on this, then from the large hold at top of that route hand-traverse to the crack of Barbizon and finish up this slightly right on big holds.

Sheltered Shuffle   14m   E3 6a * *(2003)*

Start as for Rosemary's Baby. Climb this, move right and climb the wall directly to make a committing move to the good hold right of the red thread. Move slightly left and use the crack of Barbizon, finishing up the wall above the crack. Low in the grade.

Voyage of the Lilliputs   13m   E1 6a *(2003)*

A low level girdle. Start as for Rosemary's Baby, then follow the obvious line of handholds left to the quartz flake ledge. Start moving up and left to below the thread. Move left of the tree to finish right up the slab to walk off. A lot easier after the initial moves.

CLYNDER MAIN QUARRY

(NS 245 836)   East & South facing

The Main Quarry is rather disappointing, but the routes on the Graffiti Slab make the pleasant walk worthwhile and get the sun all day.

Approach: As for Hole in the Forest Quarry. Continue up the path until it turns up and right following some steps, to a clearing below the Main Quarry. The track contours the bottom of the screes then leads up scree to a big grassy flat section.

Scary Monsters   23m   E2 5b/c *(2004)*

Start left of the arete at the back of the quarry. Follow a slabby rib right, to below the arete and climb it to a block with a thin crack. Pull up and right and use a good hold to step up and left into a groove. Face right and layback over the tree stump. From the highly polished slab follow the right arete to the top. Move left to finish at a tree in the wet gully or pull a rope through and belay on the trees well back.

GRAFFITI SLAB

South Facing

This slab is unbelievably polished and poorly protected. A mat is probably more use than a rack. From the flat grassy section of Main Quarry a lone oak tree can be seen on the left; Graffiti Slab lies below it. There is a stake at the top of Autograph Hunter.

The Scribe   12m   E2 5a/b *   *(2004)*
Low in the grade but unprotected. Start just below and left of an obvious flake with a hole. Climb the short slab to a good but loosish quartz pocket. Move right onto a spike and from the right side of this climb straight up using the borehole until below a yellow bulge in the slab above. Pull directly over this and move left to finish.

Trance Fusion   15m   E1 5b   *(2004)*
Follow The Scribe to Connect Three, then that route to the move onto the quartzite band. Move right and up to the good borehole. Traverse right until above the Mega Flake and finish as for Mutiny....

Calligraphy   11m   E1 5a   *(2004)*
Badly protected lower down. Follow The Scribe to the loosish quartz pocket. Move onto the slab above and diagonally right to the quartzite band. Follow this then up to the good hold on Doomsday Book. Use this to gain the top of Mega Flake.

Book of the Dead   11m   E3 5c **   *(2004)*
Start for The Scribe. From the big hole move right onto the slab and using the foot hole and corner above move right to gain the small footholds above the crux of Autograph Hunter. Move right again to the quartz band then up and right to a committing move into the groove of Mega Flake at half height. Follow this past poor thread to the top. A diagonal traverse slightly below the previous route.

Connect Three   14m   HVS 5a *   *(2004)*
Unprotected. Start at the obvious flake with a hole up and right of The Scribe. Climb the right-hand side of this to the top, move left and climb the slab above using a good borehole for the right hand. Up the slab past another borehole until at a small spike type hold and small pocket. Using the quartzite flake on the right move up to finish on bigger holds.

Even the Midges Have Droont   14m   E2 5c   *(2004)*
Unprotected. Start as for Connect Three. Climb to the top of spike, then move up and diagonally right to the good holds in the quartzite vein. Move right for a move then climb the slab centrally, avoiding holds on adjacent routes.

Keeh   9m   VS   *(2004)*
Start at Connect Three. Follow the obvious left sloping diagonal fault to the big hole. Up the slab and corner above moving slightly left to finish on loose edges.

Autograph Hunter   11m   E3 6a/6b **   *(2004)*
Unprotected. Start just left of the Billy Irvine graffiti at the bottom of the slab. Move up using a one finger pocket and a high sidepull until it is possible to slither onto the small holds on the right (crux). Gain better holds in a small niche and climb up left to a good sidepull, then up and right to a good borehole. Finish left.
Variation: **Billy Bunter   E3 6b**   *(2004)*
Climb straight up through the Billy Irvine graffiti.

Doomsday Book   15m   E4 6b ***   *(2004)*
Unprotected. Start just right of the previous route at a good small ledge just below an obvious hole. Climb the slab above the hole moving slightly right once established. Using a good dink high up left, gain the horizontal band on the right. Move left then gain a good but slightly loose hold on the wall above and using this gain good holds and traverse left to finish up Autograph Hunter.

Jonah   14m   E2 5c/6a *   *(2004)*
Start just right of the hole at the start of Doomsday Book on a downward sloping foothold. Move up and right to a good small hold on the quartzite band, just below the bottom of the hanging flake arete. Move into the slim groove right of Mutiny... and just right of the arete and climb this past a peg to the easier wall.

**Every Trick in the Book   14m   E4 6a/6b ** **   *(2004)*

Unprotected. The quartz band traverse, without using the flakes of Yosemite Sam. Start at a small hairline crack right of the obvious flake system. Ascend the slab to the band and using a good small foothold to get some height, follow the band left.

Lost in Translation   11m   HVS 5c   *(2004)*

A low level right to left girdle. Start just left of Yosemite Sam at a black foothold. Traverse left using all the holds available to gain the corner flake of Connect Three.

**Yosemite Sam   15m   E1 5c ** **   *(2004)*

Follows the obvious quartz band which girdles the middle of the slab. Start below the flake system on the right. Ascend and undercut the flakes left using the band for the feet. Traverse left to a point where the flake leads upwards. Care should be taken here as the protection pulls out after the crux move. Traverse the band to the small niche of Autograph Hunter. Unusual climbing.

Mega Flake   15m   E1 5a * **   *(2004)*

Wobbly holds and the gear is hard to place. The obvious flake system on the right of the slab. Follow Yosemite Sam until below the obvious corner continuation. Climb this and move left past the borehole to finish.

Mutiny on the Submarine Bounty   15m   E2 5b   *(2004)*

Follows the right-hand side of the mega flake. Follow Yosemite Sam until below the flake continuation, poor peg high right. Follow the edge to the top of the flake and finish direct with care.

Lost in Space   16m   E3 5c *   *(2004)*

Unprotected until after the crux. Follow Yosemite Sam to half way along the undercut flake traverse. Pull over and slightly right to a line of flakes and follow them to a borehole. Traverse hard left using small holds on the slab above and make a hard move to gain the short banana shaped groove, hard to clip peg. Up the corner, thread, then more easily left to the top.

Boletus   14m   E3 6a   *(2004)*

Unprotected. Start as for Yosemite Sam. Move up and follow the obvious line of flaky holds to the borehole of Lost in Space. Move past this on the left and pull over a small bulge onto the slab above using some looosish flakes and small holds. Continue up and right to a big hold. Traverse left to finish up Mega Flake.

Numpty   14m   E3 5c   *(2004)*

Unprotected, awkward and insecure. Follow Yosemite Sam to the end of the undercut flake traverse. Using holds in the groove of Mutiny... cross the overlap and gain footholds on the right. Move up the left side of the obvious cleaned slab, then right across it to good footholds in a small niche. Move left and up to finish.

Liberty Cap   13m   E3 5c   *(2004)*

Unprotected. A more direct on the previous route. Start for Yosemite Sam. Follow a short slabby ramp on sidepulls to gain the flakes of Numpty. Traverse right and climb the slab directly on small edges, avoiding the good big foothold on the right.

Brinjal   16m   E2 5c   *(2004)*

Unprotected. Follow the previous route from the start of Yosemite Sam until at the flakes. Instead of traversing right follow the line of obvious holds until at the good high sidepulls on Boletus. Traverse left to finish as for previous routes.

ROSNEATH QUARRY

(NS 257 824)   North, South & East facing

This slate quarry lies approximately 500m south of Rosneath in Camsail Wood and offers a variety of routes on north, south and east facing slabs and overhanging walls. The rock does not run to much protection, although a number of pegs have been placed, and the routes are quite serious as a result. Nut and camming device protection can be found, but placements are few and far between and both size and type specific. Selecting a rack is hard, but carrying nuts and cams is recommended for all routes. Routes were rope soloed or soloed on the first ascent and are published here unchecked, so grades should be approached with caution. Spring and autumn are the best times to visit as midges, mosquitoes, clegs and flies make Rosneath a hellhole in summer.

Approach: Park at the lay-by at Camsail Bay, the first bay south of Rosneath. Cross the road, and follow the faint track to the quarry (5 mins). The quarry is full of water and marshy, so the best approach is by abseil off the many trees. Climbers should keep a low profile as the owner does not want large groups visiting. Go through the rusty gate, and then contour round to the right.

Routes are described from right to left. Trees at the top provide lower-offs.

SOUTH FACE

At the extreme right-hand side of the quarry are short walls and an obvious arete, taken by Poison Dwarf.

Gloog Gloog   5m   Very Difficult   (2003)
The short slabby wall right of the arete. Gain the ledge without using the crack of Atlantis and climb the wall to traverse left to a tree.

Atlantis...5m   VS 5b   (2002)
The slab right of the arete has a boulder problem start. Continue to a finger slot, then straight up the middle of the slab.

Scrog   15m   VS 5b   (2003)
A pointless, scrappy traverse. Start as for Atlantis, then follow the obvious horizontal ledge left to Snafu.

Poison Dwarf   5m   E2 6a *   (2002)
The obvious arete without using the slab or corner crack on the left.

Cocopop   5m   Severe 4b   (2002)
The short corner crack.

Screwball   5m   VS 5a   (2003)
The slab is more of a boulder problem.

After the Flood   5m   Severe 4b   (2002)
The crack in the slab is hard to start.

One Move Wonder   6m   E1 5c *   (2002)
Gain the crack of After the Flood and move left to gain the slab above.

Touch and Go   6m   E4 6b   (2003)
Gain the crack of After the Flood and move left to stand on the sloping hold, without using the two small holds on the other routes. Make a strange foot move, then step onto the slab (crux). Gain the horizontal and ascend right to a tree.

Son of Chalkstorm   6m   E4 6a *   (2003)
Unprotected with a bad landing. Gain the crack of After the Flood and move left to stand on the sloping hold. Use the right-hand of two small holds in the horizontal crack to gain the slab and a long reach to the glacis.

Ba Boo   6m   E3 6a   (2003)
The blunt rib between Bhoona Baby and One Move Wonder. Follow Bhoona Baby

to the good big hold in the corner. Traverse right onto the rib and make committing and poorly protected moves to gain the slab above the small overlap.

Bhoona Baby   6m   E1 5a   *(2003)*
Climb the next corner groove above a short slab. Gain the slab above and move right to tree. Poorly protected, with some wobbly holds.

Pay Now or Die Later   8m   E3 5c   *(2003)*
The left arete of the blank wall above a murky puddle. Start as for Footless Crowbar, and using the undercut and hold above, move right to gain a good foothold on the arete. Once on the arete, move up and pull over onto the easier slab above to finish right to a tree. Awkward and poorly protected.

Footless Crowbar   8m   E2 5c   *(2003)*
The route right of Snafu. Starting from a corner on the right, move left on undercuts to an undercling. Pass two pegs, the left one is better and the right-hand one is easiest clipped from above, to finish at Snafu. High in the grade.

Eliminate   8m   E3 5c   *(2003)*
The slabby wall between Snafu and Footless Crowbar. Follow your nose, utilising the peg on Snafu.

Snafu   10m   E4 6a ***   *(2003)*
The slabby bulging wall below the overhanging top wall. Finish direct up the overhanging wall just left of the pegs to tree lower-off.

No Place for a Bunter   E4 6a *
Start as for Snafu. Move left to a shallow groove with a poor peg. Pass this using some awkward pinches to the glacis, poor peg high on the right. Pull through the overhang above, move left to a good hold, protection and easier slab.

Lola   12m   E2 5b   *(2002)*
The wide V-groove with a block low down. From the tree gain a good hold just behind the right of the block, then move left to stand on the block. Gain a massive jug for both hands, peg on left, and crank right onto a slab, over a bulge. Once established on the jug use the good jam crack, protection, to shuffle left using low holds to a crack. Awkward, with a necky start.

Revelations   8m   E2 5c *   *(2002)*
The left side of the arete, left of the previous route. Climb the arete to a peg on right and move up to a good flat hold and crack in a bulge, protection. Pull over and clip a peg on left before moving onto the slab above, from the right-hand side of big ledge.

Triangulation Point   8m   E2 5b   *(2002)*
Starts about 2.5m right of Voodoo Child. Move up the overlapping slab to a peg. Undercut up and right to a hold on the arete from where an amazing triangular hold can be used to gain easier ground, peg.

Village of the Dammed   8m   E3 5c   *(2004)*
The wall just right of Voodoo Child. Climb straight up the wall just right of the corner to pull over the bulge left to good holds, pegs on left. Pull centrally over the small bulge to gain the slab; some loose holds.

Voodoo Child   10m   E2 5a   *(2002)*
Climb the big corner groove with a capping overhang past pegs and a dodgy big flake. Move left onto a slab and using holds high up, step left to lower-off.

Zeeg Zog Zeeg   8m   E2 5b *   *(2003)*
The small inset wall right of Zook Pa Rook, left of Voodoo Child. Climb a short crack

to a good horizontal break. Using the arete on the left, step up, layback onto the left arete and pull onto the ledge, peg. Finish up the left-hand corner.

Zook Pa Rook   11m   E3 6a   (2003)
Follow Reek Pa Reek to the good horizontal break. Using a high left sidepull step right onto a sloping ledge. A high pinch then a hold in the glacis leads to two pegs. Move right and make an awkward move up onto the slab.

Reek Pa Reek   11m   E3 5c   (2001)
Start as for Voodoo Child. Make an awkward hand-traverse left to a flaky undercut spike, dodgy, and a good slot. Ascend left to follow Spear Chukka to the peg, move right to gain the left of the two obvious short slabby grooves, using a thin crack.

Spear Chukka   11m   E2 5c **   (2001)
Just left of previous route is an obvious buttress with a lot of overlaps. Start centrally and using the left arete get established on wall, then move hard right and up to in-situ thread and peg. Ascend right to a big ledge hold, peg. Using high holds on the arete step left onto the slab, poor peg, to finish left to Swamp Fever.

Swamp Fever   11m   E1 5b   (2001)
Just right of the slabby arete climb the obvious groove and crack to a bulge. Pull over using a weird big hold, move slightly right then back left past poor peg.

Tatless   7m   E2 5a   (2003)
The slabby arete left of previous route. Start up and left on a boulder in a corner. Move hard right, over two overlaps and right to a lower-off; unprotected with some loose holds.

More Intense than a Bummer on Mushrooms   9m   E2 5c   (2003)
Start as for Tatless. At a short layback crack, attain the ledge, some poor gear, and make committing moves right onto the slabby arete and up to a poor peg. Move left round the arete on good, but awkwardly-spaced, holds, then up and left to a poor lower-off, large Friend back-up.

West Coast Suntan   6m   VS 4c   (2003)
The obvious yellow wall and ramp left of the previous route. Using a big hidden hold to start, follow your nose to the poor lower-off.

Quasimodo   37m   E2 5b   (2003)
A two pitch traverse of the right-hand section. Start as for West Coast Suntan.
1. 17m Move onto the ledge, then right round the corner past a poor peg. Climb left and up to the lower-off on Swamp Fever. Traverse up and right to a step down onto the slab and hanging belay under the obvious roof.
2. 20m Move down and right to an awkward step down to a good ledge below the slab, crux, and traverse right along the ledge, past a peg. Follow the obvious traverse line past pegs to large loose blocks. Finish easily right to lower-off.

West Nile Virus   12m   HVS 5a   (2001)
The first route on the main slab. Start as for SV1417 and move right to a ledge at about 5m. Move right to a shallow corner and follow this to an awkward mantel onto a polished ledge; poorly protected.

Herring Bone   12m   E1 5b *   (2003)
The slab with a hairline fracture in its middle section. Start at a tree. Climb the slab to a mantel onto the glacis. Move right to protection, then loft and follow the hairline crack to a second glacis to finish right to a tree.

The next few routes start in the vicinity of a big spike, an obvious feature on the right-hand section of the slab.

SV1417   13m   HVS 5a *(2001)*
Start just right of the spike. Some loose and green moves lead to a good ledge, peg. Move up onto the slab using a pinch and move rightwards and up to good flat holds (wires). Move left to a large triangular hold, then down and rightwards to lower-off tree. A good middle section spoiled by the lower choss.

The New Hyksos   12m   E2 5c * *(2004)*
Start just right of the spike in a small niche. Pull onto the slab, cross an overlap, and move slightly right to the break; poorly protected. Clip the peg on Lupin and make a couple of moves up the SV1417 slab. Pull onto the slab above a small overlap, ascend to the next break, peg, and follow it right to a lower-off tree.

Lupin   12m   E2 5b ** *(2001)*
Follow Dicentra Spectabilis to top of the spike. Move slightly right and follow the two thin cracks up the slab, peg, to a move left, peg, below a tree stump to join Dicentra Spectabilis.

Dicentra Spectabilis   18m   HVS 5c ** *(2001)*
Climb the big spike and follow the crack above to a peg. Move up to a good ledge and using a loose spike on the left gain a good small hold at the top of the slab on the right. Finish right to a tree, crux.
Variation: **Alternative Finish   VS 5a ****
From the ledge above the peg move right to the tree.

DNA   20m   E3 5c ** *(2004)*
Climbs the slab between Stag and Dicentra Spectabilis; if dry. Start left and down from the big spike. Pull over the bulge, peg, and climb the slab rightwards to triangular foothold. Move up and right over a small bulge to a polished ledge just left of the crack of Dicentra, peg. Avoiding the crack, gain the next good ledge from where a peg can be clipped. Move hard left and using a low handhold, climb the slab past a crumbly hold to better holds. Move right and up to the big ledge, peg. Stand on the loose block, and climb the slab to a V-slot and an awkward traverse right to a hidden hold at top of the right arete of the slab.

Stag   13m   E2 5b * *(2001)*
Follow Habanero to the good ledge, pegs, move into a niche on the right and cross the overlap. Ascend to the pink holds and traverse right to the big ledge on Dicentra Spectabilis. Move slightly right and finish up the right edge of the slab.

Seven Pillars of Wisdom   22m   E2 5c * *(2001)*
This girdle the lower glacis fault is one of the best protected routes in the quarry. Start as for Dicentra Spectabilis from the top of the spike utilising all the available pegs. Traverse left to the ledge on PLXD Double Zero. Do the weird crux move then continue to the niche on Kiya, move up and left, high peg, then left to the arete. The poor peg on Death Wish protects the moves down into the Deus Liberatus corner.

Habanero   19m   E2 5c * *(2001)*
From the big spike and follow the left-hand crack to a niche just left of the spike top. Move left then up and left onto a good ledge, two poor pegs. Move into a small sloping niche above the lower peg to reach a good hold. Using this move hard left to two pegs. Step onto the good hold and traverse left to a yellow niche and Kiya.

PLXD Double Zero   19m   E2 5c *(2001)*
Follow Habanero to the big ledge and the two pegs. Move down and left onto the good ledge under the overlap, peg. Traverse left and use a good flat foothold low on the left to make baffling moves left through the overlap. Move left to a good hold and follow the slabby fault rightwards to the two pegs; traverse left to Kiya.

Stone of Destiny   20m   E2 5c *** *(2001)*
Start left and down from the big spike. Pull straight over a bulge to a massive jug,

peg up left. Move right then back left to a peg at the big ledge and ascend to the Habanero ledge, poor pegs. Once established on the slab above the bulge, peg, sustained moves lead left then straight up to the pegs on Habanero.

Kiya 13m E3 5c ***   (2001)

When dry, one of the best routes in the quarry. Start below a niche with a crack and peg on its left wall. Gain the undercut, then loose the two-finger pocket by bridging. Step onto the arete and move onto a bulging, slabby rib. Make committing moves to gain the downward sloping spike and move into a niche. Traverse right, step left onto the slab above, peg, and make a long reach to a good slot below the lower-off.

Variation: **Scota E2 5b**   (2001)

A harder finish. From the niche on Kiya pull left onto a big ledge, pegs. From its left side make a high step onto the slab and ascend to the pegs on Death Wish.

The 18th Dynasty 16m E3 6a *   (2004)

Good slab climbing up the green streak between Kiya and Scota. Start in the impressive corner of Deus Liberatus. Gain the good hold on the arete on the right. Traverse right, step onto a flat block foothold, then up to a good ledge on the right, just left of the niche on Kiya, various pegs. Step onto the slab and avoiding the bigger holds on the left on Scota, ascend to two pegs.

Death Wish 15m E2/3 5b   (2001)

A serious route following the left arete of the main slab. Start at right-hand side of the Deus Liberatus slab. Move up and right onto the arete, then up and right again to a poor peg, some loose holds. Move left onto the arete via a slabby hanging groove and gain a huge jug. Move right past two poor pegs to Kiya.

Deus Liberatus 13m E2 5c   (2001)

An impressive corner and good top slab offer a committing route, spoilt only by a band of loose rock. Follow the easy slab to a move right onto the arete. Hard moves left gain a loose ledge in the corner, crux, poor peg. Lunge left to a very good jug, gain the slab and finish more easily.

Variation: **Slab Variant E2 5c ***

From the good jug hand-traverse left to the arete of Trials and Tribulations.

Hiram Key 13m E5 6b ***   (2003)

The hardest route in the quarry and unprotected. Climb the wall left of the Deus Liberatus corner using the spike at foot of the slab to gain a small hold below the overlap. Pull left and gain a good jug under the overlap, tied off peg. Gain a small hold at the bottom of the short groove above and make a long reach to gain a small but positive two finger hold. Pull over the overlap to finish up the easier slab.

Seqenenra 11m E4 6a ***   (2003)

Unprotected local test-piece. Follow Hiram Key to the small hold at the bottom of the short groove above the overlap. Move hard left to a smear and a final tricky move onto the arete. Finish up this at 5b.

Trials and Tribulations of a Village Idiot 10m E2 5b   (2001)

Unprotected. Start left of Seqenenra and ascend onto boulders in a corner. Step onto the arete and ascend to the big hold of Meet yer Maker. Step left onto the slab and make thin moves left to better holds.

Guantamalan Insanity Pepper 12m E2 5b *   (2001)

Unprotected. Start as for Meet yer Maker. Gain a ledge on the arete. Follow the slab up and right using a thin crack to a good pocket/edge. Mantel this to gain good hold on the right and finish left.

Meet yer Maker 10m HVS 4c   (2001)

Unprotected. Climb the short corner at the right-hand side of the next slab and pull onto a slab on right using big holds and a flake-crack. Follow the crack to big holds, finish left past two pegs.

Baloo   13m   E2 5c * *(2004)*
A high girdle of the Triple Triangle Insignia slab gives good climbing and the easiest route at its grade on the slab. Start in the corner of Meet yer Maker. Climb the wall on the left to a ledge and foot traverse it left to Triple Triangle Insignia. Follow this to the big holds and traverse left under the peg. Move left for a few feet then diagonally up and left to The Boy Bisto lower-off.

The Five Keys   11m   E3 6a * *(2001)*
Unprotected. The most right-hand route on this slab starts just left of Meet yer Maker. Ascend the wall, cross the overlap on the right-hand side and finish direct.

Forest Fire   11m   E2 5c/6a * *(2001)*
Thin and unprotected. Start 1.5m up and right of Triple Triangle Insignia. Gain the triangular niche at the right side of a big ledge. Climb straight through the overlap and slightly right to finish on Triple Triangle Insignia.

Khallill   12m   E2 5c ** *(2001)*
A good but sparsely protected route. Follow Forest Fire to the big ledge. Move 2m left and gain the yellow rock scar using undercut below overlap. Pull straight through, poor peg, to easier sustained climbing using holds in the thin left crack, peg.

Laws of the Cosmos   10m   E3/4 6b *** *(2004)*
On the Triple Triangle Insignia slab is a small triangular niche. Gain this from the left using a good small undercut spike type hold to finish up various routes.

Forest Fire Direct   10m   E3 6a/b *(2001)*
Start as for Triple Triangle Insignia but move over the overlap on the right.

Triple Triangle Insignia   11m   E1 5a *** *(2001)*
The easiest route on the slab should become a classic. From a plinth move left using the overlap to a slot in crack (hidden) which is used to surmount the overlap. Continue to the big ledge and move right. With a high step gain a V-shaped pinch hold and cross a small overlap to better holds and a peg.

The Boy Bisto   12m   E2 5c * *(2004)*
Hard slab climbing. Follows the left-hand corner of the Triple Triangle Insignia slab. Start just left of Triple Triangle Insignia below a triangular slabby niche. Climb this using the left arete, and the small finger slot high on the right above the overlap. From the ledge move up and slightly left to climb the green slab direct. From a good pinch near the top of the chimney, go right to a tree.

Third Degree   11m   E3 5c *(2001)*
Unprotected. Start just left of Triple Triangle Insignia. Layback wide crack then step right onto slab and up to big ledge. From its left side move onto a good hold, then up and right to a good hold, followed by a hard move to get the right foot onto the good foothold on Khallill.

Red Beusant   11m   E2 5b * *(2001)*
Poorly protected. Follow Third Degree to the big ledge. From its left side move up and onto a slab which is followed leftwards on well spaced holds, then rightwards to a right traverse, peg, and tree.

True Colours   13m   E2 5b * *(2003)*
A right to left girdle of the Triple Triangle Insignia slab. Start as for Meet yer Maker and hand-traverse the obvious fault to the far side of slab. Follow the Red Beusant to finish, first left then rightwards along top of crag, peg, and tree.

**High Girdle 37m E1 5b ** * *   *(2003)*
Do Triple Triangle Insignia. Belay on tree. Move right then down to the peg on Deus Liberatus. Move round corner past two pegs to a hanging belay on the Kiya lower-off. Follow the traverse right to the tree lower-off in the corner. The longest route in the quarry.

**Route 66 8m Very Difficult ** *   *(2002)*
Left from the slab and down slightly is a boulder split by a thin crack (Smear or Disappear). Start directly below this in a small cave. Move right into a strange diagonal chimney fault and slither up this (very entertaining) to a small slab. Move left then traverse right to pull onto the slab above at the lower-off.

**Dwarf People 6m E3 6b ** *   *(2003)*
The line right of Smear or Disappear. Start at a small cave, move left to gain the good two-finger slot, then move onto the slab rightwards utilising a high sidepull. The obvious tapered hanging nose on the right is 5b **.

**Smear or Disappear 6m HVS 5c ** *   *(2002)*
The thin crack avoiding holds on the left.

Tarasbulba 8m Severe   *(2002)*
The easy left edge of Smear or Disappear, move left onto the slab from blocks and abseil off the big spike.

Frogmella 5m Very Difficult   *(2002)*
Up and left from the previous routes are some big blocks and a slabby section beyond. Start in the middle of the slab at a block belay. Step onto the block, move into a slabby groove and pull out right to a big tape. Abseil off.

Boke till you Choke 6m VS 4c   *(2002)*
Low in the grade. Start just right of the left arete; If 6 was 9. Move up and slightly right to a good horizontal crack. At a spike move right and up a slabby wall to a big hold at the back of the flat top. Move left over a bulge to finish. Abseil off.

**If 6 was 9 5m Difficult ** *   *(2002)*
The slab and edge 3m left of Frogmella, starting from a large blocky hold. Lower-off or pull onto the block and traverse right to Frogmella.

The next eight routes are best approached by abseil. Magnum is the first route on the last south facing slab.

**Magnum 17m VS 4b ** *   *(2001)*
Climb the slab left of the chossy corner past a huge jug to the top of a slabby corner. Traverse left and finish up Sobek.

Happy Valley 12m HVS 5b *   *(2004)*
Follow Magnum to the spike. Move slightly right and pull onto the headwall using a triangular hold and pinch undercut on the left. Lower-off or top-out.

Cleopatra 20m E1 5c *   *(2004)*
A right to left mid-height girdle. Start at Magnum. Follow this to the good big triangular hold and traverse left to Heron. Move left to a big ledge, then follow the foot-crack to the peg on El Thumbo. Traverse across the slab to the arete and finish up the corner of Lilith.

**Careless Talk Costs Lives 11m E4 6a ** *   *(2004)*
Follows a black streak in the slab between SLIX 220 112 and Magnum. Start as for Magnum. Ascend the slab to a steepening, pull over slightly leftwards, then climb the streak directly on poor slaps, crux, to the big hold and gear. Move left to a niche, then right to the tree. Unprotected.

SLIX 220 112 15m   E3 6a   (2001)
Start as for Magnum. As soon as possible move up from a good foothold leftwards on smears to a good hold (crux). From here move right to the tape runner on Magnum and finish up that.

Heron   11m   HVS 4c   (2001)
The next crack-line fault on the left is followed by this route.

Sobek   11m   Very Difficult *   (2001)
The obvious crack left of the previous route. Move left at top to finish as for the next route. A good wee route.

Crocodilopolis   10m   Severe   (2001)
This crack can be seen from the opposite side of the quarry. An obvious feature. Follow the crack to the top.

El Thumbo   10m   E3 6a *   (2001)
The slab left of the previous route. Start in the middle of the slab or directly below the peg. Move right onto the slab, peg , then up and left on smears to a small corner and easier finish.

Sandwich   10m   E3/4 6a **   (2003)
Climb the centre of the unprotected slab, without using the left arete.

Rosneath Riviera   10m   E2 5b/c **   (2001)
Gain the El Thumbo slab and ascend using the left arete; unprotected.

Lilith   11m   VS 4c *   (2001)
In the left-hand corner of the slab is an inset slab with a thin crack. Follow the well-protected crack-line, passing a loose spike at the top and move right onto the slab. Follow the crack in corner above, then move right to finish at the wide crack.
Variation: **Butlins   VS 4c**   (2004)
From the move right onto the slab follow the easiest line rightwards to the spike/block on Magnum.

Girdle   15m   E1 5b   (2003)
Start as for Lilith. Up a few feet then hard right to below the peg on El Thumbo. Follow the short horizontal crack and use the slot on Heron to pass the two thin cracks to a good jug. Using the next good jug move right on smears then up to the horizontal break which is followed to the big spike! Traverse back left to finish.

The Turnip   6m   Severe   (2004)
The arete right of Glucosamino. Climb the arete to a good hold up and right, then up and left to finish.

Glucosamino   6m   VS 5b   (2004)
Unprotected. Gain the slab right of the previous route by a high step. Straight up to big holds and finishing jugs.

Glucosamine Sulphate   6m   VS 4c *   (2004)
The short clean slab just right of Glucosamino. Start just right of the crack and gain the slab without using it (crux). Follow the slab to a thin crack and follow this to big holds. Move right to finish up Glucosamino. Low in the grade.

Soap Dodger   6m   Very Difficult   (2004)
The obvious dirty crack-line and short rightwards curving continuation.

The following routes are on the wall right of the seasonal waterfall at the back of the quarry.

Kamikaze 5m E3 6a *(2004)*
Short, devious and poorly protected. Climb the centre of the short steep wall up and right of Torra Torra Torra to a hard pull onto the slab above and finish left.

Monkey Position 5m E2 5c *(2004)*
The arete left of Kamikaze. Start just left of Kamikaze and climb the short slabby wall. Pull over the overlap and finish right up the slabby ramp and arete on the left. Scary!!

Torra Torra Torra 6m VS 5a * *(2003)*
Start at the arete and climb past a tree and hollow flake to a crack. Up and right to finish up a slabby ramp, crux.

Zero 5m Severe *(2003)*
Left of Torra Torra Torra. Start centrally, pull onto slab and gain the crack.

Govan Googly 6m Severe *(2004)*
Traverse left to the right arete of Kamikaze, step round the corner to the big flake and move left to finish up Zero.

EAST FACE

The next routes are on the small east-facing wall at the back of the quarry.

Approach: By abseil.

Chossville 12m E1 5a *(2002)*
Start down and right of the obvious smooth, polished groove under an obvious bulge at the left-hand side of slab. Undercut right to a crack, move right and up on good but wobbly holds. Move up and left avoiding loose blocks, then left to finish

Smeero 10m E2 6a *(2002)*
Start as for Chossville and move awkwardly left round the overlap to the big ledge. Move sharp right to a foothold on the edge of the overlap, gain a crack in the slab and ascend to a horizontal hold. Go slightly right then left to finish on good ledges.

Clegso 8m HVS 4c/5a *(2002)*
The obvious smooth, polished groove is poorly protected and slippery.

Gethsemene 7m E4 6b * *(2003)*
Start just right of the obvious left-hand corner. Climb past a peg to finish in the shallow groove above, right. Easy for the grade.

Wee Polaris 6m E1 5b * *(2002)*
Unprotected. The obvious left-hand corner, moving up right past the big spike. Best leave rope in-situ in case of failure.
Variation: **Variation Start E1 6a**
Follows the slab just right of the corner to the big blocky hold.

Gorilla Warfare 6m VS 4c *(2003)*
The left arete of Wee Polaris is climbed directly to finish left.

Urban Gorilla 6m VS 4c * *(2003)*
Left again. Climb up to block on good holds and finish right.

**Fingers like Toes 6m HVS 5b ** ** *(2003)*
Just left of Urban Gorilla, finishing directly up the capping block's right hand side.

Le Cube 5m E2 6a * *(2004)*
Start just right of a thread. Climb the wall directly and pull straight over the cubelike overhang. Strange.

Toes like Fingers   7m   E2 6a   *(2003)*
Follow Ape Man then move right to gain the crack. Climb this and use holds above
the block to swing into the groove on left. Poorly protected and awkward.

Ape Man   6m   VS 5a   *(2003)*
Climb the obvious slabby arete on the small wall between the Clegso slab and the
main back wall, finishing up the tree branch.

X.T.C.   6m   E2 6a *   *(2003)*
The wall left of Ape Man. A poorly protected lower part, leads to good wires at the
top.

White Man Sambo   5m   Very Difficult   *(2003)*
The Wall left of X.T.C.

Gorilla Wall Girdle   10m   HVS 5a   *(2003)*
Start as for X.T.C. Follow the rising traverse right to gain the corner, move onto the
wall beyond and traverse right to the arete left of Wee Polaris. Entertaining.

The following routes lie on the main east-facing back wall.

Kek   9m   VS 5a   *(2003)*
Start just right of the obvious long slabby buttress on the right (Flat Top). Climb the
obvious groove until it is possible to traverse right across a slab using a slot. Follow
the slabby groove to a big loose blocky hold; a pile of ...

Nefertlti   10m   E3 5c *   *(2003)*
Start at toe of the obvious long slabby buttress on the right. Climb up and right
into the obvious flaky groove. As soon as possible move slightly right following
holds just right of the groove, without using any of the big holds in the groove, to
the mantel move. Up onto the block on the left, pegs, and follow Flat Top until
standing in the big hole above the pegs. Move right using the top of the crag and
past a good peg, to finish up the groove of Kek.

Flat Top   11m   E2 6a **   *(2003)*
Follow Nefertiti to the obvious flaky groove and follow it to a mantel onto a ledge,
pegs on right. Move up and right attain a standing position in the hole above the
pegs. Up the groove above, crux, to a flat finale.

Hanging Garden   14m   E1 5b   *(2003)*
Follow Flat Top to just below the mantel and move left on a hidden foothold past
a thread to finish up the slabby arete.

Run Like the Wind   11m   E4 6a   *(2003)*
Follow Wild Wild Wood to just below the slabby corner. Using the slot in the back
of the slabby groove, gain a foothold on the right and use a two finger sidepull on
the slab to gain a small hold on the arete. Move onto the bigger foothold, ascend
to the thread, and finish up the ramp.

Wild Wild Wood   10m   VS 4c ***   *(2002)*
One of the best protected routes in the quarry and worth looking for. The obvious
central weakness, following a slabby ramp. Gain the slabby corner and follow this
to the top. One of the best protected routes in the quarry and worth looking for.

The Land that Time Forgot   12m   E2 5c **   *(2003)*
Start as for Wild Wild Wood. Follow the diagonal crack left to gain holds above a
peg. Move right and follow the wall to a thread and peg, finishing direct.
Variation: **Direct Start   E2 6a ***
Start just left of the normal start, just left of the peg. Ascend to gain a triangular

hold for the right toe. Up to good sidepull gain the main route. The peg can't be clipped until after the crux.

Sitka   16m   E2/3 6a *   (2003)
Follow the direct start to The Land that Time Forgot, then that route right and up to the corner of Wild Wild Wood. Move right and down past the thread and reverse The Hanging Garden to the big hold on the right. Clip pegs and move up and right to the hole above the pegs. Move right using holds at the top of the crag, past a good peg, to the easy groove.

Bin Diver   8m   E1 5b/c   (2003)
Just to the left is a small buttress with a ledge at half height. Ascend using a loose spike to the ledge (crux). Follow holds until it is possible to make a move onto the arete near the top to finish.

A chossy fault is then followed by a wall.

Nylorac   7m   Hard Severe 4b   (2002)
The obvious short slabby wall on the right-hand side. Follow this and finish right.
Variation: **Left-hand Finish   VS 4c**
Follow the original route until it is possible to move left at some slots to large spiky holds. Finish left.

Slippery Jim   7m   E2 5c   (2003)
Start on the first big hold of Nylorac, peg. Move up and left using a tiny toe hold and smear to gain horizontal moves and holds on the ramp above. Using these move right to finish.

Stick like Evo   7m   E2 6b *   (2003)
The slab left of Slippery Jim. From the good flat hold gain a standing position on the high foothold to gain holds above, peg. Finish more easily right up the ramp.

Flying Teapot   7m   E1 5c   (2003)
Start just left of Nylorac at a small flat foothold. Move up and left using a small pocket, then the holds above to gain the large hold on Bokerama. Poorly protected.

Bokerama   9m   E2 5b   (2002)
The obvious line at the left-hand section of the back wall. Using a loose large block gain the finger-crack and move right to better holds. Pull over a couple of bulges, then easier left to the top. Poorly protected in the lower half.

Dem Elves   9m   E2 5b   (2003)
Follow Bokerama to the move right to better holds. Step slightly down right and finish up the ramp of Slippery Jim.

Bokerasmus   9m   E2 5c   (2003)
Start as for Bokerama but move up and leftwards past a large ledge to an area of blocks. Using the right arete of the large boulder above move left to gain a good hold at the bottom left side of the block. Move up to a polished hanging ramp and use this to gain a good hold at the top, finishing via a small tree stump.

Boke   9m   E3 6a   (2003)
Follow Bokerasmus to the area of blocks. Move left until it is possible to gain the ramp. Step onto the slab without using the foothold on Bokerasmus and finish up and right.

City of the Tiny People   6m   HVS 5a   (2003)
The wall with the blue paint just right of Jeepster. Climb to the horizontal break and pull straight over to finish, avoiding the big jug on the right.

NORTH FACE

High up on the right, facing in, is a sloping ledge. For Jeepster and many of the following routes it is best to find the cleaned block at top of that route, abseil in and use the rope as a belay.

Jeepster 6m E2 5c   *(2002)*
The first route on the overhanging north facing wall. High up on the right (facing in) is a ledge. Best to find the cleaned block at top of route, abseil in and use the rope as a belay. Using a good triangular jug on the right, pull into the niche to gain good holds. Short and serious.

Zak Zobar 6m E1 5a *   *(2003)*
Start 3m left of Jeepster at a spike hold. Follow the obvious line of good holds, two pegs. Finish just left of Jeepster, passing a poor peg. Better protected than most in this area.

Space Cadet 7m E1 5c   *(2004)*
Follow Zak Zobar to the last holds, then traverse left to finish in the groove of Captain Barabas.

Wambler 12m Very Difficult   *(2004)*
The following route is a good start to routes around Jeepster. Below the sloping ledge on the right of the North Face. Start at the lowest section of rock, just right of Captain Barabas. From a small tree climb the slabby groove to just below the bulge on the arete. Turn this on the left and move up to the big loose ledge, peg on wall above. Move right until below the tree and finish up the wall above, via the groove right of the tree.
Variation: **Wambler Extension VS 4b**
Follow Wambler to the groove below the tree, move right and finish up the wall past a flake. Low in the grade.

Breakfast Barabas 9m E4 6a *   *(2004)*
Follow Captain Barabas to the top groove. Instead of moving left climb direct up the groove with one long reach to finish at the tree.

Captain Barabas 10m E4 6a   *(2003)*
The fault just right of Coffin Dodger.

Coffin Dodger 12m E4 5c/6a   *(2003)*
Start just right of Death Comes on Swift Wings. A loose start leads to a peg. Follow the groove to a large spike hold. Ascend left for a couple of moves, then follow the hand-traverse at the top of the crag rightwards.

Sidewinder 16m E2 5b   *(2003)*
A well-protected right to left girdle of the north face via the lower fault. Start as for Captain Barabas. Follow the fault past a loose block to some wobbly holds in a bay. Step down and follow the continuation hand-traverse to the end, finishing up Soap Dodgers and Submarines.

Death Comes on Swift Wings 13m E3/4 5c   *(2003)*
Move off the rocking plinth to good holds, two pegs. Move left and up to a niche and pass a poor thread. Clip a poor peg and moving right past a loose hold into the top groove; best to belay off the abseil rope.
Variation: **For Whom the Bell Tolls E4 5c ***   *(2003)*
Easy for the grade, but with some loose holds. From the jugs and pegs move directly up, passing a thread, to a good large hold and easier ground.

Captain Kirk   12m   E3 5c   *(2003)*
Start just right of Death Comes on Swift Wings at orange graffiti. Move up the wall
and clip a second peg on the left. Move right into pod on wobbly holds and gain
a big hold up left. Not recommended.

Snerk   13m   E3 5c/6a *   *(2003)*
Follow Death Comes on Swift Wings to the niche and two pegs. Clip the poor peg
and thread, then move slightly down and left to a big juggy spike, peg. Ascend the
overhanging wall using the crack, to a good hold, then up and right on good holds
to pull over the overhanging flaky pedestal at the top of Niche Direct.

Jingo Wobbly   11m   E5 6b *   *(2003)*
The obvious line on the left-hand side of the north face. Start just right of Midgefest
and climb the wall to a dyno to gain the horizontal break. Gain a standing position
on the fault, then easier to the top via juggy wobbly flakes.

Midgefest   11m   E1 5a   *(2003)*
Start just right of Shuggie and Duggie, just below the flake. Use this to gain the big
ledge, poor peg, and move right past the pointed block. In an area of red rock use
the obvious flaky holds to the top of the big block, passing a loose block en route.
Airy.

Shuggie and Duggie   12m   E2 5b **   *(2002)*
Start at the left-hand side of the north face. Follow a short wall on loose large
flakes to a large ledge (gear). Also possible to clip the poor peg from here. Traverse
right using a pointed block and pull up under the bulging wall to a poor peg. Pull
over the bulge and better holds lead up to good gear and a nice finish. Easy for the
grade.
Variation: **Left-hand Finish   E3 5b/c ****
An excellent harder finish to the route. Follow the route till feet are level with peg.
Move leftwards to a hold on front of the exposed hanging block and finish directly
up this. Airy.

Bubble Language   13m   E2 5b   *(2003)*
Start as for Shuggie and Duggie. Traverse the obvious fault with some loose holds.
The last move is the crux and the arms are tired.

Soap Dodgers and Submarines   8m   VS 4b **   *(2002)*
Start as for Midgefest then follow the groove right of the large hanging flake. Up
the steep groove past a strange flake to a small tree. Move right across the void to
the projecting block to finish.

Mongol   5m   Hard Severe 4c   *(2002)*
The short corner left of Soap Dodgers and Submarines.

Dead Ant   5m   Very Difficult   *(2002)*
The obvious blocky rampline left of the previous route.

Belly Full of Ants   6m   E1 5a   *(2002)*
The hanging crack in the bulging short wall a few metres left of Soap Dodgers and
Submarines.

Glen Fruin   6m   HVS 4c *   *(2002)*
The obvious short corner, just right of a spike. Move up and right to a slot. Move
up the corner, finishing right. The right arete direct is **Peaton Glen** (E2 5b).

Gonksville   6m   E2 6a   *(2003)*
The wall right of Gonk. Start left of the spike at the start of Glen Fruin. Climb the
wall and the wall above, avoiding the good finishing hold on Gonk.

Gonk   6m   E1 5b/c *   (2002)
The unprotected wall left of Glen Fruin.

Son of Gonk   4m   Very Difficult   (2002)
The wall left of Gonk.

Gonkerama   6m   E2 5c *   (2003)
Poorly protected with a sequency crux. Start as for Son of Gonk, or follow the
obvious traverse line from the left end of the crag, and traverse right using the
sloping holds at the crag top. After the good jug on Gonk gain the corner of Glen
Fruin and finish up this.

HMS Nugget   20m   VS 4b   (2003)
A low level traverse of the Gonk wall. Start on the left and finish up Soap Dodgers
and Submarines. Low in the grade.

The following routes lie in the overhanging pinnacle area. The short dirty groove
right of Evil McEvil is **Bleeb** (HVS 4c).

Evil McEvil   7m   E2 5b/c   (2002)
The wall with two pegs in the horizontal break, has an obvious crack on the right.
Follow this and finish directly.

Their Satanic Majesties' Request   7m   E3 6b   (2003)
The wall just left of Evil McEvil. Start just left of the crack and gain the horizontal,
peg. Attain a standing position and gain the crack just below the top.

Belly-flop Finale   7m   E2 5c   (2002)
What the previous route should have been named. Follow Evil McEvil to the top,
then traverse left to the niche on the following route.

Dazed and Confused   8m   E3 6a ***   (2002)
Start as for previous routes. Gain the horizontal fault, peg, then traverse left to
second peg. Move slightly left and finish up the wall direct to a good crack well
back over the top.

Stone Circle   8m   E3 5c **   (2003)
A strange route starting at the top of the crag. Reverse the top niche of Dazed and
Confused, peg, and traverse left to the arete, peg. Continue left to finish on the big
ledge of Pingu. Follow Pingu to top of pinnacle and back to where you started.

The Light of Venus   7m   E2 6a *   (2003)
Follow Pingu to the big ledge, then launch out right and round corner, peg, to
finish directly up the front of the pinnacle. Airy.

Dolmen   6m   E3 5c *   (2003)
Follow Pingu to the big ledge. Move down and right to traverse past the in-situ
peg, and round the corner on good holds (peg). Lower down to gain a foothold on
the arete, then traverse right past a peg (possible friend) to finish just short of the
crack. Easy for the grade.

Pingu   7m   Severe 4b   (2003)
Start at obvious shallow chimney-crack. Climb up and right, avoiding any holds left
of the wide crack, to a big ledge. Move right using a big foothold to pull over the
top onto the pinnacle.

Gong   7m   Hard Severe   (2002)
Start at Pingu and climb onto a large hold without using the crack. Ascend to pull
onto the hanging ledge to finish. Loose start – better finish.

Myopia   8m   E1 5b   *(2003)*
The arete just left of Gong. Start at the obvious chimney (Xthenoraz) and follow the obvious hand-crack right and round the corner onto a ledge, pegs. Without using the big flake mantel onto the ledge to finish up the edge.

Fub   8m   E3 6a   *(2003)*
Start right of the obvious chimney (Xthenoraz). Move onto the face, then right to the arete. Gain the holds above, pegs and thread, and climb the arete.

Leg-over   8m   E2 5c   *(2003)*
Follow Myopia to the ledge, pegs. Pull left onto the overhanging face, make a hard move onto the ledge and finish more easily.

Lard Bambino   8m   E3 6a   *(2003)*
Climb the right-hand side of the obvious chimney of Xthenoraz, up the arete direct to the good jug (pegs). Traverse right to the middle of the pinnacle, attain a standing position and finish left by a sit move at the top of the wide crack.

Xthenoraz   8m   E3 5c *   *(2003)*
Steep, with the hardest moves at the top. Follow the outside edge of the obvious chimney leading to an off-width crack and move up and right to a good jug, two pegs. Pull over to finish.

Seal of Solomon   8m   VS 4c *   *(2003)*
The back of the chimney gives a caving experience with little room for harness or rack.

Subterranean Homesick Blues   9m   E2 5c   *(2003)*
Follow Xthenoraz to the second break and pull left around the corner, thread. Continue left round the arete and finish as for Left Foot First.

Aqualung   9m   E4 6a *   *(2003)*
Follow Ali Baba past the crux move, then traverse right onto the overhanging face on good holds, thread. Heel hook the horizontal crack to gain the long reach finishing moves up the shallow overhanging groove. Way out there.

Ali Baba   9m   E3 6a *   *(2003)*
Climb the right-hand side of the Left Foot First arete, past a peg onto a good ledge and finish up the slab on the left.

Left Foot First   7m   E1 5b/c   *(2002)*
Start up and left on a chossy ledge. Move onto the arete and follow it to a big ledge, mantel this and climb the middle of wall above.

Mama's Little Ray of Sunshine   4m   Moderate   *(2003)*
The obvious chimney-groove left of Left Foot First is the easiest route on the crag.

Air   13m   E2 5c **   *(2003)*
Climb Left Foot First to the break and move right past a thread to the chimney. Ascend to the good hold on Xthenoraz, two pegs, then hand-traverse right past a thread, round the corner, to finish easily.

Like a Rolling Stone   9m   E3 5c *   *(2003)*
A girdle from Air to the good jug on Xthenoraz, finishing up that route.

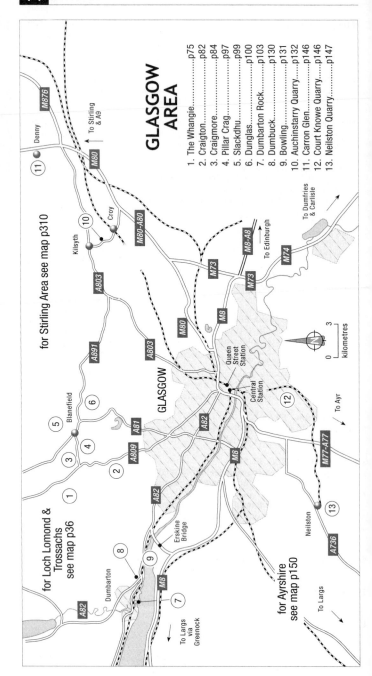

GLASGOW AREA

for Stirling Area see map p310

To Stirling & A9

Denny

Kilsyth

Croy

GLASGOW

Blanefield

Queen Street Station

Central Station

To Edinburgh

To Dumfries & Carlisle

for Loch Lomond & Trossachs see map p36

Dumbarton

Erskine Bridge

To Largs via Greenock

Neilston

for Ayrshire see map p150

To Largs

To Ayr

0   3
kilometres

M876 · M80 · M80-A80 · M73 · M8-A8 · M74 · M8 · A803 · A891 · A81 · A809 · A82 · A736 · M77-A77

GLASGOW AREA

This chapter describes the climbing in and around Glasgow, north and south of the River Clyde. The crags are ordered approximately north to south, starting with The Whangie and Craigmore and progressing via Dumbarton, Dumbuck and the Kilsyth quarries, to finish with the quarries of Neilston and Court Knowe.

THE WHANGIE

(NN 496 806)   Alt 300m   West facing   Map p74   Diagrams p76, 79

Situated on the flanks of Auchineden Hill in the Kilpatrick Hills, The Whangie has a sunny, open aspect and fine views over Stockie Muir to Loch Lomond and the Southern Highlands. Like Craigton and Slackdhu the rock is basalt. Unlike these areas, the faces have been cleaved from the hillside to form interesting pinnacles and ridges. In 1892 the cragging pioneer Gilbert Thomson described the rock as "rather treacherous, being mainly shaky" and his words ring true today.

The popular routes are generally the better protected and more stable crack-lines, the faces often being steep, friable and bold. All the hard routes should be approached with great caution and soloing is not recommended. Unfortunately a lack of finishing belays can make top-roping extremely difficult.

Approach: From the Queensview car park (NN 511 807) on the A809 follow the path up and around the hillside to a highpoint at a small tree and a rock-step. Descend to a lower path (muddy) to reach the crag; 30mins.

THE GENDARME

This is the first group of pinnacles met when approaching on the path from the north. In 1892 Gilbert Thomson and companions made the 'first ascent' of The Whangie by throwing a rope over The Gendarme and 'ascending' the wall right of Heartbreak Corner. The first routes are on the Inside Face and are described from right to left. The face gets some sun at midday and the rock is slabby and pleasantly solid, but a bit polished in places.

1 Spider Slab   4m   Severe 4a
Rather artificial climbing up the short slabby wall at the north end of The Gendarme.

2 Blaeberry Crack   4m   Very Difficult
Climb the line of polished holds left of Spider Slab.

3 Mossy Slab, Right   4m   Severe *
A deceptive route, climbed mainly on small holds.

4 Mossy Slab, Left   4m   Difficult **
Straightforward and pleasant.

5 Staircase Crack   4m   Easy
A convenient descent route.

6 The Bulge   4m   Hard Severe 4b *
The small bulge left of Staircase Crack gives a technical high step.

7 Bird's Nest   5m   Very Difficult ***
An obvious line of good holds lead left above the prominent slanting corner.

8 Red Crack   5m   Very Difficult
Follow the slanting corner to an awkward steepening and finish right. A direct start can be made up polished red holds below the steepening **Red Slab** Very Difficult, or to the left again, **Windswept Wall** Severe 4a, or via the corner left of Upturned Flake and a right traverse **Upturned Left** Very Difficult.

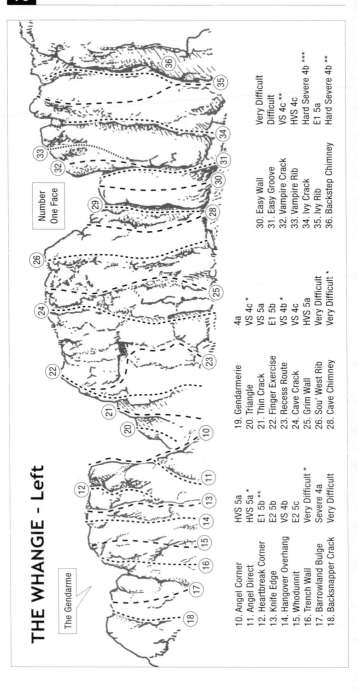

THE WHANGIE - Left

The Gendarme

Number One Face

10. Angel Corner — HVS 5a
11. Angel Direct — HVS 5a *
12. Heartbreak Corner — E1 5b **
13. Knife Edge — E2 5b
14. Hangover Overhang — VS 4b
15. Whodunnit — E2 5c
16. Trench Wall — Very Difficult *
17. Barrowland Bulge — Severe 4a
18. Backsnapper Crack — Very Difficult

19. Gendarmerie — 4a
20. Triangle — VS 4c *
21. Thin Crack — VS 5a
22. Finger Exercise — E1 5b
23. Recess Route — VS 4b *
24. Cave Crack — VS 4c
25. Grim Wall — HVS 5a
26. Sou' West Rib — Very Difficult
28. Cave Chimney — Very Difficult *

30. Easy Wall — Very Difficult
31. Easy Groove — Difficult
32. Vampire Crack — VS 4c **
33. Vampire Rib — HVS 4c
34. Ivy Crack — Hard Severe 4b ***
35. Ivy Rib — E1 5a
36. Backstep Chimney — Hard Severe 4b **

9 Upturned Flake   5m   HVS 5a *
Start immediately left of the edge. Thin moves lead to a good undercut, then climb the smooth wall and crack in the headwall.

The next routes are on the Outside Face of The Gendarme, again described from right to left. This face gets the afternoon and evening sun, but the rock requires care.

0 Angel Corner   7m   HVS 5a
Climb the right arete of The Gendarme.

1 Angel Direct   6m   HVS 5a *
The corner left of the arete gives a short sharp shock.

2 Heartbreak Corner   5m   E1 5b **
Smear and layaway up the fine corner in the middle of the face, until it is possible to move right and up past loose rock. Steep and technical.

3 Knife Edge   5m   E2 5b
A long reach and crank should solve this problem up the arete immediately left of Heartbreak Corner.

4 Hangover Overhang   5m   VS 4b
Poor climbing up the poorly-defined curving corner left of Knife Edge.

5 Whodunnit   5m   E2 5c
Not many and not surprising. The steep blocky wall left of Hangover Overhang may have already lost all the essential holds.
Variation: **5m   5c**
Climb the bulging broken rib to the left, avoiding the boulder and holds on the left.

6 Trench Wall   5m   Very Difficult *
A slabby start up the detached flake leads to a steep juggy finish on the wall above.

7 Barrowland Bulge   4m   Severe 4a
Athletic moves overcome the bulging wall left of the gap.

8 Backsnapper Crack   4m   Very Difficult
The wide crack dividing the two small pinnacles gives a poor loose route.

9 Gendarmerie   25m   4a
A low-level circumnavigation of The Gendarme, clockwise from Spider Slab.

NUMBER ONE FACE

The west face of the main crag faces Loch Lomond and has some excellent steep routes and a number of horror shows. The Lomond faces of the boulders in front of the cliff have a few short problems.

) Triangle   3m   VS 4c *
At the north end of the face is a small triangular wall. A good finger pocket starts a strenuous sequence.

Thin Crack   4m   VS 5a
Right of Triangle is a thin finger-crack. A difficult start leads to a loose finish.

2 Finger Exercise   8m   E1 5b
Climb the blunt arete to finish just left of Recess Route.

23 Recess Route   8m   VS 4b *

A good exciting line, though with some loose rock. Gain the obvious recess and swing left and up.

24 Cave Crack   10m   VS 4c

Follow the chimney, which narrows to a crack. Climb a gently overhanging wall to finish more easily.

25 Grim Wall   10m   HVS 5a

From the lowest point of the wall climb up and right to a ledge. Gain the arete, then swing left and finish up poor rock.

26 Sou' West Rib   10m   Very Difficult

Loose rock abounds on the rounded arete at the end of this section of the face.

27 Snowy Traverse   12m   4a

A low-level traverse going left from the start of Sou' West Rib.

28 Cave Chimney   10m   Very Difficult *

The wide chimney right of the arete leads past a small cave and chockstone.

29 Easy Chimney   8m   Difficult

To the right is a large open chimney.

30 Easy Wall   7m   Very Difficult

Climb the short wall right of the chimney by a choice of lines.

31 Easy Groove   7m   Difficult

Useful for beginners or as a descent route. Climb the polished left-slanting groove.

32 Vampire Crack   10m   VS 4c **

Start up Easy Groove, but continue up the curving hand and fist-crack. Popular and well protected.

33 Vampire Rib   10m   HVS 4c

Climb to the base of Vampire Crack, place a high runner, then traverse right onto the arete and continue to the top. Short and a bit eliminate.

34 Ivy Crack   10m   Hard Severe 4b ***

A superb route, one of the best climbs at The Whangie. The prominent steep corner-crack capped by a chockstone is technically interesting, sustained and well protected.

35 Ivy Rib   10m   E1 5a

Serious climbing on poor rock with little protection. Follow Backstep Chimney for a few moves, then make a committing traverse left on rattly holds and follow a wall and rib of deteriorating rock.

36 Backstep Chimney   12m   Hard Severe 4b **

A classic of its kind, the key is in the name. The moves are polished and a bit brutal, but thankfully quite short! Finish up the pleasant chimney.

37 Backbreak Wall   13m   VS 4c

Gain the small sloping ledge on the wall to the right. Climb the bulge above on creaking holds, traverse left and finish up Backstep Chimney. Continuing up the poorly protected exfoliating wall pushes the grade to E2 5a (horror route!).

38 Bluebottle   15m   E3 5b

The thin crack in the steep bulging wall offers good but poorly protected climbing, followed by a death finish of exfoliating flakes and steep grass.

THE WHANGE - Right

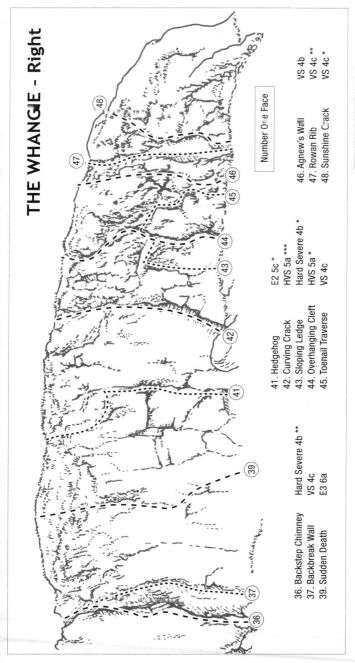

Number One Face

36. Backstep Chimney	Hard Severe 4b **
37. Backbreak Wall	VS 4c
39. Sudden Death	E3 6a

41. Hedgehog	E2 5c *
42. Curving Crack	HVS 5a ***
43. Sloping Ledge	Hard Severe 4b *
44. Overhanging Cleft	HVS 5a *
45. Toenail Traverse	VS 4c

46. Agnew's Wall	VS 4b
47. Rowan Rib	VS 4c **
48. Sunshine Crack	VS 4c *

39 Sudden Death 15m E3 6a   (1985)
Rarely climbed, let alone led. Steep, strenuous and friable with poor protection, what more could you ask for? About 6m right of Backstep Chimney is a thin curving crack with a peg stump in it. Follow this for about 4m to a move left on dubious rock to a high jug. Continue up the crack-line, past a sapling to a loose rightward finish. Belay on the pathetic 'tree'.

40 Flakealong 10m Severe 4a
A low-level traverse going right from the foot of the large prominent flake right of Sudden Death.

41 Hedgehog 15m E2 5c *
The crack to the right is the most amenable of the hard route. Strenuous climbing leads past a reasonable peg to a suspicious spike. Commit yourself to this and continue up protectable cracks to pegs. Grunt past another peg to the top. Belay on the right (Friend 3.5 useful). The second is advised to stand well back from the route.

42 Curving Crack 15m HVS 5a ***
Good climbing. A corner leads to the striking curved crack. Step right onto the white rib, move up to a ledge, then go left and over a bulge to finish (Friend 3.5 useful for belay).

43 Sloping Ledge 15m Hard Severe 4b *
A crack splits the white wall right of Curving Crack. Climb this to the sloping ledge, traverse right and climb the exposed left-slanting fault on dubious holds.

44 Overhanging Cleft 10m HVS 5a *
Jam and bridge up the technical bulging crack. Move left and finish up the left-slanting fault of Sloping Ledge.

45 Toenail Traverse 12m VS 4c
Climb ledges on small holds and move left to finish as for Overhanging Cleft.

46 Agnew's Wall 10m VS 4b
Start as for Toenail Traverse, then climb a right-trending crack to a holdless slab. Finish up the bulging wall.

47 Rowan Rib 8m VS 4c **
Dynamic climbing up the rib left of Sunshine Crack leads to a traverse right to finish.

48 Sunshine Crack 8m VS 4c *
A deceptive little number. Enter the recess and climb the crack above.

NUMBER TWO FACE

Although the rock is quite solid, the sunless 'back side' of the main crag is dark and dank, and understandably the least popular bit of rock at The Whangie.

Be-Bop 7m Very Difficult *
Starting about 4m in from the south (left) end of the passage, climb a small wall on good holds to a groove.

Monk's Wall 7m E1 5b
Climb the steep wall on the right to a sharp pocket, the finish up and left.

*Roadkill Recipies, F7a, Crystal Crag. Climber Craig McCallum
(photo Dave MacLeod)*

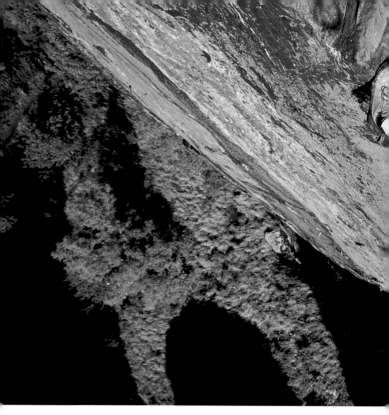

Requiem, E8 6b, Dumbarton Rock. Cliimber Dave MacLeod (photo Nick Tarmey)
Sabotage, 7a (Font 8a+), Dumbarton. Climber Dave MacLeod (photo Cubby Images)

hemin de Fer, E5 6a, Dumbarton. Climber Mark Garthwaite (photo Cubby Images)

Ladybird Layback   8m   Very Difficult *
Follow the obvious right-slanting ramp.

Ladybird Direct   7m   E1 5b
This climbs the left arete of the large overhung recess, finishing as for the normal route (a bit artificial).

Militant Tendency   7m   E1 5b
Follow the crack at the back of the large overhung recess to a roof, pull left and finish up Ladybird Layback.

Nocibur Wall   10m   VS 4b **
A good interesting route. Bridge up between the two walls at the narrowest part of the passage, transferring onto the left wall to finish.

Ruth's Route   10m   VS 4c **
About 2m right of the narrowing, where the path rises, a line of holds lead to a thin crack. Step left and up to finish.

Whippenwoof Wall   10m   Severe 4a *
Starting just right of the last route, climb a shallow groove to a ledge, followed by a wall.

Gremlin Groove   10m   Very Difficult *
Pleasant climbing up the obvious groove 5m right of the narrows in the passage.

Mantelshelf Wall   10m   Severe 4a *
To the right, the path starts to level off. Climb the broad rib, with an interesting move to gain a large hold on the left a few moves up.

Varsity Groove   10m   Very Difficult
Start at the same place as Mantelshelf Wall, but move right into a shallow groove. Follow this to a grass ledge finishing up poor rock.

McBain's Wall   10m   VS 4c **
Some 10m right of the narrows in the passage is a steep crack. Gain a handhold with difficulty and climb slabby rock on the left past a spike to easier ground. The easier original line started to the left.

Rowan Tree Groove   12m   Difficult *
Good holds lead up the obvious right-slanting groove on the left side of an arete.

Fallen Tree Arete   12m   Very Difficult *
Make a difficult move onto the right-facing arete to finish more easily.

Fallen Tree Groove   12m   Severe 4a
Above where the path starts to descend and right of the arete is a corner. Climb it, awkward at the top, finishing through vegetation.

Young's Route   12m   Severe 4a *
About 3m right of Fallen Tree Groove is a nose of rock above smooth wavy rock. Climb the slabby wall to the left of the nose, step right and finish up the wall.

Allison's Route   12m   VS 4b *
The path starts to level out about 5m to the right of the nose of Young's Route. This route climbs the steep wall between the sections of wavy rock, moving right at the top to a vegetated finish.

Gorilla, 6b (Font 6b), Dumbarton Rock. Climber Tim Morozzo
(photo John Watson)

Ripple Wall   12m   HVS 5a
Start as for Allison's Route. Climb the left edge of the smooth wavy rock to join Allison's Route at the top.

Long John's Wall   12m   HVS 5a
Sustained climbing on small holds up the steep wall with a thin crack, where the path starts to rise towards The Gap.

Hutch's Route   8m   Severe
Right of Long John's Wall the angle eases; climb the wall.

Needle Route   7m   Moderate
Climb the arete left of the wide crack which forms the descent route from Backstep Chimney.

The following routes lie on the buttress right of The Gap.

Novice Overhang   6m   Difficult
Climb the steep rib left of a prominent recess on good holds.

Novice Crack   6m   Moderate
Grassy climbing up the wide crack on the left side of the detached pillar.

Jughandle Arete   7m   Moderate
Pleasant climbing on good holds up the prominent arete 6m right of the recess.

Arrowhead Arete   15m   Difficult
Follow the arete dividing Number One and Number Two Face.

Tidemark   45m   E1 5a
A girdle of Number Two Face.

NUMBER THREE FACE

A number of routes have been recorded on the loose slimy front face of Auchineden Hill. They were fully documented in a previous edition of this guide, but the wall is best left to the adventurous or sad of heart. However, a low-level traverse of the face gives some 60m of 5b entertainment.

CRAIGTON

(NS 517 766)   Alt 250m   North-East facing   Map p74
Craigton is a pleasantly situated escarpment of rough basalt similar to Craigmore above the A809 Glasgow to Drymen road, on the east side of the Kilpatrick Hills. It takes a couple of days to dry after summer rain. Most of the climbs are short, but seem longer due to the steep bank below. Unlike nearby Craigmore, peace and quiet are guaranteed. The shorter routes have become neglected in recent years.

Approach: Park at a layby on the A09 at the bottom of the hill, just south of the entrance to Hilton Park Golf Course (NS 526 773). Walk across fields and braken slopes to the crag. It is closer than it looks.

CRAIGTON QUARRY

The quarry at the left end of the crag contains one route.

Chasing the Dragon   E2 5c
The obvious finger-crack in the steep slab in the top right-hand corner of the quarry.

MAIN CRAG

Jughandle Corner   4m   3b
At the left end of the outcrop is a small buttress topped by a wind-swept tree. Climb the short corner-crack left of the alcove.

Elbow Crack   4m   4c
The crack in the alcove's left wall. Better in autumn!

Machiavelli's Crack   6m   5c *
The steep crack in the left side of the next buttress.

Jam Crack   4m   4b
The cracked corner on the right.

The Rasp   5m   4a
The painful wide crack on the left side of the next buttress.

Mantelshelf Wall   6m   5c
The mantelshelf and slab.

Hairy Mary   6m   5a *
The left-hand groove topped by a chockstone.

Easy Lady   6m   3a
The right-hand groove.

Two Hand Crack   4m   4b
Twin cracks up and further right.

Far from the Maddening Crowd   6m   7a (Font 7c) **   *(1998)*
The bald and very rounded Gritstone-like arete has a desperate bouldery start followed by a bold finish.

Boa Constrictor   10m   4c
A tight off-width behind the flake.

Farewell Groove   10m   4c
The narrow ramp behind the flake.

The Screaming   12m   E2 6a *
This takes the obvious line of weakness up the smooth wall left of The Clam. Start beside a boulder and climb to a horizontal break. Continue up the crack (crux), then go direct to the top. An easier variation avoids the crux by traversing the break (5c).

The Clam   12m   5b **
The chimney-crack through the overhang.

Octopus   10m   5c **
The right end of the overhung recess leads to an off-width crack. Or, traverse into the crack from the right (5b).

Chockstone Groove   4m   4a
The V-groove on the right.

Lone Tree Groove   3m   4a
The next crack.

Gremlin's Groove 10m 5b *
The overhanging groove further right. A bit nasty.

Lazy Layback 10m 3a
Some broken rock leads to the next buttress. This takes the broken groove and wide layback crack.

Affront 10m 4c
Climb the rib and cracked arete further right.

Sidestep 10m 4c
Climb the crack on the left, step right and climb the crack above.

The Groove 10m 4c
Climb the big groove.

The Doddle 10m 5c **
A bulging wall is split by a sloping ledge. Climb the centre of the wall direct.

Two routes climb the broken rock to the right: **Isolated Buttress** (4b) is a thin groove, and **Deception** (4c), a small wall.

Deceiver 4m 5b
This is the obvious deep groove in the large block separated by deep cracks.

Shield Right Edge 4m 5b *
The right edge of the obvious shield like flake gives surprisingly good climbing.

The small walls and cracks to the right are taken by: **Route 1** (4b); **Route 2** (2a); **Twisted Crack** (4c); **Black Crack** (5b); **Ledge Wall** (4a); **Small Wall** (4b) and **Small Wall Groove** (4c). Their names are description enough.

OTHER KILPATRICK CRAGS

Various routes have been done at **Loch Humphrey Head** (NS 453 745) and **Lang Crags** (NS 433 767), but the rock is structurally unsound on a major scale; (see SMCJ 1973, 1974). A number of 8m-15m routes from Difficult to Severe have been recorded on the pillars of **Dunellan Crag** (NS 494 758), overlooking Jaw Reservoir. Old chisels hammered into some of the cracks indicate the interest of previous generations. Approach from West Muirhouses farm (15mins, parking charge) or via the car park on the Cochno road (NS 503 739) and the fisherman's path beside the Cochno Burn (1hr 5mins).

CRAIGMORE

(NS 527 797) North-East facing Map p74

Solid rock, numerous routes and a wide variety of grades make this 10 to 15m escarpment one of the most popular outcrops in the Glasgow area. The rough basalt gives excellent friction (although some routes are becoming quite polished) with generally positive face holds but rounded cracks.

However, it can be quite slippery when wet and the routes can get a bit dirty if neglected for a few years. The crag can be slow to dry in winter and midges are rife later in the summer. The longer routes have been given route grades in this edition of the guide as they are often led, but top roping or soloing/bouldering is more common on the shorter climbs.

Approach: Park by a stile on the north verge of the B821, about 1km east of its junction with the A809 Glasgow to Drymen road. The crag is visible among trees to the left. The local farmer is understanding; please help to maintain this state of affairs. The Drymen bus from Glasgow's Buchanan St will take you to the Carbeth Inn, just before the junction.

CHIMNEY AREA

Diagram p87

Following the path through the field, this is the first area reached and it marks the furthest left end of the crag. The most obvious feature is a body-sized chimney. Some poor and now overgrown routes have been made to its left, but the real climbing starts with the arete.

1 Chimney Arete   8m   4c
The left arete of The Chimney.

2 The Chimney   8m   4a *
Climb the body-munching chimney, staggering leftwards to finish.

3 Polo   8m   5b
A problematic start gains the short crack right of The Chimney.

4 Polover   8m   6a *
Climb the wall just right of Polo via thin cracks and a long reach to finish.
Variation: **Tanktop   5c** *
Eliminate: From small fingerholds in the horizontal break, gain the blunt arete and climb its left side to join the next route.

5 Silver Arete   8m   4a *
Follow the arete right of Polo direct, then go up a slab and exit left.

6 Glug   8m   3b
The groove adjacent to Silver Arete, finishing up that route.

7 Grooved Arete   10m   Severe 4c *
Climb into the hanging groove right of Glug and gurgle up the arete to exit at tree. Or, if you've got an itch to scratch, start up the wide crack to the right (4b).

8 Totem   3m   5c **
Climb the obvious totem-like block from horizontal break undercuts. Use a devious heel-hook or simply dyno for the top and slide down Kit Kat to finish.

9 Kit Kat   10m   Difficult 3b
Follow the obvious curving groove right of the block to a ledge, then the continuation groove above.

0 Legless   10m   6b *
Start just right of Kit Kat and make hard moves up, then right, to join Wide Eyed.

1 Wide Eyed   10m   6b ***
An excellent route up the zigzag crack. A long reach gains a horizontal break, marginal laybacking up the crack brings better holds, but not that quickly.

2 Harmless   10m   6a *
To the right a short crack leads to a rounded spike. Finish up the ramp of Arrowhead Left-Hand.

3 Arrowhead Left-Hand   10m   Severe 4b **
Right again is a small pinnacle. Start on its left side and climb the left-slanting ramp to finish with a short left traverse. Continuing up the outside of the pinnacle from the ramp is 4a.

14 Arrowhead Right-Hand 10m 3b
Climb the wide crack on the right side of pinnacle.

15 Chimney Area Girdle 30m 4c
A low-level traverse starting at Chimney Arete and finishing by a hand-traverse of the block of Kit Kat.

MAIN AREA

Diagram p89

This extends from the corner with what was once a healthy holly tree and is now just a stump, past a number of grooves to an obvious undercut boulder next to the path. The first route starts on the left wall of the corner with the tree stump.

16 Cariad 15m HVS 5b
Takes the first crack-line right of the pinnacle. Go up the wall to gain a shallow groove, climb this and the crack on the right, avoiding grass ledges.

17 Magic Crack 15m HVS 5b *
The prominent crack in the wall left of Holly Tree Corner. An enjoyable direct finish is possible through the overhang on the right at the top of the corner.

18 Holly Tree Corner 15m 4b *
Climb the corner to the tree stump, step left onto the wall, then go diagonally left until it is possible to traverse right on the slab above the overlap. A fine airy finish can be had by traversing horizontally right below the overlap to finish up a short arete (4c).

19 The Beast 15m E2 5c ***
Start below the groove in the arete of Holly Tree Corner. Pull directly into the groove and follow this to a slab, finishing up the wall on the left, avoiding the right arete.

20 Slingsby's Crystal 15m E2 6a **
Climb the wall between the start of The Beast and Jolly Green Dragon (eliminate). Continue up the slab above (treating the eponymous crystal with care) without using the arete of the groove of The Beast. Finish directly up the upper wall using as few holds as possible. Amazingly, climbed by Slingsby in the early 1900s, but never recorded.

21 Jolly Green Dragon 15m E1 5c **
Start 2m right of The Beast. Gain the shallow groove without using the boulder and pull round right into a short finger-crack. Make a hard move onto the ledge and finish up a short groove.
Variation: 15m E2 6a
Using any start that seems appropriate, climb the arete between Slingsby's Crystal and Jolly Green Dragon via a superb and unlikely rock over. Done properly it is quite independent.

22 Craigmore Corner 15m HVS 5b ***
The classic of the crag, taking the big corner capped by an overhang. Climb the corner to the overhang, trend right and go up to a ledge, then finish up a groove. Alternative finishes go left of, or straight over, the overhang.

23 Tom and Jerry Wall 15m VS 5a ***
Another very fine route, with a problematic start. Start below the arete. Move up and left to reach a good pocket, then continue more easily up the wall to reach the arete. Finish up a short groove.

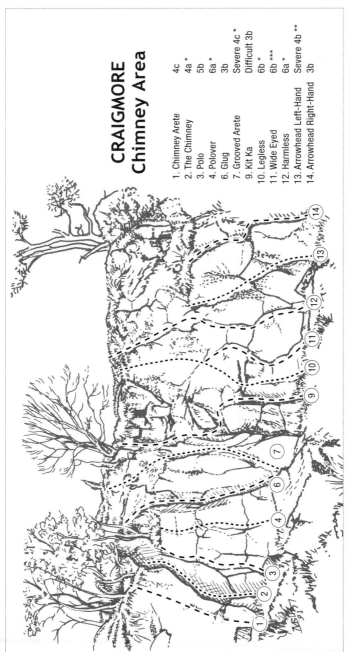

CRAIGMORE
Chimney Area

1. Chimney Arete — 4c
2. The Chimney — 4a *
3. Polo — 5b
4. Polover — 6a *
6. Glug — 3b
7. Grooved Arete — Severe 4c *
9. Kit Ka — Difficult 3b
10. Legless — 6b *
11. Wide Eyed — 6b ***
12. Harmless — 6a *
13. Arrowhead Left-Hand — Severe 4b **
14. Arrowhead Right-Hand — 3b

**24 Rampage   15m   Hard Severe 4b ** **
Start below a curving crack right of the arete. Go up and left to cracks, climb these and the ramp above to a large ledge overlooking Craigmore Corner. Traverse left to the arete on the skyline and finish up this.

**25 Curving Groove   15m   HVS 5b ** **
Gain and climb the groove direct to join Rampage. Follow this and the groove above.

26 Hamilton's Arete   15m   E4 6b ** *
Climb the arete between Curving Groove and Daylight Robbery on its left side, finishing by a short crack. Delicate, fingery, technical and strenuous.

27 Daylight Robbery   12m   VS 4c
The next mossy groove along is climbed all the way.

28 Basil Brush   12m   HVS 5b
Just right of the last route is an overhung vegetated niche. Climb this leftwards, then go back right into a narrow mossy groove. Or, from the slim groove on the ordinary route pull into and follow the slanting crack on the right to finish at the same grade.

29 The Niche   10m   Hard Severe 4c ** *
Start just right of the last route below an obvious niche. Climb up into the niche, pull out right and climb cracks to a block, then layback to easier ground. An inferior finish is possible out left from the niche to join a sloping crack (5a).

30 Crib   10m   VS 5a
Start below the small overlap right of The Niche, behind a flat block. Climb the arete above on its steep side, avoiding the crack on the right. Finish up The Niche.

**31 Rampant   10m   Very Difficult 4a ** *
Follow the ramp throughout; popular, polished and dirty.

32 Grotty Groove   10m   Very Difficult 4a
Climb Rampant for 3m then go right onto a ledge, then climb the groove to the top. Not as popular or as polished, but dirtier!

**33 Sunday Wall   12m   VS 5b ** **
Start 2m right of Rampant. Climb the wall direct to a horizontal crack, then pull up the wall to the top. The horizontal crack can be traversed right (5b) to finish up the arete of Hot Dawg.

34 Hot Dawg   10m   HVS 5c
Right of Sunday Wall is a block. From the top of this gain a hold on the arete, then balance precariously up.

To the right is a horrible green groove, **Gregor's Groove** (4a), and right again a smaller pinnacle like buttress. **Mirage** (4b) takes the crack on the left side of the buttress, and **Solo** (4b) the right arete and the arete above. The dirty broken groove to the right is **Nap** (3b).

LAYBACK CRACK AREA

Diagram p91

Right of the undercut boulder is a fine wall which extends rightwards to a pinnacle split by an obvious hand jamming crack.

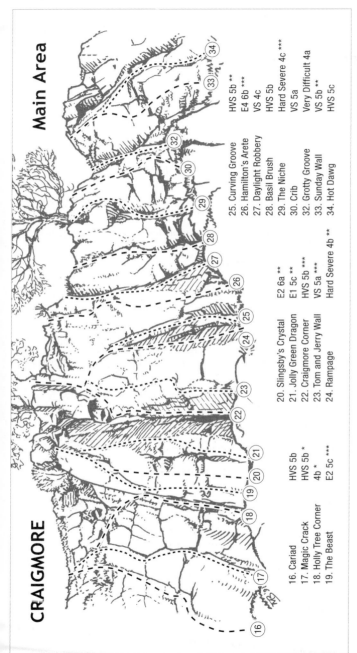

CRAIGMORE

Main Area

16. Cariad — HVS 5b
17. Magic Crack — HVS 5b *
18. Holly Tree Corner — 4b *
19. The Beast — E2 5c ***

20. Slingsby's Crystal — E2 6a **
21. Jolly Green Dragon — E1 5c **
22. Craigmore Corner — HVS 5b ***
23. Tom and Jerry Wall — VS 5a ***
24. Rampage — Hard Severe 4b **

25. Curving Groove — HVS 5b **
26. Hamilton's Arete — E4 6b ***
27. Daylight Robbery — VS 4c
28. Basil Brush — HVS 5b
29. The Niche — Hard Severe 4c ***
30. Crib — VS 5a
32. Grotty Groove — Very Difficult 4a
33. Sunday Wall — VS 5b **
34. Hot Dawg — HVS 5c

35 Terror 5m 5c **

A good problem up the overhung right arete of the boulder. A sitting start to this problem is 6b (Font 6c+).

36 Bwana 13m HVS 5b

Above the boulder and below and right of the beech tree is a wide blocky overhanging crack.

37 Spinal Wall 15m E2 5c **

Climbs horizontal cracks in the often mossy wall right and above the overhung boulder and left of the White Hope groove. The bulging cracked wall just to the left is taken by **Inverlussa Crack** (E2 5c).

38 White Hope 15m E1 5c ***

The groove to the right is climbed until it is possible to move right to finish up the slanting crack of Layback Crack.
Variation 1: **15m E1 6a**
It is possible to climb the wall between the arete and the groove direct from ground level. A sitting start to this problem is 6c.
Variation 2: **6b **
Climb the left arete, near the Terror boulder from a sit start to a good letter-box, then traverse into White Hope.

39 Layback Crack 15m E1 5c ***

A popular classic taking the fine crack in the centre of the wall. Climb the strenuous flake-crack, then make a hard move up and left for a jug. Finish up the left-slanting crack above. The **True Finish** takes the right-slanting finger-crack at E4 6a, from where the normal route escapes left. The **Super Direct** is E3 6a.

40 Craig's Wall 15m E7 6c ***

This fine piece of rock has been led to give a bold and ferocious test piece. Climb the wall right of Layback Crack on edges to a break. Fill this with small RPs, move slightly left, and climb the desperate wall above to easier ground and the top.

41 Crag Mate 12m VS 5a

About 5m right of Layback Crack is a brown sentry box with a crack. Follow this and the left-slanting groove above.

42 Salamander 10m HVS 5b *

Start just right of Crag Mate. Climb into the scoop without using holds on adjoining routes, step up left and ascend the wall on the right to a rib and finish up this.

43 Not Another Eliminate 10m E2 6a *

Start as for Salamander, then go straight up over the overlap.

44 Samson 10m HVS 5b

Start 2m right of Salamander, below a crack. Climb the crack to an inverted-V then go up into a groove.
Variation: **6b **
An excellent problem. Gain the inverted-V from the right.

45 Sabre Crack 8m VS 4c **

Climb the crack above the boulder and finish up the arete. The grade is lowered to 4b if the boulder is used.

46 Stiletto Crack 8m VS 4c **

Hand jam the crack to the right of Sabre Crack.

47 Rapier Arete 8m E1 5b

Direct up the arete just right of Stiletto Crack, avoiding both adjacent cracks.

CRAIGMORE
Layback Crack Area

35. Terror	5c **
36. Bwana	HVS 5b
37. Spinal Wall	E2 5c **
38. White Hope	E1 5c ***
39. Layback Crack	E1 5c ***
39a. True Finish	E4 6a ***

40. Craig's Wall	E7 6c ***
41. Crag Mate	VS 5a
42. Salamander	HVS 5b *
43. Not Another Eliminate	E2 6a *
44. Samson	HVS 5b
45. Sabre Crack	VS 4c **
46. Stiletto Crack	VS 4c **
47. Rapier Arete	E1 5b

BLADE AREA

Diagram p93

Right of Stiletto Crack is an area of more broken rock, then a large elliptical boulder known as The Blade, whose left and right sides have been climbed at 4a and 2a. Right again is another boulder taken by Tae a Moose, then an area of higher rocks bounded on the right by an arete.

48 White Streak   5m   5b
From the top of the Blade, climb the wall above trending left.

49 Preliminary Exercise   10m   E2 5c
Climb the overhanging twin cracks right of White Streak without using the pinnacle.

50 Tae a Moose   3m   4a *
Climb the crack on the boulder below and right of The Blade. The short wall and arete just left of this is a good 6a (Font 6a) from a sitting start.

51 Tic Tac   3m   5b
Climb the wall right of the previous route, only using the right-hand rib.

52 Bugs Bunny   6m   3b
Climb the foul gully behind the last two routes. For the desperate only.

53 Weasel   10m   HVS 5b
Start in the niche at the left end of the area of higher rocks. Pull up onto the left-sloping ramp. From its end move right onto the wall and go up to a ledge. Finish up the wall above.

54 Stoat   10m   HVS 5b *
Follow the previous route to a ledge above the niche, step right then go straight up to a ledge. Finish up the rib.

55 Autobahn   10m   VS 5a **
Climb the nice groove in the centre of the wall to its top. Move left to another groove and finish up this.

56 All Hope   10m   VS 5a **
Start just right of Autobahn at a crack. Climb this to a ledge on the right, step left and climb the groove and crack to the top.

57 Hendo's Obsession   8m   5c
Climb the arete then follow All Hope to the top.

58 Elk   6m   3a
Climb the mossy groove to the top.

59 Ell   6m   4a
The crack and wall just right of the previous route; dirty.

60 Tarantula   6m   5b **
Just right of Ell is an obvious nose of rock above a steep scooped wall. Climb to the nose, pull over and continue up the groove above.

61 Leech Arete   6m   6b **
Pull onto the steep arete from the right using small holds and climb the arete.

CRAIGMORE
Blade Area

48. White Streak		5b
50. Tae a Moose		4a *
53. Weasel		HVS 5b
54. Stoat		HVS 5b *

55. Autobahn	VS 5a **	
56. All Hope	VS 5a **	
57. Hendo's Obsess.	5c	
58. Elk	3a	
59. Ell	4a	
60. Tarantula	5b **	
61. Leech Arete	6b **	
65. Coal Face	4b *	
66. Charcoal Chim.	4a **	
67. Black Beauty	5a **	
68. Black Power	4c	

62 Leech Direct   5m   6a *
Round and right is a short vertical wall. Climb the centre of this wall direct, avoiding holds on adjoining routes.

63 Leech   5m   5b *
The original line. Start up the corner of Eel, then hand-traverse left to finish above the crux of the Direct.

64 Eel   5m   4c
Climb the corner to a hard finish.

65 Coal Face   5m   4b *
The cracked wall right of Eel.

66 Charcoal Chimney   5m   4a **
The prominent chimney.

67 Black Beauty   5m   5a **
The cracked wall right of the chimney, avoiding holds on that route.

68 Black Power   5m   4c
The arete right of Black Beauty.

69 Mat Black   3m   4b
The wall immediately right of the arete.

Going uphill from here the height of the crag decreases to about 3m. At the highest point of the path is a useful descent route. The small walls and corners give a variety of short problems as easy or as hard as desired.

LITTLE BUTTRESS

The path then leads downhill to the foot of a small buttress with two wide blocky cracks. The first route starts at the left side of the buttress halfway up.

East Wall   3m   5a
Move right onto the buttress from the grass, then go up to the top.

Pinnacle Wall   7m   4c **
Climb the face of the buttress, left of the double cracks, without straying from the straight and narrow.

Donald Duck   5m   4a
The left-hand crack.

Mickey Mouse   5m   4b
The right-hand crack.

Piglet   5m   5a
Climb the wall just right of Mickey Mouse, avoiding all holds on that route.

Pig's Ear   6m   5a
Start as for Piglet. After 1m move right to the arete and finish up this.

Silk Purse   6m   5b
Climb the start of the arete to Pigs Ear and finish up a slab; dirty.

West Wall   6m   5b
The wall right of the last route, finishing up the slab.

To the right are some unappetising vegetated grooves, best left to herbivores.

EXTREME RIGHT-HAND SLAB

Continuing rightwards a small buttress is passed

Extrarete　5a
Climb the shallow groove in the arete, finishing up the right-hand side of the arete.

Sunshine Arete　5a
The Wall right of Extrarete.

More broken rocks lead rightwards until an obvious slab left of a pinnacle is encountered.

Tree Wall　5m　5a
Climb the short wall left of the slab, avoiding the right arete and the tree above.

Left Arete　10m　4b
Start left of the obvious crack in the slab. Pull up to gain the left edge of the slab, then follow the edge and the short wall above.

Cracked Slab　10m　3b *
Climb the obvious crack splitting the slab, taking the right-hand branch to finish up the wall above to the left.

The Slab　10m　4a **
Climb cracks in the slab right of the large crack of Cracked Slab, avoiding the right edge and the crack on the left. Finish up the wall above at its highest point.

Right Arete　6m　4a
Pull up to gain the right edge of the slab, then climb this direct.

Cave Route　5m　3a ***
Just right of the slab is a short chimney. The cave inside gives an underground excursion, or you could just climb the chimney. No place for fatties.

Slab Traverse　12m　4a
Start as for Tree Wall. Climb the wall for a few moves, gain the arete on the right, traverse right across the slab to Right Arete and finish up this.

The Wizard　6m　6b (Font 6b) ***
Powerful and impressive climbing up the left arete of the flat-topped pinnacle right of the slab. Starting from the top of the chockstone in the short chimney reduces the grade to 6a.

Wizard Sit Start　7m　6c (Font 7b) ***
The best hard problem on the crag on excellent rock. Sit-start at a low break. The short arete to the right is not allowed!

Tarot　6m　3b
The right edge of the pinnacle.

Right of the pinnacle is an unattractive short wall with some routes recorded at 4a and 3b; climb at will.

Suzy Q　6m　5b
Some 4m right of the pinnacle is an arete right of an obvious wide crack. Step on to the ledge from below, then follow the crack above.

Victory V   5m   4c
About 3m right of Suzy Q is a grotty crack with boulders at its base. Pull out onto the capped block on the right of the crack (without using the back wall or standing on the block), then go up and over the block above. A sit start is possible at 6a, without using the wall of Wopitee. Undercut up to the crack, swing left to the arete and finish up Suzy Q.

Wopitee   5m   5b
Start below the obvious roofed niche to the right of Victory V. Bridge up and gain the wall above the roof, then continue directly to top.

Expo   5m   5b
Follow the right edge of the niche to reach flat holds above. Finish up the left edge, avoiding vertical cracks. Or start in the niche and traverse horizontally right (5b), or climb the wall below the tree stump, avoiding the left arete and the crack on the right (5a).

Toad   8m   4c
Climb the crack below and right of Two Tree Wall to reach a ledge. Finish up the wall above.

Rizla   3m   3a
Just right of the final wall of Toad is a groove. Climb it.

Amphitheatre Girdle   15m   5a
This wall has been girdled starting from the short wall right of Tarot, crossing Suzy Q and going below the roof of Wopitee (crux), then round the corner and right below the tree stump.

PINE TREE BOULDERS

Some 15m right is a pile of scattered boulders below a Scots Pine, which give good if short problems.

Vanguard   3m   5a
Climb the narrow wall just left of the wide crack above the three tiered slab.

Sunshine Arete   3m   5a *
Below the Scots Pine is a fine arete which is climbed direct. The slabby left wall of the arete gives a thin and fingery 6a if holds on adjoining routes are avoided.

Sunburn   3m   3a
The pile of blocks right of Sunshine Arete is climbed on the left-hand side.

The next five problems all climb the small overhanging face with a rounded top-out opposite Sunshine Arete.

Jamie's Overhang   6a *
The original line. Start standing up using an incut on the centre of the rounded lip. A problem with a secret! The overhanging nose to the left is 5c.

Nice Guys Finish Last   6a (Font 6b+) **
A sit start to Jamie's Overhang. Start at the twin crimps in the centre of a break, get the good hold on the left and pull up into the slopey lip jug of Jamie's Overhang.

Flesh for Fantasy, F7c+, Dumbuck. Climber Neill Busby
(photo Tim Morozzo)

The Art of War   6b (Font 6c+) *
An eliminate based on Nice Guys avoiding the slopey lip jug by lunging direct from the good hold to a sloper to the right of the slopey lip jug and pulling over.

Surprise Attack   6c (Font 7b) *
From a sit start at the twin break, crimp and dyno desperately to the lip sloper right of the slopey jug.

Sanjuro   6b (Font 6c+)
Sit-start at the right edge of the low break and traverse this leftwards (desperate first move). Move up slightly to the good hold, pull round the left edge (avoiding boulder below), gain a sidepull on the lip and pull over.

PILLAR CRAG

(NS 541 795)   North facing   Map p74

This small but enjoyable crag of columnar basalt offers generally well protected crack climbing. Although a good alternative to crowded Craigmore and quick drying, it is not popular and had become very mossy. In spring 2004 the routes received a good brushing.

Approach: The crag lies in trees on the south side of the B821 about 1km east of Craigmore. If approaching from Craigmore, park 100m before the entrance to 'Braehead', at the edge of a fir plantation on the south side of the road. The crag is reached by crossing a marshy field and scrambling through the trees.

In the Groove   4m   5a
The first groove at the left-hand end.

Moss Crack   5m   2b
The broad crack.

Keystone Corner   4m   2a
The jammed boulder corner.

Serpent's Chimney   6m   4a
The obvious chimney, finishing left,

The Ride   6m   5a *
The arete to the right of the Serpent's Chimney.

Twin Roots Chimney   6m   3b
The next chimney on the right, with a low chockstone.

Club Foot   10m   6a *
The thin cracks right of Twin Roots Chimney.

Butterfingers   10m   5c *
The fine thin crack.

The Slot   10m   5a *
Right again is a corner-crack with a hard start.

Sidestep Wall   10m   5a
The next thin corner.

Backstep Chimney, Hard Severe 4b, The Whangie. Climber unknown
(photo Tom Prentice)

The Horror   10m   5b
Climb one of two jam cracks to a ledge, then the groove above on the left.

Melting Pot   12m   4c *
An expanding jam crack on the right leads to a higher ledge and a chimney.

Pinnacle Chimney Direct   10m   4b
A groove followed by a crack on the left.

Pinnacle Chimney   10m   3a
Climb the right side of the pinnacle and the groove above.

Damocles Groove   10m   4c *
Follow the groove below the single poised block. This is a good reference point for starting to locate the climbs.

Pillar Groove   10m   5a *
The groove right of the poised block.

Candle Snuffer   10m   3b
An apt name for the chimney formed by three large sections of column.

Pillar Front   10m   5a
Climbs the front edge of the fallen column.

Chockstone Chimney Direct   10m   4b
The left of two cracks leads to a chimney right of the fallen column. The right-hand crack is 5a.

Mick   10m   3b
A wide pod-shaped crack.

Lurcher's Chimney   10m   4c
The nasty looking inverted-V groove.

Manky Crack   10m   4b
A crack with a small tree.

The broken area on the right contains; **Grand Slam** (5a) and **Fingerlicker** (5c).

Avalanche Chimney   10m   4c
A wide crack right of the broken rock, with a tree at the top.

Cracker Crack   10m   4c *
A cracking jam crack.

Hiroshima Groove   10m   5b *
The smooth groove.

Twiggy's Crack   10m   3b
Climb the crack right of the tree, then the cracked groove on the left.

Up and right are three dirty grooves: **Woody Groove** (2a); **Thunder Block Groove** (2b); and **Pinnacled Groove** (4a).

Right-Hand Crack   4m   4b *
A good short jamming crack.

Right-Hand Wall   4m   4c
The wall right of the crack.

SLACKDHU

(NS 558 816)   Alt 496m   South facing   Map p74

The crags on this dolerite escarpment provide the only worthwhile climbing in the Campsie Fells. Like The Whangie, much of the rock is inherently unstable, but it gets much less traffic, so very great care should be taken. **Coffin Gully** is the deep black cleft in the centre of the main face above Blanefield. Lower and to the right is a small compact crag, Jenny's Lum, which offers the most stable rock. The outlook is suburban stockbroker belt, but very fine. Worth a visit on a lazy Sunday afternoon.

Approach: Park at the war memorial in Blanefield, near the start of Campsie Dene Road (NS 556 767). Follow the road to open hillside, and the crag can be seen up and on the right at the lowest part of the escarpment. The prominent two tier crag at the right end is The Black Craig; it is very loose.

Jenny's Lum Arete   10m   Hard Severe 4b *
The arete and crack to the right give an excellent route.

Tendons   10m   HVS 5a   *(1992)*
Follow the broken twin cracks in the wall 2m right of the arete.

Rusty Pegs   10m   HVS 5a
About 2m left of the waterfall is an obvious crack come –chimney-line, normally fern filled in summer.

To the right of the waterfall are broken buttresses, then a prominent pinnacle with an obvious block filled chimney on its left.

Blocker   8m   Severe 4a   *(1992)*
Bridge up the large chimney, climb the pinnacle on the right and make an exciting step back to terra firma.

Classic Crack   8m   Severe 4a   *(1992)*
The crack in the pinnacle right of the chimney.

Pinnacle Arete   8m   Severe 4a *
Climb the arete face of the pinnacle.

About 40m further right is another smaller tower called Jacob's Ladder.

Jacob's Crack   5m   VS 4b
The mossy crack.

Moss Kills   5m   Very Difficult   *(1992)*
Climb the broken right side of the pinnacle.

A number of routes have been climbed in this area over the years, but only the best are described above. Other scrambling and bouldering possibilities exist. Two traditional routes, which combine loose and wet rock and turf in equal measures, climb the main face left of Jenny's Lum. **The Long Gully** (135m Moderate) takes the first prominent gully right of Dumgoyne. **Coffin Gully Buttress** (75m Very Difficult) takes a line to the left of Coffin Gully (see intro).

Apart from Jenny's Lum crag on Slackdhu there is little worthwhile climbing in the Campsies. A few routes have been done on **Crichton's Cairn** near Campsie Glen (NS 610 800), and the north facing **Corrie of Balglass** (NS 589 849) has some impressive crags, plus a lot of steep grass and loose rock.

DUNGLAS

(NS 575 789)   North-West facing   Map p74

This conical volcanic plug is situated 2km east of Blanefield in open countryside at the foot of the Campsie Fells. The rock is micro-porphyritic basalt with marked hexagonal columns on the north and east faces. Most of the climbing is on the west face where the rock takes a sheet like structure. The routes are up to 30m high and take about two sunny days to dry, although the sport routes often remain dry. In previous years, only the West Face was popular, but more recently, the imposing black overhangs on the North Face have given unusual and serious routes. Belays are sometimes awkward to locate at the top of the crag, but are usually found well back.

Approach: The crag is visible south of the A891 east of Strathblane. Park on the right at one of the lay-bys several hundred metres further east along the A891, not at the farm track. From these walk back along the road then down the track leading directly to the crag. The farmer objects to climbers walking across the fields, but climbing is tolerated.

EAST FACE

This is the left-hand face, as seen from the approach path. It is large and rather featureless, with a big corner in the centre. The unsoundness of some of the rock and areas of steep grass have restricted development. The first two routes are on an easy angled rib of reasonable rock left of the corner.

Rubbish   30m   Difficult   (1977)
Climb the groove left of the rib to finish on easy ground.

Ribbish   30m   Severe   (1977)
Start below the rib at a boulder. Climb the rib to a small overhang and take this by a groove on the right, past a spike. Continue up the slabby rib to a grass ledge, step right and go up slabby rock to a steeper exit.

Dunglas Corner   30m   Severe   (1975)
Climb the central corner left of the broad rib, trending right at the top past small trees to finish by the loose corner above.

Overlord   30m   E1 5c   (1982)
This takes the prominent nose formed by the junction between the east and north faces. Start 10m right of Dunglas Corner and climb a shattered rib into a scoop and go up to a peg runner. Move left and up to bulging rock, then go right to gain a corner-crack. Wend through bulges, step right and move up to the top.

North-East Arete   25m   E2 5c   (1976)
The steep edge bordering Dunglas Corner. Start right of the edge then climb it trending right beneath an overhang and a jug. Surmount the overhang (crux), then follow easier rock to join Dunglas Corner.

NORTH FACE

A rather menacing part of the crag with much unstable ground. A large scree covered ledge splits the face into two tiers, with impressive black overhanging walls on the left and a smooth wall bounded by corners on the right.

Drink Up for Tomorrow we Die   25m   E7 6b *   (2001)
This dangerous route is the first to breach the upper of the two black overhangs on the left of the face. Start near the left of the face, just right of a recess. Climb rightwards to a protruding block below some smooth overlaps. Step right and climb

the overlaps (crux) to better holds and protection. Move up left to a large detached block below a roof and pull directly through the roof to easier ground leading to the top, passing a tree on the left.

Unnamed   10m   E2 5b   *(1998)*
Climb the short steep wall at the left end of the lower overhanging wall with no protection.

Don't Wake Up Now   20m   E5 5c *   *(1998)*
An unprotected and serious route which follows the left-hand weakness in the lower black wall. Climb up into the scoop and follow a flake rightwards. At the end of the traverse, climb steeply to a long reach (crux) on the lip. Continue more easily to the top.

Dream Delirious   20m   E5 6a *   *(1998)*
A direct line up the centre of the lower wall. Start below a niche in the centre of the wall. Make difficult moves to gain this (good rest). Continue directly with exhilarating steep moves through the roof on big holds to gain easier ground. Unprotected.

Joker's Groove   25m   VS 4c   *(1975)*
This climbs the corner right of the overhangs. Climb the rib and enter the corner. Trend left past flakes and finish up the wall on left (crux). The rock is loose.

Bite them Bequerels   20m   E3 5b   *(1987)*
Serious and exciting. Start at the obvious rock scar right of the massive scar. Pull up on large holds to a foot-ledge and poor peg runners on the left. Move right across the wall and up on better holds to the trough. Follow this leftwards and up to below the overhangs. Traverse right, taking care with the rock to old belay pegs. Abseil descent.

The Nightmare   20m   E2 5c   *(1976)*
This takes the hexagonal slabs right of the massive rock scar. Start at the inset corner on the left of the slabs. Climb this and a steeper corner over slabs above (crux) to a small ledge and shattered blocks. Traverse left along shattered rock to the edge. Move up to a ledge and climb the wall above. An apt name.

WEST FACE

This sunny wall contains some of the most solid rock and has the most popular routes on the crag, although lack of traffic has allowed the moss to reclaim many of the easier lines. The obvious features are a right-slanting ramp, Curioser and Curioser, and a cross shaped crack in the centre, The Cross. At the left end there is the remains of an old fence; the first route starts about 40m left of this.

The Gentle Touch   20m   HVS 5b   *(1976)*
A rib, about 8m left of the shallow corner of Pullover, marks the start. Move up shelves past a spike and surmount an overhang (crux) to reach a belay. Traverse right to a break and climb the centre of the arete on large holds to an awkward exit.

Pullover   20m   VS 4c   *(1976)*
About 5m left of the remains of the fence is a shallow corner. Climb the corner past a peg runner, pull up and traverse a few metres left along a shelf. Continue up and right past blocks to exit up the groove above.

Curioser and Curioser   40m   VS 4c   *(1975)*
This follows the slanting ramp, starting as for Pullover. Move up then across right to a small ledge. Cross the wall to a second ledge, then up right to basin hold.

Traverse right past a narrowing to the second cave. Step right, surmount the overhang and finish up a crack.

Skirmish   25m   VS 5a   (1975)
The original route on the crag has some bold climbing. Climb the wall about 5m right of the remains of the fence, trending slightly left to a ledge and caves. Go through the overhang left of The Cross and continue leftwards to a thin crack and horizontal break, traversing left (crux) to finish. A direct start climbs the wall above the old fence at the same grade.

The Cross   20m   E1 5b *   (1975)
Good climbing. Follow Skirmish to the cave. Move right and follow the crack through the overhang to the top.

A Feet of Arms   20m   HVS 5b   (1976)
Some athletic moves in well protected situations. Start below a slanting crack about 8m right of the fence. Climb a wall to the base of the crack, then go up this and the wall on the right to a ledge, finishing up the deceptive wall.

Downfall   35m   HVS 5b   (1975)
This follows the obvious left traverse line about 10m right of the old fence. Climb up to the traverse and follow it to the cave. Traverse right past a narrowing and a ledge and go over the overhang right of The Cross. Climb the wall trending left to finish by a V-break and drooping spike.

The Ramp   13m   Moderate   (1975)
The slanting break right of Downfall provides easy access to the upper wall.

Deviant   15m   E1 5b *   (1987)
Interesting climbing. Follow The Ramp for a few metres until it is possible to get established on a parallel ramp-line above, which leads to a second cave. Traverse right across the horizontal break to a niche, finishing above.

Steel Finger   15m   E3 6a *   (1991)
Start 2m right of The Ramp and climb the strenuous steep wall and thin crack.

Negotiations With Isaac   15m   F6c **   (1992)
Climb directly up the left end of the overhanging wall via two bolts and a stuck wire. Good climbing, easing towards the top.

The Beef Monster   15m   F6c+ **   (1989)
Start right of Negotiations With Isaac at the base of a left-slanting crack. Climb straight up past a horizontal break, move up and right, continue up a thin crack to gain the niche-break, then go right and up the wall to the top.

Political Legacy   15m   F7b   (1992)
Start up The Beef Monster, then step right and climb to a good but loose hold. Finish trending slightly left.

Airhead   15m   F7a **   (1992)
Tackle the bulging wall left of Wall of Horrors past two bolts.

An eliminate may be climbed at F6b between Airhead and Wall of Horrors, reaching left to clip the bolts.

Wall of Horrors   10m   E3 5c *   (1977)
Near the right-hand end of the face is an overhanging wall with a thin crack. Climb up very steeply on good holds to a small niche and a jug. Continue past a flake and through the easier overhang at the top.

Little Gripper   10m   VS 5a   *(1975)*
The overhanging rib right of Wall of Horrors. Climb the bulging wall to exit via a
jammed flake on the right. Traverse left, go up the wall to a ledge, then move up
and left to finish at a break.

Moss Flop   8m   Difficult   *(1976)*
The shallow corner right of Little Gripper, finishing right.

Last Grasp   8m   Severe   *(1976)*
Start at the blunt rib right of the last route. Climb the wall, step left to a block and
finish up grass shelves.

A Dream of Brown Trousers   VS 5b   *(1976)*
A low-level left to right girdle with interesting moves in entertaining positions.
Climb to a height of 5m at the extreme left end. Follow a line to The Ramp then
past shelves to some difficulties by Little Gripper and the crux beyond Moss Flop.
Finish on grass.

DUMBARTON ROCK

(NS 400 745)   West facing   Map p74

Sitting by the river Clyde near the town of Dumbarton, this 70m volcanic plug is
one of Scotland's finest low lying outcrops. Combining excellent bouldering on the
huge basalt boulders with spectacular positions on the main North-West Face, it
offers varied and exhilarating climbing. On summer evening the crag is a sun trap
and often buzzing with climbers. Climbers will also be found in the depths of
winter due to Dumbarton's quick drying and accessible nature.

Dumbarton Rock is arguably Scotland's finest and most intense bouldering
venue, ranking among the best areas in the UK. The boulders dry very quickly after
rain, as do most of the routes. March and April are excellent months for friction,
but conditions are frequently good all year. Midges are rarely experienced, except
during very still summer evenings. 'Dumby' has always retained a reputation for
danger and seriousness. The previous edition of this guide mentions that "some
climbers' blood runs cold at the mere mention of the place" and this still rings true,
despite the considerable development which has taken place in the past decade.

There is a good mixture of bouldering, sport climbing and traditional lines and
almost all the routes feature spectacular exposure disproportionate to their length,
with a very pleasant outlook to the Clyde estuary. Many of the older bolts have
recently been replaced.

Approach: Entering Dumbarton from the A82, take the second left after
Dumbarton East train station. Follow this to a small car park on the right. From
here an alleyway leads round the rock to the boulders. Frequent trains run from
Glasgow Central to Dumbarton East, (25mins).

Descent: Descent is generally by abseil from the top of nearby sport routes. Do
not climb inside the castle grounds as this will lead to a fine and will threaten
access to the crag. Keep a low profile while moving around at the top of the main
face routes.

The bouldering is described first (numbered 1 to 148), followed by traditional and
sport routes (numbered 1 to 87), which start on p121.

EAGLE BOULDER

Map p104   Diagrams p106, 125

This huge boulder is the first to be reached from the approach path. The routes are
described from left to right, starting at the easy descent route, which is the arete
facing the castle, on the left of the large slab.

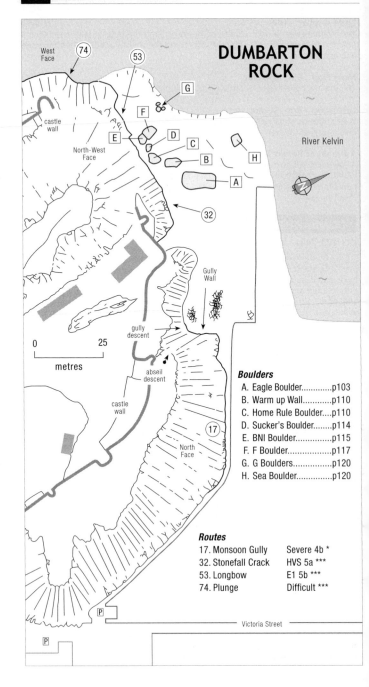

West Face

74

53

G

F

DUMBARTON ROCK

castle wall

North-West Face

E

D

C

B

River Kelvin

H

A

32

Gully Wall

gully descent

abseil descent

castle wall

North Face

17

0   25

metres

Boulders

A. Eagle Boulder.............p103
B. Warm up Wall............p110
C. Home Rule Boulder....p110
D. Sucker's Boulder........p114
E. BNI Boulder...............p115
F. F Boulder...................p117
G. G Boulders................p120
H. Sea Boulder..............p120

Routes

17. Monsoon Gully	Severe 4b *
32. Stonefall Crack	HVS 5a ***
53. Longbow	E1 5b ***
74. Plunge	Difficult ***

P

P

Victoria Street

1 Rankin's Bajin **4a**
Start 1m right of the descent route and climb straight up the slab.

2 Soixante Neuf **4b** *
Climb the slab direct on good holds, starting 2m right of the descent route.

3 Pas Mal **4a** *
Climb the slab just left of No.1 Route, joining that route at half-height.

4 No. 1 Route **3a** *
The large left-slanting ramp gives the easiest route on the slab.

5 Left Direct **4a** **
Start up Pas Mal, then climb rightwards from the ramp on good holds.

6 Centre direct **5a** *
Delicate climbing up the centre of the slab between Left and Right direct.

7 Right Direct **4b**
Climb straight up from the flake of No. 2 Route.

8 No. 2 Route **3a** *
The right-trending ramp and flake gives a pleasant problem.

9 No. 2 Direct **4c**
A tiny problem, climbing the small white groove at the start of the overhanging wall.

0 Pullover **5a** *
Start 1m to the right. Reach the jug on the lip and pull over using a flat hold up and left. Short and sharp.

1 Runs on Potato Power **6c (Font 7a)** *   (1998)
Start on two undercuts. Slap with the right hand to the finger hold directly above. Rock over leftwards to the long, vertical sidepull then slap for a sloper on the lip and pull over.

2 Kev's Problem **6c (Font 7a)** *   (1996)
Start on the twin undercuts and slap with the left hand to the finger hold. Continue straight up into Pullover.

3 Bust My Chops **6b (Font 6c+)** **   (1998)
Start 2m right of Pullover at the hip height break. Move up to two small crimps in the next break and make a hard slap left for a large, right-facing sloper. Finish directly. Footholds on the right are allowed.

4 Bust My Chops **(right-hand) 6c (Font 7b)** *   (2001)
Follow the above problem to the second break, then use minute holds on the lip of the overhanging wall to move up right to a flat hold in a horizontal, near the crack of Zig Zag. Finish up this.

5 Zig Zag **5b** ***
This classic, varied problem weaves through the stepped roofs at the right end of the wall. Start left of the bush and climb steeply to a jug. Move immediately left, then layback upwards until a rock over left onto the slab is possible. Finish directly. A good variation climbs this problem to the jug, then traverses the lip leftwards into Bust My Chops at 6a. Another variation starts lower, at an undercut (good footholds) moving up with a slap for the slopey break (6b). A sit down start is also 6b, and it is possible to finish right onto the small slab of Shadow at 6a.

DUMBARTON ROCK
Eagle Boulder

22. Gorilla — 6b (Font 6b) ****
27. King Kong — 7a (Font 8a) ***
29. Shin Sekai — 6b (Font 6c+) *
30. Hoop — 7a (Font 7c) ***
31. Unnamed — 6c (Font 7b+) **
33. Supinator — 6a *
34. 2HB — 6a ***

36. Oceans — 6c (Font 7b+) ***
38. Snappy — 6b *
39. Unnamed — 6b *
40. The Blue Meanie — 5c ***
41. PTO — 5a *

16 Fouk Yee   6c (Font 7b) *   *(2001)*
A good but slightly eliminate problem climbing the short arete right of Zig Zag.
From the large sloper use a two finger sidepull, and edges on the arete to reach
the sloping ledge above. Mantel onto this and finish up Zig Zag.

17 Tam's Route   5c
Climb the stepped overhanging groove 5m right of Zig Zag, just round the arete.
From the sloping ledge at 3m, finish leftwards.

18 Shadow   E3 6c **   *(1992)*
Round to the right is an intimidating overhanging wall. On the left of this, is an
extremely overhanging black groove. Climb the groove with difficulty to its top.
Make a hard and technical move up and left to a good hold and finish up the small
slab. Committing and scary, get some good spotters!

19 Trick of the Vale   E5 6c **   *(1992)*
Climb the groove as for Shadow, and move right onto a ledge. This provides a good
rest, but also a good place to get scared! (retreat possible to the right or by
jumping). Continue up the centre of the wall direct, heading for the apex, to a
difficult mantelshelf on to the dirty slab.

20 High Flyer   6b/c (Font 6c+)   *(1980s)*
From a ledge on the left side of the cave, make a ridiculous leap for a good hold
and continue to the lip of the overhang. Desperate high jumping for the short!

21 Firestarter   7a (Font 8a) ***   *(2004)*
On the lip of the black roof are two jugs. Start on these and climb diagonally
rightwards on micro crimps into the hanging groove to gain a good slanting hold
at its top. A wild dyno gains the top.

22 Gorilla   6b (Font 6b) ****   *(1978)*
A brilliant classic, climbing the wildly overhanging arete to the right of the cave.
From the starting crimps, slap for the large, smooth layaway above. Make a long
reach left to a jug on the lip, then swing! Use a hold up and right to rock over onto
the slab. Jumping off from the lip definitely doesn't count!

23 Gorilla Warfare   6b (Font 7a+) **   *(2000)*
From the jug of Gorilla, hand-traverse the lip of the boulder leftwards to pull over
on good jugs.

24 Gorilla Hanging Start   6c (Font 7a)   *(2000)*
Use the finger edge under the lip and the lowest edge on the wall (just above
Gorilla's starting foothold) to pull on. Make two hard moves to gain the starting
edges of Gorilla and finish up this. Now attempt the unclimbed start from the big
sloper further back in the cave.

25 Neil's Extension   6c (Font 7b)   *(2000)*
An alternative start to the above problem, sit starting from the right at a low crimp
and sidepull (under roof). Gain the finger edge of the hanging start by a blind slap
and make more hard technical moves into a finish up Gorilla.

26 Silverback   7a (Font 7c) ***   *(2001)*
An awesome and desperate problem climbing the true line of the arete. From the
starting holds on Gorilla, move left on tiny edges to the obvious lone crimp on the
arete. Lunge to the protruding hold at the top and pull over.

27 King Kong   7a (Font 8a) ***   *(2002)*
Link Neil's start into Silverback into Gorilla Warfare! The big finishing jug on Gorilla
is out of bounds.

28 Cautious Lip   6b *
Climb Gorilla to the layaway, then slap directly upwards to the hold on the lip.

29 Shin Sekai   6b (Font 6c+) * (1999)
A reachy problem, climbing the wall just right of Gorilla. Start at an edge and sidepull and make a rather long stretch to an obvious hold just below the lip. Watch those ankles if you miss!

30 Hoop   7a (Font 7c) * *** (2001)
Start 2m right of Shin Sekai. Move up to a finger jug and make a very long rock over to the crimp on top of the 'ear' feature. Move left on the lip to finish at better holds.

31 Unnamed   6c (Font 7b+) * ** (2001)
Start 5m right of Gorilla below a jug on the wall. Jump for the jug and move right to another jug. Use a small crimp above to make a huge span left to a hold on the lip. Desperate for the short.

32 Dressed for Success   6c (Font 7b+) * ** (1999)
An excellent, sustained traverse. Start at the jugs left of Supinator and traverse right, past Supinator. A difficult sequence leads to a finish up 2HB.

33 Supinator   6a * (1978)
The obvious overhanging crack in the centre of the wall is bold, with a difficult move at the top (crux).

34 2HB   6a * *** (1978)
Another classic. Start just left of (or in!) the tree at an undercut. Move up and make a difficult rock over for a small undercut beak-like hold in the crack. Thankfully, good edges and thank god jugs lie above the bulge. A sitting start to this from a sharp crozzly sidepull is a good 6b.

35 A Ford Flash   6c
This problem is currently inaccessible due to the tree, but has been included in case it one day disappears (hopefully not). Climb a small groove right of 2HB and make a long reach left to a good hold.

36 Oceans   6c (Font 7b+) * *** (2001)
Climb the first couple of moves of the shallow groove of 1990 Traverse then move left to an undercut. Use this to reach holds up and left (crux). Slap upwards on crimps, then make a long and bold reach left to a protruding edge to finish.

37 1990 Traverse   6c (Font 7b) * (1990)
A hard and technical traverse which has seen few repeats. Start in a groove to the right of the tree right of 2HB. From the lowest holds, layback up, then traverse right on small edges (crux) to better holds. Continue right, finishing up The Blue Meanie.

38 Snappy   6b * (1996)
To the right of the tree is a steep, blank wall. This problem climbs the wall above the sharp, threatening, ankle height ledge, left of The Blue Meanie. Climb up and make a difficult move left to a jug. Finish straight up, with a long move to another jug. Bold.

39 Unnamed   6b *
Start 1m left of The Blue Meanie, heading directly for a large undercling pinch. Use this to boldly go where few have gone before!

40 The Blue Meanie   5c * ***
This problem climbs the wall above the slabby rock at the top of the path. Start at

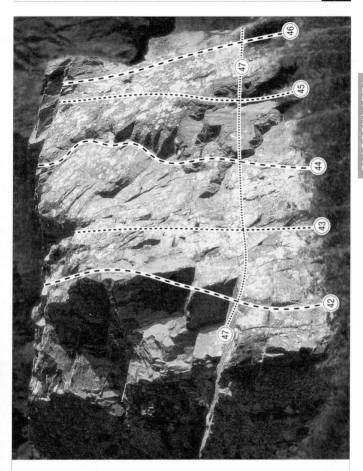

DUMBARTON ROCK
Warm Up Wall

42. Left Edge   4a *
43. Friday's Fill   4a **
44. Friar's Mantle   5b ***
45. Urgava   5a *
46. Right Edge   4c *
47. Low Traverse   6a *

a jug and use one of 2 or 3 different ways to gain an inset sloper below a bulge. Finish leftwards on good jugs. A little unnerving, spotter useful.

41 PTO   5a *
Climb the short wall and bulge a few metres left of the descent route, with a long reach from an undercut.

WARM UP WALL

Map p104   Diagram p109, 125
The wall down and to the right of the Eagle Boulder (below Home Rule Boulder) has a vertical wall which faces down the Clyde. This has good problems and is also an excellent spot for warming up circuits.

42 Left Edge   4a *
Climb the stepped left edge of the wall.

**43 Friday's Fill   4a ** **
The crack on the left is awkward to start and often a little wet, but has an excellent finish. Very popular.

44 Friar's Mantle   5b * **
The obvious stepped central line has one tricky move on slopers. Brilliant!

45 Ungava   5a *
The wall just right of Friar's Mantle, using a small sidepull, but not the right edge.

46 Right Edge   4c *
Layback up the right arete of the wall.

47 Low Traverse   6a *
Traverse from right to left just above the ground with some technical moves.

HOME RULE BOULDER

Diagrams p104, 111, 125
This sits on top of the Warm Up Wall and is characterised by a smooth, graffiti covered wall, facing Dumbarton. The descent is by the arete facing the castle (The Beast). Routes are described from left to right, starting with the descent.

48 The Beast   4b
This is the arete facing the castle, climbed on the left-hand side, and then reversed.

49 The Brute   5a
The wall just right of the arete is gained from the smaller of two rocks below the boulder.

50 Valkyrie   5a
Climb the shallow corner above the two rocks and finish up the slab.

51 Pas Encore   5b *   (1960s)
A good problem, if a bit dirty. Climb the strenuous bulge above the larger rock and finish up the slab.

52 Crimp!   6a *   (2000)
Start below the obvious jutting nose. From the right side of the larger rock, gain a slot hold under the roof. Climb straight up, just left of the arete and use a flat hold and small crimp on the slab to pull over with difficulty.

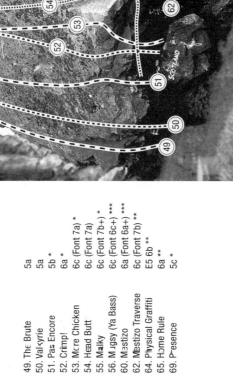

DUMBARTON ROCK
Home Rule Boulder

49. The Brute	5a	
50. Valkyrie	5a	
51. Pas Encore	5b *	
52. Crimp!	6a *	
53. Mcre Chicken	6c (Font 7a) *	
54. Head Butt	6c (Font 7a)	
55. Malky	6c (Font 7b+) *	
56. Mingsy (Ya Bass)	6c (Font 6c+) ***	
60. Mastizo	6a (Font 6a+) ***	
62. Mestizo Traverse	6c (Font 7b) **	
64. Physical Graffiti	E5 6b **	
65. Home Rule	6a **	
69. Presence	5c *	

53 More Chicken   6c (Font 7a) *   (1999)
An eliminate problem climbing the actual arete left of Head Butt, Starting as for the previous problem. From the slot hold, Use a tiny edge on the nose to slap desperately up the edge of the nose. Holds to the left are out of bounds. Good if brushed, poor if not!

54 Head Butt   6c (Font 7a)   (1993)
Start at Pas Encore, but traverse right, and pull round into the corner on the right of the nose. Slap awkwardly up this (head used on the first ascent!) to finish. Give it a brush first.

55 Malky   6c (Font 7b+) *   (2000)
Start just left of Mugsy. Use a sloping edge over the lip on the right (common to Mugsy Traverse) to make a long reach to the obvious sloping shelf. Once established on this, climb direct on small edges without recourse to the incut on Mugsy. Heel-toe useful.

56 Mugsy (Ya Bass)   6c (Font 6c+) ***   (1980s)
The classic at the grade. Start at a good jug (good for one arm pull ups!) on the lip of the cave. Jump for a sloping hold and use a left foot heel-hook to gain an excellent incut. Finish leftwards on small edges.

57 Spam   6c (Font 7c) *   (2002)
A good problem with a cramped start. Start by lying down on a small boulder come ledge below Mugsy. A desperate deep egyptian allows the twin crimps above to be reached. Slap for the starting jug of Mugsy and finish up this.

58 Dweller   6b (Font 6c+)   (2002)
Another eliminate variation in the roof. Start sitting on the ridge shaped rock in the middle of the through route below an inset flat crimp. Use this (foot allowed on jammed block to the right) to move right into Spam. Follow this to the lip and finish up Mestizo.

59 Mugsy Traverse   6c (Font 7b) ***   (1993)
Start at the left of the cave. Traverse the handrail in the roof rightwards and use a heel/toe lock to move up into Mugsy, finishing up this. To extend the fun even more, this problem can be started from a line of good holds behind the rocks in the depths of the cave (7b+).

60 Mestizo   6a (Font 6a+) ***   (1985)
A brilliant problem climbing the left arete of the graffiti covered wall. Climb the arete to a good hold and move left on edges. A thin but excellent rock over leads to the easy groove and the top. Good landing.

61 Mestizo Sit Start   6c (Font 7a+) **   (2000)
Start at sidepulls and make two slaps to gain the handrail. Use heel-hooks to make improbable moves on poor holds, and finish up Mestizo. Mat and spotter useful.

62 Mestizo Traverse   6c (Font 7b) **   (1997)
Start as for the Mugsy Traverse, but continue along the handrail to the arete. A hard move allows a finish up Mestizo.

63 Knowledge is Power   6c (Font 7b/7b+) **   (1998)
A good, sustained problem. Start at two small crimps in the roof of the cave, below the starting jug of Mugsy. Make a desperate slap and swing onto the jug, then follow the Mestizo Traverse to the hard move on the arete. Now reverse the Home Rule Low Traverse and finish up Home Rule.

54 Physical Graffiti   E5 6b ✱✱   *(1985)*
Bold and fingery climbing up the left side of the smooth wall, moving slightly
rightwards near the top. Committing if you climb past the good hold at half-height.
The first few moves up to the good hold make for a worthwhile 6a problem.

55 Home Rule   6a ✱✱
Climb the right side of the wall to the left end of a handrail. Move right along this
and finish past the jammed block. A long rock over, which is a little bit harder for
the short. Awkward landing. The dirty direct finish is also 6a.

56 Home Rule High Traverse   6a ✱✱
Fingery, sustained and technical. Start up Home Rule and traverse left along a line
of crimps and make a perplexing move to gain Mestizo. Finish up this.

57 Home Rule Low Traverse   6c (Font 7a) ✱   *(1995)*
From the arete right of Home Rule, traverse left with increasing difficulty to a cross
through move to gain Mestizo (crux) and finish up this. Thin climbing.

58 Bob's Problem   6a ✱   *(2000)*
Start just left of Presence on the horizontal edge. Pull up and catch the sloper
beside the arete then continue to the handrail.

59 Presence   5c ✱
Climb the bold arete on the right of the graffiti covered wall, with one scary move
to reach the handrail. Will your spotter have the courage to catch you if you fall!

70 Route Royale   E3 5c ✱✱   *(1960s)*
An intimidating trip across the wall to the right of Presence. The climbing is never
hard or committing, but is technical and very bold. Start on the edge of the
platform. Traverse right across the wall past a groove and move up right to the
arete. Rock over into a niche on the arete and continue easily to the top. The
traverse can also be gained from directly below (6a). The groove itself has also
been climbed direct at E4 5c.

1 Royal Arete   6a   *(1996)*
Climb the blunt arete directly to join Route Royale near the top. Bold.

2 The Whip   E2 5b ✱✱
Climb the right side of the blunt arete until it is possible to use good holds to move
rightwards into the obvious shallow groove. Climb this until a scary, thin move left
leads to ledges and the top. Guaranteed to raise the pulse, especially if you take
the direct finish over the bulge (5c).

3 Unnamed   6b ✱
Start hanging from a good hold in the roof under the start of The Whip (or sitting
down on the left). Move to a hold on the lip, then slap right to a huge and good
sidepull. Use this to climb the small arete, and pull over on small crimps.

4 The Switch   5a   *(1960s)*
A left-slanting line between The Whip and Valhalla, 5b if finished by the bulge on
the right. The first ascent was done in Vibrams!

5 Valhalla   4c ✱
The shallow fault above the junction of the two boulders. Bridge up the gap and
use a good jug to pull onto the wall. Climb the groove to a technical exit. Another
very bold problem.

76 The Beauty   5a
Climb the bulging wall just left of the descent arete.

SUCKER'S BOULDER

Map p104   Diagrams p118, 125

The boulder to the right of the Home Rule Boulder. The problems are described from left to right, starting on the smooth overhanging wall facing the distillery.

77 Unnamed   6a *
Start sitting down at the left arete of the smooth wall (at the entrance to the cave). Climb up left into the darkness and through the gap above without putting your back on the other boulder.

78 P.S.   5a
Awkward clambering up the cleft between the C and D boulders.

79 Unnamed   6a
Start just left of Toto and climb direct to the jug, using a couple of small edges.

80 Toto   6a (Font 6a) *   (1985)**
Another Dumbarton classic not to be missed. Originally given 6b, but much easier than many of the 6as! Climb the left-slanting crack, then use a high pinch to gain the jug on the left. Finish here or climb the right-hand finish at 6b. Every ascentionist seems to use a different sequence!

81 Toto Sit Down Start   6b (Font 7a) **   (1994)
Start 3m to the right of Toto in a crossed over position. Follow the line of edges leftwards and finish up Toto. Sustained, but no stopper moves. A variation, **Totality** (6c, Font 7b+, 2003), moves diagonally righwards across the wall once established in the crack, with long reaches between sidepulls.

82 Toto Traverse   6c (Font 7a+)   (1996)
Start as for the sit down to Toto and follow this to the good hold at the start of the crack. Make a very long reach left (crux) and continue to finish up P.S.

83 The Shield   7a (Font 7b+) *   (1994)**
This hard test piece climbs the obvious shield feature in the centre of the wall. Desperately pull on the sidepulls and slap for the top with the left or right-hand, or both at the same time! Pull awkwardly onto the ramp above and finish. The top sloper is frustratingly hard to hold.

84 The Shield Sit Down Start   7a (Font 7c) **   (1997)
Use the pocket and undercut to gain The Shield with difficulty.

85 Shield Right-hand   6b/c *   (1999)
Use the good undercut at the base of the shield feature, and a poor sidepull on the right to slap up for the sloping ramp on the right. Move left and finish as for The Shield.

86 Power Pockets   6b *
At the right-hand margin of the wall there are two shallow, sharp finger pockets. Use these, and the small, square toe edge to slap for a sloper on the lip and pull over 6b/c if done foot off. A true 'one move wonder'.

87 Power Pockets Sit Start   7a (Font 7c) *   (2000)
Use the two parallel sloping edges (foot in pocket to the right) to desperately gain the power pockets. The right arete is out of bounds.

88 Redpath's Problem   7a (Font 7b) *

A hard eliminate. Use the left-hand power pocket and a pinch on the left for hands, and the square foothold and a tiny pocket just above the ground for feet. Make a desperate blind slap for a tiny edge above the Power Pockets sloper (the one with a tiny pocket just above it) and pull over.

39 Railing 6a (Font 6b+) ** (1999)
Start up large pockets on the blunt arete and follow a hand-traverse leftwards along the lip, to finish up The Shield. Technical footwork, high in the 6a grade. The rail has also been climbed in its entirety at an even more sustained 6a.

40 Snooker Shelf 5a
Start at the right end of the face. Climb up onto the big left-slanting ramp and follow it without much difficulty to its end and finish up a groove. Much better than it appears.

41 Kneebar 6a * (1999)
An unusual problem! A sit-start to Snooker Shelf (sort of), starting at a big sidepull. Pull on and use a bizarre kneebar to climb past slopers to snooker shelf.

42 Mosca 4a
The left arete of the slab above the overhanging wall, approached from the rear side of the boulder. Dirty.

43 Antimatter 5b
An eliminate with thin smearing up the slab left of Sucker's. Has benefited from a recent wire brushing.

44 Sucker's Slab 5b * (1960s)
A friction problem on tiny holds up the centre of the slab.

45 Volpone 4a *
The thin crack gives a good problem, but with the obligatory poor landing.

BNI BOULDER

Map p104 Diagrams p118, 125

This is the tall boulder to the right, partially sitting on top of the Sucker's and F boulders. Some of the problems here really do feel like routes, and would not forgive a fall. The problems are described left to right, starting at the cave path between the D and F boulders.

46 Chahala 5c **
This steep problem starts just right of Snooker Shelf, on the roof of the cave, below a trio of good incuts. Jump to the first, then campus upwards to the top one. Reach right and pull round the arete onto the ledge.

47 Harvester of Eyes 4a
The next four problems start from the ledge on top of the F Boulder, which is reached by squeezing up through the gap right of Juggie, on the F Boulder. This problem climbs the open groove on the left of this face.

48 Astronomy 3b
The ribs and grooves in the centre of the face are straightforward, and give the best descent route from this boulder.

49 Deo Gratis 5b *
The wall left of the arete is straightforward, apart from one hard, and bold move to stand on a tiny foothold.

100 Imposter Arete   4c **
The high arete on the left of the huge slab gives excellent, steady climbing on small, but good holds.

101 B.N.I. Direct   5c **   (1994)
Traverse across the slab to the sharp foothold as for BNI, then move up and left, and finish easily up the centre of the slab.

102 B.N.I.   5c ***   (1960s)
Start at the base of Imposter Arete and traverse across the slab to the obvious good foothold. Make a difficult move to swing right onto a small flake, then continue up and right to finish up Pendulum. Delicate and committing.

103 Very Ape   6b   (1998)
Start up the squeeze descent route, then pull out right on big undercuts. Reach over the lip to a small finger hold and pullover onto the BNI slab using mono pockets. Finish up B.N.I. Direct.

104 B.N.I. Direct Start   6c (Font 7b+) *
Use two small crimps on the very base of the slab to make a hard reach to the sharp hold above on the slab. Finish up BNI. Desperate for the short.

105 Sabotage   7a (Font 8a+) ***   (2003)
An outstanding line with devious and powerful climbing across the roof below the B.N.I. slab. Sit start at a small slab at the back of the roof. Move directly up to gain an incut undercut in the roof. Use this to awkwardly gain an edge on the right wall. Slap outwards and use the superb sloper on the right to gain the lip and a technical rock over come mantel onto the B.N.I. slab.

106 The Elbow Basher   6c (Font 7b+) **   (1997)
A brutal traverse across the cave under the slab. Start spanned between a big flat edge on the left, and an incut crimp on the right. Use a small pinch to reach undercuts at the top of a tiny slab. Traverse these rightwards round the corner with difficulty (bruised shins likely). In a very cramped position, reach sidepulls (head jam useful!) and use these to finish up the crack of Good Nicks.

107 Good Nicks   6a ***   (1970s)
The test piece at this grade. Start underneath the right arete of the B.N.I. slab. Climb the short finger-crack to its top, then make a difficult span left to an edge on the arete. A brilliant move to match the edge permits a swing round to the small flake on the slab. Finish up B.N.I. Jumping from the arete is fine, but try not to fall backwards! The sit start to the crack is 6b and it is also possible to continue up the arete after the span at 6a.

108 You're Nicked!   6c (Font 7b) **   (2001)
A direct version of Good Nicks. From the fingerlock pull up to small edges directly above and make a hard move to the nick on the arete. Finish up Good Nicks.

109 Pedulum   4c ***
Excellent climbing up the big flake right of the arete. Pull onto a ledge and climb the flake steeply on jugs. Use the block at its top to pull round onto the slab. Pause for a minute to take in the situation (are you bouldering or soloing!) then rock over to reach the top. Popular, but still deserves more attention. It is possible to finish right, into the black V-groove. The previous guide gave this variation 5a, but frightening 5c is more appropriate! Span right from the top of the flake.

110 Revalation   E4 5c **   (2004)
Climb the V-groove from directly below via a terrifying dyno.

1 Nadjilation   E6 6b ** (1998)

This intimidating route climbs the grossly overhanging wall round to the right of Pendulum. Start standing on the razor sharp boulder under the right-hand side of the wall. Climb the wall aggressively, using a fin hold to make a big lunge to the top (crux). Only a few moves, but falling off could be catastrophic!

2 Jump **

A more exciting (and rapid) descent of the B.N.I. boulder. Jump from the top of Nadjilation to ledges on the main face.

3 Jump II **

Not as long as the above problem, but much scarier! Jump across the gap between the D and E boulders to the top of Sucker's Slab. If you actually enjoyed this, then proceed to the next problem!

4 Jump Challenge III **

Unclimbed. Jump from the slabby main face to the top of the arete right of Pendulum, or from the top of Pendulum to Fever Pitch on the main face.

F BOULDER

Map p104   Diagrams p118, 125

This is the boulder to the right of the Sucker's Boulder, underneath the B.N.I. Boulder. It features a very steep, smooth wall facing Dumbarton, and a slabby face looking down the Clyde. This boulder has some of Dumby's (and Scotland's) hardest problems. The problems are described from left to right, starting at the cave between the D and F boulders.

5 Skint Knuckles   5b *

Start at the entrance to the cave and use a good sidpull on the right wall to layback rightwards until it is possible to pull over on to the big ledge.

6 Slap Happy   6c ** (1993)

This problem, along with Toto, must be the most frequently attempted (and failed on) problems at Dumby. From the good hold on the left of the overhanging wall, reach the slopey edge and make a hard move to the top edge. Reaching it is easy, but holding it is a different story. If you can not hold it, carry on flying to the top ledge in one move, which is easier, even though it feels harder.

7 Hap Slappy   7a (Font 7c) (2000)

An eliminate based on Slap Happy. Take the small hold with your lefthand and then twist...

8 In Bloom   6c (Font 7c) *** (1998)

This hard and powerful problem is now a classic test piece, requiring an aggressive approach. Start at Slap Happy and traverse right along the poor, sloping handrail and span out into Pongo. Finish up Pongo.

9 Pongo   6b (Font 6c) ***

Climb the grossly overhanging crack on the right of the wall, starting by swinging in from the left. A hard move at mid-height is eased by a foot-hook on the right arete. Classic!

10 Pongo Sit-Start   7a (Font 8a) *** (1998)

From two holds below the start of the crack, 6b moves lead to two frustratingly desperate moves off the jammed block. If you get past this, cruise to the top of Pongo and celebrate!

DUMBARTON ROCK
F Boulder

87. Power Pockets S.S.   7a (Font 7c) *
96. Chahala   5c **
115. Skint Knuckles   5b *
116. Slap Happy   6c **
118. In Bloom   6c (Font 7c) ***
120. Pongo Sit Start   7a (Font 8a) ***
121. Andy's Arete   6b

21 Andy's Arete 6b (2004)
The arete right of Pongo, climbed on the overhanging side. A sitting start is Font 7b.

22 Sorcerer's Slab 5a
This problem climbs the left side of the slab round to the right, on the other side of the large bush.

23 Magic Wand 5b
Climb straight up from the start of Sorcerer's Slab.

24 Slant 5b
This climbs the small, steep groove just right again.

25 Nemesis 5b * (1960s)
This problem climbs the bulging arete and easy angled groove on the left of the west face of the boulder. Use a poor finger jam in a small crack to slap up left to a jug and pull over to finish up the easy groove.

26 Narcosis 5b *
Rather blind climbing up the wall to the right of Nemesis. A sitting start from the huge, hidden undercut is 6a.

27 Lunik 5b **
A good technical problem which climbs the shallow groove in the centre of the face. Use a hidden incut to pull into the groove, then continue directly to finish up the technical arete.

28 Cheddar Direct 4b ***
An excellent varied problem, with a good landing. Start at a blunt arete with a little niche in it. Climb past this until standing on the slab above. Move rightwards across the slab to finish.

29 Hard Cheddar 5c ****
Start at the same point as Cheddar Direct, but follow holds on the lip of the hanging rib rightwards to finish up Juggie.

30 Big Cheese 7a (Font 7c+) (2003)
Below the hanging rib of Hard Cheddar is a bottomless groove. Sit start at the right side of this on two very poor pinches (the right-hand one is on the lip). Desperately pull up and slap left to an incut sidepull and finish up Hard Cheddar.

31 Juggie 4c
Steep climbing up the arete just left of the descent passage leads to good jugs.

32 Consolidated 6b (Font 7b+) **** (1994)
A classic not to be missed by any dedicated boulderer. Sustained and technical, but with no hard moves. An eliminate problem which is somewhat difficult to describe, but a good rule of thumb is if you think it might be too high, it probably is! Start at the arete just left of Nemesis on a sidepull and undercut. Traverse right on small holds on the lip and then drop down to better holds. Follow the line of parallel holds or ramps to the blunt arete of Cheddar Direct. Pause here for a moment on an upside down rest on a toe-hook, then layback past the niche and continue right past a complex sequence of holds below the lip, to reach triangular hold below the arete of Juggie. Finish up the arete, which will now feel rather uphill!

33 Consolidated Extension 6b (Font 7c) *** (1995)
An extension to the above traverse which is even more sustained. Follow the previous problem to the triangular hold, then continue dynamically rightwards on sidepulls to finish on jugs at the descent route.

134 The 8b Traverse 6c (Font 7c/7c+) *   (1998)
A harder, eliminate finish to the extension. From the triangular hold, use only a long thin crimp and a further small crimp to the right to reach the descent route.

G BOULDERS

Map p104   Diagram p125

This is the trio of small boulders below the F Boulder. All three problems climb the seaward face of the largest central boulder.

135 Short Sight 4a
Climb the short east facing wall. Green.

136 Short Notice 5b
The bulging nose of rock facing Dumbarton. Start on the slab and make an interesting move using a hidden sidepull to finish. Don't bounce backwards if you fall off!

137 Long Reach 5c
Climb the scooped wall to the right (facing the Clyde), avoiding using the arete on the right. Eliminate.

138 Reducer 6c (Font 7b) *   (2001)
The obvious and enticing one move problem on the smooth leaning face of the smallest boulder. Start on the very sloping ramp and if you can pull on, jump for sharp jugs on the top (without using the sides of the boulder for hands or feet).

SEA BOULDER

Map p104

The obvious lone boulder on the shore has several good problems in the easier grades and is also a good spot to warm up. The seaward face is tidal (just) and its base is finely polished by the action of the sea. Problems are described left to right, starting at the side facing Dumbarton.

139 White Streak 6a *
An eliminate problem climbing the narrow wall between the right arete and the short crack. Climb the wall using some very sharp holds, without using the aretes to either side.

140 Steptoe 4c *
Climb the right arete without using the lump of lead.

141 Red Streak 5c
Climb the wall just right of the arete, avoiding the lump of lead hold, and holds on Chowbok.

142 Chowbok 4c **
Climb the centre of the seaward face, via a thin crack.

143 Erewhon 5c **
The right arete of the seaward face is very smeary and polished to start, but easy to finish on good holds.

144 Commercial Route 4c **
The corner to the right of the arete, finishing rightwards.

45 Wednesday Wall   4c
Climb the technical slab just to the right of the corner.

46 Silver's Route   4c *
Use sidepulls to pull onto the slab and finish more easily.

47 Silver's Route Sit-Start   6b (Font 6c+)   *(2000)*
This is an excellent problem, starting on poor slopey opposing sidepulls, and a heel-hook.

48 Gardner's Girdle   5a **
An excellent, exciting traverse when the tide is in. Also good for warming up. Watch out for the pull round past Erewhon, it seems to catch people out with amusing regularity.

EVER DRY WALL

The small overhanging wall below Appliance of Violence (always covered in chalk) on the North-West Face gives some ever dry bouldering, but it is not as good as it looks and is rarely used. However, the wall below Longbow (to the left) is good for warming up.

BLACK WALL

The overhanging wall down to the right (left of Benny's Route) is also ever dry, and gives good shelter from the rain. This wall is brilliant for doing stamina circuits, which can be tailored to the correct difficulty by missing out holds or sections.

NORTH FACE

Map p104

This is the wall above the alleyway path leading from the car park to the boulders. The wall is very dirty and almost all of the routes here have been ignored for years and are in a poor state. A few of the routes are good though and are worth doing. Belays are generally well back from the top of the crag.

1 Alpha   20m   HVS 5a
Climb the twin cracks high on the left-hand end of the face to a belay well back.

2 Beta   20m   E1 5b
The central crack to the right is approached by sloping rock, belay well back.

3 Gamma   20m   E1 5c
Climb sloping rock to the steep crack just left of the left-hand of two right-slanting mossy ramps.

4 Uisge Beatha   25m   HVS 5a
The left-hand of the two slanting ramps gives a botanical romp.

5 Rising Power   35m   E2 5b   *(1984)*
Start as for Uisge Beatha, but follow the obvious right-slanting fault to the foot of the Antigrav crack. Climb the crack to the good hold and continue traversing right to finish up Crackerjack. Good climbing but quite mossy and eliminate.

6 Bohert   30m   HVS 5a
Sloping rock leads to the right-hand slanting ramp which gives mossy climbing. Finish up a crack.

7 Antigrav 30m E3 6a *   *(1970s)*
This is the smooth wall and thin hanging finger-crack towards the left of the face.
Climb the unprotected wall direct to the crack. Climb the well protected crack with
difficulty and continue to belay (very) well back.

8 Slainte 30m E2 5c   *(1970s)*
This follows the right-hand of two hairline cracks, right of Antigrav. Climb the wall
to the crack, and up this turning the small overlap on the right.

9 Crackerjack 30m E1 5b *   *(1970s)*
The main feature of this route is an entertaining well protected crack after a bold
start. Start immediately below the vertical finger-crack right of the hairline cracks
of Slainte. Go up the wall to a small ledge at about 8m. Step left and follow the
crack and its continuation.

10 Drizzle 30m E1 5b *   *(1970s)*
Another good route. To the right, an obvious left-slanting crack starts from a small
recess. Follow this to an awkward move onto a sloping ledge below a shallow
corner. Climb the corner for a few moves, then left to the arete.

11 The Neilweg 30m E1 5b *   *(1964)*
Climb the corner above and right of the slanting crack of Drizzle, with a mossy exit
onto a ledge and possible belay. The crack above provides an airy finish.

12 Big Ears 35m E1 5b   *(1981)*
A poor route taking the rock right of The Neilweg. From the ramp, enter the
triangular niche and climb the groove above, finishing by a thin crack.

13 Boulevard 30m VS 5a *   *(1963)*
Gain the obvious ramp below the triangular niche with difficulty, then climb
rightwards to a grassy finish.

14 Hailstone Climb 30m Severe 4a   *(1960s)*
Climb the wall to the right via corners, grooves and the line of least resistance to
a grassy finish. Not recommended.

15 Left Edge Route 30m VS   *(1960s)*
This takes a line up the left edge of Monsoon Gully. Start at the middle of a short
wall and follow a direct line, aiming for the arete above. Climb the arete until a
steep section forces a move out left to a finishing crack. This route has been
affected by rockfall (2002) and may contain further unstable rock.

17 Monsoon Gully 35m Severe 4b *   *(1963)*
A delightful neo-Victorian gully for sub-aqua devotees and ecologists. At the top of
the gully move left to gain the grass. The direct finish gives HVS 5a climbing up the
steep crack on the right wall at the top of the gully.

18 Supple as a Brick 35m E4 5c   *(1988)*
Steep, technical and serious. Start up the huge gully (Monsoon Gully) then move
out right to a good jug on the right wall (Friend 1.5). Climb the steep groove above
(poor RPs) then use a small overlap to reach better holds. Continue to a ledge and
belay. Move 2m left and climb interesting grooves to the top.

19 Nameless Crack 25m Very Difficult   *(1964)*
Start 10m right of Monsoon Gully and climb the pleasant grassy left-slanting crack-
line.

20 Alleyway 25m VS 5a   *(1960s)*
Start at the base of Nameless Crack, but climb the narrow right-slanting shelf to

grass. Step left and finish up mixed ground.

21 Sunset Groove   30m   VS 5a   (1970s)
At the right end of the face is a foul-looking chossy groove. Climb it if you dare.

22 Angel's Pavement   90m   5a   (1964)
A low-level girdle of the complete face, usually less than 3m up, gives pleasant bouldering with little chance of breaking an ankle. However, there's a high chance of being stung to death. The section below Boulevard provides the crux.

GULLY WALL

Map p104

To the right is a grassy gully. High in the gully is a west facing wall, recognised by the large mass of ivy on its left. Descent is by traversing right from the top of the routes and carefully down the gully.

23 Ganglion Grooves   20m   VS 4c
This route lies at the left edge of the west facing wall above the trees at the end of the alleyway. Start just right of the ivy covered wall and follow cracks and grooves to the top.

24 Ciamar a tha Sibh   25m   E2 5b *   (1970s)
The short corner on the left side of the wall gives enjoyable open climbing. Follow Ganglion Grooves for 5m, then go up the narrow slab on the right (poor protection) to the short corner, which is climbed until forced left to the arete.

25 Snowhite   20m   E2 5b **   (1970s)
This good route climbs the thin crack in the centre of the wall. Start right of a corner and pull left onto a slab. Climb steeply towards the base of the crack and finish up this. Bold and strenuous.

26 Rag   15m   Severe 4a   (1970s)
Climb the large grassy groove right of Snowhite.

27 Tag   15m   HVS 5a   (1970s)
Up and right of Rag is a series of short discontinuous cracks. Climb the twin left-hand cracks and the wall above, then finish up the groove on the left side of the block overhang.

28 Bobtail   12m   HVS 5a   (1970s)
Start at the far right-hand end of the face. Follow a short crack to a groove, make an awkward move to gain the continuation groove and step left at the top.

NORTH-WEST FACE

Map p104   Diagram p125

This awe-inspiring face is home to some of Scotland's finest crack climbs, as well as numerous other classic traditional and sport routes, which have a reputation for being bold, exposed and intimidating.

29 Stonefall Wall   10m   E4 6a   (1990s)
This climbs the steep, cracked wall on the extreme left of the face.

30 Eliminator   15m   E6 6a/b *   (1993)
Start at the same point as Route Three. Climb up and turn a small roof on the left. Move right to the arete and boldly climb this to a horizontal break. Climb a faint crack in the headwall to the top.

31 Route Three 15m HVS 5b * (1965)
At the left side of the wall is a crack topped by a square roof. Climb the crack to the roof, traverse left, and finish up the chimney.

32 Stonefall Crack 20m HVS 5a ** (1963)
The wide crack below the chimney is climbed either direct, or with a deviation out left at mid-height to finish up the chimney. Big cams or hexes useful.

33 The Big Zipper 30m E3 5b ** (1983)
After the serious first section, the corner above the ledge gives an excellent pitch of bridging and finger jamming with good protection. Climb Stonefall Crack until it is possible to traverse right along the ledge to the base of the corner. Continue up the excellent corner (bolt belay).

34 Payback Time! 15m F7b+ (1990s)
This is the bolt line on the wall to the left of The Big Zipper. Either abseil down the corner and belay, or climb a small groove (RPs) left of Woops to reach the start.

35 Woops 30m E4 6a * (1980)
Difficult technical climbing up the short overhanging finger-crack right of Stonefall Crack. Climb the crack to the ledge and finish up Big Zipper.

36 Omerta 30m F7c *** (1980)
The stunning and exposed left arete of the main wall. Climb the direct start to The Big Zipper via a desperate move then continue up the technical arete.

37 Chemin De Fer 30m E5 6a **** (1980)
One of the finest crack-lines in Scotland and a test piece at the grade. The crack has hard moves in the first half, then eases very slightly towards the top. However, there is excellent protection. Bolt belay at the top.

38 Achemine 30m E9 6c *** (2001)
A spectacular line on the headwall above Chemin De Fer giving desperate and very bold climbing. Scotland's first E9 trad climb. Follow Chemin de Fer to where the crack bends left. Move up through a small overlap and traverse right to a tiny groove. Climb rightwards using the groove with desperate moves to gain a rounded sidepull. Use this to rock over back left and follow a desperate sequence leftwards (crux) to gain a half moon shaped edge. Move up and left to a good finishing jug.

39 Requiem 35m E8 6b **** (1983)
The awesome central crack-line remains one of the hardest routes in Scotland. By 2002 the route had been lead placing all gear on the redpoint (all previous ascents had involved yoyos or preplaced gear). Requiem may have been the world's hardest route when first done! From a bolt belay on the ledge, climb the crack with hard moves at its top, then follow the line of holds leading right on the headwall (bold). If you get that far, do battle with the crux last move.

The impressive blank walls to the left and right of Requiem have been bolted but remain projects with projected grades in the mid F9s!

40 Rock of Ages 20m E3 6a * (1983)
The rising traverse line from below The Big Zipper to the base of Requiem is now rather bold since the pegs have rotted away (RP3 in flake at the crux). Finish at the bolt belay on the ledge.

41 Dumb And Dumber 20m E7 6c ** (1999)
An extremely thin wall come slab climb. Start up the slab just right of Chemin de Fer to stand on an obvious perched block. Place a good nut at hip height in the groove on the left, take a deep breath, and teeter boldly up the blank slab above direct. A razor thin move leads to a finish up Rock of Ages.

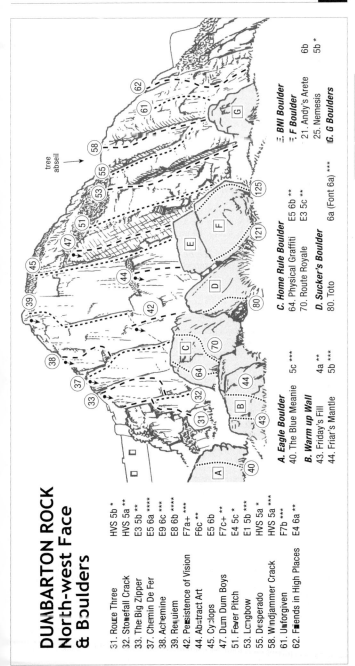

DUMBARTON ROCK
North-west Face
& Boulders

51. Route Three · HVS 5b *
32. Stonefall Crack · HVS 5a **
33. The Big Zipper · E3 5b **
37. Chemin De Fer · E5 6a ****
38. Achemine · E9 6c ***
39. Requiem · E8 8b *****
42. Persistence of Vision · F7a+ ***
44. Abstract Art · F6c **
45. Cyclops · E5 6b
47. Dum Dum Boys · F7c+ **
51. Fever Pitch · E4 5c *
53. Longbow · E1 5b ***
55. Desperado · HVS 5a *
58. Windjammer Crack · HVS 5a ***
61. Unforgiven · F7b ***
62. Fiends in High Places · E4 6a **

tree abseil →

A. Eagle Boulder
40. The Blue Meanie · 5c ***

B. Warm up Wall
43. Friday's Fill · 4a **
44. Friar's Mantle · 5b ***

C. Home Rule Boulder
64. Physical Graffiti · E5 6b **
70. Route Royale · E3 5c **

D. Sucker's Boulder
80. Toto · 6a (Font 6a) ***

E. BNI Boulder

F. F Boulder
21. Andy's Arete · 6b
25. Nemesis · 5b *

G. G Boulders

42 Persistence of Vision   15m   F7a+ *** *(1990s)*
This recent addition is now the most popular sport route in the area. Follow the line of bolts on the slab directly below Requiem to a lower-off. Moving out left then back right at the fourth bolt is the crux.

43 Requiem Direct Start   15m   E3 5b *(1983)*
This serious pitch up the lower wall is now very dirty and ignored.

44 Abstract Art   12m   F6c ** *(2004)*
Balancy climbing on the slabby grey wall.

45 Cyclops   35m   E5 6b *(1981)*
This technical route up the big corner on the right of the main face is also very much in need of a brushing to restore its quality. May be E6 in the near future when the peg rots down.
1. 20m 5b Climb the virtually unprotected lower corner past some dubious rock to a bolt belay on the ledge.
2. 15m 6b Difficult bridging leads to the poor peg. More hard moves lead to an easier finish up the well protected crack. Either abseil off from here or climb the small (dirty) corner leading left to the top of the face.

46 Calm Before the Storm   35m   E6 6c * *(2003)*
A sparsely protected and technical pitch. From the Cyclops belay, place a Friend 2m up the corner and step back down. Climb diagonally across the wall on small edges with increasing difficulty to a hard sequence leading to a huge diagonal 'thank god' jug. Much easier, but very poorly protected climbing leads directly to the top.

47 Dum Dum Boys   23m   F7c+ ** *(1995)*
An excellent sport climb running the height of the smooth right wall. Move up the corner and onto the right wall. A hard move gains the base of the long ramp which is followed (sustained) to the ledge. Continue up the easier upper wall past another shake out to the top.

48 Sufferance   21m   F8a *** *(1993)*
A first class sport route up the very smooth wall just to the right. The route is sustained and technical on small edges, with a traverse at half-height being the crux.

49 Tarrier   24m   F7c+ ** *(1993)*
The line of bolts just left of the arete gives technical and cruxy climbing, finishing at the same point as Sufferance.

50 Tolerance   30m   F8b ** *(2003)*
The obvious linkup to give a superb, sustained pitch with some new climbing. Follow Tarrier to the end of the initial undercut flake. Break out left on sidepulls and make a hard lunge to a handrail (crux). Traverse left along the handrail past Sufferance to join Dum Dum Boys just before its crux. Finish up this.

51 Fever Pitch   25m   E4 5c * *(1970s)*
An exciting but serious pitch with some dirty rock and the odd rattling hold. The crux is much harder than anything else on the route. Start just right of the left arete of the buttress. Climb straight up to a resting place at the horizontal break (large friend). Climb past the thin crack beside the roof (crux) and finish rightwards up the wall above.

52 Fatso   30m   E4 5c * *(1998)*
An exposed and bold wall climb, but not too technical. Follow Fever Pitch to the horizontal break then take a rising traverse across the wall to the right pointing spike. Move up and right then back left across the wall (crux) to finish as for Fever Pitch.

53 Longbow   30m   E1 5b *   *(1960s)*
Exhilarating and well protected climbing up the steep left-hand corner. Much better than it looks from below. Exit right at the top.

Project   10m   F8b
Start up Alliance of Violence but break out left onto the leaning black wall. Move up to large sidepulls on the left and make a desperate sequence leading back right to finishing holds on the ledge. Grabbing the belay reduces the grade to F7c.

54 Appliance of Violence   10m   F7b+   *(1993)*
The bolted overhanging arete to the right of Longbow has a hard crux.

55 Desperado   30m   HVS 5a *   *(1970s)*
Good climbing in the central hanging corner, but poorly protected in the middle section. Climb Windjammer for 10m, traverse left and climb the central corner. The traverse line can also be reached by a direct start just left of the initial groove of Eh Gringo **Eldorado** (E3 5c).

56 Eh Gringo   30m   E4 5c *   *(2003)*
A serious lead on the green arete left of Desperado. Climb a shallow groove 3m left of the start of Windjammer then move leftwards on big holds to the slabby section. Boldly climb the steep wall immediately right of the arete, heading for a good undercut in the overlap above. Pull slightly right through this, then easily back left to finish at the same point as Longbow. Supersedes the eliminate **Gaucho** (E2 5c, 1970s) which avoided the crux wall with an excursion into Desperado.

7 Blackout   30m   E6 6a **   *(2003)*
The soaring black arete left of Windjammer gives a scary lead. Follow Windjammer to the base of the arete. Follow the corner for another 3m (good gear) and move out to the arete on undercuts. Boldly launch up the technical arete, with a crux near the top.

8 Windjammer Crack   30m   HVS 5a ***   *(1964)*
A classic sustained pitch up the soaring right-hand corner. Again the climbing is considerably better than it looks. Well protected (large Friends useful for the lower section).

9 Bad Attitude   18m   F7b *   *(1993)*
On the wall to the right of Windjammer, the left-hand bolted line gives technical climbing.

10 Half Breed   18m   F7b **   *(1993)*
The central line takes the shallow groove, pulling leftwards from a flat hold to join Bad Attitude above the roof.

11 Unforgiven   18m   F7b ***   *(1993)*
The right-hand line is the best of the three, with blind, technical climbing.

12 Friends in High Places   35m   E4 6a **   *(1993)*
This technical and sustained route starts down to the right of the ever dry wall below an overhung niche. Climb leftwards from the niche, then back right past a series of overlaps to a difficult exit right (crux). Move right then finish up a series of easy vegetated grooves. May have been climbed before.

13 Benny's Route Left-hand   10m   F7b   *(1994)*
The overhanging wall at the right end of the grass shelf has two bolt lines, diverging at the third bolt. From here, move left and climb the blunt arete before moving back right (crux) to the lower off.

14 Benny's Route Right-hand   10m   F7c *   *(1993)*
From the third bolt make hard moves rightwards then follow the faint fault to the lower-off.

65 Natural Born Drillers   12m   F7a *   *(1996)*
From the edge of the shelf, follow the diagonal line of bolts across the wall to a
crack. Climb this and use a fingerlock over the bulge to pull over (crux) and reach
the lower-off. Regularly failed on.

66 Knees and Toes, Knees and Toes   40m   E4 5c   *(1998)*
Technical and pumpy. From the edge of the shelf (no clipping any bolts!) traverse
horizontally right to a tiny pod (Friend 0.5). Climb straight up almost to Drillers
(Friend 5 useful), then traverse right and climb the arete until it is possible to
traverse left on a slab into a steep corner. Climb the corner, then finish up
vegetated grooves.

WEST FACE

Map p104

This section of the crag, like the North Face, is broken and gives generally poor
routes by comparison to the North-West Face. To the right of and below
Windjammer Crack a short ridge of poor rock leads to the beach. West Face Gully
is the large grassy cleft below and left of the castle wall.

67 Dumbarton Chimney   30m   VS 4c
The obvious chimney left of West Face Gully gives a disgusting climb.

The left wall of West Face Gully contains a few routes.

68 Silly Thing   40m   HVS
This climbs the rightmost corner in the wall.
1. 25m 4b From the gully traverse easily left to the foot of the corner and follow
it to a block belay at the foot of a steep crack.
2. 15m 5b Climb the crack and belay well back.

69 Frendo   30m   VS 4c   *(1963)*
Higher up the gully is a slab bordered by a narrow ramp. Climb the ramp for 10m
or so. After a short section of mixed ground make a short right traverse over loose
blocks to another slab. Easy for the grade.

70 Grey Slab   25m   VS 5a   *(1964)*
Above and right of Frendo, near the finish of the gully, is a steep slab. Climb it
direct to finish up Frendo.

71 Easter Rib   20m   Severe *   *(1999)*
On the left side of the gully as you approach Casanostra, there is a rib on the left
side of a small corner with a roof in it. Climb the rib direct on good holds, finishing
slightly left at the top. Brilliant!

72 West Face Gully   30m   Severe 4a   *(1965)*
The overgrown gully – yuck.

73 Casanostra   10m   F6c+ *   *(1997)*
This good little route can be found hiding on the right wall of the deep gully. It was
very popular for a while but people seem to have forgotten it's there! Interesting
laybacking leads to a hard move followed by an easier finish on good holds.
Starting from further left up the gully reduces the grade.

74 Plunge   30m   Difficult *   *(1960s)*

Cave Crack, HVS 4c, Loudoun Hill. Climbers Dave McGimpsey & Jim Blyth
(photo Tom Prentice)

An excellent climb in a good situation and on good rock. Also a handy access route to the top of the crag. Best done when the tide is in. Start at the large mooring ring and follow steepening grooves in the clean rock rib to the castle wall. Avoid this on the right and finish on the balcony. Abseil off or continue up and left and abseil off the main face for extra enjoyment!

5 Red Slab   10m   Hard Severe 4b
To the right of Plunge is a cracked red slab, bulging at the top.

6 Old Socks   10m   VS 4c   *(1965)*
Takes a direct line up the crack and overhang, about 4m right of Red Slab.

7 Poison Ivy   10m   VS 5a   *(1964)*
Delicate climbing up the steep red slab, topped with ivy, some 7m right of Old Socks.

8 Sea Traverse   140m   4c   *(1960s)*
This traverse lies between the foot of West Gully and the park railings on the south side of the Rock. The route is usually less than 5m above the beach. For most of its length the traverse is about Difficult, but about mid-way there is a 10m stretch containing the crux. More enjoyable at high tide!

9 Pinky   12m   VS 4b *
About 20m to the right is a small crag below the castle wall with a central overhang and grooves to either side. This route climbs the left-hand groove.

0 Still Going   12m   VS 5a *
This route climbs the lower right-hand groove and the overhang from the right. Much easier than it looks.

1 Perky   12m   Hard Severe 4b
This route follows the right-hand groove all the way.

2 Banana Rib   15m   Very Difficult
Further right at the same level is another crag with a prominent black groove on the left and a grey coloured wall to the right. This climbs the straightforward rib left of the black groove.

3 Banana Groove   15m   VS 4c
Climb the black groove, moving right at the top.

4 Banana Slide   15m   E1 5a
An eliminate line. Start just right of the black groove and climb the wall until forced on to the arete. Make a few moves up the arete then traverse right to finish.

5 Grey Wall   15m   E4 5c *   *(1983)*
A serious solo up the grey wall to the right. There is no protection and the crux is at the top. High in the grade and is being reclaimed by ivy.

6 Datura   12m   E3 5c   *(1980)*
Start about 3m uphill from Grey Wall, below a small downward-pointing flake. Climb the wall direct past two ledges.

7 Samora   12m   E3 5c   *(1984)*
Start a few metres right of Datura and follow holds to gain the ledge at its right end, then finish directly. This and the above route are almost reclaimed by Ivy.

Pulpit Arete, Severe 4a, Loudoun Hill. Climber unknown
(photo Tom Prentice)

DUMBUCK

(NS 420 748)   West facing   Map p74

This good sport climbing venue lies 1.6km east of Dumbarton Rock, on the large quarried basalt plug above the junction of the A82 and A814 on the outskirts of Dumbarton. The routes are on the large overhang on the craggy face to the right of the huge quarry. Climbs are mainly in the harder grades, although the easier routes are well worth doing, and have excellent climbing, which stays dry in heavy rain. Most of the routes are climbable during dry periods in winter, but the crag suffers from some seepage. The routes are generally short, powerful and very sustained, being about 45-50 degrees overhanging.

Approach: Continue on the A82 dual carriageway past the quarry entrance and turn right at the traffic lights opposite the Abbotsford Hotel. Drive up the hill through the housing estate and park. Walk across fields then slant up right through trees to reach the crag.

Filth Infatuated   8m   F5+   *(1997)*
This uninspiring route climbs the bolted groove to the left of the overhanging face.

Project   12m
The left-most line of bolts on the overhanging face, finishing into the easier scoop above.

**Happiness in Slavery   10m   F8b+ ** **   *(2004)*
The faint groove gives a short and fierce route. Very sustained and powerful with several deep egyptian moves.

**Voodoo Magic   10m   F8b ** **   *(1996)*
This excellent sustained route has become harder and better since the loss of a jug at halfway and the ledge at the start.

Awaken   10m   F7c+ * **   *(1992)*
The classic of the crag. Powerful moves lead to the obvious spiky jug. A hard move from a sloper gains easier climbing and the amazing 'thank god' finishing jug. The second and third bolts are very difficult to clip.

**Flesh for Fantasy   10m   F7c+ ** **   *(1994)*
Another excellent sustained climb with no hard moves but good climbing.

**If Six Was Nine   10m   F7c ** **   *(1992)*
Powerful undercutting leads to a hard move near the top. Harder since the loss of a resting jug.

Parallel   10m   F7c   *(1995)*
The line just to the right of If Six Was Nine has a powerful start on undercuts and a technical finish.

**House of Pain   10m   F7c+ ** **   *(1996)*
The line through the curious scoop. Thin climbing leads to a hard jump for an undercut in the roof. The finish is easier but brilliantly steep.

Dirty Sanchez   10m   F7c+ *   *(2001)*
Start up Gentle Mass, follow the scoop rightwards with unusual contortions to finish into House of Pain.

Gentle Mass   10m   F7c *   *(1992)*
This climbs the wall just right of the scoop. Rather longer than most of the Dumbuck routes, but it eases towards the top.

Project
This looks desperate, and loose.

Devastation Generation 10m F8c ★★★ (2004)
The small scoop and faint crack is an outstanding line of great difficulty and the
hardest climb in this guide.

So Be It 8m F8a+ ★★★ (2000)
The rightwards slanting ramp is a brilliant power route. Straightforward climbing
gains the obvious jug. From here, traverse the ramp rightwards and make desperate
moves on tiny edges and pinches. The line directly above the jug is a desperate
project.

Second Sights 7m F7c+ ★ (1998)
Another short but very sharp power route which is essentially a direct version of
Tragically Hip. Desperate bouldering.

Twister 8m F7a+ (1997)
A hard move at the start leads to a difficult traverse left on undercuts. A good
variation is to carry on upwards finishing up the next route at F7a.

Tragically Hip 12m F6c+ ★★ (1997)
A good route which works its way leftwards across the short overhang into a niche
and then finishes up the wall with good varied climbing.

Breathe the Pressure 12m F6b+ ★ (1998)
A difficult, blind starting move over the bulge leads to pleasant climbing up the
slab.

Call of the Wild 25m HVS 4c (2000)
Loose (on a grand scale!) and mostly unprotected. From the lower-off on the
previous route, traverse right then follow a ramp to beneath an overhang. Pull over
this and continue easily to the top of the rock.

GLASGOW AREA

BOWLING

(NS 443 738) South facing Map p74

This small venue on the Glasgow-Loch Lomond cycle route has a few worthwhile
problems on smooth quarried basalt at an off vertical angle. The crag is a bit high
for bouldering and the climbs are mostly given route grades. The routes can either
be boldly soloed (they generally ease towards the top) and down-climbed until it
is safe to jump off, or just climbed for as far as you like. It is not possible to top-
out due to the brambles; take a rope and abseil from the in-situ bolt lower-offs.

Approach: From Bowling train station follow a path into the woods directly across
the road. This leads in 20m to the cycle path. Turn right under the bridge and the
crag is on the left.

Tom's Chimney 10m VS 4c
Bridge up the chimney using natural rock and the wall to a brick ledge. Continue
more easily to the left-hand lower-off.

Yogi's Wobble 10m HVS 5b ★ (2000)
Climb the left arete of the slab past a peg then make an interesting step up the
shallow groove to gain the lower-off. Worth finishing for the move in the groove.

The Pastor's Dirty Daughter 10m 6a (2001)
Climb the face right of Tom's Chimney directly. Powerful moves gain a block. Step
onto the face, jump to a handhold and continue more easily to the left-hand bolt.

Booboo's Knob   15m   5b   *(2000)*
Start up the left arete then foot traverse this rightwards across the slab to gain Yosemite Crack Jump off or climb to the right-hand lower-off at E1.

Astroboy   10m   6a (Font 5) *   *(2000)*
Climb the technical thin crack in the centre of the slab to a small ledge in the break. Jump off or continue at E1 to the left lower-off.

Yosemite Crack   10m   6a (Font 6a)   *(2000)*
The obvious fingerlock crack on the right of the slab is strenuous. Either jump off at the ledge or continue with a long reach to the right-hand lower-off.

The Thin White Line   6m   6c (Font 7a) *   *(2001)*
This climbs the smooth wall just right of the crack. Use a long thin sidepull to gain edges in a faint groove. Gain the flat hold at the top of this and crank past a protruding hold on the wall above to the ledge. The ripple just right of the crack is out of bounds.

The Fold   6m   6c (Font 7a+) *   *(2002)*
This desperate and bold problem takes the obvious vertical ripple running up the smooth wall. Gain an incut sidepull in the ripple and make hard moves past this to gain a two finger press in the groove up and left. Desperately use this to stand up and reach the break and ledge above. Holds in the faint groove of The Thin White Line are strictly out of bounds.

Eiger Suction   11m   E4 6b   *(2000)*
Probably best to take a rope. Climb the corner behind the tree (in-situ RP0) and move left along the break to gain Yosemite Crack.

AUCHINSTARRY QUARRY

(NS 719 771)   South facing   Map p74

This extensive quarry offers a wide range of routes throughout the grades. It remains the best of the central belt dolerite quarries and is popular with locals and visitors. Protection is generally good and the quarry dries quickly, making some climbs possible throughout the year.

North Lanarkshire Council have carried out stabilisation measures, but areas of unstable rock remain. Climbers must use their own judgement to assess the risks intrinsic to the sport and climb at their own risk. The quarry remains popular inspite of this stabilisation work which has damaged or destroyed many of the best climbs over the years. On the bright side, some fine routes have escaped the crowbar, while the damaged ones are soon re-climbed and become popular once again.

Once the ground at the top of the crag has dried out there is a tendency for sand to trickle down some areas and collect on the holds. For this reason, a few of the harder climbs are best brushed before an attempt. Helmets are recommended; as well as loose rock, the younger locals frequently toss stones over the top.

General Approach: The quarry is on the southern outskirts of Kilsyth and is easily accessed from the large and obvious car park at its base. The nearest rail station is at Croy (2km), while Kilsyth is served by bus from Glasgow's Buchanan Street.

Approach: Climbs in the main section of the quarry are accessed from above, via the path which ascends the left side of the quarry from the car park, followed by a scramble down the broken ground left of Stir Crazy and the slopes to the right of Dream Machine.

CAR PARK AREA

Diagram p134

This section has some fine routes and some of the most stable rock in the quarry. The climbs are described from the small, sometimes overgrown wall in the trees at the far left end of the car park, below the top access path. The first real route (Green Onion) is the corner at the junction of the tapering wall and what becomes the main face.

1 Undercut Wall   5a
Near the left end of the tapering wall. Start 1m left of the juggy flake on an undercut. A long reach or thin move gains a break.

2 Easy Flake   4a *
Climb the pleasant juggy flake.

3 Crimpy Wall   6a
Climb the thin wall right of the flake without deviation to a nose grinding mantel onto the finishing slopers.

4 Thin Crack   5b *
Climb the good thin crack and top-out with the aid of a sapling.

5 Pod and Wall   5c
Start up the pod but use a rail on the left to make a long span into Thin Crack.

6 Pod   5c
Climb the pod come groove until forced by ivy to traverse right on undercuts into Green Onion.

Bruddaz Gonna Work it Out   6b (Font 6c) *   (2003)
A low-level left to right traverse of the face from the left edge to Green Onion. The crux is the wall between Thin Crack and Pod.

Green Onion   10m   HVS 5b   (1980)
Climb the groove and corner. An alternative eliminate start climbs the left wall of the corner on small holds to the ledge **Teardrops** (2000).

I-Spy   10m   E2 5c *   (1980)
Start up Green Onion, then gain and climb the curving flake. Subtract one point if you touched the ledges on the left.

Mr Men   10m   VS 4b **   (1980)
A serious lead up the delightful short arete on good holds.

Mister, Ye Can Walk up Roon the Back   10m   Severe   (2003)
Start at the bottom of Mr Men. Climb a flake-crack immediately to the right. Follow a right-trending ramp come groove to finish at a big tree.

Mister, You're On Fire Mister   10m   VS 5a   (2003)
Just right again is a crack in an open groove. Climb the crack and continue past two trees to the top.

First Footer   15m   E1 5c **   (1978)
The fine clean open groove to the right of Mister, You're On Fire Mister gives an enjoyable problem with a delicate reach in the lower section.

No Stone Unturned   10m   Severe 5a   (2004)
Scramble easily up a staircase of ledges then climb the crack leading from the right end of the top ledge.

Just Stand Up   10m   E1 5a   (2004)
Clamber onto a big ledge below a lichen coated slab. Climb a blind crack till it

AUCHINSTARRY QUARRY - Car Park Area

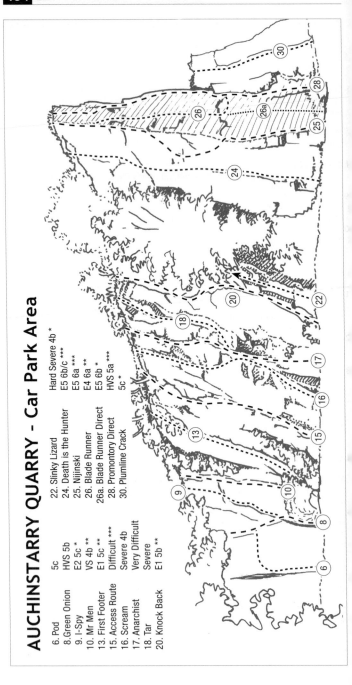

6. Pod	5c	22. Slinky Lizard	Hard Severe 4b *
8. Green Onion	HVS 5b	24. Death is the Hunter	E5 6b/c ***
9. I-Spy	E2 5c *	25. Nijinski	E5 6a ***
10. Mr Men	VS 4b **	26. Blade Runner	E4 6a **
13. First Footer	E1 5c **	26a. Blade Runner Direct	E5 6b *
15. Access Route	Difficult ***	28. Promontory Direct	HVS 5a ***
16. Scream	Severe 4b	30. Plumline Crack	5c *
17. Anarchist	Very Difficult		
18. Tar	Severe		
20. Knock Back	E1 5b **		

peters out, then two curved ledges, a bulge and a careful top-out over a rock-fall scar.

6 Access Route   15m   Difficult *
The rib and groove left of the smooth slab gives a splendid climb, popular with beginners.

The smooth slab itself can be climbed direct at 5c by those with blinkers. The flake-crack to its right is taken by:

7 Scream   15m   Severe 4b   (1977)
The crack gives interesting and well protected climbing.

8 Anarchist   15m   Very Difficult
The obvious line up the broken buttress right of Scream, passing a small tree.

9 Tar   15m   Severe   (1976)
Climb Anarchist for 5m, then trend right to the top.

10 Three Cheers for Yer Uncle Bob   15m   VS 5a   (1992)
Between Tar and Knockback is a steep wall with a large protruding jug in the middle. This route is an eliminate line on the wall. Follow Slinky Lizard to a spike (loose), then climb the wall on the left to the jug. Climb directly until forced onto Tar and finish up this.

11 Knock Back   15m   E1 5b **
The slabby corner right of Tar is climbed to an overhang at half-height. Break left and follow the shallow groove and crack with interest.

12 Slinky Lizard   15m   Hard Severe 4b **   (1977)
This steady route follows the slabby corner all the way to the top.

13 Cubigoruasry   15m   HVS 5a   (2004)
Start just right of the last route. Climb a short slab then pull up right, into a groove come pod. A hard move at the top gains a niche then a finish up a ramp.

The buttress on the corner provides some of the best and most technical routes in the quarry. The most prominent line is the fine arete of Nijinski. The two converging crack-groove lines **CP1, CP2** (1992) behind the tree are both VS.

14 Cat's Whiskers   15m   E2 5b
Start below the large tree, 5m left of the arete. Climb cracks to a step right near the top. A couple of thin moves gain the top. Traversing right to the arete before finishing reduces the grade to E1 5a.

15 Death is the Hunter   15m   E5 6b/c *   (1980s)
Brilliant technical climbing. Start at the bottom of the faint arete. The fun soon begins. A series of humorous bold moves up the apparently blank wall (stiff rock shoes help) may lead to an awkward mantel onto the first real holds. Climb the thin crack above (numerous small wires) and finish direct; 6c for the short.

16 Nijinski   15m   E5 6a *   (1982)
Another tremendous route. Balance up the bold arete to a good hold, then move up and left to the thin crack of Death is the Hunter. Fill this with small wires, step back down, then move up and right to the arete. The bold and committing climbing above (crux) is best finished direct.

The next four routes share a common start up the V-groove some 4m right of the arete.

**27 Blade Runner   15m   E4 6a ** ** *(1980s)*

This takes the wall right of Nijinski. Climb the short jamming groove to a good ledge at its top. Continue briefly up the wall of Promontory Direct to arrange protection, then descend to just below the good ledge. Swing left below the small overlap and mantelshelf with difficulty to a rest. The short thin crack above takes up to five good micro-wires. A difficult sequence leads to much easier climbing for the last few feet. An almost circular variation is **Promontory Runner** (E4 6b 1989) which follows Blade Runner to the rest by the small wires, then cranks up and right to join Promontory Direct.

Variation: **Blade Runner Direct   E5 6b *** *(1980s)*

A thin direct start to Blade Runner without the side runner to protect its crux. Follow the thin crack with difficulty (RPs) to join Blade Runner at the overlap.

28 Promontory Direct   15m   HVS 5a * *** *(1976)*

An excellent route. Follow Blade Runner to the good ledge, then make a couple of awkward moves up the wall above. Step left and climb the prominent hand-crack, which is set in a little corner in its lower half.

29 Spirogyra   15m   VS 5a *(1976)*

Follow Blade Runner to the good ledge, climb the short wall of Promontory Direct, then move up to ledges which lead right across the overhanging wall. Where they stop, climb a short awkward groove to the top. The initial groove is slightly harder due to the loss of a block.

30 Plumline Crack   5c *

A thin crack just right of the V-groove gives a good extended boulder problem which leads to the good ledge of Promontory Direct.

**31 Carouselambra   15m   E5 6b ** ** *(1980s)*

The obvious crack in the overhanging wall below Spirogyra gives a desperate problem. Balancy and powerful laybacking (placing protection is hard or impossible) gains the huge hold at half-height, somewhat easier climbing leads left and up to the last moves of Spirogyra.

32 In Through the out Door   15m   E5 6a *(1993)*

This route starts from the platform at the top of the V-groove. Hand-traverse right to join and follow Carouselambra for a short distance, then finish up and rightwards up the wall. The route has lost holds since its last ascent.

To the right of Carouselambra the rock becomes greener and poorer. While the older climbs here may once have been fine outings, they are in a poor state and may now be much harder than when they were first graded (which was presumably after a thorough cleaning). Public spirited enthusiasts are invited to return them to their former glory.

33 Fish Rising   E2 5b

Climb the green arete right of the open groove right of Carouselambra.

34 Twilight Zone   15m   E4 6a * *(1992)*

This route climbs the sharp arete right of Fish Rising directly past a peg runner, making the crux move to finish onto an easy slab.

35 Tit for Tat   E2 5c

Climb the shallow groove capped by an overhang, just right of Twilight Zone.

36 The Surf Shack   15m   E5 6b *(1992)*

Start next to the corner of the old building. Climb with difficulty past two peg runners to reach a jug. Make another hard move to reach better holds and a welcome runner. Finish awkwardly and strenuously. Hold loss may have affected the grade and re-cleaning is necessary.

The dank overgrown section behind the building has been climbed by a number of routes, but they are in such a poor state that they are not worth describing. A rather better buttress lies about 20m to the right, right of a steep sharp arete.

37 Newcastle Brown   15m E1 5b *(1978)*
A steep slabby wall is split by two cracks. Climb the left-hand crack and the awkward groove above to finish on recently exposed rock.

38 Roll Up   15m   VS 4c
The layback flake-crack to the right, joining Newcastle Brown for a step before finishing on the right.

To the right is a large area of recent excavation, with debris descending to the water's edge.

39 Soft Machine   20m   E2 5c *(1978)*
Scramble a few metres at water level to a ledge beneath a shallow groove. Climb the groove (poorly protected) to a roof, then step right to join Maypole. A serious route, at the upper limit of its grade.

40 Maypole   20m   HVS 4c *(1976)*
Right again is a short vertical groove. Climb it to a ledge, over an awkward bulge to a small ledge. Move left to finish up the groove above. Poorly protected.

41 High Dive   25m   E3 5c * *(1980s)*
Gain the slim groove starting at water level at the left end of the smooth wall. Climb the groove to a ledge (RP2) then make a very long and frightening reach up and right to better holds. Finish directly.

BACK WALL AREA

Diagram p138

This area comprises a number of buttresses and walls including and to the right of Mascarade Buttress, the smooth wall rising straight from the pool. The climbs are approached by walking over the top of the quarry and scrambling down various decent routes, described with the routes below.

The first seven routes lie on Mascarade Buttress and are approached by a low-level traverse from the right.

42 Dwr Budr   25m   HS 4c *(2004)*
Move onto the low-level traverse then immediately start climbing the right side of the buttress, into a chimney groove and onto a grassy ledge. Walk past a narrow chimney then climb a good clean jamming crack.

43 Surface Tension   25m   E5 6b *** *(1980s)*
An awe-inspiring pitch taking the centre of the smooth wall, which is best brushed on abseil before an attempt. Traverse in above the water to a tiny stance and belay at the foot of a long groove (Mascarade). Move left below an overlap, and make hard moves up to a peg. Lunge up and right to a resting place. Step left and up (small wires), then climb the centre of the wall to the top. Local urchins have been known to jump from the top, but what reassurance is that?

44 Mascarade   25m   E1 5c * *(1975)*
Approach as for Surface Tension and climb the long vertical groove in the centre of the buttress. Variations are possible on the right wall.

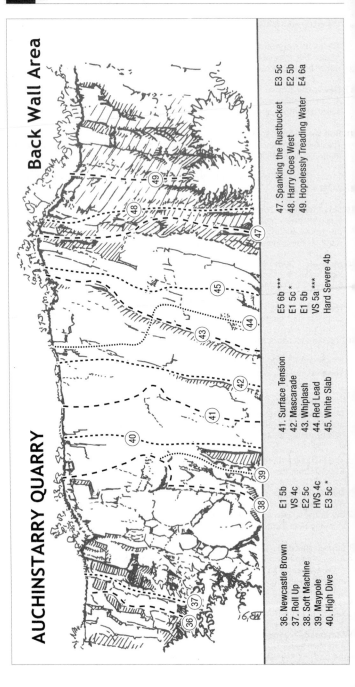

AUCHINSTARRY QUARRY

Back Wall Area

36. Newcastle Brown   E1 5b
37. Roll Up   VS 4c
38. Soft Machine   E2 5c
39. Maypole   HVS 4c
40. High Dive   E3 5c *

41. Surface Tension   E5 6b ***
42. Mascarade   E1 5c *
43. Whiplash   E1 5b
44. Red Lead   VS 5a ***
45. White Slab   Hard Severe 4b

47. Spanking the Rustbucket   E3 5c
48. Harry Goes West   E2 5b
49. Hopelessly Treading Water   E4 6a

45 Whiplash   25m   E1 5b   (1976)
The smaller bottomless groove right of Mascarade. Climb to the top of a pinnacle, then follow the groove and shallow scoop above.

46 Red Lead   25m   VS 5a ***   (1977)
An enjoyable route with a finely placed crux. Climb the centre of the white slab to a horizontal break. Step down and left to a hidden layback crack. Follow the crack and traverse left across Whiplash to a thin diagonal crack. Climb this (crux) and the vertical crack above, finishing at the same point as Mascarade.

47 White Slab   25m   Hard Severe 4b   (1977)
Traverse left just above the water to the foot of the white slab, crux. Climb up to a hand sized crack, continue to a ledge and finish up the shallow scoop of Whiplash on the left.

48 Demons and Dead Lizards   30m   HVS 5a
Follow the thin crack right of White Slab to a ledge, then climb newly exposed rock to the top.

The area right of Mascarade Buttress is known as Little Amphitheatre. The next three routes take lines on the steep left wall. The top sections of the first two have been severely affected by the council trundlers, but they should still be possible at their original grades.

49 Spanking the Rustbucket   25m   E3 5c   (1990)
Climb the obvious awkward clean-cut white groove just right of the water's edge (bold and difficult) until moves up left gain a steep wide crack. Climb this to a ledge, then continue up the rock scars to the top.

50 Harry Goes West   25m   E2 5b   (1990)
Follow the cleaned line of good holds up the wall right of the white groove (bold) to gain a small pillar. Climb the crack on the left to the large ledge of the previous climb, then finish up newly exposed rock.

51 Hopelessly Treading Water   10m   E4 6a   (1990)
A serious route on less than perfect rock. Start at the left end of a higher ledge at the junction of the left and main faces. Climb to and past a poor, old blade peg at 4m, using hidden holds in a slanting line just left of the peg. Gain a small ledge (sideways Rock 5) and continue with difficulty to the top.

The back wall of Little Amphitheatre was severely affected by stabilisation work and is now smaller and scarcely more stable. Most of the routes were destroyed, but a few remain or have been replaced by new routes. Approximately in the middle of this sector, a rather better piece of rock is taken by the following climb:

52 The Seven Year Plan   10m   E2 5c *   (1992)
Climb a short grey wall to a grassy ramp (peg runner). Finish directly over an overhang.

53 Cracked Arete   10m   VS 4c **   (1977)
Climb the fine arete in the buttress which marks the right end of Little Amphitheatre. Finish up the prominent crack.

54 Cruiser's Creek   10m   E1 5b   (2003)
An eliminate line starting in the middle of the smooth wall right of Cracked Arete. Mantel onto a small ledge at head height, then go up a thin seam near the arete. Crank up left to a ledge on the arete, the back right to a mantelshelf.

The obvious corner to the right was Fourth Wave, until destroyed by the council. The remaining rock has been re-climbed to give:

55 Orange Flash   12m   HVS 5a   *(2003)*
Start at the foot of the corner. Climb cracks in the left wall, then move right into the corner which is followed with a few tricky moves.

56 Danger! U.S.R.   14m   HVS 5a *   *(2003)*
Climb onto the warning sign, then up the grey wall to a ledge. Finish up the excellent crack.

57 Caftan   15m   HVS 4c   *(1977)*
There are three vertical bore holes in the wall right of the warning sign. Climb the bold wall to a good hold at a protruding block. Step left and climb the wall to the top.

58 Bazaar   15m   HVS 4c   *(1977)*
Climb Caftan to the protruding block, then step right and go up right to the top.

Solstice Slot   13m   VS 4c   *(2004)*
Starts as a seam and ends as a finger-crack.

59 Ice Edge   10m   VS 4c
Start up Mastalgia and climb its left arete. Rather artificial.

60 Mastalgia   10m   VS 4c *
The steep corner with a smooth right wall right of Bazaar gives good climbing.

61 Higher Beginning   10m   Very Difficult
Climb the short wall right of Mastalgia, finishing near the top of the descent route.

The area to the right provides the easiest descent into the quarry. The next climbable feature, a smooth slabby wall to the left of a deep corner, is most easily reached by traversing in from halfway down the descent.

62 Bouldermouse   10m   HVS 5a   *(2003)*
Scramble up the short corner on the left to a niche, then layback the left arete.

63 Stir Crazy   10m   HVS 5a
Climb the centre of the slab left of Lion Cub.

64 Lion Cub   10m   VS 4b *   *(1977)*
Climb the right edge of the slab, bold at the top.

65 Lion   10m   HVS 5b **   *(1977)*
Climb the obvious corner right of the slab. The top section gives technical but well protected bridging.

66 The Return of the King   14m   E2 5c ***   *(2003)*
Sustained and technical bridging up the prominent groove 3m right of Lion leads to a small overhang. Step onto a small ledge on the left, then climb the shallower groove using holds on the right wall.

67 Sunshine   HVS 5a †   *(1993)*
Start just left of the toe of the buttress. Climb steep rock on the left-hand side to a flake-crack. Step right to a ledge then move over the overhang to deep cracks. Step left to climb thin cracks before moving back right to finish on the arete. Has been severely altered since the first ascent.

68 Kelvin Way   25m   E1 5a †   *(1976)*
This route has also been severely damaged by stabilisation work and its description may not be accurate. Start up the grey wall at the foot of the buttress, then move right into the open groove. Move up, then take the left wall for a few feet (or

direct, 5c) before returning to the groove for an overhanging sand exit.

The next three routes start from a terrace, reached by a scramble up blocks 15m right of Kelvin Way.

69 Auch! 20m HVS 5a *(2003)*
A direct start to Mac's Wall. Start 6m right of Lion. Climb a groove using the arete to a ledge directly below a progressively widening crack. Climb the crack.

70 C.K.D.C.F.U. 25m V3 1a *(2004)*
Follow Auch! to the top of the groove then go right and up a wide chimney to finish up cracks.

71 Mac's Wall 20m HVS 5a
From the terrace, scramble carefully over blocks to the crest of the prow which overlooks Kelvin Way. Climb the crack in the prow directly to the top.

72 Short Reach 15m E1 5b ** *(1976)*
Start up a wide chimney right of Mac's Wall, then climb the thin groove to a small overlap, step right and go for the top.

73 Pigeon Hole 15m VS 4c *(1977)*
Starting 4m right of Short Reach, climb blocks to a ledge and finish up the corner above.

74 Exorcist 5m HVS 5b
Below the terrace a short overhanging crack faces the pool. Climb the crack to an awkward mantel finish.

75 Separated Edge 25m HVS 5a *(1977)*
Further right a long groove runs up to a fine prow. This route climbs its left arete. Climb the wall left of the groove to good holds, then continue more easily to below the prow. It is probably easiest to step into Pigeon Hole to finish.

The long groove used to be Talisman, but the top section has been removed and a hideous earth cornice remains. The right arete of the groove was the start of Knife Edge, which finished up the fine prow. Most of the other climbs in this area have been demolished; the only survivor takes the next obvious groove which runs the full height of the quarry.

76 Christmas Corner 25m HVS 5a * *(1976)*
The corner left of a smooth slabby arete gives a varied and interesting climb.

The buttress to the right once housed some of the finest routes on quarried dolerite. Stand on the pile of rubble and inspect the thin and frightening crux of **Balance of Power** (the smooth blank looking arete) at close quarters. It would still be possible to climb this to ledges in the middle of the wall, and a possible finish up Christmas Corner, but the runner placements are no longer high enough above the ground to prevent a Desmond. The new smooth corner to the right has been revealed by the complete removal of Fusion and Sandman.

77 Glass 25m E1 5c *(1993)*
What you get when you fuse sand! A hard start leads to better holds and an interesting excursion on the right wall to gain the upper groove. Scrabble past another hard reachy move to an exit on the right arete. Loose and vegetated at present.

78 Dream Machine 25m E4 6a/b *** *(1983)*
This fine problem takes the right arete of the buttress. Although the upper section is on newly exposed rock, the climbing there is straightforward. Even before the bogeymen came, a crucial foothold had disappeared from the lower section,

turning a hard problem into one that is very difficult to flash. Swing onto an obvious good sidepull on the arete to start. Place a vital Rock 2 in the thin crack above with care, then make a series of hard moves up the arete. It is possible, but extremely precarious and strenuous, to place excellent protection. Do not place a Friend behind the good hold, as a fall will snap it off.

Further right the cliff becomes broken, and there is an easy descent at the top right-hand corner of this section. At the top of the quarry, just right of the descent, is a short problem up a blunt arete left of a vertical bore hole **Model T** (HVS 5b). The other climbs further right on this upper wall have been destroyed, but it may be possible to find some short but worthwhile replacements. The next prominent feature is a square-cut pinnacle, one of the most obvious landmarks of the quarry. Its left side used to have a steep corner, the fine Think of England. This is now rubble. The right arete of the front face is a worthy recent replacement and the quarry's hardest route:

79 Think of Scotland   10m   E6 6b ** (2003)
Climb onto stacked blocks and make a series of desperate moves above a horrible landing to gain a good finishing rail. The fall has been tested!

80 Quick Buck   10m   VS 5a *
The leftmost of the cracks in the pinnacle's right wall.

Right again a splendid slab descends to the edge of the pool. This provides some of the best middle grade routes on dolerite. Although the routes can be finished via any of the easier obvious lines in the upper section, it is common to traverse off left along the ledges at two-thirds height. There is a rather pointless girdle traverse at about half-height of the lower wall, going from left to right and finishing up Gold Rush; **Southern Man** (E2 5b 1981).

81 Glasgow No More   20m   VS 4c (1999)
Climb the left-slanting groove at the extreme left end of this section of cliff, just left of Replicant, moving right at an overlap to finish.

82 The Javelin   20m   E2 6a* (1999)
The short left arete of the white speckled prow. Start up Glasgow No More until level with the arete (good runners). Move out right with a tricky move to swing round onto the front face and finish up the arete.

83 Replicant   30m   E3 5c
Start at the far left side of the slab below a steeper prow. Climb up and boldly right below a white speckled wall to easier ground to the right of the prow. The crux holds come to light only at the last moment.

84 Trundle   30m   VS 4c *** (1977)
The crack up the left side of the slab is enjoyable and well protected.

85 Walk on the Wild Side   30m   HVS 5a *** (1980)
The faint crack-line in the slab right of Trundle gives a steady lead. After an initial bold section the micro-wire protection is excellent.

86 Midas Touch   30m   E1 5b *** (1980)
Climb the right edge of the slab to a faint groove in the arete, which is taken direct, with runners in the crack on the left.

87 The Gold Bug   30m   E3 5c (1988)
Climb the wall left of Gold Rush by a boulder problem start, then by using the left arete. Pull left onto Midas Touch 5m from the top.

88 Gold Rush   30m   E1 5b *** (1975)

Another outstanding climb which takes the striking groove right of Midas Touch.

89 After the Gold Rush   30m   E2 5a †   *(1977)*
Mantelshelf onto the ledge just right of the corner, then climb the centre of the wall direct on creaking flakes. The upper section has been 'stabilised' and is now in a more dangerous state than before! Best inspected before a solo.

**90 After the Grave Dig   30m   VS 4c ** **
A more sensible alternative to the above with pleasant climbing. From the ledge, trend up right to the arete and climb cracks in its left side.

91 Golddigger   20m   HVS 5a   *(2003)*
To the right of After the Grave Dig is a slim black groove. Climb the groove with few holds but excellent friction to join the previous route to finish.

About 20m further right is another fine buttress. Although all the climbs have been affected by recent excavation, the best of them are still possible.

92 Deep Throat Revived   30m   E5 6a * **   *(1977/91)*
A climb with a history of hold and peg loss. It is now stable but a bold proposition with sparse protection. Start at the foot of the left arete of the buttress, and climb to a step right into a vague niche at 10m. Move left beneath the overhang, then make a series of precarious hard moves on slowly improving holds to a good ledge. Climb the left arete of the wall above.

93 Power Play   30m   E1 5b *   *(1976)*
Start in the overhung bay right of the corner to the right of Deep Throat (currently overgrown). Climb up awkwardly through a small overhang to easier ground and a block belay. Continue up the groove slightly to the right, then traverse left below the final overhangs to the top of Deep Throat Revived.

**94 Foxy Woxy   15m   E3 5c ** **   *(1976/93)*
From the belay of Power Play, place a Friend 3 in the bore hole then step down and onto the wall. Balance precariously left (nasty fall potential) to holds in the groove on the left. Climb the groove to join and finish up Deep Throat Revived.

95 Shiny Happy People   15m   E3 6a **   *(1999)*
From the Power Play belay, place the same runners as Foxy Woxy in the bore hole but climb it as well. A hard move to leave the bore hole leads to a direct finish up the slab and arete above (RPs).

Right of Power Play is a smooth wall with strange circular striations. Some 4m to the right is an area of rock like a smaller tapering version of the Trundle slab. Above it is a bulging wall and a series of grooves.

96 Kein Trink Wasser   25m   HVS 5a   *(2004)*
Climb the corner at the right edge of the slab to a ledge at the apex. Go directly up the central black groove through two overhangs.

About 10m right of the smooth wall with circular striations, twin cracks can be seen high on the lower section of the quarry.

97 Crazy Daisy   25m   HVS 5a
Climb a grassy groove and move right to climb the cracks. Find a way through the recent debris to reach the top, or face a horrible scramble back down to the left.

98 Think Positive   5m   E2 6a
A good little problem which smears up the slabby arete right of Crazy Daisy. Finish up the cracks of Crazy Daisy.

99 Shot in the Dark   15m   E1 5a *   *(1986)*
Start up the centre of the white speckled slabby wall about 10m further right.
Trend right to an interesting finish up a small groove.

100 Evasive Action   15m   VS 4c
Climb the corner groove just right of Shot in the Dark, exiting right.

The area to the right is The Right-Hand Amphitheatre, which is split into three
distinctive sections: the lower cliff right of Evasive Action, identified by the 'ear' of
Urea, the upper cliff above the terrace and the wall at the far right of the quarry.
The routes on the lower section degenerate into vague scrambling at half-height.

101 B.C.'s Return   25m   E1 5b   *(1981)*
Left of Urea lies a squat pinnacle. Climb the blunt arete to a horizontal break.
Move up and step right onto the prow, then continue to easy ground.

102 Urea   25m   VS 4c   *(1976)*
Climb the diagonal crack on the right of the prominent 'ear' (about 10m right of
B.C.'s Return), to a wide crack and easier ground. Climb a slab and scramble
through the upper walls.

The climbs further right on the lower tier have all been substantially modified and
are probably not worth re-investigating. The next routes are on the upper tier, best
reached by taking the path round the top of the quarry on the right and then
scrambling down with care (to the west of the climbs) to good ledges at half-
height. The rock here is intrinsically loose. Ironically this part of the quarry (except
for the descent) has not been much affected by the stabilisation work.

103 Stool Pigeon   15m   E3 6b
The left side of the upper tier wall is defined by an orange groove, the result of
recent excavations. To its right is a smooth convex wall. Climb the centre of the
blank wall, with side runners in the next route.

104 Both Toes Burning   15m   E2 6a   *(1986)*
Start at the right side of the convex wall. Climb a short groove and vertical crack-
line through two small roofs, finishing up an easier groove.

105 The Color Purple   15m   E1 5b   *(1986)*
Climb the obvious jamming crack about 5m left of the corner. The top section has
been affected by council crowbars.

106 Red Snapper   15m   E2 5c   *(1986)*
A technical and poorly protected route up the corner, where the crag turns right.

107 Band Aid   15m   E3 5c   *(1986)*
Climb the thin crack in the white wall with difficulty, past a peg runner, to a loose
finish.

108 Race Against Time   15m   E3 5c   *(1986)*
Step right from the foot of Band Aid into a shallow corner. Layback this, surmount
the roof and continue up the wide crack to another loose finish. Use of holds on
Band Aid makes this easier, and vice versa.

109 Footloose   20m   HVS 5a
Start on terrace down and right of Race Against Time. Climb the crack-line to the
right of the smooth open (unclimbed) corner. Great care is needed at the top.

The buttress to the right is one of the largest and loosest in the quarry. Climbs have
been found starting from water level on the left-hand side, and also up the ramp
on the right-hand wall. Both are dangerously loose and best avoided.

BOULDERING WALL

A collection of good problems can be found on a vertical wall on the south face of a landscaped hump adjacent to the car park (hidden from view).

Diagonal Crack   4a
Climb the diagonal crack at the left end of the main wall.

Zigzag Crack   4a
Climb the zigzag crack-line just left of the tiny arete come corner.

Tiny Arete   5a
Eliminate. Climb the tiny arete without using the Zigzag Crack for hands.

Spiderman   6b
Climb the narrow wall left of the central wide crack via a tiny square crimp and a high flake.

Wide Crack   4a
Swim up the central off-width.

Team Ascent   6b (Font 6b+) **   (1999)
This problem climbs the above thin seam but comes in from the right, starting up the next problem.

Finger Flakes   4a
A pleasant series of flakes at the right end of the wall.

JACKDAW QUARRY & CROY QUARRY

(NS 722 761)   North facing   Map p74

Both of these quarries have been largely ignored – probably with good reason. Jackdaw is now fenced off and Croy, while containing a lot of rock, is generally unappealing. Their inclusion here is more for the record. Both can be accessed from the path to Croy Hill.

JACKDAW QUARRY

This is the hole in the ground beside the B802 on the outskirts of Croy, 1km south of Auchinstarry.

The Dispossessed   20m   E2 5c   (1985)
Climb the left-hand of two cracks in the steep black wall.

The Trouble   20m   E2 5c   (1992)
The right-hand crack.

CROY QUARRY

The large two tier quarry behind Croy has lots of rock, but is north facing and rather lichenous.

Lazy Lady   15m   F3 5c   (1987)
Climb the obvious line in the slabby rectangular wall in the middle of the upper tier, starting at the bottom left-hand end of the buttress. Move up and right to a horizontal crack. Make a hard move up and right to gain a standing position in the horizontal fault. Follow the obvious ramp up and left to a good foothold. Make an awkward move up and right to a horizontal crack, then follow this to the right to

good Friends. Climb up and right to a vague scoop. It is best to leave a rope in position for the easy but loose top section.

Crojan Horse 10m Severe   *(1992)*
At the far left end of the quarry is a wall above a scree slope. At the right-hand side of this is a jamming crack in a groove.

CARRON GLEN - KAMIKAZE SQUIRREL CRAG
(NS 783 835) Map p74

Approach: From the M80 turn off at junction 1, take the A883 into Denny, at the traffic lights turn right, continue to the B818. After leaving Fankerton park on the right, take the Carronglen footpath. In 15 minutes the crag is visible on the right.

The Carronade 9m E1 5c   *(2003)*
A slim groove through the roof, finish left of a projecting rock.

Carron Crack 10m E1 5c   *(2003)*
The finger-crack.

The Fankerton Flyer 10m E1 5b   *(2003)*
The left-hand side of arete using a crack.

Carronbridge 10m Severe 4b   *(2003)*
The wide scoop and chimney.

Tak' Mi' Up 7m Hard Severe 5a   *(2003)*
Scramble onto boulder and climb the crack.

Wee Chimney 4m 4b   *(1995)*
The chimney-groove.

COURT KNOWE QUARRY
(NS 588 600) South-west facing Map p74

Pleasant entertainment can be had in this tiny dolerite quarry facing Linn Park. The rock is generally sound, although a bit lichenous and trees can delay drying after rain. The crag lies within a public park.

Approach: By car or train from Glasgow to Cathcart. Follow Old Castle Road uphill to its junction with Seil Drive. Court Knowe is behind railings on the left.

LEFT WALL

The left wall has two chimney-lines. The left-hand one below the tree is **Grotty Groove** (4a): the right-hand off-width is **Chockstone Crack** (5a). The wall between the two can be climbed at various points.

MAIN WALL

Blue Tit's Nest Crack 5a *
The cracked arete at the left end is deceptively hard.

Wullie's Crack 5a
Start right of the previous route, make a hard balance move onto a hold and continue up a small corner

DF 118'S 6a
The wall and crack right of Wullie's Crack. Gain a hole and dyno for a sloping ledge, finish left.

Layback Crack 4c
The crack left of the central crack.

Coleptera Crack 3b
A botanical excursion up the obvious central crack.

Thin Finger's Crack 5c
Technical moves up the thin crack to the right.

Mountain Climber Route 4c
Start below the last route and climb the wall, trending up and right.

Last Route 4a
Follow the right edge of the Main Wall, starting left of the large tree and finishing by a left traverse.

SMALL WALL

Up and right of the tree is a small wall with various routes. **Andrew's Wall** (4c) follows the thin crack splitting the wall right of the tree; **Everest Corner** (3b) is the corner behind the tree; **Right Wall** (3b), not as fierce as its more famous namesake, takes the wall right of the corner; **Easy Arete** (3a) lies right of the corner; **The Long Reach** (4a) takes the wall and slab left of the muddy crack; **Mudcrack** (4b) is the crack, and **Consolation** (3a) climbs the right edge of the blank wall.

Ten Year Wall 6a *
The blank wall between Mudcrack and Consolation.

Girdle Traverse 5b
From Blue Tit's Nest Crack to Consolation.

Snowy's Big Traverse 6b
From Thin Fingers Crack to Coleptera Crack.

NEILSTON QUARRY

(NS 474 558) South-West facing Map p74

This small quartz dolerite quarry offers pleasant climbing and a sunny aspect. There are two main buttresses; a broken wall and slabs on the left and steep grooves and cracks on the right.

Approach: The quarry is easily accessed from the left-hand side of the back road to Dunlop, about 500m south-west of Neilston village. A regular rail service runs from Glasgow Central to Neilston.

LEFT BUTTRESS

Descriptions for this broken and rather confused buttress are not definitive and climbers should follow the lines of least or most resistance as seems most appropriate. There are three small hawthorns at the base.

Right-Angled Corner 10m Difficult
Left of the first tree a small square buttress leads to grassy slabs.

Corner and Groove 10m Difficult
Take the corner on the right and grassy slabs above.

Flake Route 10m Very Difficult
The indefinite flake-line between the first and second trees.

Pinkerton's Corner   10m   Severe
Climb the wall just right of the second tree, past a break. Continue above from the recess.

Corner Arete   10m   Severe
Climb the broad arete on the right, followed by a line to the left.

Kristeen's Crack   10m   Very Difficult *
Climb cracks in the left wall of the deep Y-shaped recess, 7m right of the second tree.

Polish Direct   4m   Hard Severe
The short steep wall just left of the third tree.

RIGHT BUTTRESS

This part of the quarry starts with the Strawberry Tower, an obvious large block above a curving crack.

Juggy Crack   10m   Very Difficult
The short crack on the left side of the tower.

Strawberry Direct   10m   E2 6a
Steep and dynamic climbing up overhanging face left of Strawberry Crack with side runners in that route

Strawberry Crack   10m   Severe **
The fine curving crack below the tower.

Spiney Boulder   10m   Very Difficult
The indefinite crack in the wall of Strawberry Crack. Finish straight up.

Easy Gully   10m   Difficult
The grassy trough on the right, finishing right or left.

B.N.I.   10m   Severe
A small black streaked wall left of the arete.

Broken Arete   10m   Very Difficult
Obvious!

Y-Crack   10m   Very Difficult
The short loose looking crack.

Stephen Slab   10m   Hard Severe *
The short reddish wall.

Crack Corner   10m   Very Difficult *
Start about 8m right of Strawberry Crack where the main face begins and climb a right-slanting corner-groove, left of a stepped overhang.

Polish Hangover   10m   VS 4c *
Climb the steep arete and overhang to finish up Crack Corner.

Intrusion Line   10m   Very Difficult
The left-curving groove and crack right of Polish Hangover.

Punk Rock   15m   HVS 5a *
Follow Intrusion Line until it is possible to move right to a crack. Climb the wall above.

The wall to the right has been top-roped at 5c.

Curving Crack   15m   HVS 5a *
Climb the long left-curving crack, finishing up the wall just right of Punk Rock.

Twisted   12m   E3 5c*   *(2004)*
Climb the twisted slab just right of Curving Crack and 2m left of the E2 variation
to Willie's Route to poor protection at half height. Step left to gain slopers and
sidepulls on the tiered overhang.

Willie's Route   15m   Severe **
Start at the broken crack-line to the right, finishing on the right.
Variation: **E2 6a**
The slab can be climbed direct without touching neighbouring routes but with side
runners in them.

Fornication   15m   VS 4c
Climb cracks in the left side of a white speckled wall, round the corner from Willie's
Route.

Hyper-reality   15m   VS 4b   *(1998)*
The undercut slabby wall immediately right of Fornication. A scoop leads to an
overlap at 3m, followed by the wall above and a bulge (crux) which is taken direct.

Grassy Crack   15m   Severe
Start 2m right of Fornication. Climb the mossy crack to an overhang, move left and
climb the broken crack in the speckled wall.

Jig-Saw Jive   10m   Very Difficult
The mossy crack-line passing the overhang of Grassy Crack on the right.

Whitehorse Rib   15m   Severe 4b   *(1998)*
Right of Jig-Saw Jive is an undercut blunt rib. Gain the slabby rib and make
unprotected moves to easier ground (but no protection). Finish left up the upper
groove of Jig-Saw Jive.

Grot Gully   10m   Moderate
Yuck.

Peg Leg   2m   HVS 5b
The short crack in the quarry's right wall was once pegged.

OTHER CRAGS

One climb has been recorded in **Johnstone Quarry** (NS 429 613), the higher of
two off Craigbog Road opposite the public park. **Tom's Crack** (20m E3 6a **) is an
esoteric gem taking the obvious crack on a compact buttress of quartz dolerite in
the trees above and overlooking the forecourt. Approach through the wood to the
left. The overgrown north facing **Windyhill Quarry** (NS 435 614) holds some
potential for the green fingered. **Hide-and-Seek** (12m E2 6a) climbs the obvious
cleaned crack and groove line in the middle of the wall. The groove on the left is
a poor VS, and the small tower on the right is VS 4c. On the north side of the road
is a small bouldering cliff. Approach from the road. **Craig Minnan** (NS 641 322) is
a steep little outcrop in a fabulous setting. Approach from Muirshiel Country Park,
3km north-west of Lochwinnoch. Follow the signs to Windy Hill from where the
crag can be seen. Climb at will.

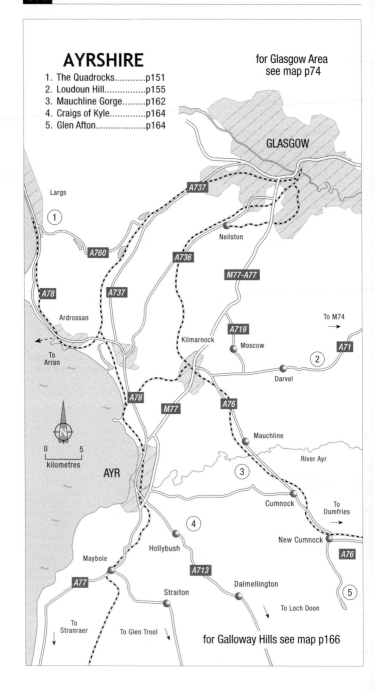

AYRSHIRE

for Glasgow Area
see map p74

GLASGOW

Largs

① A737

A760

A736

Neilston

M77-A77

A737

To M74 →

A78

Ardrossan

A719

Kilmarnock

Moscow

② A71

To Arran

Darvel

A78

M77

A76

Mauchline

River Ayr

AYR

③

0   5
kilometres

Cumnock

To Dumfries →

New Cumnock

④

A76

Maybole

Hollybush

⑤

A77

A713

Dalmellington

Straiton

To Stranraer

To Glen Trool

To Loch Doon

for Galloway Hills see map p166

AYRSHIRE

The natural crags of The Quadrocks and Loudoun Hill offer excellent short routes on natural rock in fine settings. Of the other crags in this chapter the granite crags of Glen Afton offer the most interest, although seepage is a problem and some of the routes are grassing over. Mauchline remains an esoteric backwater.

Nesting birds have resulted in occasional seasonal restrictions to parts of Loudoun Hill and Glen Afton and have led to climbers being prosecuted (but not convicted). Climbers are urged to look out for posted restrictions and follow them. Be assured that there will be a zealous twitcher behind a bush watching you through binoculars. If in doubt contact the MCofS (see Environment).

THE QUADROCKS

(NS 220 605)   Alt 250m   West facing   Map p150   Diagrams p152

These crags of sound rough basalt lie on the hillside about 1km north-east of Largs town centre and are visible from the town (marked as Cauld Rocks on the OS map). The climbing isn't extensive, but enough to occupy a sunny afternoon or evening and there is a fine view across the Firth of Clyde to Great Cumbrae, Bute and Arran.

Approach: Just north of Largs town centre, turn into Burnside Road by following signs for the Inverclyde National Sports Training Centre. This leads in under 1km to a large car park outside the centre. Walk onto the hillside behind the centre, avoiding a shooting range to the south; 15mins.

LOW CRAG

1 Far Groove   6m   Very Difficult
Climb the open groove directly.

2 Far Wall   7m   Very Difficult
Follow a cracked wall to below an overhang, turn this on the left by a slabby shelf, or better, climb the overhang directly.

3 Boulder Rib   7m   Very Difficult
Go directly up the rib on good holds and gain a sloping shelf at the top. Pass a large boulder on the right.

4 Dank Chimney   7m   Difficult
The messy chimney immediately right of Boulder Rib.

5 Boulder Problem   7m   Very Difficult
Easy climbing leads to the boulder, whose stability is in some doubt, then make an awkward move to gain its top followed by a short steep wall.

6 Choc-Chimney   7m   Severe *
The strenuous, deep chimney-crack which contains a swinging chockstone.

7 Sentry-Box Crack   6m   Severe *
Climb easily to the sentry-box, then make a hard move to gain the ledge above. Finish up a short wall.

8 Fingers Wall   6m   VS 4b
This brutal little wall problem joins Curving Crack at two-thirds height.

9 Curving Crack   6m   Very Difficult **
A good route which takes the crack direct.

0 Curving Crack Wall   6m   Very Difficult **
Climb straight up the attractive wall on good holds.

THE QUADROCKS
Low Crag

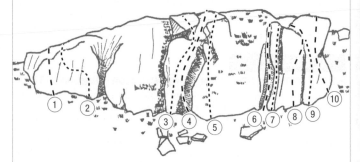

1. Far Groove	Very Difficult	6. Choc-Chimney	Severe *
2. Far Wall	Very Difficult	7. Sentry Box Crack	Severe *
3. Boulder Rib	Very Difficult	8. Fingers Wall	VS 4b
4. Dank Chimney	Difficult	9. Curving Crack	Very Difficult **
5. Boulder Problem	Very Difficult	10. Curving Crack Wall	Very Difficult **

High Crag

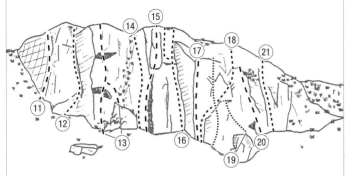

11. Easy Face Groove	VS 4a	17. The Arete	E3 5b **
12. Green Corner	Very Difficult	18. The Traverse	VS 4c ***
13. Overhang Route	VS 4b *	19. Traverse Face Direct	VS 4b **
14. Flake Wall	HVS 5a	20. The Nose	VS 4a
15. Vee Groove	VS 4b	21. Slab and Corner	Severe
16. Big Corner	Severe **	22. Sunburst Red	E3 5c **

MAIN CRAG

The largest face has been girdled from left to right, finishing up The Traverse.

11 Easy Face Groove   7m   VS 4b
The right edge of the easy face is followed by awkward moves directly up the shallow groove.

12 Green Corner   10m   Very Difficult
At the left end is an obvious large corner which is climbed exiting directly or by an easier shelf on the left.

13 Overhang Route   10m   VS 4b *
Step left from a convenient boulder then right to below a small roof. Climb the roof by a slot high up for the right- hand, strenuous. The first overhang can also be climbed direct, raising the grade.

14 Flake Wall   10m   HVS 5a
This steep route climbs the tall narrow wall. Gain a foothold in the middle of the wall, then make some hard moves up and left to better holds.

15 Vee Groove   12m   VS 4b
Climb the green groove, step right then left into a V-groove and climb this directly to a hard finish. A variation finish is to step left to another groove on the upper wall.

16 Big Corner   12m   Severe **
Climb directly up the very obvious corner running almost the full height of the crag. It is possible to move left near the top and finish up an open groove.

17 The Arete   12m   E3 5b **
Protectionless climbing up the right- bounding edge of Big Corner. Start in the corner and as soon as possible make a hard move right onto the face and continue up the arete.

18 The Traverse   12m   VS 4c ***
Probably the best route on the crag. Make a rising traverse across the steep face to a flake, gain its top and enter a bay above, exiting left or right.

19 Traverse Face Direct   10m   VS 4b **
Various starts lead to the middle of the traverse, from where it is possible to climb straight up very steep rock to a small niche and an easier finish.

20 The Nose   10m   VS 4a
Climb the edge forming the right-hand end of the traverse face, starting round the corner.

21 Slab and Corner   10m   Severe
Starting right of The Nose, follow a slab in the corner until the rock becomes vertical, then reach for holds high on the left.

22 Sunburst Red   10m   E3 5c **
The short wall at right end of crag, starting at a prominent hole in the rock.

HIGH CRAG

This is the outcrop well up and right of Low and Main Crag. The main line is quite long, very pleasant and about Difficult in standard; it follows a direct line from the lowest rocks. Other short problems can be found.

AYRSH RE

LOUDOUN HILL - Pulpit Rock & The Amphitheatre

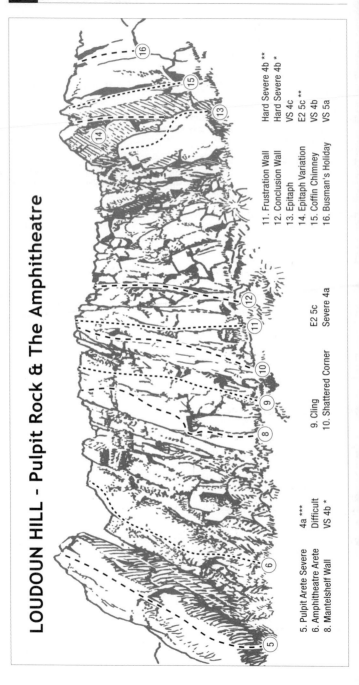

5. Pulpit Arete Severe   4a ***
6. Amphitheatre Arete   Difficult
8. Mantelshelf Wall   VS 4b *

9. Cling   E2 5c
10. Shattered Corner Severe 4a

11. Frustration Wall   Hard Severe 4b **
12. Conclusion Wall   Hard Severe 4b *
13. Epitaph   VS 4c
14. Epitaph Variation   E2 5c **
15. Coffin Chimney   VS 4b
16. Busman's Holiday   VS 5a

LOUDOUN HILL

(NS 609 379) Alt 250m   South facing   Map p150

This prominent landmark provides some excellent climbing on steep, rough and generally sound trachyte. Popularity is assured by a variety of quality routes at all grades, on walls, cracks and chimneys. The crags dry quickly, but are quite lichenous, so care should be taken after rain. Access to parts of the crag are sometimes restricted due to nesting birds. Please follow details on the posted notices.

Approach: From the car park at (NS 614 379) go through the gate to a gravel track then head straight down beside the fence, cross the burn and ascend.

The approach path leads past the distinctive large roof of the Eastern Buttress, to the Central Wall opposite an old stone wall and characterised by ribs and steep walls above mossy lower walls, to reach the trees at Pulpit Rock.

PULPIT ROCK

Diagram p154

This large isolated pinnacle lies at the far left-hand end of the crags. The left wall is split by the curving Pulpit Crack, while the prow forms the impressive Pulpit Arete. Although the face gives quality climbing, the rock is rather lichenous.

1 Pulpit Chimney   12m   Moderate   *(1960s)*
Climb cracks immediately left of Pulpit Rock to a ledge, then move right past chockstones to the top.

2 Slings   12m   E4 5c **   *(1978)*
The groove in the left face of Pulpit Rock gives sustained and strenuous climbing with improving protection.

3 Lunge   15m   E3 6a ***   *(1960s)*
An excellent technical route requiring commitment and a cool head. The undercut nose leads past good runners to a small spike in the groove, poor nut runner. Levitate into the groove and continue for some distance to protection. Finish up the crack.

4 Pulpit Crack   20m   HVS 5a **
The steep curving crack gives a classic climb, or a character building thrash, depending on your skill with hand-cracks. Finish up the bulge and crack to the left (E1 5b) or up the arete further right. The wall to the right of the crack can be climbed on small flake holds at 5c.

5 Pulpit Arete   20m   Severe 4a ***   *(1930s)*
Tremendous airy climbing up the arete dividing the two faces, but it's getting a bit polished. From the gully on the right traverse left past a thin crack and climb the arete direct to the top. A direct start coupled with the thin crack direct pushes the grade to Hard Severe 4b.

Cleaner rock can be found on the right face of Pulpit Rock. The steep slabby wall rising from the gully gives an entertaining but rather artificial route; **Senile Slab** (E4 5c 1978), which is usually top-roped.

THE AMPHITHEATRE

Diagram p154

Curving gently right from the Pulpit Rock is The Amphitheatre. The left-hand side

LOUDOUN HILL - West Face

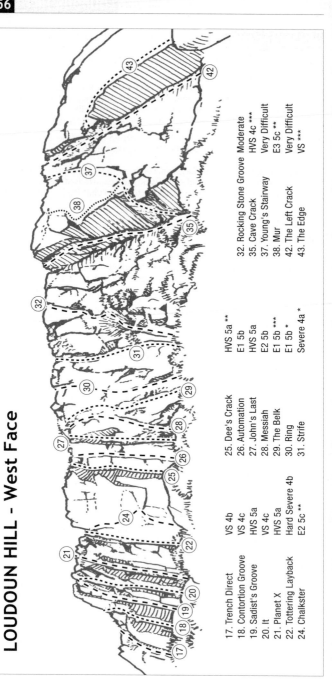

17. Trench Direct   VS 4b
18. Contortion Groove   VS 4c
19. Sadist's Groove   HVS 5a
20. It   VS 4c
21. Planet X   HVS 5a
22. Tottering Layback   Hard Severe 4b
24. Chalkster   E2 5c **

25. Dee's Crack   HVS 5a **
26. Automation   E1 5b
27. John's Last   HVS 5a
28. Messiah   E2 5b
29. The Belk   E1 5b ***
30. Ring   E1 5b *
31. Strife   Severe 4a *

32. Rocking Stone Groove   Moderate
35. Cave Crack   HVS 4c ***
37. Young's Stairway   Very Difficult
38. Mur   E3 5c **
42. The Left Crack   Very Difficult
43. The Edge   VS ***

is characterised by the small rectangular buttress taken by Mantelshelf Wall and Cling, and the right-hand side by the flake-crack of Epitaph Variation.

6 Amphitheatre Arete   15m   Difficult *(1960s)*
Right of Pulpit Rock is a clean arete, which after a steep start leads to easier climbing.

7 Gorse Route   10m   Difficult
Climb cracks on the left side of the small rectangular buttress.

**8 Mantelshelf Wall   10m   VS 4c ** ** *(1960s)*
Technical climbing. The left edge leads to a ledge, move right and go up with difficulty to finish on the right edge.

9 Cling   10m   E2 5c *(1960s)*
Steep, technical moves up the right arete of the buttress lead to better holds, but still no protection.

10 Shattered Corner   10m   Severe 4a *(1960s)*
The corner forming the right-hand side of the small buttress.

**11 Frustration Wall   10m   Hard Severe 4b ** **
To the right of Shattered Corner, climb twin cracks to a niche. Continue up the groove, taking care with the rock to step left, then go up the wall above. Or, step right and climb the steep crack (VS 5a). Popular and well worn.

12 Conclusion Wall   10m   Hard Severe 4b * *(1960s)*
Just to the right, an inset groove gives easy climbing to steep bulging cracks at the top.

Mossy rock to the right can be climbed in various places at Moderate to Very Difficult.

13 Epitaph   10m   VS 4c *(1960s)*
Short but fun. Start below the obvious flake-crack. Climb to the niche, take a deep breath, then... delicately left.

**14 Epitaph Variation   10m   E2 5c ** ** *(1960s/74)*
Follow Epitaph to the niche, then power up the crack before the barn door opens.

15 Coffin Chimney   10m   VS 4b *(1960s)*
The evil looking green slot right of the flake-crack gives a surprisingly good climb.

16 Busman's Holiday   8m   VS 5a *(1993)*
The cleaned crack right of Coffin Chimney gives a short, well protected problem.

WEST FACE

Diagram p156

Below and right of The Amphitheatre is another long wall with a prominent hand-crack and corners at its left-hand end, a steep wall with a small roof in the middle and the prominent chockstone-capped crack of Cave Crack at the right-hand end. The face has been girdled at E2 5b.

17 Trench Direct   12m   VS 4b *(1960s)*
At the left end a short jamming crack gives pleasant climbing. Finish up the crack on the right.

18 Contortion Groove   10m   VS 4c   *(1960s)*
Just to the right is a constricted, dirty V-groove with a mossy patch on the right wall. Grovel up the groove and finish up Trench Direct.

19 Sadist's Groove   10m   HVS 5a   *(1960s)*
This climbs the obvious corner leading to a prominent spike. Traverse right to a grass tuft and up.

20 It   10m   VS 4c   *(1995)*
Awkward bridging in the shallow V-chimney between Sadist's Groove and the prominent corner of Planet X further right.

21 Planet X   12m   HVS 5a   *(1994)*
The larger corner right of Sadist's Groove has a dubious looking plaque like block at two- thirds height.

Right of the corner is a green wall with vertical grassy cracks.

22 Tottering Layback   8m   Hard Severe 4b   *(1960s)*
The right side of the green wall is a flake-crack overhung by a blocky roof. Layback the crack, move round the hollow roof with trepidation and dance through gorse bushes to the top.

23 Quick Skive   10m   VS 4c ★★   *(1993)*
Exciting and surprisingly independent laybacking up the crack in the wall right of Tottering Layback.

24 Chalkster   12m   E2 5c ★★   *(1981)*
A fine crack and flake-line cuts the left wall of the next steep buttress. Dangle right along the horizontal break to a runner (Rock 6), lunge for the flake and swing up the cracks. Great for gorillas.

25 Dee's Crack   10m   HVS 5a ★★★   *(1960s)*
Awkward climbing up the off-width and finger-crack on the right side of the steep wall. A memorial to a certain Professor of Physics whose classes were skipped for the first ascent.

26 Automation   8m   E1 5b   *(1960s)*
Immediately right of Dee's Crack is a thin crack with an old peg. Independent and hard at the start, but a bit artificial higher up. If you can avoid touching any holds on other routes, the grade is E2 5c/6a.

27 John's Last   10m   HVS 5a
Loose rock and lichen mar the large overhung groove 2m right of Dee's Crack.

To the right is a bulging wall.

28 Messiah   10m   E2 5b   *(1995)*
Climb the V-niche forming the left side of the wall and the crack direct to the block. Sustained.

29 The Belk   10m   E1 5b ★★★
Superb well protected climbing up the groove and crack-line in the left-hand side of the bulging wall. Finish up the crack, trending left to the block.

30 Ring   10m   E1 5b ★   *(1960s)*
The shallow groove right of The Belk gives good climbing when clean. Protection is adequate if tricky to find. Finish right from the ledge below the top.

1 Strife   10m   Severe 4a * *(1960s)*
This takes cracks up the right side of the bulging wall. Climb up to the large semi-detached block on the right. From its top, step left and climb cracks on good holds to the top.

2 Rocking Stone Groove   13m   Moderate
Behind the semi-detached block is a short grassy groove with two gorse bushes at its base. This can be used as a descent, once you can find the top.

Further right, the West Face curves downwards to a wall with a prominent hand-crack topped by a chockstone.

3 Evening Groove   10m   Severe 4a *(1960s)*
The wall left of the prominent crack is climbed to finish up the left-hand groove – dirty.

4 Slab and Groove   13m   Hard Severe 4b *(1960s)*
Start as for Evening Groove, but finish up the obvious slabby groove on the right.

5 Cave Crack   10m   HVS 4c *** *(1960s)*
Sustained and sometimes painful jamming leads to a spectacular finish over the chockstone. Deduct points if you try to escape through the hole.

6 Hobbit Crack   15m   E1 5b * *(1995)*
Climb Cave Crack to two-thirds height. Step right under the large block and traverse right under and around the block and finish more easily up the wall above. Strenuous placing gear.

7 Young's Stairway   16m   Very Difficult *
Start just right of Cave Crack, and follow the obvious traverse line up and right across the face to above the pinnacle on the Central Wall. Finish by the easiest line above. A direct start is possible at the same grade.

8 Mur   12m   E3 5c ** *(2002)*
Climb the arete directly above the start of Young's Stairway, finishing as for Hobbit Crack.

9 Leftover Crack   10m   HVS 5a * *(1995)*
From the start of Young's Stairway use the arete of Mur to gain the thin diagonal crack.

CENTRAL WALL

Diagram p160

The lower tier of this face lies above the old stone wall on the approach path and is generally mossy and grassy. The upper tier is dominated by the Edge, the impressive knife edged pinnacle on the left. The steep central wall is climbed by The Splits and to the right is a series of corners and overhangs. The better climbing on the upper tier can be accessed by an exposed scramble down and round from the base of Cave Crack. This approach combines grass and rock and requires great care.

For those wanting a longer route, or unwilling to make the scramble, the first pitch of The Edge leads to the ledge below the upper tier from where all the routes can be accessed.

0 The Cat   15m   E1 5b *(1998)*
Start above and 6 metres left of the old stone wall. Climb the crack and corner in the lower tier with difficulty, pull over a loose block and continue to a belay at the start of Young's Stairway.

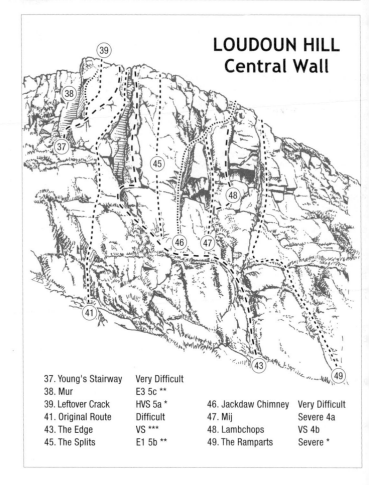

**LOUDOUN HILL
Central Wall**

37. Young's Stairway	Very Difficult		
38. Mur	E3 5c **		
39. Leftover Crack	HVS 5a *	46. Jackdaw Chimney	Very Difficult
41. Original Route	Difficult	47. Mij	Severe 4a
43. The Edge	VS ***	48. Lambchops	VS 4b
45. The Splits	E1 5b **	49. The Ramparts	Severe *

41 Original Route   45m   Difficult

Down and right of the old stone wall is a grassy area and then a large mass of moss.
1. 30m Climb the dirty wall left of the moss to the mid-way terrace. Ascend rock and turf up the left side of the pinnacle to below the upper tier.
2. 15m The right-slanting grass filled diagonal fault is followed to a finish behind the pinnacle.

42 The Left Crack   20m   Very Difficult   *(1930s)*

The wide chimney-crack between the left side of the pinnacle and the face gives good climbing.

43 The Edge   45m   VS *

The knife edged pinnacle on the upper tier gives a wild, wild route with a minimum of protection.
1. 25m Right of the mossy wall on the lower tier is a fairly clean open groove with a large block on the right at the top. Ascend rock and turf up the left side of the

pinnacle to below the upper wall.
2. 20m 4b Traverse right onto the arete and, with some trepidation, climb the knife- edge to the top. A direct start has been made at 4c.

The left and right faces of The Edge have been top-roped at 6b/6c and 5c respectively.

4 Foxglove Chimney 20m Severe 4a *(1930s)*
Grunt up the chimney-crack on the right-hand side of the pinnacle, threading the chockstones as you go.

5 The Splits 20m E1 5b **
Fingery climbing up the centre of the upper tier, right of The Edge. Climb the thin crack to a small ledge, then move right and up to the top.

6 Jackdaw Chimney 15m Very Difficult *(1930s)*
The groove forming the right edge of the wall gives pleasant but wandering climbing. Climb the corner-crack to a ledge, then traverse right past a loose flake to the top.
Variation: **Direct Finish Severe 4a**
From the ledge follow the right-slanting crack directly above.
Variation: **The Vein VS 4c** *(1995)*
From the ledge follow the left-slanting crack out onto the face, bridging off the arete.

7 Mij 15m Severe 4a
The wide crack and groove splitting the left-hand end of the overhangs down and right of Jackdaw Chimney.

8 Lambchops 15m VS 4b *(1995)*
Ascend a groove to below the main overhangs and pull over into a shallow, mossy corner.

9 The Ramparts 40m Severe *
Pleasant climbing leads to an exposed crux at the top of the shocking green inverted V-groove, right of the overhangs.
1. 25m Right of the mossy wall on the lower tier is a fairly clean open groove with a large block on the right at the top. Climb the grassy groove right of and below the block, then go up and right to belay below the groove.
2. 15m 4a Climb the groove – lethal when damp – and make an energetic move over the intimidating bulge on surprising holds. Continue by a choice of lines above.

The cracks on the left wall of the crux of The Ramparts give a short and artificial route **Short Term Effect** (HVS 5a).

Staircase Crack 40m Very Difficult
About 30m right of the old stone wall on the path is a clean rib. Climb the left side of the rib, continue up the short wall above, then left and up corners, grooves and short walls of good rock about 100m right of The Ramparts.

EASTERN BUTTRESS

A large roof characterises this buttress, the first crag met on the approach path. The face gets less sun than the rest of Loudoun Hill and the routes tend to be short, very lichenous and mossy. The best climbs take the ribs left and right of the roof. The face has been girdled at Severe.

The Hand Traverse 10m HVS 5a
Down and left of the roof is an overhanging wall split by a horizontal crack.

Traverse strenuously left to a ledge, then climb the shallow scoop above, or the blunt rib directly above the wall.

Nose Rib   15m   Severe 4a
A mossy and often wet rib bounds the left side of the large roof.

Painless   25m   A1   (1995)
Follow the crack-line through the left side of the large roof.

Suicide   25m   Hard Severe 4b
Start below the right side of the roof. Broken ground leads to a crack and a large flake. Stand on the flake and make a hard move up the crack to join Dusk Route. Rather artificial.

Dusk Route   25m   Very Difficult ∗∗   (1930s)
Start at the lowest part of the crag below the roof. Climb a short wall to a slabby corner, which leads to ledges right of the large roof and below a small overhang. Climb the obvious left-trending flakes across the wall.

Further right the grassy corner is climbed by **Spitfire** (Severe); **Wall and Groove** (Severe), takes the groove to the right and **The Blitz** (VS), the wall left of the overgrown zigzag crack right again. The wall right of the crack is **SCC Wall** (Severe). **Breakfast Route** (Very Difficult), climbs vegetated ground to the right.

Boulder Suicide   15m   E2 5b   (1995)
Right and uphill about 80m from the large roof of Suicide is a clean wall forming the left end of a big mossy boulder topped by a tree. Climb the centre of the face, turning the lip by a crack.

MAUCHLINE GORGE

(NS 510 253)   South facing   Map p150

These red sandstone cliffs on the banks of the River Ayr are best visited in spring or early summer before they become too overgrown. The rock is generally solid, but a bit friable and the crags have a distinct Lost World atmosphere, similar to Roslin Glen. The only climbing of note is on the impressive River Buttress.

Approach: Follow the A76 south from Mauchline to make a hidden turn right, just before the sign for the golf club and the bridge over the River Ayr. Follow the road to a parking place on the right (NS 512 255). Cross the field and follow the path to the river. 5mins.

BOULDER CRAG

This is situated in the trees on the right of the approach path to the river. It has some bouldering, traverses and short routes.

RIVER BUTTRESS

Follow the approach path down to the river. This impressive buttress overhangs the river on the right. It has a prominent corner and roof in the centre.

Games of Chance and Sandancing   20m   E2 5b ∗   (1988)
The obvious steep crack-line left of the prominent corner of Bridge Over Troubled Water gives a good route. Traverse right to finish at the same place as Ayrheid.

Bridge Over Troubled Water   25m   E4 5c ∗   (1988)
Well out there; some of the rock in the upper corner is thrillingly poor. Start in the centre of the buttress below and right of the corner. Climb a small corner and

traverse left below roofs into the main corner-line and follow this to a bay. Climb the overhanging corner above passing a peg runner. A very well hidden Rock 7 can be placed just before a step right to a resting place. Climb over two further roofs to a small ledge and runner. Traverse left and up to trees.

Ayrheid   25m   E2   (1988)
Generally good rock and very exciting climbing. Start in the centre of the buttress.
1. 10m 5b Climb a small corner and traverse left below roofs into the main corner-line. Follow this to a bay and belay.
2. 5m 5c Traverse right and pull round the bulge to a good thread belay.
3. 10m 5a Climb the wall above and move left to finish.

CHIMNEY CRAG

This is the large, wet and rather vegetated crag approached by turning left at the river and walking upstream from River Buttress.

The Chimney   20m   HVS 5a   (1970s)
Fight your way up the loose sandy fault and finish out left. It's a long time since it was climbed and it will probably stay that way!

SPHINX ROCK

Further upstream and beside the river is Table Rock, a large and very steep crag marred by its extremely soft lower section. Sphinx Rock lies to the left of Table Rock and has a large overhang on its left and a small slab on its right.

Corner Root   5m   Severe 4a   (1986)
Climb the corner to the right of the slab.

MAIN QUARRY

The quarry in the woods above Chimney Crag is very overgrown, although the underlying rock is quite good.

Bowman's Corner   10m   Severe 4a   (1986)
The dirty corner on the left.

Mossy Wall   15m   E2 5a   (1989)
The dirty wall right of the corner, finishing between the two trees.

Purism Personified   15m   E2 5a   (1986)
Start behind the puddle at a faint crack. Climb this and the steep wall above to finish left of the tree; unprotected.

Gardener's Corner   15m   VS 4b *   (1986)
Reasonable protection can be found for this shallow left-facing corner.

Board Walk   15m   E2 5b   (1987)
The clean wall between the two corners has been led with peg runners (not in-situ).

Y Bother   12m   E3 5c   (1987)
Climb the left-hand crack of the Y-crack in the large square-cut corner. Hard to protect and climb.

Bye Eck   12m   E4 6a   (1987)
Unprotected climbing up the arete to the right of the corner. Tall and strongies should climb it direct, short and less strongies to the right (technical).

AYRSHIRE

Green Machine **15m** **VS 4b** *(1987)*
Climb the dirty wall between the two aretes, then the slab above.

Dredge Bog **15m** **VS 4b** *(1986)*
The blunt arete to the right may be easier when clean!

Monstrously Horrible **15m** **Very Dirty** *(1986)*
Slither up or down roots to the right. Several alternatives are possible, the best being to avoid it altogether!

Lightning Crack **6m** **E2 6a** *(1989)*
The very far right end of the quarry is crossed by the path. This clean route lies on the small buttress forming the continuation of the quarry wall on the right, overlooking Table Rock, and is approached by a scramble down through bushes. Start with boulder problem moves up the left-hand crack, traverse right and finish up the crack.

BRIDGE BUTTRESS

This buttress lies downstream beyond River Buttress and directly below the viaduct. It can only be reached when the river is very low, or by an abseil from under the viaduct.

Bushwhacker **20m** **E1 5b** *(1989)*
Start below the viaduct at the right end of the crag. Climb up and past a tree root to a pocketed wall, then up and left to a ledge. Continue up a crack to a tree and a small slab.

OTHER CRAGS

East of Ayr, the small crag at **Craigs of Kyle** (NS 428 155) offers some entertaining and popular bouldering. Leave the A713 south of Hollybush and continue to an old quarry on the left, parking below it. Cross the gate to the right of the quarry and walk uphill into a small valley which leads to the crag in about 5mins. Two routes have been recorded on the loose dolerite quarry at **Tappet Hill** (NS 533 128) above the large open cast mine. **Tap Dance** (VS 4c), takes the prominent arete and **Cumnock Wall** (VS 4c), the wall to the left. A number of routes have been recorded on **Benbeoch** (NS 495 083). However the crag is now part of a big quarry and is likely to remain an unattractive climbing location for some years to come.

GLEN AFTON

(NS 629 054) **Alt 400m** **North facing** **Map p150**

A scattering of granite crags lie on the north-west spur of Craigbraneoch Rig, just north of Afton Reservoir. The most obvious feature is the 25m lower wall, known as Stayamrie. Although the underlying rock is excellent, seepage and the north facing aspect have returned many climbs to their natural state. At least three or four days are needed for the crag to dry. There is a seasonal climbing restriction from February 15 to June 30 due to rare birds nesting.

Approach: From the car park at the end of Glen Afton (NS 628 053). The crag is easily seen on the left across the burn.

STAYAMRIE

This is the smooth steep buttress at the foot of the crag, identified by a prominent right-curving crack at its left end.

Magic Carpet   30m   VS 4c   *(1992)*
The wide crack at the extreme left end of the wall. Start 3m right of the crack and climb past an awkward ledge to a grass ledge at the start of the main crack. Exit left to finish.

Midnight Express   25m   E1 5b *   *(1992)*
Follow the thin crack in the wall left of the curving crack. A fine climb, but often wet.

Stone Circle   30m   E1 5b **   *(1992)*
Exciting, sustained and unusual climbing up the prominent curving crack.

The Crack of Doon   30m   HVS 5a *   *(1991)*
When dry and clean this route gives excellent climbing up the obvious vertical crack leading to and joining the top of the conspicuous curving crack.

Hyacinth House   25m   E2 5b   *(1992)*
Steep and uncompromising climbing right of the blank section of the wall. From a small niche, climb up and right into a large niche at 5m and continue, finishing up the wall to the left of the top grass ledge.

Sweet Liberty   25m   E3 5c   *(1992)*
Thin and delicate climbing up the thin right-trending ramp right of Hyacinth House and below an overhanging tree. A small corner leads to a ledge, then up the ramp right to finish.

Grass Roots   30m   VS 4c   *(1977)*
Start a few metres right of the smooth wall. Ascend a line of good holds trending right to a perched block. Surmount this with care and follow awkward vegetated ramp and rock steps. A direct start (E1 5b, 1990) climbs straight up to the right end of the grass ledge.

Delirium   30m   E4 6a *   *(1992)*
A technical, sustained and quick drying climb. Start at the foot of Grass Roots and climb directly up the wall to an overlap and peg. Climb up to twin pegs and move leftwards up the thin ramp- line to finish.

The next two routes lie on the buttress up and right of Stayamrie.

Rehabilitation Route   40m   Very Difficult   *(1977)*
Start left of the vague central mossy groove and climb straight up on good holds, by-passing the overhang on the right. Move left then up the edge to finish.

Two Plus Two   35m   Severe 4a   *(1978)*
Start a few metres right of the mossy groove and climb the rib to a perched block. Turn bulging rock above by a corner on the right.

Deception Slab   30m   HVS 5a   *(1978)*
This route is on the narrow slab to the right of the previous routes and about 250m right of the Main Wall. The central line is sustained, but a bit dirty.

Raven Slab   25m   HVS 4c   *(1978)*
The last route is on the large slab above and left of Stayamrie. Interesting but unprotected climbing leads up a central line on the slab.

AYRSHIRE

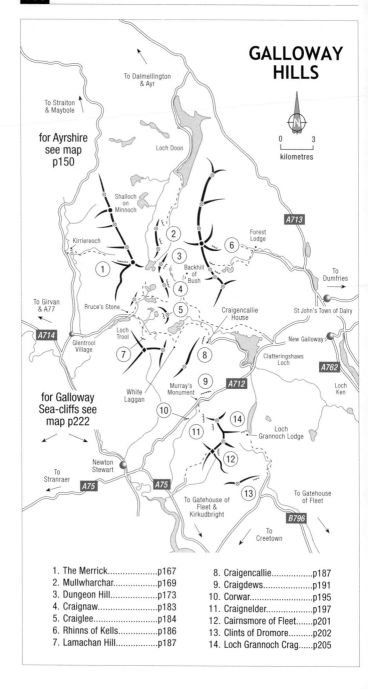

GALLOWAY HILLS

To Dalmellington & Ayr

To Straiton & Maybole

for Ayrshire see map p150

Loch Doon

A713

Shalloch on Minnoch

Forest Lodge

Kirriereoch

To Dumfries

To Girvan & A77

Backhill of Bush

A714

Bruce's Stone

Craigencallie House

St John's Town of Dairy

Glentrool Village

Loch Trool

New Galloway

Clatteringshaws Loch

A762

for Galloway Sea-cliffs see map p222

White Laggan

Murray's Monument

A712

Loch Ken

To Stranraer

Newton Stewart

A75

A75

Loch Grannoch Lodge

To Gatehouse of Fleet & Kirkudbright

To Gatehouse of Fleet

B796

To Creetown

0   3 kilometres

GALLOWAY HILLS

The mountain crags in this chapter offer some wonderful climbing, particularly to lovers of remote solitude. Approaches are generally long and the going extremely rough and boggy. A mountain bike, wellies and a cheerful disposition solve these problems to some extent. It should be noted that the term 'lane' in the Galloway Hills means a large and often unfordable burn, rather than an easy means of passage, though the real path may not be any drier, if it exists at all.

The rock climbing is on granite, usually solid, clean and quick drying. It is seamed with cracks, often rounded ones, so that on many pitches a double rack of cams is well worth carrying. In winter many of the larger granite cliffs offer some good lines, as do the metamorphosed cliffs of Black Gairy on The Merrick.

Many birds nest on the quiet crags of the Galloway Hills and climbing is restricted at certain venues during this period. These restrictions are detailed where known, but restrictions come and go as nesting locations change. If in doubt contact the MCofS (see Environment).

The Merrick, Dungeon Range & Rhinns of Kells

North of the gap that runs between Glen Trool, Loch Dee and Clatteringshaws Loch is found the most wild and remote climbing in the Galloway Hills.

The Merrick is the highest summit in the Southern Uplands. The mountain is composed of metamorphosed sediments which offer some good winter climbing on the large north facing Black Gairy.

The Dungeon Range is the long broken ridge that bisects the Galloway Hills from Loch Doon to Loch Dee. The major summits are, starting from the north, Hoodens Hill, Mullwharchar, Dungeon Hill, Craignaw and Craiglee. The rock here is granite, clean and solid on the south-east facing crags of Dungeon Hill but more vegetated on the north-east corries of Hoodens Hill and Mullwharchar.

The Rhinns of Kells define the northern Galloway Hills to the east. They are composed of metamorphosed sediments and so far have offered only a little winter climbing.

General Approaches: The Merrick is best approached from Kirriereoch to the west, on the minor road north of Glentrool Village. The track followed by The Southern Upland Way links Glen Trool to Craigencallie. The main access points for The Dungeon Range are from Loch Doon off the A713 to the north or Craigencallie (see Minigaff Hills) off the A 712 in the south. The Rhinns of Kells are best accessed from the A713 to the east. For those equipped with a mountain bike, forestry tracks currently provide the easiest means of access and full approach details are given in the introduction to each crag.

The 8m high south-west facing **Gaw Glen Crag** (NS 483 025) has five routes between Difficult and Hard Severe, with bolt belays. It is situated on the east side of the Loch Doon road, 2km south of its junction with the A713.

THE MERRICK

(NX 427 855)   Alt 843m   Map p166

The usual route to the highest summit in southern Scotland, starts in Glen Trool and is very popular. It is also one of the few reasonable paths in the Galloway Hills.

BLACK GAIRY

(NX 415 856)   Alt 600m   North facing

This crag has the most reliable winter climbing in the area, though it still requires snow, followed by a good freeze.

Approach: Although the crag can be approached from Glen Trool to the south, the approach from Kirriereoch farm to the west is quicker. From the car park

(NX 358 866) follow the forest track to the gates of Kirriereoch. Turn right here then right again to a fork just before a bridge over Kirriemore Burn. Take the right fork, cross the bridge and turn left immediately. Follow this track (not marked on the map) until it ends, then continue across unpleasant felled forestry on the right (south) side of Kirshinnoch Burn to gain open ground. The crag lies on the right shortly after the second stone wall is crossed, while the third stone wall leads to the foot of the Black Gutter (1hr 45mins).

Descent: Westwards, following the stone wall at the top of the cliff, dropping back down to the Kirshinnoch Burn once clear of the crag.

The large gully of the Black Gutter, with the wall leading to its foot, is the most obvious feature of the crag. The steepest section of the cliff lies to the right, with the icefall of Interstellar Overdraft another landmark. In mist, the shallow burn or icefall of The Kyle Gully, immediately to the left of Interstellar, can be a useful identifying feature. Routes are described from right to left.

150m to the right of the conspicuous icefall of Interstellar Overdraft is a recess. Taking left and right exits, are **Kenny's Folly** (III 1996) and **Chippy's Downfall** (III 1996).

Interstellar Overdraft   150m   V/VI **   (1993)
Takes the obvious and intimidating vertical icefall in the centre of the steep wall 200m right of Black Gutter. Start directly below the icefall.
1. 50m Climb mixed ground to a peg belay on the right of the fall.
2. 40m Climb the 30m icefall directly, then trend up right to a poor belay.
3 and 4. 60m Continue up easier ground for two pitches to the plateau.

The Kyle Gully   150m   III/IV **   (1987)
This takes the shallow and stepped gully/icefall immediately to the left of Interstellar Overdraft. Two fine ice pitches lead up past the Interstellar icefall, above which the route eases.

Several other routes were climbed in this area in the 1970s and '80s, but were not properly recorded. These may take a similar line to the upper part of the following route.

The Lang Scots Miles   156m   IV **   (2003)
A fine long ice route. 150m right of Black Gutter (and 50m left of the icicle of Interstellar Overdraft), at mid-height on the face is an overhanging square black wall. Start below the right end of this, mid-way between a shallow groove and a large spike at 3m.
1. 30m Climb iced walls directly to an ice screw belay beneath a short steep chimney.
2. 26m Climb the bulge to the left of the chimney, then easier ground to belay below the square black wall.
3. 50m Climb the icefall corner on the right of the wall, then continue up the hidden gully above.
4. 50m Continue by icefalls to the top.

Right Rib of the Gutter   150m   II   (1987)
The rib bounding the Gutter on its right side.

Black Gutter   200m   III **   (1970s)
A classic. The main gully on the left of the crag gives four good pitches but is hard to protect in places. It branches near the top and either fork may be taken. The left branch is III/IV (1985). It is a greasy, grassy, Very Difficult in summer (1920).

Left Rib of the Gutter   250m   II   (1970s)
The rib on the left of the Gutter.

HOWE OF THE CAULDRON

(NX 430 857)   Alt 600m   North-East facing

This is the atmospheric corrie on the north-eastern side of The Merrick.

North-East Couloir   200m   II/III *   *(1996)*
Follow the obvious steep snow and ice ramps, the grade depending on line and conditions. Finish straight up to the summit, or go left beside a rock band, or go directly over the steep rock, snow and ice rib.

MULLWHARCHAR

(NX 454 866)   Map p166

This hill has a lot of rock and a lot of vegetation. The crags get little sun and seepage can be a problem. However, there are some good routes in a wild setting.

Approach: Park at the locked gate at (NX 476 942) one mile past Loch Doon Castle, at the bridge over the Carrick Lane. Follow the track south for 2.5km to the head of Loch Doon where a further track branches right (south) into forestry. Follow this to its end, then continue on a footpath rightwards for 150m to a bridge over the Gala Lane and follow its west bank upstream. The Wolf Slock is the first cliff on the right (2hrs – 1hr with a mountain bike), while The Tauchers lie under the summit of Mullwharchar another 1.6km (30mins) further south. The approach from Loch Trool via Loch Enoch and Mullwharchar is 3hrs 30mins, and from Craigencallie via Backhill of Bush the same or 2hrs 30mins with a mountain bike.

WOLF SLOCK

(NX 457 894)   Alt 350m   North-East facing

This large rambling cliff lies on the north-east end of Hoodens Hill, a northerly outlier of Mullwharchar. It contains **The Gullet** (70m Very Difficult 1992), which is the right-hand of the two vegetated parallel gullies situated at the left end of the cliff.

THE TAUCHERS

(NX 458 874)   Alt 525m   North-East facing

Pronounced 'Talkers' (almost!), this north-eastern corrie of Mullwharchar gives remote and occasionally idyllic climbing on good granite in a wild and romantic setting. It is generally rather slow to dry, although some routes such as the classic Behind the Mask, come into condition fairly quickly. There is a seasonal climbing restriction from February 15 to July 31 due to rare birds nesting.

There are two main crags, visible from the path. The Giant's Stairway is immediately south of the two burns in the corrie, with the Organ Pipes up and to the left.

The Tiers

These small crags lie to the right of the Giant's Stairway on a broken area of hillside situated between the two burns. Among these there is a clean white slab low down and a tiered headwall higher up.

Concave Slab   30m   HVS 5a   *(1994)*
This demanding route takes the shallow corner immediately left of the smoothest part of the white slab reached by the wall directly below the corner. Quick to dry.

GALLOWAY HILLS

The next routes are on the tiered headwall that looks across towards the Giant's Stairway. This is reached by scrambling 300m up the hillside to a short wall with a huge poised boulder.

Tiers before Bedtime   50m   Severe   (2001)
An enjoyable series of quicker drying variations on Tiers for Fears. Start 20m left of the huge boulder at a short blocky wall.
1. 35m 4a Climb the wall to a terrace below a wall with a small poised boulder on top of it. Climb the shallow groove 3m to the left of the boulder, moving up right to a ledge and an awkward move onto another terrace. Climb a curving groove to yet another terrace.
2. 15m 4b   Ahead are two thin cracks. Cunningly avoid these by climbing a rightward-trending series of steps on their left to an impasse. Hand-traverse left to a scoop and so the top. A nice pitch.

Tiers for Fears   45m   E1   (1994)
Interesting but avoidable climbing. Start above the first short wall of Tiers before Bedtime and 2m left of the small perched boulder.
1. 30m 5b Climb the thin slab to gain a finger-crack and the top of the first tier. Climb the thin crack in the next wall.
2. 15m 5a The left-hand crack of the pair.

Where Beagles Dare   15m   VS 4c   (1994)
About 100m down and left of the headwall is a smaller steep wall. Climb the left-hand crack system.

Giant's Stairway

(NX 458 874)   Alt 425m

This rather rambling cliff just left of the central burn in the corrie offers good rock separated by rather too much heather and scrambling. The main face looks north-east towards Loch Doon and is more continuous at its right end. Routes are described from right to left.

The Raiders   105m   E1 *   (1992)
Worth doing. Towards the right side of the crag at about one-third height, and above the large tree in the burn, is a pale slabby wall. Scramble to its foot (crux!).
1. 35m 5a Climb steep parallel cracks to a ledge, then go boldly up right to finish up a corner. Easier ground leads up right to a block belay. A serious lead if wet – which it often is.
2. 35m 4c Descend slightly right and follow a rib to finish up an awkward and unprotected flared chimney. Two short walls lead to a belay in a grassy bay below a steep wall.
3. 35m 4a Skirt the wall on the right and continue left via short walls to finish.
Variation: **Dry Variation 1   5b**
Avoid the wet twin cracks of the first pitch by starting on a heather ledge up on the right. Traverse into the middle of the wall and make hard moves up to gain the corner.
Variation: **Dry Variation 2   4c**
Avoid the greasy flared chimney at the end of the second pitch by traversing to a heather bay on its left and climbing the well protected wall and arete.

Bugle   150m   HVS   (1992)
A reasonable but serious first pitch, after which the climbing deteriorates. Slightly below and left of the pale slabby wall of The Raiders is a slab with a right-slanting corner in its middle section.
1. 30m 4c Boldly follow the main corner up then right to exit via a short crack.

Climb the wall above and take a stance immediately (poor belay – look for a crack up right).

2. 50m Move left up heather to a short wall which leads to a large heather terrace. Scramble up this and belay to the right of a layback crack and under a blunt cracked arete. (It is possible to walk off left here, or scramble up to Solstice – either of which is a good alternative to continuing.)

3. 35m 4b Either climb the layback crack and move right, or climb the arete to a steep wall with two parallel cracks. Up these, moving right to the arete and up to a grassy ramp, which leads up right to a short chimney by a small tree. Climb the chimney then more grass to a short groove.

4. 35m 4c Climb the groove by its right edge to a terrace, then an overhanging groove up left leads awkwardly to easier ground.

Solstice   20m   E2 5c *   (1992)
An excellent sustained pitch up the obvious crack in the wall high on the left side of the crag.

Switchback   115m   Very Difficult *   (1992)
A pleasant but escapable route taking the clean rib towards the left side of the crag. The climbing, though quite bold, is easy enough and the rock is delightful and very quick to dry. Start at the lowest point of the crag at a wide vegetated corner containing a small sapling.

1. 50m Gain the clean rib on the right of the corner and follow it to a large heather terrace. Traverse left immediately to slabs and climb these to a stance below a short wall.

2. 30m Move rightwards to overcome the wall then move back left to slabs and follow these to a heather ledge below a steep wall. Walk right to a pair of shallow right-facing corners with a larger left-facing corner to the right.

3. 50m Move further still along the terrace to the right to a long easy corner which is climbed by its right rib to slabs. Follow these leftwards to a broad heather terrace. Either walk off to the left, or climb several further pitches of heathery scrambling to the top.

Variation: **Original Finish Pitch 3   15m**
Climb the left-facing corner and steep chimney-groove above to finish on slabs.

The Couloir   200m   Moderate *   (c1909)
The deep gully on the left-hand side of the crag is notable for being Galloway's first recorded climb and an excellent scramble.

Winter: **I/II ***   (1970)
A good route that may be harder in lean conditions.

Organ Pipes

(NX 459 872)   Alt 500m

Up and left from the Giant's Stairway, this aptly named crag abounds with impressive fluted corners and ribs. On the left-hand side of the crag is a large deep vegetated corner, with an even larger and deeper corner (Brigadoon) to its right.

Phoebos Mask   45m   E3 5c **   (1995)
The cracked face just right of the vegetated corner and left of Behind the Mask provides a fine, quick drying and sustained but well protected pitch that just merits the grade. Climb parallel slim grooves to some cracks high and right. Pull out left to gain the roof (crux) and climb the crack in the arete to a ledge. Easily to the top.

Behind the Mask   45m   E1 5b ***   (1992)
Excellent, well protected, and reasonably quick to dry. Climb the fine groove in the blunt rib between the two large dank corners on the left side of the crag. The crux arrives just when you think it's all over.

GALLOWAY HILLS

Brigadoon   45m   El 5b *   *(1995)*
The huge groove just right of Behind the Mask proves a somewhat gothic experience. Follow the groove until it eases. Continue up the easier continuation groove, taking care with Damoclean spikes.

Yucatan   50m   E1   *(1995)*
Probably a good route when clean – unfortunately it isn't. Start 15m right of Behind the Mask below vegetation leading to a vegetated corner capped by a large block.
1. 20m 4c Heave yourself up vegetation to the dirty corner and climb it, turning the block on the left to gain a short groove leading up and right to a narrow terrace.
2. 30m 5b Move rightwards into the rightmost and most pronounced groove and follow it to a large overhang which is avoided on the right. Continue up the sustained crack above to a poor belay.

The Pagan   50m   E1 5b   *(1995)*
Start 30m right of Behind the Mask, round under the next bay from Yucatan. Swim up vertical vegetation, a few metres left of a small rowan, to the central and deepest groove in the buttress above. Climb the groove, either direct, or moving right into the right-hand groove in the upper half, to a ledge. Climb up the left side of the arete above to below a roof. Move right onto ledges and make hard layback moves up to regain the arete which is followed to the top - all rather artificial unfortunately.

At the bottom right of the crag is a buttress with two steep corners and, to their left, a searing finger-crack. For the shorter routes, the best belay is to scramble a further 20m to a flat grass platform above which is a short wall containing a good spike.

Dragonslayer   30m   E3 *   *(2002)*
1. 20m 6a The sustained finger-crack leads to a grass ledge.
2. 10m 5b Traverse horizontally right under the upper groove of Dungeonmaster to a second slimmer hanging groove which is followed to a ledge.

The Dungeonmaster   75m   E1 *   *(1992)*
Good climbing at the top end of the grade.
1. 30m 5b Climb the left-hand corner to where it splits into three. Follow the leftmost corner and belay immediately.
2. 45m 4b Step down and traverse left to a grassy ledge. From the left end of this follow the left-hand of two grooves to easy ground on the right. A good spike belay lies 5m above. Walk off right or finish up slabs and walls on the left.

Smaug   30m   E2 5b   *(2002)*
The right-hand groove gives a rather grubby pitch with a worrying feel. A Rockcentric 9 is useful to protect the crux.

The Throne   20m   E1 5b *   *(1995)*
A fine wee pitch, much better than it appears from below. Start 15m right of and up from the Dungeonmaster at a short yellow groove leading to a long narrow roof. Climb the groove to the roof. Traverse left to a curving crack. Use this to gain the wall above and climb it straight up the centre of the wall on superb holds until forced left to finish up a hanging groove.

Goat Rock

This two-tiered crag lies on the ridge on the very left of the corrie, left of The Organ Pipes. The rock is good, but the climbing is limited. **Kid's Stuff** (25m Severe 4a 1992) takes the right-slanting slab on the right side of the upper tier. **The Nose** (15m Severe 4a 1992) climbs the nose on the upper tier by the easiest line.

DUNGEON OF BUCHAN - DUNGEON HILL

(NX 462 848)   Alt 450m   South-East facing   Map p166

Technically the Dungeon of Buchan encompasses Dungeon Hill and Craignaw and their corries and lochs, but the name is now synonymous with the superb crags of clean granite that lie in splendid isolation on Dungeon Hill.

The arduousness of the approach is somewhat mitigated by the quality of the climbing and the rugged beauty of the surroundings, and though seepage can be a problem early in the season, by mid-summer the crags take only a day or two to dry after rain. The bird ban mentioned in the previous guide has been removed, making this a fine venue throughout the year. The many jamming cracks warrant doubling, or even trebling, up on Friends.

Approach: Just beyond the Clatteringshaws Loch dam, leave the A712 for the single track road on (NX 545 749), signed Craignell and Loch Dee. Follow the road round the loch, then inland to where it ends under Craigencallie crag (see below) at a car park next to the forestry gates. Continue on foot or bike, taking a right over the River Dee after 1.5km, followed by a left turn immediately thereafter. Bear left at the next major junction, to the Backhill of Bush bothy. This makes a good base for this crag, being just a 45min walk away.

Opposite the bothy, take either of the firebreaks in the forest to the edge of the marsh known as the Silver Flowe. This is a SSSI and climbers are requested to skirt the boggy central area slightly to the north; 10.5km, 2hrs 30mins from Craigencallie (1hr 30mins using a mountain bike). Walking from Glen Trool takes 3hrs.

DUNGEON BUTTRESS

Diagram p174

This is the small but steep rectangular buttress on the far left-hand side of the hill. Belays are well back, but an intermediate belay can be taken on a terrace which splits the crag near the top.

1 Galloway Grooves   35m   Very Difficult *   (1991)

Enjoyable climbing. Start in the gully at the left end of the crag and traverse right along a shelf. Swing round onto the face, move up to a right-slanting diagonal groove and follow this to a detached block. Gain the slab above and move rightwards to a short open chimney.

2 Battle Axe   35m   Hard Severe   4b   (1991)

Climb the crack just right of the edge of the gully to a wide crack and a grass ledge. Stretch up the groove behind to finish up the arete.

3 Carrick Corner   35m   VS 4c **   (1991)

The obvious corner on the left side of the crag leads to an awkward exit and the detached block of Galloway Grooves. The slab slightly left is climbed to an overhung niche and a skin-rasping finish.

4 Bruce's Stone   35m   E1 5b *   (1991)

A fine, if artificial, route with a desperate start. Climb the right arete of the corner direct to a tiny ledge. Continue straight up the arete to a slab, move left and finish up the blunt arete between the finish of Carrick Corner and Galloway Grooves.

5 Scots Wha' Hae   35m   HVS 5b **   (1991)

Excellent climbing. Right of the arete is a steep crack with several large half jammed flakes. Climb the crack to the tiny ledge of Bruce's Stone. Make a hard move up and right to a shallow niche and pull left over the roof to regain the arete, which is followed to slabs. Trend right then left to finish.

GALLOWAY HILLS

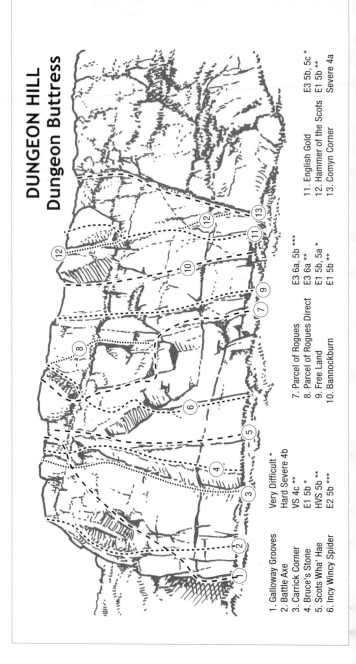

DUNGEON HILL
Dungeon Buttress

1. Galloway Grooves — Very Difficult *
2. Battle Axe — Hard Severe 4b
3. Carrick Corner — VS 4c **
4. Bruce's Stone — E1 5b *
5. Scots Wha' Hae — HVS 5b **
6. Incy Wincy Spider — E2 5b ***

7. Parcel of Rogues — E3 6a, 5b ***
8. Parcel of Rogues Direct — E3 6a **
9. Free Land — E1 5b, 5a *
10. Bannockburn — E1 5b **
11. English Gold — E3 5b, 5c *
12. Hammer of the Scots — E1 5b **
13. Comyn Corner — Severe 4a

6 Incy Wincy Spider   35m   E2 5b * **   (1991)

A superb route, strenuous and intimidating. Climb the steep jamming crack 2m right of Scots Wha' Hae to a niche. Reach over the roof and hand-traverse right to grasp a reverberating pinnacle. Pull over the roof leftwards using the pinnacle (!) and step left. Go up the unlikely wall to a thread and continue to the terrace, finishing up the corner right of the cracked arete.

7 Parcel of Rogues   35m   E3 * **   (1991)

Technical, strenuous and sustained climbing with good protection. Start below a crack leading to a huge overhung niche 10m right of Incy Wincy Spider.
1. 30m 6a Climb up to the crack and follow it as far as a small ledge. Make a difficult jamming traverse left and climb the clean undercut groove, exiting right at the top. A bold move leads to the terrace.
2. 5m 5b Climb the prominent impending right-slanting crack in the narrow arete.

**8 Parcel of Rogues Direct   35m   E3 6a ** **   (1994)

The obvious challenge of the hanging niche, when dry, is a little easier than the original way. Climb the original route to the small ledge at the top of the crack and make hard moves into the niche above, then struggle up the impressive overhanging slot. Finish as up the open corner above (as for Incy Wincy).

**9 Free Land   35m   E1 * **   (1991)

Good hard jamming.
1. 30m 5b Climb the left-hand crack in the wall 2m right of Parcel of Rogues to a small ledge. A short groove leads to a belay on a huge block.
2. 5m 5a The cracks in the right side of the arete.

**10 Bannockburn   35m   E1 5b ** **   (1991)

Another sound test of jamming technique – or lack of it. Climb the triple crack system in the centre of the wall to a ledge on the left. Force yourself back into the cracks and make hard but well protected moves to gain the large heather ledge. The final impending off-width is a piece of cake (by comparison).

**English Gold   35m   E3 * **   (1991)

A harder variation to Hammer of the Scots, starting 2m left of the right-slanting groove on the right side of the crag.
1. 25m 5b Climb a crack and where it closes hand-traverse diagonally right into the crack of Hammer of the Scots, then go up this to belay in the niche.
2. 10m 5c Traverse horizontally right under a hanging beak of rock and pull over the roof to finish up twin cracks. A well protected but strenuous pitch.

**12 Hammer of the Scots   35m   E1 5b ** **   (1991)

A good route but slower to dry than its neighbours. Start at the base of the right-slanting groove on the right side of the crag. An awkward crack leads to the huge niche which is surmounted by difficult bridging.

13 Comyn Corner   35m   Severe 4a   (1991)

A doddle compared with most of the other routes. Climb the right-slanting groove, or its right arete, finishing up the wall above.

SILVER SLAB

This clean slab is situated up and right from Dungeon Buttress, above the descent ramp from Cooran Buttress, and provides some good climbs in the lower grades.

**The Scrieve   50m   VS 4c ** **   (2002)

Start at the lowest point of the slab and follow the rib and twin cracks of Wee Slanter until just below the grass ledge where it is possible to move left into a scratch like crack in the slab. Follow this with interest to a good flake and then continue directly through bulges, crossing Wee Slanter, to a bold direct finish. A fine pitch.

15 The Wee Slanter   55m   Severe 4b *   (2001)
1. 25m Start at the lowest point of the slab, just right of a large overhang. Climb a crack in a rib to a horizontal grass ledge, then follow the obvious large twin cracks to the left end of a larger grass ledge and belay below a large flake.
2. 30m Climb the leftward-trending flake above on good holds, steeply at first and then make an airy step left at the top to finish up the easy angled rib on the left.

The remaining routes start from the large grass ledge that cuts in from the right at half-height, or can be reached by climbing the first pitch of the Wee Slanter.

16 Sprauchler's Groove   30m   VS 4b **   (2002)
Climbs the obvious thin dog-leg crack in the upper slab. An excellent sustained pitch with some highly unusual moves. A good selection of Friends is worth having. Follow the second pitch of Wee Slanter for 1m, then step right and pull up to the foot of the crack. Climb elegantly up this or sprauchle your way to the top.

17 The Big Smirr   30m   Severe 4a *   (2002)
Only Very Difficult except for one tricky move early on. Start 3m right of the left-hand end of the grass ledge and below the central crack in the upper slab. Climb up rightwards, then back leftwards (crux), past a small flake, to reach the crack which is followed to the top.

18 Pembroke Mist   30m   Severe 4b *   (2002)
Start about 3m left of the lowest point of the grass ledge on the right-hand side of the upper slab, at a fist sized crack. Climb this to the heather ledges, cross these leftwards, and climb the thin crack in the slab above with a choice of three finishes, all good; the left-hand crack, the right-hand crack, or pull out rightwards to the arete and finish straight up on jugs.

19 Stairway to Heather   35m   VS 4c *   (2004)
With apologies to Led Zeppelin! Start at the lowest point of the grass ledge on the right-hand side of the upper slab at a miniature staircase. Climb the fluted staircase to the heathery ledges, then the right-sloping finger-crack under the overlap to a square grassy ledge. Finish awkwardly up a groove to a giant detached block belay.

COORAN BUTTRESS

Diagram p178

This buttress runs the full length of the hillside to the right of Dungeon Buttress and has numerous good routes, though all are split by heather ledges. The obvious huge corner on the right side of the buttress is The Colonel's Corner.

Descent: By an easy grass ramp on the left that finishes at Dungeon Buttress.

The first routes tackle the broken ridge of clean rock that bounds the far left-hand side of the buttress.

20 Traitor's Gait   115m   VS **   (1984)
Fine pleasant climbing and very quick to dry. Start at a crack splitting the slab at the toe of the ridge. Low in the grade.
1. 25m 4b Climb the crack to a ledge on the left at 8m, then continue up leftwards to the left edge and either finish up this, or toe-traverse right and move up. Belay on a large ledge.
2. 30m 4a Cross the slab on the right for 5m to a vague ridge and follow it to a terrace and thread belay on a leaning block. A lovely pitch.
3. 20m 4b A few metres left of the leaning block are two short steep cracks. Climb

the left-hand one directly (or move onto the left arete at 5m) to a terrace below the headwall.

4. 40m 4b Follow the cracks directly above which lead up to parallel cracks just to the right of the left arete of the final wall (and a few metres to the left of the long overhang). Move left to the arete and climb it to easy ground. Alternatively finish up the cracks direct at VS 4c.

21 Snakes and Ladders   120m   E1 *   (2002)

Four good technical pitches though little in the way of a line. Start just right of Traitor's Gait where two ragged cracks split the sidewall of the buttress.

1. 25m 5a Climb the right-hand crack to a large ledge stance on Traitor's Gait.
2. 30m 5b Climb the short crack on the back wall to a rib on the left and follow this boldly to a ledge which is traversed right past a spike to a block in the gully. Climb the crack system above, moving left to the arete near the top, and belay at a wide crack at the back of a commodious grass ledge.
3. 35m 5a Climb the crack to a footledge and traverse this left to a crack in a rib which is followed to grass. Scramble up a few metres to a square tower. Follow a groove on the front face to a ledge on the left then step right onto the slabby upper face and go up to belay in a paddock under an attractive blocky grey pillar.
4. 20m 5a The pillar.

To the right are two grassy fault-lines separated by a broken buttress.

22 Cooran Buttress Direct   120m   VS *   (2001)

This series of variations on Cooran Buttress provides some good pitches. Start down and right of the left-hand grassy fault at a clean slab, 10m left of the start of Cooran Buttress. Hard for the grade, but the protection is good.

1. 25m 4a Climb the slab, moving left to its arete, and mantelshelf onto a large grass ledge. Step down left and climb directly up to heather. Climb straight up the front of the pinnacle above to a pile of blocks and a belay.
2. 35m 4c Climb the overhanging groove on the left, passing a precarious block to a ledge. Continue up the awkward groove to a slab which is climbed on the right to a leaning block belay. A fine pitch.
3. 15m 4b A few metres left of the leaning block are two short steep cracks. Climb the left-hand one (as for Traitor's Gait), for 5m, until it is possible to climb diagonally into the right-hand crack (5b direct) and so to a terrace below the headwall.
4. 40m 5a Follow the slab, then cracks, directly to under the overhang near its left-hand end. Step right across a mossy streak into the crack of Cooran Buttress. Move up and then climb up left (crux) to overcome the overhang. Finish up an easy groove.
5. 5m 5b The desperate short crack on the right makes a fitting finish – or walk off abjectly.

23 Cooran Buttress   115m   Hard Severe *   (1955)

The original route of the crag, incorporating parts of Roraima, makes a good climb with a great finish. Start at a short easy right-facing corner at the foot of the right-hand grassy fault-line.

1. 25m Climb the corner a few metres to a large grass ledge on the left. Avoid the steepening continuation crack (5a direct) by climbing the easy wall 4m to its left leftwards to heather and a pile of blocks belay up on the left.
2. 35m 4b A vague arete with cracked white holds (right of the groove of Cooran Buttress Direct) is climbed for 6m then, moving to the right, continue up the wall until easier slabs are reached which lead to a leaning block belay.
3. 15m 4b Climb the awkward groove immediately behind the block to a terrace below the headwall.
4. 40m 4b The final wall has a long narrow overhang in its centre. Climb a crack system that leads up to the overhang just right of a mossy streak, then avoid the overhang by making a rising traverse rightwards to a groove on its right. Climb the

DUNGEON HILL
Cooran Buttress

Silver Slab

descent

leaning block

20. Traitor's Gait	VS **	27. Monkey Puzzle	VS **
21. Snakes and Ladders	E1 *	28. The Highway Man	HVS **
22. Cooran Buttress Direct	VS *	29. Heir Apparent	HVS **
23. Cooran Buttress	Hard Severe *	30. The Colonel's Corner	HVS ***
25. Bickerdike's Buttress	VS *	31. Cyclopath	E1 **
26. Castles in the Air	HVS *	32. Cooran Chimney	E1 *

groove moving right to spikes near the top. If this is wet, as it often is, the fluted cracks to the right (Monkey Puzzle) make a fitting finish at the same grade.

Variation: **Pitch 2** Roriama returns rightwards to the grassy fault and follows it via its left fork to the leaning block belay.

Variation: **Pitch 3** Cooran Buttress Original Route avoids this pitch by a long traverse out left to avoid the wall altogether.

24 Hell Freezes Over 120m IV,5 *** (2001)

A classic turf climb that is hardly ever in condition, requiring at least one week's hard freeze followed by snow. It follows the right-hand grassy fault more or less in its entirety. Start as for Cooran Buttress. Climb up the easy right-facing corner to where the fault steepens and move left onto a large ledge (5m). Climb the rock wall 4m left of the corner with difficulty, then move right across turf to regain the corner. Follow this over bulges to belay in an alcove (25m). Climb up and over the chockstone, to where the gully forks. Take the right fork to a terrace (30m). 2m right of the top of the gully (and 10m right of the large leaning block), climb the line of maximum turf and continue to the foot of the headwall, belaying beneath the fluted cracks and perched block of the top pitch of Monkey Puzzle (30m). Climb a turfy groove 2m right of the fluted cracks to a steepening, traverse 2m left, and make difficult moves up the Monkey Puzzle cracks. Climb more easily to the top (30m).

25 Bickerdike's Buttress 120m VS * (2002)

A pleasant meandering route slightly spoilt by some vegetated areas. However it is quick to dry and the technical difficulties on each pitch are brief and well protected. Low in the grade. Start as for Cooran Buttress.

1. 25m 4c On the right is a prominent left-leaning jamming crack with a wedged spike at its base. Gain the crack and climb it (Friend 3.5) and the vegetated rib above for a few metres to a point where you can step left across the grassy fault to the base of a buttress on the left (good stance but poor belay) Climb directly for 5m to a square sloping ledge with a corner-crack belay.

2. 30m 4b Traverse leftwards 2m to cracks which are followed through a bulge. Easier rock leads directly to a heather terrace and a leaning block belay.

3. 30m 4c Start just right of the block and climb rightwards up and across a slab to a large dubious spike on the right, at the left end of a shelf. Traverse right along the shelf to a hidden groove which is followed to a terrace. Scramble up to belay at the foot of a long narrow clean slab that leads up to the left-hand side of the roof.

4. 35m 4c A good pitch. Climb up the centre of the clean slab to the base of a thin crack that just skirts the left edge of the roof. Follow this crack (with assistance of the wider crack on its left) to an easier groove and the top. This is all about 2 or 3m right of the Direct Finish of Traitor's Gait.

26 Castles in the Air 130m HVS * (2002)

A fine series of variations on Monkey Puzzle. Start as for The Highway Man.

1. 45m 5a Climb a shallow groove to the central crack but quit this at 6m for a leftward-slanting crack system (this may also be reached rather unpleasantly direct from below). Follow the cracks up and left to an impasse below a smooth slab. Boldly climb this direct and scramble up and rightwards up heather to belay at an obvious wide crack (pitch 2 of Monkey Puzzle).

2. 25m 5a Climb a slim rightward-slanting groove just right of the crack, to step left onto a slab. Go up to flake-cracks and pull up these to the right-hand end of an overhang. Scramble up heather to the obvious crack of The Highway Man in the short wall above.

3. 30m 4c One metre right of the crack is a line of jugs up the wall. Follow these to a slab and more heather.

4. 30m 4b Although slow to dry this is still a good pitch in the wet. Down and well left of the main crack of Cyclopath and of the cracked groove finish of The Highway Man are some fluted cracks leading to a perched block (Monkey Puzzle

takes the right-hand crack). Climb the wide left-hand crack almost to the block, but then follow holds up leftwards into a crack 2m to the left (and 2m right of the spike finish on Cooran Buttress). Finish up this with interest.
Variation: **Pitch 1** The bold slab can be avoided by traversing left along a ledge 3m and climbing up a blocky gully. This reduces the pitch grade to 4c.

27 **Monkey Puzzle** 130m VS ** *(1991)*
Four engaging pitches filling the gap left of The Highway Man and starting as for that route.
1. 45m 4c Climb a shallow groove to the central crack which is followed to slabs. Continue directly up the crack onto the upper slab and the terrace.
2. 25m 4c Starting about 4m left of the tiny roof, climb a wide crack cutting through a bulge with difficulty. Follow it to a steepening, then take an obvious traverse right to a terrace.
3. 30m 4a Ahead is a short wall with a short wet chimney on the left and the obvious crack of The Highway Man in the centre. Start 1m left of this crack and climb a right-slanting line up the wall to heather. Scramble up leftwards to the final wall.
4. 30m 4b Down and well left of the main crack of Cyclopath and of the cracked groove finish of The Highway Man are some fluted cracks leading to a perched block. Climb the right-hand crack carefully avoiding the block (unless it is gone by the time you read this). Carry on up the continuation crack above.

28 **The Highway Man** 130m HVS ** *(1968)*
The original hard route of the crag is actually quite easy for the grade. Start below cracks at the lowest point of the buttress, mid-way between the right-hand grassy fault-line and The Colonel's Corner.
1. 45m 5a Climb a shallow groove to the central crack which is followed to slabs. After about 2m, traverse 3m right under a bulge, then climb a groove to a large spike. Move left onto an upper slab and climb a crack just left of the rib, then go left and over a bulge to a heather terrace (or climb the arete direct). Belay at the right-hand end below a tiny roof.
2. 25m 4c Climb directly up a crack just left of the roof to a narrow terrace and belay at the obvious short crack in the centre of the wall.
3. 30m 4a Climb the crack and scramble up heather to just below the final wall.
4. 30m 4a Climb the crack-groove line a few metres up and left of the impressive central crack of Cyclopath.

29 **Heir Apparent** 130m HVS ** *(1991)*
A fine sustained way up the crag and at the top end of the grade. Start at the foot of The Colonel's Corner.
1. 45m 5a Climb steeply up the left wall to a good flake, then swing up left and make an awkward pull onto a small ledge. The groove above leads to an easier groove in the left arete of the corner. Follow this and then go up and left to a large spike. Stand on this and swing back right into a corner which is followed to a belay under a tiny roof at the right-hand end of the terrace.
2. 25m 5a Pass the roof on the right and continue, moving slightly right to a very awkward move onto a sloping ledge. Easier climbing via a niche leads to a heather ledge.
3. 30m 4c Climb the wall above, via a crack in the rib 2m right of the short central crack taken by The Highway Man (and just down and left of the wide crack taken by The Colonel's Corner and Cyclopath), and scramble to a belay under a blunt nose at the right-hand end of the final headwall, 5m right of the impressive crack of Cyclopath.
4. 30m 5b Just up and left on the smooth wall is a long thin flake. Gain it directly with difficulty (or cheat by climbing the blunt nose above the belay and traversing left), then follow it past a small ledge until just below its top, where a step right onto a sloping foothold can be made. Swing right into the groove of The Colonel's Corner and climb the overhanging jamming crack direct.

Variation: **Direct Finish   30m   E3 5b** ******* *(1991)*
"Excellent climbing but leave your brain at home". Follow the long thin flake to its top (last runners), swing up left to holds, stand on them, and then go straight up the slight flake above to good handholds. Hand-traverse left into a scoop and finish more easily. Add a technical grade if you are short, maybe even two if you are very short.

30 The Colonel's Corner   130m   HVS *** *(1991)*
A popular classic – at the top end of the grade, particularly if you find jamming a challenge. Take lots of Friends and start up the huge corner on the right of the crag.
1. 45m 5b Climb the corner to a steep finish and exit left by a poised flake. Cracks above lead to a finish up the left-hand of two short V-grooves and a good stance (as for Cyclopath).
2. 25m 4a Follow the right-slanting groove above to a narrow ledge which is traversed rightwards to its end. Move up left to a square grass ledge, then go up a short crack to a higher ledge and belay under the obvious wide crack at the far right end of the wall.
3. 30m 4c Follow the crack for a short distance before quitting it for the arete on its right. Climb this rightwards in an unlikely and sensational position before moving up to a spike. Scramble up to a belay under a blunt nose at the right-hand end of the final headwall, 5m right of the impressive crack of Cyclopath.
4. 30m 5a On the right is an overhung groove with two large poised blocks. Climb the groove with trepidation to the top of the second block. Either climb the jamming crack of Heir Apparent above (5b) or avoid it by stepping right into either of twin grooves and an awkward finish.

31 Cyclopath   130m   E1 ** *(1982)*
Bold slab climbing (and/or desperate jamming) on the first pitch just pushes this fine route into the Extreme grade. Start at the foot of the slabby right wall of The Colonel's Corner.
1. 45m 5b Climb a groove in the slab, move left onto the wall and go up flakes to the start of a crack. Follow this widening crack to the right-hand of twin V-chimneys, which is followed to a belay on the right. An excellent pitch.
2. 25m 4c Climb the wall behind the stance to a blunt spike in the right-slanting groove of The Colonel's Corner. Follow a thin crack through the bulge above and move up to a belay as for Colonel's Corner under a wide crack at the far right end of the terrace.
3. 30m 4c Climb the wide crack direct, then scramble up to the obvious central crack in the final wall.
4. 30m 5a The fine crack, which will be found to have a sting in its tail.

32 Cooran Chimney   135m   E1 * *(1993)*
The obvious capped chimney high on the right side of the buttress proves to be a fine example of its type. Start in a grassy bay slightly down from and 20m right of The Colonel's Corner.
1. 50m 5b Scramble across a slab and up grass to a notable rock fin. Climb this to a terrace, then traverse left to the buttress proper. Follow a long groove to the base of the chimney which is climbed with difficulty to a roof (much harder, if not impossible, for the tubby). Traverse left to a belay.
2. 25m 4b Move back right above the roof and climb an easy groove to a shelf below a wall (junction with The Colonel's Corner). Traverse right along the shelf, past where The Colonel's Corner moves up, to a short corner. Climb this, pulling out left to easier ground.
3. 30m 4c Traverse 5m right to a lichenous V-groove splitting the arete. Climb this on excellent holds past a hollow flake, then follow slabs and grass to belay at the right end of the upper terrace.
4. 30m 4c Climb the obvious rightmost groove in the headwall.

The open gully to the right of the buttress is **Cooran Gully** (110m Difficult 1976) which offers various vegetated possibilities to those that like that sort of thing. To the right again are many small and broken outcrops. High in the centre of this area is a prominent hanging arete which is well worth seeking out and is best gained by traversing from the top of Cooran Buttress. **Buchan Arete** (20m HVS 5a * 2002) takes a crack in its left side, passing two large blocks with care.

LION'S HEAD

300m to the right of Cooran Buttress the rock becomes more continuous. This area derives its name from its supposed resemblance to a lion's head and mane when viewed from a distance. Two heathery terraces split the highest part of the crag into three walls, the headwall of which is impressively smooth. To the right of the headwall the crag slopes down to the right, gradually reducing in height. A descent can be made to the left from 50m or so above the finish of the climbs, down a short chimney and thence into the lower reaches of the vague open grassy **Lion's Head Gully** (Moderate c1909).

Horns of a Dilemma   57m   HVS ** (2002)

Excellent slab climbing with some hard moves on both pitches. At the left end of the crag the lower heather terrace peters out. Start 10m left of the left end of this terrace, beneath the left end of the headwall, at the right-hand of two vertical hairline cracks.
1. 22m 5a Make a rising traverse up into the left-hand crack and pull over its first bulge to a slab. Traverse the slab rightwards and round into a niche. Move up and step right onto a sloping ledge, then continue to a belay on the heather terrace. A sustained and complex pitch.
2. 35m 5b (just) Scramble up the terrace to a short chimney. Climb this with interest to more heather and traverse right onto the headwall. Climb up rightwards to gain two parallel, rightward-trending cracks. Superb climbing up these (the dilemma and crux) gains a good stance. Either walk off right, or, better, move back left and follow the upper part of the ramp finish of Aughty Star (4c).

Saddle Tramp   75m   E2 ** (1982)

An enjoyable climb at the lower limit of the grade. The major difficulties are concentrated in the last few moves of the final pitch. Start 30m down and right of Horns of a Dilemma at a prominent convex white slab below and slightly left of obvious twin diagonal cracks at 45m.
1. 40m 5a/b Climb more or less directly up the middle of the slab, the technical grade depending on the directness of the line. Climb up over grass and follow a crack on the left side of the second slab, through a bulge, to belay on a bilberry ledge below the upper right-slanting crack in the steep wall.
2. 20m 5a Climb a groove left of the crack to a horizontal break, then follow this right to a large triangular niche. From the top of the niche, a crack leads to a large sloping ledge.
3. 15m 5b Move left to a thin crack and finish boldly up this, exiting via an open niche. A flake belay lies well back to the right.

Aughty Star   115m   E1 ** (2002)

A fine series of sustained pitches, with the option of a fiercesome finale on the third. Start at the right-hand side of the initial slab of Saddle Tramp.
1. 40m 5a Scramble rightwards to gain and follow a thin crack up the right side of the slab to grass. Follow the continuation crack in the upper slab, overcoming a bulge with difficulty, to belay on the bilberry ledge on the right below the lower of two diagonal cracks.
2 20m 5b Make a rising traverse rightwards along the crack to a shallow niche. The awkward crack above leads to an easy left-leaning scoop and a rib on the left which is followed to a large ledge.
3. 45m 5b Ignore the final pitch of Saddle Tramp above left, and follow the ledge leftwards, with interest where it narrows, to join the twin right-slanting crack-lines

of Horns of a Dilemma. Make a very puzzling move up the left-hand one, exiting leftwards and follow a leftward-rising ramp to a crack on the left. Climb the crack to an overlap and step down and right to belay on a slab.

4. 10m 4a Overcome the overlap directly to finish up slabs. Alternatively, continue to follow the narrowing ramp-line leftwards (5a). Run the rope out to a good belay.

Variation: **Direct Finish   15m   E2 5b ***   *(2002)*

On gaining the ledge at the top of pitch 2, belay on a flake over to the right, below an overhanging off-width that cuts through the left end of the impressive roof of Aslan. This skin-rasping cleft succumbs only to the most masochistically determined. A Friend 5 is a useful booster of determination. Flake belay, well back.

Aslan   107m   VS   *(2002)*

A worthwhile route, better than appearances suggest, and worth doing for its unusual final pitch. It climbs walls to the right of the headwall, aiming for the obvious vertical clean crack which is situated 8m right of the conspicuous twin rightward-slanting cracks at the foot of the headwall. Start 30m down and right of Saddle Tramp, above a steepening in the grass gully beneath the crag and just next to some big granite blocks. This is 6m left of a small tree some 12m up.

1. 40m 4a Climb into a short corner and follow this to heather left of the tree. Take the short chimney 5m left of the tree to a heather ledge, then move up left to climb a wide crack. Continue to a ledge, then traverse leftwards, then up, to belay in a heathery niche.

2. 22m 4b Tricky moves up flutings on the left of the niche lead to a narrow heather ledge. Move up left onto the headwall, and continue up left a couple of metres to gain the thin vertical crack (described at the start) at its mid-point. Climb this to ledge and belay under a huge roof.

3. 45m 4c Pad right across slabs to reach and climb the crack at the far right end of the roof. From the heather ledge above, climb a short wall to finish.

In the low wall well down to the right is a very prominent short off-width crack. Immediately left of this is a curving handjam crack. This is the excellent **Jaw Jaw** (10m HVS 5b* 2002) which is hard to start, strenuous in the middle, and puzzling to finish. The off-width itself is **War War** (10m E1 5b 2002) – extra large Friends required. Right again, and just right of a pinnacle, is another short crack.

The Lion's Mane   150m   Hard Severe   *(2002)*

An interesting route on top quality heather with a little rock in places.

1. 45m 4c Climb the short crack past an awkward chockstone to slabs. Follow these leftwards and up to a horizontal break just below a rounded boss of rock. Avoid this by traversing leftwards and go up to a stance.

2. 55m 4a Traverse right 5m across grass to a clean slab and follow the left-facing corner which curves up leftwards to more grass and a large pinnacle (possible belay). Climb into a groove on the right of the pinnacle and follow it to a double bulge on the right. Hand-traverse the upper bulge with feet on the lower until it is possible to mantelshelf onto the slab above. Move up to a large area of heather and belay on a wall on the right some 15m below a double band of overhangs.

3. 50m 4a Climb the wall on the right, then cross grass diagonally rightwards to gain a clean slab. Follow the left edge of this to a huge detached flake. Tiptoe carefully rightwards onto the flake and climb the crack to the top.

To the right of the Lion's Head is the large boulder-strewn corrie known as the Cauldron of the Dungeon, an atmospheric area containing several interesting looking crags. However close approach reveals these to be of the shrinking and broken variety, and the only route recorded is **Brishie Buttress** (25m Severe 2002) which climbs the longest area of rock on the crag at the very far right-hand side of the corrie, just below the crest of the ridge. On the flat land below this corrie lies the Dungeon Stone, by repute the biggest boulder in the Galloway Hills.

In the area of minor hills between Dungeon Hill, The Merrick and Craignaw there are numerous small outcrops including the famous Devil's Bowling Green, a vast granite slab scattered with round boulders. **Craig Neldricken** (NX 447 843) is a south facing crag of excellent granite but unfortunately only 20m high and 2hrs hard walking from Glen Trool. So far it boasts only one pleasant route, **Red Otter Day** (Severe 1994) which takes the grooved rib to the left of the gully towards the left end of the crag.

CRAIGNAW

(NX 463 833)   Alt 450m   East facing   Map p166

A few climbs have been found among the large but rambling cliffs of the east face. They all rely on water ice or frozen turf to form so a good freeze is essential.

Approach: Just beyond the Clatteringshaws Loch dam, leave the A712 for the single track road at (NX 545 749), signed Craignell and Loch Dee. Follow the road round the loch, then inland to where it ends under Craigencallie crag (see below) at a car park next to the forestry gates. Continue on foot or bike, taking a right over the River Dee after 1.5km, followed by a left turn immediately thereafter and bearing left at the next major junction to about 2km before Backhill of Bush bothy where a very short track branches leftwards and leads to a nature reserve sign on the bank of the Cooran Lane. Ford this to gain the Silver Flowe and cross this in 30mins to reach the climbs.

Descent: With adequate care Shot Cleugh (see below) makes a reasonable descent in winter. Descend the Left-Hand Finish to the basin. From there, traverse horizontally right (looking in) until a rightward-trending descent can be made.

Three vague short gully lines cut the upper section of the broken face immediately under the summit. They are difficult to spot unless viewed from the north-east as they all face in that direction. The right-hand is **Goat Track Gully** (2003) which gives 150m of Grade II with an optional 15m **Direct Finish** (IV 4) up the final rock buttress. The central line is Drainpipe Gully.

Drainpipe Gully   90m   Very Difficult   *(1981)*
Climb the interesting chockstone-strewn gully in two main pitches, followed by steep grass.
Winter: **III, 4 ***   *(2002)*
Follow the summer line but quit it just before easy ground and finish up icy slabs on the right.

Silver Flow   90m   IV 4 **   *(1994)*
The deep right-facing gully, about 50m left of Drainpipe Gully, is climbed in three fine pitches. Follow the groove to a stance on a huge chockstone, then chimney up the gully making liberal use of its ice glazed right wall to a second stance. Continue up to a steep icefall which is climbed direct, though it can be avoided by traversing rightwards to a fault-line.

100m left of Silver Flow is **Broad Gully** (2003) an open grassy gully that cleaves the face from bottom to top and provides 150m of II. 100m left again is a dramatic deep break in the cliffs which bifurcates in its upper half.

Shot Cleugh   150m
Gain the basin at half-height via either of two shallow icy groove lines (II). There is now a choice of finishes. **Full Metal Jacket** (II/III 2003) takes the right-hand gully – steep ice to start but it soon eases. The **Left-Hand Finish** is a Grade I scramble. Halfway up the Left-Hand Finish on the right is:

Hidden Chimney   50m   IV 5 *   *(2003)*
Follow steepening ice to a block overhang which is awkward to overcome and leads to more steep ice. A good pitch.

Silver Sliver   50m   IV 3 *   *(2003)*
Follow Hidden Chimney for a few metres and then boldly follow an ice smear up right, then more ice and turf to the top.

The Sleigh Team   120m   III 4 *   *(2003)*
A steep and satisfying turfin' and torquin' climb, somewhat better than appearances suggest. The difficulties are largely on frozen turf and snowed-up rock and it does not require a build up of ice. High on the crag, some 75m left of Shot Cleugh, and immediately above a lone tree, is a chimney-line. Start down and slightly left of the chimney, at a small gully. Climb this over a bulge, then move up and right across easy ground to the foot of the chimney (45m). Climb the steep chimney above by excellent torquing (30m). Continue up the chimney, taking the right-hand of two steep, sloping cracks at the top (45m).

Dow Spout   250m   II/III **   *(1991)*
This classic icefall of sustained interest lies at (NX 464 829) and requires rain followed by at least a week of sub-zero temperatures to come into condition. Easy iced slabs lead to a steepening from whence a further four pitches attain the top. Descent can be made carefully by either flank and is worth spying out from below first. It is a very wet Difficult (2003).

The southern end of Craignaw is known as Snibe Hill (NX 464 816) where two Difficults were climbed in the '50s but not recorded fully. A more recent addition, **The Arete** (VS 4b, 4c, 4c 1987), follows the longest line possible on the crag in three pitches. Climb up broken rocks to a good stance and flake belay (10m). Climb the slanting slab just left of the arete via a corner-crack to a good edge then left (13m). Climb back to the arete and up to a ledge, and follow a crack for 15m to a left-trending ramp and so to the top (30m).

CRAIGLEE

(NX 462 802)   Alt 531m   Map p166

This picturesque hill is situated immediately north-east of Loch Dee.

Approach: From the car park at Bruce's Stone (NX 415 804) in Glen Trool, follow the Southern Upland Way to its high point overlooking Loch Dee, where a vague boggy path leads to the summit (1hr 45mins, 1hr 15mins by bike).

SOUND CLINT

(NX 461 797)   Alt 475m   West facing

This small wall of fine granite is situated just south of the summit. Although the climbs are short (nowhere more than 13m), the flat grassy base, good sustained climbing, superb views and excellent rock make it a worthwhile venue. A double rack of camming devices is recommended, and belays are fairly well back, so it is worth setting one rope up as a belay rope and climbing on the other doubled. The routes are described with reference to Hoo-Haa, the obvious central crack.

Pecher's Redemption   13m   E1 5b/c   *(2003)*
The thin crack 3m left of Hoo-Haa gives a good hard start but then deteriorates rather. Climb the crack to a shallow scoop. Traverse right for 2m and pull up to the top (finishing direct would require very dry conditions).

Hoo-Haa   12m   Severe 4a *   *(1994)*
The obvious central crack.

Pauchler's Wa'   12m   HVS 5a *   *(2003)*
2m right of Hoo-Haa is a short vertical crack. Climb the crack to a shallow triangular niche and finish more easily.

Caw Canny   12m   VS 4c *   (2003)

2m right again is an short vertical crack. Climb the pock marked wall between the two cracks to the break, step right and finish up the vague bulging rib (a direct finish looks possible at a similar grade).

Skelf Wa'   12m   VS 4c   (2003)

The short crack to the break. Step left to finish up the vague rib of Caw Canny.

Pernicketie Wa'   12m   E1 5b *   (2003)

Just right of Skelf Wa', climb the wall to the break via two vague potholes. Gain the shallow scoop above by a difficult move and finish boldly up the centre of this.

Keep yer Heid   12m   VS 4a *   (2003)

A bold little number, with no gear above the break. Start just right of Pernicketie Wa' below a distinctive triangular pocket and climb to the break. Go directly up the wall above on good holds but without runners.

At the right end of the main wall are a series of 'steps' below a jutting nose formed by a large bloc.

Tak a Brek   20m   HVS 5a   (2003)

Traverses the obvious wide break at two-thirds height. Start just left of the 'steps' and gain the break. Hand-traverse this for 3m then move up and make a bold and delicate foot-traverse to easier climbing and a finish up Hoo-Haa (the obvious continuation pitch is yet to be done).

Neb o' the Clint   10m   VS 4c   (2003)

Climb the 'steps' and wall to the nose and pull directly over it. Better and harder than it looks.

Right again the easy left-trending ramp-line finishing behind the block is **Heeliegalerie** (Moderate). It can also be climbed direct from its right end at Difficult.

RHINNS OF KELLS

(NX 505 954 to NX 518 829)   Map p166

This long hill ridge lies to the east of the Loch Doon – Loch Dee valley, and forms the eastern edge of the northern Galloway Hills. The rock is metamorphosed sediment and offers little in the way of rock climbing, although the eastern corries contain a fair amount of rock. Several Grade I open snow gullies were climbed one hard winter in the 1970s, in the north-east facing corrie of **North Gairy Top** (NX 512 865) on Corserine. There are also rumours of a steep metamorphic cliff hereabouts, possibly **Craigbrock**, east of North Gairy Top (NX 522 869).

On the north-east side of **Millfire** (NX 508 849) are two good icefalls of grade III/IV (1996). South of them the broad **Central Gully** gives a straighforward grade I. Further south, the north-east corrie of **Milldown** (NX 514 844) has some winter routes. Near the centre of the corrie an old drystane dyke runs up towards the col between Milldown and Millfire. **Biggar Gully** (II/III 150m 2004) climbs the gully above the dyke in a series of short pitches, including a through route behind a large chockstone near the top. **Better Gully ** (III 150m 2004) lies 250m to the right (north): it holds more ice and gives a more continuous and interesting climb. Milldown's broken east-facing flank has numerous grade I/II routes (1990s).

Approach: All these climbs are best approached from the car park at Forest Lodge (NX 553 863). 4km of forest road lead to the north side of Loch Dungeon, from where a path leads to a memorial and over the Hawse Burn. The corrie lies about 1km to the south, total walk about 2hrs from the car park, less if using a mountain bike to the memorial. The climbs could also be approached from the bothy at Backhill of Bush in about 1hr 30mins.

Minigaff Hills

South of Loch Trool and Loch Dee and north of the A712 lie the Minigaff Hills. The northern and southern sections are granite, but the hills in between are metamorphosed sediments. The best cliffs lie at the east and south of the range and are granite.

General Approach: The main access point for the northern Minigaff Hills is Glen Trool. The southern and eastern parts of the hills are accessed from the A712 to the south. The Rhinns of Kells are best accessed from the A713 to the east.

MULLDONOCH & LAMACHAN HILL

(NX 426 786) and (NX 435 770)   Map p166

Various winter routes have been recorded in the northern Minigaff Hills on the south side of upper Glen Trool. They are easily accessed in about 1hr from the Bruce's Stone car park in Glen Trool via the Southern Upland Way. The waterfalls just above the tree-line in the **Shiel Burn** (NX 435 788) are Grade III and two icefalls have been climbed on the northern flank of **Bennanbrack** (NX 439 784). **Tack it Easy** (60m II/III 2003) takes the main fall, while **Bit o' Fun** (60m II 2003) is the lesser fall slightly lower down and 100m to the right.

CRAIGENCALLIE

(NX 500 783)   Alt 350m   East facing   Map p166   Diagram p188

Craigencallie is one of the few easily accessible Galloway mountain crags. Although the rock is superbly solid epidiorite, a much finer grained granite than found elsewhere, the crag suffers from an excess of moss and vegetation which, coupled with the lack of traffic, means that only a few of the routes are really worth doing. Those few however make for at least one fruitful visit for any party whatever their ability. There is a seasonal restriction from February 15 to June 30 due to rare birds nesting.

Approach: Just beyond the Clatteringshaws Loch dam, leave the A712 for the single track road at (NX 545 749), signed Craignell and Loch Dee. Follow the road round the loch, then inland to where it ends under Craigencallie at a car park next to the forestry gates. The crag lies 15 grueling bracken-bashing minutes up the hillside to the west – watch out for adders.

ARROW BUTTRESS

This is the small steep white buttress capped with trees that lies about 80m down and left of Main Wall.

Decaffenator   12m   VS 4c *   (1991)
Near the right-hand side of the buttress is a right-trending steep slab with a crack on its right-hand side. After a hard start, climb the crack. A good little pitch.

The Grey Man   20m   HVS 5b   (1993)
Beneath the large oak tree in the centre of the crag is a horrible green undercut corner-crack. A titanic struggle to overcome the initial bulge gains the corner which is followed to grass. Either finish up broken rock on the right, or better, climb the wall on the left via a broken groove.
Variation: **The Original Way**
Quit the groove for a thin crack in the slab on the right – now totally overgrown.

Across the Barricades   20m   E4 6a **   (1992)
Good climbing, both technical and sustained, but the lack of decent gear makes it very serious and high in the grade. Start at the stepped overhanging corner in the

CRAIGENCALLIE

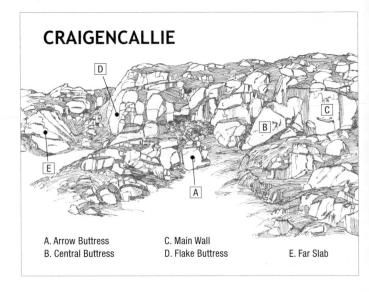

A. Arrow Buttress
B. Central Buttress
C. Main Wall
D. Flake Buttress
E. Far Slab

centre of the steep white wall forming the left side of the buttress. Follow the corner to a right-trending overlap and traverse below it to the right edge of the buttress. Move back left and overcome the overlap with difficulty. Climb directly to a small tree at the break and finish up the crack splitting the headwall to the left.

Tree Sanctuary   15m   VS 4c **   *(1993)*
Short but of great character. At the left end of the buttress is a very clean cracked wall which leads past a small tree to an overlap. Climb the intimidating cracked upper wall to a difficult finish.

CENTRAL BUTTRESS

This is the long slabby buttress which lies 30m up and right of Arrow Buttress, and is passed on the walk up to Main Wall.

Descent: By easy abseil down a grassy gully to the right.

Alligator   35m   Very Difficult **   *(1991)*
A lovely climb on excellent rock, with spaced but good protection. Start at the lowest point of the buttress at a white slab. Climb directly up the slab to a pillar and use this to surmount a bulge. Avoid the overlap above by traversing right 3m, then climb directly up slabs to spike belays.

The Scream   55m   HVS   *(1984)*
1. 35m   4c Start as for Alligator at the white slab. Climb the slab diagonally rightwards to a grass ledge. Climb straight up the black wall above until it eases, move left and climb up through the overlap. Keep moving left and go up via a scoop, then follow the left edge of the buttress to spike belays. A serious lead, the hard start of which can be avoided by climbing a few metres up Walkabout and traversing left. Either descend as above, or:
2. 20m   5a The water worn slab above, with a finish over steep blocks, is only worth doing if bone dry.

Walkabout   35m   Severe 4a *(1985)*
A potentially fine climb lurking under greenery. Start as for Alligator at the white slab. Climb the slab diagonally rightwards to a grass ledge. Continue up rightwards up a groove in the same line to a grass ledge on the left. Step back right and follow another groove to a larger grass ledge. Move left and finish up the arete. Low in the grade.

MAIN WALL

Above and right is the steep Main Wall, with a huge roof to its right. Main Wall has two large vegetation covered ledges, one up and right of the other.

Descent: Immediately to the right of Old Mortality.

Deviator   40m   VS 4c *(1977)*
A circuitous route. Start below the overhang of the lower veg-ledge, just right of a smooth black wall where it's all mossy. Gain the left-slanting chimney-groove from its right-hand end and traverse it leftwards. Take the easiest line up grass and occasional rock above until confronted by a steep wall. Avoid this by traversing diagonally rightwards, around a bulge and across a scoop until it is possible to break through the overhang via a pointy block and stupendous holds. Probably worth three stars if clean: as it is – nul points!

Eliminator   35m   E1 5b *(1977)*
Starts up the left-slanting finger-crack just right of Deviator and immediately under the left-hand end of the upper right vegetated ledge. Climb thin flake-cracks up the mossy wall to the left-hand vegetated ledge. Move up and follow the crack above (more moss) to a prominent triangular niche, then continue to gain an easier right-trending rock ramp. Go up the ramp to a horizontal flake runner, then pull left and break through overhangs. Another route that would be worth several stars if cleaned up.

Delta of Venus   30m   E4 6a *** *(1993)*
The only truly clean line on the face gives sustained and technical but reasonably protected climbing up the thin finger-searing crack 3m right of the upper right vegetated ledge. Climb past a small triangular niche to the start of the crack. The crux is reaching the first ledge, although the climbing above is hard right to the top. Quite low in the grade.

Heinous Venus   25m   E3 5c *(1994)*
The blocky shallow edge 3m right of the crack of Delta of Venus. A steep but civilised lower section leads to a blind, poorly protected, precarious and now very overgrown crux.

The Heretic   25m   E3 6a *(1995)*
Start just right of the arete, and just left of the huge overhang, at a prominent finger-crack. Climb the crack to gain a large horizontal spike. Finish up the off-width, moving leftwards for good gear. All rather dirty.

To the right of Main Wall is a huge roof, immediately to the right of which is the smooth corner of Old Mortality.

The Whirling Dervishes   30m   E2 5c * *(1998)*
Weird and wacky! A sustained and very technical, not to say contorted climb, but the gear is good. Climb Old Mortality to just below the smooth corner where a thin left-slanting crack strikes out to the arete. Traverse left with difficulty to a jug on the arete. Continue left with even more difficulty, across the slab to a pointy block on the left. Move up and back right (still difficult!) to a break in the overlap and continue more easily to gentler ground.

Old Mortality   25m   E2 6a * (1994)
Technical, well protected, and thankfully whistle like. Climb the corner. Trickier than it sounds.

FLAKE BUTTRESS

This is the slabby wall forming the right side of the obvious short grassy gully on the left-hand side of the hillside and identified by a large semidetached flake on its right flank. Climbs are described from right to left.

Descent: With care down the grassy gully.

Cranium Edge   60m   VS 4c (1977)
Exciting and worth doing despite the horrible start. Begin about 5m left of the edge beneath an obvious unattractive green chimney.
1. 30m 4c Climb the chimney to a frightening detached flake and traverse rightwards to cleaner rock. Move up rightwards and surmount the cracked overhang (crux), then go up the groove to the top of a huge flake. Move left and up to the top of another flake.
2. 30m 4b Climb up the centre of the wall (3m right of the wide crack) to a large grass ledge. Climb the steep wall at the back of the ledge, then slabs to the top.
Variation: **Corbie Steps   HVS 5a** (1994)
A direct line on the first pitch starting up the scoop 3m right of the chimney and climbing directly to a steep corner. Surmounting this gains a leftward-trending grassy crack which is soon quitted for the wall above and a belay on the huge flake. Both these climbs would merit a star if gardened.

Raven Seek thy Brother   45m   HVS (1985)
Pleasant and mainly clean but rather artificial climbing avoiding the vegetated crack as much as possible. Start about 2m further up the gully from the chimney at a large spike.
1. 35m 5a Climb the crack on the left side of the spike, pull over the bulge, move left onto the open slab and follow it until forced back into a crack. This leads to a ledge.
2. 10m 4b Finish up the wall via two jammed blocks.

Just to the left is an undercut slab rising to a wall, the steepest feature on the buttress.

The Empty Quarter   50m   E2 *** (1994)
A superb pitch, giving fine climbing up the undercut slab. Protection is good but spaced. Start directly under the centre of the overhang at a slim pillar with a square hold.
1. 30m 5b Using the pillar, make a difficult move to gain a good hold over the roof and pull up onto the slab (alternatively take the Original Start to reach the same point from the left and deduct an E-point). Climb the slabby wall until it eases, move right and then up to a ledge.
2. 20m 4a From the left end of the ledge, traverse 5m left and climb a cleaned crack and slabs to the top.

Talk to the Wind   25m   HVS 5a (1985)
A bold and very mossy route. About 15m up the gully is an open groove left of an obvious flake. Climb the groove to an ear-shaped flange of rock and continue rightwards up the slab above to avoid the overhang.

Thumbs Up   25m   VS 4c * (1993)
Delightful and, more importantly, clean. Start about 20m up the gully and about 3m right of a triangular chimney, at an overlap and three thin cracks. Follow the cracks to a large flat hold below the overlap. Step right and pull onto the upper slab which is followed to the top.

FAR SLAB

The slab to the left of the gully has a number of bold routes which despite the vegetated appearance, are on excellent clean rock.

The Cry   35m   Severe 4a *   *(1984)*
Climb the left side of the slab to a hairline crack at 20m.

The Shout   35m   Severe 4a *   *(1984)*
From the lowest point of the slab, follow the best rock to a suspect flake. Continue up the slab to a long thin crack.

Secret Garden   25m   Very Difficult *   *(1984)*
Start 5m right of The Shout. Follow the clean slab exiting rightwards past a large shallow pot-hole to another slab which is climbed to a horizontal band of quartz cracks. Step left and then go up to finish, or finish direct at Hard Severe (4b).

CRAIGDEWS

(NX 497 723)   Alt 200m   South facing   Map p166   Diagram p194

These south facing granite terraces near Murray's Monument on the A712 have been out of bounds to climbers until recently. The crag, though broken and vegetated, is bigger than appearances suggest and gives some good pitches which would benefit from more traffic. Despite proximity to the road, Craigdews feels very much a mountain crag with all that implies, good and bad! It is quite a suntrap and quick to dry. The crag lies in a goat park and the goats may take an unwelcome interest in the contents of your rucksack though they are more likely to be begging sandwiches from passing tourists. The goat park is also a nature reserve and gardening should be kept to a minimum. There is a seasonal restriction from February 15 to June 30 due to rare birds nesting.

Approach: The climbs are reached in 10 minutes from the main Goat Park car park and are described from right to left.

TREE WALLS

These lie are on the right and consist of short, steep, tree studded walls, bounded on the left by slabs overlooking the left-sloping bracken covered 'Ramp'.

Descent: The climbs end on a narrow terrace from which a careful descent may be made leftwards down the right-hand side of the Ramp Slabs. Alternatively, climb easily up the wall above and descend via the Ramp.

Cemetery Goats   27m   HVS 5a *   *(1984)*
A nice little route with a hard bouldery start. The largest, right-hand buttress has a steep corner on its left side, distinguishable by an overhang at 7m and holly tree above at half-height. Climb the corner past the overhang, moving right onto the wall at the top and so gain the bottom of the holly. Move down and right for 2m then climb the wall, squeezing painfully past the holly, to finish up a prow.

The buttress to the left, between Cemetery Goats and the leftward-sloping bracken Ramp has an obvious central depression leading to overhangs.

Vorsprung Goat Technique   27m   HVS 4c   *(2000)*
A spectacular but somewhat Fowleresque climb. Start up the central depression, until it is possible to move up right onto a ledge, or, more solidly, gain the ledge direct via cracks just left of a holly. Climb up the huge detached flake, past a small tree, to the overlap – try to avoid touching anything hereabouts. Pull through the bulge on superb holds and gain the belay terrace.

GALLOWAY HILLS

3 Amazing Technicolour Dreamgoat   27m   E1 5b ✱✱   *(2001)*
Quality, strenuous climbing. 5m left of the central depression is an overhung niche. Climb this using both cracks, then go up the left crack, with final moves right to gain a ledge. Follow the crack above to the belay terrace.

RAMP SLABS

Left of the Tree Walls is the leftward-trending, bracken covered Ramp. On the right of this and extending the full length of the Ramp is a very obvious slab. Both the following climbs are serious, and wandering from the easiest line would make them more so.

4 Dirty Old Raingoat   44m   VS 4a   *(2001)*
A very bold and rather mossy climb, which takes the centre of the right-hand, lower slab.

5 Capricorn Relish   25m   Hard Severe 4a ✱   *(2000)*
The upper pale slab is climbed directly at its cleanest point. Steady, continuous climbing with very widely spaced protection.

CENTRAL SECTION

The highest area of the crag lies directly under the summit and has two large bays at its base. Flat Boulder Bay is broad with a large flat boulder on its floor and lies to the right. Central Bay is directly under the summit, more square-cut and bounded on its left by an easy white slab. The wide bracken covered Halfway Terrace divides the Central Section horizontally at 45m. Above it the largest section of rock is Main Wall which is split by a distinctive thin crack and has a small overhang (the Nose) on its left.

6 Das Goat   108m   Very Difficult ✱   *(2000)*
This pleasant route follows the easiest line up a poorly defined rib leading from Flat Boulder Bay to the summit. Start in the bay beneath its steep central wall.
1. 23m Climb a short rib just left of the steepest part of the slabby wall to a white scoop, then traverse left under a heathery chimney to a juggy rib and climb this to the left end of a thin grass terrace.
2. 30m Traverse 2m right, then take a rising line rightwards up the wall until it is possible to gain a ledge on the left from where a scramble leads to Halfway Terrace (it is also possible to gain the wall further right, and also to climb the rib to the left of the stance).
3. and 4. 30m, 25m Either traverse off right to descend via the Ramp, or continue more easily up the broken rib to the summit in two pitches.

7 Up Perisgoat!   53m   VS ✱   *(2002)*
Good climbing via direct variations on the first two pitches of Das Goat, starting as for that route.
1. 23m 5a Follow Das Goat via the short rib to the white scoop. Make hard but well protected moves up rightwards from this to a bald slab, then follow the crack above, finishing boldly up the juggy wall. Traverse left to belay at the end of the thin grass terrace.
2. 30m 4c Traverse 2m right, then take a rising line rightwards up the wall until it is possible to step down left onto a large patch of heather. Leave this via its left rib to gain the obvious central groove which is followed to an exciting exit and a scramble to the terrace. Traverse right to descend via the Ramp.

8 Goathouse of Fleet   52m   VS 4c   *(2001)*
Although the main difficulties are avoidable, this route has some good moves and

The Colonel's Corner, HVS, Dungeon of Buchan. Climber Chris Bonington
(photo Stephen Reid)

provides access to Halfway Terrace. Climb a rib on the left-hand side of Flat Boulder Bay to its top, then follow slabs above on the right (without deviation into the adjacent undergrowth). Bypassing the slabs by undignified heather-pulling lowers the grade to Severe.

9 Goats of Delirium   110m   HVS *   (2000)
Three good but disjointed pitches give an enjoyable route to the summit at the top end of the grade. Although it is still a bit vegetated, a little traffic should soon improve this, and an extra star would become due. Start in Central Bay, just right of the easy slab. Hard for the grade.
1. 45m 4c Climb the middle of the steep wall at the back of the bay, then move left at the steepening to gain a grassy groove. Move up this a little and then move right with difficulty to gain a flake. Continue up, and then right to a small ledge. Climb a groove just left of this with difficulty to Halfway Terrace. Belay beneath a small isolated buttress down and right of Main Wall.
2. 35m 5a Climb the small isolated buttress leftwards to the foot of Main Wall (underneath the thin crack). Follow parallel cracks on the left side of the wall, either by foot traversing the lower crack into a groove (easier but bolder) or moving up to the upper crack and following this (5b, but better protected) to the Nose. Boldly overcome the Nose (crux) and follow the right-trending ramp above for 7m to gain a horizontal crack. Difficult moves straight up lead to the Upper Terrace.
3. 30m 5a Above is a smooth upper wall. Climb the slim right-facing groove at its right-hand end to gain a grass ledge on the right. Climb a groove above until it is possible to move up right and onto the top of a large detached flake, from which a rib leads to the top.

0 Central Route   110m   VS *   (ca 1959)
A fine route to the summit. Start in Central Bay as for Goats of Delirium.
1. 45m 4c Climb the easy slab on the left and then follow the rib above to a small sapling. Make a hard bold move left and continue up the rib to Halfway Terrace. Belay down and right of Main Wall under a small isolated buttress.
2. 35m 4c Walk left some 5m to just left of the Nose and climb a mossy wall for 4m until it is possible to step right onto a ledge. Move up right again, on top of the Nose, and follow a right-trending ramp to a horizontal crack. Traverse right with difficulty into a grassy chimney and avoid this via a large flake on its right. Belay on the Upper Terrace to the right of the smooth upper wall.
3. 30m 4b Climb a grassy left-facing corner 3m to the right of the smooth wall, to a smaller terrace. Go 1m up a wide corner, then foot traverse left along a huge flake to gain the right-hand side of a large unstable looking flake. Climb this and the rib above. Scrambling remains.
Variation: **Original Finish   VS 5a**
Pitch 3 of Goats of Delirium.

1 Nanny State   15m   E2 6a **   (2004)
Start from the Halfway Terrace and climbs the prominent thin crack in the slab to the right of pitch 2 of Goats of Delirium. Exit via pitch 3 of Goats of Delirium.

2 Astrogoat   48m   VS 4c *   (2001)
A long, sustained pitch. A second star may be due once it has had a bit of traffic. Start from the left end of Halfway Terrace, 10m left of the Nose (this is just right of a long low mossy wall and about 10m up bracken from a large rock spike). Follow an obvious line of handholds up the clean wall for 15m until a step left leads to a grass ledge. Above, follow cracks on the left side of a flake through a bulge, then continue to the Upper Terrace which has a smooth upper wall on the right. Climb the wall directly above, then a final wall of dark metamorphic rock. Easy but unprotected metamorphic slabs lead to the top.

The Spout of the Clints, V,5, Cairnsmore of Fleet. Chris Bonington on the first ascent.
(photo Stephen Reid)

CRAIGDEWS

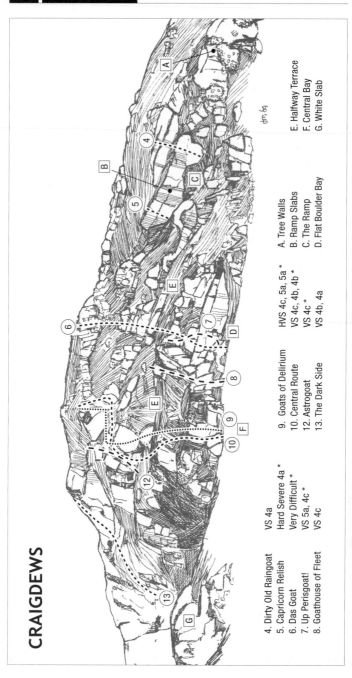

4. Dirty Old Raingoat   VS 4a
5. Capricorn Relish   Hard Severe 4a *
6. Das Goat   Very Difficult *
7. Up Perisgoat!   VS 5a, 4c *
8. Goathouse of Fleet   VS 4c

9. Goats of Delirium   HVS 4c, 5a, 5a *
10. Central Route   VS 4c, 4b, 4b *
12. Astrogoat   VS 4c *
13. The Dark Side   VS 4b, 4a

A. Tree Walls
B. Ramp Slabs
C. The Ramp
D. Flat Boulder Bay
E. Halfway Terrace
F. Central Bay
G. White Slab

13 The Dark Side   100m   VS   *(2004)*
About 100m left of Central Bay is a fallen tree and 7m right of this a small rock
pedestal abuts the cliff. Start at the base of this, 3m below an easy right-slanting
rock ramp.
1. 50m 4b Step up and follow a line of square jugs rightwards to a rib. Go up this
and over a bulge to a grass ledge. Climb short slabs above to grass and run the rope
out to a belay well left of the upper buttress at a small roof.
2. 50m 4a Traverse right on grass until under a roof at the left side of the upper
buttress. Climb the obvious diagonal line up rightwards to a small grass ledge.
Continue straight up to the summit ridge and continue to a thread belay. Techically
easy, but virtually devoid of protection.

WHITE SLAB

A small white slab of glacier scoured granite stands alone some way below and left
of Central Bay. The rock is excellent but the belay abysmal (0.5 Friend).

Three Men in a Goat   12m   Severe 4a   *(2001)*
Mantelshelf onto the very left end of a long ledge and climb up to a small
triangular ledge under the overlap. Pull over this rightwards to a crack which leads
to the top.

One Man, One Goat   12m   Very Difficult   *(2001)*
Start as for Three Men in a Goat, but climb up leftwards to a short black chimney.
Up this to a black roof on the right. Avoid this on the right via a crack and so to the
top.

Just Kidding   8m   Hard Severe   *(2004)*
The fine little rib on the left of the buttress is hard to start. Finish up the short
groove on the left.

Cairnsmore of Fleet Range

The Cairnsmore of Fleet Range are the southernmost of the Galloway Hills and lie
south and east of the A712. They are bordered to the north-east by the Palnure
Burn and the Minnigaff Hills and extend almost to the Solway Coast in the south.
The most significant summits are Craignelder and Cairnsmore of Fleet. While the
crags hereabouts are not as dramatic as those further north, they still offer
worthwhile granite routes in fine remote settings, and with good icefall potential
too.

CORWAR

(NX 483 705)   Alt 100m   South facing   Map p166

This small but steep buttress of compact granite lies sandwiched between the A712
and the Palnure Burn, on the northern edge of the Cairnsmore of Fleet Range. It
is quick to approach, fairly fast to dry, catches plenty of afternoon sun, and has a
beautiful outlook south-east over Bargaly Glen. The area is seriously midge ridden
in summer but makes a good venue at other times. The Forestry Commission has
kindly felled numerous trees around the crag to improve the climbing. Protection
can be tricky on some of the routes and a good selection of small camming devices
is recommended.

Approach: Park in the large lay-by near the weird lookout platform at the Glen of
the Bar (NX 479 707) on the A712. Follow a trail down and across a stream, then
take a bearing of 120 degrees (east by south-east) through woods (paint marks on
trees indicate the way) to the crag (10mins). The crag sits above a forest track
which can be accessed 2km further south along the A712 (signed Corwar and

Dallash). The Forestry Commission allow pedestrian and bicycle access along this track, but no vehicles please (25mins on foot).

The most prominent feature of the crag is the shallow chimney-groove of Bigger Than Tigger on the left. Further right, the obvious right-to-left slanting break, passing a smooth black niche (which at the time of writing contains a small birch sapling), is taken by Ruta Aurelio. The lengths given are the route lengths – a further 10m is required to belay.

Pinus Worship   30m   Very Difficult * (1998)

Good but contrived climbing at the left-hand end of the crag. Climb the rib on left side of the slab beneath the huge overhang left of Bigger Than Tigger, then the left wall of the overhang itself, finishing on an excellent hold. Climb the slab above (possible tree belay), move right and climb the blunt rib above on good holds.

Bigger Than Tigger   23m   Severe 4b * (1998)

The obvious chimney-groove near the left-hand end of the crag, stepping left at the top to finish up the steep wall on excellent holds.

Alpamayo no More   25m   VS 4c * (1999)

Follow the groove of Bigger Than Tigger for 7m, then step out right. Climb the wall above, via a shallow cave, straight to the top, passing right of two small trees.

Variation: **Direct Start   E1 5b** (2000)

Climb the steep fingery wall and lichenous bulge above, just right of Bigger Than Tigger to join the ordinary route. Continuing via the FRCC Finish gives a good pitch.

The Prune   30m   VS 4b ** (1998)

An excellent sustained route that is low in the grade. Follow the groove of Bigger Than Tigger for 5m, then follow the diagonal crack-line out rightwards across the face for about 5m to join the Peach. Either finish up the shallow groove of the Peach directly above, or, better, make one move up and continue rightwards to the dark blocky scoop on the right and then move back up the left-slanting ramp finish of Ruta Aurelio to the top.

The Peach   25m   HVS/E1 5a ** (1999)

A climb with a hightist crux! Start at the stump 5m right of Bigger Than Tigger. Climb directly up the wall until it eases and move up slightly right to a shallow groove and finish up this. The crux is low down and is protected by a peg runner. For anyone much under 6 feet however, the crux is clipping the peg and is rather serious – a cunning shallow nut placement can be found on the right by the diligent.

Variation: **FRCC Finish   VS 4c ** (2000)

Artificial but excellent climbing; perhaps more in keeping with the hard start. From above the peg, move up and left into the shallow cave on Alpamayo No More. Leave this on the right and climb directly up the wall above on excellent holds.

Plum Line   30m   E2 5b *** (1999)

A direct line up the highest section of the crag taking in the obvious short open pink groove at half-height. Superb and not too technical – take the grade as a reflection of the quality of the pegs. Start at the lowest rocks and climb the slabs above until stopped by a smooth bulge. Move left and up (very shallow peg runners) and make a difficult mantelshelf into the pink groove above where wire a low on the right helps to calm the nerves. Climb out of the groove on its right and make a long reach to gain easier ground. Move 1m up the leftwards-slanting ramp of Ruta Aurelio, step right onto the impressively bulging but easy headwall, and saunter to the top.

Corwar Wall   23m   HVS 5a ** (1999)

An excellent and well protected route with an exciting finish, taking the easiest line up this part of the crag. Start near the left-hand end of a narrow vegetated ledge directly beneath the smooth black niche containing a small birch sapling. Climb up a short blocky corner and move right to, and up over, a small overhang, then climb up to the left-slanting break of Ruta Aurelio. Follow this up left to just before the smooth niche containing the sapling, reach upwards for a jug and hand-traverse (rapidly) rightwards to finish up easy slabs.

Nutcase 22m E2 5b ** *(2000)*

Good but bold and intimidating climbing directly up the wall between Corwar Wall and Tutti Frutti. Start at the right-hand end of the grass ledge, 3m right of Corwar Wall and directly under the point of the 'V' formed where the left and right-slanting overlaps meet. Climb a slim fault to a ledge on the left and junction with Corwar Wall. Pull directly over the overhang above, 1m to the right of Corwar Wall, and go up to a dubious block under the overlap. Move onto this from the left, place your last gear, make a wish, and go for it.

Tutti Frutti 22m E1 5b ** *(2000)*

The obvious right-slanting fault provides a super little route, quite hard for the grade but with gear where it matters. Start 2m right of Nutcase and 2m left of the stump at the right end of the crag. Climb straight up the wall to a short, shallow groove and up this to the dubious block under the overlap. Follow the rightward-slanting overlap to a thin crack and climb this to a well earned rest. Search fruitlessly for a well earned runner and then make the last few moves without one.

The Harvesters 20m E4 5c * *(2000)*

Seriously bold climbing up the wall to gain the thin crack-line just right of Tutti Frutti. Start at the large tree stump near the right-hand end of the crag. Climb straight up the wall to a small overlap (assorted small wires in slanting cracks above). Move up to a sloping foothold, then straight up the wall above to a good hold and an obvious wire in the crack. Climb the short rib and crack above, right of the top crack of Tutti Frutti, to gain a slab which leads more easily to the top.

Ruta Aurelio 35m E1 5b ** *(1999)*

A good climb, low in the grade, taking the obvious right to left-rising traverse in its entirety. The crux is short and well protected. Start 2m right of the stump, and 1m left of the pink streak at the right-hand end of the crag. Make a bold rising traverse leftwards up to the break and follow this to the smooth niche with the birch sapling. Cross the blank slab just left of the small birch (crux) to a dark blocky niche and an easy finish up the leftward-slanting ramp.

The Midge 10m HVS 5a *(2000)*

Makes the best of the rock on the far right of the crag. Start as for Ruta Arelio. Climb directly up the wall to a good nut in a short crack. Traverse horizontally right 3m and move boldly to the top. The obvious direct finish is unclimbed.

200m further up the glen, and visible from the forest road, is a 5m slab of granite which gives some good bouldering.

CRAIGNELDER

(NX 505 698) Alt 601m Map p166

This northern outlier of Cairnsmore of Fleet exhibits lots of excellent granite – unfortunately little is joined together in any way meaningful to the rock climber. The slabby crag overlooking the A712 and facing Murray's Monument is Big Gairy, while the much better Craig an Eilte lies much higher, and slightly further to the south but is hidden from view. Both crags require some effort to reach.

Approach by foot: Park at the Talnotry Forest Trail car park (NX 487 716) on the A712. Walk south past a disused campsite and follow a new forest track that branches off right to a new bridge. Cross the bridge and turn left immediately up the bank of the stream, until the edge of the forest can be followed round (rough

(GALLOWAY HILLS)

going). From the top of this Big Gairy is across and right (45mins); alternatively, as the forest has recently been cleared, follow the forest track until directly under the crag and then strike directly up to it (also rough going). Craig an Eilte lies up the hill to the right (a further 45mins).

Approach by bike: Using the forest tracks can shorten this approach a little. Park as above and bike along the forest track over the bridge and downhill to eventually reach a T-junction. (The same point can be reached by following the Corwar bike approach but turning right over a bridge just before the crag). Turn left and follow the track which first winds and then zigs right and zags left up the hill. At the end of the zag, quit the track for a forest ride that crosses Crochan Burn and leads to open hillside from which either crag can be reached in about 30mins – 50mins in all if you're fit. Keep an eye out for adders.

Talnotry Trickle (NX 492 707, II 2003) is the obvious 80m icefall situated on the hillside to the left of Big Gairy. It is quickly reached from the road by following either of the Big Gairy approaches.

BIG GAIRY

(NX 492 701)   Alt 325m   West facing

This area of vegetated terraces and slabs is split by a grassy gully. Apparently, starting immediately left of this, at the lowest rocks, lies **Pale Face** (65m VS 1984). From the right toe of a band of light coloured slabs, climb easily to a ledge beneath a short crack (15m). Climb the wall above leftwards (crux) to a ledge and belay (15m). A delicate pitch. Twin cracks lead to a ledge (5m). Climb the slabs on the right to a bulge, move left and climb a short corner. Take a final slab and bulge direct to easier ground (30m). If you succeed in locating this climb the guidebook writer would like to hear from you.

CRAIG AN EILTE

(NX 498 698)   Alt 450m   West facing

This long cliff forms an escarpment above, behind and slightly south of Big Gairy, not far from the summit of Craignelder. The crag's alternative name, The Flesh Market, derives from the number of sheep that fell over it to their doom in the days when there were sheep on these hills rather than trees.

Though much of the cliff consists of vegetated slabs, high on the left-hand side above a large boulder scree slope, is the prominent Eilte Tower which has clean rock and the dramatic hanging arete of Gloom Super Direct. A few further climbs lie above the tower and more to its left and right. Although the routes are short, the magnificence of the remote surroundings, the absence of bird restrictions, the quick drying nature of the crag make it worthwhile.

In winter the crag can offer a few icy lines though its aspect and proximity to the sea mean that a prolonged freeze and an alpine start are essential

Eilte Slabs

These routes lie left of Eilte Gully, the gully left of Eilte Tower and are described right to left. Some 5m left of Eilte Gully is **Dream of Grey Mares** (II 2003) which follows a thin icy groove line. 30m left of Eilte Gully is Hind Gully, a grassy gully with a short wall at its top. Although the following routes are short, nowhere more than 20m, they are very quick to dry and on excellent rock. **Snozzle** (VS 4b 2002) climbs directly up the rib on its right. **Slab-u-Like** (HVS 4c 2002) boldly climbs the centre of the slab on its left via a fluted scoop to finish just right of a poised block, and **Slabadabadoo** (VS 4c 2002) follows cracks on the left via a dodgy block, to finish just left of the poised block. **Rock Lobster** (Severe 1990) takes a slabby line in between Hind and Eilte Gullies but its exact whereabouts is uncertain.

Eilte Tower

The first route starts left of the hanging arete, in the entrance to Eilte Gully, the gully left of the tower.

Flowers of the Forest   45m   III 4 **   *(2003)*
Just left of the initial chimney of Gloom is a rock groove. Climb this on turf, then continue up the mixed ground above (as for Gloom) to belay on the neck of the tower at 25m. Traverse rightwards across icefalls (line may vary) to exit from an icy niche (20m).

Gloom   25m   Severe 4a   *(1984)*
Atmospheric and awkward climbing. Start at the left edge of Eilte Tower, directly under the blade like roof. Thrutch up the off-width to the roof, or, more elegantly, climb the rib on its left, and move up left to a large ledge. Traverse left again and finish up greasy grassy corners.
Variation: **Direct Finish   HVS 5a**   *(1992)*
A better finish. From the large ledge, mantelshelf onto a small ledge and move boldly up onto the wall. Toe traverse right to the arete and finish up this.
Variation: **Super Direct   E2 5c ***   *(1992)*
From the large ledge, stride right onto a good foothold on the lip of the roof and follow the arete, mainly on the right. Good bold climbing.

The Original Route   20m   Hard Severe 4b **   *(1978)*
An obscure gem. Start just right of Gloom at a narrow crack. Follow this and the prominent right-trending groove system to a steep finish up the impending crack.

The Flesh Market   25m   HVS 4c   *(1992)*
Climb the steep wall 1m right of the Original Route crack on good holds to a slim block ledge. Traverse right over a large flake, then go slightly downwards onto footholds on the wall. Move right and follow the wide jamming crack past a worrying flake to the top.

Eilte Pinnacle Rib   25m   Difficult   *(1982)*
Just right again, a short chimney with huge poised blocks leads to a ledge. Follow a second chimney on the left of a large pinnacle, to a rib which is climbed on good holds mostly on the right.

Gogledd Tower

The upper right wall of Eilte Gully, above the finish of The Original Route etc. contains a couple of nice climbs.

Guledig   20m   Severe 4c   *(1992)*
A useful finish for the lower routes. Start at an overhung groove in the arete on the right of the tower. Make a difficult move to good holds, then follow the arete above to the top.

Gwry Y Gogledd   20m   E2 5b *   *(1992)*
The impressive north facing wall overlooking Eilte Gully gives a fine sustained and well protected route. Start at the right-hand side of the wall and climb to a shallow V-niche in the centre of the face. Traverse right to footholds on the arete, then go up and left up cracks to the top.

No Hawkers or Campbells   20m   HVS 5a   *(1992)*
The left-hand side of the wall is harder than it looks. Climb strenuously up cracks to the large depression, then go up the left-hand crack to the top. A good little pitch.

GALLOWAY HILLS

Weeping Wall

This is the pale, moss flecked (and usually wet) wall immediately right of Eilte Pinnacle Rib. At the base of the right-hand side of this wall is a shallow cave. The routes, though rather mossy and slow to dry, are on good granite and provide some atmospheric long pitches.

Adder Country   30m   VS 4c   *(2000)*
Start round to the right of Eilte Pinnacle Rib, at the left-hand side of the wall. Climb a short blocky pinnacle to gain a short chimney on the right of Eilte Pinnacle. Climb the chimney for a few metres and then leave it for the wall on the right. Climb up this moving leftwards to a steep wall (crux) which leads further leftwards. Climb through the juggy bulge on the left and go up easier ground to finish via a wide crack.

Kerb Crawler   30m   Severe 4b *   *(1991)*
A good route with some airy climbing. Start at an open corner in the centre of the wall, 9m left of the cave. Climb the corner to a ledge. Step left and climb a second corner to another ledge. Move left and climb steep cracks to finish via ledges and large granite blocks.
Variation: **Original Start**   Climb the short blocky pinnacle 2m left of the groove and gain the right-slanting ramp that leads to a junction with the direct start at the top of the first groove.

Y Geifr   40m   HVS 5a *   *(2000)*
Good climbing taking a direct line up the wall at its highest point and passing through the huge square-cut scoop high on the crag. Start at the blunt, cracked rib in between the groove of Kerb Crawler and the stalactite of Hall of the Mountain King. Climb the cracked rib and wall above to a ledge. Traverse left to a fine rib, which is climbed on superb holds to another ledge. Climb up the steep slab above into a short groove on the left side of the square-cut scoop and leave this by means of a half-nelson on the left followed by a strenuous mantelshelf. Weave strenuously through blocky corners directly above.

In the Hall of the Mountain King   40m   VS 4b *   *(2002)*
A pitch of some character following the obvious line of weakness via niches up the centre of the wall. Start at a crack with a stalactite hold some 6m left of the cave and 3m right of the open groove of Kerb Crawler. Climb directly up to a narrow ledge, then make a rising traverse to the right up stepped holds to a flake-crack which leads to a huge slabby niche. Traverse left across this and gain a rib on the left which leads back right to a steep groove. Go up this to a grass ledge and continue up a crack and bulging ledges above until it is possible to step left onto a large sloping ledge and a puzzling finish up the hanging arete.

Diagonal Route   40m   VS   4c *   *(1997)*
Another good route taking the obvious diagonal line rising from left to right. At the upper end of the grade. Start as for Hall of the Mountain King. Climb up a few metres to a ramp-line rising to the right and follow this until it runs out, then move directly up via a short crack (crux). Continue straight up to finish via ledges.

Coel Fain   40m   E2 5c *   *(2000)*
Takes in the prominent hanging arete on the right of the square-cut scoop of Y Geifr. Low in the grade. Start in the cave. Climb the overhanging left arete of the cave to a jug below a sloping ledge. Make a long reach left for a good hold and pull up to easier ground. Climb directly up the wall above onto the rightward-sloping ramp of Diagonal Route, then move up and surmount a hollow hanging shield of rock. Continue directly up the clean wall above (crux) to a large grass ledge (the original way (E1 5b) avoided this wall by climbing a mossy overhanging

groove on the left). Traverse left a few metres until above the square-cut scoop, and climb a steep mossy crack (just right of the finish of Y Geifr) through bulging rock to the top.

Some 100m to the right of Eilte Tower are a pair of similar but lesser towers. **Minas Tirith** (VS 4c 2002) is the left-hand and better of the two and gives a good steep 25m pitch following the undercut rib up into a blocky niche from the top of which a hand-traverse right gains a V-groove splitting the top of the tower. **Minas Morgul** (Severe 4b 2002) on the right is longer but more broken. The blank upper wall is avoided by a crack on the right. Right again some 150m is a vague turfy open corner that gives some good ice in a hard freeze. This is **Hinkes's Downfall** (50m III 2003). Some 500m down and right of the main cliff, at the lowest point of the escarpment, is a deeply recessed corner-bay. **Gorm** (25m III,3 2003) climbs the back of the bay, the lower bulge being climbed by steep ice, just right of centre. A walk of 150m uphill from this climb leads to a 20m icefall (II/III).

CAIRNSMORE OF FLEET

(NX 502 671) Alt 711m Map p166

This massive whaleback of a mountain, a graveyard to aircraft during WWII, possesses disappointingly little climbing though it does boast two of the best winter routes in the area, and, on its outlying spurs, the useful practice outcrops of the Clints of Dromore and Loch Grannoch Crag.

CLINTS OF THE SPOUT

(NX 509 667) Alt 450m East facing

Very remote with a wonderful atmosphere.

Approach: Leave the A75 5km south-east of Newton Stewart at the white farmhouse of Muirfad (NX 457 628). Follow the road to a three way junction under the disused sandstone railway viaduct. Turn right off the tarmaced road and follow the track through the centre of the viaduct into the Cairnsmore Estate. Continue on this track alongside the Cairnsmore Burn, to skirt the large white estate building on the left. Turn left to a small car park (NX 472 641).

Follow the track to its end and cross the field to a gate hidden by gorse bushes, in the far left-hand corner. Follow the path to the summit of Cairnsmore of Fleet (NX 502 671). Descend north-east to the Nick of the Saddle (the col between Cairnsmore of Fleet and Meikle Mulltaggart) and then, southward to the cliffs (2hrs).

Due to their aspect the routes catch the sun all morning; a prolonged and severe freeze of at least a fortnight and an alpine start would seem to be essential for good winter conditions.

The Spout of the Clints   160m   VS *   (1992)
The obvious watercourse in the centre of the crag may become easier in a drought.
1. 50m 4b Scramble up the gully bed with a hard move to overcome a chockstone.
2. 60m 4c Can be split. Climb the waterchute first on the left, then on the right, then scramble up the gully.
3. 50m 4c Climb the left wall of the gully, well back from the fall, to gain a right-slanting ramp. Follow this back into the gully and the top.
Winter: **V,5 ****   (1997)
A superb sustained climb. The final pitch is the crux and not too well protected.

Smoar Tort   120m   IV,4 **   (1997)
The spectacular icefall on the right of the crag gives an excellent climb in three or four pitches with the final thin smear up the top slab being the crux.

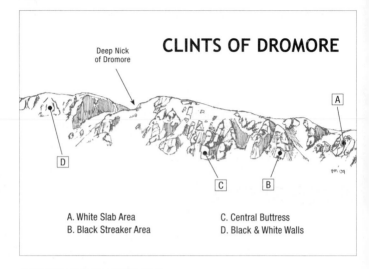

CLINTS OF DROMORE

Deep Nick
of Dromore

A. White Slab Area
B. Black Streaker Area

C. Central Buttress
D. Black & White Walls

CLINTS OF DROMORE

(NX 547 641)   Alt 200m   South facing   Map p166   Diagram p202

The impressive towering pillars of this extensive crag mysteriously vanish when approached, to be replaced by broken and easy angled heathery slabs. Nevertheless this is a good, exceptionally quick drying, sunny and sheltered venue, particularly suitable for those looking for lower grade routes. Only the main lines are described and many other variations have been climbed over the years.

The Clints of Dromore are part of the Cairnsmore of Fleet National Nature Reserve, and are used by several species of protected nesting birds. Scottish Natural Heritage ask climbers to observe a seasonal restriction (15th February to 30th June) to avoid disturbing them. However, the nest sites vary from year to year, so check the MCofS website (see Environment Notes), or phone the NNR office (01557 814435). Keep an eye out for adders.

Approach: The visitor centre is reached from Gatehouse of Fleet via the B796 and the minor road and track leading to the old viaduct across the Big Water of Fleet. Walk west along the old railway for a short distance to a stile. Follow the path up towards the crags to the remains of an old wall with a gate in the fence to its left. Continue to the remains of a second old wall at a point where the fence almost reaches the foot of the crag (15mins). Some 200m beyond this is a prominent black streaked slab with a large flake boulder at its foot. This is Black Streaker Slab.

To the right of Black Streaker Slab is a broad grassy gully and right of this more rock containing the prominent **White Slab** (30m Very Difficult). **Far Right Rib** (Moderate) is the rib on the right of this area. **Left Right Slab** (10m Very Difficult) is the slab on the left side of Far Right Rib. All were climbed in 1981.

BLACK STREAKER SLAB

The routes are described from right to left.

Flake Climb   45m   Hard Severe   *(1982)*
Pleasant but protectionless climbing up the white, right-hand side of the slab. Start on top of the large flake boulder, just right of the streak. Go up the slab then trend up right to the foot of the curving overlap. Step left over the lowest part of the

overlap and continue up to belay on spikes in a heather bay.

Black Streaker   45m   Very Difficult   *(1981)*
Start just left of the black streak at a rib. Climb the rib and slab to a fault-line and
follow it up leftwards, stepping right at the top, and go up to the Flake Climb
heather bay belay.

Left Rib   45m   Severe   *(1982)*
Start at the second rib to the left of the black streak and climb its right side to a
small overlap. Continue up and slightly rightwards to finish up Black Streaker.

CENTRAL BUTTRESS

Some 150m left of Black Streaker Slab lies Central Buttress which provides the most
continuous area of rock on the crag. A useful identification point is that the fence
directly below the crag drops back down to the forest. Belays need searching for –
a Hex 9 is useful.

Left Edge   55m   Difficult   *(2001)*
Start at the very left edge of the buttress. A pleasant route.
1. 35m Climb up into a scoop and follow a leftwards-trending groove, then onto
the rib on the right and up to a ledge. Ignore the crack above and instead take a
diagonal line up and then horizontally leftwards across a scoop to follow a short
crack through a bulge to a ledge (round spike high up broken rib on right).
2. 20m Climb up then traverse left to a white slab. Traverse this left to a spike.
Gain and follow the rib above or, alternatively drop down left to the foot of a fine
slab which is climbed to the top (4b).

Left of Centre   55m   Difficult   *(1981)*
Start as for Left Edge. Another pleasant route.
1. 35m Climb up into a scoop and climb up slightly rightwards, keeping to the
right of a rib above, to a ledge. Climb straight above the ledge, up a corner, passing
some prominent quartz lumps, to gain another ledge (round spike high up broken
rib on right).
2. 20m Follow the easy rib above to the top.

Just Left of Centre   50m   Difficult   *(2001)*
Very heathery, but surprisingly, not a bad climb. Start just left of Central Buttress and
follow the easiest line to a heather ledge at 10m. Climb a steepening above just right
of a pinnacle and gain a heather filled groove which is followed to the top.

Central Buttress   50m   Hard Severe ★★   *(1978)*
The original route of the crag is a pokey little number, but on excellent rock. Start
4m to the right of its left edge, just left of a narrow black streaked slab. Climb up
a rib and over an overlap to a heather ledge at 10m. Climb the steep white scoop
above with difficulty. A serious run-out up slabs followed by a bold crack in the
right side of the crest of the buttress leads to the crest which is followed to the top.

Quoth the Raven   50m   HVS 5a ★   *(2001)*
A pleasant eliminate with good protection where it matters. Start just right of
Central Buttress and climb the narrow black streaked slab to a heather ledge at
10m. Climb the crack to the right of the white scoop, moving right onto the open
face. Pull back left into the crack and follow an easier slab to a white bulge
between the ridge of Central Buttress on the left and the groove of Comfy Chair on
the right. Climb the slab above passing a poised flake near the top with care.

Just to the right and up at the level of the heather ledge is a grey and white
streaked slab. The next two routes start by scrambling up rock and grass 10m to
the base of this slab.

The Comfy Chair   50m   VS 4c *   *(2001)*
Another pleasant route, thoroughly enjoyable despite the lichen. Start on the left side of the slab, just right of a heather filled crack, and only a metre or so right of the crack on Quoth the Raven. Climb straight up for 5m to gain a flat jug on the arete on the left. Move up and left to easier slabs and then gain the upper of twin right-slanting groove-ramps. Follow this to a tricky leftwards exit. The jug on the arete was originally gained by starting as for Quoth the Raven (HVS 5a).

The Spanish Inquisition   50m   VS 4c *   *(1991)*
Very nice climbing but slow to dry. Start at the left edge of the grey and white streaked slab as for Comfy Chair. Make a rising traverse rightwards above large heather clumps and then move up to an overlap. Step right over this, then go rightwards across and up a slab to the left-hand end of a conspicuous right-trending overlap. Follow the overlap up and right, then cross it and trend right to the top.
Variation: **Direct Finish   HVS 4c**   *(2001)*
Follow the original route over the first overlap, then climb straight up, almost to the heather crack on the left. Step across right to the left end of the second overlap and climb directly to the top.

Just right again (and 25m right of Left Edge) is an enticing clean rib.

Spare Rib   30m   Severe *   *(1978)*
Start at the left edge of the rib, or directly underneath it, or (reduces standard to Very Difficult) a few metres to its right. Climb the rib, keeping to its left side throughout. Easier variations may be made to the right.

Round and up the wide gully to the left of Central Buttress are two short slabs, one above and left of the other. These give excellent short problems at Severe and VS respectively.

Some 300m to the left of Central Buttress is the Deep Nick of Dromore, an open wide grassy gully. On the right of the entrance to this is a fine short slab from whose bottom right corner starts the enjoyable **Diagonal Line** (10m Difficult 2002). The other obvious lines on this slab have also been climbed, all are of similar standard.

BLACK & WHITE WALLS

Some 100m left of the Deep Nick of Dromore, past several broken buttresses, is a steep short wall of fine clean rock. It is split by the central, left-facing, Honeysuckle Groove. To the right of this groove is White Wall, to the left is Black Wall, the latter being sub-divided into three distinct black slabs by slim grooves. Belays are scarce: the best is a crack just right of a detached block directly above Cupid's Bow.

Cupid's Arrow   13m   VS 4b   *(2001)*
Start towards the left edge of Black Wall at a vague blocky arete just right of a short raggedy groove. Bridge up the groove to gain the arete, which leads to a rounded finish.

The Climb with No Name   14m   E2 5b   *(2001)*
The slab to the left of Cupid's Bow just merits the grade. Start up a quartz seam, step left slightly and then straight up, finishing over a bulge.

Cupid's Bow   15m   E1 5a *   *(2001)*
The pink coloured left-facing groove, just left of the centre of Black Wall is followed until it steepens at a little nose, and moves are made to a jug on its left wall. Either continue up the groove, or, more easily, move left and back right. Finish up the scoop above. Technically easy for the grade, but the limited protection is worrying.

Variation: **Right-Hand Finish E2 5b**
A serious variation pulling out right below the little nose and finishing up the right arete.

Do You Feel Lucky? 16m E2 5b *(2001)*
Weigh up your chances and climb the central black slab via an obvious halfway jug. Easy for the grade.

Stupid Cupid 16m VS 4c ✱✱ *(2001)*
The slim flaky groove just right of centre is followed to a flake overhang which is avoided on the left.

Make My Day! 16m E1 5a ✱✱ *(2001)*
The right-hand slab is excellent, low in the grade and better protected than it looks. Climb up via pockets to a short crack on the left, move up this, then traverse horizontally right and finish direct.

Sheer Cupidity 14m Severe 4a *(2001)*
Follow the cracks in the left wall of the central Honeysuckle Groove and finish out leftwards.

Honeysuckle Groove 14m VS 4c *(2001)*
The obvious left-facing groove in the centre of the crag is climbed via a slim groove just right of the cracks of Sheer Cupidity to just below vegetation at the top where wild moves via a jug on the right provide a fine finish.

White Arete 14m Severe 4a *(2001)*
The arete to the right of Honeysuckle Groove is followed to a large grass ledge. Continue up the arete above. Low in the grade.

Sweet Heart 16m Hard Severe 4b *(2001)*
Mantelshelf into a niche just right of White Arete and follow stepped rock rightwards to just right of the large grass ledge. Move up and then back leftwards to finish directly up the middle of the upper wall.

White Scoop 16m VS 4c *(2001)*
A rather artificial climb taking the centre of White Wall. Start 2m right of Sweet Heart and climb the wall to a break above the large white scoop. Traverse left to just right of the large grass ledge, move up, and make a rising traverse back right to finish up a rib. Has been climbed direct at 5b.

The Notch 15m HVS 5a *(2001)*
Climb the right side of White Wall to a ledge. Steep rock above leads to an obvious large notch. Finish up the rib on the right.

LOCH GRANNOCH

(NX 535 686) Alt 300m South-East facing Map p166

Four groups of slabs lie in a fine position on the hillside above the sandy beach and old fishing lodge at the southern end of Loch Grannoch. Although the rock is good, the shortness of the climbs, the bird restrictions and the long approach, mean the routes are unlikely to prove popular except with instructors at the lodge. There is a seasonal restriction from February 15 to June 30 due to rare birds nesting.

Approach: Park as for Clints of Dromore (see above). Continue on the track, turn left and follow a forest track past Meikle Cullendoch. Take the next left and left again to the lodge (1hr 30mins, but much quicker by bike). Follow a vague path through woods to the crag (a further 15mins).

LOCH GRANNOCH

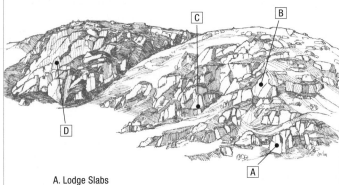

A. Lodge Slabs
B. M Slabs
C. Goat Slabs

D. Madman's Slabs

Lodge Slabs

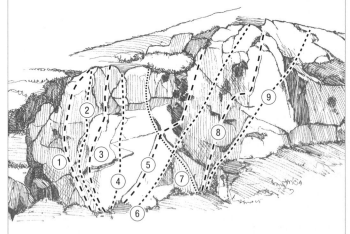

1. Spike Slab	Very Difficult	5. Diagonal 1	VS 5a
2. Wall Left	Severe 4a	6. Diagonal 2	HVS 5b
3. Wall Centre	VS 4b	7. Centre Crack	Very Difficut
4. Wall Right	Hard Severe 4b	8. Diagonal 2.5	E1 5b
		9. Diagonal 3	Hard Severe 4b

LODGE SLABS

Diagram p206

The left-hand slab is climbable anywhere at about Difficult. The right-hand is more interesting. **Spike Slab** (Very Difficult) gains and climbs the ramp above the big spike. **Wall Left** (Severe 4a) takes a vague crack, **Wall Centre** (VS 4b) goes via a niche and **Wall Right** (Hard Severe 4b) takes a crack to ledges and a wall. The striking right-slanting crack is **Diagonal 1** (VS 5a) which crosses the obvious central crack-line of **Centre Crack** (Very Difficut) before finishing up slabs on the right. **Diagonal 2** (HVS 5b) gives a hard start up a faint line of tiny flakes before crossing Centre Crack to finish up the upper of two diagonal faults. **Diagonal 3** (Hard Severe 4b) starts at the foot of Centre Crack and follows the lower fault, and **Diagonal 2.5** (E1 5b) climbs boldly and slightly artificially up the slab between the two faults.

M SLABS

Diagram p206

These lie 60m up the hillside above Lodge Slabs and give some very clean but short (8m) routes. The centre of the white left-hand slab is the very bold **Kid's Stuff** (E2 5c). **Kids R Us** up the arete to the left is Very Difficult and **Kid You Not** (Severe 4a) climbs the short wall to the right. The remaining routes lie to the right of the vegetated central groove. **M1** (VS 4b) takes the thin wiggly crack on the left and **M6** (VS 4c) the right-slanting diagonal crack starting at the same point, while **M62** (HVS 5a) follows M6 until it is possible to step left into the upper crack and boldly follow this. Right again, **Bypass** (HVS 5a) takes an unlikely line up the blank looking slab, and at the far right, **Detour** (Difficult) follows the clean cracked slab.

GOAT SLABS

Diagram p206

These are 50m to the left of M Slabs. **Stemlines** (E2 5b) gives a sustained pitch up the thin triple crack system on the right of the main slab, while **Goat Slab** (Hard Severe 4a) climbs the unpleasantly vegetated left-hand side to finish up the wall and arete. The inaptly named **Goat Grooves** (Severe 4a) starts up a subsidiary slab on the left, before crossing heather to finish up the pleasant upper slab. All these routes are 25m long.

MADMAN'S SLABS

Diagram p206

This is the rather broken area of slabs at the far side of an open gully some 200m to the left of Goat Slabs. **Black Ball** (25m Severe 4a) gives somewhat vegetated climbing up the centre of the large dark convex slab on the right. To its left are two prominent clean ribs. **Right Rib** is an 8m Difficult, while **Left Rib** (10m Very Difficult) starts up a steep crack then more easily follows the rib above. Up and right of the ribs, **Shortie** (Severe) is a pleasant if heathery 12m wall leading to the foot of the upper slab where **Captain Madman** (VS 4c) gives a good 25m pitch up the thin right-slanting crack just right of the vegetated crack.

OTHER CRAGS

There are no climbs recorded in the unattractive quarry opposite Clatteringshaws Dam, but on the hillside above this lie the easy angled vegetated slabs of **Clatteringshaws Crag** (NX 549 754) which is best reached by taking the first left turn 100m down the Raiders' Road and then striking directly up the hillside. The sole climb is the pleasant **Dam It** (25m Moderate 2002), which takes the rib formed by fallen blocks on the left of the crag.

GALLOWAY HILLS

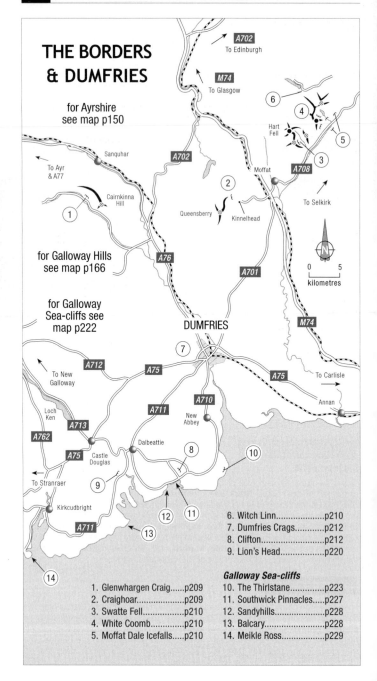

THE BORDERS & DUMFRIES

for Ayrshire
see map p150

A702
To Edinburgh

M74
To Glasgow

6

4

Hart
Fell

5

3

A708

Moffat

To Selkirk

Sanquhar

A702

To Ayr
& A77

Cairnkinna
Hill

1

2

Queensberry

Kinnelhead

for Galloway Hills
see map p166

A76

A701

for Galloway
Sea-cliffs see
map p222

0   5
kilometres

M74

DUMFRIES

7

A712

A75

To New
Galloway

A75

A710

New
Abbey

A711

To Carlisle

Annan

Loch
Ken

A713

A762

A75

Castle
Douglas

Dalbeattie

8

10

To Stranraer

9

Kirkcudbright

A711

13

12   11

14

THE BORDERS & DUMFRIES

Save for the granite outcrop of Clifton, this area has few inland crags of note outside of the Galloway Hills p166. Winter climbing is largely confined to the Moffat Hills.

The Borders

The border hills and dales have yielded little rock climbing, and none of much worth. In winter a sharp freeze will bring many burns and falls into condition, though only the Grey Mare's Tail is likely to draw the crowds.

GLENWHARGEN CRAIG

(NS 763 031)   Alt 400m   South-west facing   Map p208

This impressive mountain crag lies in the glen of the Scaur Water in Nithsdale. Unfortunately the rock isn't above suspicion. Five routes graded from Easy to Difficult and from 15 – 100m high were climbed here in the '50s and a diagram published in the 1958 SMC Journal. The crag has only received passing attention since. **Fraser's Second Climb** (70m Difficult 1979), starts at the lowest point of the lowest left-hand part of the crag. Follow a rib to the right of the lower rib, then go right across a grass ledge to belay. Climb the wall by a rising left traverse and follow a small spur and a crack on the left to a belay on a ledge. Scramble to the top. **Gibson's Climb** (33m Very Difficult 1977), is on the white crag at the bottom right corner of the cliff. Follow a groove up left, then go up a gully to easier ground. **Fraser's First Climb** (10m Severe 1977), takes a mossy groove in the centre of the top buttress. An additional VS has been climbed on one of the lower tiers.

CRAIGHOAR

(NT 008 022)   Alt 400m   South-east facing   Map p208

Situated above Annandale on the eastern side of the Lowther Hills, this steep little crag has reasonable rock and adequate protection. A metal stake is in place for belaying at the top. The farmer requests no dogs please, even on leads.

Approach: Park beside the bridge (NT 033 016) at the start of the private road to Kinnelhead Farm, accessed from Junction 15 on the M74. The crag can be seen high on the hillside on the far right. Walk through the farmyard and follow the track for 1km before heading directly for the corner of the wood below the crag. Allow 45mins. The climbs are described from left to right.

Silence of the Ram   12m   VS 5a   (2002)
Start just right of the lowest point of the crag and climb up to a short crack. Follow this to beneath a block (crux), struggle up on to it, have a rest, and finish directly.

Scobie-Doo   12m   HVS 5a   (2002)
Takes the dark coloured wall 2m right of Silence of the Ram. A steep and fairly sustained route. Climb directly up the wall passing the right end of a ledge.

Hoar Crack   12m   VS 4b   (2002)
Start beneath the high vertical crack. After a hard start, climb up to the crack and finish directly above tending to the right side of the crack. Low in the grade.

Hoar Cleft   12m   Severe   (2002)
The obvious groove on the right half of the crag. After a hard start, climb directly up with a steep pull to finish.

Crooked Brae   12m   VS 4c   (2002)
Follow for Hoar Cleft for 6m, then traverse rightwards across the short wall to a series of almost vertical cracks. Climb these to the top.

SWATTE FELL

(NT 118 114)   Alt 500m   North-east facing   Map p208

This southern outlier of Hart Fell lies north-east of Moffat and offers a number of easy winter routes on the large craggy faces above Blackhope Burn.

Black Crag Gully (I 1979) is the largest most obvious gully on Black Craig (NT 135 110). To the north are two large corries. Nether Coomb Craig (NT 126 113) is the most southerly and has a number of gully and buttress lines at Grade I.

Upper Coomb Craig (NT 123 118) has **Central Gully** (150m, II 1979). To the left of this lies **Blackout Gully** (160m, III 2003), which starts from the left-hand side of the second bay left of Central Gully and gives a 30m water ice pitch followed by easier climbing up the left-hand fork, and **Paok!** (140m, II 2003), which starts about 40m left and higher than the previous route and follows water ice to the end of the gully, followed by turf up and left to the top. **Coomb Craig Ridge** between the two corries is a good winter scramble.

Approach: From Capplehill on the A708, follow the west side of Blackhope Burn up the valley.

WHITE COOMB & MOFFAT DALE

Map p208

Assorted winter routes have been recorded here, the best known being the Grey Mare's Tail, the impressive waterfall on White Coomb's eastern flank.

Carrifran Glen (NT 152 130) provides a few routes. **Shortfall Gully** (180m, II 2000) is the obvious shallow gully on the left side of Raven Craig (NT 144 137) and is started via a 35m icefall. Several finishes are possible. To the north-east (NT 148 145) a good 10m II/II icefall forms, **Raven Craig Fall** (1996). Firthope Burn (NT 153 146), the easterly tributary of the Carrifran Burn, has the atmospheric **Firthhope Falls** (II *, 2000) following a series of falls up the bed of the burn. Two gullies giving 150m of Grade I climbing (1990) have been recorded on the east face of **Firthybrig Head** (NT 158 172) at the far western end of Loch Skeen.

Grey Mare's Tail (NT 183 149) is the only major ice-climb in the area but nearly a fortnight of prolonged low-level night frost is needed to bring it into condition. The ice forms quickly at the sides of the fall but the central cascade is so voluminous that it rarely freezes completely. Both sides are Grade **III/IV** ** (1969), depending on the solidity – be warned, there have been fatalities here. Above the initial steep section the fall continues in a series of steps which decrease in size as height is gained. There is also a shallow Grade III gully to the right, which comes into condition more readily.

Broken Cleugh (NT 185 135) is a Grade II/III * (2000) situated on Mirk Side on the northern flank of Bell Craig and gives 500m of short stepped pitches and is only 400m from the road. This is almost opposite the Grey Mare's Tail and forms much sooner. **Dob's Linn** (NT 196 158) lies just to the north-east of the Grey Mare's Tail and provides two routes: a Grade II (1987) up frozen mixed ground to the left side of the falls and the falls themselves at Grade III * (1995).

OTHER CRAGS

Witch Linn (NT 133 202) is the northern of two streams at the southern end of Talla Resevoir, on the west flank of Garelet Hill which gives a good Grade II (2002) after several day's freeze. The main Talla Falls are thought to have potential in a longer freeze. **Bitch Craig** (NT 199 266) below Dollar Law is rumoured to contain some interesting pinnacles and may warrant further exploration.

FATLIPS CRAG

(NT 581 207)   South-east facing

Marked on the map as Minto Craig, this whinstone crag is prominently situated in wooded surroundings to the west of the A698 Hawick to Jedburgh road in Teviotdale. The rock is somewhat dubious, lichen and gorse can be a problem, and protection is adequate rather than brilliant, but it is the only major crag in the area.

Approach: Leave the A698 at Denholm for the B6405 and cross the River Teviot. Turn immediately right and follow a minor road below the crag until 100m past a small gate lodge. A left turn gains a forest track with a wooden gate. Park here and follow a good path as though going to Fatlips Castle but take the left fork and then cut through the trees 100m up. A rough track climbs steeply up to the crag starting from a pile of boulders (ignore the boulder field visible from the track as this leads to the broken right-hand crag). Alternatively, from the castle, walk a few metres towards the river and descend a hidden stone staircase to reach an overgrown path which leads via serious nettle beds to two Scots Pines at a view point above the crag.

Descent: A gully on the left of the crag makes an unpleasant descent and it is perhaps better to take a spare rope and abseil down Minto.

Minto   15m   Severe 4a   *(2002)*
Just right of the gully at the left end of the crag is a short wall. Climb the red groove on the right of the wall to a small roof. Move left under this and up to a pine tree. A pleasant but rather artificial pitch.

The next five routes all start 2m to the left of the main tower at a vague groove leading to a prominent roof formed by a detached block.

Fatlips Rib 35m VS 4a   *(2002)*
From just left of the groove, climb slabby rock to a diagonal, left-trending stepped overlap. Follow it up and left to its end, then move up and step right onto a clean rib and join Whin Some, Lose Some which is followed to the top. Low in the grade.

Whin Some, Lose Some   30m   HVS 5b   *(1997)*
Follow the groove up to the roof, make a hard move left and up, and then traverse left to a broken rib which is followed to the top. An interesting route, though the block is rather worrying.

Hotlips   30m   VS 5a   *(1997)*
Follow the groove of Whin Some, Lose Some to the roof, make an awkward move right to surmount the bulge, and then go up, slightly leftwards, to an overlap, which is overcome directly. Continue in the same line to the top. Another nice climb except for the worrying nature of the roof.

Fatlips Corner   30m   VS 4c *   *(1993)*
This is the main corner immediately left of the steep tower – a much better route than it looks. Start up the groove of Whin Some, Lose Some, but traverse right at 5m to gain the main corner/groove which is followed to the top. Better still, do the bold Direct Start (HVS).

Big Fella   30m   HVS 5a   *(1997)*
A rising traverse. Follow Fatlips Corner into the main groove until below a roof on the right. Traverse right under the roof, crossing Crest of a Knave and Who Youse Callin' Fatlips?, and continue rightwards to join Top Lip which is followed right and up into a big open scoop, before battling with rope drag and loose rock up the left-trending groove.

Crest of a Knave   30m   E3 5c *   *(2000)*
Good climbing, but a serious undertaking with no gear for the first 15m. Start in the middle of the steep wall 3m left of the crack start of Who Youse Callin' Fatlips? at a flat round stone. Boldly climb up the wall and slabby groove above until under the overhang at some dodgy blocks. Take the overhang direct and then climb the left arete of the tower on its right-hand side.

Who Youse Callin' Fatlips? 30m   E1 5b *   *(1993)*

A good sustained climb which takes the tower direct. Hard for the grade. The impending wall at foot of the tower is broken on its right side by a short wide crack. Climb the crack with difficulty, then step up and left to a small ledge. Follow the obvious line above, over several bulges, then moving slightly right, until awkward moves up and left surmount the final bulge. Follow the easy groove to the top, passing a large block with care.

Top Lip   25m   VS 4c   *(1996)*

Start as for Who Youse Callin' Fatlips? by climbing the short wide overhanging crack: this succumbs best to a bold approach. On recovering, step left and climb up an easier broken line for a few metres to where the wall steepens (junction with Big Fella). Traverse right and up into a big open scoop, to finish up a loose left-trending groove.

Situated near Earlstown, **Craighouse** (NT 604 356) is a 10m high, 25m long, whinstone crag giving short routes up to 5a/b and good bouldering. Permission to climb should be sought at the neighbouring quarry.

Dumfries Area

Of the few inland crags in the area, Clifton, situated above the Solway coast south of Dumfries, offers a variety of quality routes on superb granite, with an attractive outlook and southerly aspect. The other crags described, though by no means totally worthless will probably only to be of interest to locals. The coastal cliffs near Dumfries are described in the Galloway Sea-cliffs chapter, p222.

DUMFRIES CRAGS

Georgetown Quarry (NX 998 742) is a large dank hole with a sandstone wall 10m high and 30m long rising from the nettles on the right. Unfortunately it is mostly devoid of protection and lines. From Dumfries follow the old A75 Carlisle road (not the bypass) and turn right at a mini-roundabout down Georgetown Road and continue for about 1.4 miles, through a housing estate, to a short track on the right leading to the quarry (opposite a house called 'The Knowe'). The routes are described from right to left. **Route 1** (8m, HVS) follows a line of shot holes up the right wall of the groove of **Route 2** (8m, VS). **Geronimo** (12m, E2 5b) is the left-slanting crack with in-situ pegs just left of Route 2. To the left again, the obvious challenge of **Main Wall** has been top-roped at 6b. **Maidenbower Craigs** (NX 988 745) are 15m conglomerate crags overlooking the Georgetown area of Dumfries and 800m from Georgetown Quarry. The prominent chimney at the left-hand end of the left main buttress gives a VS and there are a couple of Severe chimneys, one in the centre of the right-hand buttress and the other to the right again. The rock needs careful handling.

CLIFTON

(NX 909 571)   South-west facing   Map p208   Diagrams p216

Clifton is one of Southern Scotland's best kept secrets. Sunny, quick drying, close to the road, and in a beautiful location: its only weak point is the diminutive stature of the climbs. However, these pack sufficient punch into their short length that they will leave you just as drained as a 50m pitch would on many other crags.

Approach: About 2km south-west of the junction between the A710 and the B793 at Caulkerbush, and 2km north of Sandyhills Beach, a narrow lane goes inland, signed variously to Southwick Cemetery, Nether Clifton and Clifton Farm. Follow the lane for about 500m to Upper Clifton Farm; there is room for a few cars hereabouts. Just past the farm is a small passing place on the left and opposite this a granite stile leads into a paddock. Squelch straight across this (wellies advised), well to the left of the farm buildings, to an angle in the far wall. A second stile is hidden some 15m to the right, just before a fence. Cross the next field, keeping an eye out for the occaisional bull, to a gate in the far corner, under Hollowstones Wall. Please keep dogs on a lead when in the fields. There is a possibility of bird restrictions on part or all of Clifton crag in the spring (February 15 to June 30) and visitors are strongly advised to check with the MCofS (see Environment Notes) prior to visiting.

HOLLOWSTONES WALL

At the far left-hand end of the crag, not far above the field-gate, is a yellow wall, flanked on the left by a hawthorn tree, and with a pleasant gearing up area below. A scrambling descent can be made a few metres left of Sideshoot.

1 Sideshoot   15m   VS 4b
Pleasant but slightly artificial. Start just left of the tree. Gain the undercut slab directly and follow it, finishing up a shallow groove in the wall above.

2 Sideshow   15m   E1 5b   (2002)
Contrived fun. Start directly behind the tree and (avoiding use of the tree with difficulty) climb the arete direct to a ledge. Continue up the blunt nose between the groove of Sideshoot and the crack of Sidekick.

3 Sidekick   15m   Hard Severe 4b *
Take the groove behind the tree, finishing up the steep crack, or wimp out by moving right and finishing up Jeune Ecole.

4 Aquiline   15m   E1 5b
Artificial, but still enjoyable nonetheless. Start as for Jeune Ecole at the shallow, blocky chimney-crack just right of the tree. Start up the crack, but move left immediately and up to a hollow below the upper crack of Sidekick on the left side of the arete. Move horizontally round the arete to the right and climb it via a short groove on the left of Jeune Ecole's ledge to a junction with that route.

5 Jeune Ecole   15m   Severe 4b **
Superb. Start at a shallow, blocky chimney-crack just right of the tree and climb the crack to a platform on the right. Climb the steep crack in the wall to gain a standing position on a ledge on the left. Traverse to the arete and finish up a groove.

6 Overground   15m   Severe 4b *
Start just right of Jeune Ecole and climb the wall to the platform. Climb the crack of Jeune Ecole to the ledge and grovel directly up the crack and groove above.

7 Outcast   15m   HVS 5a
A strenuous one move problem. Follow Overground to the platform. Climb the thin overhanging crack 1m to the right of Overground, to pull out left onto that route. Easily rightwards to finish.

8 Infill   10m   E1 5b   (1997)
The thin crack-line between Outcast and the upper section of Hollowstones Chimney is climbed by devious means. Start from the grassy platform as for Outcast, gained by climbing the first easy section of Jeune Ecole. Climb 2m up Hollowstones Chimney and make a technically bewildering move leftwards across a slab to gain a short slanting crack and ultimately easier ground to the top.
Variation: **Infill Direct   E2 5c**   (1997)
The direct start is extremely strenuous.

9 Hollowstones Chimney   15m   Hard Severe 4a   (1975)
A good if worrying climb. The open, briar-filled groove right of Outcast proves more difficult than it looks (particularly if the brambles are at their most magnificent). The chimney above is aptly named and disconcertingly awkward.

DIRL CHIMNEY AREA

A path leads up and rightwards to a bay behind an oak tree. Alternatively it can be reached from above Hollowstones Wall by a brambly traverse rightwards.

10 Gramercy   13m   Severe 4a * (1980)

An enjoyable pitch gained either from the foot of Dirl Chimney, or from the top of Jeune Ecole. Climb the short crack on the very left edge of the bay (to the left of the start of Dirl Chimney) and follow an easy ramp up left to a huge block. (The same point can reached from below the short wall above Jeune Ecole by traversing rightwards 5m.) Climb the crack forming the left side of the block to a small ledge. Follow the crack on the right onto the front of the buttress and either climb directly to the top with difficulty when it peters out, or continue the traverse rightwards, finishing as for Dirl Chimney (just as good and reduces the grade to Very Difficult). Taking the crack on the left from the ledge also reduces the grade to Very Difficult.

11 Dirl Chimney   13 m   VS 4c ***

A classic! Dirl means "a tremulous stroke; a sharp blow; a resonating sound; an anxious haste or hurry; a twinge of conscience; an exhilarating pleasure of mind and body". All these, and more, may happen when you undertake this interesting exercise in back and footing up the chimney on the left-hand side of the bay. Start below and left of the chimney, at a crack with a wobbly block in it. Climb the crack without hesitation, repetition, deviation or repetition and move rightwards into the chimney. Follow it over a roof to easier slabs.

12 Monkey Business   13m   HVS 5a (1995)

Start under Dirl Chimney. Climb the corner-crack on the right and fight up leftwards via brambles and dubious rock to a junction with Dirl Chimney. Fix a runner and swing sensationally right via a worryingly hollow flake to pull round into the top section of Lemur. Leftwards to the top.

13 Lemur   13m   E3 6a * (1979)

Spectacular strenuous climbing up the sharp arete and through the slim groove in the roof right of Dirl Chimney, finishing right then left. Hard for the grade.

14 Gibbon in Wonderland   13m   VS 5a **

The obvious handjam crack through the roof is made considerably less daunting by modern camming devices. Start opposite the oak tree. Climb a short way up a groove and avoid loose debris above by taking the slab on the right to finish up the blood-stained crack. Probably HVS if you don't know how to jam!

15 Blazing Apostles   15m   E1 5b **

Extremely strenuous climbing up the twin cracks in the overhanging arete just right of the oak tree. If you make the first part, finish up the awkward overhanging groove, just right of Gibbon's crack. Top end of the grade.

16 Tour de Force   15m   VS 4c **

Well named. Start as for, but thankfully avoid, Blazing Apostles, by traversing rightwards along a large flake for 2m until a series of mantelshelves lead to a bulge. Surmount this and finish up a short corner.

17 Owl Cave   15m   Difficult

The off-width crack to the right is reputed to be a convenient descent if you can brave the brambles. A through route is rumoured to lead to the top of Lipstick.

JIGSAW BUTTRESS

This small square buttress lies 20m right of the Dirl Chimney Area. The arete at the left-hand end of the wall has been recorded as **The Sucker** (E1 5a) but appears both artificial and impossible at this grade without using Owl Cave or Lipstick.

18 Lipstick   10m   Hard Severe 4b *
The crack just right of the arete is hard to start.

19 Stiff Upper Lip   12m   Severe 4a *   *(1997)*
A rising girdle. Start as for Lipstick. Climb up to below the main crack on Lipstick and traverse right to gain a rightwards-slanting line of jugs that leads to a finish at the top of Liplet. Huge block belay.

20 Lip Service Direct   10m   VS 5a   *(1998)*
The main groove, 1m right of Lipstick, is gained by strenuous swearing to get over the roof and into a briar. Disentangle yourself and finish easily up the chimney-groove above. The original route started via Lipstick (Hard Severe).

21 Hotlips   10m   VS 4c **
Good climbing up the wall 3m to the right of Lipstick. Climb up right past a huge thread to a ledge. Go up left past an undercling to finish by a thin crack.

22 Labrum   10m   E1 5a *
An interesting route up the wall to the right, just near a step up in the path. Climb steeply to an obvious plate of rock (or gain it more easily from the right) and make a petrifying layback to a much needed resting place. Follow flakes to the top.

MAIN WALL

A large beaked roof dominates this area which is defined by a steep corner behind a tree on the left and a fine arete on the right. Gain the foot of the wall by scrambling up from the right to a lower ledge known as Coffin Stone Ledge. Another move up and left leads to Main Wall Ledge from which the main routes start. It is also possible to gain Main Wall Ledge by scrambling up rightwards from the foot of Jigsaw Buttress. Alternatively the following 6m climbs (all done in 2000/1) take the wall below the ledges: **Long Ears** (Hard Severe) takes the awkward crack on the left and makes a good start to Liplet, **Le Tour** (Very Difficult) starts 2m to the right and passes to the left of the hanging block (the direct start up the slab is 5a), and **Le Coin** (Very Difficult) starts just right again and passes to the right of the block. **Easy Street** (VS 4b) starts 2m right of Le Coin at the lowest point. Climb up rightwards to behind the obvious pillar and continue up the blunt arete to finish with difficulty. **Bright Eyes** (VS 4c) follows a crack on the right and then a hand traverse right across the wall to gain Coffin Stone Ledge.

23 Liplet   10m   Severe 4b **
Short but sweet. Start to the left of the tree on the left end of Main Wall Ledge, and climb a short groove to a roof. A good and longer variation is to climb Long Ears to Main Wall Ledge, and gain the groove direct rather than from the right (VS 4c).

24 Ratten's Rest   10m   HVS 5b *
The short corner behind the tree is said to be worth the considerable struggle.

25 Wall Street   13m   E1 5b ***   *(1977)*
Easy for the grade and possibly only sustained HVS. Nevertheless a truly superb route – strenuous, technical and well protected. Follow the thin crack just left of centre of the wall to a break and then finish up the awkward hanging groove immediately left of the roof.

26 The Groove   13m   VS 4c
The V-groove just right of centre, exiting rightwards, is not as good as it looks. Beware of dubious blocks at the top of the groove.

CLIFTON
Left

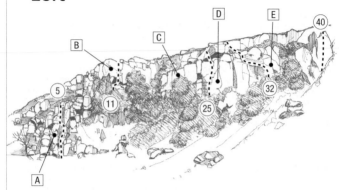

5. Jeune Ecole	Severe 4b **	A. Hollowstones Wall
11. Dirl Chimney	VS 4c ***	B. Dirl Chimney Area
25. Wall Street	EI 5b ***	C. Jigsaw Buttress
32. The Esplanade	Difficult	D. Main Wall
40. Fingerlust	E4 6a ***	E. Red Slab

Right

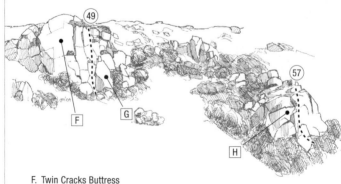

F. Twin Cracks Buttress
G. Clifton Pinnacle
H. Jugular Vein Buttress

49. Twin Cracks	VS 4b **
57. Jugular Vein	E1 5b ***

The next four routes finish on The Esplanade, which makes a convenient descent.

27 Novice Crack   12m   VS 4b *   *(1976)*
Start as for The Groove, but follow the awkward crack rightwards into the top of Kenny's Chimney. Better and longer if started up Bright Eyes.
Variation: **Tiger Finish   E1 5c**   *(2002)*
Follow Novice Crack to the point where it steps right into Kenny's Chimney. Hand -traverse left instead and make a hard pull up a thin crack (bridging out across The Groove is cheating!).

28 Kenny's Chimney   8m   VS/E2 4b/5b *
A classic thrutch and entertaining (at least for spectators) wet weather route. The grade is dependent on one's girth and the crux is avoiding getting one's head stuck.

29 The Arete   15m   E2 5b ***   *(1978)*
Exciting climbing up the arete with the prominent knob on it and quite easy for the grade. Start down and right from Coffin Stone Ledge at the foot of Elders Crack. Climb up to a roof and traverse left under it. A difficult move leads round the arete and into a groove on the left. (Many parties start from Coffin Stone Ledge and gain this groove easily but thus miss out the first of the climb's two cruxes – deduct one E-point for this). Climb the short corner until it is possible to reach right to grasp the knob and swing right. Move up with difficulty and finish by a short crack up on the right. It is also possible, but difficult and serious, to climb the arete direct without moving into the corner (E4 6a).

30 Elders Crack   15m   VS 4b *
A great little climb up the crack to the right of The Arete. Start down and right of Coffin Stone Ledge directly under the crack and just left of some elders.

31 Muckle Knob   20m   Very Difficult   *(1991)*
Reasonable climbing despite a heavy coating of bryophytes. Start at the foot of The Esplanade. Traverse horizontally left 1m to a wide crack and climb this to a junction with The Esplanade. Go directly up the mossy wall to a roof. Traverse right to a short groove and climb this, moving left and up to a heather ledge. Finish directly up the shallow scoopy groove above.

32 The Esplanade   20m   Difficult
Some 10m right of Elders Crack is a left-slanting gangway which forms a good easy descent route, except for the last 2m.

33 The Red Slab
To the right of The Esplanade is a complex area of walls and roofs half hidden behind some pinnacles.

34 Pegasus   20m   Hard Severe 4b
The wall right of The Esplanade is split high up by a left-slanting crack. Follow the crack to a ledge at the left end of an oak bush, and finish up a groove with jammed blocks. A direct start (1995) has been climbed, starting from The Esplanade.

35 Red Slab   13m   VS 5a
After a hard start, this climb deteriorates rapidly. Climb the left side of the red slab to battle through an oak tree, then climb the unpleasant upper wall, traversing sharply right to finish.

36 D.I.Y.   15m   HVS 5a *
Climb the crack flanking Red Slab on its right, followed by a hand-traverse right to finish up an awkward break in the roof. Surmount this by use of a dubious block which in retrospect you would probably much rather not have touched. It is also possible to start via the crack of Nebula and hand-traverse leftwards to the break at the same standard.

BORDERS & DUMFRIES

37 Toddamundo   15m   E4 6a ** *(1984)*
Climb the blunt arete right of D.I.Y. to the break. A thought provoking reach from a sharp fingerhold on the roof's lip gains a strenuous and exposed upper wall on the left of D.I.Y's crack. A further hard move (crux) leads to a jug at the top. Very serious, and hard for the grade.
Variation: **Finish   E2 5b ***
From the break finish up D.I.Y.

38 Nebula   20m   E1 5b
Climb the corner right of Toddamundo, then follow a disconcertingly loose rising traverse rightwards beneath the roof to a cursingly awkward finish.

39 Crosswires   12m   E1 5b
More awkward and bold than it looks. Just right of Nebula is a thin green groove in the left wall of the leaning tower. Finish up the hardest bit of Nebula for good measure.

40 Fingerlust   12m   E4 6a *** *(1979)*
The thin crack in the leaning tower gives tremendous route; short, but very strenuous and technical, with excellent protection (but only if you can hang around and place it).

The broken rib down and right of Fingerlust gives a pleasant Difficult. At its top a traverse left can be made on grass to finish up the short arete (Severe).

41 Dulce Cour   110m   HVS * *(2003)*
The girdle traverse of Main Wall is artificial certainly, but has some good exciting pitches nonetheless. Climb Jeune Ecole, or any other pitch to the top of Hollowstones Wall.
1. 30m 4c Follow Gramercy until just below the mantelshelf, then traverse right along the flake and step across Dirl Chimney. Descend down rightwards with difficulty and traverse the lip of the roof, to gain the crack of Gibbon in Wonderland. Use this to gain a platform up on the right, and traverse right to the top of the groove of Tour de Force. Descend this for 2m and step right awkwardly onto a heathery ledge with a block thread belay.
2. 20m 4b Traverse rightwards across a slimy slab into Owl Chimney, and step out right onto a platform. Descend the crack of Lipstick for 2m and then follow the rising traverse of Stiff Upper Lip to belay on a huge block at the left-hand side of Main Wall.
3. 35m 4c Descend slightly the corner of Ratten's Rest, and traverse the break under the roof taking care with loose blocks to pull out at the top of The Groove. Descend half way down the Esplanade and then make a slightly rising traverse across the mossy wall, and go up to a hanging belay on a small oak tree, just left of Red Slab.
4. 25m 5a Cross the slab to join D.I.Y. and finish up this. Alternatively continue the traverse to an awkward finish up Nebula (E1 5b).

In between The Red Slab and Twin Cracks Buttress is a grassy ramp which forms the best descent from routes hereabouts.

TWIN CRACKS BUTTRESS

About 100m right of the Red Slab is a buttress marked by a blasted tree in the centre near the top, and a large detached pinnacle below.

42 Horner Corner   8m   Very Difficult
The short but strenuous crack on the left side of the buttress.

The following routesl start from a ledge up under the left-hand side of the buttress.

43 Crawl Wall   14m   VS 4c *
A good route. Climb the wall just right of the left arete of the buttress until it is possible to move right into a crack which leads to a ledge. Finish up the wide crack on the right as for The Direct.

44 Wiggle   15m   HVS 5b *
Start under The Direct and climb strenuously up the thin left-slanting crack to join Crawl Wall.

45 The Direct   15m   HVS 5a *
The straight crack succumbs to gritstone tactics for those who have them. Elastoplast might be handy for the rest.

46 Crackshot   15m   HVS 5a *
From the foot of The Direct, step right and move up to a ledge. Go boldly up to a second ledge and, stepping up left, finish up the wall above.

The next routes start down and right; from near the Pinnacle.

47 Revolver   15m   E1 5b *
Play Russian Roulette up the left-hand side of the obvious revolver-shaped flake to the scrawny tree. Make a hard move up left and then go right to the top. It is also possible to climb the arete behind the tree. Quite bold.

48 Bullet   15m   HVS 5a   (1995)
Takes the thin crack up the right-hand side of Revolver's flake. Starting as for Twin Cracks, climb up to the crack, and struggle to its top. Avoid the tree on the right and continue more easily.

49 Twin Cracks   15m   VS 4b **
Fine climbing up the twin crack system starting just left of the Pinnacle. The best route on the buttress.

50 Clifton Pinnacle   15m   Severe 4a   (2000)
The large detached flake just right of Twin Cracks gives a disappointing climb. The Pinnacle can be gained via its right arete or chimney (crux is avoiding the gorse bush), its left arete (no gear), or more easily via the chimney on the left. Step off the Pinnacle and climb to the top making the best of the dodgy rock and spiky vegetation.

JUGULAR VEIN BUTTRESS

A short bushwhack down and to the right leads to a steep buttress with a double tier of roofs on the left.

51 The Pinnacles   15m   Severe 4a   (1995)
At the left-hand side of the buttress is a series of blocky pinnacles. Climb the pinnacles to a steep wall. Surmount this via a spiky block.

52 Essence of Giraffe   15m   E1 5c   (1995)
Immediately right of The Pinnacles is a slim lichenous groove. Climb the groove to below the steep wall on The Pinnacles. Traverse rightwards under the overlap with a hard move to gain a foothold on the arete (tiny wires useful). Make a strange move right to gain a large block near the top of The Slash. Finish up this. Alternatively the diagonal crack in the headwall above the initial groove can be taken. This reduces the grade to HVS but is rather artificial.

53 Beyond the Terminator   15m   E3 6a ** (1984)

At the left side of the buttress, 3m left of the central crack-line of The Slash, is a slab topped by a crescent-shaped roof. Make hard moves to a rest at the top of the slab then swing out left to gain the obvious good hold. Continue directly to the top surmounting a small roof.

54 Moonshine   15m   E2 5c ***

Start as for Beyond the Terminator and climb the desperate slab rightwards under the first roof to a resting place. Continue rightwards, crossing The Slash and stepping onto Jugular Vein, to finish up a short crack in the right arete.

55 The Slash   15m   HVS 5a **

The central crack is a classic of its type, and those who like that sort of thing will find that this is the sort of thing they like.

56 Slashshine   15m   E1 5b **

This combination misses out the 5c start of Moonshine and gives a good pitch. Climb The Slash for 5m, step right onto Jugular Vein, and continue traversing rightwards to finish up a short crack in the right arete.

57 Jugular Vein   15m   E1 5b *** (1977)

Fine climbing up the wall to the right of The Slash and quite low in the grade. Start up and right of that route. Puzzle your way up the wall leftwards to a resting position on the arete. Take deep breath, step right, and climb the intimidating crack above.

Two further routes lie to the right. **Loneliness of the Long Distance Runner** (E4 6a 1984) is described as 'a serious undertaking up the right arete of the buttress', which it no doubt is so long as one does not bridge across into the grass and holly-filled groove on its right which reduces the grade to VS. **Little Wall** (E1 5a) takes the cracked wall to the right again and is very grassy and unpleasant. Some 300m to the right lies **The Slab**, an attractive feature when viewed from the road. Unfortunately it is not as quite good as it looks but has a few pleasant pitches: **Crack Up** (12m, Hard Severe 4a) takes the crack on the left; **Sunset** (15m, VS 4c *) climbs the slab trending rightwards (small cams recommended), and **The Corner** on the right has also been climbed (Difficult). A hanging belay start to avoid the sea of gorse bushes may be required.

LION'S HEAD

(NX 822 581)   South-east facing   Map p208

This buttress of blocky mica schist stands clear of the trees above the A711 north of Palnackie. The crag is hard to see from the road, but it is up high, almost at the left-hand edge of the woods on the right, just after Kirkennan Cottage, where trees give way to open fields. Unfortunately the quality of the crag is nowhere near that of the scenery, but if you can take friable holds, loose rock, and poor gear in your stride then a reasonable pleasant day's climbing may be had.

Approach: Parking is impossible anywhere remotely near the approach without risk of arrest. From near the left end of the wood, follow the main track up and right but quit it after about 100m and scramble up leftwards through conifers and then deciduous woodland to the crag. All save one of the routes are on the Upper Tier.

LOWER TIER

Snout Direct   50m   VS (c1960)

Good in parts, but not many of them. Start behind the large pinnacle.

1. 20m 4b Climb the pinnacle and step across to the brambly groove which is

followed direct to the terrace and a tree belay.

2. 30m 4c Traverse horizontally left from the tree and climb the wall to a grass ledge. From here, either climb the flake-crack above, or climb the rather worrying cracked face to its right, or (best), traverse up right past a big detached block and go round right to finish up a steep crack. Yet another alternative finish traverses right from the tree to gain a pinnacle and takes the wall and green groove above.

UPPER TIER

Two unsatisfactory routes have been climbed on the steep loose sidewall on the left. Moving rightwards there is a prominent rock scar groove – this was the line of the **Slant** (HVS) – then a smooth face containing a small bonsai tree, and the large corner on the right taken by Twinkletoe Wall. The routes are described from left to right.

Catspaw   25m   HVS 4c   *(1976)*
Climb the wall left of the corner, past the 'bonsai' and wend your way to the top. Easy for the grade and relatively sound.

Twinkletoe Wall   25m   HVS 4b   *(1976)*
Solid but serious. Climb the large corner; tiny wires needed.

Sheer Can   25m   E1 5a   *(1976)*
Scary. Follow Twinkletoe Wall for 2m and then step right onto a small ledge on the arete. Traverse diagonally right into a groove and pull out right to gain the shattered rib which only becomes less so for the last metre or two.

Claustrophobia   25m   E2 5b   *(1976)*
Extremely scary. The bold arete right of Sheer Can leads to the small ledge on that route. Move diagonally right into a groove and follow it up leftwards to a cracked roof. Move over the roof on dubious holds and finish up the groove above and then left. Alternatively start directly up the black groove to the right of the arete – very technical and bold.

Snout Indirect   30m   VS 4c
It is possible to traverse right from the foot of Twinkletoe Wall, under Claustrophobia, and climb a large flake to gain the ledge on pitch 2 of Snout Direct from which the various finishes can be taken.

BOULDERING

The following areas may be of interest to boulderers. **Screel Hill** (NX 785 553) is a pleasant walk. Its small granite outcrops give some bouldering on its north-east and south faces. **Clawbelly Hill Slabs** (NX 882 609) are two granite slabs situated at the bottom of dense forestry plantations. The 17m left-hand slab is the better and is climbable anywhere at Difficult to Severe, although it is devoid of protection. Pine needles add to the interest, if not the friction. Nearby **Little Cloak** (NX 865 595) is an area of granite boulders developed in the late '70s – also known as the Khumbu. **Millour** (NX 953 596) at the base of Boreland Hill is a southern outlier of Criffel. Unfortunately though granite, the short ribs are only of Moderate or Difficult standard and are hardly worth the walk. The extensive boulder field on nearby **Airdrie Hill** (NX 947 590), an outlier of Criffel may prove more rewarding. A number of hard modern problems have been done among the granite boulders below **Clifton**.

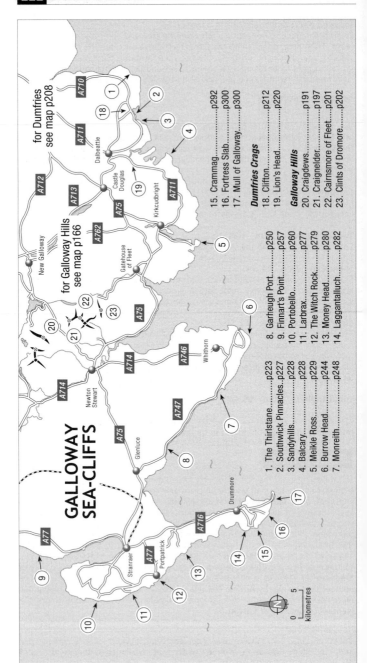

GALLOWAY SEA-CLIFFS

for Dumfries see map p208

for Galloway Hills see map p166

A710
A711
A712
A713
A711
A75
A762
A714
A746
A747
A75
A716
A77

Dalbeattie
Castle Douglas
Kirkcudbright
New Galloway
Gatehouse of Fleet
Newton Stewart
Glenluce
Whithorn
Stranraer
Portpatrick
Drummore

N

0   5
kilometres

GALLOWAY SEA-CLIFFS

The 320km Galloway coast contains a wide variety of climbing, from beachside bouldering to adventurous routes on wild headlands. It is an area of considerable beauty, unspoiled and surprisingly unfrequented with a milder climate than the rest of Scotland. With the exception of The Thirlstane, Finnarts Point and the granite cliffs of Laggantalluch and Crammag, greywacke is the principal rock. This finely bedded sediment varies in quality from immaculate to appalling, sometimes on the same crag. When sound it provides superb and intricate balance climbing.

Although many of the cliffs in this chapter are affected during the seabird nesting season, there are no official restrictions on climbing. Any dates are purely to help the climber gauge the level of noise, smell and guano. However, it should be noted that the intentional disturbance of nesting birds such as razorbill, guillemot, puffin, fulmar, kittiwake and cormorant is a criminal offence. If in doubt contact the MCofS (see Environment p29).

The cliffs have been divided into three areas; The Eastern Coast around Dumfries, the Central Coast around Kirkcudbright and Whithorn and The Rhinns around Stranraer.

Eastern Coast

This includes the cliffs near Dumfries, between The Thirlstane and Balcary Bay. With the exception of Balcary, these are more in the nature of crags on the beach, rather than true sea-cliffs. They are short and non-serious, and many can be combined with a visit to nearby Clifton, see The Borders & Dumfries p208. Camping is possible at the busy Southerness (NX974 549), Sandyhills (NX 891 550) and Rockcliffe (NX 853 530).

THE THIRLSTANE

(NX 993 568)   Tidal (outer cave only)   West facing   Map p222

This lovely small sandstone crag rises from the beach and provides the odd combination of easy routes and fine, hard bouldering. The easier inland wall is connected to the main beach by a roofless tunnel, wherein lies the bulk of the bouldering. The outlook across the sands to the distant Lake District is superb. The crag is not extensive and is best visited for an evening or half day.

Approach: The crag is marked Thirl Stane on the OS Landranger. Leave the A710 at (NX 968 579) signposted for Southerness. Take the first left signed Arbigland/Paul Jones Cottage. After 1km, opposite further signs for Arbigland/PJC, take a right turn to the sea and car park The crag is a short walk east (left looking out) along the shell strewn beach.

At the left edge of the cliff is a fine arete. The following routes are round the corner to the left, overlooking a narrow gully.

In the Gulch   7m   Severe 4b
Above the boulders blocking the gully is a left-trending and slightly loose corner.

Left Wall   9m   Severe *
The wall starting 1m left of the arete provides a more sustained version of the arete with some dubious rock and a nastier landing.

Left Arete   9m   Very Difficult **
Climb the left arete of the crag by its right edge. Steep and juggy, with a rattly hold at half-height. A variation is to start 2m to the right and climb to join the parent route at the top at the same grade.

Goodnight Irene   10m   E2 5b *   (1901)
A fine sustained climb with spaced gear. Start 2m left of the cave. Pull over a small roof, and then move up to, then left underneath the larger roofs (Friend 3 to 4), to finish up a short groove (crux).

Thank You Irene   10m   E5 6b *   *(1990)*
A sensational eliminate on the previous route, with poor protection. Follow Goodnight Irene to the large roof, then cross the widest part of the main roof using a pinch for the left-hand and a small hold on the lip.

THIRL WALLS

These are the walls forming the inside of the cave. The routes here have always been considered extended boulder problems and, as a consequence, are given technical grades. The older problems retain UK grades, while the newer ones have been given Font grades.

Left Wall (East)

Routes are described from left to right, landward to seaward. An unfinished problem is the traverse of the wall at low-level. The initial section from the cave mouth to Route 1 is 6a.

Route 1   8m   5c **   *(1976)*
About 4m into the cave is a smooth groove, formed by a series of sloping holds.

Craig's Wall   8m   6c (Font 7b+) **   *(1985)*
The impressively smooth wall to the right, started by a rectangular slot.

To the right the cave diminishes in height with a long, two-tier roof. This gives a number of small, but beautiful problems.

Endrina   6m   Font 7a   *(2000)*
Start under the left edge of the roof, to the right of Craig's Wall.
Pull up at the back of the roof on sloping holds, move round to the front (difficult), slapping footless right to good holds that lead into the tight groove.

Lateral Thinking   6m   Font 6b   *(2000)*
Start to the left of Easy Roof, under the widest part of the roof. Pull up footless, get foot on, then finish on crimps to better holds.

Insect Kin   8m   Font 7a   *(2000)*
Start as for Route 2, traverse the break leftwards under the roof following Hardcore Superstar until good crimps are reached and a top-out is possible to the right of the tight groove finish of Endrina.

Route 2   6m   6a (Font 6c) *   *(1980)*
Start in the niche at the very back of the roof, with both feet on the slab, on an obvious pocket and crimp match. Make blind moves right to slots around the roof lip, and then heel-hook to good break.

Easy Roof   4m   5c *   *(1980)*
Climb the roof left of the flake-crack on good holds

Hardcore Superstar   9m   Font 7c *   *(2000)*
An eliminate, but fine climbing. Start at the sea entrance on good pockets, come in footless along the good break, drop down to slots and crank under the roof to a pocket continuing well into the cave. Once a blank wall is reached, span across on bad crimps (crux) and finish up the tight groove of Endrina

Stephen Reid on the first ascent of Smear Test, IV,4, Cairnsmore of Fleet
(photo Doug Scott)

Shrinking Violet   3m   Font 7a+/7b   (2001)
The blank wall at the sea entrance to the cave is climbed directly.

Right Wall

Routes are described from left to right, seaward to landward. Left of the sea entrance is a smooth sloping shelf at 3m, around which the following six problems are located.

Chinese Democracy   9m   Font 8a ***   (2001)
Starting in a near sitting position, traverse right from the sea entrance on edges and pockets until the sloping shelf is reached, then up Tied up and Swallowed.

Route 6   4m   6a   (1980)
This climbs the wall immediately left of the sloping shelf. Take obvious pockets with the right-hand, and slopey pocket with the left, pull up footless and cross over for a good foothold on top of the break to top-out.

Tied Up and Swallowed   6m   Font 7c *   (2000)
A direct onto the sloping shelf. Start from obvious hold on the sloping shelf, take bad crimp with right-hand, rock over and grunt to the break.

Jihad   6m   Font 7a+ **   (2000)
Start to the right at the beginning of the sloping shelf. Traverse left to a good pocket for the left-hand, go straight up, and then traverse left to finish.

Nitro   6m   Font 7b+ *   (2000)
As for Jihad to the shelf, then climb the wall directly above.

Crack House   6m   Font 7b   (2000)
Start as for Jihad, but keep traversing left at the same level to the sea entrance of the cave.

The blank wall between Jihad and Route 5 is an obvious, and so far unclimbed, last great problem.

Route 5   9m   5c **   (1980)
In the middle of the right wall inside the cave is a niche, left of a corner. Climb to the niche; break out left and up the gradually steepening wall on dramatically improving holds. Strenuous and extended.

Route 4   9m   5c *   (1980)
As for Route 5, but exit right from the niche and follow the crack past the large chockstone.

Route 3   9m   5b *   (1976)
Climb the steep corner near the landward entrance to the cave, past a prominent protruding block (opposite Route 1).

Back on the landward face of the crag, leading right from the cave.

Cave Route   14m   Severe 4b
Start on the right of the cave mouth. Climb a groove and move left to bridge across the cave. Swarm into the constriction and eventually emerge on the other side.

Cupid's Bow, E1 5a, Clints of Dromore. Climber Chris King
(photo Stephen Reid)

GALLOWAY SEA-CLIFFS

The mouth of the cave can be traversed at **4b** * by a swing from Cave Route onto good handholds on top of the first overhang of Goodnight Irene.

Zig-Zag   12m   HVS 4c *
Surprisingly intimidating. Start as for Cave Route but continue directly into the recess above. Climb the crack above and finish by the slab on the left, immediately above the cave (the odd shaky hold).

The Rib   10m   VS 4c *
An eliminate but good climbing. Climb the rib to the immediate left of Catechumen Groove, avoiding using the groove until the top.

Catechumen Groove   10m   Severe 4a *
The large open groove between the cave and the overhangs. Good bridging.

The Overhang   10m   HVS 5b
Climb the overhang to the right at its widest point (holds a bit loose following recent rockfall), moving slightly left to climb the steep nose directly to the top of the Ramp.

The Ramp   9m   Difficult
The obvious right to left ramp.

Colourful and Carefree   8m   VS 4c *
To the right of the Ramp is a vegetated and gorse filled groove (a one time 4a). Start up this, move left across a slab to gain the left edge of a prominent prow. Climb the arete to finish.

The small roof below the slab can be taken direct at 5a. It has no gear and an uncharacteristically nasty landing.

Rough Buttress   7m   Very Difficult
Start at a metal post and climb the buttress to the top.

To the right the crag diminishes in height. The following are boulder problems of particular note.

The Hole   4m   5b *
The short wall with the prominent hole. Climbed direct without using either the hole or the smaller hole to its right is 6a *.

Yellow Slab   6m   4b *
At the right end of the crag is a yellow slab. Climb this directly, then over the roof above.

The Traverse   4b *
The traverse of the crag, from right to left, provides a pleasant diversion. Keep at mid-height for the first part, descend Rough Buttress to its foot, and then keep at low-level until the finish up Left Arete. The crux is the swing across the cave.

EAST BUTTRESS

About 65m east along the beach (or up the steep path from Left Arete) is a smaller crag with boulders at its foot.

Overhanging Crack   8m   E2 5c   (1984/5)
The obvious crack in the overhanging wall.

To the left are a Difficult crack, and a 5a wall facing east. To the right is a wall with two Very Difficult cracks.

SOUTHWICK PINNACLES

Map p222

These greywacke pinnacles and slabs overlook the coastal merse near Southwick, below the raised section of the A710 between the turn off to Clifton and Sandyhills Bay. The climbing is radioactive, due to the presence of a nearby vein of naturally occurring material, but otherwise undistinguished!

Approach: As for Clifton along the A710. Southwick Needle's Eye is situated below the end of the Clifton turn. About 1km after the Clifton turn, the road leads downhill to a bridge. Park just before the bridge and descend steep grass to the pinnacle of Lot's Wife.

For the Lookout, continue on the A710 for a further 200m, to a wooden cottage on the left (The Lookout). Concrete steps lead down to the coast from The Lookout. At low tide the coast can be traversed between the two crags, but the mud is fairly unpleasant.

SOUTHWICK NEEDLE'S EYE

(NX 916 561)   Non-tidal   South-East facing

Included more as a warning, this pinnacle is the most easterly of the three areas. It has been climbed by its seaward face (Moderate); by its east face on steep vegetation (ungradeable); and by a crack just left of the south-west corner, at the right end of the overhanging face. This latter route is Very Difficult, thoroughly rotten and totally unjustifiable.

LOT'S WIFE

(NX 909 558)   Non-tidal   South-East facing

Lot's Wife   30m   *(1970s)*
This is the largest of the pinnacles. The seaward face is moderate, the buttress at the left (west) end of this face is Difficult, and the north-east arete is a loose, vegetated Difficult.

The smaller pinnacles have all been climbed at Moderate or Difficult.

Lot's Wife Slab   40m   Very Difficult   *(1979)*
Climb the slab to the left of the waterfall. Pleasant when it was clean, the upper section has now been reclaimed by vegetation.

THE LOOKOUT

(NX 907 557)   Non-tidal   South-East facing

The first two routes are on the slab immediately to the left (west) of the steps leading down from the Lookout

The Watchtower   13m   Severe 4a *   *(1980)*
The crack up the buttress on the left side of the slab.

Lookout Slab   13m   Severe 4a   *(1980)*
The slab to the right of The Watchtower is climbed centrally, being reached by vegetated steps.

The Tombstone   13m   VS 4b *   *(1982)*
This route climbs the next clean slab east of the previous two routes. The top of the slab is separated from the main coastline.

SANDYHILLS

(NX 890 546)   Tidal   South-East facing   Map p222

The large crags to the west of the beach at Sandyhills Bay are loose in their upper reaches. Lower down they provide some excellent bouldering with sandy landings. The main bouldering is situated underneath a large overhang, which stays dry in all conditions except when rain is driven by a strong south wind.

Approach: Park in the main beach car park NX 892 552 (charge). Walk west (right facing the sea) along the beach (signposted Coastal Path), go over a footbridge, then continue west over grass then more beach until, just after nets, a large overhang is reached, just before the prominent arch of the Needle's Eye. At high tide it will not be possible to reach the crags by the coast. Instead, after the footbridge, follow the coast path uphill above the cliffs to the first turn of the fence 100m into the first field. Here a vague path leads painfully through gorse to gain the bays before the overhang. At full tide the overhang may still be inaccessible
.

SANDYHILLS - BOULDERING

The best bouldering is in the small bays immediately east of the overhang, and beneath the overhang. The traverse of the bay underneath the overhang is a particularly fine and long problem (6a). Also of note is **My Evil Twin** (Font 8a/8a+) reckoned at the date of writing to be Scotland's hardest boulder problem. This starts at the back of the cave behind the overhang, and climbs out on the bottom of the undercut nose splitting the entrance to the cave. It then climbs the arete (of the nose) direct (avoiding the big sidepull on the left, and the foot jam/heel in the juggy break on the left). The main overhang has been led up to the final loose roofs but remains uncompleted

NEEDLE'S EYE

The obvious crack inside the arch on its seaward side is **Needle's Eye** (30m E3 5c 1990). It starts well but soon deteriorates into a loose and dangerous struggle.

IVY WALL

About 150m past the Needle's Eye, a large ivy covered wall stretches up the hillside, providing one route.

Amethyst Crack   40m   E1 †   *(1978)*
A strong line on interesting, but suspicious, rock. Start just right of the ivy below an obvious pothole at 20m.
1. 20m 5a Climb a series of short walls, intersected by slanting ledges, to a quartz intrusion. Move up a groove on the left, then move right to belay in the pothole.
2. 20m 4c Move left to gain a left-slanting groove and crack-line, which is followed to the top on variable rock.

The semi-tidal island of **Gutcher's Isle** (NX 864 527) provides bouldering above a beach, in a very pleasant location. From Dumfries, follow the A710 to Rockcliffe. Park in the main car park and follow the coast east for 2.5km.

There are two groove-lines above the beach just east of **Castlehill Point** (NX 845 525). The easier groove has been climbed at Very Difficult/Severe. The cliff is situated 1km before Gutcher's Isle, on the Rockcliffe side.

BALCARY

(NX 824 487)   Tidal   South-East facing   Map p222

This is a large and extensive greywacke cliff, scenically located. That development has been very limited is probably due to two factors. Firstly, the crags bottom directly into deep water, making it difficult to see them from above. Secondly, the cliff tops are often loose and vegetatious, making for unattractive abseils or major gardening. Those in search of the truly bizarre are pointed to the World Flounder Tramping Championships, held in nearby Palnackie. The area is affected by nesting seabirds from mid April to early August.

Approach: From the Balcary Bay (NX 820 497) car park follow the path straight ahead, aiming for a low depression on the skyline. The Cave Traverse starts in the bay immediately to the left, while Lot's Wife is in the next main bay to the left (2km, 15min).

The Cave Traverse   150m   Very Difficult *   *(1978)*
A traverse through impressive scenery into a cathedral-like cave, somewhat marred by loose rock. Low tide needed to enter the cave. Start in the large and easily accessible bay at the west end of the main cliffs. The peninsula on the east side of the bay is reached by easy traversing from caves at the back of the bay, then a 30m climb leads to the saddle at the left end of the peninsula (30m). From the peninsula, traverse round the corner to the top of a chimney (50m). Descend the chimney to the cave (30m). The tantalising but water filled tunnel exiting the cave is unclimbed.

Lot's Wife   25m   VS 4c *   *(1990s)*
Towards the east end of the crags is a sea-stack, named on the OS 1:50k map, which gives a good climb. The most obvious access is by abseil down very loose and dangerous ground. The stack can then be reached by a jump across a narrow channel.

High in obscurity value are the Black and White Caves of **Barlocco** (NX 786 466). The White Cave is easy of access, while the Black is tidal and requires an abseil, at anything other than low tide. While the rock is an uninspiring conglomerate, the thirsty should note that the caves were used for smuggling and that a cache of brandy was found nearby.

Central Coast

This includes Meikle Ross near Kirkcudbright and the cliffs of the Whithorn peninsula, being Burrow Head, Monreith and Garheugh Port. With the exception of Garheugh, these are some of the largest and first developed greywacke cliffs. While giving some classic routes, the rock is occasionally not the best and some routes can be serious. Camping is available at various locations including: Brighouse Bay (NX 630 454), Mossyard (NX 549 519), Newton Stewart (NX 414 654), Burrow Head (NX 451 346) and Glenluce (NX 200574).

MEIKLE ROSS

(NX 652 433)   Non-tidal   South and East facing   Maps p222, 230
This extensive greywacke cliff was the first of the major sea-cliffs to be developed. While the Ross cliffs are only a small part of the Galloway sea-cliff experience they have, for good or ill, been responsible for much of the area's reputation. On the plus side, the climbing is often excellent, the cliff dries quickly and much of it is sheltered from the prevailing south-west wind. Scenically it is one of the finest in the south-west, with outstanding coastal scenery.
    The down side is that lack of traffic on some routes has allowed loose holds to develop, particularly at the cliff tops. However, there are more than enough totally sound routes to occupy a day, particularly in Little Zawn. A helmet is recommended. With the exception of the Red Slab, Old Zawn and parts of Little Zawn the cliffs are also affected by nesting seabirds from mid April to early August.

Approach: Leave the B727 south of Kirkcudbright at NX 647 475 and follow the

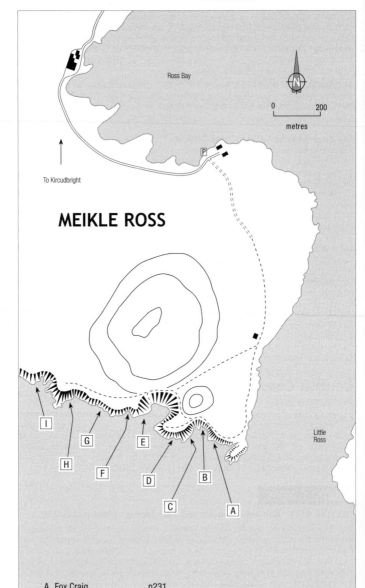

Ross Bay

0   200

metres

To Kircudbright

MEIKLE ROSS

Little
Ross

road to Brighouse Bay, then left on the road and track to Ross Bay. Park at far side of the bay at NX 651 443. Follow the track on the right up the hill to a barn. From there, for Fox Craig, Limehouse Blues Cliff and Little Zawn skirt the beach on the left, then follow the fence to the top of Fox Craig, or, for the other cliffs head right uphill through a depression to the crags surrounding Slack Heugh Bay (10mins).

FOX CRAIG

Non-tidal   South facing   Map p230

This is an impressive crag of steep cracks and corners formed by upturned beds in profile.

Approach: Access to all, except the final three routes, is best made by descending a steep grass ramp on the west side (facing Limehouse Blues Cliff), to ledges above a slabby wall. Descend the wall at its seaward end to the rock shelf above the sea. Routes are described rightwards from the grass access ramp.

Promontory Wall   15m   Severe 4a   *(1975)*
An innocuous but pleasant and clean route. This climbs the stepped corners high on the right side of the slabby wall, below the descent ramp. Start 5m left of the grotty chimney-corner and climb the wall to a ledge, then go up the corner to finish directly.

The impressive overhanging wall to the right is characterized by a fine hanging arete and is breached by one excellent route.

Corridor of Power   30m   E3 5c ** **   *(1984)*
Strenuous and atmospheric climbing up the curving crack-line and hanging groove 5m right of the hanging arete and 4m left of the right edge of the wall (Ken's Groove). The climbing is much better than it looks; take a good selection of Friends. At the top of the crux, hanging groove, move right to finish up a groove on the left.

Ken's Groove   30m   VS 4b   *(1976)*
Reasonably worthwhile if unexceptional. At the right edge of the wall is a shallow groove and corner. Follow the groove to a ledge and finish up the corner on the left.

Crack and Corner   30m   VS 4b *   *(1975)*
A fine crack climb. Climb the crack to the right of Ken's Groove to join it at the ledge and finish up the same corner.

Dolphin Groove   20m   HVS 4c   *(1976)*
An attractive looking, but possibly unrepeated, route. Start on the right of Crack and Corner. Scramble to a ledge on the right, follow a shallow groove on the left to a break, then step into a steep groove on the right to a ledge (ancient peg runner). Finish boldly up an overhanging flake.

Curving Arete   15m   Severe 4a ** **   *(1975)*
One of the best of the easy routes. It takes the obvious stepped and curving arete and gives pleasant climbing.

Round the corner are two small walls, a higher one on the left, flanking the top of Curving Arete, and a long one on the right. The easiest access is from the east end of the crag, facing towards Little Ross Island (the scene of a notorious murder of one lighthouse man by the other in the 1950s). From this direction, the longer wall with Alligator Crawl will be encountered first.

Fats Waller   15m   E1 5b   *(1984/5)*
On the higher wall, climb a crack for 7m, go slightly right, and then go over the small overhang. This route is increasing by a grade per guide.

**Rez Route   10m   Hard Severe ** ** *(1996)*
A nice slab route taking the sinuous crack system left of Alligator Crawl.

Alligator Crawl   10m   HVS 5a * *(1984/5)*
Good, slabby climbing up the middle of the right wall.

Shark's Tooth   10m   Very Difficult *(1984/5)*
Innocuous. Climb the cracks up the rib on the right of the longer wall.

CROW'S NEST CLIFF

Tidal   South facing   Map p230

West of Fox Craig is a hideous mass of twisted and decomposing beds of grey-wacke. Left of the large cave, a disturbing fault-line crosses the cliff from bottom left to top right. The hanging slab further to the left is an unclimbed but frightening possibility.

Approach: As for Fox Craig (above).

The Battle of Osfrontalis   45m   HVS *(1977)*
An epic undertaking (as in undertaker) climbed on-sight and most justifiably unrepeated. Start left of the cave where a small promontory meets the cliff.
1. 20m 4c Climb left of a chimney to a ledge. Make a precarious move up the wall and continue to a large bower.
2. 25m 4b Move right to join the main diagonal fault and follow this to a finish up short groove. The holds on this pitch are entirely disposable, and are best used as pressure holds.

LIMEHOUSE BLUES CLIFF

Non-tidal   East facing   Map p230   Diagram p234

The main cliff at the Ross offers a number of excellent crack and face climbs in the middle grades. The routes tend to pack in a lot of climbing and feel bigger and harder than their lengths might indicate. Lack of traffic has allowed some superficial vegetation and occasional loose rock to accumulate, and particular care should be exercised at the top. The arch below and right of the terrace is tidal.

Approach: There are four alternatives. In order of safety they are; 1) At low tide the crag can be approached from the beach below Crow's Nest Cliff; 2) By a scramble from Little Zawn; 3) By abseil. There has been one very bad accident due to loose rock being dislodged when the abseil rope was pulled down. It is recommended that caution is exercised and the abseil rope is left in-situ; 4) By descending Exit Groove. This is the quickest descent, but the easiest and soundest line is not particularly obvious from above. It can only be recommended to those familiar with the route.

The first route takes the wall left of the obvious triangular pinnacle forming the left end of Limehouse Blues Cliff.

1 Ancient Mariner   44m   E2 * *(1991)*
The steep pillar left of Pigeon gives varied climbing with a serious upper section. Start about 7m left of the chimney.
1. 4b 15m Climb the grey wall to a prominent twin niche. Leave this on the left and follow easy ground right to belay in a large overhung niche.
2. 5b 30m Move right out of the niche, then go up to twin overhung corners. Climb the left-hand corner to a large ledge, and then go rightwards to a thin undercut slab, crux (low runner immediately after slab). Continue boldly rightwards up easier slabs to exit at a small pinnacle.

2 Meikle Gorbachov   40m   VS 4c   *(1988)*
A fine finish, but dirty in the easy middle section. Start at the foot of the Pigeon Chimney. Climb a flake on the left wall of the chimney, then continue along this above the chimney. At its end (overlooking the pinnacle) climb the tower above.

3 Pigeon Chimney   20m   Difficult   *(1975)*
Climbs the chimney to the left of the triangular pinnacle, going below a huge chockstone. Pleasant early in the season, by August it has deteriorated into a brutal struggle up greasy bird shit.

4 Groovey   15m   Very Difficult   *(1975/7)*
Wander up the left edge of the pinnacle.

5 Compulsion   15m   E1 5b   *(1980)*
A stocking filler. Follow the left-hand crack in the front face of the pinnacle for 8m, then move right on pockets to the top.

6 Zugsfang   15m   E2 5c   *(1981)*
A good problem up the thin crack just right of Compulsion. Climb the wall at first on the right, then on the left of the crack, until forced right to a good pocket. Continue direct to the top. Harder for the short-arsed.

7 White Out   15m   Severe 4a   *(1975/7)*
The groove in the right-hand arete of the pinnacle.

8 Exit Groove   15m   Difficult   *(1975)*
Above the pinnacle at the left side of the main face is a groove; follow the main groove, exiting left at the top. This is a quick descent to the terrace, but only recommended with prior knowledge. There are a number of grotty alternatives to this route. The **Right-hand Finish** is (Difficult 1975); the arete to the left is **Exit Arete** Very (Difficult 2000); while the groove to the left again is **Grass Groove** (Very Difficult 1975). The first two are innocuous although the hardcore rubble enthusiast will particularly appreciate the latter.

9 Seadog   25m   HVS 5a *   *(1977)*
A sustained and intricate wall climb with spaced gear. Start at a thin crack below a shallow recess capped by a roof on the wall about 3m up and right of Exit Groove. Gain the crack and follow it and the wider continuation to a junction with Dogleg.

0 Argus   25m   E1 5b *   *(1978/80)*
A good but rarely climbed route, starting just right of Seadog. Strenuous moves lead to a rectangular niche, then follow the continuation crack leftwards to a shallow recess. Climb the left edge of the recess, or better the finger-crack in the recess to a roof.

To the right, two prominent crack-lines meet at the top of the crag to form the letter A. The next three routes start at the crack forming the left side of the A.

1 Dogleg   25m   HVS 5a **   *(1977)*
An excellent steep climb with the crux high on the crag. Start up the crack, but move immediately left and follow the left-slanting crack to the top.

2 Akela   25m   HVS 5a   *(1978/80)*
Follow Dogleg for 3m, then step right to a good jug and follow the crack above.

3 Salty Dog   25m   HVS 4c **   *(1975)*
A popular clean trade route. The left-hand crack of the "A" gives a fine strenuous route with the hardest moves in the first 4m.

MEIKLE ROSS
Limehouse Blues
Cliff

descent

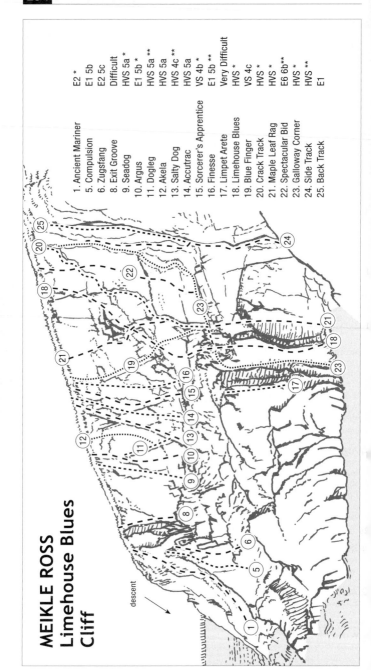

1.	Ancient Mariner	E2 *
5.	Compulsion	E1 5b
6.	Zugsfang	E2 5c
8.	Exit Groove	Difficult
9.	Seadog	HVS 5a *
10.	Argus	E1 5b *
11.	Dogleg	HVS 5a **
12.	Akela	HVS 5a
13.	Salty Dog	HVS 4c **
14.	Accutrac	HVS 5a
15.	Sorcerer's Apprentice	VS 4b *
16.	Finesse	E1 5b **
17.	Limpet Arete	Very Difficult
18.	Limehouse Blues	HVS *
19.	Blue Finger	VS 4c
20.	Crack Track	HVS *
21.	Maple Leaf Rag	HVS *
22.	Spectacular Bid	E6 6b **
23.	Galloway Corner	HVS *
24.	Side Track	HVS **
25.	Back Track	E1

14 Accutrac   25m   HVS 5a *(1978)*
From a crack mid-way between the left and right cracks, climb directly to the apex of the 'A'.

15 Sorcerer's Apprentice   25m   VS 4b * *(1976)*
The easiest line on the face gives a good, sustained climb, now marred by some vegetation. Follow the right-hand crack to within a few metres of Salty Dog. Traverse right past a small ledge and climb direct to the top (or continue to join Salty Dog's finishing crack)

16 Finesse   30m   E1 5b ** *(1978)*
Bold balance climbing up a nice piece of rock. Start just right of the right-hand crack below a rectangle of light rock. Climb over a small overlap to a ledge, then move up past a hinged spike to an inverted V overlap. Follow the fine wall above, moving right to an indefinite crack, which leads to a ledge. Step left and follow a crack to the top.

The terrace below the foregoing routes continues right and narrows to a ledge. Below this the cliff extends to the sea. The following routes all have lower pitches lying adjacent to the arch at sea-level. These lower pitches are not of particularly good quality and, as they are only accessible at low tide, are usually missed out. The second pitches are easily gained by traversing the ledge above the arch.

17 Limpet Arete   20m   Very Difficult
The left edge of the slabby wall left of the rock arch and below the terrace has a pleasant arete. Climb to a ledge and continue above. The corner to the right gives a Hard Severe.

18 Limehouse Blues   60m   HVS * *(1972)*
A bold airy finish enlivens the original route of the cliff. Start from sea-level, below the slabby wall left of the rock arch and right of a narrow chimney.
1. 20m 3b Climb the middle of the slab to the belay on the terrace below a grassy flake-crack. (The narrow chimney can be climbed at 4c and the right edge of the slab at 4a).
2. 20m 4b From the terrace, gain the prominent right-trending flake-crack and follow it to the prominent large niche.
3. 20m 5a Step down and climb the fine slab right round the edge to a short crack, then to a thin ledge. From the right-hand end of the ledge, climb a crack to gain a small ledge on the right (crux). The wall above leads to the top.

19 Blue Finger   30m   VS 4c *(1976)*
Now dirty and loose. To the right of Limehouse Blues second pitch is a bulging crack leading to two niches. Start at the belay at the right end of the terrace above the rock arch and below the two niches. Climb the steep wall on the right, left of a crack, to the left-hand niche. Follow a crack leftwards to a junction with Limehouse Blues. Move up and left to finish up the left-slanting crack.

20 Crack Track   60m   HVS * *(1975)*
Delicate climbing in a good situation. Start at sea-level as for Limehouse Blues.
1. 20m 3b As for Limehouse Blues, but belay at the right end of the terrace, above the rock arch and below two obvious niches.
2. 20m 5a From the terrace, follow Blue Finger, but gain the right-hand niche. Traverse right to a crack and follow it past a small spike to a ledge and belay on the left.
3. 20m 5a Traverse right to the base of an edge and follow this boldly to a junction with Galloway Corner. Move up, traverse 2m left and climb good holds to the top.

21 Maple Leaf Rag   60m   HVS * *(1978)*
A good route with a surprising and superb last pitch. Start under the arch, just right of the Limehouse Blues slab.

1. 20m 4b Climb the slab to the roof, move left across shaley rock, and climb a groove to the terrace. Belay at the right end of the terrace below the two obvious niches.
2. 20m 5a Start as for Blue Finger. Climb steeply on the right of the crack to the right-hand of two niches. From the top of the niche, climb thinly up the slab to a good resting place. Step left, and climb the front face of a large flake to belay in the large niche of Limehouse Blues.
3. 20m 5a Move left to reach a curving crack and a ledge with a horizontal crack, then climb the apparently blank wall above.

22 Spectacular Bid 40m E6 6b ** (1997)
A last great problem, taking the blank wall between Crack Track and Galloway Corner. Start mid-way between these two routes. Step off a boulder into a horizontal break, then move up to a good hold (possible skyhook). Make a committing thin traverse right for 3m, then climb up until a traverse left leads to a break (Friends 1, 1.5). Step off a rib on the right and move leftward up the wall to an intimidating rock up into a small niche (poor Wallnut 3 in slot on left). Climb out of the niche on small edges (crux) to mantel onto a ledge, then ascend a fine thin rightward slanting crack on fingerlocks to finish.

23 Galloway Corner 60m HVS * (1975)
The main pitch takes the huge corner at the right of the face. A good route, slightly easier than Side Track.
1 20m As for Limehouse Blues pitch 1. At the top traverse the ledge right to belay 3m from the corner.
2. 40m 5a Layback up the left-hand stepped corner, then follow the main corner to the top.

24 Side Track 60m HVS ** (1975)
An interesting sustained route, following the true corner-line just right of Galloway Corner. Again, the first pitch can be avoided and is rarely climbed.
1. 20m 5a Start at sea-level, right of the cave recess. Move up a slab to the groove and follow it to a belay on the large ledge.
2. 40m 5a Move 2m right and layback the main corner-line until it joins with Galloway Corner.

25 Back Track 60m E1 (1977)
A powerful line of some historical interest which takes the groove then thin slab on the wall immediately right of the main face. The top pitch is presently loose, vegetated, badly protected, dangerous and would probably be quite memorable.
1. 20m 5a Side Track, pitch 1.
2. 40m 5a Regain the groove and follow it to the top.

26 Rhythm n' Blues 60m HVS ** (1977)
An enjoyable girdle with considerable atmosphere. Start 6m up the right branch of Exit Groove, at a ledge and thread belay.
1. 30m 5a Traverse right, passing a small roof to a spike. Then, either climb a further 3m and descend Dogleg to a ledge, or harder, immediately descend a finger-crack then traverse right to the same point. Step down, and traverse right to a crack, then gain a traverse line leading to Salty Dog. Continue in this line to a ledge and horizontal crack.
2. 30m 5a Move right to the ledge on Limehouse Blues, then follow Crack Track pitch three to Galloway Corner.

LITTLE ZAWN

Non-tidal East facing Map p230

These steep walls and corners of generally good rock are found to the left of Limehouse Blues Cliff. Little Zawn is the ideal introduction to the Ross, and the depression above the crags is a sheltered spot to leave sacks. Continue down the hill behind Limehouse Blues Cliff to a flat area of grass above the crag.

Approach: Descend the grassy bank to the west (right looking out) of the crag and make an exposed traverse above the sea onto the platform below the routes.

Steve's Route   12m   VS 4b   (1979)
Start at a square recess where the airy traverse ends and about 4m left of the chimney. Make a long reach and continue direct.

Spectrum Wall   12m   E1 5b   (1979)
Start just left of Orange Chimney at an inverted V recess. Climb through the recess then up the wall above; serious.

Orange Chimney   15m   Difficult *   (1975)
Climb the chimney, finishing either on the left or, better and harder, direct over the bulge.

Green Wall   15m   Hard Severe 4b **   (1976)
Good climbing. Follow the left-slanting crack 2m right of the chimney to a horizontal break. Move right and climb the right-leaning niche until a step left can be made to finish.

Clockwork Orange   15m   Very Difficult *   (1975)
Right again is a corner-crack, which is climbed on the left wall.

Pinking Sheer   20m   HVS 5a ***   (1977)
The arete right of Clockwork Orange gives an excellent route with surprisingly good protection. Start just right of the corner, climb the first bulge and make a move left to a ledge. Take the second bulge on the left, move right up a crack and finish up the wall above on good holds.

Mellow Yellow   20m   VS 4c ***   (1975)
A South-West classic giving excellent climbing up the clean-cut crack splitting the yellow wall right of Pinking Sheer. Neither of the overhangs is the crux.

Sunshine Superman   20m   E4 6a *   (1984)
A sustained eliminate gaining independence with height. Start just right of Mellow Yellow and climb a short wall to the roof, move over this then make a hard move up the wall to a small spike. Move right, then left to gain a crack above the bulge, then go right again to the top. Runners in Mellow Yellow reduces the grade to E3 6a.

Stepped Corner   20m   Hard Severe 4b   (1975)
Better climbing than expected up the corner right of Mellow Yellow.

Bloody Crack   15m   E1 5b ***   (1976)
An excellent sustained route taking the crack right of Stepped Corner. The crux is passing the first roof.

Fil d'Or   15m   E3 6a **   (1979)
Beside Bloody Crack is an alarmingly smooth corner with a peg runner at half-height. A technical test piece, high in the grade. The peg can be backed with a small friend, the crux lying in wait just above.

The left-hand and right-hand cracks at the back of the zawn are both Severe and slightly better than they look; **Left Corner** (1975) and **Right Corner** (1976).

Amnesia   25m   VS 4c   (1975)
It is said that the reason forf memory loss is to forget the pain. The right wall of the zawn has an obvious, long, stepped corner, which starts just right of the green tongue of moss. The holds and gear are all in the disintegrating shale at the back of the crack, providing an unforgettable experience.

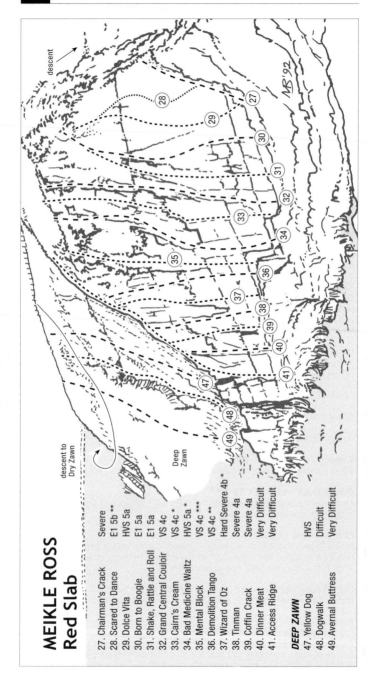

MEIKLE ROSS
Red Slab

27. Chairman's Crack	Severe	
28. Scared to Dance	E1 5b **	
29. Dolce Vita	HVS 5a	
30. Born to Boogie	E1 5a	
31. Shake, Rattle and Roll	E1 5a	
32. Grand Central Couloir	VS 4c	
33. Cairn's Cream	VS 4c *	
34. Bad Medicine Waltz	HVS 5a *	
35. Mental Block	VS 4c ***	
36. Demolition Tango	VS 4c **	
37. Wizard of Oz	Hard Severe 4b *	
38. Tinman	Severe 4a	
39. Coffin Crack	Severe 4a	
40. Dinner Meat	Very Difficult	
41. Access Ridge	Very Difficult	

DEEP ZAWN

47. Yellow Dog	HVS	
48. Dogwalk	Difficult	
49. Avernal Buttress	Very Difficult	

Headace 15m VS 4c *(1975)*
The steep corner right of Amnesia; swing right to finish onto steep mixed ground.

**A Walk on the Wild Side 50m E1 ** *(1979)*
A girdle traverse starting as for Steve's Route. Excellent climbing compensates for the understandably odd line.
1. 25m 5b Follow the initial steep section of Steve's Route, then take a rising line right, past Orange Chimney, until an overhanging arete blocks progress. A hard move round the arete leads to Mellow Yellow. Continue in this line to a small spike, then descend into Stepped Corner.
2. 20m 5b Climb the pocketed rib on the right, then hand-traverse right under a roof to Bloody Crack. Follow this, over its crux, to a ledge. Move right on excellent incuts, then go round a corner to a foot traverse which leads into Left Corner.

To the north-west lies Slack Heugh Bay, with a Red Slab on its far side.

Non-tidal East facing Map p230 Diagram p238
The northern side of Slack Heugh Bay gives some enjoyable slab routes, generally on good rock.

Approach: If approaching directly from the walk-in, take the right-hand path after the barn and follow the shallow depression up to the top of the bay. Access to the base of the crag is by descending the grassy bank on the right.

The climbs are described from right to left. Belay on a stake.

27 Chairman's Crack 10m Severe *(2002)*
Climb the obvious loose corner formed by a pinnacle at the right end of the crag.

**28 Scared to Dance 25m E1 5b ** *(1979)*
A satisfying slab route, with spaced protection from small wires. Start just left of Chairman's Crack. Climb up for 15m, traverse left 4m, then go straight up to a break. Move up and left to finish.

29 Dolce Vita 25m HVS 5a *(1979)*
An excellent but bold climb when clean. When gritty it requires a steady head. Start left of Scared to Dance, below a lyre shaped mark in the rock. Climb up to the mark, move diagonally up and left for 5m, then continue direct to the top.

30 Born to Boogie 25m E1 5a *(1999)*
Climbs the blank-looking slab just left of Dolce Vita. Start below the centre of the jagged overlaps and climb into a small sentry box. Pull out leftwards on to an obvious large foothold, step up, then make thin moves back right to a thin crack and incut holds. Continue straight up, with poor protection, to a horizontal break (good Friend protection), before the final wall leads to the shattered scoop at the end of Dolce Vita/Scared to Dance.

31 Shake, Rattle and Roll 25m E1 5a *(2000)*
Start just left of Born to Boogie, at the right side of Grand Central Couloir. Climb up to the overlap, where it forms a curved arch. Move up its left side as far as a thin diagonal crack, then pull back right on to the left edge of the smooth slab. Follow a thin crack up the rounded rib to a resting-place out left, then step back right into a groove. Up this, passing a vegetated ledge, to a horizontal break (good Friend protection). Continue up the easier but bold wall to the shattered scoop at the end of Scared to Dance, etc.

32 Grand Central Couloir 35m VS 4c *(1978/83)*
The central depression immediately left of Dolce Vita gives good climbing in its

first half, but the rest can be loose and dirty. Traversing left onto the final rib of Cairn's Cream gives a more pleasant finish at 4b.

33 Cairn's Cream   35m   VS 4c * (1979)
Left of the Couloir is an obvious tongue of rock. A crack leads to the right-hand side of the tongue, which is followed until it becomes an overlap. Cross the overlap to a ledge and finish up the blocky rib on the left.

34 Bad Medicine Waltz   35m   HVS 5a * (1981)
Climb a crack 3m left of Cairn's Cream to the left side of the tongue. Step right on to the tongue, then go boldly up its centre to a ledge, finishing up the twin cracks.

35 Mental Block   30m   VS 4c ***   (1979)
A classic, giving good clean fun. Left of centre is an area of slab between two tongues of rock, notable for an obvious block sticking out of the slab. Take a choice of lines up the slab, past a break, to gain the block. Move left, go up 3m, and then climb right to finish up a corner next to a rib.

36 Demolition Tango   30m   VS 4c **   (1983/4)
Another excellent route with a distinctly nippy crux. Hard moves up the thin twin cracks left of Mental Block lead to the right side of the overlap. Surmount the overlap and climb the thin crack to a ledge, finishing on the right.

37 Wizard of Oz   30m   Hard Severe 4b * (1980s)
A tongue of rock descends to the left of the overlaps. This worthwhile climb, previously climbed in error for Tinman, takes cracks to the right of the tongue, then continues directly

38 Tinman   30m   Severe 4a (1976)
About 13m right of Access Ridge is a coffin shaped recess. Start 3m right of this. Climb up the diagonal crack, to the left of the overlapping tongue of rock and continue to join the top of Access Ridge.

An eliminate **Glenfinnan Hotel** (Hard Severe 4b 2002) climbs the initial slab between Tinman and Coffin Crack to join Tinman after 9m.

39 Coffin Crack   30m   Severe 4a (1976)
Climb into and out of the coffin shaped recess in the black wall 3m left of Tinman and continue through the overlap to the ridge.

40 Dinner Meat   30m   Very Difficult (2002)
Pleasant climbing up an obvious crack 1m left of Coffin Crack.

41 Access Ridge   30m   Very Difficult (1972)
The left edge of the slab gives a route of variable difficulty depending on the state of the guano. Worthwhile early in the season.

42 Fiona's Folly   30m   Severe (1970s)
Omitted from the previous two guides for reasons of good taste and public safety, this folly climbs the grooves round the corner and 4m left of Access Ridge. Where the wall gets steeper, traverse right to a large ledge on Access Ridge.

DEEP ZAWN

Tidal   East facing   Map p230

Left of Red Slab lies the area's only tidal cliff, Deep Zawn. It is characterised by a gash on its right, The Rift (which almost runs the height of the crag), and the prominent corner of Dogwalk on the left. Though the angle is pleasantly slabby, the top 15m steepen dramatically.

Approach: Save for K9, the best approach is by descending the ramp forming the left edge of the crag, then by a fine traverse right (looking in) to ledges below the routes (Very Difficult). The climbs are described from right to left.

**43 K.9. 50m HVS ** ** (1972)
This climbs the face to the right of the Rift. The second pitch presents exciting and exposed situations. Access by traversing left from Access Ridge (Moderate).
1. 20m 4b Steeply past a large ledge until a traverse right can be made to another ledge.
2. 30m 5a Move left to a small groove bordering The Rift. Climb delicately up this to a resting place, then continue in the same line, through the bulges, to the top. An easier finish traverses right from below the final bulges and finishes up a green slab.

Between K9 and Rift Route is the major sea-cave of the Rift. The jump across from the base of K9 to Rift Route has been done but is only safe at three-quarters tide – an impressive leap of faith.

**44 Rift Route 50m Severe 4a ** ** (1972)
An excellent outing when combined with the access traverse. Only the last moves are severe. From ledges left of The Rift, traverse right to The Rift edge and follow it to the top.

**45 Eminence Grise 40m Hard Severe 4b * ** (1981)
Start for Rift Route, but climb up right to a deep recess and at the top pull out right to a ledge. Follow the thin crack in the slab above, pull over the overlap on the left and thence to the top. Somewhat eliminate, but good climbing.

46 A Sop for Cerberus 40m Hard Severe 4b (1981)
From the ledges, move into the recess on the left and exit 2m left of the previous route. Climb slabs, moving left, to a ledge below the roofs then go back right across the overhanging wall on huge holds.

47 Yellow Dog 40m HVS (1973)
An attractive looking early route, probably in need of a comeback. Start from the left end of the ledges.
1. 20m 4a Climb the slab, trending left to a ledge and nut belay 3m below the roofs.
2. 20m 4c Go up right to the first overhang, then move left to a ledge. Continue left and layback the second bulge, then go right and up grooves to the top.

48 Dogwalk 30m Difficult (1973)
This is the prominent corner on the left of the cliff. Start at the same place as Yellow Dog. Traverse left to the prominent corner and climb it to a roof, exiting left to a ledge. Continue to the top. Much guano after the nesting season.

49 Avernal Buttress 30m Very Difficult (1981)
Follow the arete left of Dogwalk, just left of the edge. Pleasant if combined with the access traverse.

DRY ZAWN

Non-tidal East and South facing Map p230
This cliff forms three sides of a rectangle and can be quite sheltered from the wind.

Approach: Descend the ramp at the left end of Deep Zawn to the sea, then traverse left (facing in) to the floor of the zawn.

The following routes are on the left-hand wall.

Route One   25m   Severe 4a *   (1978)
Good climbing up cracks at the left-hand end of the cliff.

Route Two   15m   VS 4c   (1983/4)
A once worthwhile, but now licheneous line up the wall in the centre of the cliff.

Route Three   10m   Very Difficult   (1981)
It's turf at the top. The right-hand corner.

Pinko-Subversive   20m   Severe 4a   (1987)
The short, steep corner on the right-hand side of the zawn.

About 3m left of Dry Zawn is a groove-line.

Manic Nirvana   25m   HVS 5a *   (1991)
Steep technical climbing. Climb to the overhang, then traverse right and go up the
right-hand groove. Follow this back left and climb a short crack to a large ledge and
easier ground.

The next climbs lie on **The Slabs** and can be found by following the cliff top
westward until a stake is located at the top of a pointed headland. The cliff below
is extensive but quite loose. Access is by abseil, or via a pleasant traverse leftwards
from Dry Zawn. The climbs are all non-tidal and south facing.

Bumper Dumper   30m   HVS 5b   (1982)
Once upon a time a fine well protected slab climb, now gone back to nature. The
smooth sound face at the right-hand side of the cliff is split by two cracks. Climb
the left-hand one to a ledge, step right to a crack and follow it to the top.

The Moosetrap   30m   VS 4c   (1982)
A 1.5m sword of rock lies precariously balanced across the upper wall, one of
several delights in store on this deathtrap. The crux corner is mild by comparison.
Start 3m left of Bumper Dumper. Climb a wall then the corner, say a prayer, and
tackle that top wall.

Poison Ivy   30m   Difficult   (1982)
Left of The Moosetrap is a chimney whose left wall and upper section gives a turfy
escape. Only mildly poisonous.

Further west, immediately below the headland, and above a pinnacle, is the
biggest slab, bounded on its right by a steep wall and split by an easy angled
groove. Sea grass has reclaimed a number of formerly good routes and they can
only be recommended after gardening, or with a tractor. Descent is by abseil. Do
not descend the groove in the middle as this is spectacularly loose.

Titan's Corner   40m   E1 5a   (1982)
A one time excellent undertaking, both delicate and bold; it is now badly in need
of resurrection. It climbs the right-hand corner, taking the overlap to finish.

Marie Celeste   40m   VS 4b   (1982)
Another fine route, now with mixed winter potential. Start mid-way between the
central groove and Titan's Corner. Follow the prominent cracks up the slab, then
continue through the overlap as for Titan's Corner.

Blistering Barnacles   40m   Severe 4a   (1982)
Pleasant climbing up the middle of the slab left of the groove.

Barnacle Bill   40m   Severe 4a   (1982)
The left arete of the slab gives a mediocre climb.

The next corner is **Dogday Blues** (Very Difficult 1981). The clean slab up left of this is a pleasant Severe.

OLD ZAWN SLAB

Non-tidal   South-East facing   Map p230

Even further west is a bay with a pinnacle. Past this, at the very end of the cliffs is a small bay with a short clean slab above a platform. The area is pleasant and non-serious by Ross standards, and, while the climbs are short and often eliminates, they are on good rock.

Approach: It is best to abseil, although at low tide it is possible to scramble down the gully to the right (facing out).

Nursery End   8m   Very Difficult   (2000)
The corner at the right end of the slab, finished on the left.

Silly Mid-On   8m   Very Difficult   (2000)
One metre left a diagonal crack slants up from right to left. Climb up to the start of this, but continue straight up to the left end of the horizontal break on Nursery End.

Silly Mid-Off   8m   Severe   (2000)
1m further left, thin twin cracks are followed until they intersect the diagonal crack. Finish straight up.

Grapeshot   9m   Hard Severe 4b   (1987)
Climb the slab to the right of the upper overlap.

Mid-Wicket   10m   HVS 4c *   (2000)
Between Grapeshot and Old Zawn, a thin crack-line leads to the middle of the overlap. Finish straight over.

Old Zawn   12m   HVS 4c   (1990)
Start below the right end of the overlap. Follow thin cracks diagonally left to gain the left end of the overlap.

Evens   9m   VS 4c   (1990)
The left of the two cracks to the left of Old Zawn. Worthwhile.

The Slips   10m   HVS 5a   (2000)
The left side of the slab has a horizontal crack at half-height forming a tiny overlap. Starting 1m left of Evens, climb up to the right end of the horizontal crack, and finish direct with delicacy.

Left of the slab is a deep gully (the scramble descent at lowish tide). The left wall of the bay consists of some steep black walls.

Whale Meat Again   15m   Severe   (2002)
Start as for The Slips and climb the slab leftwards to the chockstone in the gully. Cross the gully and climb the stepped corner to the right of the steep stratified wall. Finish by the left of two easy ramps.

A Wee Cracker   15m   VS 4c *   (2000)
Below and left of the steep stratified wall is a large right to left slanting flake-crack. Immediately below this is a thinner and parallel flake-crack. At low to mid-tide, step across the inlet to climb the thinner flake-crack to the break, then finish more easily up the arete above.

The Meikle Ross Traverse   VS/Ungradeable   *(1999)*
The full sea-level traverse of the Meikle Ross. This scenic undertaking is mostly
scrambling with some 4c moves between Poison Ivy and Titans Corner. The crux is
most definitely the leap of the Rift, from K9 to Rift Route, only safe at three-
quarters tide.

The 30m cliff at **Ringdoo Point** (NX 596 458) is situated on a remote section of
coast west of Meikle Ross. It is best approached from Borness Farm, south of
Borgue. The main section, above a pinnacle, is unfortunately marred by much
loose rock. To the east of this are some mediocre but sound 10m Difficult and Very
Difficult slabs.

BURROW HEAD

(NX 458 340)   Non-tidal   South facing   Map p230

Burrow Head has acquired something of a reputation as a fearsome deathtrap and
those in search of horror and human sacrifice need look no further. It was here that
the burning of the eponymous Wicker Man, the finale of that occult movie, was
filmed.
   More prosaically, it is the furthest of the sea-cliffs from the main climbing
centres and has seen little traffic since the routes were first climbed. This has
allowed superficial loose rock, guano and serious adventure potential to
accumulate, particularly on the Main Cliff. This should not disguise the fact that
many of the routes, when first gardened were excellent and most of them could be
returned to their former glory by a quick clean. The star ratings reflect the present
condition of the routes. The cliffs are affected by nesting seabirds from mid April
to mid August. Camping is available at Burrow Head caravan site (NX 451 346).

General Approach: Follow the A750 to Isle of Whithorn village (NX 476 365).
From the village follow the sign to Burrow Head Holiday Village and park beside
reception. This is the start of the coastal walk to St Ninian's Cave. Please inform
reception between March and October.

Approach: For the main crags walk through the site to the coast and follow it east
over some awkward fences to the first stakes (abseil and vampire deterrent), which
are located where the path turns a sharp corner to the east (5mins from the
caravan site and just past the cairn on the hill summit).

CAMP SITE WALLS

Tidal   East facing

Various routes have been done in the coves underneath the caravan site.

The Fin   30m   HVS 4c *   *(1980)*
The sea-stack below the caravan site can be climbed to the left end of the flat
narrow arete down right of its summit. Relatively sound rock.

The bay immediately east of The Fin contains a small tidal cliff with two routes.
Approach by abseil from a large spike near the left end of the cliff (above the first
route). The most prominent feature is a left-slanting crack in the middle.

Goblin's Eyes   25m   HVS 5a   *(1991)*
Good steep climbing, starting about 6m left of the left-slanting crack. Climb up and
through two niches, then go directly up, finishing to the left of the top of the
slanting crack.

Killer on the Loose   25m   VS 4b   *(1991)*
Start below the left-slanting crack. Climb the twin crack-lines and walls above and
slightly to the right. Low in the grade but well named.

FLENSING KNIFE CLIFF

Non-tidal   South facing

This and the following cliffs lie about 4mins walk east along the coast from the campsite. Flensing Knife Cliff lies below the first stakes and is identified by a smooth wall, flanked on the right by a slim corner (Flensing Knife) leading to the right-hand end of a quartz flecked roof.

Approach: Scramble down the grass and rock to the west (right-facing out) and then traverse east to below the cliff.

Run Rabbit Run   20m   VS 4b   *(1980)*
Start left of the smooth wall below a short groove, which leads to a corner. A juggy but unprotected wall leads to the crux groove, which is difficult to protect. Move left to a longer easier groove and a good steep finish. Low in the grade.

Lemming's Wall   20m   HVS 5a   *(1981)*
Immediately right of Run Rabbit Run, taking the left edge of the main wall. The name records Burrow Head's golden years when a party of seven made the first ascent.

Watership Down   20m   VS 4b **   *(1980)*
An excellent and clean wall climb, a recommended introduction to the crag. Start just right of Lemming's Wall below a crack high on the wall. Climb up past an undercling, move right to a ledge, and then regain the original line at the crack.

Prometheus (on his crag)   20m   E1 5b   *(1980)*
Delicate, and bold climbing leads to a strenuous roof. Start 3m left of the prominent corner of Flensing Knife. Move left over quartz flecked rock to gain a shallow scoop, then go up and right to a ledge. Climb the roof on the left by twin cracks.

Flensing Knife   20m   VS 4c   *(1980)*
A fine route spoilt by the easy but loose finish. Climb the corner to a bulge, then either layback left (strenuous) or bridge right (technical) to gain a ledge. Follow a diagonal line of loose flake holds leftwards to finish.

Yellow Crack   20m   Severe 4a   *(1980)*
The wall right of the corner has a good crack. Finish up a shallow scoop.

DIAMOND BUTTRESS

Non-tidal   South-East facing

Further to the right is a yellow, lichen covered, diamond shaped face, streaked with guano like streaks of quartz. It has two good but hard climbs. The cliff is marked at the top by a stake.

Naked Fun   35m   E2 5b ***   *(1980)*
Magnificent, when clean, and a then contender for best route in the South-West. Sustained and well protected above the difficult lower section. It roughly follows a line of quartz up the middle right of the face. A grooved ramp left of the toe of the buttress leads right to a foothold on the edge of the wall. Make a hard reach to a horizontal crack, then traverse right to a jug. The ramp above leads delicately right to a small ledge (crux). Climb up left to a good jug, then traverse right until it is possible to go directly up the wall to a small ramp, which leads to the finishing cracks.

Adventures in the Skin Trade   30m   E3 5c **   *(1982)*
Another excellent route, high in the grade and with a thin bold crux. It climbs the

left side of the face, crossing Naked Fun. Start at the toe of the buttress, right of Naked Fun and climb direct to the small foothold on that route. Move up to the horizontal crack, step left and climb straight up (crux) to a line of good holds. Follow these right until a flake-line leads back left and up to a finishing crack.

Round the corner to the east, at a higher level, is a small triangular face.

The Changeling   15m   Scottish VS †   (1981)
The centre of the triangular face. Originally a sandbag at Severe, it is likely to be considerably harder.

Boozers Chimney   15m   Very Difficult   (1981)
The left-hand chimney is shaped like an upside down bottle. Climb the initial chimney, then the left branch of the chimney. The right branch is **The Newt**, and provides better laybacking at the same grade

The Python   15m   Severe 4a   (1981)
Pleasant juggy climbing up the right chimney.

Continuing east is a 20m split wall seamed with grooves.

The Beastie   20m   E1 5b   (1981)
A bit of a beast and not to be underestimated. It starts at the left side of the cliff and climbs a crack through a small roof and the groove above.

GUARDIAN ANGEL CLIFF

Non-tidal   South facing

Hidden from above, this cliff lies about 75m east of the previous routes, mid-way between Flensing Knife Cliff and the pillbox. A solitary stake marks the top.

Approach: Steep grass on the west leads down to the start of the climbs. A prominent left-facing stepped corner identifies the cliff.

All of the routes here were good at one time and it is likely that an abseil garden would quickly resurrect them.

Mephistopheles   20m   HVS 5a *   (1980)
Climb a crack left of the stepped corner, with a hard move above the corner to a ledge. Finish up and left to the top.

Wild Horses   20m   E1 5b   (1981)
Climb the stepped corner, with an excursion on the right-hand wall to gain a crack at its top. Continue directly for 10m, stepping right to a ledge below the final wall. Climb this using an edge on the left.

Guardian Angel   20m   HVS 5b *   (1980)
Well protected, with a sharp start and finish. One of the classics if clean. Start immediately right of the stepped corner. Make a strong pull up right to a ledge and climb the steep crack above to a circular bulge, which forces the climber left then right to cross the slab above to a ledge. Step left and climb the fingery wall to the top.

Devil's Daughter   20m   HVS 5a   (1980)
Start just right of Guardian Angel, below a steep finger-crack. Climb the right-slanting crack, step left then move up to a ledge. Climb the groove on the left to its top, then go direct to the top.

MAIN CLIFF

Non-tidal   South facing

The Main Cliff is located below the pillbox, 75m east of Guardian Angel Cliff. It is an impressive cliff, with a big feel, but is unfortunately now spoilt by loose rock, fish bones and guano.

Approach: The best descent is via a worn V-groove about 50m east of the pillbox (not obvious), that leads to a grassy spur and the base of the cliff. Routes are described from right to left.

East Buttress

On the right side of this buttress there used to be a 15m high by 7m wide detached plinth at mid-height on the crag. Some time in the late 1980s this fell, leaving a long pale and unclimbed groove in the centre right of the crag. The following routes are left of this.

The Shootist   30m   VS 4c   (1983)
A one time enjoyable climb with an exposed finish. Start 1m right of Bright Eyes. Climb a good steepening crack to a ledge. Traverse right for 2m to a small footledge: climb directly to the top on good holds. Strenuous.

Bright Eyes   30m   VS 4c   (1980)
Start at the obvious crack in the yellow wall left of the large rock scar and climb to a ledge. Finish up the twin finger-cracks to the right of the upper right-facing corner.

Waiting for Godot   30m   HVS 4c   (1981)
An unexceptional, albeit bold route, with a sting in the tail. Start just right of the left edge of the face. Climb flakes to a ledge, then the wall left of the upper right-facing corner (crux). Change into winter climbing gear for the final 10m of high angle guano and shale.

Central Buttress

Moving left, assorted rubble leads to the Central Buttress, flanked on the left by a grim looking vertical trench in the bedding planes.

The Cutter   45m   HVS   (1980)
Perhaps the cleanest route on the Main Cliff, with a fine first pitch.
1. 25m 5a Start just right of the trench and climb flakes to a small stepped corner and a ledge.
2. 20m 4b Climb the slabby arete on the right edge of the face.

The Cut   35m   Severe 4a   (1980)
The loose trench between the Central and West Buttresses. Recommended for those in search of a near death experience at a reasonable grade

West Buttress

This is the biggest cliff, noted for a series of hanging overlaps on its left side. The obvious crack-line springing from these overlaps is unclimbed, one of Galloway's last great problems. The following routes are all on the wall to the right of the overlaps.

Mirror, Mirror   45m   E3   (1981)
A serious climb up the centre of the fine wall. Steep fingery climbing on dubious

flakes but with reasonable protection leads to structurally unsound rock on a much grander scale. The start described here was previously described as a direct variation, but the original first pitch seems to have lost vital holds and is no longer possible at this grade. Start below the twin cracks.
1. 15m 5c Climb the cracks gently and flop on to the ledge. The climbing would be good but for the tendency of the flakes to shear off.
2. 10m 5b Place gear behind the booming flake above the belay and gibber upwards to a good Friend placement. Move right over a bulge and up to a ledge.
3. 20m 5a Finish up the arete, as for Conquistador.
Variation: **Pitch 2 25m 5b**
From the ledge, traverse right and grovel up the crack past an in-situ Friend to the top - a bit safer.

Conquistador 45m E2 * *(1980)*
Probably the best route on the Main Cliff if cleaned. Start at the left end of the wall, below a right-slanting crack at half-height.
1. 30m 5b Climb a distinct finger-crack for 3m, move left and climb a deceptive crack to the ledge. Above is an overhanging finger-crack. Climb this rightwards to a ledge and belay. A strenuous pitch.
2. 20m 5a Climb the "cleaned" arete above.
Variation: **Variation Start 4c**
It is possible to climb the groove left of the wall to join the route under the overhanging finger-crack. Dirty.

MONREITH

(NX 370 393) Tidal South-West facing Map p222

South of Monreith the coast rises up to form a small headland above an attractive sandy beach. This is the only sea-cliff where the greywacke is horizontally banded, resulting in a steeper, juggier style of climbing, altogether different from the norm. While it has a lovely beach and nice scenery, the routes are uninspiring and it is deservedly unpopular. The cliffs are affected by nesting seabirds from mid April to mid August. The base of the crag is tidal, and a lack of suitable abseil points means that the routes are best reached by traverse.

Approach: About 1km south of Monreith, leave the A747 opposite the campsite and follow the road to St Medan's Golf Course and the large car park beside the beach. At low tide the beach leads south-east to the crags.

The 500m girdle traverse of the coastline gives a worthwhile expedition, with a 5b crux at the start of Do Barnacles Bite.

MAIN CLIFF

This is the crag first encountered when traversing from the beach and lies behind the prominent pinnacle. Right of the pinnacle is a large slab with three grooves topped by overhangs.

The Big Dig 35m HVS 4c *(1987)*
Probably not as ghastly as it looks. The central groove, or the arete just to its left, leads to the large groove running down from the roof. Traverse right across the slab and climb an awkward crack on the left of the large blocks to a stance. Continue right until a short slab and arete lead to a grassy bay.
Variation: **St Ninians Groove 5a**
A variation start up the right-hand groove and slab directly to the blocky crack.

THE PROMONTORY

Further right the crag becomes more vegetated, then a large gully is reached. Right of the gully is a series of easy angled slabs and right again is a small zawn of sea sculptured rock with quartz veins.

Hack Crack   15m   VS 4c   *(1987)*
The obvious crack in the back of the zawn, reached from the left corner by a layback move.

Do Barnacles Bite?   15m   HVS 5b   *(1987)*
The slanting crack right of Hack Crack.

Between the small zawn and the tip of the promontory lies a steep wall with an obvious groove just left of centre. The next two routes lie between the small zawn and the groove.

Stingray   15m   VS 4c   *(1987)*
From the centre of the wall, climb to the overlap above the previous route. Pull over this to a large ledge and a variety of exits.

Fireball XL 1.5   15m   VS 4b   *(1987)*
Start as for Stingray and climb up and slightly rightwards to reach a right-facing groove at half-height. Finish up the groove or to the left on big holds.

Soup Dragon   15m   Hard Severe 4b   *(1987)*
The barnacle covered wall leads to the main groove, traversing off right at the top. The groove can also be reached from the left.

Mobile-Bat   15m   VS 5a   *(1987)*
This climb takes a left then right-facing groove about 3m right of Soup Dragon.

Mobile-Kack   15m   VS 4c   *(1987)*
Climb the easier angled wall to the right.

Past the promontory the coast turns inland towards two large caves in the back of the bay.

CAVE TWO

This is the second of the two large caves.

Iron Age Crack   18m   Very Difficult   *(1987)*
The slimy crack out of the right side of the cave, finishing up the vegetated groove

CAVE THREE

This lies approximately 25m right of Cave Two. On the left of the entrance to Cave Three is a grey wall with a hanging corner on its left side, clearly visible from the promontory.

Satori   30m   E3 6a *   *(1987)*
An impressive line, in a different class from the other routes. Climb the grey wall into the central groove and go up this to a good resting place above the overlap. A hard and sensational traverse out to the right gains a good jug at the bottom of the thin hanging groove, which is climbed to the top.

A further 300m on is a small, west facing red wall, visible from the top of the promontory

Jelly Fish   15m   Severe 4a   *(1987)*
Climb obvious flakes up the seaward arete of the red wall.

GALLOWAY SEA-CLIFFS

GARHEUGH PORT

(NX 268 501)   South-East & North-West facing   Map p222

This rocky headland offers a variety of traditional routes and bouldering on fins of greywake, with a pleasant, sunny aspect. Most of the rock dries quickly after rain and nesting seabirds are not a problem. The bouldering areas are encountered first, followed by the Main Crag further north-west along the shingle and rock beach. The Roadside Crag is located on the landward side of the road, and north of the hill above the beach crags, when approaching from the Cock Inn and Glenluce.

Approach: Although the second layby passed on the hill above the cliffs (when approaching from the Cock Inn and Glenluce) provides the quickest access to the Main Crag, the best parking is probably on the verge on the seaward side of the road directly opposite the turning to the B7005 to Wigtown. From here, take the track down to the beach and follow it north-east round a field to the Approach Slab.

GARHEUGH PORT - BOULDERING

The boulder problems are situated on a series of crags and sea sculptured outcrops south-east of the Main Crag. A few loose holds remain on some problems, although in general the rock is good quality and there are a few classic problems. The sunny aspect makes Garheugh a good winter venue. Problems are given British technical grades and Font grades where possible.

Approach Slab

Non tidal   South-East & West facing

The first decent rock reached on the approach has an easy angled slab surrounded by gorse bushes on its right-hand side, and a steeper seaward face with a prominent hanging crack. Problems are described from right to left and are rather highball.

A Sense of Danger   5b **
The faint curving ramp near the right edge of the slab.

Afterlife   6b (Font 6c+) ***
A superb bold problem taking the smooth slab just left of Sense of Danger and right of the ivy patch.

Mr Prickles   6a (Font 6a) ***
Another great problem up the left arete of the slab from a sitting start.

Princess   4a **
A highball problem up the bulging right to left crack about 5m left of Mr Prickles.

Suck My Woolie   6b (Font 6b+) **
The short arete at the left-hand edge of the outcrop,right of the wall. Sit start at a jug, move up and swing onto the arete. Finish up Princess.

Un-named   5b
Eight metres left of Suck my Woolie is a short wall. Traverse this from left to right, below the lip, starting from pockets under the left arete.

Sheep Pen 2

Non tidal   West facing

About 25m left is a prominent undercut grassy corner. Left of this are two diagonal right to left crack-lines, above another stone wall.

High Heels, Low Lives   5b *
Sit start left of the right-hand crack and climb the arete without using holds on the right.

Un-named   5b
Sit Start on a low sidepull, left of the left-hand crack. Climb diagonally leftwards.

Some 60m to the left, upturned beds of greywacke extend seaward in a line of waterwashed outcrops. They present characteristically slabby bedding planes to the south-east and steeper cross sections through the beds to seaward.

Sheep Pen 3

Non tidal   South-East & West facing
The landward mass comprises two ivy covered sections of rock, one in front of the other. The first three routes lie on the higher rear section which has another wall at its base.

Snowhite and the Seven Dwarfs 6b (Font 6c) ***
Sit start at a boss in the overhang just right of the arete. Lunge to the excellent sloper on the lip, then pull directly onto the upper slab with difficulty. A classic.

Stretch Armstrong   6c (Font 7a+) **
An innocuous but hard problem up the left arete. Sit start at the same point as Snowhite, move left into an undercut and gain the upper slab with more difficulty.

Eat My Greenie   5b *
Climb the left wall from a sit start, via slopey crimps and a ramp. Finish rightwards.

The lower frontal section is waterwashed and bulging.

Repentance   6b (Font 6c)
The rounded arete. Sit start and climb directly past a circular crimp.

Don King   6b *
Start left of the arete of Repentance and lip traverse rightwards, missing out the big foothold just round the arete. Continue all the way to the diagonal crack before topping out.

Darkness Falling   5b
Sit start on the big undercut right of a small cave and climb the left to right diagonal crack on the right side of the wall.

Un-named   5b
Climb the slab right of the diagonal crack of Darkness Falling and left of the ivy.

Point 1

Non tidal   South-East facing
Left of Sheep Pen 3 is a long easy angled slab which is well seen from the road. The problems are described right to left.

Tied and Bound   5b *
The slab, avoiding the large triangular jug for hands and feet. Aim for the apex.

Rib Tickler   5a *
Start just right of a small arete. Move up the slab till it is possible to reach the slopey pod. Finish up the crack, no escaping up the arete.

Missing Rib   5c *
Climb the slab to the left with a tricky move high up. Avoid using any of the jugs to the left.

Broken Rib   5a
Follow the line of jugs, running slightly leftwards.

Nuclear Puppy   6a ***
Start left of a short crack which runs up to the ramp. Gain a standing position on the crack, now rock up left to a long crimp, and the ramp.

The Ramp   5a
Climb the ramp in the centre of the slab.

Dumby Boys   5b **
Start left of the 'jaggies' on jugs, move up then right to some good holds. Climb up and left to finish.

Lizard Line   6a/b
A bold line can be pushed directly up from the starting pod of Dumby Boys.

1.1   5a
The left arete of the slab is easy, except the start.

Scream Slab

Non tidal   South-East facing
The small slab directly behind Point 1 is flanked on its right by a curving grassy bed of fractured rock.

Robocop   5a
Layback up the sharp left arete.

Robotica   6a *
Sit start feet on jug, layaway of arete. Now pull around onto slab to finish as above.

Screamers   5b *
Start just right of the arete, using tiny holds pull on and move up to catch the apex.

Dreamers   5a
Climb the slab on good holds at its highest point.

Manky Boulder

Tidal   South-East & North-West facing
Seaward from Point 1 wall, three boulder like outcrops emerge from the beach. This is the solitary outcrop; the first reached on the approach. The problems don't get much traffic and have remained a bit lichenous. The problems start on the north-west face (away from the approach), split by an horizontal break.

Puma   5b *
Gain the horizontal break near its left end, then mantel.

Reebok   4c
An almost identical problem just to the right.

Shadow Dancer   6b (Font 6c) *
Sit start on a sloper, slap up to a ledge, climb the arete following holds. No flake

or juggy foothold to left allowed for hands or feet. The first move may not be possible if the pebbles are washed too high.

Nike   5a
Climb the bulging wall just left of the seaward arete from a sit start.

Boy Racer   5b
The shallow scoop come groove on the landward face of the boulder.

States Boulder

Tidal   South-East & North-West facing

A short distance further north are two boulder like outcrops, divided by a cleft. They offer the best bouldering at Garheugh, on excellent clean rock. The bases are sea-washed at high tide.

The first problems are on the south-east face (facing the approach) of the landward outcrop. Right of a leaning vertical crack is a scooped wall cut by a low left to right break come crack, which ends below a prominent beak.

Cutaway   5b
Sit start at base of the diagonal break come crack, move up left to a pocket then over the lip.

Life is Beautiful   6a/b ***
Sit start at the left end of the break come crack, swing powerfully up right to a small ledge on the right arete. Finish up the slab above.

Bowfinger!   6a/b (Font 6c) ***
Climb the central face of the boulder via a thin seam to gain the diagonal break. Classic of the crag.

Curmudgeon   7a (Font 7c) ***
Sit start at a juggy slot and climb an innocuous looking thin crack to gain the ledge. Finish as for Life is Beautiful.

Pirates 6a *
Sit start at the right-hand side of the arete on a directional flatty, pull on, swing round the arete and move up to the ledge.

The following lie on the undercut north-west face (away from the approach) of the seaward outcrop.

Mike's Traverse   6a/b (Font 6b+) ***
A superb traverse. Start at a break near the left end of the face and climb the ramp-line rightwards with great moves until it is possible to climb a groove to the top.

Slap and Go   6b *
Below the right hand end of the ramp is a smooth steep wall (offering a hard sit start project). Pull on from a standing start on small holds, gain the ramp and finish directly.

Altered States 6c (Font 7b) ***
Another superb problem taking the undercut flake. Sit start, undercut rightwards to a hard finish on small crimps and slopers.

Changling States 6b (Font 6c+) *
Climb leftwards up the lip of the slabby groove using slopers and heel hooks from a sitting start at a good crimp behind a flake.

In a State   5b *
The slabby groove at the right hand end of the face.

MAIN CRAG

Non-tidal   South-East, West & North-West facing
This crag lies about 120m to the north. There are no sea birds and the rock dries quite quickly.

South Wall

The south-east facing wall (facing the approach) of the promontory has been beautifully undercut by the sea. The routes are described rightwards from the tip of the promontory. Descend down the tip of the promontory (the access route from the second car park on the hill above the cliff).

Secrets of the Coast   20m   Severe   *(1985/6)*
The left arete of the undercut slab. Climb the short crack at the left end of the wall, and then continue up scoops on the right side of the arete.

Battle of the Bulge   15m   E4 6a *   *(1987)*
A hard and technical problem. Start 5m to the left of the above route. Climb the bulge rightwards, making a difficult move over the bulge to a flat hold. Step right to the leftmost of two cracks which is followed to the top of the cliff.

Two Tyred   15m   E3 6a **   *(1985)*
An impressive route. To the right is a thin right-hand crack in the undercut wall. Step off a large block to reach a hold (difficult for the short) and climb to a ledge. Continue with less difficulty up the crack to the top.

Snailey-Whaley   15m   Severe   *(1987)*
Climb the crack in the right arete of the slab to gain the wide and brambly left-trending crack. Step right to finish at the top.

Flubb   15m   VS 4c *   *(1987)*
An interesting, sustained climb. Climb the large corner to the right of the undercut wall.

Deathwish   15m   E3 5b   *(1985)*
Well named. The arete right of Flubb gives fine laybacking, entirely devoid of protection. Placing a side runner above mid-height in Flubb reduces the grade to E2. It has also been climbed by laybacking the right side of the arete.

The E6 Process   15m   E1 5b   *(1987)*
Start out of a small cave 5m right of the last route at a fin-like protrusion running from halfway up to the top of the crag. Climb up to the centre of the overhang and pull over using a large jug over the lip. Move left then back right to climb the groove on the left side of the fin.

Buba Luba   14m   HVS 5a *   *(1999)*
A good sustained climb. To the right of the E6 Process are twin cracks, which are followed to the top. Utilising only the left crack is E1 5b *.

Too Cold to Chew   14m   VS 4c   *(2004)*
Two metres right of Bubu Lubu is a crack with a large thrift at about head height. Climb up past this to a ledge and spike (loose) at half-height. Continue on to the top.

The Promontory

These routes are found on the tip of the promontory, immediately left (north) of the descent. Routes are described right to left from the tip of the promontory.

My Bonny Lies Over the Ocean   23m   Severe   (2001)
A pleasant route. Start just right of Foot in Mouth. Climb the right-leaning groove to gain an arete on the right. Follow this and the slab above to a bulge. Avoid this by traversing the wall on the right to a wide crack, which leads to a slim groove and the top.

Foot in Mouth   23m   VS 4c   (2001)
A traditional but worthwhile struggle. It takes the wide crack in the centre of the green lichen covered, seaward face to a ledge, then the continuation crack above.

Cock Inn Cap'n Birdseye   22m   Severe   (2001)
Worthwhile, if somewhat lichenous. Start as for the previous route, but move left after 2m into another crack. Follow this to a ledge on the left or north wall of the promontory. Continue up left to another ledge, and then finish up a leftward sloping crack in the final wall.

Gooseberry in a Lift   23m   HVS 5a   (2001)
Climb the direct start to Cock Inn to a ledge. Climb the hairy green arete and wall above, left of Foot in Mouth, to a platform. Climb the arete just right of the finishing crack of Foot in Mouth to the top.

North Wall

This wall is steep but split by ledges. At its left end, in a brambly bay, is a steep chimney running the length of the crag.

Full Moon Fever   20m   E1 5b *   (2001)
Surprisingly fine, taking the steep, unrelenting chimney. Well protected, and worth two stars were it not for the odd loose hold.

The Fat Lady Sings   20m   E1 5a   (2001)
A good sustained climb, albeit somewhat devious and contrived in places. Immediately right of the previous route is a slim rib, bounded on its right by a steep corner leading to a grass ledge. Climb the steep corner for 5m, moving left onto the rib as soon as possible. Follow the rib up and left, to eventually stand on a ledge on the left edge of the rib. Boldly move slightly right, then up to good holds, following these back left to the edge to finish.

Pillar Area

About 100m north of the main crag, at the back of a bay, is a pillar with ivy on its right wall. Descent from this and all the following routes is by scrambling down a chimney situated on the seaward end of Smuggler's Slab.

Dr. Hemlock and Mr. Damocles   22m   VS 4c *   (2001)
A good climb with some interesting moves. It takes the groove in the arete, finishing to the left of the obvious rock swords. Belay on crash barrier.

An Idea of Excellence   22m   HVS 5a *   (2001)
Another good route with a thin crux. A roof splits the wall left of Dr. Hemlock. Climb up to the alcove below the roof which is exited at its left end. Traverse right along the lip of the roof to a thin crack. Directly up this (crux), then continue to top.

GALLOWAY SEA-CLIFFS

Smuggler's Slab

About 150m to the north of the main crag is another smaller slab of good quality rock. Micro-cams useful.

Too EC   10m   Severe   (2001)
The undercut and vegetated wall left of Smugglers Grill is better than it appears.

Smuggler's Grill   10m   Severe   (1987)
Climb the obvious wide central crack.

Bombin the L'   10m   VS 4c *   (2001)
Lovely climbing, probably the best on this face. Climb the white and green speckled slab 1.5m right of Smuggler's Grill, avoiding using that route.

Stone Crop   10m   VS 4c *   (2001)
Start 2m right of Bombin the L', and just left of Landmark. Climb straight up to a very short leftward-slanting crack. Move up to a rock flange with difficulty and then finish more easily to the top.

Landmark   10m   VS 4c   (1987)
Climb the centre of the slab past a peculiar wedged flake.

T Bone   12m   HVS 4c   (1993)
Fine climbing up the vague right-sloping fault-line at the right side of the slab.

Cash 'n' Carry   VS 4c   (1987)
Start at the far right of the slab, just left of the ivy mass and just right of T Bone. Climb straight up the wall to a left-trending fault, which is followed to the top.

Pigeons' Cave

About 170m north of the Main Crag is a medium sized cave. Some 30m further north is a smaller vertical cave partly obscured by undergrowth. It features a long black streaked, and often wet, right-hand wall.

Stop the Pigeon   5c (Font 6b) *
Start in the cave at crimps by a pile of blocks, traverse out and keep going for 15m to a big smooth foot ledge on the far right.

ROADSIDE CRAG

(NX 265 504)   South-West facing

These short cliffs lie on the landward side of the road. They are not as fine as the beach cliffs, but provide an element of variety. Routes are described from left to right and all except the last two route are contained in the left-hand of two bays. The first two routes are on the short clean wall facing the road at the left side of the bay.

Approach: From the Cock Inn and Glenluce, park in the first layby on the right at the road ascends the hill above the beach crags.

First Bay

Gorilla   8m   E1 5c   (1985/6)
Starting from the left side of the bulging central crack, use an undercut to swing up and left. Gain the arete, move to its right, and then continue to the top.

Jackdaw Crack   8m   VS 5a   (1985/6)
Take the bulging central crack direct to a slab, then a thin crack to the top.

The left wall of the bay is spotted with yellow lichen and is the largest wall.

Wee Pig   10m   VS 4c   (1985/6)
Climb the wall using the cracks on its left side.

Trainspotter's Traverse   12m   VS 4c   (1995)
Climb the centre of the wall, just right of poised blocks, until underneath the
overhang, then traverse left on good holds to finish at the top of Wee Pig.

Pause for Thought   10m   E2 6a   (1995)
This climbs the thin crack direct to gain and climb the open groove above the
overhang.

At the right end of the yellow licheneous wall there is a pillar buttress.

Catapult Suzie   10m   E3 5c   (1995)
Bold and committing with ground fall potential. Climb the shale filled crack on the
left to a handrail on the main face above a small roof (runners in the thin corner-
crack on the left). Make hard moves up using both aretes to stand on a handrail,
then straight up to finish.

Ranti Crack   8m   E2 5c   (1995)
Climb the right corner of the buttress to a ledge, then follow the thin left-trending
crack above.
Variation: **E1 5b**
Climb the crack to the sloping ledge at 5m, then step right to the holds on the
arete. Finish leftwards.

Second Bay

Nay Sweat   9m   Severe 4b   (1985/6)
Starting at the cave in the second bay, about 10m right of the yellow wall. Climb
up on the right to a niche, then move up and right to the arete at the top.

Fine Line   6m   VS 5a   (1985/6)
This is on the roadside slab at the far right of the crag. Climb either up and left
using small pockets or straight up the thin crack.

The Rhinns

This area has the largest number of cliffs. The rock is greywacke in the north and
at the Mull of Galloway, and granite at Laggantalluch and Crammag. It is here that
the bulk of good new climbing has been found in recent years. The rock is generally
the best on the sea-cliffs with a variety of routes from the lighthearted to the
remote and serious. Although Finnarts Point is on the Ayrshire coast, it is included
in this section for convenience. There is camping at Glenluce (NX 200 574),
Portpatrick (NW 007 537), New England, north of Drummore, (NX 120 425) and
Drummore (NX 136 366).

FINNARTS POINT

(NX 044 742)   Non-tidal   West facing   Map p222   Diagram p259

A series of cliffs situated on that isolated section of coast between Stranraer and
Ballantrae. The main cliff is probably the steepest in Galloway and gives power and
stamina routes reminiscent of a sports crag. While initially intimidating, the rock is
an excellent quality igneous material and gear and holds appear when required.
The cliffs are affected by nesting seabirds from mid April to mid August and some
of the ledges below the main cliff remain dirty after the nesting season. The cliffs
dry quickly after showers, but two to three days of dry weather is needed after
prolonged rain. There is a fine outlook onto the north end of Loch Ryan.

GALLOWAY SEA-CLIFFS

Approach: Leave the A77 at (NX 094 789), 5km south of Ballantrae, for a minor road signposted pottery plants. Follow the road for 200m to a junction at the pottery. Turn left and continue for 6km along a gradually deteriorating road then track, keeping left at any junctions. The track swings southwards and eventually Loch Ryan and the top of the Stranraer peninsula become visible. Shortly thereafter, there is an area of gorse bordering the track, shortly before the track swings sharply uphill to the left at a gate. Park here, and from the gate walk south-west, aiming for a small nick on the edge of the moor just below an aerial on the Stranraer peninsula. To reach this nick, it is best to remain high on the left, until a wall is reached, which leads into the nick. From the nick, go down the hillside to the left. The main cliff is straight ahead at the bottom of the slope (15mins).

MAIN CLIFF

Approach: From the cliffs southern end (left looking out), go down an easy rib on its seaward side. At low tide it is also possible to climb out from the north side of the crag at Very Difficult, although this is complex and not recommended in descent.

1 Edge of the Abyss   25m   E4 6a *** (1996)
An outstanding route, macho fantastico, and both strenuous and sustained. Protection is good if you are strong enough to place it. The route takes the overhanging grooved arete at the left end of the face. Climb the arete to a spike and step left off the spike into a hanging groove. Difficult moves up this lead to a ledge. The final wall is climbed on the arete to the left.

2 Last Night at the Prawns   25m   E3 5c ** (1997)
An excellent and varied route, where no-brain thuggery leads to a delicate and cunning crux. This is the line of mildly overhanging corners 2m right of Edge of the Abyss. The crux is the pale corner just above half-height (Rock 2 and 4 sideways near foot of corner).

3 Full Speed Ahead   25m   E3 6a ** (1997)
Technical, delicate and strenuous, with increasing difficulty. To the right of Last Night at the Prawns is an uncompromisingly steep wall, with a right-trending stepped ledge on its right. The route takes the initial step in this ledge via a wide crack in its corner, then climbs directly, then right to a slim and difficult groove on the immediate right of the uncompromising wall.

4 Red Hot and Blue   25m   E3 6a * (1996)
Another fine climb. The right-trending stepped ledge leads right to join the top of a crack. This crack runs nearly the length of the cliff and provides this climb. The crack is reached by boldish climbing, then is sustained but excellently protected. At the top of the crack, swing left to an easier finish.

5 Camp Boss, Can't Cook, Won't Cook   25m   E3 5c * (1997)
Another good route, protection increasing with height. Start just right of Red Hot and Blue. Climb up and rightwards with poor gear to gain the obvious crack up above and left of the big corner of I Should Coco.

6 I Should Coco   25m   E2 5c * (1995)
The central area of the crag is slightly easier angled, with a large corner. This climbs the corner, reached by the wall directly below. While not as sustained as some of the other routes, the top corner is technical.

7 Rhythm Nation   25m   E2 5b * (1995)
An interesting and varied route. Start for I Should Coco and climb its initial wall to the foot of the corner. Traverse right round a rib and climb up and right to gain a corner. Follow this for a few moves until it is possible to traverse left onto the arete, which is followed to the top.

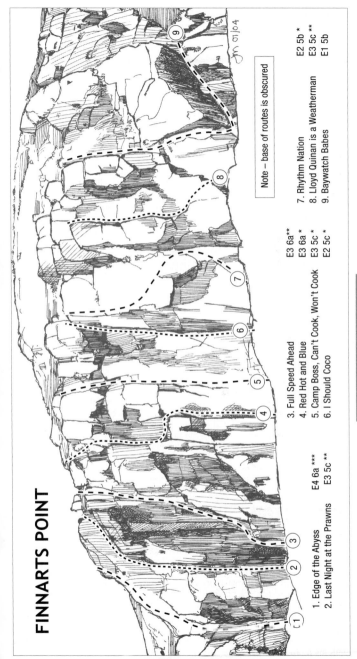

FINNARTS POINT

1. Edge of the Abyss   E4 6a ***
2. Last Night at the Prawns   E3 5c **

3. Full Speed Ahead   E3 6a**
4. Red Hot and Blue   E3 6a *
5. Camp Boss, Can't Cook, Won't Cook   E3 5c *
6. I Should Coco   E2 5c *

Note – base of routes is obscured

7. Rhythm Nation   E2 5b *
8. Lloyd Quinan is a Weatherman   E3 5c **
9. Baywatch Babes   E1 5b

GALLOWAY SEA-CLIFFS

**8 Lloyd Quinan is a Weatherman   22m   E3 5c ** *(1996)*
A fine route of contrasting styles. To the right of the previous area is a prominent hand crack high on the wall. Start 3m to the right of the hand-crack. Step off a flake and climb a short but very intimidating undercut wall on underclings, past a half-moon shaped overlap, to a flake. Traverse left along the flake to the fine fist-crack and finish up this.

9 Baywatch Babes   18m   E1 5b   *(1995)*
A good introduction to the wall. Start at the extreme right end of the crag and traverse left (this traverse line would eventually lead to the foot of the fist-crack on Lloyd Quinan) to below a short corner. Climb this, then continue to the top.

SURFIN' SEAL BAY

This is the next large bay south of the main cliff. About 200m south of the Main Cliff access is a block with a stake on top of it. The only climb to date is on the south face of this.

Approach: Scramble down to the top of the block, then either descend its seaward face (Difficult) or abseil.

Bustin' Surfboards   8m   E2 5b   *(1995)*
This route climbs the centre of the block's south facing side and, while short, has some excellent moves. Start at the left of the face and climb up to clip a peg above an overlap. Move 2m up and right to a precarious mantelshelf onto a small ledge. Continue directly to top.

SMUGGLER'S ZAWN

This is the next bay to the south, difficult of access from land or sea and with a cave at its head.

Approach: Abseil down the following route, from anchors 30m up the hill; a spare rope is required.

Electric Brae   45m   HVS 5a * *(1996)*
An interesting route in a remote setting. A further curio is the changing geology on the route. At the back of the zawn, about 50m left of the cave, is the biggest sweep of clean rock on the crag. At mid-height are overlaps, with two corners. Start right of centre, and climb up to, and up the higher, right corner through the overlaps. Above the overlap, move 2m right and continue on excellent rock to the top.

Smuggler's Ridge   40m   Very Difficult   *(1996)*
This is the ridge to the right of the cave. While useful as an escape out of the zawn, the final moves are on turf and it is not recommended as a descent.

PORTOBELLO

(NW 961 664)   Maps p222, 261

With its small bays, sunny inlets and wide range of routes at all grades, there are few better places in Galloway to enjoy a mellow and relaxed day at the seaside. Although only 10 to 15m in height the greywacke is generally sound and the climbing interesting. The rock is very quick drying and the area sheltered, making it a good early or late season venue. Climbing is also possible during the nesting season. Some of the cliffs are tidal, although with the exception of Portobello Bay Cliff it is possible to reach all routes at low tide without abseiling.

Approach: From Leswalt, north-west of Stranraer, follow the minor road straight ahead, up the hill past the monument (NX 008 646). Turn left at the T-junction with the B738 coast road. After 1km (just after Mains of Carbrock Farm) at a sharp

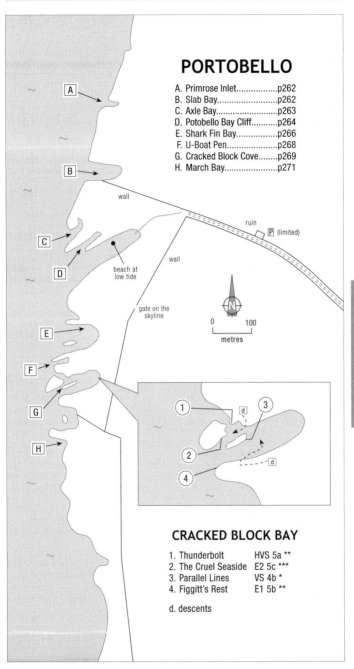

PORTOBELLO

GALLOWAY SEA-CLIFFS

CRACKED BLOCK BAY

1. Thunderbolt   HVS 5a **
2. The Cruel Seaside   E2 5c ***
3. Parallel Lines   VS 4b *
4. Figgitt's Rest   E1 5b **

d. descents

left turn, turn right onto a track, which leads down to Portobello Bay Cliff. Park at the last ruin.

There are two main areas of cliffs. Portobello Bay Cliff is straight down the track (2mins), with Primrose Inlet, Slab and Axle Bays to the right (north). Shark Fin Bay and the remainder of the crags are across fields to the left (5mins). The cliffs are described north to south.

PRIMROSE INLET

Tidal   South facing   Map p261

This long, low wall is situated 250m north of the access track and immediately north of Slab Cove. Even further north are short walls, providing pleasant and safe bouldering. In the centre of the wall, at mid-height, is a ledge, easily accessed from either side by flakes.

The Snail Trail   6m   Hard Severe 4b   (2003)
This deceptive climb takes the narrow slanting ramp 2m left of the easy flake.

Haddock's Left Fin   7m   Severe 4a   (2003)
The slanting crack just left of Fanny Haddock.

Fanny Haddock   7m   Very Difficult   (2001)
The wall to the left of the left-hand easy flake, starting up a small corner and finishing to the right.

Above the easy flake is a short wall with three cracks splitting its top.

Johnny Dory   8m   Very Difficult   (2003)
Climb the left side of the huge flake, then continue up the wall above, to finish up the left-hand crack.

Ann Chovy   8m   Severe   (2003)
Up the centre of the huge flake, to finish via the central crack.

Mullet of Cocktail   9m   Severe   (2003)
Climb the right edge of the huge flake, then the crack above, to finish up the crack to its left.

Sick Squid   10m   Hard Severe 4a   (2003)
A hard eliminate, starting up the corner on the right side of the huge flake, then climbing the wall between Mullet of Cocktail and Bottom Feeders. Finish up the short crack above.

Bottom Feeders   10m   HVS 5a   (2001)
The best route on the wall. It climbs the wall to the right of the right-hand easy flake, starting 1m to the right of the foot of the flake. Short but not to be underestimated.

Whiting For Godot   10m   VS 4c   (2003)
This climbs the wall to the right of Bottom Feeders, via a curious pancake of rock.

SLAB BAY

Tidal   North and South facing   Map p261

This bay lies about 180m north of the access track, beneath the stone wall leading from the access track.

The south side of the bay has a steep, slabby wall split by a zigzag crack with two pods; The Man from Del Monte. The north side has a long low wall with, from right to left, the following three routes.

Brain Dead Fred   10m   E3 5c   (1995)
This is the intermittent crack-line in the centre of the wall. Bold moves up the grey shield of rock gain twin pegs. Continue up on small edges to exit with difficulty.

Grim Reefer   10m   E1/2 5b   (1995)
Climbs the wall to the left via long reaches on pockets. Poorly protected.

One Green Bottle   10m   Very Difficult   (2000)
The corner to the left of Grim Reefer.

The following lie on the south side of the bay.

A Dream of White Helmets   23m   Hard Severe 4b *   (2000)
A pleasant route. The wide, low wall overlooking the easy gully that leads down to the base of The Man from Del Monte contains an obvious diagonal fault-line rising leftwards from the right-hand end of the wall. Follow this fault till it ends at a shallow scoop, then finish up short corner above.

Screamadelica   15m   E5 6a *   (1997)
Intimidating (with good cause), and difficult to read. This is the arete to the left of the Changeling, starting up the Changeling and climbing its lower crux before moving out left onto the arete.

Changeling   15m   E5 6a **   (1993)
An excellent sustained route, now serious. Climb the unprotected arete left of The Man from Del Monte with difficulty, to reach the thin crack just right of the upper arete. Pegs originally protected the lower section at E4. While the upper crack is the technical crux, the lower unprotected arete is now the overall crux.

The Man from Del Monte   15m   E3 6a ***   (1987)
Excellent, technical finger-jamming up the central zigzag crack with two pods.

Dances with Mackerel   15m   E2 5c   (1993)
Climb the cracks to the right of The Man from Del Monte. Worthwhile, and high in the grade.

AXLE BAY

Non-tidal   South facing   Map p261
This is the steep, south facing and pocketed wall situated in the small bay immediately north of Portobello Bay Cliff. The rock is good, generally better than on Portobello Bay Cliff. Routes are described right to left.

The Elle Factor   12m   VS 4c   (2001)
Well positioned with some good moves. At the right edge of the face is a slab leading to roof. Climb the slab, over the roof then straight up the hanging groove in the arete to finish.

Jack the Kipper   12m   E2 5c **   (2001)
Brilliantly devious and compelling climbing unlocks the wall right of Bootless. Start 2m left of the vegetated fault between Bootless and the right arete of the face. Climb to a horizontal fault, follow this left, then climb pockets until they disappear. Above the pockets move up and slightly left, then back right to gain a good ledge at the top right of the face.

Bootless   15m   HVS 5a *   *(1992)*
The left-trending central line gives steep, sustained and occasionally intimidating climbing.

The Dogs Pollacks   15m   HVS 5a   *(2001)*
Another steep, but better protected route, up the left-hand crack-line. Finish to the right, avoiding the final vegetation.

PORTOBELLO BAY CLIFF

Tidal   South-East facing   Map p261

Portobello Bay Cliff, Captain Pugwash's home port, is situated about 90m ahead of the end of the track, down the line of a small stream. A deep sea filled chimney divides the crag in two, with the left-hand section rising straight from the sea. Routes are described from right to left and are easily viewed from the promontory dividing the bay.

Crawford's Crackers   20m   HVS 5a   *(1987)*
Good climbing in its upper reaches. Start a few metres left of the old plaque and follow a left-slanting crack-line to an overhang, which is climbed, slightly rightwards, on good holds. Belay well back.

Underling   25m   E2 5c   *(1993)*
Bold and technical climbing up the groove in the undercut left wing of the Crawford's Crackers buttress. Climb the groove at the left toe of the buttress, then continue more easily up the left side of the main buttress.

Traverse of the Cods   40m   Difficult   *(2001)*
An easy but spectacular rising traverse. Start just left of Underling. Gain the obvious leftward-rising traverse line and follow it across Limpet Buttress and out left onto the arete. Move up to a ledge and continue traversing the rising line leftwards, around the far arete (overlooking the sea filled chimney) where a groove leads to the top.
Variation: **Direct Finish   Hard Severe**
From just before the far arete, climb directly through the bulge on dubious jugs.

The next three routes are on the buttress to the left.

Monsieur Dubois   22m   E1 5b *   *(1997)*
Enjoyable climbing up the leftward-curving corner then overlap at the right side of the buttress. Pass the overlap on the left, where it joins The Crayfish Twins, and finish up that route.

The Crayfish Twins   25m   E2 5c **   *(1993)*
Classic greywacke intricacies. It climbs the improbable wall 3m left of Monsieur Dubois. Follow flakes and pockets, moving slightly left at 8m, then go back right to cross the overlap.

Floating Voter   25m   HVS 5a   *(1987)*
Starting about 1m left of the previous route, follow a left-curving groove or corner continue up until easier ground can be reached. Continue up and right to finish. Low in the grade.

Limpet Buttress

This is the slabby buttress between Floating Voter and the deep sea filled chimney to the left.

Limpetstiltskin   15m   VS 4c   *(2001)*
The right arete is much easier and better protected than it looks. Gain a jug on the arete and pull up via a thread to a ledge. Follow the crack above or move up right to regain the arete and follow this to the top.

The next two routes take the two crack-lines on the face and are best gained from the foot of the sea filled chimney by traversing right to gain a flake at their foot (low tide only).

Thinking Man's Limpet   15m   VS 5a   *(2001)*
Start up the left-hand crack for a few moves until a thin traverse right can be made into the right-hand crack. Follow this to the ledge and finish up the wall between the two upper cracks.

Blockhead   15m   Severe   *(1987)*
Make a hard pull up into the left-hand crack and follow it to the ledge. Finish up the crack above

Sea Buttress

To the left is the deep, sea filled chimney dividing the crag. There are four routes on its left side. Access is by abseil down either side of the chimney. It is possible to step across the bottom of the chimney opposite the wide crack of Cockle Sucker. The first two routes lie to the right of Cockle Sucker, inside the chimney.

Flaked Halibut   15m   Severe   *(2000)*
From the ledges at the foot of Cockle Sucker, traverse right and slightly down to reach the right arete of the wall, and follow the prominent flake-crack up the arete to the top.

Herring Aid   15m   Severe   *(2000)*
The obvious flake-cracks directly above the belay ledge, just right of Cockle Sucker.

Cockle Sucker   15m   Severe 3c   *(1990)*
Climb the wide crack at the junction of the main cliff and the chimney, directly opposite the step across.

Shellfish Bastard   15m   Severe 3c   *(1990)*
The shallow corner right of Happy Man. Traverse left from the foot of Cockle Sucker and climb the corner. Pleasantly innocuous.

The following four routes are reached by abseil down the line of Happy Man to belay on small ledges at its foot.

The Prawnbroker   15m   VS 4c   *(2000)*
Start as for Happy Man, climb the wall to the right till near the right arete, then finish by cutting back left. Unpleasant with rock not above suspicion.

Happy Man   15m   Severe 4a *   *(1987)*
The excellent and conspicuous crack-line in the buttress rising from the sea.

Unhappy   15m   E1 5a †   *(1996)*
Climbs the wall to the left of Happy Man on fragile edges.

Soul Kitchen   15m   HVS 5a *   *(1992)*
Climb the thin corner left of Unhappy.

Horse Latitudes   15m   E1 5a *   *(1993)*
Traverse left from the foot of Soul Kitchen to the arete, which gives fine climbing with spaced protection.

The following four routes are reached by abseiling to a semihanging belay at the foot of Count Duckula.

Puffin Nuffin 12m Severe 4a *   *(1989)*
A pleasant route. Immediately to the left of Horse Latitudes is a large corner. From the start of Count Duckula, move up right and climb the corner.

Hanging Duck 12m Hard Severe 4a   *(1990)*
Start as for Puffin Nuffin, but after 3m break out and climb the steep corner which trends up left.

Count Duckula 10m Very Difficult   *(1990)*
This is the left-trending shaley groove-line about 5m left of the corner of Puffin Nuffin.

Lost at Sea 10m E1 5b   *(1993)*
Sustained edging. There is no protection for the crux and the grade reflects the soft if wet landing. From the foot of Count Duckula, traverse 2m left into the middle of the wall and climb directly to the top, with a rightward diversion at half-height.

Surfin' Safari 10m Severe 4a   *(1989)*
Pleasant. At the furthest left end of the crag is a wall with two thin, disjointed, right-trending cracks. Climb these, starting from a platform to the left. Approach by abseil to the platform.

Warsteiner 8m Very Difficult   *(1989)*
Climb the left-hand arete of the cliff above a small platform. Access by abseil, or by climbing down the climb?

SHARK FIN BAY

Partially Tidal South facing Map p261

The following three cliffs, Shark Fin Bay, the U-Boat Pen and Cracked Block Cove are close together and are the most popular at Portobello. Shark Fin Bay lies a short distance to the left of the gate on the approach, and is recognised by a pinnacle resembling a shark's fin. The U-Boat Pen is the narrow inlet immediately south again. Shark Fin Bay comprises a larger section on the right and a smaller promontory to the left. All the routes, except the first three, finish on the promontory.

Approach: From the car parking enter the field on the left, and cross it diagonally left to a gate on the skyline. Access Shark Fin Bay from the top of the U-Boat Pen (depressions in the grass here are a good place to leave sacks) down grass slopes.

At the right end of the bay, reached up a grass slope, is a buttress with a large roof at mid-height. Routes are described from right to left.

Walking the Plank 20m E1 5b **   *(1999)*
An interesting route with a sensational crux. Start at the left toe of the buttress and climb a right-curving crack just right of the left edge of the buttress and leading to the A shaped recess at the top. While it is now possible to escape up easy ground, this misses the main event. Step right into the recess, then down and out to the very lip of the overhang. Swing round this using hidden holds, then climb the headwall to the top.

The next two routes climb the highest section of cliff, right of the promontory.

Buckets of Doom 25m HVS 5a   *(1997)*
Unusual, like climbing a fossilized dinosaur. To the right of the roofs is a line of large pockets leading to a large nest. Climb the pockets to the large nest, move

right then up the wall above. The original route climbed this top wall in its entirety, following it leftwards at E1 5b. It is more obvious, although probably not as good, to follow it directly into the finishing vegetation at HVS 5a.

Silence of the Clams 25m E1 5b ** *(1992)*
A surprisingly big feel to it and a crux way out there. Above the main roofs is a left-trending diagonal crack. Start directly below this crack. Follow a dirty crack to a turf ledge, then go directly up to the roof. Move up and right to perched blocks, then go left up the diagonal crack in a fine position.

The following routes finish on the promontory. Escape from the top of the promontory is either by abseil, by descending Basking up the Wrong Tree (Very Difficult – low tide only), or by ascending the Upper Ridge. The Upper Ridge is Difficult, although climbing it round the left edge, Severe 4a, gives better climbing and is slightly more bird free in the nesting season.

Basic Instinct 15m HVS 5a *(1992)*
Reasonable climbing but poorly protected and worrying. Start 4m to the right of a large triangular niche at an undercut pillar. Gain this with difficulty. Continue boldly to finish at the right end of the promontory.

Cutty Shark 15m Hard Severe 4b * *(1990)*
One of the best of the easier routes. Start below and right of the triangular niche and traverse left into it via flakes. Continue up right to a spike in the corner, which is followed to the top.

The remaining climbs are effected by the tide to varying degrees.

Mussel Bound 15m HVS 5a ** *(1990)*
A popular and well protected classic. Climb the thin crack-line left of the niche, surmount the overhang, then go directly above, via a jagged flake. At high tide start as for Cutty Shark and traverse left into the route.

Water Dance 15m E1 5b * *(1993)*
This gives excellent climbing up the arete left of Mussel Bound, started at a left-trending undercut slab. The main difficulties are concentrated at the start, the initial overhang being climbed by a rockover move. Continue more easily up the arete above

Sanity Claus 15m Severe 4a *(1989)*
Start as for Water Dance, climb the left-trending undercut slab and prominent right-sloping corner above. Some loose rock.

Aqua Vitae 15m Severe 4a *(1990)*
Start as for Sanity Clause, but leave the main corner to follow a less obvious one on the left.

Mussels from Brussels 15m VS 4c *(2000)*
To the right of Basking up the Wrong Tree are steep parallel cracks. Climb these to the ledge. Start up the arete above then climb the wall just to the right to the top. Worthwhile

Basking up the Wrong Tree 10m Very Difficult *(1990)*
The left-sloping corner near the left end of the promontory. A possible descent for the competent at low tide.

Speed Limpets 10m Hard Severe 4b * *(1990)*
Short but sweet. Start at the foot of the corner of Basking and climb diagonal left-trending cracks.

Winklepicker   10m   Severe 4a   *(1992)*
The left-trending layback crack left of Speed Limpets is only visible at low tide.

The seaward face of the promontory has three small routes at Moderate to Very Difficult. The steep west wall of the pinnacle has been climbed at Moderate.

U-BOAT PEN

Tidal   South facing   Map p261

This is the narrow tidal inlet between Shark Fin Bay and Cracked Block Bay. The first three routes are on the slabbier right-hand buttress, the latter ones are on the steeper tidal buttress. The routes are described from right to left.

Approach: As for Shark Fin Bay.

Lurchin' with the Urchins   13m   Hard Severe 4b   *(2000)*
Climbs the obvious undercut crack, corner and slab to the right of Feeling the Pinch.

Feeling the Pinch   14m   VS 4b *   *(1990)*
A popular climb. Take the left-trending brown streak in the top half of the buttress, reached from below by a crack. Low in the grade.

The Water Margin   15m   E2 5b **   *(1991)*
Excellent climbing, with improving gear after a worrying start. Start 2m left of the last route and follow pockets (good nut in large pocket) up the thin, lower slab, then climb the upper wall to the right of its left edge. Low in the grade.

The following three routes start at the same point, and require low tide for access.

Doon the Watter   14m   Hard Severe 4b   *(2000)*
Pleasant, if totally forgettable, climbing. Start as for Dead Sea Strolls, but climb straight up the short corner above. At its end move left onto the wall and up this to the top.

Dead Sea Strolls   14m   Severe 4a   *(1990)*
A conspicuous crack slopes diagonally leftwards across the seaward buttress. Climb it for 6m, then take the corner above the coffin shaped recess.

The Ducking Stool   20m   VS 4c **   *(1991)*
A classic – the place to be at low tide. Start as for Dead Sea Strolls, then take the conspicuous, wide diagonal crack slanting left across the buttress. Finish by moving up right, to finish up a corner at the top of the crag.

The Zombie   15m   Severe 4a   *(1990)*
Creep out of the coffin-shaped, sea filled recess left of Ducking Stool, then go leftwards up the wall above, crossing a small overhang near the top. Abseil access to hanging belay. A little artificial.

Riverboat Gambler   15m   VS 4b *   *(1989)*
This takes the fine crack, which springs from the bottom of the easy, left-sloping ramp at the left side of the crag. Climb the crack to its top, then traverse up and right to a corner.

Paranoid Android   6m   E4/5 6b   *(1997)*
An extended boulder problem, climbing the small steep wall at the seaward end of the south wall of the inlet (opposite the preceding routes). Climb the right-hand overhanging crack and groove-line.

CRACKED BLOCK BAY

Partially Tidal   South (mainly), West and North facing   Map p261

This is the next bay past the U-Boat Pen, reached down grass slopes from the Pen. It is distinguished by the eponymous Cracked Block.

Approach: The quickest descent is not immediately obvious, and takes a ledge leading left (looking out) from above the Cracked Block, across the top of A Close Shave, to reach steep grass slopes.

The first routes are described by reference to the Cracked Block.

**Thunderbolt   15m   HVS 5a ** **   *(1987)*
Enjoyable climbing up the wide crack in the block. Gain the niche and follow the crack above.

St Elmo's Fire   15m   E3 5c *   *(1992)*
Excellent, bold climbing up the wall right of Thunderbolt. Follow the thin crack right of the Thunderbolt niche, move slightly right over a bulge with difficulty, then climb directly to the top.
Variation: **Right-hand Start   E2 5b ** **
The route can also be started up the wall immediately left of the gully, rejoining the parent route at the good holds immediately above the crux. This is easier and better protected, but avoids the true challenge.

Only Monsters   12m   VS 4c *   *(1987)*
A very descriptive name. It is situated on the wall round the arete to the left of Thunderbolt, and follows a line of large holds up its right side.

Carrycots of Fire   12m   E1 5a   *(1997)*
A worthwhile route, with adequate but tricky protection, which climbs a line 3m left of Only Monsters. Move slightly left at the top to cross the bulge at its widest point.

Right of the block is a horrible mass of twisted overhanging rock, which provides two surprisingly sound routes.

Tales of the Rubblebank   13m   HVS 5a   *(2001)*
Contrary to all expectations, the honeycombed pillar 3m from the left end of the face gives a reasonable climb.

A Close Shave   13m   E1 5b *   *(1996)*
Decidedly different climbing up the twin cracks at the right end of the stratified wall. Steep and strenuous, much better and sounder than appearances suggest. It is particularly sheltered and will stay dry in showers.

Left of the Cracked Block is the main wall of the bay. Descent from this is either by abseil or by descending the flakes immediately opposite Only Monsters. To the right of this descent, on the slabby seaward end of the wall facing Carrycots of Fire are three routes. From the left: **Mackerel** (Very Difficult), up slabs; **Herring** (Difficult), the left-hand of two cracks left of the deep chimney and **Goldfish** (Difficult), the thin crack in the rib right of the deep chimney. The remaining routes are described leftwards from the descent.

NRG   10m   HVS 4c *   *(1997)*
Superb positions, fine climbing, the odd dubious hold and ground fall potential add up to a memorable experience. The climb follows the arete defining the right edge of the main face, immediately above the Waster.

GALLOWAY SEA-CLIFFS

**The Waster   10m   E5 6b ** **   (1993)
A desperate and technical route. Left of the Cracked Block and to the right of the undercut sea wall is a smaller wall, seamed with faint ripple cracks. Climb the ripple cracks, using some holds on their left side. The crux is just below the small ledge at two-thirds height.

Another One Bites the Dust   10m   Hard Severe 4b   (1993)
Climb the rather scrappy corner left of The Waster.

Left of the rather scrappy corner is a fine arete which bounds an impressive south facing steep wall, undercut at its base.

**Critical Mass   15m   HVS 5a ** **   (1992)
This popular classic gives sustained climbing up the scooped arete forming the right edge of the steep sea wall. Start from the right.

**Sweaty Trembler   15m   E5 6b ** **   (1993)
At one time the hardest climb in Galloway. A superb but devious climb with just adequate protection. Start 2m right of The Cruel Seaside, below and left of an in-situ peg. Climb through the roof to the peg, then go right and up past the peg almost to the arete. Gain and follow a left-trending ripple to the top. Given the proximity to the sea, it would be wise to check the peg prior to an ascent.

The Cruel Seaside   15m   E2 5c *   (1991)
Forceful and strenuous climbing up the steep crack-line on the right side of the wall, a few metres left of Critical Mass.

Acid Test   10m   E2 5c   (1992)
Climb cornflake rock 4m left of The Cruel Seaside. The climbing eases and protection improves with height. Not a bad route, which would improve with traffic.

Pushed to the Limit   10m   E4 6a   (1992)
Bold and serious with a ground fall possible from the hard move at the top. On the left side of the wall is a left-slanting ramp. Follow the left-trending crack directly above the start of this ramp.

Ramplet   10m   VS 5b   (1992)
The left-slanting ramp is started with great difficulty and followed to its end.

The small south facing wall in the middle of the bay has three routes.

**Betty Blue   10m   E4 5c ** **   (1993)
Superb but very bold climbing up the middle of the blank wall left of Parallel Lines. Low in the grade.

Parallel Lines   10m   VS 4b *   (1990)
The parallel cracks in the centre of the face.

Return of the Limpet   9m   Severe 4a   (1990)
Climb the face to the right, with an overhang at half-height.

The south side of Cracked Block Cove, opposite all the previous routes, has a steep wall at its seaward end. This can be accessed at mid to low tide, by a traverse at the 6m level (Difficult). The wall, while seemingly innocuous, is larger and better than appearances suggest.

**Figgitt's Rest   20m   E1 5b ** **   (1992)
A merciless stamina test piece, taking the steep crack at the left side of the wall.

Finish up the easy slab above.

Portobello Belle   20m   E3 5c * **   (2002)
Sustained, technical and, on occasions, puzzling climbing up the steep wall to the right of Figgitt's Rest. Start 1m right of the start of Figgitts Rest and follow a ripple then crack rightwards to a good hold. Continue directly, then move leftwards onto the upper ledge, to gain cracks through the headwall. Finish up the easy slab above. The gear is good, although micro-wires are required low down.

**Yon Kipper (Fish of Atonement)   20m   E1 5c * **   (2002)
The black corner right of Portobello Belle is harder and better than it first appearances.

MARCH BAY

Tidal   South facing   Map p261

South of Cracked Block Cove is a bay with a pinnacle in it. Immediately to the south of this, in a small inlet, is this small, south facing crag. Routes are described right to left.

Slime Based Organism   9m   Severe   (1996)
Climbs the leftward sloping ramp/slab at the landward end of the bay.

**They're Watching Me   8m   VS 4c * **   (1996)
On the centre left of the wall above the sea is a ramp that rises rightwards from the water. This route climbs the thin leftwards-slanting crack from part way up the ramp.

Tactical Anti-Jellyfish Weaponry   8m   E1 5b   (1996)
From the start of the previous route, head leftwards across the wall come slab to finish nicely via the left arete and a good edge.

Jellyfish Szechuan Style   8m   VS 4b   (1996)
To the left of the previous route, climb a series of ledges and walls.

JUNIPER ROCK

(NW 960 649)   Non-tidal   West facing

Some 2km south of Portobello is a large cove with a striking 25m pinnacle at its southern end and a large red fin in the middle. The pinnacle has reportedly been climbed by its seaward face (VS†), although the deportation of the German poacher first ascentionists, following an appearance in Stranraer Sheriff Court means that details are sketchy. The pinnacle is affected by nesting seabirds from mid March to July.

Approach: Park as for Portobello (see above), walk across the field as for Shark Fin Bay, then follow the coast south. Juniper Bay is below the fourth field, about 2km (25mins). Alternatively, park as for Kiln o' the Fuffock (see below) and follow the coast north for 1km.

The routes are on a north facing wall at the north end of the cove, which is hidden from above.

The Beauty of Flight   15m   E1 5b   (1993)
Climb the thin and strenuous left-slanting crack.

Bridg-it   10m   Severe 4a   (1993)
This takes the chimney between the left end of the wall and a neighbouring rock fin.

FISH KETTLE

(NX 958 646)   Tidal   North-West and South-East facing

About 100m south of Juniper Rock, where the fence turns to the left, is a narrow, steep sided inlet. While not extensive, this provides fine routes in an idyllic location and is worth the walk. As the south wall is red granite, and the north wall is greywacke, there should be something for all tastes. The crag is free from nesting birds.

RED WALL

Routes are described right to left, from the sea inland. Access to the first three routes is by scrambling down the seaward end of the crag, then traversing left.

Absent Friends   15m   VS 4b * (2003)

An interesting and varied route. At the right end of the crag is a deep chimney, with a possible, although unclimbed through route. Climb the chimney to its top, then swing onto the steep right wall to finish.

Tilting at Windmills   13m   E3 5c * (2003)

The grade is due to the relentless, strenuous climbing, rather than any particularly difficult moves or protection issues. Start as for One Hand Clapping and follow the thin fault 2m to its right, finishing through the break in the roof.

One Hand Clapping   15m   HVS 5a ** (2003)

Fine steep climbing up the obvious layback crack in the red wall 7m left of Absent Friends. Start from ledges, which are accessible for a couple of hours, either side of low tide.

Rust Never Sleeps   13m   VS 4c * (2003)

A fine steep route on big holds. To the left of One Hand Clapping is a steep, blank wall, then a deep corner running the length of the cliff. Climb this by the right of two cracks. Abseil approach.

NORTH WALL

Routes are described right to left, landward to seaward.

Midshipman Hornblower   16m   VS 4b * (2003)

Fine, enjoyable climbing. This is the left arete of the inland of the two slabs. At the small roof at two-thirds height, step down left into a scoop and follow this over the roof (crux and not to be avoided on the right!). Low in the grade. Abseil approach.

Gullslinger Slab   18m   Very Difficult (2003)

The pleasant left-hand slab started centrally, then moving out to the left edge as soon as possible. Abseil approach.

To the left of Gullslinger Slab is a steep greywacke wall. The following four routes start from sea-level ledges at the left side of the crag. These are accessible at almost all states of the tide, by down-climbing flakes from the left end of the cliff.

Hanging from the Yardarm   18m   E1 5b ** (2003)

Steep and meaty. In the lower centre of the steep seaward wall, two cracks form a V, this climbs the right-hand one. From the ledges, traverse right around a rib to gain the right crack and climb this to the overlap. Surmount this with difficulty then directly up the left-hand of two slots to finish.

Trouble with the Mizzen Mast   11m   E1 5b * _(2003)_
Another fine route, which takes the left-hand crack, at the right end of the sea-level ledges. Climb the wall 1m left of the lower section of the crack to gain the break below the roof. Move through this (crux), then continue more easily to the top.

The Singing Kettle   12m   VS 4c * _(2003)_
Huge holds make this surprisingly straightforward. Start in the middle of the ledges, some 3m left of the previous route. Climb the wall, then bulge to gain the crack-line, which climbs the tower.

The Jolly Rodger   9m   Severe 4b _(2003)_
At the left side of the crag, above a huge flake, is a left-slanting ramp. Climb this, finishing right.

Magillas in the Mist   20m   HVS 5a * _(2003)_
Fine positions and interesting climbing, following the fault below the roofs that slopes upwards across the crag, from left to right. Start on the ledges at the left edge of the crag, and finish up Gunslinger Slab.

KILN O' THE FUFFOCK

(NW 959 642)   Tidal   South facing   Diagram p275

This curiously named cliff is the south facing wall of a narrow sea inlet, at the landward end of which is an arch leading to a circular depression (The Kiln). This natural blowhole gives the crag its name, and is a useful identifying feature, avoiding confusion with smaller inlets to the north.

While most of the climbing is on the wall of the inlet, there is now climbing in the Kiln itself and on two inlets to the north. The greywacke here is of excellent quality, perhaps the best in Galloway, and some of the routes are outstanding, particularly in the E3 to E4 grade. The cliff is affected by nesting seabirds from April to August and best avoided in big seas. Although quick drying, seepage can cause problems for a few days after prolonged rain.

Approach: Either park as for Portobello and follow the coast south for about 3km (40mins) or, from Mains of Cairnbrook, continue on the B738 for about 2km before turning right up the track to High Mark Farm. Park just before the farm (please ask permission), then cut across fields to the coast and the crag (15mins).

Access to most routes is by abseil and it is wise to leave a rope in case of retreat. At the left end of the cliff is the wide left-sloping ramp of Penguin Parade, beneath the left end of which lie the first three routes.

1 Seaside Buddies   7m   Severe _(1993)_
Directly beneath the top end of Penguin Parade is a shallow corner. This route takes the cracked wall 3m left of the corner. Low in the grade.

2 Water Wings   7m   Very Difficult _(1993)_
Climb the shallow corner.

3 Point Break   10m   E2 6a * _(1993)_
A test piece, with a notable crux dyno. Start 3m right of Water Wings and climb the wall via cracks and pockets.

4 Penguin Parade   15m   Difficult _(1993)_
The wide left-slanting ramp at the left end of the crag is a useful escape route, but is slightly off balance and is not a good descent.

Directly above the lower part of Penguin Parade, at the top of the cliff, is the prominent corner of the Pincer, which is a useful marker for the next three routes.

5 Body Swerve   12m   VS 4c   *(1993)*
Start on Penguin Parade, some 4m left of the corner. Climb a crack to thin left-trending ripples. Move right to the foot of the corner, then take the prominent left-trending crack to the top. Worthwhile.

6 The Pincer   15m   VS 4c *   *(1993)*
A nice civilised route. Climb directly to the corner and follow it to the top.

7 Rock Lobster   20m   E1 5b *   *(1993)*
Steep, technical and unforgiving! Start at the lowest point of the ramp and 2m right of the corner. Climb a thin crack over a bulge, then continue up and left to climb the wall right of the corner.

The next feature right of Penguin Parade is a roof with two distinctive down-pointing prongs.

8 Total Immersion   20m   E4 6a ***   *(1993)*
A magnificent route, delicate and sustained. Start just right of the bottom end of Penguin Parade. Climb up to and over the roof at the niche left of the left-hand prong. Very delicate climbing leads up the steep slab above to the top.

9 Echo Beach   20m   E3 6a **   *(1993)*
Another sustained and technical route. Protection is good but hard to place. Start 3m right of the bottom end of Penguin Parade. Take the very thin crack at the right end of the pronged roof, and once above the roof follow the crack slightly leftwards.

Right of the pronged roof is the lowest, central part of the cliff. The following two routes are immediately either side of this.

10 Abide With Me   20m   E4 6a **   *(1993)*
Sustained climbing with a delicate crux. Abseil just left of the central grassy low point to a hanging belay. Climb to a thin left-trending ledge beneath the widest part of the overhang. Traverse this delicately left to reach holds under the overhang, then move right to cross the overhang at its widest point. Continue slightly leftwards up cracks, then move right to finish.

11 Saturation Point   20m   E4 6a *   *(1993)*
A hard and serious route, particularly lower down. Start immediately below the lowest part of the cliff. Hanging belay on RPs. The line follows the slightly right-trending hairline crack which finishes just right of the central grassy low point. Climb the crack with difficulty over a bulge to a rest. Continue more easily up the better crack to the top.

The next four routes are accessed from sea-level ledges at the right side of the cliff. These are awash at high tides.

12 Burning the Boats   20m   E3 6a **   *(1993)*
A technical but well protected route, which takes the main challenge of the steepest part of the cliff. At the right end of the cliff are ledges at sea-level. Start at their left end, at the foot of a wide and prominent right-sloping crack. Climb to the foot of the corner beneath roofs. Climb the corner, stretch left to clip and check the peg, then down-climb. If the peg is not pre-clipped the route is E5. Step left onto a desperate slab, which leads to the peg and a prominent flat hold at a break in the roof. Continue to the most prominent crack in the headwall, which succumbs with surprising ease.

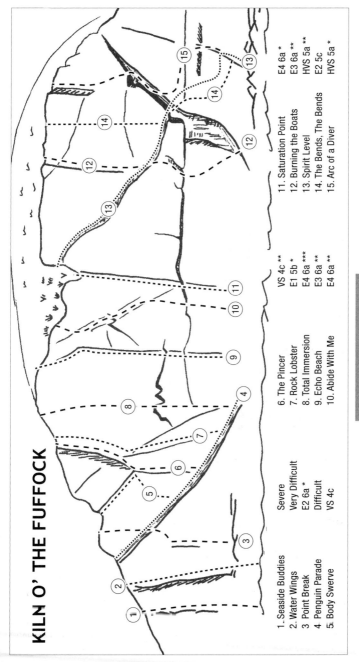

KILN O' THE FUFFOCK

1. Seaside Buddies   Severe
2. Water Wings   Very Difficult
3. Point Break   E2 6a *
4. Penguin Parade   Difficult
5. Body Swerve   VS 4c

6. The Pincer   VS 4c **
7. Rock Lobster   E1 5b *
8. Total Immersion   E4 6a ***
9. Echo Beach   E3 6a **
10. Abide With Me   E4 6a **

11. Saturation Point   E4 6a *
12. Burning the Boats   E3 6a **
13. Spirit Level   HVS 5a **
14. The Bends, The Bends   E2 5c
15. Arc of a Diver   HVS 5a *

13 Spirit Level   30m   HVS 5a ** *(1993)*
An excellent route in superb positions, somewhat reminiscent of the Carnivore traverse. Start in the centre of the sea-level ledges beneath a right-sloping crack. Climb the crack for 6m to a bulge, then move up and left to a good ledge at a niche (the mid-point of the prominent wide right-sloping crack). Traverse left and follow a superb, thin, left-trending ramp-line which traverses the headwall and finishes just right of the central low point. The crux is at the top.

14 The Bends, The Bends   20m   E2 5c *(1993)*
A strenuous climb with a hard, bold finish. Start up Spirit Level, but follow a line below it to rejoin it at the mid-way niche. Step left and climb the headwall directly to crux pinch moves just below the top.

15 Arc of a Diver   20m   HVS 5a * *(1993)*
A good route, steep but with huge holds. Start as for Spirit Level, but follow the right-sloping crack over the bulge to ledges. Move 2m left and climb the wide right-slanting prominent crack to the niche. Move up and left to gain and follow a steep corner at the top.

THE KILN

The Kiln is the grassy hole situated inland from the main cliff and separated from the sea by an arch. The following routes lie in the Kiln on the left side of the arch.

Scrounging Duma   6m   E2 5b *(1994)*
The left crack-line.

Suggestive Digestive   7m   E4 6a * *(1994)*
The right crack.

ORANGE WALL

Immediately north of the Main Cliff is a north facing steep and compact wall. The rock is of very good quality, although all routes are strenuous. Routes described right to left.

Stonehead   10m   E3 5c * *(1996)*
Takes a central line up the wall to the right of the central corner of Spinning Wheel to a rounded finish.

Ocean Colour Scene   10m   E4 6a ** *(1996)*
The left arete of the same wall, immediately right of Spinning Wheel. Excellent but poorly protected.

Spinning Wheel   10m   E2 5c *(1996)*
The crack in the centre of the wall. Climb the crack until it is possible to step right 2m below the top and finish up Ocean Colour Scene.

Hate thy Neighbour   10m   E2 5c *(1996)*
The crack left of the previous route.

Medicine Man   8m   E2 5b *(1996)*
Climbs the wall between Hate thy Neighbour and the corner at the left end of the crag.

Rubbledance   10m   Severe *(2001)*
The left corner of the crag, finishing to the left. The true finish up the slot is liable to dislodge tons of loose rock.

The north side of the bay opposite Orange Wall contains one route

Breakaway   8m   Hard Severe 4b   (1993)
This climbs the central, barrel shaped buttress by the wall just left of the obvious crack.

The inlet immediately to the north contains black slabs on its south side. The routes are best reached by abseil, although none are particularly worthwhile.

Dave's Slab   8m   Very Difficult   (1993)
This takes the middle of the seaward of the north facing slabs.

Zari's Slant   10m   Very Difficult   (2000)
A crack slants up the slab from the left edge, to finish just right of Dave's Slab.

Fuffocking Contortions   10m   VS 4c   (2000)
A deceptive climb. This route lies on the right wall of the Sea Fowl slab. Start by falling across the deep gully cleft and pulling into a short groove at the start of an overhung, left-trending ramp. Ignore the latter and swing awkwardly right across two ribs to the base of the corner, which is entered by more inelegant moves. Step up right, enter the slot, and crawl back left to finish at the top of the corner.

Sea Fowl   10m   Severe   (1993)
Climb the centre of the loose left-hand slab. Low in the grade.

LARBRAX

(NW 967 607)   Non-tidal   South-East facing   Map p222

A gem of a crag, providing inspiring routes above one of Galloway's most idyllic beaches. The climbs to date are on a series of excellent quality greywacke slabs, which give delicate edging and smearing. These include the two hardest routes in the South-West. A double set of small micro-wires is useful. An added bonus is the excellent bouldering on the beach underneath the crag.

Approach: Leave the A718 4km north of Stranraer by a roundabout for the minor road at (NX 028 635) and follow this to a T-junction with the B738 coast road. Turn right and after 2.5km turn left onto a track signposted Meikle Larbrax-Bay Lodge (opposite the ranch style house of Larbrax Lodge). Follow this track to park at the beach. Walk north for 10 to 15mins along the beach (or if the tide is in, at the edge of the grass) to a series of pinnacles on the beach. The slabs are just beyond, above a grass shelf.

SEAWARD SLAB

O'er the Dyke   17m   HVS 5b *   (1995)
A popular and hugely enjoyable route, which climbs the crack at the left edge of the slab. Start beneath the main crack, and climb the wall, then left to grass ledge. Move right onto the main crack, which succumbs to fine finger jamming.

Haste Ye Back   17m   E6 6b/c **   (1995)
A classic, taking the slab at its blankest. The climbing is excellent and thin and the gear just adequate. In the centre of the crag, where the overlap reaches the ground, is a thin crack. Climb the crack for 7m to the first overlap or ripple where a line of reasonable footholds lead leftwards towards the edge of the overlap. Move left along these for 1m or so until small finger pockets and very thin edges lead to the second overlap (RPs in the crack to the right). Move left and up (crucial RP2 on the left) until a stretch back right can be made to a good flat V shaped hold. More extended moves lead to the top on improving holds.

Ceud Mille a Failte   17m   E4 6a ***   (1998)

Another superb route, taking the most obvious weakness in the centre of the slab. After the initial bold section, gear is reasonable. Start as for Haste Ye Back and climb the initial crack of that route for 7m to the first overlap or ripple. Move 2m boldly right (crux) to a rest at a large pocket. Continue directly to the start of a left-slanting fault, then move right with difficulty to reach and finish up the top crack of Ace is Low.

Ace is Low   17m   E2 5c **   (1994)

Lovely climbing in the upper reaches. At the right side of the slab is a crack leading to a spike come pinnacle. Climb the crack to stand on the spike. Tricky although reasonably well protected moves lead into the thinner cracks and the top.

CENTRAL SLAB

A belay stake is situated above this crag.

Trapdoor Fandango   19m   E2 5c **   (2001)

Sustained and delicate climbing up the narrow slab between the Seaward and Central Slabs. Protection is good, from RPs, but is easily overlooked. Climb the left-slanting crack to its top, then traverse 2m right to a horizontal crack on the right of the slab. Climb directly up past triangular pockets, then move left to gain a slot then the arete. Continue up the arete to its top, then move up right (holds under juniper), to gain the centre of the slab which is followed to the top.

Soor Ploom   16m   E2 5c **   (1995)

Start in the middle of the Central Slab. Make a bouldery pull leftwards to start, then move up and left to the right edge of the ivy where a very thin crack splits the overlap (good wires). Climb the thin crack to reach an obvious pocket from where moves left gain a pod crack, just right of the left edge of the slab. Climb this via some odd moves and the last protection, then run it out up the easier arete and the slab.

The Lotus Eaters   16m   E1 5b *   (1999)

Fine climbing to gain, then follow the central crack on the slab.

Mealy Pudding   16m   E1 5b *   (1995)

The right-hand line on the slab, up obvious finger-cracks, via some nice finger jamming with good protection.

RIGHT SLAB

A stake belay is situated at the top of the long grass slope behind the crag.

Caledonia Dreaming   19m   E1 5b *   (1999)

Good climbing compensates for a wandering line. At the base of the left wall is a tapering slab. Climb the left arete of this, using cracks on the left to gain the ledge at the foot of the wide crack. Traverse right for 2m to a footledge. Intimidating climbing leads up to gain and climb the shallow crack just left of the edge.

Cranberry Jam   18m   Hard Severe 4b *   (1995)

The corner-crack at the right side of the tapering slab, then the wide crack above.

Elegance   16m   E6/7 6c **   (2000)

The hardest route in Galloway, taking the centre of the bald slab. Holds and gear are extremely thin and the route is serious, if superb. Start 2m right of the left arete, where a horizontal line of fingerholds leads left into the centre. Follow a micro crack up the centre (thin, sustained and hard to stop and place small RPs) until a small foothold rest can be gained on the right. Step up to gain a horizontal break (shallow Friend 0.5 on the left). Step left and go directly up the centre to the top.

THE BEACH

There is excellent bouldering to be had on and around the pinnacles at the beach. The following problems are on the large beach pinnacle.

Ship's Prow   7m   Very Difficult * (2001)
The arete bounding the steep, landward side of the largest pinnacle.

Reach or Beach   7m   E2 5c * (2000)
This takes the steep landward side of the pinnacle, climbing the overhanging left arete on its right side via obvious holds.

Summit or Plummet   7m   6a * (2001)
A fine extended boulder problem, which climbs the right side of the same face. A spotter is advisable.

The Fin   8m   Very Difficult (2001)
Immediately before the main slabs, where it is necessary to squeeze through a fence on the approach, are three pinnacles. This route climbs the concave slab in the middle of the south facing wall of the middle pinnacle, then the crack above. A number of variations have been climbed.

Mont Vin   8m   Difficult (2001)
About 200m north of the car park, above a stone dyke, is a small, steep, north facing wall. This route climbs the crack on the seaward side of the wall, above a wall. Pleasant

PORTPATRICK

Map p222

There is some good bouldering on the seaward boulders just north of the harbour.

THE WITCH ROCK

(NW 995 542)   Tidal

The Witch Rock   15m   Severe (1899)
This is the sea-stack about 500m north of the town, situated in the bay under the second wireless mast. Climbed by the obvious landward-facing groove system. The west or seaward face has also been climbed, allegedly without difficulty. Low water is required to gain access.

PORTPATRICK QUARRY

This uninspiring greywacke quarry is just south of the harbour at (NW 001 537) and the fact that it doubles as the canine toilet for the town does little to enhance it. The climbs to date are on the central section where the rock is less diabolical in quality, but where protection is worse. Care is needed with the rock, particularly on the mixed ground at the top. Routes are described right to left.

The Flight of the Falcon   30m   HVS 4c (1984/1986)
The best route here, although poorly protected. On the right side of the central section of the quarry is a quartz streaked slab. Follow this then the final 10m of rubbish above.

GALLOWAY SEA-CLIFFS

Kittiwake Ledges   30m   Severe 4b   (1984/1986)
Immediately to the left of Flight of the Falcon is a stepped rib. Climb this to the top overhang, which is climbed using high holds on the left. The final 10m is up the usual mixed ground.

Razorbill Walk   30m   Difficult   (1984/1986)
Start just left of the above route and take a leftward rising line across loose rock and grass. Looks particularly unattractive, except for squatting dogs.

Between the start of Razorbill Walk and the next route is **Chough's Landing** (Severe).

Fulmar Wall   30m   Severe 4b   (1984/1986)
This is the sound(ish) wall situated directly below the most visible part of the cliff top fence. Finish up the usual disgusting mess. Poorly protected.

Two VSs have been recorded further left but fortunately they cannot be identified.

MONEY HEAD

(NX 047 483)   Partially Tidal   South-West facing   Map p222

While not really in the same league as the best crags on the peninsula, this is a nice spot with more than enough good climbing for a day. The crags are about 15 to 25m, face south-west and are formed of clean, good quality metamorphosed greywacke with igneous intrusions. They are mainly bird free, but seepage can be a problem in the central area.

Approach: Just before Sandhead (NX 097 503) on the A716, gain the B7042, signposted Portpatrick. After a sharp right-hand bend take the first left and follow the minor road to park at the crossroads at Cairngarroch Farm (NX 059 498). Walk straight down the road ahead, to the second, new house. From here, a track on the left leads down to a house on the beach. Skirt the coast to the south for about 10mins until a steep, slanting, north facing wall with a slabby south side is reached. Continue south-west for about 10mins to the furthest point of the headland, and descend a slabby platform sticking out into the sea. Ecu Wall is to the right of the platform facing in (south), the central Bear Pit Area is on the left (north) and the Cioch Area is left again. These crags cannot be seen from above.

ECU WALL

All the routes are reached from the platform, save Insider Dealing, which is approached from the rib flanking the wall to the south. Routes are described right to left.

Insider Dealing   40m   Severe 4a   (1992)
A left-rising traverse of the wall, starting just above the initial overhang, at the right toe of the buttress. Interest and situation improves with height.
1. 25m 3b Steep ground and large holds lead left to easy slabs. Follow these left to descend a corner (Ecu Wall) to a cave belay below the large roof.
2. 15m 4a A crack leads up and left beneath the roof. Cross the corner leftwards to a ledge from which an arete leads to the top.

Ecu Wall   20m   Severe 4a   (1992)
Pleasant. Start below the cave beneath the large roof. Climb up and right via corners to a break in the roof, 5m up and right of the cave.

The Liquidator   20m   HVS 5a *   (1992)
An unusual finish. Start about 3m right of the slot of Slot Machine where the crag

is no longer undercut. Gain the short steep corner, then go right to the crack leaving the left side of the cave. Follow this for 4m, then limbo right across the undercut break in the roof to finish.

Slot Machine   20m   VS 4c *   *(1992)*
A curious slot at 5m leads to good bridging up the corner left of the large roof.

The Root of all Evil   20m   E3 5c   *(1992)*
Follow Slot Machine to the slot, then traverse left onto the steep wall, peg runner. Move up and left to a spike on the arete, then go right to the ledge. Finish up the top arete of Insider Dealing.

Cash Flow Crisis   17m   E2 6a   *(1994)*
Fine athletic climbing over the lowest part of the overhang 6m left of the corner of Slot Machine. Above the roof, finish straight up by easier climbing.

Jug Jive   20m   E1 5b *   *(1994)*
A good climb which is less fearsome than appearances might suggest. About 10m left of Slot Machine is a hanging yellow prow with a grey overhanging recess to its left. Move rightwards into the recess, then cross the overhanging right wall on surprising holds to reach the yellow prow. Traverse the lip of the roofs to gain and climb the corner which lies left of the arete of The Root of all Evil.

BEAR PIT AREA

Corners on the right give way to an impressively compact central face. A flying buttress divides this area from easier rock to the left. Access can be difficult during high tide or rough sea. Routes are described right to left.

Pay Day   6m   VS 5a   *(1992)*
Take the undercut corner left of the wide roof at the right-hand end of the crag.

Bolivars   10m   VS 4b   *(1992)*
The two left-trending corners just to the left of Pay Day. Low in the grade.

High Finance   10m   VS 4c   *(2000)*
Left of Bolivars there is an obvious triangular niche 5m up the crag. Start below the left end of this and climb easy rock, before harder moves gain the niche. Pull out on to the left edge, move up to a prominent jug, then up and slightly rightwards to finish.

Free Enterprise   15m   E1 5b *   *(1992)*
Steep and impressive. The left-hand side of the steep, and often wet, central face culminates in an apex. Start right of and below a small, square, black wall. Climb up to the wall, then move leftwards to the apex and finish directly.

Tumbling Dice   26m   VS 4c *   *(1992)*
The stepped rib bounding the central face on the left gives varied climbing. Start at the right end of the short wall, left of the central face. Climb an arete to a ledge. Move left, then right up a steep hanging slab to a wide ledge. Continue up steps and corners to finish right up slabs.

Cash Flow   26m   HVS 5a   *(1992)*
Nice climbing in places. It climbs the corner-line between the stepped rib of Tumbling Dice on the right and the flying buttress of Tax Evasion on the left. Climb the overhung corner at sea-level, move rightwards and up the steep corner above to an easier slab. Below the steep top wall, move right up slabs to a steep finish just left of a protruding beak of rock.

GALLOWAY SEA-CLIFFS

Tax Evasion   26m   Severe 4a   (1992)
The lichen coloured flying buttress descending into the sea is only climbable at low
tide. Start as for Cash Flow and climb the short steep corner on the left to a slab.
Traverse left to a wide crack and finish up the crest of the buttress.

Filthy Lucre   20m   E1 5a   (1992)
Approach by descending slabs to the north, followed by a sea-level, right traverse
for about 100m. Climb the steep left-slanting corner in the bulging undercut rib
with difficulty, then finish out right. Bold.

CIOCH AREA

The northern section of the cliff is characterised by an overhanging beak of rock,
left of a sweep of slabs split in two by a corner. Pot of Gold and Rainbow's End
start at the bottom left corner of the right wing of the slabs and are approached
via easy slabs to the south. Routes are described from right to left.

Martin's Bank   17m   VS 4c *   (2000)
Start up and right of Pot of Gold. Climb a short nose to overcome the initial bulge,
then move right and follow the obvious slotted corner at the right end of the slab
until under the right end of the overlap. Pull up right, then move back left, and
finish up a short hanging corner.

Pot of Gold   20m   VS 4c *   (1992)
Move up right to the overlap, cross this at its left end, then traverse right along the
lip of the overhang to easier ground – good climbing.

Rainbow's End   20m   Severe 4a *   (1992)
A good route. Climb directly for 10m, just right of the edge, before moving slightly
right and then finishing direct.

Loan Shark   21m   Severe   (2000)
Start below and just left of Rainbow's End. Climb over the initial bulge and up easy
slabs to an obvious break in the overlap that defines the left edge of the Pot of Gold
slab. Pull through on mega jugs, then move left to climb the left arete to finish up
a short hanging corner.

LAGGANTALLUCH

(NX 084 363)   Partially Tidal   South-West facing   Maps p222, 283

The cliffs on this part of the coast extend for nearly 1.5km and offer some of the
best quality climbing in Galloway. Most of this is on granite, but north of
Laggantalluch Head there are a number of fine greywacke cliffs. In many ways the
rock quality, scenery and light are reminiscent of Cornwall and a visit is
recommended.

Locating specific cliffs from above can be difficult and once parties have found
an area they tend to stay in it. Consequently Laggantalluch repays repeat visits.
While a number of cliffs are non-tidal the area is best avoided in high seas or strong
sou'westerlies. There are nesting birds in places, but they can usually be avoided.

Approach: At the top of Drummore village, take the road on the right at (NX 134
365), signed Port Logan B7065. Follow this a short way to a T-junction at
Kirkmaiden. Turn left, drive through Kirkmaiden (B7065) and take the second
turning on the right (the first is immediately after the telephone box). Continue for
4km to Barncorkrie Farm, then park with due consideration in limited space after
a further 500m. A track on the right leads down to a cottage overlooking
Portencorkrie Bay. Follow the track until near the cottage then follow the wall on
the right (northwards).

For all crags except Craig of the Stone Dyke and the Anchorage going over the

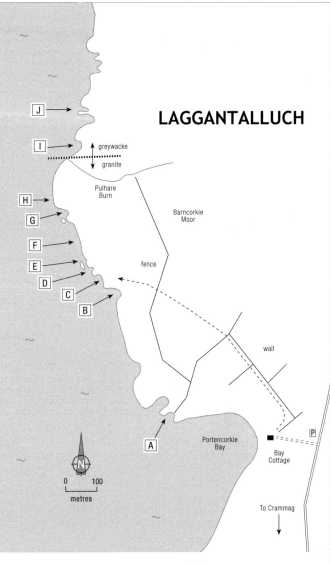

LAGGANTALLUCH

greywacke
granite

Pulhare Burn

Barncorkie Moor

fence

wall

Portencorkie Bay

Bay Cottage

P

To Crammag

0   100
metres

N

hill (Barncorkrie Moor) is easier underfoot, than following the coast. From the end of the wall, head uphill and slightly leftwards. The Main Cliff, with its distinctive large slab, is reached about 200m after crossing a fence on the crest of the hill. The most distinctive features from above are the long low island opposite the Island Walls (although only visible from lower down the hillside), and the headland of Laggantallach Head itself. Abseil ropes are useful for some of the descents.

Crags are described from south to north.

Craig of the Stone Dyke and **The Anchorage** (NX 085 359). At the north end of Portencorkie Bay, just after a stone wall, are two small bays. The first inlet has a few routes between Difficult and Severe up the slab and cracks. The next bay has a 10m south facing wall with one Very Difficult which is poorer than it looks.

SMALL BAY

Partially Tidal   North & South-West facing   Map p283

This is the deeply incut bay just south of the Main Cliff. It has two walls; a steep north-facing seaward wall with the obvious corner of Tormentil facing the ribs and platforms of the Main Cliff; and at the top of the bay, the corner of Stolen Moments.

Approach: Down grass on the north side of the bay.

Immediatly south of Small Bay is a pinnacle at sea level. The groove to its seaward side is **Bright Side of Life** (8m VS 4b 1991). The left side is Severe 4a. Further south again is another block, whose seaward crack is **Unnamed** (9m E15b 1991).

Arete   10m   Difficult (1987)
Take the wall on the seaward face, right of Tormentil.

Tormentil   15m   HVS 5a (1987)
The corner. Low tide or a calm sea needed.

The Brothers Grim   50m   E1 5a (2004)
8m left of Tormentil an innocuous slab slopes up left, setting the trap for this masterclass of loose rock and turf. Follow the slab to its apex, then climb the short desperate arete above to reach the sloping grass shelf. The grassy gully above takes craft and cunning, amply demonstrating the maxim of the great Dr Bell that 'any fool can climb good rock'.

Stolen Moments   25m   E1 5c ** (1995)
A sustained, well protected and thoroughly worthwhile route. High up at the back or landward end of this bay is a raised wall, split by a clean corner. Climb the corner.

Waiting for the Sun   12m   VS 4c (1991)
About 120m south of the main slab is a steep green wall with an easier right-trending, green lichen covered upper slab. Finish up the slab, or scramble down the crack to the left.

MAIN CLIFF

(NX 085 359)   Partially Tidal   South & South-West facing   Map p283

This consists of a large slab, undercut at its right side, and corners and fins above a rock platform to its left. Easy access can be gained by abseiling down the fins to a large platform. The first seven routes lie on the steep ribs and corners to the left of the main slab.

Aqualung   15m   HVS 5b   (1991)
The steep wall at the extreme left end of the crag. From the extreme left end of the platform, abseil down the corner immediately below Escape Route (low tide essential). Start up the corner left of Escape Route, until it is possible to move round left onto a steep fingery wall above the sea. Climb to a ledge, then go up a thin groove about 2m left of the buttress edge.

Stepped Corner   15m   Very Difficult   (1991)
Approach as for Aqualung, but continue up the corner left of Escape Route.

Escape Route   10m   Difficult   (1987)
Left of the overhanging fin is a stepped corner. Step across a gap and climb the corner. This is a possible descent route, but it is difficult to find from above.

Quick Seal   10m   E3 6a ***   (1992)
Excellent climbing up the obvious thin crack in the overhanging fin right of Escape Route.

Rogered Direct   12m   HVS 5a   (1991)
Climb directly up the corner system right of the overhanging fin. The initial difficult section can be avoided from the right (Severe).

The following three routes are on the long steep walls left of the main slab.

Seventh Wave   20m   E1 5b *   (1987)
Start below and left of Laggantalluch Corner at a diagonal crack. Follow this into the base of the corner. Move up and across the left wall of the corner to a thin crack and spike on the arete, then climb the slab above. Eliminate, but good climbing.

Laggantalluch Corner   20m   HVS 5a ***   (1987)
A classic, giving excellent climbing with good protection. It takes the obvious corner in the middle of the wall on the left of the slab.

Ape Escape   20m   E2 6a **   (1987)
Spectacular and well protected climbing through the roof-crack up and right of Laggantalluch Corner. Follow the main slab up past the corner until it is possible to step onto a steep yellow wall, which is followed to a ledge below the crack. Climb the crack to a good spike, make a long reach up and right to a good jug and continue with steep jamming to finish.

The next routes climb the main slab.

The Holy Grail   40m   HVS 5a **   (1994)
The huge corner on the left side of the slab provides unusual chimneying and laybacking. Low in the grade.

Krill Bill   50m   VS *   (2004)
Lovely positions and nice climbing on this rightwards traverse of the slab.
1. 28m 4a   A crack runs diagonally right across the slab from the foot of Laggantalluch Corner. Follow this till near its end, then move up to a higher crack and follow this right to a ledge at its end.
2. 22m 4c   Climb the wall just right of the belay ledge then continue directly to finish.

Irish Mist   40m   E1 5a   (1987)
Near the top of the large slab on the left side is a flake. Climb to the flake and from its right end climb the wall above, trending right. Spaced protection.

**Freewheeling   40m   E2 5b ** **   (1987)
Quality in climbing, but not in gear! Follow the longest central black streak on the slab to a break on the right, runner. Continue up and left to a slight bulge, then trend up and left to finish. The best route on the slab, but a serious undertaking for the grade.

Dublin Packet   40m   E1 5a   (1987)
High on the right of the slab is a black streak leading to a small grassy ledge. Climb the slab to a break below the streak and follow this past the grass to the top.

Stingray   50m   Severe 4a ***   (1987)
An enjoyable open traverse above the large roofs with the hardest moves at the end. Traverse the lip of the overhangs until a groove and corner lead to a small roof and the top.

LUNCH BAY

Non-tidal   South facing   Map p283

Immediately to the north of the Main Cliff is a small bay characterised by a south facing wall with low overhangs. The left arete of the wall is Difficult.

Fish Fingers   12m   E2 5b   (1991)
The wall between Sciatic Nerve and the left arete.

Sciatic Nerve   15m   Severe 4a   (1987)
The stepped corners left of the overhangs.

Truncheon Muncher   15m   E2 5c ***   (1994)
Thin climbing up the wall right of Sciatic Nerve. Start 2m down and left of a large boulder jammed in the gully. Climb to the left end of the roofs, move left round a rib, then climb the wall above.

Micro Niche   10m   HVS 5a   (1992)
The right side of this cliff is characterised by a long roof. Climb the overhung break in the right side of the roof directly from below.

ISLAND WALLS

(NX 084 360)   Tidal   West facing   Map p283

Immediately north of Lunch Bay are short, non-serious walls of immaculate granite lying opposite a long low island. The first routes lie on the southern wall, opposite the island.

Approach: By abseil or, by descending the small gully between the walls and traversing right (facing in), to below the wall. The northern walls are approached from the north down a sloping platform.

Routes are described right to left.

South Wall

The Fish Ladder   12m   Very Difficult   (1991)
The prominent left-slanting chimney-crack on the right of the cliff.

Fish Tales   10m   Hard Severe 4b   (1991)
A thin crack joining The Fish Ladder at two-thirds height. Nice.

Little Feat   10m   VS 4c ***   (1991)
Good climbing up the central corner, finishing just left of the top of Fish Ladder.

Bouillabaisse   10m   Severe 4a   *(1991)*
The rib to the left of Little Feat leads to a short corner at the top.

Jellyfish Jive   10m   Severe 4b   *(1999)*
The wall left of Bouillabaisse, via a flake and ledge. Finish up the cracked wall above.

Skating   12m   Very Difficult   *(1991)*
To the left are stepped corners. Climb them, finishing to the right.

A Plaice by the Sea   12m   Hard Severe 4b   *(1991)*
Start at the left-hand end of the main wall. Follow a thin crack to join Skating at half-height, and finish up the steep corner-crack above.

The following two routes are situated in the small gully which separates the two walls, lying opposite the north end of the island.

Desert Island Discs   8m   VS 4c   *(1991)*
There are three cracks on the outer gully wall. Climb the right-hand crack with a narrowing slab at the bottom. The left-hand two cracks are both Difficult.

PC Plummet   10m   E1 5b *   *(1994)*
A good although usually wet route up the steep, cracked wall at the back of the gully.

North Wall

Good Morning Ladies   8m   Hard Severe 4b *   *(1991)*
An excellent micro route up the steep right-sloping crack about halfway along the platform.

The Blind Man   7m   Hard Severe 4c   *(1991)*
Deceptive climbing up the stepped corners on the left side of the wall.

HOODLUM BAY

Non-tidal   West facing   Map p283
Continuing north is a long wall with an impressive overhanging black wall in the centre.
Approach: Scramble down slabby rock from the south.

Routes are described right to left.

The Foaming Hoodlum Traverse   Severe 4a *   *(1991)*
The traverse of the Hoodlum Walls and Foam Zawn to Laggantalluch Head gives an exciting and scenic outing. The traverse makes a fine Difficult when combined with The Shadow Line (Foam Bay).

The first two routes are to the right of the black overhanging wall.

Green Eggs and Ham   25m   E1 5b **   *(1997)*
This fine route takes the tapering steep slabby corner, which is the only break in the overhangs. Start 6m right of Sam I Am. Climb the slab corner, moving right onto the slab to finish.

Sam I Am   25m   E4 6a ***   *(1997)*
A tremendous route on flawless granite. It takes the corner immediately to the right of the black overhanging wall. Climb the initial corner (crux) to a ledge. Move

right for 1m, then climb directly up the wall above until it is possible to move back left into the corner. Climb up to a roof until it is possible to swing out left to finish. Climb an easy slab to the top.

**The Oyster Thief   20m   HVS 5a ** * *   (1991)
A fine Buddhist climb, featuring one hand clapping. Start under the left edge of the black overhangs, where a curving crack leads to up to a crack immediately left of the overhangs. Finish up the right-hand corner above.

The Clam Catcher   25m   VS 4c   (1991)
At the left end of the black wall, a white streaked wall and crack lead to a small tower. Pull round and over this to finish. The stepped wall to the left is Severe.

To the north is a small island and an obvious squat pinnacle in the sea. This marks the southern end of Foam Zawn. The bay to the south has a prominent flat topped rib, easily identifiable from above.

Mourning Rib   25m   Very Difficult   (1991)
Climb the rib to the top.

White Sauce   15m   Severe 4a   (1991)
In the north corner of the bay and 10m south of the squat pinnacle in the sea is a knife edged arete, climbed on its left side.

FOAM BAY

Tidal   North & West facing   Map p283

This small, tidal zawn is the first small bay to the south of the headland of Laggantalluch Head and lies about 650m north of the main cliff. It is partially hidden from above. A calm sea is recommended.

Approach: Descend a rock and grass rib on the left (looking out) side of the zawn. Abseil towards the island and traverse ledges to the right (looking out) into the zawn, or descend the left-slanting corner right of Tunes of Glory (Difficult – but hard to see from above). The zawn and abseil point can be seen from the large platform of Laggantalluch Head to the north. Spongonema is reached by a traverse south from Laggantalluch Head (Severe).

Routes are described from right to left; the first three routes are on the south wall of the zawn.

The Shadow Line   20m   Difficult   (1991)
Climb the buttress immediately behind the island via a crack and stepped corners. This can be reached by a traverse from Hoodlum Bay (Difficult).

Tunes of Glory   25m   Hard Severe 4b *   (1991)
At the right-hand end of the wall is a prominent steep crack to the right of the main overhangs. Climb it on good jugs, moving left in the top half.

**Davy Jones's Locker   20m   E1 5b ** * *   (1992)
Steep and strenuous climbing through the overhangs left of Tunes of Glory and facing Refusnik. Follow the corner at the left end of the overhangs into and then out of a niche, to easier ground.

The back of the zawn is an evil looking mess. The following routes lie to its left.

Toxygene   25m   E5 6a *   (1997)

*Tales of the Rubblebank, HVS 5a, Portobello. Andrew Fraser on the first ascent
(photo Ian Magill)*

The arete right of Refusnik. Although a one time last great problem with good climbing, there are a few caveats. The moves are difficult to read, the gear spaced and the upper section somewhat loose. Start to the right of the arete and climb up to a niche, then move left with difficulty on to the arete. Climb up into a shallow corner on the right side of the arete, climb this, exiting left back onto the arete. Climb to a wide ledge beneath the final arete, which is loose but 5a.

Refusnik   25m   E2 5c ** (1987)
A tremendous route with great exposure, but prone to seepage and bird nests. The grade takes account of the seep at the bottom, although it tends to dry out in afternoon sunshine. Climb the overhanging corner to a ledge, belay possible. From the ledge, climb poorer rock on the right to finish.

Pillar   25m   HVS 5a (1987)
Descend the ramp below Refusnik and make a sea-level traverse left round the arete. Climb the wall above, moving right to the arete, and make a steep pull onto a yellow slab (guano depending on the season). Continue up the slab and easier rock to a large ledge, finishing up poorer rock on the right.

Spongonema   25m   E1 5b * (1991)
The obvious hanging chimney-line, round the corner from Pillar and conspicuous from Laggantalluch Head. Technical and sustained, but with some dubious rock to finish.

LAGGANTALLUCH HEAD

(NX 084 362)   Non-tidal   West facing   Map p283
This steep little crag of fine grey granite lies immediately south of the headland of Laggantalluch Head and about 750m north of the main cliff. Hidden from above, it has a large rock platform at its base and a prominent line of overhangs at mid-height.

Approach: The crag is best reached from the headland to the north by a scramble down and along the coast.

Obliteration   15m   E3 5c (1992)
An intimidating route with nasty fall potential. The left side of the cliff drops directly into a fissure, at one point bridged by blocks. From the blocks move up left past a poor peg to a good hold. Continue up the steep crack with difficulty.

Sea Monkey   20m   E2 5c * (1999)
Start 4m left of Seal Song. Climb a steep left-slanting groove and crack system to a small rectangular overhang. Pull through its left side with difficulty.

Seal Song   20m   E1 5b *** (1987)
Enjoyable steep climbing. Start below the left end of the overhang where a line of holds lead out left to the lip of the roof. Traverse right across a small wall and round a rib. Continue up and right to finish.

Back Burner   20m   E3 6a (1987)
This breaches the line of overhangs via a steep chimney. Good technical climbing, but hard to protect as the runners fill the best holds.

First Touch   20m   E1 5b ** (1987)
Climb to the break at the right end of the overhang. Traverse left to a slim corner and climb this with difficulty to finish. Continuing straight up above the overhang gives a pleasant VS 4c.

The Water Margin, E2 5b, Portobello. Climber Dave McGimpsey
(photo Andrew Fraser)

Wave Good-bye   20m   Hard Severe 4b   *(1987)*
Right of the above route is a cave like recess. Enter it, then exit at the top and
follow easy ground above.

DRAGON'S CAVE

(NX 085 364)   Tidal   South-West facing   Map p283

Continuing north along the coast and just past a small burn is an obvious yellow
slab of metamorphosed greywacke. The roaring sea cave below gives the crag a
memorable atmosphere.

Approach: At low tide descend the seaward slab (climbed by Darwin's Waiting
Room) by abseiling from spikes at the top.

Routes are described from right to left.

Heart of Darkness   35m   HVS 5a *   *(1991)*
The large yellow slab gives a superb atmospheric route, considerably better than it
looks from above. Start near the right edge and follow a line of holds up and left
to a conspicuous spike on the left edge of the slab. Move slightly right then directly
up to the top.

Darwin's Waiting Room   35m   VS 4b   *(1991)*
Climb the corner in the seaward slab until it eases, then climb steep cracks on the
right wall of the corner. Worthwhile – low in the grade.

The Origin of Species   35m   VS 4c   *(1991)*
Fair climbing but much guano higher up – serious white-out potential. Start at the
steep left edge of the seaward slab, starting at the left end of a small platform.
Move steeply up and left into a groove and climb to a large ledge. Slightly left is a
hidden slab, which is climbed to the upper arete of the seaward slab.

AULD SHIP

(NX085 365)   Tidal   North facing   Map p283

This greywacke cliff is situated about 500m north of Dragon's Cave. While
somewhat out of the way, it is the quickest drying crag at Laggantalluch and is free
of birds.

Approach: From Dragon's Cave, continue north along the coastline until it is
necessary to climb up steeply to avoid a high cove. Descend on the far side of this
to the cliff, a narrow arete with a north facing 25m slab of excellent greywacke
falling sheer to the sea. Access is by abseil. At low tide there are ledges at the foot
of the cliff which can be traversed between routes, otherwise abseil directly.

Read the Small Print   20m   E5 6b **   *(1997)*
Technical bridging and udging, gear being good but spaced. The left corner of the
cliff, above the cave, divides into two main corners at mid-height. Between these
is a slab split by a thin blank corner, the line of the route. Due to big seas on the
first ascent the route was started from abseil at a niche about 6m below the corner.
From here climb the roof into the corner, then proceed with increasing difficulty,
using small edges on the right wall of the corner.

Optical Illusions   25m   HVS 5a *   *(1997)*
Fairly steady wall climbing, gear and holds both improving after a bold start. The
route climbs the wall between the left corner of the cliff and the obvious groove in
the centre of the cliff. Start on a ledge up and just left of the central groove. Move
out left, then directly up the wall.

The Auld Ship   25m   Severe 4b *   *(1997)*
A sheep amongst wolves. This is the central groove in the cliff, the obvious bulge
being climbed on the right.

Higher than the Sun   25m   E2 5b **   *(1997)*
A sustained and delicate route with spaced protection. Between the Auld Ship and
the right arete of the cliff are two thin cracks. The left, more obvious crack, leads
leftwards, while this climbs the cleaned strip around the right-trending right-hand
crack. Climb the crack for 5m, then move slightly out right. Continue directly above
with difficulty and follow the cleaned strip to the top. High in the grade.

Zero Tolerance   25m   E5 6b **   *(1997)*
A very thin route with just adequate RPs for the crux. The route climbs the wall just
left of the right arete of the cliff, starting as for Higher than the Sun. Follow a right-
trending diagonal crack out to nearly the arete. Place a good nut at 8m, climb
straight up from this to a good hold and small wire placements on the right. Move
slightly left, then up on small holds past a small horizontal break with a long reach
to better holds (crux). An easier (6a) but less satisfying variant is to stand on the
good hold and make a hard move up to better holds. The climbing above is easier
but not well protected until just before the finish.

POINT OF THE CLEUGH

(NX 088 348)   Partially tidal   West facing   Map p293

A small non-serious area situated on the low headland mid-way between
Portencorkrie Bay and Crammag Head to the south. Directly below a fence, is the
Cleugh Slab, a slab of pink granite similar to a scaled down version of the slab at
Laggantalluch Main Cliff, but with bigger holds.

Approach: In about 10mins by walking south from Portencorkrie Bay or north
from Crammag Head. See the approaches for Laggantalluch or Crammag.

The first two routes lie on an obvious block of pink granite with a steep landward
wall, about 100m north of the Cleugh slab.

Comatose   10m   VS 5a *   *(1992)*
Excellent climbing up the obvious crack and over the small roof on the right side
of the block's seaward face.

Corkie the Catfish   10m   Severe 4a   *(2003)*
This takes the slab, niche and green lichen slab at the leftmost end of the seaward
face. Disappointing as the rock continually forces the climber to the left.

About halfway between the block and the Cleugh slab, at sea-level and facing
northwards is a chimney about 6m deep into the cliff.

The Slot   13m   Very Difficult   *(1992)*
A traditional struggle!

The remaining routes lie on the Cleugh Slab itself.

The Chancer   15m   VS 4c *   *(1992)*
Eases after a hard start. Step off a small grey boulder and climb the steep wall
directly above to good holds on the slab. Continue up and left to brown water
streaked rock and finish straight up.

Cleugh Clamber   15m   Severe 4a   *(1992)*
Start just right of the grey boulder and climb straight up the slab about 5m right
of the previous route.

Just Friends   15m   Severe 4a   *(1992)*
Right of Cleugh Clamber is a clean slab with a small rock pool at its base. Climb the recess to the right of the slab until it is possible to swing onto the slab and follow a central line to a ledge and short wall.

CRAMMAG HEAD

(NX 089 340)   Partially Tidal   West facing   Maps p222, 293

This is the small headland with a lighthouse to the south of Laggantalluch. Excellent granite, superb scenery and a range of quality routes at all grades make Crammag one of the nicest crags in the south-west. The recent development of Crammag South has added further variety to the area. Some of the cliffs are tidal and best reached by abseil. Nesting birds can be a problem in some areas, particularly Kittiwake and Gabarunning Zawns, which are best avoided from mid April to mid August.

Approach: At the top of Drummore village, take the road on the right at (NX 134 365), signed Port Logan B7065. Follow this a short way to a T-junction at Kirkmaiden. Turn left, drive through Kirkmaiden (B7065) and take the second turning on the right (the first is immediately after the telephone box). Continue past Barncorkrie Farm and the cottage overlooking Portencorkrie Bay. At the fork in the road go right and park at Slockmill Farm. Please ask permission. The main cliffs are to the right, running from the lighthouse to the headland, and reached across fields. Crammag South is straight ahead, located in the bay between Crammag Head and the hill of Dunman to the south. Beware of bulls on the approach.

The crags and routes are described southwards from the lighthouse.

LIGHTHOUSE WALLS

Non-tidal   North, West & South facing   Map p293

The walls beneath the lighthouse give short, fun routes on superb granite. The first seven routes are located on the steep walls beneath the end of the concrete steps leading from the lighthouse. Just right of the end of the steps, is a gully

Twenty   7m   Difficult   *(2000)*
Start from the platform just right of the descent gully and 1m left of the following route. Climb up into and follow the shallow groove on the arete.

Anniversary Outing   7m   Moderate   *(2000)*
The large groove with roofs just left of Shining Path.

Shining Path   8m   VS 4c   *(1992)*
The left arete of the steep wall gives nice climbing with one nippy section.

Lighthouse Wall   9m   HVS 5a *   *(1992)*
Good climbing up discontinuous cracks and pockets in the centre of the steep wall. Low in the grade.

Firefly   9m   HVS 5a   *(1994)*
Start at the right end of the ledge. Climb the wall keeping as close to the right edge as possible.

Round the corner to the right is a black slab.

Poisoned Ocean   10m   HVS 5a   *(1992)*
Climb the black slab, exiting through the large break in the roof towards the left side of the slab.

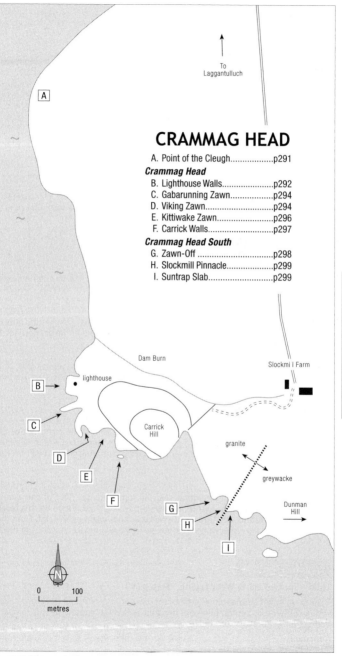

CRAMMAG HEAD

GALLOWAY SEA-CLIFFS

Little Flasher   10m   VS 4b   *(1999)*
Climbs the right arete of the black slab, finishing across the right end of the overhangs.

Round the corner to the right and directly south of the lighthouse is a slab of pink granite.

Santa's Little Helper   10m   Very Difficult   *(2002)*
Up and left of the main slab is a smaller slab. Gain this by the steep wall below, then climb the middle of the slab. Pleasant

Hourglass Slab   10m   Very Difficult ✱✱   *(1992)*
Climb the main slab slightly left of centre. A wee gem.

Razamatazz   9m   HVS 5a   *(1994)*
A direct line up the middle of the Hourglass Slab. Poorly protected.

Bully Beef   8m   Hard Severe 4b   *(1993)*
Climb the corner right of the black water streak on the slab. Delicate and poorly protected.

GABARUNNING ZAWN

Tidal   South-East facing   Map p293

South of the lighthouse is a lookout and directly below this is a bay containing a slanting overhanging south wall with a pinnacled crest.

The Pantomime Horse   35m   Very Difficult   *(2002)*
A scenic ramble. Start at the left toe of the cliff. Traverse across steep ground at sea-level for 10m, then climb diagonally right to gain and exit out of the deepest notch in the crest (third notch from the left).

The following two routes start at the right edge of the cliff, on either side of a quartz flecked block, where it is possible to lean across the zawn to gain starting holds.

Accommodations of Desire   25m   E2 5c ✱✱   *(1992)*
Steep and surprisingly good. Start 2m left of the quartz flecked block, below a small triangular niche. Lean over to good handholds below the niche. Move up past the niche into a wide crack and go up to the large square niche at mid-height on the cliff. From its right-hand side, follow the right-slanting crack to exit up the obvious corner.

Matador   25m   E1 5c †   *(1994)*
Fine climbing initially, but deteriorates at the top. Start 3m right of the quartz flecked block, at the base of a steep, rightward-trending crack. Climb up to a ledge and traverse 3m left to the large square recess at mid-height on the cliff. From the top left corner of the niche, climb an arete, swing round onto its left wall and finish directly.

VIKING ZAWN

Tidal   South-East & West facing   Map p293

The next inlet lies a little to the south of the lookout. Its north wall is a broken one, with a conspicuous central pinnacle. Its south wall is the impressive and compact buttress of Viking Wall.

Approach: Both crags are accessible at low tide via a traverse south from

Gabarunning Zawn. Access to Viking Wall at high tide is by abseil down the groove of Bjorn Again.

Orabidoo   10m   VS 4c *   (1992)
Surprisingly tricky. Left of the pinnacle on the northern wall is a chimney and left again is a buttress split by a wide sloping ramp. Climb the lower tier by a double chimney-jamming crack. On the upper tier, a steep start leads to a layback flake and short groove.

Pillage   10m   Very Difficult   (1992)
The short chimney left of the pinnacle on the northern wall.

Fallen Star   25m   VS 4b **   (1992)
Good climbing on large holds up the front face of the pinnacle, finishing up the corner behind.

Skol's Out   25m   Difficult   (1992)
Start at the outside edge of the narrow chimney at the back of the zawn and climb the stepped wall to the left. Not a good descent.

Viking Wall

While impressive, the wall on the south side of the Zawn is considerably more friendly than appearances suggest. The most obvious feature is the upper groove of Funeral Pyre/Bjorn Again, which is also the line of the high tide abseil approach.

The Four Bees   35m   Hard Severe *   (1993)
A surprisingly enjoyable excursion up the obvious huge chimney at the back of the zawn, left of Viking Wall. Traverse left at sea-level, step across the gap and climb up to an obvious handrail. Follow this to a good footledge, then bridge or back and foot up into the chimney on excellent rock. Exit left just below the top to finish up a steep corner.

The following routes are on Viking Wall itself.

Ultima Thule 30m   HVS 5a *   (1994)
A fine route tackling the steep ground at the extreme left of the face. Climb the initial 6m of the gully of The Four Bees until it widens and it is possible to step right onto a slab. Climb this, then up a left-trending corner above. Continue directly to a bulge, surmount this then up the slab to the top roofs. These are split by a leftward fault, which is climbed.

Ragnarok   25m   HVS 5a *   (1992)
Varied and atmospheric climbing just right of Ultima Thule. Start as for Soft Parade to the foot of the square niche. Traverse left and climb the upper left-slanting ramp (bold) to easier ground. Break out left onto slab as for Ultima Thule and cross the roofs at their widest part.

The Soft Parade   20m   E1 5b *   (1992)
Good climbing. Not very sustained, but quite high in the grade. Start at the left side of the buttress below a square niche. Gain the niche from the left and continue to an overlap. Cross this and follow the slab and crack to finish.

The Seven Seas   20m   E4 6a **   (1993)
This climbs the steep scooped slab and arete left of Funeral Pyre. Move left from a conspicuous pocket, then go up via steep layaways to a blind reach left to a hold in the scoop. Stand on this (crux), then move up to the right end of the overlap. Pull over and follow the left side of the arete (bold).

Funeral Pyre   20m   E1 5b *   *(1992)*
This takes the central groove of the wall. Start in a shallow scoop below a small overlap. Climb the scoop on the left to gain the central groove.

Up Helly Aa   20m   HVS 5a **   *(2000)*
A varied route with some unusual climbing. Start as for Funeral Pyre. Climb the right side of the scoop past a small overlap (2m left of the wide crack of Bjorn Again). Continue more easily to gain the foot of a rightward-curving overlap. Follow the overlap to its top. Gain the crack that springs from the end of the overlap with difficulty (the obvious one foot rest into Hagar the Horrible makes things more difficult)

Bjorn Again   20m   VS 4c *   *(2003)*
While in some ways this is merely a bjorn again Funeral Pyre, it provides good balanced climbing and is the easiest route on the main face. Climb the left-hand chimney of Hagar the Horrible, until it is possible to move left into Funeral Pyre's central groove. Continue up this to finish by the steep right-hand crack.

Hagar the Horrible   20m   Hard Severe 4b **   *(1992)*
An excellent climb. This is the large right-slanting chimney-corner on the right side of Viking Wall. It is started by the right-hand of the two chimneys.

KITTIWAKE ZAWN

Tidal   South-East & South facing   Map p293

This is the next bay to the south, with steep walls on its north side and back wall.

Approach: The steep left (south facing) wall of the zawn has a wide ledge at 8m, accessed by traversing round the corner from Viking Zawn or by abseil.

The first two routes start from this ledge.

Sid Stingray   20m   VS 4b   *(1993)*
Left of the centre of the wall is an obvious open groove-line. Climb the narrow groove on good juggy rock, then step left at the top and go up into the main upper groove. Climb a steep crack on the left wall of the groove (crux) and finish up a short loose corner.

Down Under   35m   E2 **   *(1993)*
A fine atmospheric route up the corner on the right side of the impressive overhanging south wall. Start at the grey corner, which springs, from the right end of the wide ledge, 10m right of Sid Stingray.
1. 15m 5b Climb the grey corner to a notch in the arete.
2. 20m 5c Continue up, passing a niche on the left, then move right above the niche to a spike. Continue to a recess, then traverse back left on good holds to finish direct.

To the right of the last route, where the north and back walls of the Zawn meet are two corners, the left of which starts as a wet overhanging chimney, and the right is the corner at the back of the Zawn.

Violently Happy   20m   E3 5c **   *(1994)*
An impressive and steep route on large holds. This route takes the left corner starting at the sloping ledge (reached by abseil) where the wet overhanging chimney closes. Climb the short corner to a small ledge, then up to a roof. Climb the left side of this, then move slightly right (Wallnut 3), up to an obvious hinged spike, then pull steeply up on large holds to a rest. Finish boldly up the wall above.

Beers, Smears and Queers   25m   E4 6b **   *(1995)*

A fine although unbalanced route. Though prone to seepage, direct sun will temporarily dry it. Well protected. This is the main corner-line in the back of the zawn. Access from the south by abseil. Climb a fine overhanging flake-crack for 3m then step rightwards into a niche. Make a committing high step up onto a high foothold. Using underclings, climb up the wall to some sidepulls. Hard moves gain a pocket and good flange, then move out right onto a rib. Climb this to its top, then undercling up and right until below a roof. Exit via an awkward and precarious slab, then leave this on big sloping holds to ascend the much easier, but often wet, finishing corner.

Dormouse   20m   Very Difficult   *(1992)*
Follow the obvious, rather loose, slabby chimney near the right or seaward side of the slabby south wall.

CARRICK WALLS

Non-tidal   South-West facing   Map p293
These walls lie immediately to the south of Kittiwake Zawn and have some of the best routes at Crammag. A tower (Molotov Cocktail) splits them, opposite a small offshore island.

Approach: Abseil down grooves north of the promontory to reach the first five routes. The other routes are best approached either by abseil, or by down-climbing short walls beneath the left side (looking out) of a shallow depression above the small island.

Freedom Fighter   15m   HVS 5b *   *(1992)*
The line follows the right edge of the wall at the far left end of the Carrick Walls. A right-slanting crack leads to a ledge. Make an energetic move over the bulge and continue up the right edge of the wall. High in the grade.

Fresh Air   20m   E1 5b *   *(1993)*
An intimidating but sensational finish, much easier than appearances suggest. Climb the obvious chimney right of Freedom Fighter to its top. Place runners, then descend slightly to reach a prominent hole in the leaning left wall. Move onto the wall, trending left to the overhanging arete, and finish spectacularly on good holds.

Gorilla Warfare   20m   HVS 5a   *(1992)*
Steep and intimidating, but on good holds. Start just right of Fresh Air and climb to a right-trending corner. Follow this to a ledge, then continue right to finish just right of the overhangs on dubious rock.

Kalashnikov   20m   VS 4b *   *(1992)*
Follow the prominent arete on the right, turning the overhang on the left. Continue to the upper level section of the arete. It is possible to cross the gully on the left and finish up the slabby red wall. Low in the grade.

The following two routes are located on the tower at the promontory.

Molotov Cocktail   20m   E1 5b **   *(1992)*
Good and meaty climbing – a classic. Above a small sea channel is a tower with two crack-lines. Follow the left-hand until it is possible to move left to a ledge. Climb the excellent twin cracks above, move right onto the crest of the tower (avoiding the obvious dirty escape above) and finish up the crack in the upper wall (crux).

Enfant Terrible   20m   HVS 5a   *(1992)*
The right-hand crack, avoiding any wet patches.

Yosemite Sam 15m HVS 5b *   *(1992)*
Right of the descent is an overhanging and exciting pod above a pool.

The Krapton Factor 10m Severe   *(1994)*
The short steep wall to the right of Yosemite Sam.

To the right is a slabby wall, capped by a roof.

The Ship's Cat 20m HVS 5a *   *(1992)*
Start just left of the central slanting crack, and follow easy slabby walls to below
the roof. Spectacular climbing leads rightwards through the break in the roofs to
easier ground.

The White Rabbit 20m Hard Severe 4b   *(1992)*
A good traditional route up the central crack on good holds.

Mog 20m E1 5b *   *(1992)*
The slim pillar to the right lacks independence, but gives good climbing. An
awkward undercut start leads to the pillar, which is short but unexpectedly fingery
and sustained. Finish directly up the pillar (eliminate) or up the crack of The White
Rabbit.

Anvil Chorus 25m E1 5b   *(1993)*
Start as for Mog, then climb right up an undercut slab to the right-hand of twin
grooves. At the top exit left via an obvious layback flake.

Fragile Edge 20m HVS 5a   *(1992)*
Varied climbing, but with some doubtful rock. To the right is a pinnacle. Bridge up
between this and the buttress and continue up the arete and crack.

Rocky Relations 25m E1 5b *   *(1994)*
A very good route. Start just right of the pinnacle of Fragile Edge at a pod. Climb
this, then follow cracks up the wall above.

CRAMMAG HEAD SOUTH

(NX 094 338) Non-tidal South-East & South-West facing Map p293

Some 2km to the south of Crammag is the rocky hill of Dunman. In the low lying
area of coast mid-way between Crammag Head and Dunman are a number of
crags, which are described north to south. The initial area is granite, but it soon
changes to greywacke.

Approach: As for Crammag Head. The area is 10mins from either Slockmill Farm,
or Crammag Head.

ZAWN-OFF SHOTGUN

This is the low inlet with a fine south-east facing slab of pink granite on its north
side, and Slockmill Pinnacle on its south side. Two rocky islands just offshore
provide another useful landmark.

Pink Slab

A narrow ledge slants across the lower third of the slab, and can be reached by
abseil, or by scrambling down the ridge above the slab.

Firearms Certificate 13m Very Difficult   *(2000)*
This follows the line of cracks, up the left edge of the slab.

Wi-ped Biped   12m   VS 4c *   (2000)
Climb the easy slab 1m right of the previous route, then a thin bayonet shaped crack, finishing delicately left to the top of the cracks.

The Barricades of Heaven   12m   HVS 5a **   (1992)
Lovely climbing. Start at sea-level at the leftmost edge of the platform on the right of the cliff. Climb the centre of the slab directly to a thin crack in the final smooth section. Follow this, a vague pocket on the left providing the key.

Holy Mackerel   12m   HVS 5a *   (2003)
The right side of the slab is black, separated from the pink slab by a rightward-curving fault. Start as for Barricades of Heaven. Climb up and right to ascend the black wall 1m right of the curving fault, to a point where the fault levels. Move 1m left onto the upper section of the pink slab, then directly to finish up a thin crack.

Axis of Weasels   22m   HVS 5a **   (2003)
A sustained route of great character. To the right of the Pink Slab at the inner end of the zawn, is a steep wall, the most obvious feature of which is a deep rightward-trending groove. Climb this groove to its top, then move 1m left and climb a wall to a ledge with large spike. Difficult moves above the spike lead to a ledge on the right, then the top.

The Ba'ath Party   22m   Severe   (2003)
Pleasant, if unremarkable. From the platform under Axis of Weasels, step across to the south side of the zawn. There are two bulges on this wall. Climb directly up to and over the higher, left-hand bulge, and continue directly to the top.

SLOCKMILL PINNACLE

On the south side of Zawn-Off Shotgun is a fine pinnacle of greywacke with a slabby west face split by a crack-groove in the shape of an inverted Y and an impressively steep and unclimbed south face.

Approach: The base of the west face can be reached by a short scramble just to the north.

Descent: By abseil or by down-climbing Eldora.

Custer   14m   Difficult   (2000)
This route climbs the arete to the right of the inverted Y, starting at the foot of the right leg.

Eldora   14m   Difficult   (2000)
The inverted Y, with a start up the left leg.

Old Ted   14m   Severe **   (2000)
A fine route. The slab left of Eldora has a sloping crack leading up towards an overhang. Climb the crack and pull over the overhang by a move to the right to finish up the lichenous slab above.

Just to the left (north) of the Slockmill Pinnacle is a short steep wall, with a prominent black crystalline hold, and short slanting crack at half-height.

Big Sandy   12m   Severe *   (2000)
A good little route. Climb the centre of the wall to reach a line of holds trending right where the wall steepens. Finish back left.

SUNTRAP SLAB

Just south of Slockmill Pinnacle is a slabby line of cliffs facing west. The main features of the crag are a wide crack slanting up from the left, bounded on its right by a narrow rib with an overhang low down.

Approach: The ledges at the base can be reached by a scramble at their south end, or by abseil.

Baked Potato   20m   Difficult   *(2000)*
From the ledges move left to climb the ridge that defines the left edge of the overlapping slab.

Fried   20m   Severe   *(2000)*
Climb easily up to the overlap, pull leftwards through this past a prominent spike, then move back right to follow the overlap to a prominent hold. Finish up the slab above via a thin crack.

Boiling   20m   Hard Severe 4b   *(2000)*
Start as for Fried, but take the hanging slab beneath the overlap to reach the overhang. Pull over this and follow the slab above, rightwards to the top.

Char Grilled   20m   Very Difficult   *(2000)*
The rib to the right of the wide, slanting crack. Care with friable rock is needed near the top.

Done to a Turn   20m   Hard Severe 4b   *(2000)*
Follow the slabby ramp on the right and finish up the steep headwall on the left.

FORTRESS SLAB

(NX 129 311)   Tidal   West facing   Map p222

A blank slab is situated on a remote section of coast 1km west of West Tarbet.

Approach: Leave the B7041 Mull of Galloway road at (NX 130 336), south of Drummore and follow the minor road to park on the verge at the far end of West Cairngaan Farm, just after the road turns to the right (NX128 319). A track leads to the left, adjacent to the barn. Follow this to its end, then cut diagonally right to the coast (15mins). The slab is the west face of a narrow promontory with an ancient fort (marked on the OS Landranger). Access is by abseil from stakes (50m rope needed).

Fortress Slab   50m   HVS 4c *   *(2002)*
Although a worthwhile climb, it fails to entirely live up to appearances. The lower section of the slab is bounded on its left by a corner. Gain this from the right by a rib and overlap, and follow it to some large poised blocks, at the point where it becomes vegetatious (Friend 4). Place a good RP on the slab 4m above the Friend, reverse back to the Friend, and traverse the slab to its right edge. Climb this (bold, 14m run-out), to where shallow cracks allow the right side of the slab to be climbed to the top.

MULL OF GALLOWAY

(NX 143 305)   Partially Tidal   South facing   Map p222

The Mull is Scotland's southernmost point. In folklore it is the site of the Pict's last stand, where the secret of the legendary heather ale vanished over the cliffs with the last Pictish king. These are the highest and most extensive cliffs in Galloway, high in atmosphere with some remarkable caves and coastal scenery. While the larger cliffs nearer the lighthouse are hopelessly loose (and an RSPB nature reserve), the cliffs nearer West Tarbet to the north are of better quality, relatively bird free and largely unaffected by tides. It would however be wise to avoid the cliff when windy or in big seas. There are some strong currents near the end of the Mull and caution should be exercised.

Approach: The Mull is signposted from Drummore. Park at the narrow isthmus separating the bays of East (on the left) and West (on the right) Tarbet about 1.5km before the lighthouse, at a dilapidated brick shelter.

With the exception of one route, all the climbing is situated between West Tarbet and the promontory of Carrick-kee. This latter feature is opposite Kennedy's Cairn (the stone tower between the lighthouse and West Tarbet), and a fence leads directly from the Cairn to Carrick-kee. The climbs are described from West Tarbet in the north to Carrick-kee in the south. While the Stranraer peninsula runs from north to south, the Mull actually runs west to east. To avoid confusion, the north-south references have been retained, south being towards the lighthouse.

BENWEE

Tidal   North-West and South-East facing
The first area reached from West Tarbet consists of two small inlets divided by a fence.

Approach: From the parking the fence above the left side of West Tarbet leads directly to the first cliffs at Benwee.

The first small inlet has a black, slabby north facing wall. This bay gives three routes

Bible Class   12m   Very Difficult   *(1991)*
The slabby black wall on the south wall of the inlet.

Playtime   12m   Severe 4a   *(1997)*
The right side of the slabby black wall, climbed from the sea.

Sundae School   8m   Severe 4a   *(1991)*
Climb the twin buttress at the landward end of the inlet, by a steep crack and niche. The climb is not visible from above.

Shipwreck Cove

The second inlet has a steep south facing wall with a recess near the left side and a slabby corner in the middle.

Approach: By abseil.

Wrecker's Wall   15m   E1 5b *   *(1997)*
A good climb on solid rock. Start mid-way between the recess and the corner Climb up to a spike runner just below half-height, move slightly right then directly up the centre of the wall.

Release the Pressure   15m   E3 6a **   *(1997)*
The slabby corner gives a fine and technical route, the best in the bay.

Unscathed   14m   E5 6a   *(1997)*
This serious undertaking (as in undertaker) climbs the concave wall to the right of Release the Pressure. Some of the holds are dubious. Climb up on edges to a thin ledge and good gear. Foot traverse right towards a layback flake and make a long reach for a good but slightly loose hold. Place crucial gear behind this (HB2, 3, 5 and thin sling), step left on friction using underclings (crux), then make a long reach for better holds and on to the top.

Anchor Chimney   12m   Difficult   *(1997)*
The chimney at the right or landward edge of the wall.

CARRICKCORIE

Mainly Non-tidal   Largely South-West facing

This is the name for the area south of Benwee. South of the Benwee inlets are a further three bays with no recorded climbing. The next one contains a low island (when the tide is in) and a steep black north facing wall on its south side – the start of Carrickcorie North Crag. Just to the south are some grassy depressions in the cliff top, before the fence heads off south-east. A small stream flows from first depression, dividing the North Crag and the Main Cliff.

North Crag

This stretches from this stream north to the large bay passed on the approach, and includes the black north facing crag previously mentioned. The rock is poorer than the Main Cliff.

Approach: An easy way down can be found immediately to the right (looking out) of the stream. This accesses the right of the cliff at all states of the tide, and as far as Astrofest in calm seas and lowish tide. Otherwise, abseils are available.

The easy way down starts as a ramp and becomes a slab angling right (facing out) into the first bay. Above this slab is a rounded rib split by a steep crack with a collection of pockets on its right side. Routes are described from right to left.

Slartibartfast   15m   Very Difficult *   (2000)
Climb the steep crack on good holds, and continue up the fine arete.

Zaphod Beeblebrox   19m   Very Difficult *   (2000)
Start in the gully forming the left edge of the descent slab. Climb the slab to a prominent thin crack slanting up right. Follow this and up a slab 1m left of the arete.

Marvin   17m   Very Difficult   (2000)
The arete that defines the first bay on the left, reached by a short groove and crack on the right.

Left of Marvin is a chimney come gully. The next route climbs the ridge to its left.

Constellation Prize   22m   Severe   (2000)
Start on the left edge of the arete, sea permitting, (or with more difficulty up the groove to the right), to reach a ledge below a wide crack. Bridge up and pull round the left side of the arete to reach a larger ledge, and continue to the top past some doubtful blocks.

Past another deep gully and slabby ridge the crag changes aspect, facing north. After an easy angled corner above a large ledge, it becomes less accessible, dropping straight into a short zawn. Below the easy angled corner is a short gully. The next two routes start here.

Hyperspatial By-Pass   25m   Very Difficult   (2000)
Follow the rib that defines the black north facing crag on its right. Good positions but care required with the rock at the top.

Astrofest   27m   HVS 4c *   (2000)
Climbs the right side of the black north facing crag. Start in the gully, overlooking the zawn. A line of large flakes is reached by traversing left from the gully. These lead enticingly upward, until they expire a few metres below a short, hanging layback crack. Boldly and delicately reach the crack, pull exultantly over the bulge to reach a grassy ledge, then continue carefully up left to the cliff top.

Katinka   25m   VS 4a *   *(2002)*
This route takes the obvious line of flakey cracks on the left side of the black north
facing wall. Approach by scrambling into the bay to the left, or by abseil to a ledge
at the base of a prominent corner defining the left edge of the wall. Climb the
steep wall to the obvious undercut flake, pull over the bulge on big holds, and
move right to follow the left-facing flake-crack to a careful finish on easier ground.

Carrickcorie Corner   20m   Severe   *(2004)*
This climbs the prominent corner at the left end of the crag. It provides fine, well-
protected bridging to a careful finish past some loose blocks.

Main Cliff

This cliff is defined to the north by the small stream and to the south by a long low
promontory. The rock is generally good and it is a good venue for the low to
middle grade climber.

Approach: Descend the arete to the left (facing out) of the stream, or make a
straightforward abseil down Old Whippersnappers. The latter is preferable at high
tide or in rough seas, when sections of the non-tidal ledges can be spray lashed.

Traversing rightwards (facing in) from the arete descent, the first rock encountered
of any worth consists of an easy angled buttress containing two shallow corners.

Not a Fiend in the World   10m   Very Difficult   *(2000)*
This takes the left-hand of the two shallow corners.

Hula in a Brass Skirt   10m   Very Difficult   *(2000)*
Right of Not a Fiend is a short groove with a smooth left wall. Start here, and climb
the crack in its right wall, continuing up the cracked buttress above.

I'm Sorry, I Haven't A Cleugh   10m   Hard Severe 4a   *(2000)*
A deceptively difficult route that climbs the stepped groove with an overhang on
the left wall of the shallow corner of Weigh Out.

Weigh Out   10m   Difficult   *(2000)*
The right-hand of the two shallow corners.

Happy as a Sand Martin   10m   Very Difficult *   *(2000)*
The buttress to the right, following some shallow grooves.

The crag now steepens up and curves round to face south, with a pronounced
bulge at half-height. The left end of the bulge forms an overhung niche, with a
dog-leg crack to its left.

No Tern Unstoned   15m   VS 4b   *(2000)*
Start up a thin flake in the slab, which leads to the dog-leg crack. Climb this, with
an awkward move at the top.

Still Waiting for a Bolt Hole   15m   Hard Severe 4b   *(2000)*
Start in a corner just right of No Tern Unstoned. Climb easily to the bulge, and pull
over this awkwardly on big spikes to move rightwards into the niche. Escape to a
good ledge on the right, and continue up another bulge to the top.

The bulging wall to the right contains a number of crack-lines, including two left-
facing flakes, before terminating in a clean-cut corner behind a twin headed
projection in the non-tidal ledges.

Friends in High Plaices   15m   HVS 5a   *(2004)*
The left-hand of the two flakes through the bulge. The bulge is overcome via a steep pull, then finish more easily up the short corner.

Oook   15m   VS 5a   *(2000)*
This takes the right-hand flake through the bulge. Climb easy rock then pull through the bulge on excellent handholds to a slab. Step left and take the second bulge direct (crux), just right of an easy groove.

Your Plaice or Mine?   15m   HVS 5b   *(2004)*
Takes the crozzly crack/groove at the right side of the wall, using a helpful flake hold on the right. Reach the break, traverse left, and climb over the 'erect' block to finish more easily.

Old Whippersnappers   15m   Severe *   *(2000)*
The clean-cut corner, with a good move over a small overhang, and a convenient block belay at its top.

From behind the twin headed projection the non-tidal ledges drop down into a recess overlooked by a wide, overhanging crack. Right of this is an inverted V corner with a slot at its top.

Gun Slot Wounds   20m   Hard Severe 4a   *(2000)*
Climb the inverted corner, and pull painfully through the slot on a very sharp edged pocket. Continue up the crack above.

To the right of Gun Slot Wounds is a fine projecting buttress giving two of the best routes on the crag The streaks of green weed on the ledge at the base are an obvious landmark.

Anemone Action   20m   VS 4c **   *(2000)*
Start up the left edge to a ledge, then follow the shallow groove and crack above. Finish just right of Gun Slot Wounds. Superb climbing with excellent protection.

Ruddy'ard Kipperling   20m   VS 4c **   *(2000)*
Start up the right edge to a ledge, then follow the striated crack-line near the right edge, again with delicacy and good protection.

The crag falls back to form a rocky bay with a drainage line in the left corner. On the right another buttress projects forward, with the curving crack of An Arm and a Leg starting halfway up its left flank, overlooking the rocky bay.

Outer Limpets   22m   Severe   *(2000)*
Takes a central line up the rocky bay, keeping just to the right of the drainage line.

A Pint and a Fag   20m   Hard Severe 4b   *(2000)*
Start in the second corner left of the arete of the buttress. Follow the right corner of the rocky bay on flake holds and bridging to a short chimney-slot. Exit this on the left.

A Load of Pollacks   20m   VS 4c   *(2000)*
Follow A Pint and a Fag for about 8m, then break out right to reach the ramp-line immediately below the top crack of An Arm and a Leg. Breathe a sigh of relief, and cruise up the much easier ramp.

An Arm and a Leg   20m   E1 5b **   *(2000)*
A memorable route of some character, taking the prominent wide curving crack, Start just left of the arete, and right of A Pint and a Fag. Climb the shallow corner and after 4m pull right round the arete into the thin flake-crack. Follow this to a

big ledge under the wide crack, then climb the committing wide crack.

The right side of An Arm and a Leg buttress forms the left wall of a large corner split by a chimney-crack. The next three routes take lines up its slabby face, and all start at the foot of the chimney-crack.

The Hissing of Summer Prawns   23m   Hard Severe 4b * (2000)
Superb positions. Start up the corner but traverse left after 2m to a groove system. Follow this, then up left to the more clean-cut groove above. Follow this to below the capping overhang, finishing on the left.

A Plaice in the Sun   23m   Hard Severe 4a (2000)
Start as for Hissing, but pull over the bulge to the right of that route's groove system, and follow the slab above directly to the ledge below the final overhang. Pull sensationally through this on a large wedged block.

Any Corona Left?   22m   Very Difficult (2000)
Follow the chimney-crack for 5m, then move left on to the slab to climb it easily to meet the final section of the chimney-crack again, after it has curved up leftwards. Finish steeply and carefully up the break above.

Coroner Wright   22m   Very Difficult (2000)
Climb the chimney-crack direct to the point where it curves leftwards. Move right on the slab, and back left on a good foothold, to clear the bulging finish.

The right wall of the large corner forms the left face of a projecting buttress. It has a slim right-facing corner in its lower half, and a zigzag crack towards the top. Four routes climb this face.

On Porpoise   21m   VS 4b (2000)
Climb the rib on the left of the slim corner, moving left and up to the overhang where it is split by a short quartz crack. Pull over here, and finish up the deceptively awkward corner above.

Flounders of the Baskervilles   21m   HVS 5a * (2000)
Climb the slim corner to the overhang. Pull over rightwards on excellent holds, then continue up rounded ledges to the base of the final wall. Climb this with difficulty 1m right of the final corner of On Porpoise.

Cod Moves in Mysterious Waves   20m   VS 4c * (2000)
This more or less follows the line of the zigzag crack. Climb a shallow corner to the right of Flounders, move right to a ledge then up and left to a bigger ledge just left of the crack. Make fingery moves over the next steep wall, then move right below the diagonal crack to finish steeply just left of the arete.

His Flounders to Perform   20m   VS 5a (2002)
This route climbs the right arete of the wall, starting just left of an area of loose looking projecting flakes. Climb the arete to the first ledge on Cod Moves. From here, make balletic moves up and right, using two slanting horizontal cracks, then continue up the arete to join the top moves of Cod Moves.

The buttress continues with some impressive flake-cracks on its right wall, then forms a right-facing right-angled corner. The rock is slightly suspect on this part of the crag.

Enema Territory   22m   HVS (2000)
Excellent climbing on very sharp flakes, which would merit a star when traffic has removed loose rock. Start just right of the buttress edge, below a crack in a shallow corner.

1. 6m 4a Climb the crack to the big ledge at the foot of the corner
2. 16m 4c On the left wall of the corner are three flake-cracks. Climb the right-hand, and least clearly defined, one.

Friends on the Right, Enemas on the Left   22m   Severe   (2000)
Scramble easily to the foot of the corner (or climb pitch 1 of Enema Territory), then bridge pleasantly up it, taking care with the rock in places.

The right wall of 'Friends' has a chimney in its lower half near its right side. Beyond this is an arete, and the long low promontory that terminates this section of the crag.

Mullet Over   22m   Hard Severe 4a   (2004)
This climbs the wall about 2m to the right of Friends..., following the line of a shattered crack. The rock improves as height is gained.

Absolute Crab   25m   VS 4c   (2000)
Start in the chimney and bridge up its left side to a ledge on the left below a section of very friable looking rock. Step back right on good rock, and climb up steeply on big holds to the overhang. Claw over this using a pincer movement, then scuttle sideways up a series of walls and ledges, trending left.

Awkward Bustard   25m   Hard Severe 4b   (2000)
This starts at the base of the chimney, and climbs the right arete with much greater delicacy and difficulty than would appear from below. Where the rock deteriorates under the overhang, move left and continue up into a large niche. Up this, moving left near the top to finish up a crack.

Directly opposite the long low promontory is a steep south facing wall, bounded on the right by a leftward-curving crack and overlap.

Catch the Sun   25m   E2 5c *   (1997)
Excellent and sustained climbing up the centre of the wall, marred only by the move left at half-height. Start just left of centre and climb the wall directly (initially poorly protected) on small holds and long reaches until forced out onto a ledge on the left edge at 12m. From the ledge move back right onto the wall and climb directly to the apex of the wall. Continue up and rightward to finish via a deceptively tricky final wall.

South Crag

This cliff lies between the long low promontory in the north (the south edge of the Main Crag) and the large bay to the south (Hare Bay). It comprises a west facing cliff characterised by three ridges, with two steep walls in between. The long low promontory forms a spur of the leftmost ridge (facing in).

Approach: Ledges at the base can be reached by abseil.

Ridgeard Corie   28m   Very Difficult   (1997)
The leftmost ridge starts steeply, eases to a slab, followed by a level section and a final steep wall. A mini Alpine classic.

The back wall of the bay right of Ridgeard Corie can be accessed at most states of the sea by an abseil from a large block in a shallow gully at the south end of the wall. It has two prominent grooves in its top half, and a distinct prow to the right. The first route starts a few metres to the left of an obvious niche at the base of the wall.

Fit for Nutting   20m   Hard Severe 4b   (2002)
Climb a short right-facing corner and wall to reach the left side of a prominent

block jutting from the face. Move up and right to reach a shallow left-facing groove, and follow this to the overhang. Steep pulls on big holds overcome this

A Different Kettle of Fish   20m   HVS 5a *   (2000)
This route gains the left groove with greater difficulty than expected. There is an obvious niche at the base of the wall. Start just left of this and climb up to some prominent spikes. Stand on these, then step right and up to a cruel but welcome handjam. Pull right with difficulty into a recess, then finish more easily up the left-hand groove.

Castor Oil and Pollacks   20m   Severe   (2000)
Right of the niche at the base of the wall, a crack slants steeply up to the right side of the prow. Follow this for 5m, then move left on to an overhung slab that leads left to the base of the right-hand groove. Bridge up this to finish.

Survival of the Fattest   20m   VS 4c **   (2002)
This follows the slanting crack on good hold and gear. Start up the first 5m of Castor Oil, but continue up the crack.

Fighting Fat   20m   Hard Severe 4b *   (2002)
The bulging wall just right gives some exciting moves.

Anticlimax Arete   25m   Difficult   (2002)
The middle of the three ridges, crowned by a pleasant pinnacle

To the right of Anticlimax Arete is another steep wall of twisted overhanging cracks and chimneys contained by two corners. The corner on the left defines the right side of Anticlimax Arete, and is easy angled, whilst the larger one on the right is formed by a series of steep chimney-cracks that are often wet. The right wall (facing in) of this corner features three prominent cracks in shallow corners, which are accessible in calm seas.

Neptune's Bell-Cord   21m   Severe   (2002)
Start in a large niche below the twisted overhanging wall. Climb the easy corner on the left until it is possible to move right, over the left end of the overhang into a shallow groove. Climb this to an area of shattered looking rock, then step right and continue more easily, to reach the top at the highest point of the crag.

Rhythm of the Reign   21m   Hard Severe 4a   (2002)
Start in another large niche, below the main corner. Climb the corner for a few metres, then traverse the steep slab rightwards to an easier angled corner. Climb the groove in the left edge of the corner, slanting left past a suspect block, to finish at a notch in the skyline.

The right wall of the main corner forms a steep black wall split in its lower half by three cracks.

Everest   25m   Very Severe 5a *   (2002)
The left-hand crack has a huge flake to its left, forming a narrow chimney. From Base Camp climb the crack and chimney to the top of the flake (the South Summit). Pull over the bulge above with difficulty (the Hillary Step), then follow the corner above more easily to the summit.

Chomolungma   25m   Very Severe 5a *   (2002)
The central crack-line forms a shallow right-facing corner. Start as for Everest, and climb up to an undercut ledge at the base of the shallow corner. Climb it using some delicate fins of rock in the crack and handy footholds on the walls, too difficult moves to reach a ledge. From a second ledge a shallow groove and some flakes are used to reach The Ridge, which is followed to the top.

**Sagarmatha   25m   Very Severe 4c ** *(2002)*

The right-hand crack-line quickly becomes a deep and unattractive chimney in a right-facing corner. This route climbs the left wall of the corner. Start up the corner, then move leftwards across the steep slab to holds on the arete. Continue up the right side of the arete, to reach the right end of the first ledge on Chomolungma. Move right into the top of the chimney, then up to a ledge on top of a flake. Step from this into a groove just right of Chomolungma, and continue up the short corner above to The Ridge, which is followed to the top.

Hare Ridge   40m   Very Difficult *(1997)*

The ridge separating Carrickcorie South Crag from Hare Bay to the south. It is also part of the traverse as it has so far proved impossible to fully traverse around the corner to the foot of the Black Wall. For the traverse, climb up for 20m until it is possible to traverse the easier ground at the top of the Black Wall, and so onto easier ground and back to sea-level. As a route itself, climb the full ridge.

HARE BAY

Tidal   South-East facing

The next bay is a large one and marks the point where the cliffs increase in height. In the middle of the bay is a sea cave, only passable at low tide. At the seaward end of the northern side of the bay is a small looking, but steep black wall, falling sheer into the sea, with overhangs at about half-height. The rock on the Black Wall is excellent.

Approach: Access to the routes is by abseil, then traversing left at sea-level.

The Black Wall

**Smartypants   45m   E1 5b ** *(1997)*

A sustained route with a sensational finish. The route climbs the break in the overhangs at the far left side of the wall. Start on the sea washed platform on the right of the Black Wall. Traverse left under the Black Wall to belay under the main overhang. (10m 4a) Traverse left round the corner then up right to the crack leading to the final break in the overhang. Swing over this sensationally then easier ground to belay (35m 5b). Scramble up the final arete to finish.

**Porpoise and the Hare   40m   HVS 5a ** *(1997)*

An interesting climb with much variety. The overhangs are bounded on their right by a crack leading to a mildly overhanging corner. Start on the sea washed platform as for the previous route, and traverse left to the foot of the crack. Climb this then continue up a booming flake on the right to a niche beneath the overhanging corner. This can be largely overcome by bridging to gain easier ground and belay. Scramble up the final arete to finish.

CARRICK-KEE

Carrick-kee is the narrow promontory which juts into the sea, immediately next to the junction of the coastal fence with the fence which leads from Kennedy's Cairn.

Carrick-kee   50m   VS 4c *(1997)*

This is the obvious and worthwhile slab up the ridge of Carrick-kee. The route climbs a crack on the left of the slab. It can also be used as the exit from day one of the traverse (see below).

GALLIE CRAIG

Looking north from the lighthouse car park is an obvious clean sweep of rock, above a small, pointed sea-stack, and split by a steep corner-line.

Approach: By abseil (bring your own stake but beware loose rock) or by climbing (very loose) from the wide gully leading down to the sea beneath the crag.

Vomit   50m   Scottish VS †   (1971)

An important historical route, taking some serious ground. Almost certainly unrepeated. The climb proper starts up the corner 35m right of the obvious vertical overhanging corner.
1. 20m Climb the rightwards-slanting corner by bridging, then exit up left to a large ledge.
2. 30m Climb up leftwards (above bird's nest) then climb loose rock trending left to finish with an awkward little corner.

GIRDLE TRAVERSE

This girdle traverse round the southern cliffs of the Mull of Galloway was first climbed over four days. It offers an amazing undertaking with surprisingly fine and continuous climbing and some remarkable scenery and situations. An added bonus is that the southernmost piece of land in Scotland falls somewhere along the route.

The Traverse   4200m   E1 5b **   (1997)

The traverse starts at West Tarbet bay and finishes at Seals Cave, under the foghorn just past the lighthouse. The route was originally climbed in four days and divides into three sections, which can be climbed individually according to taste, sea conditions and the state of the tide. Time taken will largely depend on the amount of soloing which parties are prepared to undertake. Careful attention should be paid to both the states of the tide and sea conditions.
1. 5b The first main section is from West Tarbet to Gallie Craig (this is the high cliff with the prominent but loose corner-line, clearly seen by looking north from the lighthouse car park). This section was originally climbed over two days, with a break at Carrick-kee. About mid-way through the first day was the cave in Hare Bay, which required low tide to cross without swimming. Accordingly, start from West Tarbet about 3 to 4 hours before low tide. It is possible to scramble out at the gully immediately to the south of Gallie Craig.
2. 4c/5a The next section from Gallie Craig onwards provides the finest climbing and the most impressive rock architecture, but is also the most serious. Low tide is essential to start this section. Farther on there are two impressive sea caves, which have to be swum. Calm seas are essential and it should be emphasised that the Mull is both exposed to big seas and prone to difficult undercurrents. It is possible to scramble out in the vicinity of the car park next to a steep yellow wall. One abseil is required.
3. 5a The final section, while worthwhile, scenic and interesting, is not as sustained and can hold much guano after the nesting season. Four or five abseils are required to pass sea caves.

GALLOWAY SEA-CLIFFS

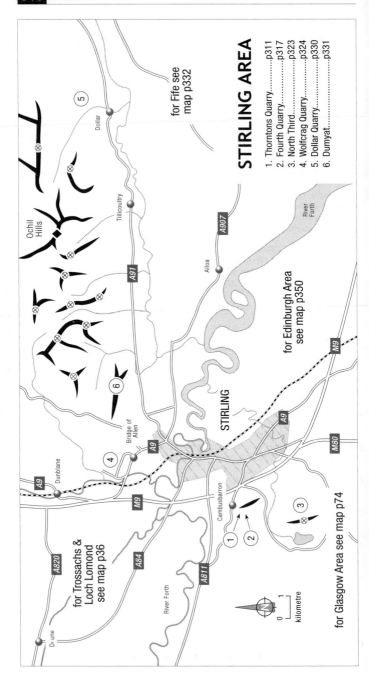

for Fife see
map p332

Dollar ⑤

Ochil
Hills

Tillicoultry

A91

A907

Alloa

River
Forth

for Edinburgh Area
see map p350

⑥

STIRLING

Bridge of
Allen

M9

A9

Dunblane

④

A9

M9

A9

M80

for Trossachs &
Loch Lomond
see map p36

A820

Cambusbarron

①
②

③

A84

A811

River Forth

Doune

N

0   1
kilometre

for Glasgow Area see map p74

STIRLING AREA

This chapter returns to the central belt to describe the crags around Stirling. These offer some good climbing and bouldering that is readily accessible from the urban areas of the central belt. The local names for the two Cambusbarron quarries have only recently come to light and are included here for the first time.

THORNTONS QUARRY - CAMBUSBARRON

(NS 772 922)   Enclosed, North & West facing   Map p310   Diagram p312

This fine abandoned quarry bowl offers a good selection of high standard routes, mostly following prominent cracks or grooves. The routes are generally well protected. The quarry is very sheltered and the main face catches the evening sun in the summer, though the routes are seldom dry in winter. More traffic would help to keep some routes a little cleaner.

Approach: The quarry is accessed from Quarry Road (about 200m after the centre of Cambusbarron village, heading west). The entrance to the quarry is at the top of the road, with limited parking next to the public information board which has a useful display map showing the various quarry trails. Walk straight ahead on the overgrown access track into the main amphitheatre.

The first lines are a series of micro route/boulder problems on the short walls at the leftmost edge of the quarry where the wall nears its lowest height. They offer good value entertainment, although some would benefit from a further brushing.

1 Bro's Arete   4m   5a   (2004)
Climb the left-hand arete via a sidepull and sloping mantel, finish easily.

2 Fast and Cheap   4m   5c   (2003)
Start in the middle of the first section of rock. Lunge for a three finger hold, pull up, rock over and go for the top.

3 Treehugging   3m   4b   (2004)
Start below the pine tree. Climb the crack easily then hug the tree and...

4 Sandal-wearing   3m   5a   (2004)
The crack immediately to the right.

5 Pebble-dashed   3m   5c   (2004)
Start with a mono then climb straight up the centre of the wall.

6 Hippy Bastard   3m   4c   (2004)
The mossy corner/groove.

7 Suck my Oil   5m   5b   (2004)
The flake-crack.

8 Withdrawal Wall   5m   5a   (2003)
Climb the wall just right of the clean-cut arete arete on positive but spaced holds

9 Feel my Vineyard   6m   5c   (2004)
A pull, a lunge and a high step lead up the centre of the slab. Exit left to avoid a loose top-out.

About 7m to the right is a blocky groove with a prominent roof at half height.

0 Grangemouth High Grooves   8m   Severe   (2002)
Climb cracks in the wall just right of the blocky groove to a dirty top-out.

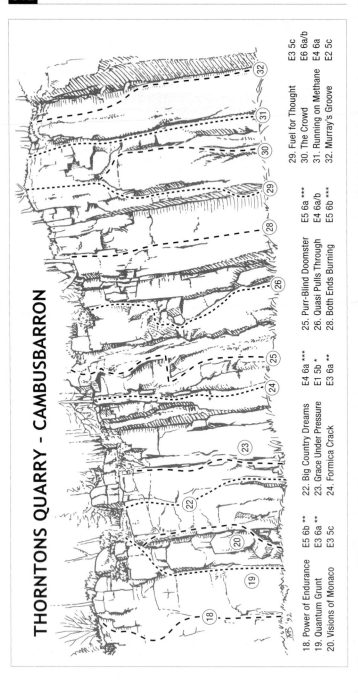

THORNTONS QUARRY - CAMBUSBARRON

18. Power of Endurance   E5 6b **
19. Quantum Grunt   E3 6a **
20. Visions of Monaco   E3 5c

22. Big Country Dreams   E4 6a ***
23. Grace Under Pressure   E1 5b *
24. Formica Crack   E3 6a **

25. Purr-Blind Doomster   E5 6a ***
26. Quasi Pulls Through   E4 6a/b
28. Both Ends Burning   E5 6b ***

29. Fuel for Thought   E3 5c
30. The Crowd   E6 6a/b
31. Running on Methane   E4 6a
32. Murray's Groove   E2 5c

Further right protrudes an obvious clean-cut arete which is home to the next three routes:

11 Bo's Groove   12m   VS 4c   *(1996)*
The groove with a thin crack to the left of the arete.

12 Bo's Arete   12m   HVS 5a   *(1996)*
From the bottom of the groove make an interesting move right to tackle the blunt arete face on. Gear out on the right, then left.

13 Bo's Arete Direct   12m   E1 5c   *(1996)*
The face to the right of the arete provides an interesting variation. Climb to the hold above the V-shaped pocket, then swing left to join Bo's arete.

The next route is identified by a large blocky corner.

14 Blockbuster   15m   VS 4c   *(1994)*
Scramble over large boulders to the wide crack at half height in the corner and climb it.

15 Three Step Corner   15m   Severe   *(pre 1984)*
Takes an obvious leftwards rising line up the series of three huge flakes.

Some 4m left of Power of Endurance is a squat, square-cut pillar, the next two routes start from its top.

16 Ballroom Blitz   20m   E2 5c   *(2004)*
Go straight up past a scoop and a projecting flake onto a ledge, then climb the overhung groove to an exit right, to avoid loose earth and tree roots.

17 Ground Force   20m   HVS 5a   *(2004)*
Climb up right into a right-angled corner and go up this to a ledge on the left. A hard move re-gains the corner to a finish on steep grass.

18 Power of Endurance   25m   E5 6b ★★   *(1984)*
A bit of a test piece, which requires a good selection of small wires and a very strong right arm. The wall near the left-hand end of the face is split by a thin crack-line which leads to an obvious small pod. Follow a line of good but quite spaced holds which lead to a thin crack. Climb this until it is necessary to crank wildly to reach the pod (crux). Easier climbing now leads to below the final wall, which is best avoided by an awkward exit right.

19 Quantum Grunt   25m   E3 6a ★★   *(1984)*
A good climb with both strenuous and technical climbing. Start below the groove a few metres right of the previous route. Make difficult initial moves to gain the groove proper (large Friend useful). Mantel into the niche using a doubtful looking flake and continue up the groove above. A thin fingery crux leads to good holds, and an awkward pull out right to finish. An alternative finish continues up the undercuts on the left (harder).

20 Visions of Monaco   25m   E3 5c   *(1984)*
This takes the obvious groove and cracked arete to the right. Start at a prominent break. Climb up and right, passing a good resting ledge, to the foot of the crack. Climb this until forced to step left into the chimney at the top. It is possible, but very artificial, to continue directly up the crack to the top (6a).

21 Cumacoma   20m   E5 6b   *(1995)*
Climb the small corner between Visions of Monaco and Big Country Dreams to a sloping ledge and up to a thin crack. Climb up to a break and traverse right to join Big Country Dreams.

STIRLING AREA

22 Big Country Dreams   25m   E4 6a *   *(1983)*
An excellent route tackling the striking S-shaped crack-line. Start just right of the
main crack-line. Climb onto a jutting block and pull up and left to follow a thin
crack which leads to a rest below the final crack. A short series of athletic moves
leads to a pumpy finish. It helps to avoid filling the best finger locks with runners.

23 Grace Under Pressure   25m   E1 5b *
The shallow flared chimney-line just right of Big Country Dreams, starting just to
its right. Follow the chimney-line past a good undercut hold to an easier finish.

24 Formica Crack   25m   E3 6a **   *(1984)*
Further right is a fine buttress with a prominent shallow pod in the lower section
on the left. Climb into the pod, then struggle up to better jams at its top. Continue
past several interesting moves to the top.

25 The Purr-Blind Doomster   25m   E5 6a *   *(1984)*
An enjoyable well protected crack contrasting with a bold upper section on the
upper arete. Start just right of Formica Crack. Climb the thin crack with difficulty
to an obvious vertical slot at its top. Move delicately right to the arete, take a deep
breath, then move up on a series of sloping holds to the obvious jutting spike.
Move back right round the arete to finish more easily.

**26 Quasi Pulls Through   25m   E4 6a/b   *(1984)*
The secret to this one is visible from the quarry floor, but not while you're climbing.
Start 5m right of The Purr-Blind Doomster, below a steep reddish groove capped
by a bulging roof on its right. Climb the difficult groove to a slanting crack, then
make a huge and strenuous reach up and left to a good hidden hold (crux) and
resting spot. Step right under a small roof to finish up a groove.

The pile of blocks at the bottom just to the right are the remains of Oink Oink. The
smooth chimney which takes its place is now the line of Pig Route.

**27 Pig Route   25m   E3 5c   *(1994)*
Climb the off-width chimney!

Right of this is another fine buttress.

28 Both Ends Burning   25m   E5 6b *   *(1984)*
Superb sustained, technical and varied climbing up the thin crack in the smooth
wall. Steep initial moves lead to a good crack. Move up, then make a short series
of hard moves to a resting foothold at half-height on the left. Step rather blindly
back into the crack, then dash past the strenuous finishing moves.

**29 Fuel for Thought   25m   E3 5c   *(1984)*
This climbs the slender groove in the arete right of Both Ends Burning, gained from
the corner on its left. Climb the corner to a flake. Move up and across right to gain
the groove. Climb this and go up right over the top of a huge block to finish.

**30 The Crowd   25m   E6 6a/b   *(1985)*
This takes a line between Fuel for Thought and Running on Methane; it has not
become popular for obvious reasons. Climb the hanging groove past 3 poor peg
runners to reach a ledge (crux). Continue boldly up the groove, with a hard move
to finish (poor RPs).

31 Running on Methane   25m   E4 6a
Another fine looking line that has been neglected and is in need of a good cleaning.
Start below the right wall of the short arete about 5m right of The Crowd. Climb
the arete (sustained, rather loose and poorly protected) to gain good holds and

runners at the foot of the groove. Follow this past a bulge with difficulty to a stopping place. Step left, then move up right to the top.

32 Murray's Groove   25m   E2 5c   (1984)
The obvious corner at the right end of the face is dirty with some loose holds. Finish on the left.

33 Auto Giro   25m   E6 6c *
Start up Adulterer's Repentance to the spike. Move round the arete and place a wire before making a desperate dyno up the left side of the arete to a ledge. Finish more easily.

34 Adulterer's Repentance   25m   E3 5c   (1985)
The bold arete and wall left of Economy Drive. Climb the arete to a spike, step right onto the wall and climb the scoop to larger holds. Move left onto a block, then finish on good holds.

35 Economy Drive   25m   E3 6a **   (1985)
Climb the thin crack up the wall just left of the large corner.

36 Contortionism   20m   E6 6c   (1996)
Climbs straight up the large corner. The route is well protected, but very sustained with a vicious crux section.

The fallen block below Economy Drive is home to three boulder problems, the first two of which are on the slabby face.

37 LDV   3m   Font 4   (1980s)
Takes the slabby right arete.

38 Spanking the Monkey   4m   Font 7b   (1984)
The very bold left arete; an intimidating friction problem, now made much safer by the removal of the rocks at its base.

39 Jerkin' the Gherkin   4m   Font 6c+   (2004)
Tackles the left arete of the overhanging face of the block, starting either from the left, or straight up with a jump.

The quarry wall then swings round through 90 degrees to form the right wall.

40 Anabolic Steroids   20m   E6 6b *   (1996)
Climbs the overhanging crack-line above the friction boulder problems at the back of the quarry. Bold dynamic climbing leads to a break at 4m. Hard and sustained, but well protected, climbing follows. Where the crack splits, follow the right hand branch to the top.

41 Tarzan   15m   E3 6a   (2001)
Right again is a strangely detached pillar on the arete. Climb the pillar and make hard moves right, traversing the seam (crux), to gain a left trending crack which is followed to the large ledge above. Finish up the line of least resistance.

42 The Bustup   30m   VS 4c   (1998)
This route tackles the large corner right of Tarzan, with well protected climbing and exciting moves on a huge detached block!

43 Sexed up   30m   F7c   (2004)
The line of bolts up the arete will be obvious for as long as they remain in place. Gently overhanging climbing on positive holds past seven bolts to a bolt belay.

The next route tackles the thin crack-line at the left end of the back wall of the quarry.

44 Nandralone   30m   E8 6c ***   (2004)
Thin climbing leads to a poor rest on the left, before continuously powerful moves up the crack. Slap out left to a jug and then climb juggy hanging blocks, before moving right, then up left, to pull over the top near a fallen tree.

45 Anger Management   20m   E5 6b **   (2004)
Make desperate bouldery moves up the left trending ramp. Rest on top of the flake before powering up the twin cracks above. Move up leftwards to finish more easily.

The start of the next route is marked by a rectangular pod, just above head height.

46 Bobbin Robin   23m   E1 5b   (2003)
Mantelshelf into the pod then move up diagonally right over blocks to the base of a shallow chimney. Make awkward moves up the chimney onto a sloping ramp then climb the left-hand corner above to a ledge. Climb the corner and off-width crack to the top.

Some 4m to the right of Bobbin Robin is a large sloping ledge.

47 Gun Fury   25m   E2 5c   (2004)
Start on the right side of the ledge. Climb the left facing corner to a ledge in a short overhanging chimney groove. Climb this, then the next one up on the right.

48 Moving Shadow   25m   E6 6b *   (2001)
The obvious V-groove on the middle of the right-hand wall. Climb the groove, with a series of desperate moves to gain the layback crack which is followed to a ledge on the right. Have a rest then lurch leftwards to make exposed moves to finish up a small headwall.

49 Trail Blazer   25m   E2 5c **   (1986)
Just to the right of the groove of Moving Shadow is a right-facing corner-crack. Climb this to a ledge on the left, then finish up the short leaning headwall. An excellent route which would benefit from more traffic.

50 Pathfinder   25m   E1 5b   (1986)
This takes a direct line immediately left of the finger-crack to climb a left facing corner-crack. Start just right of Trail Blazer. Gain the foot of the ramp on which the finger-crack finishes and climb the wide crack above, stepping up left to reach a good ledge. Climb the corner-crack to the top of a pedestal, step up right then go back left to finish using a small tree.

The obvious right, then left, slanting finger-crack gives an excellent boulder problem (4m 5c).

51 Thug of War   10m   E4 6b   (1988)
The thin crack in the wall right of the finger-crack provides a hard challenge.

The quarry wall then swings round through 90 degrees again to form the shady wall which is passed on the right when first entering the quarry. Some of the routes on this wall can be damp and are best climbed after a dry spell. Moving from left to right, about one-third of the way along this wall, is a big semi-detached pinnacle with a platform at its base. On its right is a jamming crack running up to a roof.

52 Phantom Power   20m   E1 5b   (2003)
Start on the platform at the base of the pinnacle. Layback the flared crack on the left, to an awkward mantel onto a small ledge. Move up to easier climbing in the

deep groove, leading to the top of the pinnacle. Finish up the corner on the left.

53 Dr Dre's Orgazmatron 20m E3 5c (2003)
The jamming crack. Start on the platform and pull round into the crack. Strenuous jamming leads to a roof. Move left onto a ledge and then up a short finger-crack to the top of the pinnacle. Finish up a stepped groove on the right.

54 In Hiding 10m E3 5c (1998)
Closest to the quarry entrance and starting just right of a large tree against the face, this route follows cleaned edges up the smooth mossy slab, moving right at the top to a loose finish. Low in the grade and desperately in need of another good clean.

FOURTH QUARRY - CAMBUSBARRON

(NS 770 920) South-west facing Map p310 Diagram p319

This quarry used to be known as Cambusbarron West. In contrast to Thorntons Quarry it has an open aspect with an expansive view towards the hills. It is pleasant, quick drying and can often provide year round climbing. This quarry also offers a high number of good routes in the HVS – E1 grade. A few of the routes, especially those established more recently, still suffer from loose finishes and particular care should be taken at the top of the climbs, especially after periods of wet weather.

Approach: Park as for Thorntons Quarry, continue past the barrier and follow the track up and round to the left. The first climbs are on the long left (east) wall and are described starting from the left.

Descent: Via a small track through the trees, which comes down to the left of the left-hand wall. If several routes are planned, it is generally quicker and easier to fix an abseil rope from the fence posts at the top.

1 Ninety-Five 10m E1 5b (1993)
This takes the obvious pillar on the left, as soon as one enters the quarry. Move up and foot traverse along the obvious fault. A couple of moves up gain better holds and protection. Move up to another horizontal break, then make an awkward move right to the arete. Move back left to finish up the middle of the pillar.

To the right the base of the crag is obscured by large trees. The next route climbs the slabby wall towards the right-hand end of the trees.

2 Scales of Injustice 10m F7b+ * (2000)
Sustained and difficult slab climbing up the smooth wall 10m left of Production Line. Climb up to the overlap and continue up flakes and the wall above to a lower-off. Protected by 5 bolt runners

3 Production Line 15m E6 6c ** (1993)
This hard route takes a thin crack a few metres left of the right-hand end of the trees. Climb the crack on the right placing a high side runner. Climb down and across to a horizontal crack. Move up to a small roof and make a very hard move to a triangular hold. Climb the crack above on good slots to a loose finish.

Behind the last of the trees, some 9m right of Production Line, is a large right-facing corner taken by the following route.

4 Scrubbers 14m E1 5b (2003)
Climb blocks, followed by the slab, to the corner which is climbed via ever widening cracks to a rest below the roof. Follow the crack through the roof and move left onto the face to finish.

The next route tackles the cracks in the wall immediately right of the corner.

5 Climb on you Crazy Diamond   10m   E3 5c   *(2004)*
Surmount blocks and follow the cracks, trending left. When these run out, move right and climb straight up to pass between two gorse bushes. Finish via the short corner and an entertaining top-out!

Right again is a pillar split by an obvious off-hand crack.

6 Bird's Nest Crack   10m   VS 5a   *(1996)*
Climb the crack with a tricky move at half-height and finish by the easy but loose corner above.

7 One for the Buzzards   10m   HVS 5a   *(2004)*
Struggle up the off-width chimney-crack defining the right side of the pillar. Climb a groove through a small roof to a crack, and follow this, exiting left.

Right of the pillar is a slabby, undercut buttress with two prominent converging cracks.

**8 Cross in Oz   10m   E1 5b ** **   *(1993)*
The left-hand crack, starting beneath a small roof. Pull through the bulge and follow the crack to a sloping ledge on the right. Finish straight up.

9 Cross-town Traffic   10m   E1 5b *   *(1993)*
Gain the right-hand crack by climbing the short corner and following the crack round onto the slab. Either continue along the crack to finish up the left-hand arete, or finish direct by a cleaned finger-crack in the final wall.

10 Arse on Stumps   15m   E3 5c   *(1999)*
A bold eliminate line which starts 1m to the right of Cross in Oz. Climb the short arete up to the overlap. Step left, move up and finish up the slab, stepping slightly rightwards, avoiding the right arete.

11 Cha   10m   Severe 4a *   *(1993)*
Climb the blocks left of the Cha graffiti, until it is possible to move right onto good holds. Climb to the horizontal break, then finish up the crack.

12 Looney Tunes   9m   E4 6a *   *(1999)*
A bouldery, route which climbs the front face of the Cha buttress using the right-hand arete. Starting from a tiny ledge make hard awkward moves to gain the horizontal break. From here step right onto the arete and finish straight up. Comes complete with unprotected crux and bad landing.

To the right, the base of the cliff is obscured by earth and scree. The next routes lie on Force 8 wall, about 10m up and right from Cha buttress.

13 Wind Up   10m   VS 5a   *(1991)*
The left-facing corner at the left edge of the wall offers thin laybacking.

14 Yoshimi   10m   E1 5b   *(1993)*
Climbs the left-hand arete and crack, without recourse to the previous route.

15 Force 8   10m   E1 5b *   *(1991)*
The central crack in the wall.

16 Pipistrelle   10m   HVS 5a *   *(1993)*
Start below Force 8. Follow a line of holds diagonally right to a large flat hold on arete. Follow the arete and crack to top.

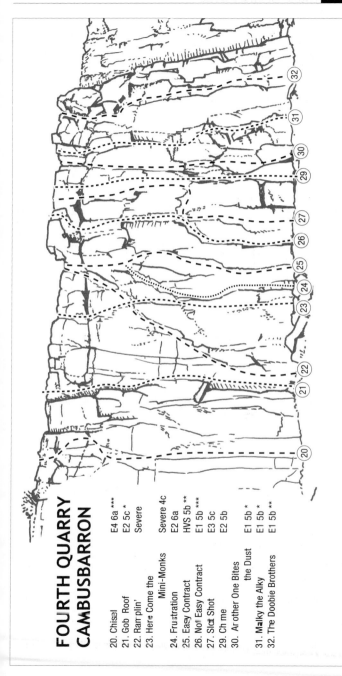

FOURTH QUARRY CAMBUSBARRON

20. Chisel	E4 6a ***
21. Gob Roof	E2 5c *
22. Rarrplin'	Severe
23. Here Come the Mini-Monks	Severe 4c
24. Frustration	E2 6a
25. Easy Contract	HVS 5b **
26. Not Easy Contract	E1 5b ***
27. Slot Shot	E3 5c
29. Ch me	E2 5b
30. Ar other One Bites the Dust	E1 5b *
31. Malky the Alky	E1 5b *
32. The Doobie Brothers	E1 5b **

17 Miss Po   12m   E2 5c   *(2000)*
Climbs the technical right-facing corner to the right of Force 8. Still a little dirty, but worthwhile.

A steep wall leads right to jumbled rocks and blocks forming a pinnacle jutting into the quarry. The left side of this promontory is Optimist's Chimney.

18 Public Spirited Individual   18m   E3 5c **
The cleaned crack system in the wall just left of Optimist's Chimney. Climb cracks on the face to obvious breaks, with the crux moves near the top. The gear is hard to place; the alternative is to make the easier finish without it.

19 Optimist's Chimney   10m   VS 4c
Climb the chimney on the left side of the jumbled pinnacle jutting into the quarry, without pushing too hard.

20 Chisel   10m   E4 6a ***   *(1993)*
About 50m right of the pinnacle is a smooth wall with a prominent thin crack. This has been extensively sculptured to produce a flawed but enjoyable piece of climbing. Climb the crack past engineered finger-locks to good holds at its top. Continue straight up the wall, past a peg runner, to a worrying last move on friable rock.

21 Gobi Roof   10m   E2 5c *   *(1990)*
Start right of Chisel at an obvious triangular recess. Climb up to a small roof, then pull over and follow the fault to the top.

22 Ramplin'   15m   Severe   *(1993)*
This takes the corner ramp-line immediately right of Gobi Roof. Climb past three small trees and finish straight up.

Just to the right of Ramplin' lies:

23 Here Come the Mini-Monks   15m   Severe 4c   *(2003)*
Climb the corner then the cracks directly above, to a ledge on Ramplin'. Follow a left-trending line of stepped holds finishing past a big block.

The right arete of Mini-Monks marks the start of a clean wall, characterised by a series of interconnected cracks, with some of the best routes in the quarry. The right arete is taken by Frustration:

24 Frustration 15m E2 6a   *(1995)*
The arete. Climb up to a small ledge in a corner and reach round to the wide crack on the face. Climb straight up, finishing up Easy Contract.

25 Easy Contract   12m   HVS 5b **   *(1985)*
Climb the leftmost of the cracks by enjoyable jamming. Where it splits, take the thinner right-hand option. Finish up the left arete of the buttress. A number of variations to this route are possible: in the lower section the wider left-hand crack of Frustration can be followed (at the same grade), whilst finishes can be made up either side of the upper arete.

26 Not Easy Contract   12m   E1 5b ***   *(1980s)*
Climb the wide crack just to the right to an awkward move onto a ledge at the foot of a short groove. Climb this steeply, then finish straight up. Good climbing.

Magillas in the Mist, HVS 5a, the Fish Kettle. Alastair Gillies on the first ascent
(photo Andrew Fraser)

Three eliminates have been squeezed between Not east Contract and Another One Bites the Dust. Although blinkers may be required, they do feature some good independant climbing. When you've done them once, try a pic 'n' mix approach.

27 Slot Shot   12m   E3 5c   *(1991)*
Climb thin cracks up the wall right of the wide crack to the ledge at the foot of the wee groove of Not Easy Contract. Make a long bridge down and right to the foot of a short crack. Climb this and continue straight up through a small niche and another crack.

28 Crack Attack   12m   E3 6a   *(1994)*
Start by a mantel onto the detached block, climb small pockets in cracks to an undercling and join Slot Shot after its rightward traverse.

29 Chime   12m   E2 5b   *(2004)*
Climb the left arete of the shallow chimney immediately to the right, then go through a capped niche and up twin cracks onto a small ledge. Move onto a larger sloping ledge on the right to climb single, then twin cracks.

30 Another One Bites the Dust   12m   E1 5b *   *(1980s)*
The large corner about 6m right of Easy Contract. Climb the corner to a ledge at half-height, then continue up the fine jamming crack above.

31 Malky the Alky   12m   E1 5b *   *(1980s)*
Start just right of the obvious central corner of Another One Bites the Dust. Climb up through a bulge to the large ledge, then continue up the corner above.

32 The Doobie Brothers   12m   E1 5b **   *(1991)*
Starting 5m right of the central corner, just left of a tottering pillar which marks the right side of the buttress, climb the obvious crack. Take care – the top was home to some very large blocks which parted company in 2002.

33 Toddle   14m   Severe   *(2002)*
Climb wide cracks on the right-hand side of the pillar to finish up a short corner. Apparently not as tottering, or as loose, as appearances would suggest.

34 Bo's Girdle   35m   E2 5b   *(1995)*
A diagonal traverse of the face. Start up Easy Contract and aim for the ledge on Not Easy Contract. Climb the layback crack until it is possible to step right. Traverse to the corner of Malky the Alky and round the arete, finishing straight up.

A few metres further on, the crag turns sharp right to form the south wall of the quarry. About 15m along the south wall is a small, charcoal grey, slabby wall covered with quartz holds and with a tiny overlap at 4m.

35 Thank God for Friends   18m   E1 5b   *(2001)*
Climb the tapering slabby wall direct.

36 Furrowed Prow   15m   HVS 5b   *(2003)*
Start just right of Thank God For Friends and climb the quartz studded wall, to a section of broken ground. Go carefully over this and move left to better rock. Follow grooves to the obvious prow which is climbed, in a very exposed position, using a crack and the arete.

Immediately right of the start to Furrowed Prow is a small black and green wall with a pointed block at its base.

The Hissing of Summer Prawns, Hard Severe 4b, Mull of Galloway. Climber Ian Magill
(photo Andrew Fraser)

STIRLING AREA

37 Smack My Birch Up   16m   HVS 5a   *(2003)*
Just right again, shallow blind cracks lead to a birch sapling at half-height. Pass this on the left and continue direct to finish up the narrow open chimney.

Right again, at about 5m height, is a smooth slab characterised by a thin lightening bolt crack.

38 Decidedly Dodgy   20m   HVS 5a *   *(1995)*
Climb up to a sloping ledge below the slab and traverse right to reach a sandwiched, vertical band of rock. Ascend to a roof which is passed on the left to finish up the large corner above.

5m right of Decidedly Dodgy is an obvious roofed V-groove.

39 Le Bal des Oiseaux Fantomes   15m   E3 5c *   *(2004)*
Good if eliminate climbing. Climb the V-groove and roof above direct to small ledges at the foot of a concave wall. Climb its left edge on layaways to reach a good handrail below the headwall. Finish via steep blocks and cracks on the right.

The next route takes the right arete of the groove.

40 Buttons   18m   HVS 5b   *(2001)*
Climb the vertical arete on somewhat loose and poorly protected rock to reach a Y-fork and good protection. Move up through the Y-fork towards a bulge and a large projecting 'shark's fin' flake (crux; Friend 4 in the parallel crack). Grab the flake and pull up over the bulge to easy climbing and a loose finish.

41 The Consolation Prize   16m   E2 5c   *(2003)*
Start 3m right of Buttons, mid-way between Buttons and Scaresville. Climb a line of sloping ledges, then a rectangular leaning block. Above on the left is an overhang split by a finger-crack. Make hard moves over this (crux) then go up to the roof which is turned on the right.

Right again is an obvious tapering slab reminiscent of the late Balance of Power at Auchinstarry. The slab faces the far end of the fenced plantation.

42 Scaresville   15m   E3 5c *   *(1991)*
Start below the left side of the slab and climb to where an awkward mantel gives access to the slab (crux). Move up and right, then back left to a large flake. Now climb slightly up and right, then go back left to finish. Necky.
Variation: **E1 5b**   *(2001)*
It is possible to avoid the crux by starting up the ramp on the right and placing gear in the corner, before traversing left onto the main face.

About 20m right is a buttress with a prominent 8 ball graffiti. The buttress is just before the start of the earth and boulder debris that lies below much of the right-hand side of the quarry.

43 The Ubiquitous Chip   15m   E4 6a   *(1993)*
The wide crack right of the arete and the 8 ball graffiti gives a hard start and some difficult jamming to a ledge at half-height. A short groove leads to a large roof, which is avoided on the right. The top section has some dangerously poised blocks.

44 Brat Attack   15m   E3 5c   *(1991)*
Thin cracks in the wall right of the start of The Ubiquitous Chip lead to the top of a small pinnacle. Follow a thin crack to the top.

The next route lies on the broken buttress above the quarry debris to the right. Clamber up the spoil to the foot of the highest part of the buttress hereabouts and the base of an undercut slab (just right of the wall with broken parallel cracks in its lower section).

45 The Cutter   12m   E1 5b
(2002)

From the left move up to a break on the slab. Move up right to a wide crack which is followed to a ledge. Climb the off-width crack and arete above onto a narrow ledge, then move left into a corner. Climb this onto a slab, move up this before finishing up a short groove. A reasonable line which would benefit from more traffic.

The spoil heap below the right-hand, west, wall is characterised by a massive boulder. To its right, when viewed from below, is a prominent squat pillar with two short but striking crack-lines on its right flank.

46 The Rock of Crack   9m   E2 5c
(1996)

The left-hand crack.

47 Confessions of a Speed Freak   9m   E1 5b
(1996)

The wider right-hand crack.

At the extreme right-hand end of the quarry, just as the path enters the woods proper, is a tiny natural bulging buttress.

48 Somnambulism   5m   HVS 5b
(1999)

Climb the bulging mossy wall with some nice moves.

NORTH THIRD

(NS 760 890)   West facing   Map p310

This extensive, though little frequented outcrop of dolerite lies about 8km south-west of Stirling, in a beautiful setting overlooking North Third Reservoir. The climbing is characterised by long straight cracks offering some fine jamming. After short periods of wet weather the cliff dries quickly. However, after longer periods the crag can take a long time to dry out. Some of the routes need of a good scrub.

Approach: The easiest approach is across the reservoir dam itself. Limited parking is possible on the verge above the dam.

Faulty Tower   12m   VS 4c

This lies on the buttress about 100m left of the Birds and Bees Buttress. Start from a cave on the right. Swing left out of the cave into a crack which is leads to the top.

BIRDS & BEES BUTTRESS

This buttress lies directly above the dam, and is easily recognised by the huge bulbous nose right of centre.

Beeline   12m   HVS 5a

Climb the obvious groove on the right side of the buttress which lies 20m left of the nose. Swing right around the overhang at the top.

Cuckoo Crack   15m   VS 5a

This lies just below and left of the huge nose. Climb the crack to a glacis under a roof, traverse right into a groove and finish direct.

RED TOWER

This area lies about 400m right of Birds and Bees Buttress. The most obvious feature is a striking red tower set in a bay, around which the climbs are situated. The best descent is down the slope to the left.

The Flying Dragon   20m   E2 5c *   (1982)
The crack in the left wall of the bay.

Jezebel   20m   E1 5b ***   (1982)
The crack right of The Flying Dragon gives superb sustained jamming. Follow the crack through a strenuous bulge then continue up the groove above. Thread belay.

Jim's Chimney   20m   VS 4b
The hideous chimney to the right of Jezebel is followed to finish up its left wall.

Red Shift   25m   E6 6b **   (1982/84)
This route climbs the fine diagonal crack across the Red Tower. Climb a bulging vertical crack (crux) to gain the diagonal crack. Follow this, with particularly trying moves round the arete, to finish straight up. Very sustained.
Variation: 6a
Slightly easier, but with poorer rock, is to start up the vague groove left of the normal start.

Beemer   15m   E3 5c   (1982)
This route takes the bulging chimney-crack 15m further right.

Sma' Gell   12m   E2 5c
Another 150m to the right is an obvious crack splitting a bulging nose. The climb gets increasingly harder and more difficult to protect as the crack gets wider.

WOLFCRAG QUARRY

(NS 789 980)   South facing   Map p310

Tucked away in Mine Woods, Bridge of Allan is a small sandstone quarry that offers good year round climbing. It is a natural sun trap and, due to its sheltered location and steepness, climbing is possible even during heavy rain. People have been bouldering at Wolfcrag since the 1980s and the quarry's greatest asset is its wealth of excellent problems and low-level traverses. Some of the traditional routes, most of which are good in their lower section, could be dramatically improved if lower-offs were installed to avoid unpleasant finishes through loose and vegetated rock.

Approach: From the M9, junction 11, take the A9 to Bridge of Allan. Turn left immediately after crossing the Allan Water, into Blairforkie Drive, then turn right up Ferniebank Brae. The quarry is straight ahead behind the trees at the top of the Brae.

As well as the more traditional lines, this guide incorporates a first attempt to document some of the many boulder problems to be found in the quarry.

Traverses – Long easier traverses can be found either side of the main faces following breaks and other obvious features, while the main faces offer more demanding traverses at various heights. A very good stamina training traverse goes in either direction across the main face with feet between 30cm and 1m above the ground. If the blob in the open groove of Experiments in Incest is avoided and the low horizontal break at the far right of the walls is not used for the feet, a trip right across the faces goes at a grade of about F7a. A very good, but contorted, technical and strenuous traverse of the main faces exists if you are strict about staying very low; grade about F7b+ to F7c.

ARETE AREA

On entering the quarry, the first obvious feature is a small isolated buttress with a sharp left arete. From the top of the good rock it is possible to down-climb the right-hand side of the face come corner using a large triangular pocket.

1 The Arete   5b   *(1970s)*
Climb the arete to an easy but loose finish.

2 Face   6a
Use rounded sidepulls at the left side of the face to gain small edges in the centre of the face. Continue trending right to finger jugs and up to a small ledge.

3 Corner   6b
Up the corner avoiding use of a large triangular pocket. At the top of the corner reach left for finger jugs on the face.

4 The Second Arete   10m   Very Difficult
Some 12m to the right is another more blocky arete. Climb this to a loose and scary finish.

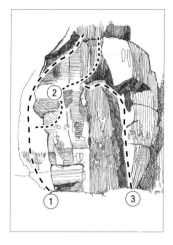

LARGE BLOCK

This lies immediately left of the main faces and is separated from them by the fist-width crack of The Outsider. The area between the start of In Trance as Mission and the crack of The Outsider has several problems.

5 Hand Traverse   5c
Left of Left-hand Crack is an obvious diagonal sloping ledge. Hand-traverse along this and continue up the wall to the left.

6 In Trance as Mission   15m   VS 4c
A poorly protected route through the roofs 12m right of the Second Arete. Start just left of Left-hand Crack, at a 'giant's staircase'. Follow this to the huge roof and traverse rightwards along ledges to escape.

7 Left-hand Crack   6a
Up the short thin crack starting with hands in two lower pockets. Gain and use one finger pocket to reach the ledge.

8 Jammed Block   6b
Start low with both hands on the jammed block. Reach left and use two edges to gain the ledge (thin crack not allowed).

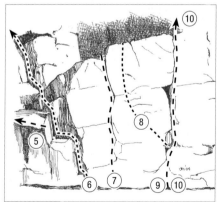

9 The Outsider   10m   E2 5c   *(1980s)*
The arete forming the left edge of the main face. A short fist-width crack leads to a ledge. A precarious mantel onto the arete gains an easier, but bold, finish leftwards.

10 Outsider Crack   4b
The initial hand to fist-width crack of The Outsider provides an easy, but pleasant, problem in its own right.

11 Up on the Catwalk   10m   E2 6a   *(1980s)*
A variation on The Outsider. Protection, once found, is good. From the precarious mantel swing right and climb the overhanging wall.

MAIN FACE - LEFT

The two central faces are separated by the open groove of Experiments in Incest. The next problems are on the gently impending left-hand face. Problems are described working left to right. If you end up at the second horizontal break this can be traversed left to the top of the Large Block without great difficulty, though the far right-hand end can feel a little fragile.

12 Dyno   6b
Use a good finger edge just right of the wide crack for both hands and dyno for the large sloping slot at the first break.

13 Sidepull   6b
Start at the same point as the previous problem, but use a poor left-facing sidepull to gain the slot.

14 First Break   6b
Start with the right hand on a small pedestal shaped hold. Pull up left for an edge and use this to gain the slot via a cross through. Traverse right along the first break on poor edges until the line of good chipped pockets can be reached. Use these to gain the second break and traverse off left.

15 Direct   6c
Start with the left hand on the pedestal hold. Above, in a left to right diagonal, are two edges and a vertical slot. Gain the slot with the right hand (via edges) and use a small sloping edge in the first break for the left hand. Use two small edges/pockets to gain the second break. Feet are restricted to hand holds above the pedestal hold, though a small edge down and left of the finger edge in the first break can be used for the feet to gain the second break.

**16 Unnamed   10m   E6 6c ** **   *(early 1990s)*
Good, but fingery climbing, between the arete and Leonardo. Difficult and bold climbing on chipped pockets leads to the second horizontal break, where a selection of cams can be placed. A brutal move off the break is required to gain the thin crack above (small wire). Finish up the crack.

The next two problems are both based around the start to Leonardo.

17 Low Pocket   6b
Start at a low pocket just left of the crack of Tribal Look. Gain the two adjacent edges above, pull through for a higher edge and use this to access a large sloping pocket with the left hand. Pull into good holds in the first break using a high rock over. Use the hand holds for the feet above the first pocket.

**18 Leonardo   10m   E2 5c ** **   *(1970s)*
Start just left of the crack of Tribal Look. Follow the chipped holds up the wall (Friends 2 & 2.5 in the first break) and past a peg protecting the final long reach. Since it's a good workout, lower-off and do it again.

19 Sit Start   5c
From a sitting start at the base of the crack pull up and left into two edges just left of the crack, before the crack proper is gained. Use these to gain the first break.

20 Tribal Look   12m   E4 6a *   *(1980s)*
A good sustained route. Climb the obvious central crack to a horizontal niche, move right then crank up to a good break. Traverse right to a flake, move up and

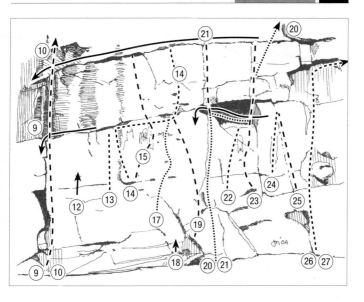

through the overlap to gain a line of hidden jugs leading right. Clip the bolt on the left and traverse left to a ledge and tree. This route is almost always dry.

1 Tribal Crack   5c
Follow the crack of Tribal Look to the second break; reachy and committing top move, then escape left.

2 Dyno   (Project)
Use sidepulls to right of the crack to gain an obvious edge with the left hand (not the higher pocket). Launch for the bottom of the sloping edge of the pod in the first break.

3 Pod   6b
Start with both hands on a large flat hold and reach up left for a pocket. Run foot onto the large flat hold and go for the sloping bottom edge of the pod. Reverse down the crack or continue to the second break.

4 Edges   6c
Start with both hands on a flat edge just above head height. Above are a diagonally sloping edge and two horizontal edges (all small and close together). Use these to gain the top of the peg scarred crack. Reach left to the pod to escape.

**5 Lock-it   10m   E4 6a ** ✱✱   *(1980s)*
A direct start to Tribal Look. Climb the thin left-slanting crack to gain Tribal Look at the horizontal niche.

MAIN FACE RIGHT

These problems start at the open groove between the two main faces (Experiments in Incest). Some may require a couple of bouldering mats, a bit of nerve, a rope, or a combination of all three. Escape is by moving right along the obvious ledge system and easily down the broken arete.

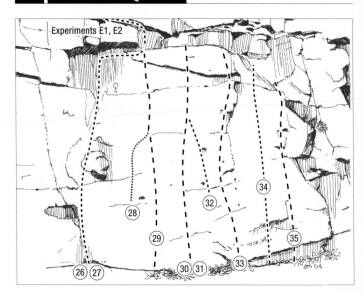

Experiments E1, E2

26 Experiments in Incest   6a   *(1980s)*
Mantelshelf the blob and climb the open groove via a shaky looking finger-jam, before making a committing pull out right onto ledges. Alternatively (for the traditionalist) from the top of the groove, traverse the break leftwards all the way across to the big ledge of The Outsider. Finish here and collect one 'E-point', or continue up the arete and claim two.

27 No Blob   6b/c
Experiments in Incest, but the blob is out for both hands and feet.

28 Oval Pocket   6b
Use an oval pocket and the larger of two low flat pockets to gain an L-shaped edge; match. Pull up for a very small edge with right. Pull through for a pair of edges above and continue to ledges.

29 Left-hand   5c
The easiest way up the left-hand side of the wall to the ledge.

30 Right-hand   5c
The easiest way up the right-hand side of the wall to the ledge.

31 Eye-shaped Pocket   6c
Start with an obvious one finger hole for the left hand and a shallow circular pocket for the right. Ascend to a tiny eye-shaped pocket and another one finger pocket. Gain a further micro edge above and on to a triangle of better edges. Restricting the feet to holds used for the hands, gain the edges just below the overlap and continue onto ledges.

32 Long Reach   6a
Start at a good flat hold (big enough for two hands) just left of the faint arete. Gain the next good pocket via a long reach and use it to gain edges above. Continue up to ledges.

33 Faint Arete   5c
Climb the faint arete come flake to ledges.

34 Slab   5c
Right of the faint arete is a slab with a series of small edges and sidepulls. Use these to gain the right end of the ledge system.

35 Slab Right-hand   5b
At the right-hand boundary of the slab are a series of right-facing flake holds. Use these to gain the left end of the ledges.

IAN'S WA' AREA

Right again, some 15m right of the open groove of Experiments in Incest, is a wall with an overlap at half-height. Escape can be made from the high ledge at the right side of the wall by means of a reverse mantel from the ledge, followed by down-climbing without undue difficulty.

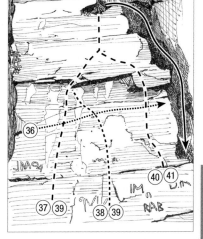

36 Corner   5c
Start at a corner and traverse the face left to right with feet in the horizontal crack.

37 Central Overlap   5c
Use small edges at the left-hand side of the face to gain good holds above the overlap.

38 Standing Break   5c
Use a shield like feature in the rock to gain a standing position in the horizontal break.

39 Ian's Wa'   10m   E1 5c *   (1980s)
Gain the overlap by either of the previous two problems, go over it rightwards and continue straight up on big chipped holds to the ledge.

40 Waterfront   10m   E2 6a   (1980s)
Gain a standing position on the low break at the right side of Ian's Wa' without using the arete. Surmount the overlap by means of a precarious layback then make a long reach left to bigger holds and finish up Ian's Wa'.

41 Overlap Rock Over   6b
Start with both hands in the head height horizontal crack just left of the arete as for Waterfront, but use edges under the overlap to make a high rockover and stiff pull straight through for a good edge above the overlap (gained with the left hand) then escape right onto the arete.

The following routes lie to the right of the Ian's Wa' Area.

42 Snakebite   15m   HVS 5a   (1995)
Climb the groove immediately left of Kalahari to a small cave. Traverse right to the top peg of Kalahari and abseil off.

43 Kalahari   10m   E1 5a *(1992)*
Start 3m right of Waterfront. Climb the arete to a ledge and thin crack (peg runner), move right, then go up and left up a crack to two pegs. Abseil off.

44 Thirty Frames a Second   12m   E2 5c *(1980s)*
Start as for Kalahari, but at the first peg reach right to gain the flake which is followed to the roofs. Swing right to gain ledges on the arete and a dangerous single bolt belay. Abseil off. Largely superseded by Kalahari and Hair of the Dog.

45 Hair of the Dog   12m   E3 6a *(1995)*
A direct line up to and over the small roof below the bolt belay of Thirty Frames a Second. Serious until the peg below the roof is clipped. Abseil off.

46 Seriously Silly   25m   E2 5b *(1995)*
A large edge is visible in the middle of the face 10m right of Thirty Frames a Second. Climb straight up this to a large roof and pull over its left side to loose ground above.

At the right-hand end of this wall is an abandoned project. Would be suitors will need to provide their own hangers.

DOLLAR QUARRY

(NS 964 991)   South facing   Map p310

This quarry lies on the southern slopes of the Ochils above the village of Dollar. It is split into two tiers, but all the climbing takes place on the upper tier. Finishes to the routes are unpleasantly loose.

Approach: Park in the lower car park for Castle Campbell, follow the road a short way uphill, then take the second track on the right into the quarry.

Climbs are described from right to left. The best descent for all routes is the earthy gully between God Nose and Modern Dance.

God Nose   15m   Very Difficult *(1980s)*
Start just left of the lowest point of the cliff. Pull over an overhang, trend right up slabs to a tree then make a rising traverse right, then go back left to finish.

Modern Dance   12m   VS 4c *(1980s)*
The slabby left wall of the V-gully 15m left of God Nose. Climb to a tiny ledge, move right, then go up a right-slanting groove. Avoid the loose finish by traversing off right. A direct start is possible at 6a/b.

Double Indemnity   15m   VS 4b *(1980s)*
Start as for Modern Dance, but move up and left to the base of a corner. Swing round the rib on the left and finish up a slabby groove. (The obvious smooth corner provides a bold direct finish at E1 5b)

D.A. Groove   15m   Severe *(1980s)*
The slabby right-slanting groove 10m left of Modern Dance.

Everyone Loves Strawberries   6m   E2 5c *(1980s)*
Start from a pile of boulders well up and left of D.A. Groove. Step off the top boulder and climb the short wall above, finishing up easier rock on the right.

Applause from the Gallery   15m   E1 5b * *(1981)*
Start at a blunt arete below some overhangs. Gain the arete from the left and climb to a big block forming the lowest overhang. Move left either below or on top of the block and climb the wall above trending right to the top.

Energy Transfer   15m   E3 5c *   (1981)
Bold climbing up the fine left-slanting groove. Start up Applause from the Gallery
then make a series of hard moves up the groove to gain a loose ramp leading back
right to the top.

Who Dares Wins   20m   E3 5c   (1980s)
A serious finish to Energy Transfer. From the top of the groove move left into a
scoop and exit leftwards to gain a horizontal crack. Follow this to a ledge and climb
straight up with a huge reach past a peg to finishing jugs.

Tent Roof   15m   VS 4b   (1980s)
Start in the centre of the slab at the top right-hand corner of the quarry. Climb a
corner to a ledge, traverse left to the cracked arete and follow this to an exit
rightwards. Easier variations exist to the right.

Electric Edge   15m   E1 5a   (1980's)
The left edge of the slab. Make a tricky mantelshelf onto the arete, which rapidly
eases with height.

OTHER CRAGS

In the mid 1970s some climbing took place on the cliffs below the **Wallace
Monument** until the threat of rock fall onto the road beneath led to stabilisation
work and a strictly enforced climbing ban. At the eastern end of the cliffs, behind
the old Acre Wood Nursery, is a disused **Quarry** (NS 810 952). Climbing is banned
here also, but those with no fear of prosecution may be attracted to **Zeig Heil** (E2
5c), the obvious arete, whilst those with no fear of death will find **Sandanista** (E3
5b) on the wall 20m to the right.

Dumyat (NS 836 977) on the western end of the Ochils is home to numerous
crags that, from a distance, look quite promising. Unfortunately, closer inspection
reveals that the rock is not of the best quality. A number of routes have been
recorded; mostly by J.H.B.Bell and by T.Low of the Ochils M.C, although a
'Raeburn's Gully' is also rumoured to be found here. The routes are left for the
adventurous to rediscover. However, one area of excellent rock does exist on the
west facing **Sherrifmuir Buttress** (NN 827 983). This has 10-15 short routes from
Severe to HVS and is approached via the Lossburn Reservoir track, then south
across the moor.

Further to the north-east lies **Craig Rossie** (NN 985 122) which, despite a
beautiful outlook across Strathearn, is probably of greater interest to the botanist
that the climber. Three routes were climbed here in 1984. **Bristler**, (30m E1 5b)
follows the large right-facing chimney come groove just below the summit and
sports some particularly fine clumps of vegetation. 100m to the left is **Blazer** (30m
E2 5c), which takes the obvious open corner on the white wall. **Fizzler** (10m E1
5c) climbs the central crack in the smaller leftmost buttress.

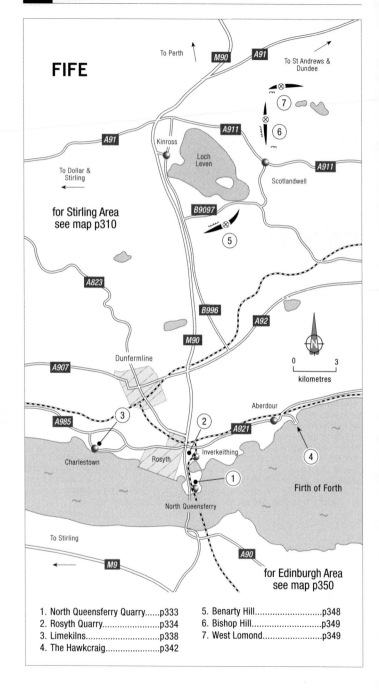

FIFE

To Perth

M90 *A91*

To St Andrews & Dundee

⊗
⑦

A911

Kinross

Loch Leven

⊗
⑥

A911

Scotlandwell

To Dollar & Stirling

for Stirling Area see map p310

B9097

⊗
⑤

A823

B996

A92

M90

N

0   3
kilometres

Dunfermline

A907

Aberdour

A985

③

②

A921

Inverkeithing

④

Charlestown

Rosyth

①

Firth of Forth

North Queensferry

To Stirling

A90

M9

for Edinburgh Area see map p350

FIFE

The Hawkcraig's outlook and ease of access from Edinburgh – Forth Road Bridge traffic jams not withstanding – guarantees its continued popularity. Rosyth Quarry is a less aesthetic location, but offers the VS leader a range of good routes. Fife's other main attractions are the limestone blocks at Limekilns, with their long history of access difficulties. With new access legislation it is hoped that an amicable agreement can be made with the landowner in the near future, and routes are described in the hope that this will occur.

NORTH QUEENSFERRY QUARRY

(NT 133 807)   South facing   Map p332

This small dolerite quarry lies just off the Fife Coastal path, east of North Queensferry. By far the best route in the quarry is the impressive corner of Scharnhorst, but there are enough other routes to make a visit worthwhile. The rock is generally quite good, although lack of traffic means the usual dusty and flaky rock and occasional loose hold. The top of the crag requires care. A top-rope can be arranged on a fence.

Approach: Follow the signs to Deep Sea World and park near the Ferrybridge Hotel. Walk uphill, turn right opposite the war memorial onto the Fife Coastal Path and follow it under the Forth Rail Bridge to an open area with a brick shelter. From its far side a path leads left into the quarry. Routes are best approached from the Scharnhorst wall.

Hidden in trees at the back of the quarry is an impressive wall with a large central corner – the line of Scharnhorst.

Bismark   20m   E3 6a *(1989)*
The big corner 5m left of Scharnhorst. Move right at 12m and climb a layback crack and a loose wall to finish.

Edge of Time   20m   E4 6a * *(1987)*
The arete left of Scharnhorst. Start at the arete and climb to a crack on the right wall. Use this to gain horizontal cracks and a rest. Continue up using holds on the arete and the left wall to reach a platform. Easy but loose climbing leads to the top.
Variation: **E3 5c** *(1987)*
Gain the horizontal cracks from a thin crack and flake on the left. Make one move up the arete, then pull left into a corner to rejoin the arete at the platform.

Scharnhorst   20m   E1 5b ** *(1985)*
The mighty corner gives a superb route, with the crux at the start. Large Friends or hexes are useful higher up.

Fleet Air Arm   20m   E4 6a *(1989)*
Climb the thin wall crack 4m right of Scharnhorst with difficulty and only adequate protection to a ledge. Easier and looser climbing leads to the top.

Nearly an Angel   20m   E3 6a * *(1991)*
Some 7m right of Scharnhorst is a large black overhang. Reach this via a tiny corner, pull over and move up to a horizontal break (rest). Climb a finger-crack on the left (crux) to another break. Move right and use large detached blocks to gain a left-trending groove which leads to easier ground.

The following routes lie about 20m to the right and are reached by scrambling up and then down at the base of the crag. The routes lie on a small graffiti daubed wall below and right of a larger graffiti daubed wall.

The Vital Spark   12m   VS 4c   *(1991)*
The right-facing corner-crack at the left-hand side of the bay. Finish up ledges on the right.

Dive Dive Dive   12m   E3 6a *   *(1986)*
The thin crack in the wall 2m left of The Boat. Climb to the second break and gain holds up on the right wall. Move back into the crack and finish more easily.

The Boat   12m   E1 5b *   *(1985)*
The curving crack at the right side of the bay. Strenuous.

INVERKEITHING QUARRY

(NO 137 824)

This large quarry on the north side of Inverkeithing Bay has one recorded climb. **Vidi, Vici, Veni** (E3 6b 1990), from R.Campbell and P.Thorburn takes a line up the cleaned slabby wall at the left side behind the pool.

ROSYTH QUARRY

(NT 125 834)   South-west facing   Map p332   Diagram p336

Like most of the dolerite quarries in this guide, Rosyth is something of a mixed bag. The urban blights of graffiti, traffic noise and local yoofs with airguns are offset by easy access from the M90, sunny aspect, quick drying rock and some good lower grade routes. As usual, some of the rock is solid and some appallingly loose.

Approach: Leave the M90 at junction 1 (the second north of the Forth Road Bridge, signed Inverkeithing and Kincardine Bridge). Turn left at the roundabout then immediately right into Harley Street and right again into Admiralty Road and parking. Follow the roundabout anticlockwise under the motorway and ascend the worn path in the bank straight ahead, up into the quarry.

The first major feature is a corner starting as a blackened recess and ending at a big tree overhanging the crag. To the left a number of short routes finish on vertical dirt and gorse. However there are some worthwhile boulder problems; the sharp arete 10m left of the corner (5c), and the bulge and thin crack (5b) just left of the corner.

1 Route to Root   10m   VS 4c   *(1972)*
Climb the obvious corner overhung by a big tree. Finish on horrendous dirt either left or right of the tree, or better, climb back down again.

2 Grot Corner   10m   Severe   *(1975)*
Climb the slim groove trending slightly leftwards in the right wall of Route to Root.

3 Skinny Lizzie   10m   HVS 5a   *(1990)*
The sharp arete right of Grot Corner, with runners and the occasional hold in that route.

4 Chemical Warfare   10m   Severe *   *(1972)*
Climb onto a block 4m right of Route to Root, then go up the deep groove between two aretes.

5 Sickle   10m   Very Difficult *   *(1972)*
The open corner with a prominent crack in its left wall, 6m right of Route to Root.

6 Wireworm   7m   Moderate   *(1972)*
Trend right up a stepped depression, finishing at some gorse bushes. Often used in descent.

7 Smith's Dilemma 6m Difficult * (1972)
The prominent curving groove widens as it rises.

8 Jack's Route 6m Very Difficult (1972)
This line goes directly through an area of quartz-faced rock.

9 Legover Groove 6m Very Difficult (1972)
Climb the bulging depression just right of the quartz-faced wall to easy ground.

10 Andy's Route 7m Very Difficult (1974)
Start at a right facing wide crack 3m right of the quartz-faced wall. Climb the crack and steps leading left to the top.

11 Drizzle 8m Severe (1974)
The steep groove immediately left of a smooth wall.

12 Philistine 8m E2 6a (1974)
Climb the smooth wall seamed with shallow cracks, using old peg pockets. Trend slightly left to a good hold in a deeper crack, then finish more easily.

13 The Waullie 10m HVS 5b * (1975)
Right of the smooth wall is a recess at ground level. Climb the thin right-facing crack above the recess to a wider horizontal break, step left and go up the crack above.

14 C.N.D. 10m Severe * (1974)
The wall just right of The Waullie, finishing up a large slabby recess.

15 Hands Off 10m VS 4c (1975)
Start just left of some loose blocky overhangs. Climb a steep blunt rib and bulge on poor rock to a slabby ledge. Finish up a crack on the left, immediately right of the slabby recess of C.N.D.

16 Suspect Device 10m E1 5b (2004)
Start just left of Iconoclast and climb the blunt rib to a small right facing corner and roof. Climb the crack on the roof's left-hand side on friable rock.

17 Iconoclast 15m HVS 5a * (1973)
Start 6m right of Hands Off at the left side of the TACK graffiti. Climb the straight crack past an awkward bulge and the short headwall above.

There is a tall blocky buttress, daubed JACK and HEATHY, behind a hawthorn tree about 60m from the left end of the quarry. The next four climbs are found here.

18 Grenville 15m VS 4b (1973)
Start just left of Heathy and climb a slightly left-trending line of cracks and grooves.

19 Heathy 15m VS 4c ** (1972)
Climb a corner-crack to the left end of a roomy ledge at 3m. Continue up the fine right-angled corner to the top.

20 Master Fwap 15m E1 5b (2000)
The hanging arete between Heathy and Cathy. One runner was placed in a triangular niche just above the overhang on the left, on Heathy. This niche was used to gain the arete and good holds.

21 Cathy 15m VS 4c ** (1972)
A slightly harder sister route to Heathy. Climb cracks to the right end of the ledge at 3m and the deep V-groove above; large Friends useful.

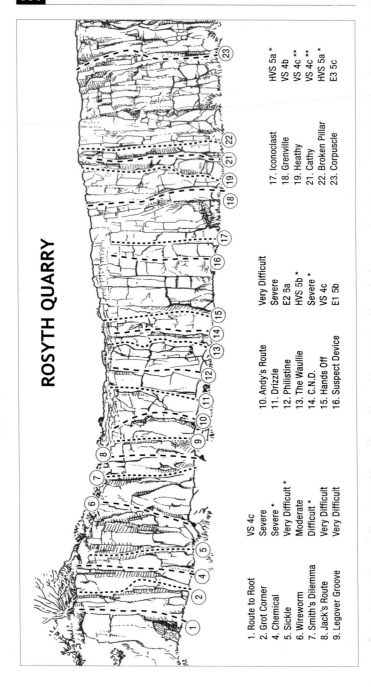

ROSYTH QUARRY

1. Route to Root	VS 4c	10. Andy's Route	Very Difficult
2. Grot Corner	Severe	11. Drizzle	Severe
4. Chemical	Severe *	12. Philistine	E2 5a
5. Sickle	Very Difficult *	13. The Waullie	HVS 5b *
6. Wireworm	Moderate	14. C.N.D.	Severe *
7. Smith's Dilemma	Difficult *	15. Hands Off	VS 4c
8. Jack's Route	Very Difficult	16. Suspect Device	E1 5b
9. Legover Groove	Very Difficult		

17. Iconoclast	HVS 5a *
18. Grenville	VS 4b
19. Heathy	VS 4c **
21. Cathy	VS 4c **
22. Broken Pillar	HVS 5a *
23. Corpuscle	E3 5c

22 Broken Pillar   15m   HVS 5a *   (1972)
Start in a corner just round to the right of Cathy. Climb cracks to a ledge on the left and continue up the awkward off-width crack above.

23 Corpuscle   15m   E3 5c   (1975)
Some 12m right of Broken Pillar is a V-groove capped by a triangular roof at 4m. Bridge up the groove, exiting left at the roof. Using poor sidepulls move right to the arete and climb this until the left wall can be regained where the angle starts to ease.

Round to the right is an area of recent rockfall. The pillar described in the last guide appears to be no more, along with its routes. To the right of the rockfall **Flakeoff** (6m VS 4c 1975) climbs a wall seamed with cracks and **Changeling** (6m VS 4c 1975), 2m to the right again, appear to have survived, but are best forgotten.

Trees, hawthorns and brambles shield the right-hand side of the quarry. However, bushwhacking will reveal a tombstone-like rock standing at the base of the cliff.

28 The Beauty   6m   HVS 5a *   (1976)
Climb the stepped arete just left of the tombstone. The second step proves troublesome until a 'secret' sidepull can be found.

29 The Beast   6m   VS 5a   (1975)
Behind the tombstone is a steep corner. Climb this to a ledge on the right, then go up the corner above.

30 The Grinder   6m   HVS 4c   (1975)
The obvious layback crack 4m right of the tombstone.

Some 17m right of the tombstone is a deep V-groove, the line of Gold Foil, with two projecting square-cut buttresses to its right.

31 Gift Horse   7m   VS 4b   (1975)
Climb the left-slanting layback crack 3m left of Gold Foil.

32 Plod   7m   HVS 5a   (1986)
The cracked wall just right of Gift Horse, finishing up the wide crack on the left.

33 Gold Foil   7m   VS 4c **   (1972)
The prominent deep V-groove.

34 The Flying Bink   7m   VS 4c   (1976)
Immediately right of Gold Foil, climb the slimmer groove formed by the right side of a pinnacle. Attain a standing position on the pinnacle and make a hard move up to finish.

35 If Pigs Could Fly   8m   E2 5c **   (1977)
The impending crack-line in the square-cut buttress 4m right of Gold Foil is strenuous and sustained.

36 The Stinking Swordsman   8m   E4 6b *   (1973)
The steep, strenuous cracks in the centre of the right-hand square-cut buttress.

37 Fat Sam   7m   VS 4c   (1974)
The groove at the right end of the buttress, 2m right of The Stinking Swordsman.

38 The Rust Bucket   7m   E2 6a   (1992)
Climb the right-hand side wall of the Stinking Swordsman buttress, without using the rock rib on the right or the tree on the left.

The last routes are about 25m from the right end of the quarry. Look for the slogan FREE LOVE; they are just right of this.

39 Late Night Final   8m   Difficult   *(1975)*
Climb the left-hand side of the flake, to finish at a small tree.

40 Jagdhond   10m   HVS 5a   *(1985)*
This route takes the face of the flake. Climb to a niche just left of a small roof, then move up and right to the top.

41 Serendipity   10m   VS 4c *   *(1974)*
Climb the crack forming the right-hand side of the flake.

42 Tiger Pad   10m   HVS 5a *   *(1975)*
Climb the tiers of small steep slabs just right of Serendipity, using the crack of Serendipity for protection only.

43 Inspiration   10m   E1 5b   *(1975)*
Climb the groove 3m right of Serendipity with an old peg at its start. Step right at a prominent undercut, then continue directly to the top.

LIMEKILNS

(NT 070 837)   Various aspects   Map p332

These two large blocks of excellent limestone are located on the wooded hill overlooking the Firth of Forth between Limekilns and Charleston. The rock is most unusual and provides some superb climbs in very pleasant surroundings. Unfortunately, Limekilns has a long history of access difficulties. With new access legislation it is hoped that an amicable agreement can be made with the landowner in the near future, and routes are described in the hope that this will occur.

Climbs are described anticlockwise around the blocks.

THE SENTINEL

This is the smaller western block, reached first on the approach.

South Face

Pickwick   12m   VS 4b
Climb the left arete of the slabby south face delicately and with no protection.

Hunter and the Hunted   12m   E1 5b   *(1983)*
A fragile and bold eliminate. Start 3m right of Pickwick at a bulge. Climb straight up with minimal holds and no protection.

Humbug   12m   VS 4c *   *(1981)*
The obvious crack in the centre of the face.

Kiln Dance with Me   12m   E1 5a
Climb the vague crack line just right of Humbug.

Empires and Dance   10m   HVS 5a
Start 2m left of the right arete and climb straight up the wall.

Dingley Dell   10m   Severe   *(1983)*
Start as for Empires and Dance but move rightwards to climb the arete on large but friable holds.

East Face

The Struggler 12m E3 6a ** *(1984)*
Start just left of Cruel Summer. Boulder up the wall until forced into Cruel Summer. Move back left to a peg runner and climb the steep crack to the top. The wall at the start can be climbed direct – slightly left, then right – to the peg at about E3 6a.

Cruel Summer 12m E2 5c *** *(1983)*
The obvious corner gives a good, well protected climb. Make some hard moves into the corner and follow it to exit left.

Colours Fly 12m E2 5c * *(1983)*
Start just right of Cruel Summer. Climb up to a tiny ledge, then go rightwards to gain a left-slanting ramp. Follow this, then finish straight up.

On the Blocks 12m E4 6a * *(1986)*
Climb directly up the wall between Colours Fly and Marley's Ghost to step left and finish up a thin crack.

Marley's Ghost 12m E2 5c * *(1983)*
Climb the right arete boldly to the ledge, move left up the ramp, then go back right to finish up the arete. The arete can be climbed all the way at about E3.

North Face

Velvet Glove 15m E4 6a *** *(1984)*
This route takes the left-hand of the two magnificent cracks on the north face. Gain the corner-crack and follow it to a horizontal break. Move right to the base of a parallel crack and follow it to the top.
Variation: **The Satin Finish E4 6a** * *(1986)*
Instead of moving right continue straight up, pulling left to a break at the very top to reach a tiny sapling to finish.

The Iron Fist 15m E5 6b *** *(1984)*
The right-hand crack.

West Face

Methods of Dance 12m E3 6a ** *(1983)*
The fine left arete provides an excellent climb. Climb up passing a tiny groove to a hanging block. Move left to the arete and climb it on good but widely spaced holds.
Variation: **Right-Hand Finish E3 6a** *
Finish up the wall right of the arete.

New Gold Dream 12m E2 5b *
The left-facing corner line.

GELLET BLOCK

This is the larger eastern block.

Descent: With care, via the stone staircase down the north face.

West Face

Slots 10m E1 5c *(1985)*
Climb the thin crack at the left end of the wall via finger slots to a ledge, then finish up the tiny corner.

Sunsetter   10m   HVS 5a *   *(1985)*
Climb the disjointed cracks right of Slots to step left and finish up either of two
short wider cracks.

Forbidden Colours   10m   HVS 5a **   *(1985)*
Climb directly up the wall right of Sunsetter, move left and finish up a wide crack
to the highest point of the wall.
Variation: **Direct Finish   E1 5c ***
Continue straight up the thin crack where the ordinary route moves left.

DT's   10m   VS 4c **   *(1985)*
Climb the short crack in the centre of the face to a ledge at 4m and finish up the
obvious twin cracks above on the right.

D-Day   10m   HVS 5a *   *(1985)*
Climb the thin crack and wall left of White Ensign to pull up into the crack just left
of that route's niche.

White Ensign   10m   VS 4c **   *(1985)*
The obvious wide crack 4m from the right arete.

VE Day   10m   E1 5c *   *(1985)*
Follow the thin cracks up the wall right of White Ensign.

Neutral Gear   10m   VS 4c *   *(1985)*
Climb the right arete, staying on the left-hand side.

South Face

Lion Rampant   10m   VS 4b *
Climb the left arete, staying on the right-hand side.

Wall Straight   10m   E1 5a *
Climb the wall 2m right of the arete. Unprotected in its lower half and serious.

Protectless   12m   E1 5a   *(1985)*
Climb the shallow groove and wall just left of Red Flag, moving right near the top
to finish as for that route. Unprotected in its lower half and serious.

Red Flag   12m   VS 4c *   *(1985)*
The obvious corner-crack, stepping out left at the top.

Grasp the Nettle   15m   E3 5b *   *(1985)*
Climb the thin crack in the wall right of Red Flag to reach a peg on the left. Move
up to another peg, then climb up and right to the top. Serious at the start.

Edge of Fear   15m   E3 5c   *(1985)*
Climb the arete to the right of Grasp the Nettle to gain a crack. Move up and right
round the arete. Finish up the right side of the arete.

Through the Motions   15m   E3 6a **   *(1985)*
Start just left of Dead Ringer. Step up to pull over the right end of the roof and
climb the crack to a break. Make a move up to a good hold where Dead Ringer
traverses in, then move left and climb the crack directly, passing a loose block, to
just below the top. Move left to finish on the arete.

Dead Ringer   15m   E1 5b *   *(1985)*
Climb the left-hand corner of the amphitheatre to a ledge, move left and follow
the thin crack past two iron rings.

Two Ringer   15m   VS 4c   *(1985)*
Follow the left-hand corner all the way to the top.

One Ringer   15m   VS 4c   *(1985)*
The right-hand corner of the amphitheatre.

Link Rib   15m   Severe   *(1985)*
The stepped rib, starting on the left-hand side.

A few short problems exist either side of the right arete to gain the first ledge of
the rib, the best being up the left wall without using the arete (HVS 5c).

East Face

**The Charleston   15m   E4 6b ** **   *(1985)*
This follows the hairline cracks right of the arete. Climb up to a thin crack, step left
then go up to the break. Step up and move across to gain flanges on the right, then
climb the thin crack to another break. Move up the wall above to the arete and
climb its right side to the top.

The Ivy League   15m   E4 6a * **   *(1985)*
Climb the obvious groove and crack right of The Charleston to gain the top break.
Move left to pull over a small roof by flake holds and continue to the top. Low in
the grade.

Yuppie   15m   E4 6a   *(1985)*
A serious route with some suspect holds. Climb the wall just right of The Ivy League
and move up slightly left past a thin crack to gain ledges. Go up to a block and
hand traverse the break to finish as for The Ivy League.

Elgin's Crack   15m   E2 5c * **   *(1984)*
The obvious crack is the best route on the Gellet Block. Low in the grade.

The Sting   15m   E2 5b   *(1985)*
Climb up to a ledge right of Elgin's Crack and follow the thin crack to a steep ramp
which trends right to the top.

Rock Around the Block   75m   E3   *(1985)*
A girdle traverse from left to right, starting across the West Face.
1. 5a Belay on the left edge on a platform. Move up and right until a step down
gains the ledge system. Follow this across the face, move round the arete and belay
in the crack of Red Flag.
2. 5c Move up and across to clip the top peg on Grasp the Nettle. Climb back
down until the lower peg can be clipped and make hard moves up and right onto
the arete. Step down to a block and traverse over to Dead Ringer. Move up to clip
the lower ring, then move into the corner. Descend to a ledge and belay. Great care
should be taken in extending runners and protecting the second on this pitch.
3. 5c Move up and across to the arete. A high runner can be placed in the top
break. Step back down and follow the obvious foot ledge across the East Face.

BELL ROCK

(NT 191 847)   South facing

This is the large sandstone tor on the coast beside the first green of Aberdour golf
course. There are almost a dozen routes of up to 10m in height on the seaward
face. The contorted rock gives interesting climbing but a band of poor yellow rock
has to be overcome to reach the better black rock above. Two smaller tors
immediately to the west also give a few short routes and problems.

THE HAWKCRAIG

(NT 200 849)   Mostly Tidal   South facing   Map p332   Diagram p344

This sea-cliff has an excellent collection of middle grade climbs in a very pleasant sunny location on the Firth of Forth. Consequently, the cliff is quite popular, particularly on warm summer evenings. The rock is a form of quartz dolerite and is sound at the sea scoured base, but requires careful handling nearer the top, particularly between Gaucho and Guano. Care should be taken in spring following winter frosts and after rain when holds can become sandy.

Approach: A regular train service runs to Aberdour, depositing the climber outside one of the area's finest bakeries. Leave the A921 around 300m east of the railway bridge in the centre of Aberdour and follow the signs to the Silver Sands and a huge car park.

Low Tide: The western end is reached via a cliff top path from the car park which descends to the right (facing out) round the back of a hotel to the boulder beach. A quicker descent involves a scramble down Moderate rock above the boundary between the hotel garden and the shore. The eastern end is reached from the car park by a scramble descent.

High Tide: During most high tides only the routes above the terrace at the west end are unaffected. Other sections of the cliff require an abseil approach or a sea-level traverse.

The obvious corner within the hotel grounds is **Cut Glass Corner** (Severe). The arete just to its left is **Crystal Arete** (E2 5b) and further left again are **Porcelain** (E1 5a) and **Crockery** (VS 4c). **Doo'cot Wall** (Very Difficult) takes the smooth wall right of Cut Glass Corner. These routes are worthwhile, but are perhaps best avoided to preserve good relations with the hotel.

The western end of the cliff, just right of the hotel grounds, is split by a terrace at half-height. Below the terrace is an obvious overhung recess.

1 Fish Head Arete   20m   Very Difficult *   *(1965)*
This is the left arete of the slabby wall which forms the left side of the recess. Climb the arete to the terrace and a tree stump belay. Continue up the crack-line above.

2 Fish Head Wall   10m   Very Difficult   *(1965)*
Start 2m right of the arete. Climb the wall trending up and left to join the arete. Finish on the terrace.
Variation: **Direct Finish   Severe**
A slightly harder alternative is to mantelshelf onto an obvious ledge and finish directly.

3 Ugh!   8m   Hard Severe *   *(1965)*
Climb the obvious crack in the slabby left wall of the recess.

4 Sacrilege   8m   VS 4c   *(1965)*
Climb straight up the bulge between Ugh and Eech to finish up the quartz corner right of them both; rather artificial.

5 Eech!   8m   VS 4b *   *(1965)*
At the back of the recess there is a quartz-filled corner-crack. Climb the corner until forced left under an overhang, then finish up Ugh. Low in the grade.

6 Squirrel Slab   12m   VS 5a *   *(1965)*
Start on the terrace, just right of the tree stump belay of Fish Head Arete. Climb a slab with 'Ken' scratched on it, and the bulging wall above to gain easier ground.

7 Weasel Wall   12m   E2 5c   *(1975)*
Start on the terrace below a white corner 3m right of Squirrel Slab. Bridge up to

below a small overhang, then move over it slightly leftwards to climb the tricky wall above via its left edge.

8 Garlic Bread   12m   E2 6a   *(1999)*
Takes the slab direct on the right of Weasel Wall.

9 Pizza   12m   E2 5c   *(1999)*
Climbs the overhanging arete to the right of Garlic Bread, and immediately left of Cranium Crack.

10 Cranium Crack   20m   VS 4c **   *(1965)*
This good strenuous route starts just right of Eech. Climb the obvious fault at the back of the recess and belay on the terrace. Continue up the corner with a white left wall.

11 Conquistador Crack   7m   VS 5a *   *(1965)*
The overhanging crack in the right wall of the recess is short but sharp.

12 The Groper   7m   HVS 5a
This climbs the left face of the pillar direct, with no protection. The rounded arete to the right of the recess is climbed without using the crack on the right at the start. Finish up the left-hand side of the capstone.

13 Stomach Ache   7m   Severe *   *(1965)*
An easier version of The Groper climbing the front of the pillar. Start just right of the arete and climb to join The Groper at 4m. Finish boldly up the right-hand side of the capstone.

14 The Beast   7m   Hard Severe 4c *
The obvious crack just right of Stomach Ache gives a short but awkward struggle.

15 Gismo   20m   VS 4c *   *(1965)*
Climb the chimney 3m right of The Groper. Move right at the top, then go up to the right-hand end of the terrace. Finish up the broken black groove above, taking care with some loose blocks.
Variation: **HVS 5a**
Climb the obvious short jamming crack above the chimney.

16 Pain Pillar   25m   VS 4c ***   *(1965)*
The local classic, giving exposed and well protected climbing. Start 5m right of The Groper and climb the tall narrow pillar, following the easiest line.
Variation: **VS 5a**
A slightly more difficult climb can be had by keeping to the left edge of the pillar.

17 Gaucho   25m   HVS 5a ***   *(1965)*
Good line and climbing up the deep groove to the right of Pain Pillar. Climb the groove to a black overhang at 15m, turn this on the right (peg runner), then move back left and continue up the groove and bulge above. An easier finish (4c) is to move left onto Pain Pillar above the overhang.
Variation: **HVS 5a**
Climb the narrow chimney below the overhang, then pull directly over it.

18 Psylocibie   25m   E2 5a   *(1990)*
A loose and poorly protected eliminate. Climb the crack in the pillar right of Gaucho to a ledge. Continue up the blunt black rib and loose wall above to reach a finger slot over a shaky flake. Use this with trepidation to surmount a bulge, then finish straight up.

19 Rebel's Groove   25m   VS 5a *   *(1965)*
Steep, sustained and enjoyable. Start 5m right of Pain Pillar. Climb an obvious

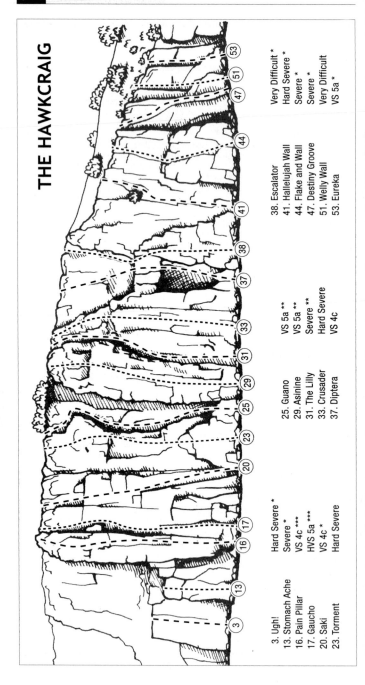

THE HAWKCRAIG

3. Ugh! — Hard Severe *
13. Stomach Ache — Severe *
16. Pain Pillar — VS 4c ***
17. Gaucho — HVS 5a ***
20. Saki — VS 4c *
23. Torment — Hard Severe

25. Guano — VS 5a **
29. Asinine — VS 5a **
31. The Lilly — Severe **
33. Crusader — Hard Severe
37. Diptera — VS 4c

38. Escalator — Very Difficult *
41. Hallelujah Wall — Hard Severe *
44. Flake and Wall — Severe *
47. Destiny Groove — Severe *
51. Welly Wall — Very Difficult
53. Eureka — VS 5a *

twisting groove to a ledge on the left, continue up the steep cracked wall above and finish up a right-facing blocky corner.

20 Saki   25m   VS 4c *   *(1965)*
Start 8m right of Pain Pillar. Climb a straight groove which slants slightly left to a ledge on the left (poor protection). Continue up the black wall above to a choice of finishes. A good start but loose higher up.

To the right of Saki there is a 6m high flake at the base of the cliff. At high tide this can be gained by abseil. It provides a useful starting point for the routes on this part of the cliff.

21 Slack Alice   20m   Hard Severe
This is the obvious wide groove starting from the left side of the flake and with tufts of grass visible higher up. Well named.

22 Brutus   20m   Hard Severe   *(1965)*
Climb the flake then the rib above, passing left of an overhang.

23 Torment   20m   Hard Severe   *(1965)*
From the top of the flake, step right, then climb a narrow rib and a wall right of an overhang to a loose and scary finish.

24 The Dwarf   20m   HVS 5a
Starting about 3m left of Guano, climb a series of shallow corners past an obvious small projecting nose. The crux is unprotected.

25 Guano   20m   VS 5a **   *(1965)*
An excellent route with a well protected crux. Start 4m left of The Chimney at an obvious overhung curving groove. Climb the groove to a peg runner at 12m. Move right, then continue up the groove passing a bush to finish.
Variation: **E2 5b**   *(1975)*
From just below the peg, step left and climb boldly up the wall above.

26 Ganja   20m   Very Difficult   *(1965)*
Follow the vague groove midway between Guano and The Chimney, to join the latter two-thirds of the way up.

27 The Chimney   20m   Very Difficult   *(1965)*
Climb the obvious deep cleft in the centre of the cliff, moving left at a bulge to finish up a wide groove.
Direct Finish: **Severe**
Climb the overhanging crack at the bulge.

28 Chimney Arete   20m   Very Difficult   *(1965)*
Climb the right arete of The Chimney on poor rock.

29 Asinine   20m   VS 5a **   *(1970)*
A good exposed route with a hard finish. Start 2m right of Chimney Arete and climb directly to an obvious jutting nose. Finish by pulling through a groove splitting the nose.

30 The Arete   20m   HVS 5a   *(1975)*
Well protected, but a bit artificial. The undercut arete right of Asinine. Start at the same point as The Lilly but climb a tiny corner to reach the arete. Now follow the arete, always keeping to the right of Asinine, to finish right of the jutting nose.

31 The Lilly   20m   Severe **   *(1965)*
Climb the obvious right-facing groove, 6m right of The Chimney, to a rounded recess. Step right and finish up easier ground.

32 Gunga Din   20m   Severe ✶✶   *(1965)*
A great route with spaced but accommodating holds. Climb the narrow groove 3m right of The Lilly, to join that route at the rounded recess.

33 Crusader   20m   Hard Severe   *(1965)*
Follow the rib between Gunga Din and Saracen.

34 Saracen   20m   VS 4c ✶✶   *(1965)*
An excellent route with continuously interesting climbing. Climb steeply up the obvious rusty groove, to finish up easier ground above.

35 Toerag's Wall   15m   Severe ✶   *(1965)*
Left of a deep overhung recess is a fine wall. Gain the wall from the recess and climb it to the left end of a large balcony. Finish easily on the left.
Variation: VS 5a ✶
A direct start is possible.

36 Hip Replacement   15m   HVS 5a   *(1998)*
Start in the recess to the right of the normal start to Toerag's Wall. Pull through the overlap without using holds to the left (on the right side of Toerag's Wall) following rounded holds on the right and a thin crack to the left. Good climbing but a bit contrived and poorly protected.

37 Diptera   15m   VS 4c   *(1965)*
Climb a crack in the right corner of the deep overhung recess, pulling over the overhang directly to gain the balcony. Finish up a shallow groove in the centre of the wall behind.

38 Escalator   15m   Very Difficult ✶   *(1965)*
Climb the wall immediately right of the deep recess and finish up the groove above the right end of the balcony.

39 Tink   15m   Severe   *(1965)*
Follow the ragged crack up left behind blocks towards the right end of the balcony. Finish up right on poor rock.

40 Aaron's Way   15m   Severe   *(2004)*
Start between Tink and Hallelujah Wall and follow a thin crack-line with three yellow lichen patches to a small dark triangular overlap. Step left to avoid loose block at the top.

41 Hallelujah Wall   15m   Hard Severe ✶   *(1965)*
Climb a crack running directly up to a gorse bush, pass this on the right and continue to the top.

42 Rib and Groove   15m   Severe   *(1998)*
Between Hallelujah Wall and The Whang. Aim for a blunt dark rib 4m up and with a thin crack in its lower half. Follow it directly to the top via a thin groove-line. Climbed before but not recorded.

43 The Whang   12m   Difficult   *(1965)*
Start at a chimney marking the left side of a huge flake. Gain and climb a flaky crack in the wall above, moving left to finish.

44 Flake and Wall   12m   Severe ✶   *(1965)*
About 15m from the right end of the cliff is a 5m high flake. Climb the face of the flake and continue up the short crack in the wall above.
Variation: **Severe**

From the top of the flake, climb the harder thin crack on the right.

45 Guillemot Head Mush   5m   VS 5a   *(2001)*
The west-facing arete of the 5m flake of Flake and Wall. Staying on the arete without using the wall to the left, pull directly over the bulge making a slap for the big ledge at the top.

46 Shadow Corner   10m   Severe   *(1965)*
The obvious three step corner to the right of the flake.

47 Destiny Groove   10m   Severe *   *(1965)*
Follow the thin left-slanting groove to finish at the top of Shadow Corner.

48 The Dreeping Beak   10m   E1 5c   *(2000)*
Start to the left of Destiny Groove on the quartz wall. Climb directly up to the porthole to the left of Destiny Groove. Step right under the overhanging nose to the left of Urmi (Friend 0.5). Pull directly over the nose and wobble upwards to finish directly at the bolt.

49 Urmi   10m   VS 4c *   *(1965)*
Between Destiny Groove and Maureen is a crack starting halfway up the wall. Gain the crack directly and follow it to the top.

50 Maureen   10m   Severe   *(1965)*
Climb directly up the groove 4m right of Shadow Corner.

51 Welly Wall   10m   Very Difficult
Climb to an obvious sloping shelf, then finish up the groove above.

52 Serendipity   10m   HVS 5a   *(1983)*
Climb boldly up the centre of the pillar between Welly Wall and Eureka.

53 Eureka   10m   VS 5a *   *(1965)*
Climb the strenuous but well protected right-facing corner 4m from the end of the cliff, passing an awkward overhang.

54 Where Were You?   10m   E2 5b   *(1990)*
Without using holds on Eureka or Termination, climb the wall to a good undercling at a small overlap. Pull over using sidepulls and finish directly.

55 Termination   10m   VS 4c   *(1965)*
Climb the crack at the extreme right end of the cliff, without using the bulges behind on the right. The top is loose.

56 The High Girdle   70m   HVS *   *(1965)*
Most of this journey is straightforward, but the crux is strenuous and exposed. The route is a lot more serious for the second!
Start on the terrace at the left end of the cliff on top of The Groper pillar.
1. 10m 4b Traverse round Pain Pillar to a small ledge on Gaucho.
2. 20m 4b Follow the ledge system down and right, belaying just before The Chimney.
3. 20m 5a Move across The Chimney into Asinine. Follow this, then make an exposed step out right round the arete to below a small roof. Swing down rather wildly to join The Lilly, and continue to a belay on the balcony.
4. 20m 4b Continue at half-height, moving slightly down to the top of the flake of Flake and Wall. Climb this to finish.

57 The Low Girdle   80m   VS 4c *   *(1965)*
Follow the line of least resistance along the foot of the cliff, solo and at high tide for maximum enjoyment.

BENARTY HILL

(NT 154 979)   Alt 300m   North facing   Map p332

The north side of this hill is characterised by a discontinuous dolerite escarpment, overlooking Loch Leven. The rock is characteristically blocky and flaky, but most of the routes follow wide jamming cracks or thrutchy chimneys.

Approach: Leave the M90 at junction 5 and follow the B9097 east to park on the verge opposite the crag. Follow the field edge and ascend the steep hillside.

Near the centre of the cliff is a gully slanting up left with a large rock jammed across it. This provides an easy descent, and is directly above a pile of boulders at the base of the cliff.

Wizard   8m   VS 5a   (1996)
Near the left end of the crag, well left of A Fist Job, is a short clean prow. Climb it directly, through a bulge, finishing with a mantelshelf onto a slab. It is possible to walk off left before the cliff top is reached.

A Fist Job   20m   E1 5c *   (1983)
The bay to the left of the gully has a chimney on the right and an obvious crack on the left. Enter the crack from the right and climb it to a roof. Pull over and layback to the top.

Treasure Seeker   25m   Severe   (1991)
This route climbs the left bounding ridge of the gully via a rattly chimney-crack, gained from the right.

Dolly Parton   15m   E3 6a   (1983)
This is the straight wide crack between two tall smooth bulges, just right of the entrance to the gully. Descend by abseil.

Pamela Anderson   15m   E4 6b   (1996)
The curvaceous off-width crack right of Dolly Parton is harder than it looks, even more so in the nesting season. A car-jack runner was employed.

Hot Potato   15m   HVS 5a *   (1991)
The obvious jamming crack in the narrow slab up and right of Dolly Parton. High in the grade.

Cubism   20m   E3 5c   (1982)
Start 4m up, on the left side of the long, narrow square-cut buttress to the right of Dolly Parton. Climb a crack to a ledge on the right side. Step left and go up to a horizontal break. Climb up and right to a ledge, then follow a crack until it is possible to step left into the centre of the buttress. Climb up the right-hand side (crux) to the top.

Ram   12m   E4 6a   (1983)
Scramble up rough ground to the foot of a short steep wall towards the right-hand side of the cliff. Climb a crack on the right to an undercut flake. Traverse left to a thin crack, then climb it until it is possible to step right and move up to the top.

The end of the cliff, well right of Ram, is split into two tiers. At the right end of the lower tier is a knobbly prow of good rock.

Demerara   12m   Severe   (1991)
The thrutchy chimney left of the prow leads to a roof, which is turned on the right.

Goblin   10m   Hard Severe 4c   (1991)
Climb the wide fault in the right-hand side of the prow.

Oat Flake   10m   VS 4b   *(1991)*
This is the right-hand chimney-line in the upper tier, above the previous two routes.

BISHOP HILL

(NO 185 044)   Alt 400   West facing   Map p332

This hill forms the continuation of the dolerite escarpment above Loch Leven. White Craigs and Carlin Maggie are best approached by the hill path near Scotlandwell Church car park (NO 183 019). **Kinneston Craigs** (NO 194 023) lie in woodland north-east of Scotlandwell and have lots of extended boulder problems and short routes of all grades up to 6b. **White Craigs** (NO 183 033) lie at the southern end of the escarpment above Kinnesswood. There are a few routes, including an E2 6a up the thin peg-scarred crack on the highest section of rock. The face below the summit includes the pinnacle **Carlin Maggie** (NO 183 044), first climbed in 1951 by I.Oliver, I.Brown and A.Grieve up the short side at Very Difficult with a point of aid, now free at VS 5a. The 15m long side was first climbed with aid by N.MacNiven and freed at E1 5b by J.Andrew and D.Kirk in 1993. About 20 climbs have been done on the cliff behind the pinnacle.

WEST LOMOND

(NO 197 066)   Alt 400m   North & West facing   Map p332

The northern continuation of the escarpment above Loch Leven contains dolerite mixed with cleaner, friable white sandstone. **Glenvale** (NO 189 058) separates West Lomond and Bishop Hill and has a few routes on the largest white sandstone outcrop on the north side of the glen. **Craigengaw** (NO 200 071) lies north-east of the summit and is split by a wide gully, where several routes have been recorded including the loose **The Split Nose** (40m VS), to the right of the gully.

ISLE OF MAY

(NT 655 995)

10km off Anstruther in the Firth of Forth, the west coast of this small island presents a spectacular cliff coastline. Unfortunately it is also a breeding ground to more than 80,000 seabirds. A number of routes were climbed at Pilgrims' Haven in the 1930s including a 25m sea stack. Access by boat is straightforward, but the island has been a National Nature Reserve since 1956 and is owned by SNH.

CRAIGLUG

(NO 404 183)

This fine little crag near the village of Dairsie north-east of Cupar has about 20 routes of all grades up to HVS and some good bouldering. Take the road north at the west end of the village and the crag is visible straight ahead. Take care not to leave cars obstructing the road or gates. The first recorded ascents were by J.Baines and T.Wilkinson in the late 1950s.

ST ANDREWS COAST

The coastline east from St Andrews offers some minor rock entertainment. **Maiden Rock** (NO 527 158) is a sandstone tower about 1km along the shore from the east sands and has more than a dozen routes varying in length from 7m to 14m, some pioneered by Harold Raeburn in 1901. **Rock and Spindle** (NO 538 157) is a seriously loose 10m pinnacle 1km further east, which becomes a sea-stack at extremely high tides and **Buddo Rock** (NO 563 150) is an isolated lump of very sandy sandstone with a strange semi-detached pillar on the south side, some 2km further east along the coastal path.

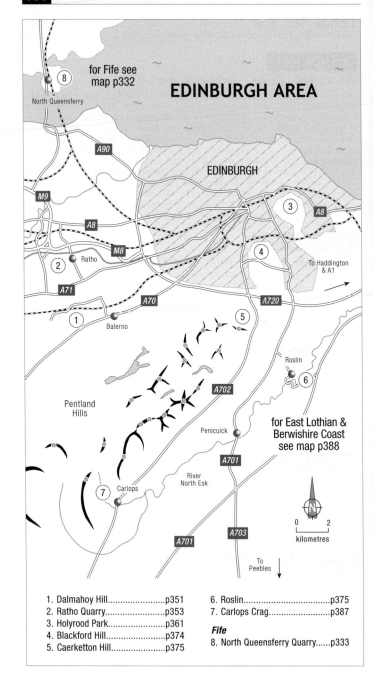

for Fife see
map p332

EDINBURGH AREA

North Queensferry

A90

M9

EDINBURGH

A8

M8

Ratho

To Haddington
& A1

A71

A70

A720

Balerno

Roslin

Pentland
Hills

A702

Penicuick

for East Lothian &
Berwishire Coast
see map p388

A701

River
North Esk

Carlops

A701

A703

To
Peebles

0   2
kilometres

EDINBURGH AREA

The major development in this chapter has been the creation of the Adventure Centre in Ratho Quarry. Details of this superb climbing wall complex can be found in the Climbing Walls section p34. At the time of publication many of the climbs in the quarry outside the centre had not received repeats after lying unclimbed for a number of years. Grades and descriptions are as the previous edition and should be approached with caution.

At Salisbury Crags, climbers have been using the South Quarry for a number of years and it is hoped that access will be extended to other crags in Holyrood Park in the near future.

WEST LOTHIAN MINOR CRAGS

The small east facing cliff in **Beecraigs Country Park** (NT 008 739), near Linlithgow, is useful only for learning abseiling or self-rescue techniques. Permission, upon payment of a small charge should be obtained from the visitor centre (01506 844516). The west-facing crag on **Binny Craig** (NT 043 735), the prominent little hill between Broxburn and Linlithgow, has a few reasonable VS routes down to the left on and around a big slab above a pond. Drive to Oatridge Farm, turn right and park beside the crag.

DALMAHOY HILL

(NT 136 671)   Alt 200m   North-west facing   Map p350

The cliffs on the northern side of Dalmahoy Hill provide some good climbing in the lower and middle grades. The rock is columnar dolerite giving rise to a uniform series of grooves and ribs and the climbing is located on the largest and cleanest section of cliff. Unfortunately a huge quarry now lies below the crag and the resulting noise and dust have not helped Dalmahoy become popular. The rock is rather green and lichenous, although many of the routes are better than they look.

Approach: Access is possible from the A70 to the south but the laybys have been blocked and parking is very difficult. Accordingly, access is probably better from the quieter minor road to the north which serves the quarry. Park on the wide pavement near the rail bridge at NT 136 675. From here a signposted Right of Way leads to and through the quarry before skirting rightwards (west) below the crags. This path then goes south to meet the A70 at NT 135 659. Alternatively, follow the quarry access road to where it divides and cross fields south to gain the Right of Way.

The Arete   8m   Difficult
The short arete above a rowan tree at the left-hand end of the crag. A useful descent route once identified.

Professor Groove   8m   Mild Severe
The mossy groove in the slab right of The Arete.

The Corner   8m   Severe
The grassy corner right of Professor Groove.

Ivy Tower   10m   Severe
The rib right of The Corner.

Lightning Groove   15m   VS 4b *
The first long groove on the left-hand side of the crag. It is split by an overlap at half-height.

Munich Climb **15m** **VS 4b** *
The obvious corner right of Lightning Groove. Go up a broken groove to below diamond-shaped overlaps, move left and climb the corner to the top.

Grass Widows **15m** **HVS 5a** *
A short technical problem taking the double overlap to the right of Munich Climb. Follow Munich Climb to the overlap, then gain the slabby groove above. Climb this to finish.

Curving Groove **15m** **VS 4c**
Follow Munich Climb to the overlaps, then move right round the bulges to finish up the rib on the left.

Resurrection **15m** **VS 4b** *
Climb the groove immediately right of a vegetated bay, then go up the wall above into an upper slabby groove. Move left to small ledges and finish up the groove above.

Midgy Gem **15m** **VS 4c** * (1991)
Start 3m right of Resurrection at the left end of some clean slabs. Climb the slab, passing left of an obvious triangular overlap, to the big overlaps at 7m. Traverse 2m right and follow left-slanting grooves and ribs to the top.

Elation **15m** **HVS 5a** * (1991)
Start up a left facing groove about 3m right of Midgy Gem. Use a loose looking block to pull through a break in the overhangs, then follow the groove above until forced right onto a rib. Finish up the groove above. A good route, high in its grade.

Frustration **20m** **Mild VS 4b** *
Start at the right end of the clean slabs, 4m right of Elation. Climb an easy groove to an obvious diamond-shaped overlap at 4m. Move left then up until forced right by the overhangs. Continue up a pleasant open groove to the top. A harder direct finish is possible.

The Lemming **20m** **HVS 4c** * (1992)
Follow the open slabby groove, midway between Frustration and Cleaned Sweep, to a steepening finish. Exit by Cleaned Sweep (or directly through the bulge, 5b).

Cleaned Sweep **20m** **VS 4c** (1991)
This takes the prominent left-facing hanging corner 4m right of Frustration. Follow a scrappy groove to an overlap. Move up and right into the corner, and follow it to a choice of hard or easy exits.

Triad **20m** **HVS 4c**
Dangerously loose. Start in a large overhung niche just left of Roots. Pull over the overhang onto a slab and surmount a further steepening to reach a small ledge. Continue up the groove above to the top.

Roots **20m** **Very Difficult**
This route starts at an obvious narrow rib near the centre of the crag. Climb the rib and the mossy wall above via a twisting groove, to finish up a short slab.

Insertion **20m** **VS 4b**
Just right of Roots are a series of slabs leading to a wall with a down-pointing flake. Climb the slabs to the base of the wall. Climb this to footholds on the flake, then move diagonally left to join Roots.

Pop-it **20m** **HVS 5a**
This route climbs through the overlap to the left of Jack of Hearts. Scramble up

slabby grooves to a steep wall. Gain the upper groove with difficulty, then continue to the top.

Jack of Hearts   25m   VS 4c **

This fine route climbs the prominent long clean groove towards the right end of the cliff. Climb the groove to two overlaps. Surmount these directly, then continue up the slab above. It is possible to slant left after the first overlap and climb diagonally right to the upper slab at the same grade.

Fine Escape   25m   Hard Severe

The groove immediately right of Jack of Hearts. Climb to an overhang and walk right to a break in the wall above. Climb up a twisting groove to slabs which lead leftwards to the top.

Draconian   20m   Very Difficult

The groove left of Father's Day.

Father's Day   20m   Very Difficult

Start at a tree below a triangular overhang. Go up through a notch right of the overhang and follow the groove above to the top.

Rearguard   20m   Severe

Some 4m right of Father's Day is a rib. Climb this to a mantelshelf move left at 7m, then follow an open-sided groove to the top.

Cake Walk   20m   Severe *

A good route taking the square-cut groove and prominent hanging rib near the right end of the crag. Climb the groove and a slab, then go directly up the rib over two bulges.

Birthday Party   20m   VS 4c *

The obvious groove and right facing corner in the upper slab at the right end of the crag. Climb the long groove over a steepening and mantelshelf on to a broad ledge below the final corner. Climb the corner to finish.

Scree Surfing   70m   E1   *(1987)*

A high-level left to right girdle traverse, starting at The Arete. Three pitches were climbed (4c, 5b, 4b) but details are lacking and the route length would suggest that the traverse was not completed.

RATHO QUARRY

(NT 128 709)   Map p350

Ratho re-opened for climbing in 2004, after being closed for a number of years during the building of the Adventure Centre. The quarry is likely to regain some popularity as it continues to offer a good range of extremes close to Edinburgh. It is very sheltered and catches the sun and most routes dry quickly after rain in summer and winter.

The left end of the West Wall and the routes in the vicinity of the Godzilla corner have been incorporated into the main climbing arena. The floor is now some 5m below previous ground level, but it is hoped that this rock will be climbed in the future to offer sport routes on natural and artificial rock in the arena. However, at the time of publication, the future of the Adventure Centre, the indoor climbing arena and the climbing in the quarry outside remained uncertain.

Ratho is no longer the quiet haven it was with traffic noise from the M8 extension to the north competing with music from the Adventure Centre to the south. Climbing in the quarry is free of charge but please report your presence to reception and to staff on the desk in the main arena. For details of the indoor arena see the Climbing Walls section.

354

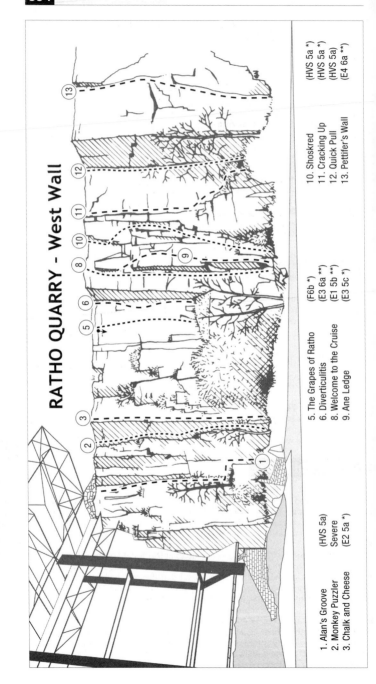

RATHO QUARRY - West Wall

1. Alan's Groove   (HVS 5a)
2. Monkey Puzzler   Severe
3. Chalk and Cheese   (E2 5a *)

5. The Grapes of Ratho   (F6b *)
6. Diverticulitis   (E3 6a **)
8. Welcome to the Cruise   (E1 5b **)
9. Ane Ledge   (E3 5c *)

10. Shoskred   (HVS 5a *)
11. Cracking Up   (HVS 5a *)
12. Quick Pull   (HVS 5a)
13. Pettifer's Wall   (E4 6a **)

Approach: From the Newbridge Roundabout at the junction of the M8/9 and the A8 (NT125 727), follow the signs for the Adventure Centre. The centre is sign-posted from all directions on the M8 and M9.

Descent: The top of the quarry is surrounded by a barbed wire fence with a gate above the right end of the East Wall. The quickest descent back into the quarry bowl is via the fire escape between the East Wall and East Bay.

WARNING: The following descriptions are from the previous edition of this guide and most have not been specifically re-checked due to Ratho's recent opening and ensuing complications. Blasting for the M8 extension is known to have destabilised some areas and others have been heavily rock scaled during building work. Added to this the dolerite is notoriously blocky, highly susceptible to weathering and has not been climbed on for four years.

If a route is believed to have been re-climbed since Ratho re-opened then this is mentioned in the text. This does not guarantee that descriptions, grades or stars are as stated, although they should be similar. For all other routes, and those which have been re-climbed but grade and stars have not been confirmed, this data has been placed in brackets. Until traffic increases, climbers are advised to approach routes with caution. The mention of any fixed protection does not mean it is in place or in good condition. The Adventure Centre has placed signs in the quarry indicating climbers use it at their own risk.

WEST WALL

Diagram p354

This is the continuation of the quarried face within the main arena. The first route climbs the obvious groove behind the tree above the exit stairwell and below the wall supporting the right-hand end of the roof. Two routes were recorded to the left **Scotty Arete** (20m Severe * 1976) and **Spiny Norman** (20m Severe 1976), However both are very close to the structure of the main climbing arena and are probably best avoided.

Further right, the wall becomes more broken until, near the centre, it rears up into a series of steep grooves and aretes before finishing in a very impressive smooth wall on the right. Landscaping means that getting a belay at the top of routes 1-12 may be difficult. Hopefully some belay bolts will be placed at the top in the near future.

1 Alan's Groove   20m   (HVS 5a)
Gain the ledge and tree below the groove with care, and climb the long left-hand groove above.

2 Monkey Puzzler   20m   Severe
Start at a tree immediately left of a sharp arete. Climb a wall, then a left-trending groove and grass to the top. Re-climbed and grade confirmed.

3 Chalk and Cheese   20m   (E2 5a *)   (1992)
Climb directly up the sharp arete. Poorly protected but good.

4 Jungle Rock   20m   (Very Severely Vegetated)
An arboreal adventure up the wall and corner right of Chalk and Cheese.

5 The Grapes of Ratho   10m   (F6b *)   (1998)
Climbs the obvious bolted wall left of Diverticulitus, starting from the big ledge. Six bolts to a lower-off. The ledge is probably best gained by abseil.

6 Diverticulitis   15m   (E3 6a **)   (1980)
Halfway along the West Wall there is a prominent left facing corner, starting from a platform 7m above the quarry floor. This gives a superb sustained route. Climb it direct except for a few moves on the left wall at 12m.

7 Alopecia 20m (E4 6a *) (1993)

Although escapable, this route has good situations on the final leaning prow. Climb the arete between Diverticulitis and Welcome to the Cruise, passing two peg runners.

8 Welcome to the Cruise 25m (E1 5b **) (1983)

This route is reported as having been re-climbed at a possible grade of E2 5c. A justly popular route up the series of grooves right of a big leaning arete. Start at some large boulders and climb the grooves direct, moving left into the final steep corner which provides the crux.

9 Ane Ledge 25m (E3 5c *) (1983)

This is the sharp arete which ends 15m up the cliff. Start immediately right of the previous route. Climb the arete and a thin crack on its right to a tiny ledge. Step left and layback boldly up the top part of the arete to a larger ledge. Finish up either Welcome to the Cruise or Shoskred.

10 Shoskred 25m (HVS 5a *) (1976)

This route is thought to have been re-climbed at a similar grade. The grooves just right of Ane Ledge. There is a choice of lines in the central section.

11 Cracking Up 25m (HVS 5a *) (1976)

This route is thought to have been re-climbed at a similar grade. Scramble up vegetated ground past a tree towards the corner of Quick Pull. Move left to gain and climb the wide crack near the arete.

12 Quick Pull 25m (HVS 5a)

Scramble up as for the previous route and climb the deep corner.

The arete to the right was **Slow Strain** (25m E2 6a* 1982). However, rockfall appears to have altered the start. The next two routes have a large bank of each at the top of them. This is likely to cause problems for anyone trying to finish these routes, and may do so for some time to come.

13 Pettifer's Wall 25m (E4 6a **) (1980)

A fine, serious route up the impressive face at the right end of the West Wall. Start 4m right of Slow Strain. Climb an open black groove to a small triangular overhang (peg runner). Move rightwards over this and continue up a shallow groove to the top.

BACK WALL

The left-hand side is loose and grassy but to the right is a tall square buttress with a prominent left arete. This area was seriously destabilised by blasting for the M8 cutting to the north. However, subsequent rock scaling appears to have revealed solid rock.

14 Sedge Warbler 20m (E2 5b **) (1981)

This route has been re-climbed, although the finish is described as 'odd and roundabout'. Scramble up to the left-hand side of the arete. Step up and swing round the arete to gain a narrow ramp. Climb this rather precariously, then follow the cracks above to a large ledge. Climb the cracked wall above to finish.

15 Time's Last Gift 20m (E2 5c **) (1983)

This route has been re-climbed. Start below an obvious groove 5m right of the arete. Climb the groove until a move right can be made onto a ledge, move up to a higher ledge and continue up the groove on the left to a large ledge. Finish up the steep crack in the final wall (crux).

RATHO QUARRY – East Wall

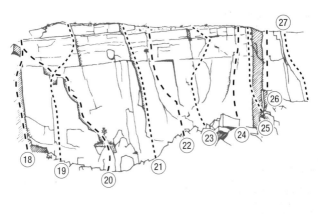

18. Artho	(E4 6a/b *)	23. Wally 3	(E4 6a *)
19. Ouroborus Eliminate	(E3 5c)	24. Wally 2	(E4 5c *)
20. Ouroborus	HVS 5b *	25. Wounded Knee	(F7a+)
21. Shear Fear	(E2 5c **)	26. Cornered	(E1 5c)
22. Strongarm	(E3 6a *)	27. So it Goes	(E2 5c)

16 Up the Creek   12m   (E1 5b) *(1981)*
The repulsive wide crack 5m left of Artho.

17 Pete's Wall   10m   (E1 5b) *(1981)*
Start up in the corner as for Artho. Step left and climb a shallow left-facing groove and the short wall above. Often wet.

18 Artho   10m   (E4 6a/b *) *(1983)*
This short but action packed climb takes the black-streaked corner in the angle between the back wall and the east wall. Start in the corner but move left and up as for Pete's Wall to a small roof under a block. Step right and climb the corner to the top.

EAST WALL

Diagram p357

This is the long wall stretching rightwards from the back of the quarry. It starts off quite tall but reduces in height above a huge pile of boulders, where there is an arete and corner daubed with graffiti. To the right of this there is a long series of broken walls, corners and ribs ending at the fire escape.

19 Ouroborus Eliminate   20m   (E3 5c) *(1981)*
Start 4m right of Artho. Climb a thin crack to a ledge and continue up a short ramp on the right (peg runner). Climb the wall above, trending right to the arete, then finish up a groove on the right. Very necky in the upper section.
Variation: **E3 5c ***
After climbing the initial thin crack, escape leftwards up Ouroborus.

20 Ouroborus   25m   HVS 5b *   *(1976)*
This has been re-climbed. Start at the lowest point about 10m right of Artho. Climb up to a small tree, then follow a flake away up to the left to the top of Artho. A good route with a perplexing crux.

21 Shear Fear   20m   (E2 5c ** **)   *(1976)*
This has been re-climbed, but a fair amount of flight time has been clocked too. The fearsome flake-crack 6m right of the start of Ouroborus and just left of the pile of boulders.

**22 Strongarm   15m   (E3 6a ** *)*   *(1992)*
Right of Shear Fear are two thinner flake-cracks. The left fades away at the bottom and the right ends in an overlap. Move up and place a high runner in the right-hand crack, then make a difficult move to the left-hand crack. Climb this to a ledge and the top.

A line of bolt studs of uncertain origin ascends the wall directly from the start of Strongarm.

**23 Wally 3   15m   (E4 6a ** *)*   *(1983)*
Start from the huge pile of boulders 6m left of the arete. Climb some flakes to reach a shallow groove, then follow this, exiting right at the top. Traverse left and finish up a small corner.

**24 Wally 2   15m   (E4 5c ** *)*   *(1983)*
Not quite as hard as its neighbour but a more serious lead. Start just left of the arete. Climb the wall, moving left to a shallow groove. Climb this to a large hold, then move right to finish up the wall just left of the arete.

25 Wounded Knee   15m   (F7a+)   *(1994)*
Climbs the excellent bolted arete between Wally 2 and Cornered. Start on the right side. At the second bolt, move awkwardly round to the left side, ascend, then swing back onto the arete to finish on large blocks. The rock scar dates from the first ascent.

26 Cornered   10m   (E1 5c)
The smooth, short corner right of the arete. Peg runner at 3m.

27 So it Goes   10m   (E2 5c)   *(1989)*
Climb the crack-line right of Cornered.

28 Fledge   8m   (VS 5a)   *(1993)*
Climb the corner-crack 10m right of Cornered.

About 20m to the right are two obvious grooves left of a rusty wall.

**29 5000 Christmas Trees   10m   (E2 5c ** *)*   *(1991)*
The left-hand groove gives good strenuous back and footing.

30 Business as Usual   10m   (E3 6a)   *(1991)*
The right-hand groove yields to crotch splitting bridging.

31 Danger No Entry   10m   (VS 4c)   *(1991)*
Start at the foot of Business as Usual. Pull out right round the arete onto a ledge and finish up over blocks.

Towards the right end of the East Wall there is a pea-pod groove starting from a ledge a few metres up. The following three routes take lines up the wall left of this.

32 Fairy Feat   12m   (VS 4c)

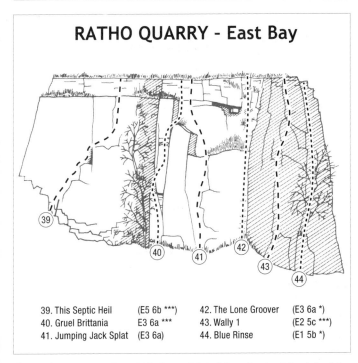

RATHO QUARRY - East Bay

39. This Septic Heil	(E5 6b ***)	42. The Lone Groover	(E3 6a *)
40. Gruel Brittania	E3 6a ***	43. Wally 1	(E2 5c ***)
41. Jumping Jack Splat	(E3 6a)	44. Blue Rinse	(E1 5b *)

The unpleasant corner-line which slants slightly leftwards, about 8m left of the pod-shaped groove.

33 Mon   12m   (VS 4c)
Start just right of Fairy Feat and climb a right-trending line up the wall.

Two routes have been found about 6m left of Beanpud. **Zam Zam** (12m E2 6a) has hard moves to gain a crack, which is followed to the top. The other route (E2 5c) follows an obvious line just to the right. A lot of rock scaling took place in this area and a number of routes are thought to be affected.

34 Pull the Other One   12m   (E1 5b/c)   (1990)
The crack 3m left of Beanpud, joining Mon near the top.

35 Beanpud   12m   (E1 5b **)   (1976)
The pea-pod shaped groove gives an excellent and interesting problem.

36 Election Sickness   12m   (VS 4c)   (1992)
The crack-line between Beanpud and Rock-a-Boogie.

37 Rock-a-Boogie   12m   (VS 4c *)
This route has been re-climbed. Start 4m right of Beanpud and climb the straight crack at the back of a V-groove.

38 Rebel Without Claws   12m   (E2 5c **)   (1983)
A good short route which climbs the smooth curving groove just right of Rock-a-Boogie. Gain the groove and climb it using the right arete.

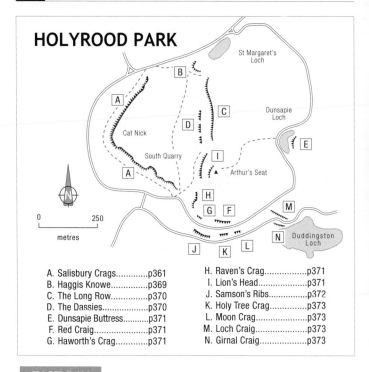

HOLYROOD PARK

St Margaret's Loch

Dunsapie Loch

Cat Nick

South Quarry

Arthur's Seat

Duddingston Loch

0 250 metres

EAST BAY

Diagram p359

The south-east section of the quarry is dominated by the stairs forming the rear fire escape for the Adventure Centre. To the right is a shady bay with some fine routes on excellent rock. A good brushing might be in order before re-climbing.

39 This Septic Heil   20m   (E5 6b ***)   (1983)
The overhanging wall on the left-hand side of the bay gives a brilliant test piece. Gain a series of steps which are followed up and right to a resting place (2 peg runners). Traverse right, move up, then continue up the wall to a ledge (peg runner). Finish up to the right.

40 Gruel Brittania   15m   E3 6a ***   (1982)
This route has been re-climbed. A great little route taking a mixture of the thin crack and sharp arete in the left wall of the East Bay. Make a few hard moves up a thin crack just right of the arete and swing up left onto a ledge. Regain the crack and follow it to a flat hold. Finish by making some interesting moves up the arete. (It is also possible to finish up the crack).

41 Jumping Jack Splat   15m   (E3 6a)
Gain the stepped groove in the wall right of Gruel Brittania (peg runner) and follow it to a grassy ledge. Go left and up to finish. Necky.

42 The Lone Groover   20m   (E3 6a *)   (1983)
The clean-cut groove at the back of the bay leads to a grass ledge and an unpleasant finish. Much harder than it looks.

Variation: **Alternative finish   (E3 6a *)**   *(1988)*
Hard, but it avoids the unpleasant finish. From the grass ledge move up and right into a groove, then step right to climb a thin crack just left of Wally 1.

The following two routes finish on a narrow ridge with belay bolts.

43 Wally 1   20m   (E2 5c ***)   *(1983)*
Fine technical climbing. Start 2m right of the Lone Groover. Climb a thin flake to a small ledge then continue up the cracked wall above.

44 Blue Rinse   20m   (E1 5b *)
Climb up past a tree, just right of Wally 1, and continue up the groove and flake-crack to the top.

EDINBURGH CASTLE ROCK

(NT 252 735)

Climbing here is illegal and it is not exactly a secluded crag, so count on appearing in court if the temptation prooves too much. Two routes have been recorded; **The Closet Climb** (Severe 1958), takes the Princes Street Face and was done by R.Smith and A.Fraser. **Breach of the Peace** (III 1987), takes the smear of ice which forms down the Princes Street Face once in a blue moon. It was climbed at 10pm on Jan 16 by G.Taylor and J.McKeever, who were charged accordingly!

HOLYROOD PARK

Maps 350

Prominent, extensive and accessible, the cliffs surrounding Arthur's Seat have attracted rock climbers for more than a century. Although there are areas of loose rock, there are also many good routes in pleasant sunny situations on rough solid basalt. All of the cliffs in the park are covered by by-laws outlawing climbing. However climbing has been tolerated in the South Quarry for a number of years. For the rest of the crags, the 2003 Land Reform Act states that all existing by-laws restricting access must be reviewed by 2006. It is hoped that when the Holyrood Park by-laws are reviewed, climbing will be allowed on more crags.

   The crags' proximity to the new Scottish Parliament building may complicate matters, but there will be certain irony in a Scottish Executive which opens access to all, spends millions on health education and then restricts recreation in its own backyard; time alone will tell.

Approach: Parking is available at Dunsapie Loch and Duddingstone Loch east of Arthur's Seat, at Meadowbank near St Margaret's Loch, at the parliament visitor centre to the north, and at numerous other locations.

SALISBURY CRAGS

(NT 267 733)   North-west & South-west facing   Maps 360
Diagrams p362, 368

This is the long line of imposing cliffs which dominates much of the Edinburgh skyline. Parts of the cliff face have been quarried and these sections have the soundest rock and the best routes. The cliffs are described from right to left.

Pinnacle Quarry

This is the deep bay at the right-hand end of the crags, just left of The Hawse, (the gap between Arthur's Seat and the crags). On the left and rear walls are many short routes; the pinnacle itself is the obvious buttress on the right.

SALISBURY CRAGS - South Quarry

12. Black Chimney	Severe *
13. Roofer Madness	HVS 5a
14. Hanging Slab	Severe *
15. Sentry Box	Severe *
17. Graham's Route	Severe *
18. Recess Climb	Severe *
20. Spike Fright	HVS 5a *

21. Idle Gossip	E3 5c *
22. Black Slab	Severe **
24. Red Slab	Difficult *
26. Initial Route	VS 5b *

27. The Lift	Moderate *
30. Rotten Overhang	HVS 4b
31. White Slab	Very Difficult

1 Pinnacle Corner   10m   Very Difficult   *(1944)*
The right side of the pinnacle. Turn an overhang on the right and climb up left of some gorse bushes. A prickly route.
Variation: **Severe**
Turn the overhang on the left.

2 Pinnacle Face   12m   Very Difficult *   *(1946)*
The front face of the pinnacle. Start 10m right of Falseface. Start up the middle of the obvious slab, then climb its right-hand side until a small projecting overhang is reached. Move left around this and go up to easy ground.

3 Falseface   12m   Severe
Start at the left side of the pinnacle and gain a sloping ledge above a bore mark. Make a rising traverse right and pull over a black bulge into a slabby recess. Finish out left.

4 The Conflict with Temptation   12m   Severe   *(1946)*
Start as for the previous route, but after a few moves up the rising traverse climb to a smooth mottled slab. Move right and climb a corner to finish at the same point as Falseface.

Middle Quarry

This is the less well defined bay, some 100m left of Pinnacle Quarry.

5 Centre Slab   15m   Moderate *
Start 2m left of a prominent slab of white rock. Climb a groove, then a red slab rightwards to finish past some white rocks.

6 The Slant   20m   Difficult
The obvious left-slanting line starting 5m left of the white slab.

7 Tournez en Face a ma Gauche   20m   Severe   *(1946)*
Start in the centre of the quarry and climb to a block overhang halfway up the face. Pull over, then traverse left and finish straight up.

8 Toujours Tout Droit   15m   VS 4c   *(1946)*
Start just right of Butterfly. Climb a groove and at 6m turn a projection by a delicate move left. Finish up a groove on the left.

9 Butterfly   15m   VS 4b
Look for two black block overhangs forming the shape of a butterfly. Climb up to and over the blocks to finish rightwards on poor rock.

Eastern Buttress

The projecting section of crag between middle and south quarries, easily identified by the huge boulder leaning against the face at the right-hand end. The rock is loose above half-height but there are some excellent boulder problems and low level traverses.

10 Eastern Buttress Face Route   20m   Very Difficult   *(1897)*
Left of centre is a thin rib projecting into the grass. Climb the rib, then trend right up to a grassy ledge. A friable wall leads to the top.

11 Black Chimney Buttress   20m   Very Difficult *
The left edge of the buttress provides a good line but is loose in the upper half. Climb the smooth wall right of the arete to a large block on the left. Step right (peg runner), then continue up the exposed but broken arete to the top.

South Quarry

Diagram p362

Previously known as Little Quarry, this is the most deeply recessed section of the crags. It has always been the most popular cliff in the park and provides many good short routes on solid rock, as well as the best bouldering in the area. The climbs tend to be fairly serious due to a general lack of protection and scarcity of belay points at the top. Many variations to the routes have been climbed.

To the right of Black Chimney, towards the arete, is a steep black wall. The traverse is a very polished 6b, and to climb straight up left of some old bolts is 6a.

12 Black Chimney   15m   Severe *

The open groove in the right-hand corner of the quarry. Climb the steepening groove until it is possible to pull into a short steep corner. Finish left of a large projection at the top.

13 Roofer Madness   15m   HVS 5a

A somewhat loose climb through the roofs about 6m left of Black Chimney. Start just left of a low overhang. Go up until it is possible to step right into a groove. Climb this and pull through the roofs at their narrowest point to gain the top.

14 Hanging Slab   15m   Severe * (1946)

Start 8m left of Black Chimney, above a large boulder. Climb up onto a hanging slab, then move up and left to a small triangular niche. Continue up to the overhang and pass it on the left.

15 Sentry Box   12m   Severe * (1935)

Some 12m left of Black Chimney is a slab with a sentry box recess just below its top. Start to the left of an overhang directly below the sentry box. Climb a shallow groove, moving right to gain the recess. Finish direct.

16 Rib and Mantelshelf   12m   Severe (1946)

Start immediately left of Sentry Box. Climb directly up a narrow steepening rib. At the top mantelshelf onto a large hold and finish more easily.

17 Graham's Route   12m   Severe * (1946)

Climb the left side of the smooth red slab, just right of Recess Climb, finishing rightwards.

18 Recess Climb   12m   Severe *

Start at some boulders where three grooves slant up the cliff, the left one being less well defined. Climb the right-hand groove.

Variation: **VS 4c**

It is possible to climb directly up the right edge of Recess Climb, keeping left of Graham's Route.

19 Notch Climb   12m   Severe

Climb the central square-cut groove.

20 Spike Fright   12m   HVS 5a *

In the centre of the quarry is an overhang with a large square-cut recess in it. Climb to a hanging block right of the recess. Pull up to its right, stand on it, then find a way up the slab above. (Sometimes called Great North Road).

21 Idle Gossip   12m   E3 5c * (1992)

Left of the square-cut recess is an overhang with a cluster of down-pointing red spikes below it. Climb a groove to the spikes, pull through the overhang using a flake hold and continue through the overhangs above on good holds.

22 Black Slab   12m   Severe ★★
An enjoyable climb, possibly the best in the South Quarry. Start 7m left of Spike Fright below a series of black overhangs. Climb to a block at the left side of the lowest overhang, pull up and hand traverse right, surmount the bulge above and finish up an exposed wall.

23 Hyphen Route   12m   HVS 5a ★   *(1944)*
Start 2m left of Black Slab and climb a straight crack to a slab and bore hole. Step right and pull over a bulge to finish up the black wall above.

24 Red Slab   12m   Difficult ★
The groove left of the previous route leads to the left side of a red slab. The black groove above then leads to the top.

25 Horrible Hook   12m   VS 4c
Climb a black corner-crack below a small quartz mark, then pull up left by pinching a hooked block. Continue directly to the top.

26 Initial Route   10m   VS 5b ★   *(1936)*
Start at a 2m long boulder in the grass. Climb a short smooth corner, moving out left at the top (crux). Go up and traverse right to a prominent projection, then finish up the wall above.

27 The Lift   10m   Moderate ★
The obvious right-facing corner-line some 15m from the left-hand corner of the quarry provides a good descent route and a worthwhile climb in its own right. Climb the corner to gain some ledges on the right. Move up and left back into the corner, then follow it to the top.

28 The Lift Arete   10m   Very Difficult   *(1945)*
The arete immediately left of The Lift.

29 The Splits   10m   Severe
Climb the corner 2m left of the Lift, and 8m right of White Slab.

30 Rotten Overhang   10m   HVS 4b
Climb the corner left of The Splits past a great rotten overhang at half-height (if it's still there).

31 White Slab   8m   Very Difficult
Near the left end of the rear wall is a white-flecked slab. Climb this at the left-hand flecks.

32 The Long Stride   8m   Moderate ★
Start at the twin corners left of White Slab. Climb the left corner for 3m, then stride left to a small ledge. Finish up the easy wall above.
Variation: **VS 5a ★**
A short crack provides an interesting direct start.

33 Athlete's Arete   8m   HVS 5a   *(1945)*
Climb the bold arete between the Long Stride and Original Route as directly as possible.

34 Original Route   8m   Moderate
Gain a shelf left of an orange slab with a bore hole, step up then traverse right across a bulge until it is possible to gain the easy wall above. No less than five variations to this climb were recorded in the 1940s, at grades up to VS 4c. Take your pick.

35 Wicked Lady   10m   VS 4c ✶✶   (1946)
Left of Original Route is a sloping shelf under a black overhang. Climb easily to the left end of the shelf, then traverse awkwardly right past the bulging overhang until it is possible to get established above. Continue to the top on good holds. So named because 'She tries to cause your downfall just as you're getting round her'. Beware!

36 Archie's Slab   12m   HVS 5a ✶   (1945)
Start as for Wicked Lady, then traverse left passing the base of two corners to a scooped slab. Climb this with difficulty. (The corners have also been climbed).

37 Harrison's Climb   15m   Severe ✶✶   (1945)
A steep route with some unusual moves. Start just left of a square cave. Climb the rib for 7m, then step right onto a small ledge. Pull up to a higher ledge and finish up the exposed wall above.

38 Doubledecker   20m   Severe   (1947)
Starting from the boulders at the left side of the quarry, climb slabs leftwards towards the arete then directly to the top, keeping just right of the edge.
Variation: **Very Difficult**   (1952)
Start from the right end of The Platform (see below). Climb slabs rightwards to join the normal route at the arete.

Western Buttress

This is immediately left of South Quarry. A broad level ledge, The Platform, runs across the base, and a broken ledge, The Terrace, runs the length of the face just below the top.

39 Slab and Wedge Route   25m   Very Difficult
Below the right-hand end of The Platform is a short steep corner. Start up this, then climb the left side of the slab above. At its top go left, then back right to easy ground and the top.

Several lines are possible between Slab and Wedge Route and Wall Route.

40 Wall Route   20m   Severe   (1937)
Start at the left end of The Platform at a steep corner. Climb the corner with a wide excursion to the right to pass a black overhang.

41 Groove Route   20m   VS 4c
Start as for Wall Route, but where that route moves right continue up the groove, turning the overhang on the left.

42 Black Corner   25m   HVS 5a ✶   (1960/91)
Climb the prominent black corner to the left of The Platform past two triangular shelving overhangs. Previously aided.

43 Horne's Slab   20m   VS 5a   (1945)
Some 8m left of The Platform is a red slab with a groove on its left which leads to a large ledge at 12m. Climb the slab to a layback hold, step up then move left and climb the groove. Scramble to the top.

44 Hewit's Groove   20m   VS 4c   (1933)
Round the rib to the left of Horne's Slab is a short twisting groove. Climb this to the ledge at 12m, then scramble to the top.

Left of Western Buttress the cliff rears up into a series of steep loose bays and buttresses. The leftmost of these, about 80m from Western Buttress, is called Great Buttress. Beyond this the cliff steps sharply back into the Great Quarry. Two very loose routes have been done up the right side of Great Buttress and are not described.

**45 Great Buttress   35m   Very Difficult ** *(1902)*
A classic route in a magnificent situation. The rock requires care. Start slightly right of centre at a broad pillar. Climb the pillar to a terrace at 4m, follow this up and right then traverse left along a ledge round a nose. At its end climb a short corner (crux), then follow another ledge to the left. Mantelshelf and climb a 'staircase' to a wide recess and the top. A more direct line can be taken at little increase in grade.

Great Quarry

Diagram p362

This is the long section of cliff set back from the path to the left of Great Buttress. In the centre is a terrace at three-quarters height. Below the left end of the terrace is a deep right-facing groove (Steeplejack's Staircase), with two bolts obvious on the wall to the left.

46 Walk On By   30m   E2 5a *(1991)*
Start just right of the only tree at the foot of the cliff. Climb up to a groove and follow this to exit right onto a ledge. Continue up leftwards via loose ledges to the top. The name gives good advice.

The following nine routes finish on the terrace from where a loose scramble leads to the top. Routes are described right to left.

47 Ped Xing   20m   E1 5b * *(1992)*
Good climbing marred by a worrying poised block. Start below the right end of the terrace, under some blocky quartz overhangs. Climb a rib to a niche left of the overhangs. Swing right round the arete of a block and pull through the overhang above. Finish left or right.

48 Second Offence   20m   E3 5c *(1991)*
Start as for Ped Xing but step left to climb a vertical crack through black rock. A hand-placed peg was used for protection behind a flake at the crux.

49 The Blackdance   20m   E2 5c ** *(1983)*
Start 6m right of Steeplejack's Staircase below a triangular overhang. Climb past the overhang and go up a groove (peg runner) to a sloping foothold on the right. Move up the groove then out right (peg runner) and continue up the wall to finish.

50 After the Axe   20m   E2 5b/c * *(1983)*
Climb The Blackdance to the first peg. Traverse left across the wall and go round the arete to the base of a shallow groove. Climb this to finish.

51 Ginger Nympho's Lust   20m   E2 6a * *(1982)*
From the right-hand end of the ledge below Steeplejack's Staircase climb a crack rightwards (peg runner) to gain a shallow groove. Climb this (peg runner), then traverse left to the base of a smooth groove. This provides a technical finish past two peg runners.

52 Election Special   20m   E2 5c *(1987)*
Climb the left-hand crack directly to the third peg on Ginger Nympho's Lust, clip the top peg as well, then move left and go up to finish.

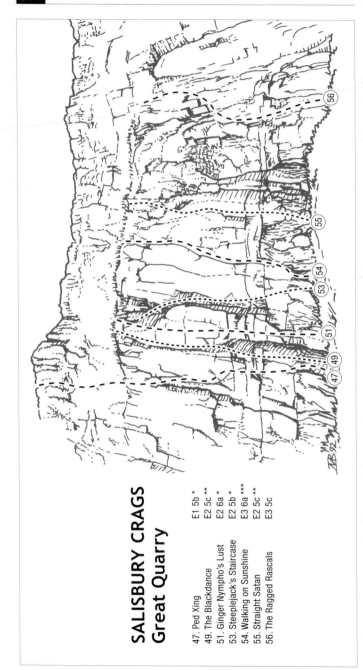

SALISBURY CRAGS
Great Quarry

47. Ped Xing	E1 5b	*
49. The Blackdance	E2 5c	**
51. Ginger Nympho's Lust	E2 6a	*
53. Steeplejack's Staircase	E2 5b	*
54. Walking on Sunshine	E3 6a	***
55. Straight Satan	E2 5c	**
56. The Ragged Rascals	E3 5c	

53 Steeplejack's Staircase   20m   E2 5b *   (1946)
The deep groove gives a classic climb, bold and technical for its time.

54 Walking on Sunshine   20m   E3 6a ***   (1983)
The smooth wall left of Steeplejack's Staircase provides one of the best climbs in
the area. Climb the wall (two bolt runners) to gain a standing position on a long
narrow hold. Move up and right to finish in an easy groove. Ignoring the bolts
pushes the grade to E5.

55 Straight Satan   20m   E2 5c **   (1982)
This takes the vertical quartz crack left of the previous route. Climb the rib to the
left of the crack until it is possible to step into the crack just below a peg runner.
Continue up the crack to the terrace (peg runner).

56 The Ragged Rascals   30m   E3 5c   (1991)
Start just left of Straight Satan and climb pleasantly up a black groove to a ledge
left of the terrace. Climb the final wall (crux, skyhook runner) to the top. Then,
presumably, run round and round the Radical Road.

57 Transatlantic Trip   30m   E3 5c   (1983)
The obvious right-facing white corner 50m left of Straight Satan. The route finishes
on a ledge about 6m below the top; the final wall is fairly easy but extremely loose.

The next important feature is the Cat Nick, an obvious deep gully about 80m left
of the Great Quarry.

58 Cat Nick Buttress   30m   Very Difficult   (1900)
The loose buttress immediately right of the gully. Climb over easy ledges to gain a
chimney, then climb this to the top of a prominent block. Cross slabs on the left to
a right-angled corner, then move up this (crux) to reach a shallow chimney in the
far wall. Follow the chimney to the top.

59 The Cat Nick   30m   Moderate **
The superbly positioned gully in the centre of the crags. A vintage route, which
even in 1897 was 'well worn and polished by the hands, feet, and knees of generations of youthful climbers'. In winter it gives 'the finest snow climb in the park. In
1947 the cornice was some six feet thick, with an overhang of ten feet, and lasted
for many weeks, despite much tunnelling'.

60 Cat Nick Arete   30m   Difficult
Start up the rib left of the Cat Nick then trend right up the left wall of the Cat Nick
to the top. Crumbly rock.

The crags to the north of the Cat Nick have seven routes, dating back to the 1890s.
Recent ascents have confirmed they are dangerously loose and worthy of XS 4b.
Historians wishing details can find them in the SMCJ Vol. IV, (1897) p335.

Opposite Holyrood Palace, near the north end of the crags is the pinnacle of **Pic
Robbieson**. Like the Inaccessible Pinnacle on Skye it has a short side (Moderate)
and a long side (Difficult). Both are very exposed. **The Great Electrocardiogram
Traverse** gives a 1km VS 5a excursion across the crags, first explored in 1946. Start
just beyond Pic Robbieson and continue across Great, South, Middle and Pinnacle
Quarry to The Hause, if daylight permits!

EDINBURGH AREA

HAGGIS KNOWE

Map p360

The isolated hillock north of the Long Row has a crag which is not high, but the rock is solid and there is good bouldering. No climbs have been recorded on the larger loose and vegetated crags to the east, near St. Anthony's Chapel.

LONG ROW

Map p360

The long line of cliffs overlooking Hunter's Bog, the deep depression behind Salisbury Crags, has good rock and many more worthwhile climbs than those described.

Fallen Column Climb   10m   Severe *   *(1897)*
The 'column' is a conspicuous feature near the left-hand end of the cliff. Climb the outside face of the column and continue up the wall above.

Waverley Crack   10m   Difficult   *(1946)*
The crack in the wall to the right of the previous climb.

Stomach Layback   10m   Severe *   *(1946)*
A further 7m right of the column is a corner-crack. Climb the corner, which curls right around an overhang.

Editor's Crack   7m   Difficult   *(1947)*
Some 50m right of the column, right of some easy slabs, is a buttress with two adjacent cracks. Climb the left-hand crack.

Reporter's Crack   7m   Very Difficult
Climb the right-hand crack.

THE DASSIES

Map p360

These are the three small outcrops in front of Long Row. The left and right-hand Dassies provide some short routes and problems on poor rock and the central Dassie contains the following problems on much better rock.

Question Mark Crack   6m   Very Difficult   *(1945)*
Climb the obvious crack 3m left of a green recessed slab.

Black Heart   6m   VS 4c *
The thin bulging crack splitting the left side of the central buttress.

Vague Arete   6m   E3 6a *   *(1987)*
The blunt arete 2m right of Black Heart. The crux is near the start but there is no protection and a bad landing.

Black Edge   6m   E2 6a *
Start on the left side of the arete immediately left of Raeburn's Crack. Make a few bold moves up and right to better holds near the arete. Climb this to the top. Unprotected.

Raeburn's Crack   7m   Severe *
The wide corner-crack to the right of the central buttress.

Cracked Slab Crack   7m   Difficult   *(1946)*
The crack-chimney immediately left of Cracked Slab.

Cracked Slab   7m   Very Difficult   *(1946)*
Climb the slab on the right side of the central Dassie via two short cracks. Finish directly above.

DUNSAPIE BUTTRESS

Map p360

This is the small crag overlooking Dunsapie Loch. No doubt routes have been climbed but no records can be traced.

RED CRAIG

Map p360

This is the line of crags about 40m above the road with a clean red wall at the left end and a red buttress with a prominent overhang at the right end.

Eureka   20m   Hard Severe * *(1946)*
This takes the centre of the right-hand buttress. Start at the lowest point and zigzag up between two bulges to finish above the prominent overhang.

Red Buttress   20m   VS 4c *(1945)*
Climb the left edge of the buttress via large steps overlooking a gorse and ivy chimney (Ivy Cleft). Finish at the same point as Eureka.

Pentland Slab   20m   Very Difficult
At the extreme left end of the crag is a slab with a steep red wall above and to its right. Climb the slab, keeping as close in under the wall as possible.

HAWORTH'S CRAG

Map p360

A tiny outcrop of red and black rock and with ivy at the top, halfway between Red Craig and Raven's Crag.

Wee Chokestone Crack   8m   Severe *(1947)*
The prominent right-facing corner-crack at the left end.

RAVEN'S CRAG

Map p360

The large crag to the right of the Guttit Haddie (the big earthy gully) has an impressive bulging black buttress on the right, which unfortunately consists of equally impressive loose rock. However, a low level traverse gives good training.

The Gutter   40m   VS 4b
The long left-facing corner on the left side of the crag. Horrific! (Sometimes called Vertical Sand).

Bacchus' Buttress Route   30m   Very Difficult *(1946)*
The first buttress left of the Gutter. Start just right of the foot of the buttress. Climb up 6m, then traverse left onto a good ledge. Continue to another ledge, then go directly to the top.

LION'S HEAD

Map p360

This is the sprawling crag on the north-west flank of Arthur's Seat, and includes the short tier of rock immediately under the summit. Most of the longer rock routes are appalling and best forgotten, however they have attracted some attention in winter.

EDINBURGH AREA

Red Chimney   20m   IV,3   (2001)
This route lies on the Lion's Head, towards the left end of the rocks overlooking
Hunter's Bog and was climbed at night to avoid attracting attention. Where the
chimney was blocked by a sapling, a move out right was made, followed by a very
difficult move on turf before regaining the chimney.

The following route lies on the West Face of Lion's Haunch, the col between
Salisbury Crags and Arthur's Seat proper. Traverse along a path below the gully of
the Gutted Haddie to a buttress about 270m from the col. It is the rightmost of two
or three spurs and lies directly above a small signpost. Gain access from a small
wooden scree barrier.

Excalibur   150m   III   (1996)
This grand outing was climbed at night to avoid alarming the locals and is possibly
the longest urban winter climb in Britain. A pentorch may be useful to examine
deep cracks for runners, but there is generally sufficient artificial light.
1. 27m Turn the steepest part of the front of the buttress (a direct attempt on the
rocks failed) on the right and follow turfy grooves to a belay
2. 46m Easy for half a pitch, then bear left to the skyline and gain a shallow gully
on the prow of the buttress in a fine position to gain the top of the lower difficulties.
3 and 4. 77m Ascend slightly leftwards through gorse (animal tracks) to snow
slopes and gain the final headwall at Nose Chimney, which appears as a notch from
below. The chimney does not hold much ice but gives a magnificent finish in a
splendid position. A long stretch allows a belay from the summit indicator.

The short upper tier immediately under the summit has three reasonable rock
climbs.

Hanging Over Gladys   10m   Very Difficult   (1946)
At the right end of the tier of rock just below the summit, not far left of the top of
the Gutted Haddie, are three black ribs. This route takes the right-hand rib, which
has an awkward overhang at the start.

Gladys' Rib   10m   Difficult   (1946)
The central rib.

No Love Rib   10m   Difficult   (1946)
The left-hand rib.

SAMSON'S RIBS

Map p360
The finest cliff in the park. The unmistakable ribs of red basalt would provide
superb climbing, however the conspicuous position of any climber would result in
certain arrest, justifiably so, because of the danger of rocks falling onto the road.

Left Ribs   45m   Scottish VS **   (1956)
Near the top left corner of the line of red ribs is a large overhang formed by the
hexagonal sections of broken ribs. Find a way up to the overhang, escape left, come
back right over the top of the overhang and finish straight up. A fine-looking route.

Grand Finale Route   60m   Hard Severe *   (1947)
Left of a bulging black wall (Evil Wall) is an isolated gorse bush. Climb up on vegetated rock, passing left of the bush, to a terrace. Continue up and right to another
grassy terrace below some ribs with overhanging tops. Belay. Traverse up left,
crossing the base of seven ribs, to reach a grass ledge. Ascend the rib above until
it becomes broken near the top, then move left to a belay on the adjacent rib.
Scramble to the top.

Scuttle   60m   Scottish VS   *(1960)*
Right of the centre of the bulging black Evil Wall is a small grass ledge at 10m.
Climb to this, then go up and right on rotten rock to escape onto easy ground.
Belay. Find a way through the tangle of ribs above.

HOLLY TREE CRAG

Map p360

Right of Samson's Ribs, above a roadside bench, is a large crag with a weather-
beaten holly at the top.

Holly Tree Slab   45m   Very Difficult
Start right of a black wall at the right edge of the crag. Climb to a ledge, then take
a wall leftwards to reach easy ground above a recess. Continue in this direction
over slabs to finish at the holly tree.

MOON CRAG

Map p360

About 100m right of Holly Tree Crag is a small black crag with overhangs on its
left side and a slabby wall on the right. The crag is apparently named after a
certain Doctor Moon, but why, and who, what or when he was remains obscure.

Overhanging Route No.2   15m   Severe   *(1946)*
The big bulge on the left-hand side of the crag is split by a crack. Climb to the
bulge and pull through a bush to gain the crack. Follow this to the top.

Zigzag Route   30m   Difficult
Climb the obvious pillar to a ledge, then traverse 8m left below the bulge and pull
over to a slab. Climb this diagonally right to the top.

Overhanging Route No.1   15m   Hard Severe *   *(1945)*
Climb the pillar as for the previous route and continue up the steep right-facing
corner above, passing a prominent overhang.

Short Slab Climb   10m   Severe
Climb the left wall of a right-angled corner near the right end of the crag.

LOCH CRAIG

Map p360

The long crag stretching diagonally from the low road to the high road above
Duddingston Loch is broken at its left end and rarely exceeds 8m in height. Not
worth the bother.

Moonlight Traverse   200m   Hard Severe   *(1946)*
A complete traverse of the crag from right to left. Loose rock and death by gorse
bushes.

GIRNAL CRAIG

Map p360

This is the secluded crag below the road, which forms a promontory into
Duddingston Loch. On the left-hand side of the cliff a buttress, above some large
boulders, abuts the main face. The following routes start from the top of this
buttress; no doubt others have been done. Gorse and other jaggies restrict access
to the routes.

Barbed Wire Route   15m   Very Difficult *(1946)*
Starting from the highest point of the buttress, move to the left of a small overhang then climb to the top.

Red Slab   15m   Hard Severe
Some 5m right of Barbed Wire Route is a prominent red slab. Gain this from the left and climb it to the top.

BLACKFORD HILL

This prominent hill lies on the south side of the city, just north of the Braid Hills and is topped by various masts and the Royal Observatory. Climbers have used these small crags for many years, although they have fallen out of fashion in modern times.

Approach: Via Hermitage of Braid to the west, Braid Hills Drive to the south, Blackford Glen Road to the east and Observatory Road to the north.

BLACKFORD QUARRY

(NT 261 703)   South & West facing   Map p360

The main west-facing wall can be climbed pleasantly anywhere, increasing in difficulty from Difficult on the right to HVS on the left and is often used to introduce novices to climbing and abseiling. Protection is sparse but there are bolt belays in place at the top. At the quarry entrance is a pinnacle with one recommended route.

Quarry Pinnacle   10m   Difficult * *(1896)*
The west-facing crack. There are belay stakes at the top.

Komik Kuts   10m   Difficult *(1950s)*
Facing the pinnacle, to the west, is a miniature buttress. This route takes the corner left of the nose.

Elsewhere in the quarry there is plenty of scope for short routes and bouldering.

CORBIE'S CRAIG

(NT 256 705)   South facing   Map p360

This is a pleasant sunny crag which has lots of good incut holds. However, the climbs tend to be quite serious due to the lack protection and the loose nature of the harder routes. It is well defended by ferocious gorse bushes.

Slab and Tower   12m   Difficult * *(1950s)*
Start below a green slab at the extreme left end of the cliff. Climb the right corner of the slab then traverse right on sloping holds under an overhang to finish up the steep final tower.

Moderate Route   15m   Moderate *(1950s)*
Take an indefinite line up the left flank of Retromingent Ridge.

Retromingent Ridge   30m   Moderate ** *(1950s)*
The ridge forming the left edge of the front face of the cliff. Climb straight up to a large block at 10m, then trend right and finally back left near the top. Good climbing, but with little protection and no belay at the top.

Sunny Scoop   30m   Difficult *(1950s)*
The gorse-filled groove right of Retromingent Ridge can be climbed avoiding most of the gorse, with care! There are a choice of finishes.

Queasy Slab   30m   HVS 4c   *(1950s)*
Right of Sunny Scoop is a big undercut slab. Climb the right edge of the slab round an overhang. Move right past a small gorse, then go straight up to finish up the open groove above. A good start but loose higher up.

Whinchat   35m   VS 4b *
From the elm tree at the foot of the crag climb up and left under overhangs and over a large gorse to a hanging slab. Move right across this to the arete and finish directly. Poorly protected. Starting about 2m left and slightly above the ele tree to meet the route before the gorse avoids the brambles at the base. It is also possible to finish boldly straight up from the gorse at the same grade.

Burning Bush   35m   HVS 4c
Start just right of the elm tree. Climb an orange slab for 3m, then climb the obvious left-trending line to a small pinnacle. Finish easily up a corner.

La Folie   30m   HVS 4c
Climb a black slab 2m right of Burning Bush to a gorse bay. Stand on a block on the right and step onto the slab above. From the top of the slab make a scary swing right onto the arete, where Fast and Loose is joined at the peg.

Fast and Loose   25m   Very Difficult   *(1950s)*
At the right side of the crag, where it starts to turn uphill, are two 2m walls one above the other. Climb these, then ascend diagonally left to reach an arete (peg runner). Finish up the obvious groove above.

The Trap   20m   Very Difficult
From midway along the diagonal traverse of Fast and Loose pull out right at an ivy and continue by slabs and grooves to finish trapped in gorse bushes.

CAERKETTON HILL

(NT 237 663)   Map p350

This Pentland hill has some climbing high up and to the west of the Hillend Ski Slope. The routes are rather discontinuous, vegetated and of an easy nature, however the situation is highly attractive. Some of the great names in Scottish mountaineering have climbed here, so it is hoped that would-be explorers will bring a suitably reverent approach.

ROSLIN GLEN

(NT 280 632)   Maps p350, 376

The deep tree covered glen of the River North Esk lies some 10km south of the centre of Edinburgh, between Penicuik and Loanhead. Hidden among the trees on either side of the glen are several sandstone outcrops which provide a large number of mostly short hard routes.

   Unfortunately, a number of factors have limited the area's popularity. The rock varies from solid, knobbly and pocketed to frighteningly friable and sandy, while the dense undergrowth and thick summer foliage makes finding and accessing some crags difficult and can give the glen an oppressive and midgy atmosphere. Finally, the cliffs on the East Bank of the river can be awkward to reach and there have been access problems on some of them.

WEST BANK

General Approach: Leave the A701 for Roslin. At the village continue straight ahead down Chapel Loan, signposted for Rosslyn Chapel, to various car parks. Continue along the road past the caravan site, fork right onto a track and follow

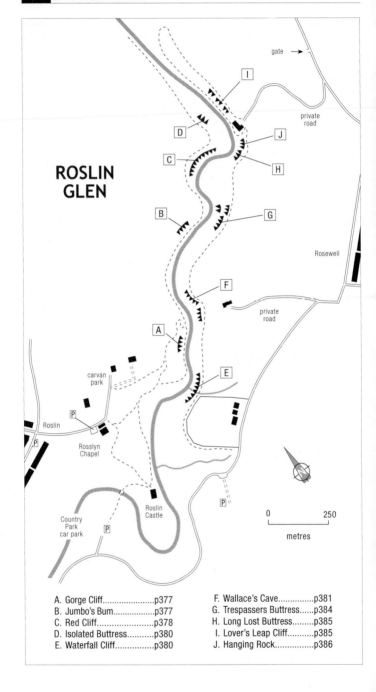

ROSLIN GLEN

A
B
C
D
J
H
G
F
E
I

gate →

private road

private road

Rosewell

carvan park

P Roslin

P

Rosslyn Chapel

Roslin Castle

Country Park car park

P

P

0   250

metres

the path to the woods at the top of the glen. Follow the path which zig zags straight down to the river bank. On the descent, Wallace's Cave can be seen on the opposite bank. Cliffs are described south to north.

Gorge Cliff

Map p376

This scrappy crag rises straight from the path and is characterised by a large roof.

Approach: From the riverside turn right (upstream) and follow the riverside path for about 100m.

Absentee Landlord   15m   HVS 5a   (1991)
Scramble over subsiding sods and brambles to the left side of a projecting wall below the roof. Climb up on pockets, then go over ledges trending left to pull over the final roof at its left end.

The Slater's Revenge   15m   Severe   (1985)
Start 4m right of Absentee Landlord at the right side of the projecting wall. Climb up on pockets to an overhang, step left and continue up to surmount the final roof at the right-hand side.

Jumbo's Bum

Map p376   Diagram p379

The first crag downstream is open and sunny and one of the more popular in the glen. The corners at either end of the left-hand buttress have been climbed at Severe. The small upper buttress has various short problems.

Approach: From the riverside, turn left (downstream) and follow the path to the crag.

1 Rock All Over Me   10m   E4 6a   (1985)
Climb the arete right of the corner at the left end of the buttress to three large pockets. Pull up and make awkward moves round the left side of the bulge above to reach good holds.

2 Bum Fun   10m   E5 6a   (1988)
Climb the wall just left of Centre Line and, using a large pocket, climb into a runnel and finish out left. Serious.

3 Centre Line   10m   HVS 5a *   (1976)
Follow a line of holds in the centre of the buttress to a crack splitting the final bulge.

4 The Forty-Twa   10m   E4 5c **   (1985)
Start just right of Centre Line. Climb 3m to reach a smooth scoop and continue with difficulty to a recess right of a projecting flange. Either finish directly or traverse right and climb a groove in the arete. Low in the grade.

5 Monodoigtism   10m   E2 6b   (1988)
Climb the hanging pillar immediately right of The Forty-Twa using a one finger pocket and a pebble on the right wall. Finish more easily up the wall on the right. Escapable.

6 Dangleberries   15m   E4 6a   (1988)
A girdle of the left-hand buttress. Gain the ledge above the crux of Monodoigtism from the right, move up and left under the bulge of Centre Line and continue left to finish up the crux of Rock All Over Me.

7 Jumbo's Proctoscopy   10m   E3 5c   *(1992)*
Climb the central corner to below the overhang. Move left to get established above
the bulge and finish up the short crack capped by a tree. A sandy route suitable
for beach bums.

8 Turn the other Cheek   10m   E3 5c   *(1992)*
Climb the left side of the right arete (buttock) to ledges, then pull through the
centre of the bulge and finish leftwards at a crack.

Red Cliff

Map p376

This is the long line of red cliffs on a bend in the river beyond the Jumbo's Bum.
Although the cliff is large and reasonably solid, the rock has a very sandy surface.

Approach: From the riverside, turn left (downstream) and follow the path past
Jumbo's Bum to where it starts to rise above the crag, which can be seen ahead
through the trees. Either bushwhack unpleasantly along the river bank or abseil
from above via any convenient tree, about 20m before reaching a fence and stile.
The first three routes start from a grassy ledge high up at the left end of the cliff.
Abseil from a tree below a small rock outcrop with a rounded black recess, 40m
before the fence, and belay on the ropes.

Red Face   10m   E2 5c   *(1985)*
Gain and climb a short right-facing corner-crack 3m above the ledge, then trend
left to the top.

Gruesome Gamboge   10m   E4 5c   *(1985)*
Start 3m right of Red Face. Climb 3m to a small pocket, reach a jug above, pull up
and traverse right to a ledge. Step back left to gain a thin curving rib and use this
precariously to reach the ledge above and the top.

Pinky and Perky   10m   E2 5c   *(1985)*
From the start of Gruesome Gamboge follow a line of holds up and right to sloping
ledges. Climb the thin rib above to a ledge and pull onto grass above.

Incarnadine   15m   HVS 5a   *(1991)*
Right of the previous three routes is an unpleasant corner. Climb this moving right
near the top to finish as for Panama Red.

Panama Red   20m   E3 6a *   *(1985)*
This route takes the obvious wide crack through the overhang just right of the
corner. Climb a green groove and mantelshelf onto a ledge on the left. Struggle up
the wide crack above, then head to the infirmary for a skin graft.

Brown Sugar   20m   E3 5c   *(1985)*
About 5m right of Panama Red is a flake. Climb the crack on its left until it is
possible to step onto the steep wall on the left. Make an awkward move to reasonable holds, pull over a bulge on the left to reach a ledge and continue more easily
to the top.

Red Ringer   20m   E2 5b   *(1985)*
Climb the thin groove 3m left of Old Red Eye to the top of a large flake and
mantelshelf onto a ledge above. Pull up and right, then step left and pull onto a
ledge. Climb more easily to the top.

Old Red Eye   20m   E2 5c   *(1985)*
The obvious left-facing corner with a tiny beech tree at the start.

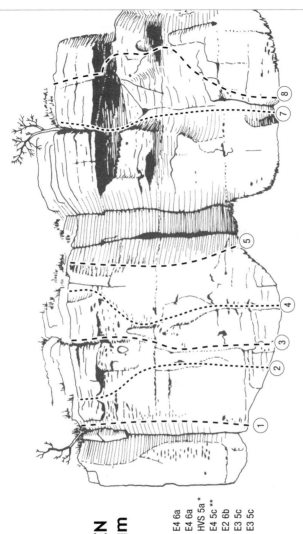

ROSLIN GLEN
Jumbo's Bum

1. Rock All Over Me — E4 6a
2. Bun Fun — E4 6a
3. Centre Line — HVS 5a *
4. The Forty-Twa — E4 5c **
5. Mortodoigtism — E2 6b
7. Jumbo's Proctoscopy — E3 5c
8. Turn the other Cheek — E3 5c

Red Wedge   20m   E3 6a   *(1985)*
Climb the slim groove 10m right of Old Red Eye to a ledge. Traverse right and move up to a corner, which is followed to a larger ledge. Easy ground leads to the top.

Dusty Road   20m   E4 6b *   *(1985)*
At the right end of the cliff are a series of corners. Approach by walking down from the path and upstream along the river bank. This route takes a short wide corner below and slightly right of a large fir tree which overhangs the cliff. Climb to a ledge on the right, then the groove above.

The short tier above the Red Cliff sports two micro routes. The central slabby arete with a break at one third-height is **Veg-hog** (E2 5b), and the rightmost arete is **Time Waster** (VS 5a).

Isolated Buttress

Map p376

Beyond the Red Cliff a buttress with a prominent overhanging nose can be glimpsed down to the right.

Approach: From the riverside, turn left (downstream) and follow the path past Jumbo's Bum and the Red Cliff.

Faustus Entor   12m   HVS 5a *   *(1985)*
The wall left of the overhanging nose. Climb up left until the right wall can be gained. Continue up and right, passing a ledge with a rounded spike, to the top.

Ham Jam   6m   VS 4c   *(1980)*
The obvious short jam crack right of the overhanging nose.

EAST BANK

Approach: From the West Bank it is possible to wade across the river in the vicinity of Wallace's Cave and south (upstream) of Gorge Cliff when the water is low, but this is often not an option. Fallen trees sometimes span the river at this point, aiding a crossing, but again this is often not an option.
   However, the most reliable approach for cliffs on the East Bank is to continue through Roslin village to a left turn signposted Rosslynlee and Rosewell. Wind down to the river then up the other side to park in the layby on the right at the Scottish Wildlife Trust Roslin Reserve (NT 278 626). Walk a short distance towards Rosewell, then follow a path on the left round a field to a faint path in the trees high above the river. Cliffs are described south to north.

Waterfall Cliff

Map p376

This atmospheric cliff lies about 350m south (upstream) from Wallace's Cave and is in several sections with the waterfall obvious in the centre.

Approach: The cliff is difficult to locate from the high path. If the river in the vicinity of Gorge Cliff is low enough to wade, then this might be the easiest approach.

Rufus   6m   E2 6a   *(1985)*
Some 80m left of the waterfall is a long low roof. Start below two obvious pockets near the right end. Gain the lip, move right and mantelshelf onto the ledge above. Scramble up to a belay.

Praying Mantel   12m   E2 5a/b   *(1986)*
Climb to an obvious circular recess above the right end of the long roof. Step right

and climb up left to an awkward mantelshelf onto a ledge. Pull over a bulge to the top. Often dirty.

Last Slap　6m　HVS 5a *(1986)*
Gain the shelf 3m left of Aficionado, then traverse left and pull onto the next shelf. Finish by climbing onto the big tree on the left.

Aficionado　12m　HVS 5a * *(1991)*
The cliff stretching left from the waterfall has a prominent left-facing prow and corner. Climb the corner and traverse right to the prow. Finish straight up.

The next four routes take the grossly overhanging cliff right of the waterfall. The finishes to these climbs tend to become dirty and will probably require cleaning before an ascent.

Edge of Darkness　15m　E3 6a * *(1985)*
In the gloom immediately right of the waterfall is an overhanging crack, gained by traversing left along a shelf. Much better than it appears.

Walk On By　15m　E6/7 6c ** *(1992)*
Rather steep. Start on the shelf as for Edge of Darkness and climb up to where Survival of the Fattest moves right. Undercut left and make very powerful moves on tiny holds (passing an in-situ nut) to gain a break. Move up and right onto the slab to finish up easier ground.

Survival of the Fattest　15m　E5 6a ** *(1992)*
Equally steep but on larger holds. Start on the shelf as for Edge of Darkness. Climb to the start of a flake handrail leading right, then move along it until moves can be made straight up (via a letter box handhold) to join Piano Player. Finish up this.

Piano Player　20m　E5 6a ** *(1985)*
A wild traverse across the most overhanging part of the cliff. Climb a short corner at the right-hand side to a tree, then follow a line of small holds on the left to large breaks and the arete. Have a breather then set off on a horizontal traverse, exiting with difficulty onto the ledge at the far end.

Syzygy　6m　HVS 5b *(1991)*
About 30m right of the waterfall is a damp overhung bay. Climb the stepped groove at its left-hand side, then escape out left at the top.

The Flying Start　10m　VS 4c * *(1991)*
Gain the upper part of Syzygy by hand traversing from halfway up Mein Sumph.

Mein Sumph　8m　HVS 5a *(1985)*
Climb the left-trending overhanging corner in the centre of the bay.

Ruff Stuff　6m　E3 6a *(1985)*
Pull over the bulge right of Mein Sumph to gain and climb a tiny crack on the left. Make an awkward move to exit.

Wallace's Cave

Map p376　Diagrams p382

This cliff is in two sections separated by a muddy overgrown gully. The right-hand cliff contains the cave (used as a hideout during the Wars of Independence in 1330 by Sir Alexander Ramsay and 65 soldiers!).

Approach: Follow the high path past the top of the Waterfall Cliff to a better path and descent to Wallace's Cave.

ROSLIN GLEN
Wallace's Cave – Left

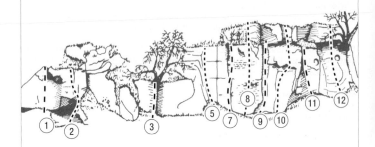

1. Scotch Corner	E2 6a *	8. The Wrinklies	E3 5c **
2. Cave Crack	HVS 5a	9. Robin Hood	VS 4c *
3. Basil Brush	VS 5a	10. Hezbollah	E6 6b **
5. Rampo	E2 5b *	11. Little John	VS 5a
7. Claymore Crack	E1 5c	12. Belly Bulger	HVS 5b

Wallace's Cave – Right

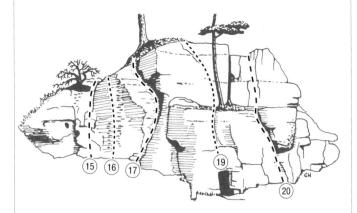

15. Dougie's Route	HVS 5b *		
16. Day of the Jockal	E2 6a *	19. Duncrankin	E4 6a **
17. Gorton Crack	Very Difficult *	20. Harry Dodder's Crack	E1 5b *

From the cave entrance continue left and cross the unpleasant gully to reach the left-hand cliff.

Left-Hand Cliff

Diagram p382

1 Scotch Corner   7m   E2 6a *   (1992)
About 10m left of a shallow cave at the left end of the cliff is a clean open groove. Climb this on small edges and undercuts.

2 Cave Crack   8m   HVS 5a   (1985)
Near the left end of the cliff is a shallow cave. Climb the crack springing from the roof and transfer into the left-hand crack above.

3 Basil Brush   6m   VS 5a   (1991)
The short mossy open corner 7m left of Rampo has a few moves on rock.

4 Gadaffi's Ear   8m   E2 5b   (1992)
Just down and left of Rampo is a curving flake-crack. Climb this to a grass ledge. Step up and right and make a 'cosmic rockover' to finish as for Rampo.

5 Rampo   8m   E2 5b *   (1985)
Climb the obvious left-trending scooped groove, stepping left near the top.

6 The Thin Crack   8m   E1 5c   (1985)
The thin crack immediately right of Rampo. Often dirty.

7 Claymore Crack   10m   E1 5c   (1991)
Climb the crack behind a tree to a ledge on the right and fight through bushes to finish. The grade is reduced to VS 4c if the tree is used.

8 The Wrinklies   10m   E3 5c **   (1985)
Boldly climb the wrinkled wall right of the tree to a ledge on the right. Gain a larger ledge on the left and finish up a short wall. Superb.

9 Robin Hood   10m   VS 4c *
The obvious chimney above a sandy terrace.

10 Hezbollah   10m   E6 6b **   (1989)
Climb the open groove and overhang 3m right of the obvious chimney with increasing difficulty. Unprotected.

11 Little John   8m   VS 5a
The shorter wider chimney 5m right of Robin Hood.

The facet of rock left of Little John has been climbed at 6b with runners and easy escape into that route.

12 Belly Bulger   10m   HVS 5b   (1986)
Near the right end of the cliff is a large bulge high up. Surmount this on the right, using a runner on an obvious branch.

Right-Hand Cliff

Diagram p382

13 The Climbist   6m   VS 5a   (1985)
Pull over a roof at the extreme left end and continue to the top.

EDINBURGH AREA

14 Ruggosities   8m   HVS 5b   *(1986)*
Start at an obvious oval hole. Pull over a bulge, climb a steep pocketed slab and
surmount an overhang using a tree.

15 Dougie's Route   10m   HVS 5b *
Climb the shallow groove 3m right of the oval hole to reach an overhang. Pull out
right and climb a wide crack to the top.

16 Day of the Jockal   8m   E2 6a *   *(1985)*
Climb directly up the wrinkly wall just right of Dougie's Route.

17 Gorton Crack   12m   Very Difficult *
Climb the corner-crack which trends right then left to finish at a big pine tree.

18 Robert the Moose   12m   E4 6a *   *(1985)*
Start up Gorton Crack and climb to an obvious hole on the wall above. Pull out
onto the front face and climb boldly to the top. Low in the grade.

19 Duncrankin   20m   E4 6a **   *(1986)*
Start at the entrance to Wallace's Cave and climb 10m to a ledge. Excellent thin
face climbing up the wall left of the wide crack leads to the top. Easier for the tall.
Bold climbing; a belay is often taken at the pine tree ledge.

20 Harry Dodder's Crack   15m   E1 5b *   *(1985)*
Start 4m right of the cave. Follow a flake-crack to the ledge, then climb the short
crack and wall above.
Variation: **HVS 5a**   *(1989)*
Climb to the ledge then finish up the wide crack on the left.

21 Scots Wha Hae   15m   E3 5c   *(1985)*
This is the right arete of the buttress. Climb an orange pillar above a roof for 2m
to reach holds on the front face. Continue up the arete (crux) until good holds can
be reached on the left. Easier climbing leads back to the arete to finish.

22 Hoppy's Least Favourite   8m   Hard Severe   *(1991)*
The chimney right of Scots Wha Hae, finishing direct.

Trespasser's Buttress

Map p376

Halfway between Jumbo's Bum and the Red Cliff, on the East Bank of the river, are
a number of crags known collectively as Trespasser's Buttress.

Approach: Follow the high path past the descent to Wallace's Cave, until the crag
is glimpsed down to the left. Descend at the far end, about 15m before a stile.

Just below the path is a short wall giving a number of extended boulder problems.
The first of these is **Feel Free** (HVS 5a), the crack at the left-hand end. The twin
cracks 3m to the right are taken by **Precious Groan** (VS 5a); the crux is the bulging
start. Another 5m right again is **Lazy Diamond** (VS 5a). The obvious open corner
is **Stem Gem** (E2 6a *), again with the crux at the start, and immediately right is
Cruel Jewel (E2 5c). The groove with a rounded recess is **Diamond Punters** (VS
5a) and the wide crack is **Welly Boot Crack** (VS 5a).

About 10m below and right is the start of a much larger wall with a gnarly tree

Decidedly Dodgy. HVS 5a, Fourth Quarry, Cambusbarron.
Climbers Alan Pert & Eddie McHutchison
(photo Chuck Pettigrew)

overhanging a gloomy recess in the centre.

Shinbones Field   12m   E1 5c   *(1986)*
Start at the left side of the wall, well left of the tree. Climb a thin crack to a ledge,
step right, gain a second ledge and climb a short wall to reach a crack which leads
to the top.

The Shouting Man   20m   E5 6b *   *(1990)*
This takes the smooth wall left of the gnarly tree. Starting from a holly bush, hand
traverse right and pull over an overhang. Climb up and right, then using flakes and
a pocket gain the break. Finish straight up.

Strange Apparatus   10m   VS 4c   *(1991)*
Start just right of the gloomy recess. Gain the obvious flake-crack from the left and
climb it, passing a small cave.

Two Tier Crack   10m   E1 5c *   *(1986)*
This route lies on the small buttress below Stem Gem. Climb the obvious layback
crack, step left and climb a similar crack to the top.

Long Lost Buttress

Map p376

This is the cliff with a metal fence at the top, about 50m south from Lover's Leap
Cliff.

Approach: Follow the high path past Wallace's Cave and Trespasser's Buttress.
Abseil from a fir tree to a vegetated ledge below a wrinkled wall on the right side
of the buttress and belay on the abseil rope.

The Chocolate Orgasm   15m   E1 5a *   *(1993)*
Climb a scoop on the left side of the wrinkled wall (bold) until it is possible to pull
left onto a slab. Climb the crack above and pull onto another slab, and so to the
top.

Lover's Leap Cliff

Map p376

This is the big cliff overhanging the river just south of Hawthornden Castle. There
is a metal fence at the top. In the past the landowner has not permitted access, but
it is not yet known how this will be affected by improved rights of access under the
2003 Land Reform Act. The routes are described in the hope that access will
become possible in the future.

Approach: Follow the high path past Wallace's Cave, Trespasser's Buttress and
Long Lost Buttress. On the right side of the cliff is a large rock ledge with a smaller
pepermint covered ledge below. Abseil to the peppermint ledge and belay.

Always the Sun   30m   E5 6b *   *(1992)*
The route awaits a first pitch! Move left off the ledge onto a narrow red ledge.
Climb an open green groove and step right to gain the large rock ledge. Step left
onto a rib and climb this (poor rock) to a thin crack (runners). Go up this then move
left onto wrinkled rock where a hard move gains an awkward rest below the big
overhang. Use a large hold on the lip to gain the vicious finger-crack in the back of
the bottomless corner above and left. Wriggle up this to a small ledge and finish
up the fine strenuous jam crack above.

Pain Pillar, VS 4c, The Hawkcraig. Climber Chris Anderson
(photo Cubby Images)

Hanging Rock

Map p376

These three separate buttresses near Hawthornden Castle have the best climbing in the glen. In the past the landowner has not permitted access, but it is not yet known how this will be affected by improved rights of access under the 2003 Land Reform Act. The routes are described in the hope that access will become possible in the future.

Approach: Across fields from the road between Poltonhall and Rosewell, starting at two metal gates. Alternatively, approach along the high path as for the other East Bank cliffs to pass below Hawthornden Castle.

Left-Hand Buttress

Rock Lobster   15m   VS 4c   (1991)
The zigzag line of wide cracks on the left-hand side.

Hanging Rock   20m   E4 5c *   (1985)
Bold climbing up the gobsmacking arete. Climb the left wall of the arete to the first break. Above, the arete forms a flat frontal face. Climb the left edge until it is possible to pull onto the front and go up to a second break. Climb up and right (crux) to gain and climb a wide crack. Finish more easily.

Give 'em Enough Rope...   20m   E5/6 6b **   (1992)
This takes the middle of the steep right hand wall of the buttress. Climb a hollow flake to the break. Move left to a wedged block before climbing the shallow runnel above. Move back right and go up to a better hold, then make a long reach to join Deep in Diana.

Deep in Diana   15m   HVS 5b *   (1988)
Start well up right of the arete and climb a dirty groove to a bush. Now make a spectacular hand traverse using a monster juggy flake on the left wall, to finish up an awkward wide black crack.

Central Buttress

There is good all weather bouldering here.

No Picnic   12m   E2 6a *   (1985)
On the left side of the buttress is a wrinkled wall. Climb a shallow groove on the left to a small roof, pull over to a recess and continue to a ledge. Finish up a thin crack.

Plunging Neckline   15m   E3 5b **   (1985)
Climb the right edge of the wrinkled wall for 6m to reach a poor spike (Friend runners on the right). Step right onto the front face, move up, step right again and boldly climb a steep slab to a tree. The crux is just below the top (make sure it's clean!).

Beyond Traprain   20m   E4 6b **   (1980)
The prominent crack splitting the big roof in the centre of the buttress provides Roslin's answer to Separate Reality. A groove leads to the roof and gymnastic climbing leads out and around the lip into the groove above.

The Cue   15m   E2 5c/6a *   (1985)
Gain and climb the right edge of the short wall below the big roof. Reach right and pull over into a peapod groove. From the horizontal break above, move left and finish up a steep slab.

Enzyme   12m   VS 5a   (1985)
The short overhung chimney on the right leads to a corner-crack and a dirty finish.

Right-Hand Buttress

Roslin Roulette   20m   E6 6b ***   (1988)
An audacious route up the left wall of the buttress. Start at a square recess and climb to a ledge at 5m. Move left and climb the right-trending arete until a step right can be made onto a steep ribbed scoop. Climb up (possible runners in Gaping Gab) and pull out left onto the steep slabby headwall using a good hidden flake. Make hard moves up then left to finish at a welcome branch. Excellent bold climbing.

Gaping Gab   20m   E2 5c ***   (1980)
Continuously interesting crack climbing. Start as for Roslin Roulette and climb 5m to a ledge and recess left of a large roof. Climb a crack up and right to a small ledge above the roof, then continue up until a move left can be made into another crack on the crest of the buttress. Follow this to the top.

Eddie the Eejit   20m   E3 6a *   (1988)
This is the big roof overhanging the path. Place runners in Gaping Gab, then traverse right under the roof. Make some powerful moves out and over the roof, then climb a short crozzly wall to the small ledge of Gaping Gab. Move right up a slab to finish at the same point as Voice in the Dark.

The Golden Apple of Eternal Desire   20m   E4 6b *   (1991)
The widest part of the roof right of Eddie provides a hard problem. Climb to a hidden thread under the roof then make a huge reach to the lip, cut loose and power up and over. Finish up Eddie or go straight up the arete above. (A skyhook runner was placed on the jug above the right end of the overhang on the first ascent). So named because it goes way over the top!

Voice in the Dark   15m   E3 5c *   (1987)
The obvious slabby corner and chimney right of the nose of the buttress gives a strenuous but well protected struggle.

Under Pressure   15m   E3 6a   (1986)
High on the right is a smooth corner. Climb past a holly bush to enter and climb the corner, exiting left at the top.

Life in the Bus Lane   12m   E3 5c   (1988)
Climb the arete at the right edge of the buttress, with an excursion left to place runners at the holly bush.

CARLOPS ROCK

(NT 162 557)   Map p350
The village of Carlops is 25km south of Edinburgh on the A702. The rock is a prominent feature in the centre of the village. It is often used for abseil practice and, although the rock is fairly loose, it also has a few climbs. The best of these is the obvious line up the front face, **Pentland Squire** (E2 5b).

EAST LOTHIAN & BERWICKSHIRE COAST

0 — 5 kilometres

for Edinburgh
Area see map
p350

To Edinburgh

EAST LOTHIAN

More than 60 new routes have been done in this area and almost all are in the lower grades. Of the new venues, Craigy Hill is worth a visit, while some of the routes at North Berwick Quarry are useful additions for climbers looking for some evening entertainment. The massive quarry at Traprain Law offers routes of a more adventurous nature altogether. Of the long established areas, Traprain Law remains popular, as do the sports routes at North Berwick Law. The former are as polished as ever, while the latter have recently been re-equiped and lower-offs added.

YELLOW CRAIGS

(NT 512 757)   West facing   Map p388

This small compact crag lies in the Garleton Hills north of Haddington and offers a nice view and pleasant evening cragging in the lower grades. Unfortunately the base of much of the crag is guarded by gorse bushes.

Approach: The crag is right beside the Drem road, north of Haddington. Drive past the crag and park with care in a lay-by on the right, just after the brow of the hill. Cross the stone stile, turn right and descend the field to the crag.

The right-hand side of the crag is clear of gorse at the bottom and all the routes lie to the left of this clearing, just into the gorse. Routes are described from right to left.

Introductory Slapping   10m   Very Difficult   *(2003)*
Just inside the gorse on the left edge of the clearing is a small rock ledge. From here pull over a steep section to a nice clean ramp with a runner at half-height, moving left at the bulge.

Slippers and Slopers   10m   Very Difficult   *(2003)*
Start as for the previous route, then move left to the centre of the slab. Go directly up the V-groove to finish as for Introductory Slapping. Hard for the grade.

Left of the slab is a blunt arete, not to be confused with the steeper brownish arete of Attack of the Gorse Fairies which has a curving crack in its left wall, Spike's Downfall.

Prickly Heat   12m   Hard Severe 4b *   *(2003)*
Either battle through the gorse and climb the steep lower section to the blunt arete, or traverse awkwardly in from the right. Move directly up the arete which gives surprisingly good climbing with few positive holds and no runners.

Attack of the Gorse Fairies   14m   VS 4c *   *(2003)*
The steep brownish arete is the crag's best line, with only a small gorse bush to spoil the fun a third of the way up. Go directly up the arete using lay-aways. A runner can be placed in the lower part of the crack at half-height. Low in the grade.

Spike's Downfall   5m   VS 4b   *(2003)*
The same shenanigans to get to the start of the route must be endured, then go up to the curving crack and ascend it directly, reaching out to the arete makes it a tad easier. Low in the grade.

CRAIGY HILL

(NT 510 765)   South-east facing   Map p388

Lucky Buttress is the obvious crag facing the road through the Garleton Hills. Natural protection is not abundant and some pegs have been placed for protection and belays. The crags are quick drying and the hill has fine views.

Approach: Further north along the Drem road from Yellow Craigs. Park in the large lay-by on the left, with Lucky Buttress obvious ahead, above the road. Walk down the road, cross over the gate on the right and ascend the bank to a natural traverse line; right to Lucky Buttress and left to Red Rocks.

LUCKY BUTTRESS

South facing

The left side of the crag is characterised by a bay of unappealing rock with an old horizontal hawthorn tree. The right side of the bay forms a stepped blunt arete; the line of the first route.

Lucky Dip   10m   Difficult *   (2002)
Pleasant climbing up the stepped blunt arete.

Lucky for Some   10m   Very Difficult   (2002)
Start just to the right and climb the centre of the steeper slab and wall to finish as for Lucky Dip.

Lucky B...   12m   VS 4c   (2002)
About 3m to the right. Climb a bulge between gorse bushes to small hawthorns where some tricky moves take you out onto a left-sloping ramp and a steep finish; take care at the top.

Lucky Break   12m   Hard Severe 4b   (2002)
To the right, a large block projects from the base of the crag. This route follows the line of ledges and niches directly above the block, until forced out and right with a strenuous move to finish.

Do You Feel Lucky?   12m   VS 4c *   (2002)
A second projecting block lies about 4m further right. The wall above the block leads to a gorse covered ledge. Climb the left-curving crack, peg runner, trend left and then direct to the top. Low in the grade.

Lucky Star   12m   VS 5a   (2003)
Start just right of the previous route below the obvious horizontal break in the lower wall. Climb short steep wall via a flake-crack to the gorse covered ledge and finish up and right.

Easy Rider   12m   Hard Severe 4b   (2004)
The broken rib 3m right of Lucky Star gives poorly protected climbing. Follow the rib until forced left to a good hold and easier ground. Ascend directly to the top.

Lucky I Only Tore my Ligaments on This   12m   VS 4c * (2003)
Some 4m right of this and right of a shattered flake-line, there is a bulge in the lower part of the wall. Climb the bulge direct, or easier to the right or left, and ascend directly past a peg runner, keeping to the left of the gorse, to climb a tier of blocks with several pockets and a sharp large hold to the top.

Nay Luck   12m   Hard Severe 4c   (2003)
Start as for the last line but move steeply up and right below the gorse to a large foothold and a finish on good holds.

Lucky Ticket   10m   Hard Severe   (2003)
To the right an arete juts out from the crag, forming a prominent groove on its left side. Grovel up the groove until forced left onto the face.

Un Lucky Arete   8m   Severe 4b   (2003)

The arete is festooned with runners (in your dreams).

Un Lucky 13   10m   Severe 4b *(2003)*
A straightforward wall leads to a steeper friable finish,

Lucky the Cat   10m   Very Difficult *(2003)*
Up a steep short wall to a harder more delicate finish.

Lucky Traverse   100m   5a *(2003)*
Traverse the entire crag, rarely more than 2m from the ground.

Little Black Roof   12m   Hard Severe 4b *(2004)*
The last steep wall before easy slabs at the far right side of the crag gives an unprotected route. Climb to the obvious black overlap and ascend on positive small holds to the top.

RED ROCKS

North-West facing

The north side of the hill has a striking boulder sitting on top of a short vertical wall. The following routes are described from right to left. The first three are boulder problems.

Scum Bag 1   5m   6a * *(2002)*
Climb up the steep wall and the right side of the block.

The Tomb Stone   5m   6c ** *(2003)*
Climb directly up the centre of the block using the break for your feet and hands, then up for a small pinch to gain the large finishing holds.

Scum Bag 2   5m   5c * *(2002)*
Climb the left side of the block with a long reach to the crucial right hand hold.

Lothian Crack   10m   VS 5a ** *(2002)*
This is the central line. A slabby wall leads to horizontal breaks, followed by a short steep crack to a ledge. Finish up the blunt arete above. Low in the grade.
Variation: **Lothian Crack Variation   4c *** *(2002)*
Takes the ramp leading right from the steep crack and the wall above.

Lothian Arete   10m   VS 4c *(2002)*
Follow the arete left of Lothian Crack finishing up the blunt arete.

To the left several short steep walls and aretes give bouldering, mostly around 4b to 4c.

NORTH BERWICK LAW

(NT 554 839)   South facing   Map p388

The impressively pointed hill just south of North Berwick offers a selection of routes in very different styles and traditions. Most of the routes are in the quarry on the south side of the law, which is characterised by a steep Main Face and a slab, at right-angles to each other.

Further right lie a number of other walls and slabs to which various traditional routes have been added, mainly in the mid to lower grades. The rock is generally not as good as on the Main Face and routes have not had much traffic; the tops need particular care. Routes have also been added to buttress above and left of the car park. The crags, especially the quarry Main Face, dry quickly after rain.

Approach: At the south end of the town, beyond Law Primary School a narrow, signposted road leads to a car park. Car Park Buttress lies above and to the left, Middle Buttress is next and Skyline Arete some 500m left and above the car park. For North Berwick Law Quarry walk to the right around the base of the hill until the quarry comes into view on the left.

CAR PARK BUTTRESS

Seismic Activity   20m   Very Difficult *(1997)*
Start at the lower left side of the crag below a crack. Move up to the crack for a few moves then follow the good footholds up and right to the next route. Instead of topping out below the bulge go across the face at three-quarters height and finish up the left-hand crack.

A Right Crack   10m   Difficult *(1997)*
At the right side of the crag go up the easy slabs to gain the big crack, follow this to the top.

MIDDLE BUTTRESS

The Advocate   15m   VS 4c * *(1997)*
Start a couple of metres right of the arete, up the wall to the bulge, move left with difficulty into the V-groove. Go up this to a steep finish below a gorse bush, climb over the top to a nice stake belay.

The following route is some 500m left of the car park. Go directly up the hill from a large old silver trunked tree to where two aretes are separated by a grassy gully.

Skyline Arete   25m   Difficult *(1997)*
The right-hand blunt arete is always escapable but gives a fine easy outing with magnificent views across the forth. Simply follow the cleanest line of rock to the top. A spike belay can be found 10m over to the left. Go up the grass to the path off to the left and descend only when past the clump of trees.

NORTH BERWICK LAW QUARRY

Main Face

Overhanging and clean, this face offers a number of strenuous sports routes, whose bolts were replaced shortly before this guide was published, and lower-offs added. Lawbreaker Slab to the right also has a couple of bolt protected routes.

Necktie   10m   F6b+ *(1989)*
The right-hand side of the left arete of the steep wall past five bolts to a lower-off.

Fogtown   10m   F7a ** *(1989)*
The next line right of the arete past four bolts to the Necktie lower-off.

Eliminate Law   10m   F7c *(1992)*
Climb the narrow strip of rock between Fogtown and Law of Gravity, protected by the bolts on these routes. Almost too contrived to exist.

Law of Gravity   10m   F7a ** *(1989)*
The line of five bolts, starting at a short corner and climbing direct to the lower-off. Not the most technical route on the wall, but very sustained. The fingery start, coming in from the left boosts it to 7a+.

Jaws of the Law   10m   F6c ** *(1989)*
The left-hand of three routes, starting from a ledge 3m up, has some reachy initial moves. Four bolts to a lower-off.

Law of the Flies   10m   F7a ** *(1989)*
Anyone under six foot tall will find this tough. Four bolts and a lower-off.

Law and Disorder   10m   F6a+ * *(1989)*
At the right-hand end of the wall, a dynamic start gains a line of four bolts passing a niche to a lower-off.

Law of the Rings   25m   F6c *
A left to right girdle. Start up Necktie, then take the obvious traverse line clipping the second bolts of the routes to Law of the Flies. Climb this to its third bolt, then finish up Law and Disorder.

Lawbreaker Slab

This is the red slab right of the Main Face.

Darkness Falling   10m   F6a+ * *(2003)*
This route takes the line left of the slab.

Igneous Intruder   12m   F6c *(1993)*
The left-hand route on the red slab had its two bolts missing at the time of publication and the route appears harder than the given grade.

Old Lawbreaker   12m   F6b ** *(1989)*
Climb to the right of the first two bolts at the start, using the ledge. A harder variation climbs to the left of the first two bolts at F6b+.

Wild Iris   12m   F5+ ** *(2003)*
The slab's blunt right arete, avoiding the difficulties on Old Lawbreaker.

To the right of Lawbreaker Slab the cliff is broken and dotted with gorse bushes. Two unpleasant routes have been recorded here at Severe, **Diarrhoea 1** and **Diarrhoea 2**. Right again is an obvious chimney-corner behind a sapling; the line of the next route.

Up the Spout and Out   12m   Very Difficult *(1996)*
Climb the chimney then straight up the small wall behind, stepping left at the top, or move left and go up juggy blocks. High in the grade.

Obelix Goes North   15m   Very Difficult * *(1996)*
About 9m right is a right to left broken slanting arete bordered on the left by an overhang at half-height and a sapling near the top.

The Menhir   5m   Very Difficult *(1996)*
Climb the short, outstanding arete immediately left of the big bushes to a large grass ledge.

Eejit's Wall

Right of the big gorse bushes is a seamed slab with a large grass ledge above an obvious stepped overhang just off the ground to its right. The red wall above the overhangs contains prominent parallel cracks.

Bored Stupid   15m   Severe 4b   (1996)
Climb the middle of the slab or start further right and go over a small overlap to gain the slab. Above, move left at the grassy shelf, make a long reach left and ascend blocks. Move right onto the last slab, (easy escape left), to a difficult finish.

Sod's Law   20m   VS 5a *   (1996)
A varied route in three sections following the cleanest line to the top. Start at the base of the slab and follow the left to right diagonal line. Move up, step right and ascend the short wall to a ledge. Climb the crack to the top passing a peg.

Eejit's Wall   15m   VS 5a   (1996)
Start at the shallow corner forming the right end of the stepped overhangs. Climb the wall past the grassy ledge, continue to the next grassy ledge to finish up the parallel cracks.

Needs Gear   15m   VS 4c   (1996)
Climb the narrow slab just right of Eejit's, crux, to the big ledge. Ascend just right of the grass to the block and climb wall right of the parallel cracks.

Short   5m   VS 5b   (1998)
The right edge of the short red wall to the right to the large ledge. Walk off right or finish up Needs Gear.

Sharp   5m   VS 5b   (1998)
Right again is a pale hanging wall with a horizontal overhang at the start. Climb the right edge to the large ledge.

Westy Slab

The fine slab of rock is named after the graffiti. Ropes and racks serve little purpose – there is virtually no protection – but a top-rope can be arranged by utilising a metal spike and the wobbly fence.

Technical Ecstasy   15m   VS 4c   (1996)
Thin slab just right of WESTY leads to a good ledge. Climb the arete following a line of holds just to its right to finish carefully up steep mud.

Mr Slappy   15m   VS 4c *   (1996)
Steeper and harder than it looks, the little holds appear just at the right time. Climb the centre of the thin slab, left of the features and right of Technical Ecstasy, trending very slightly right at the top to finish up turf.

Neck It or Deck It   15m   HVS 4c **   (1996)
A direct line up the right side of the slab. Move up following the small pockets to a large hold, then straight up to a well brushed hold to finish.

The large vegetated slab to the right gives the following lines

Traverse of the Sods   20m   Severe 4c   (1996)
Start at the lowest point of the slab and traverse up and right to the far end, rather green and vegetated with little to recommend it.

The Path   5m   Moderate   (1596!)
From the top of the grassy mound large holds lead to the top.

Parallel Lines Buttress

This buttress borders the grassy mound on the right and can be identified by a parallel right to left seam running its full length and a central grassy ledge near its base.

Jennifer 20m VS 4b *(1996)*
Start at the lower left side of the buttress and follow the blunt arete left of the gorse. At three-quarters height move right to clip the peg then back left to finish direct. Low in the grade.

Grasp the Nettle 20m VS 4b * *(1996)*
The thin left-hand seam is followed past the grassy ledge to the top. Finish straight up from the peg. Low in the grade.

Sarah 20m VS 4c * *(1996)*
The right-hand seam. An easy start leads to thinner moves on small holds. Low in the grade.

Peglust 18m Severe 4a *(1996)*
The right arete. Move left to the grass ledge near the top, go around it, then back right to finish.

Brutus Minimus 18m Hard Severe 4c *(2000)*
Start to the right of the last route on the steep side of the arete, left of the red wall. Climb up just left of the dodgy looking block to join the arete.

The arete right of the steep red wall becomes progressively harder to a finish on poor holds and a loose finish. The route is far worse than it looks and has been top-roped at 5b.

Overlap Buttress

To the right is a yellow and black slab with a central grassy seam, capped by earth, bush covered ledges and a rock overlap. The routes have interesting friction, but lack protection.

Slab and Tickle 8m Very Difficult *(1996)*
A poor route up the left side of the slab.

Vital Statistics 10m E1 5b * *(1996)*
Ascend just right of the vertical grassy seam to the undercling. Move right then up to a scoop and left of bushes to a split in the overlap. Finish using this. More strenuous than its neighbours.

Statistical Variations 10m E1 5b * *(1996)*
Start just right of the last route and climb directly up to the scoop to finish up the blunt arete just right of the earthy ledge.

Alderbaran 10m E1 5a * *(1996)*
Start at the right edge of the slab before the undercut base and ascend via small pockets to finish as for Statistical Variations.

The Grim Rurper 10m E1 5a *(1996)*
Gain the dark slab forming the right end of the undercut base and ascend to grass. Continue up the right side of the slab to a scoop, reach for a high pocket or a mantel to gain easier angled rock. Finish as for Statistical Variations.

Left Overs 10m HVS 4c *(1996)*
The blunt arete to the right is climbed on small incuts, a Friend can be placed at the top to protect the long traverse left to finish as for Statistical Variations.

Hadrian's Walls

To the right broken rock leads to a piece of graffiti shaped like a star, or the initials DK. A few metres up and right of this graffiti is a small wall with a bush and an earthy ledge near the top, the location for the following route.

Crescent Moon Rising   6m   Very Difficult   *(1996)*
The obvious lay away is used to gain a ledge and follow the ramp up and left to the bush and earthy ledge and a juggy finish.

A Gauling Crack   7m   Severe 4c   *(1996)*
Climb the awkward crack just to the right, via a niche near the top.

Gettafix   7m   Severe 4b   *(1996)*
Follow the left-trending line – tricky.

Hadrian's Wall   6m   Severe 4a *   *(1996)*
The wall to the left of the blunt arete is climbed on nice small holds. Low in the grade.

Caesar's Nose   7m   Very Difficult   *(1996)*
Follow the blunt arete direct to the top, a long reach right enables protection to be placed in the crack.

Finis Horriblis   7m   Very Difficult   *(1996)*
The green left-trending ramp is climbed, large Friend, to an awkward dirty finish.

To the right the wall steepens and leads round to the graffiti GBH. The steep crack-line just left of GBH has been top-roped at 5c. The climbing is good but the finish is appalling.

Solitary Soul   F6b **   *(2000)*
This route climbs through the GBH graffiti; 2 bolts to lower-off.

Anarchic Law   6m   E1 5c *   *(1996)*
Right of GBH and behind the gorse bushes, is a wall with a graffiti 'A' at its base. Climb the short wall to a peg, step right and go over the bulge. Harder than it looks.

Further to the right and round the corner is a short steep wall guarded by gorse bushes with two routes of no particular merit; **Red Wall** (Severe 4b), the cracks and **Right Red Wall** (Severe 4b).

DUNBAR

(NT 675 793)   Tidal   North facing   Map p388

This sandstone sea-cliff lies 500m west of Dunbar harbour. The rock is soft and sandy and the climbing is slightly disappointing as a result. The bolts on the projects and Celebration Day are old and should be treated with caution. The crag has seen a little renewed interest in recent years with the addition of some easier lines. These routes have fixed stainless steel bolts, coated with an anti-corrosive paint. There are belay bolts at the top.

Approach: At the end of the high street in Dunbar, turn left and continue for 200m, passing a garage on the left. Park just beyond this. Steps lead down to the coast walk. The crag is directly below and is reached by walking down and right.

Hoochie Coochie Man   8m   F5 +   *(2002)*

The obvious corner at the left end of the wall; four bolts.

Flown Back from Boston   8m   F5+   *(2001)*
The leftmost route on the wall following many pockets past four bolts. A pleasant introduction.

Reaching for the Pilot   8m   F6a+   *(2001)*
Just right of Flown Back form Boston. Climb the reachy wall past three bolts.

Aching Arms and Dragging Heels   10m   F6c+ *   *(2001)*
Follow the overhanging lip using heelhooks. At the end of the lip, crank up and follow pockets up the headwall; five bolts.

To the right, the rock becomes more sandy and the routes are rarely attempted. There are two projects before you arrive at the following route.

Celebration Day   12m   F7b   *(1991)*
The bolts on the right-hand line look old and in poor condition.

TRAPRAIN LAW

(NT 582 745)   South-East & North facing   Map p388

This is the prominent isolated hill 6km east of Haddington. It is well known both for its rock climbs and its archaeological importance; ancient settlements and Roman silver have been discovered here. The slabby cliffs of the South-East Face have been climbed on for generations and offer some excellent routes in the lower and middle grades. The North Face Quarry is quite a different proposition. Here, some impressive multi-pitch routes follow lines of least resistance, surrounded by vast areas of unstable looking ground.

SOUTH-EAST FACE

The best climbing is found on two high-angled slabs, Overhang Wall and Lammer Wall, on the south side of the hill. Here the sunny aspect, pleasant rural situation and good climbing, combine to make an attractive venue. The rock is trachyte, a fine-grained volcanic rock which is generally very solid. However, the popularity of the cliff has resulted in the rock becoming extremely polished and care must be taken to avoid sudden unexpected slips.

Approach: Leave the A1 at the Haddington turn off and enter the town. Take the first main turning on the left and cross over the River Tyne. After about 2km take a right turn signposted to Garvald and Stenton, and after another 3km turn left at a cross-roads. Park just beyond a sharp right bend and follow the field-edge path to a wooden stile.

In 2003 a severe brush and grass fire stripped much of the vegetation from above, and to the right and left of Overhang Wall and Lammer Wall, leaving little but scorched earth. This will re-grass in time, but the unstable soil and rock that has been exposed requires care.

EAST LOTHIAN

Overhang Wall

Diagram p398

This is the left-hand of the two main lower faces. It has a band of overhangs at mid height and some large flakes leaning against the face at the left end. Descent is best made on the right-hand side of the cliff.

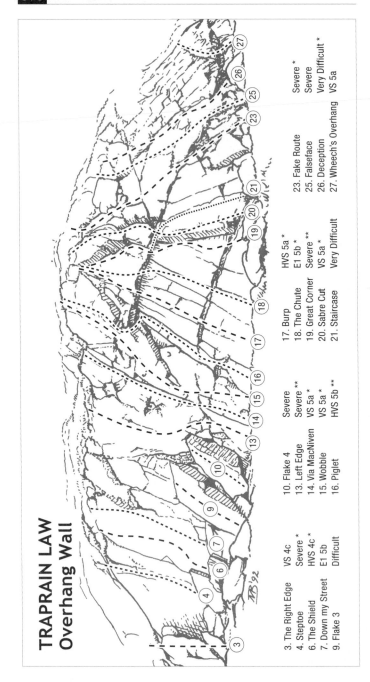

TRAPRAIN LAW
Overhang Wall

3. The Right Edge	VS 4c	10. Flake 4	Severe	17. Burp	HVS 5a *	23. Fake Route	Severe *
4. Steptoe	Severe *	13. Left Edge	Severe **	18. The Chute	E1 5b *	25. Falseface	Severe
6. The Shield	HVS 4c *	14. Via MacNiven	VS 5a *	19. Great Corner	Severe **	26. Deception	Very Difficult *
7. Down my Street	E1 5b	15. Wobble	VS 5a *	20. Sabre Cut	VS 5a *	27. Wheech's Overhang	VS 5a
9. Flake 3	Difficult	16. Piglet	HVS 5b **	21. Staircase	Very Difficult		

1 Flake 1   6m   Severe
The front face of the left-hand flake. Pull over a bulge above a recessed black boulder, then climb up and right to the top.

2 Flake 2   6m   Difficult
Climb the left side of the front face of the second flake.

3 The Right Edge   6m   VS 4c
Climb the right edge of the second flake.

4 Steptoe   15m   Severe *
Climb the prominent narrow strip of clean rock right of Flake 2.

5 Moss Groove   15m   Very Difficult
Climb the left-facing groove starting 2m right of Steptoe.

6 The Shield   15m   HVS 4c *
Start below the right arete of Moss Groove. Climb up and right into a scoop, then go up this until it is possible to pull out left onto a ledge to finish. Bold.

7 Down my Street   15m   E1 5b
A nasty route up the mossy rib right of The Shield.

8 Flake Wall   15m   Difficult
A poor climb taking the wall above Flake 3.

9 Flake 3   6m   Difficult
The slabby face of the third flake. Follow a slim right-facing groove.

10 Flake 4   5m   Severe
The triangular front face of the right-hand flake.

11 Torque   15m   HVS 5a *
The soaring corner above Flake 3. Move out right at the top.

12 Swingin'   15m   VS 5a
Follow Torque to a ledge on the right wall. Swing right round the arete to gain a sloping ledge, then follow the arete to the top.

**13 Left Edge   20m   Severe ** **
A fine route. Start just right of Flake 4 and climb up until it is possible to move left onto a sloping ledge at 10m. Continue up the obvious crack to the top.

14 Via MacNiven   20m   VS 5a *
Start 4m right of Flake 4. Climb a short wall to a small ledge, then go straight up the long slim groove which slants slightly rightwards to the top.
Variation: **VS 4c ***
From the small ledge, bridge up and move left to below a black bulge. Pull over this and climb directly to the top.

15 Wobble   20m   VS 5a *
Follow Via MacNiven to the small ledge, or better, gain it from the right. Step right and go diagonally right to a small black overlap. Climb over this, then go up and right to a sloping ledge. Pull over a bulge to another ledge, then finish more easily.

**16 Piglet   20m   HVS 5b ** **
A fine strenuous route, sadly becoming very polished. Climb the leftmost groove below the band of overhangs, then step left onto a glossy rib and pull up left over the bulge to finish up easy slabs.

EAST LOTHIAN

17 Burp   20m   HVS 5a *
Climb the next groove right of Piglet. At the overhang step onto the rib on the right, which has as much friction as a bar of soap, and make one hard move to surmount the overhang. Finish up an easy groove.

18 The Chute   20m   E1 5b *
Climb the first groove left of Great Corner to the band of overhangs. Step left and make a hard and committing move to get established on the slab above. Finish easily.

19 Great Corner   20m   Severe **
The obvious left-facing corner gives an excellent but highly polished climb. Gain the corner from a slanting shelf on the left and follow it up to a ledge on the right. Climb a groove until it is possible to regain the corner, which is then followed to the top.
Variation: **Direct Start   Hard Severe 4c**
It is possible to start directly up the corner.

20 Sabre Cut   20m   VS 5a *
Climb the arete right of Great Corner to a ledge at 10m. Finish up the short groove left of a clean nose of rock.

21 Staircase   20m   Very Difficult
Start 3m right of Great Corner. Climb a crack until it is possible to move onto the slab on the right. Climb this on good holds to the ledge at 10m, then finish up Great Corner.

22 Slab and Tickle   20m   HVS 5b
A contrived route but with some interesting moves. Climb the slab right of Staircase, moving right at the top. Go back left to below a clean nose of rock. Pull over this and finish straight up.

23 Fake Route   15m   Severe *
The left-slanting crack-line starting below some ivy. Follow the crack over an overlap to a steep flake-crack. Go up and left to gain a rib on the left and finish straight up.

24 Cat's Paw   15m   HVS 5b
Basically a variation start to Falseface. From the slab below the ivy pull rightwards over the overhang and continue up the slabs.

25 Falseface   15m   Severe
The overlapping slabs left of the twin cracks of Deception.

26 Deception   15m   Very Difficult *
The obvious twin cracks, passing left of a large flake.

Between Deception and Wheech's Overhang there are some short interesting problems.

27 Wheech's Overhang   5m   VS 5a
The large overhang low down at the right end of Overhang Wall. The initial footholds are polished to a smooth sheen.

28 The Western Girdle   60m   VS *
A traverse of Overhang Wall from left to right. It gives some good climbing but is best avoided when the crag is busy.

1. 20m 5a From Flake 3, climb up and right as for Swingin' then go horizontally right to a stance on the sloping ledge of Wobble.
2. 20m 4c Continue right below the band of overhangs to belay on the ledge at the top of the arete of Sabre Cut.
3. 20m 4a Continue rightwards to the end of the crag.

Between Overhang Wall and Lammer Wall there are some slabby ribs. Two are worth climbing.

29 Ripple Rib   15m   Severe
Climb the clean rib, skirting the small black overhang on the left.
Variation: **VS 4c**
Climb the small black overhang direct.

30 Via Dolorosa   15m   Hard Severe
Climb the clean strip of rock in the mossy face about 10m left of the deep chimney bounding Lammer Wall on the left.

Left of Overhang Wall and above a fence between two fields is a cliff with several routes of an easy nature. Above it lies a short steep wall with a few problems.

Lammer Wall

Diagram p402

This is the right-hand of the two main crags. Although it is small there are many climbs crammed onto its slabby face. Descent is by a deep chimney on the left or by some large ledges on the right, just left of Queue Corner.

31 Retard Arete   12m   VS 5a
This is the right arete of the deep chimney. The initial blunt nose can be climbed from several directions, the easiest being from the left. Continue up the groove above to the top.

32 The Direttissima   12m   VS 4c
Below and right of Retard Arete is a smooth wall. Climb a short black crack in the left side to the left-hand of two black niches. Pull out left, then step right and go up to join Tiger Wall.

33 Tiger Wall   12m   HVS 5b *
Make some hard moves up the middle of the smooth wall below and right of Retard Arete to gain the triangular niche above. Pull over the overhang and finish straight up.

34 The Vertical Ladder   15m   Very Difficult *
To the right of Tiger Wall is a wide fault jammed with blocks. Climb this and exit either left or straight up.

35 Double Stretch   15m   Severe *
Start at a shallow left-facing groove just right of the Vertical Ladder. Climb the slab to the top of the groove and continue up to a wide crack. Follow this to the top.
Variation: **The Keystone Variation   Hard Severe**
Left of the wide crack is a projecting rock rib. Gain it direct and climb it to the top.

36 The M.S. Route   15m   Hard Severe **
An excellent route, giving sustained and delicate climbing. Start immediately right of Double Stretch. Climb a bulging slab for 6m and gain a small ledge on the left (crux). Continue up the slab above to the top.

EAST LOTHIAN

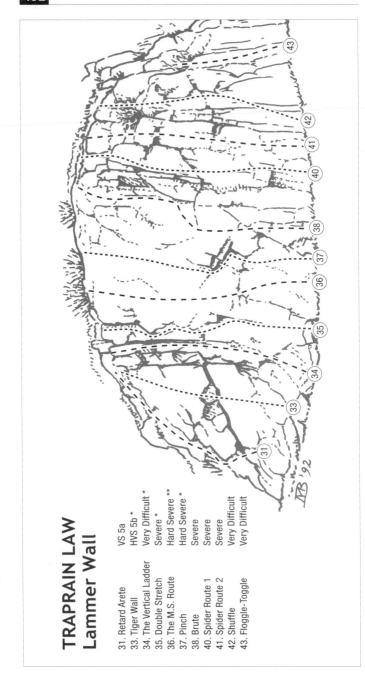

TRAPRAIN LAW
Lammer Wall

31. Retard Arete — VS 5a
33. Tiger Wall — HVS 5b *
34. The Vertical Ladder — Very Difficult *
35. Double Stretch — Severe *
36. The M.S. Route — Hard Severe **
37. Pinch — Hard Severe *
38. Brute — Severe
40. Spider Route 1 — Severe
41. Spider Route 2 — Severe
42. Shuffle — Very Difficult
43. Floggle-Toggle — Very Difficult

37 Pinch   15m   Hard Severe *
Near the centre of the face is a shallow left-facing groove leading to three small overhangs side by side. Climb the groove, turn the overhangs on the left, then trend up and right to the top.
Variation: **VS 5a**
Climb the overhangs.

38 Brute   15m   Severe
Start just right of Pinch. Climb up until it is possible to move right onto a ledge at 7m. Continue up the crack and groove to the top.

39 Pedestrian   15m   Hard Severe
Start 3m right of Pinch at some tiny black grooves. Climb up, keeping left of black rock, to the ledge at 7m. Finish directly up the slabs on the left.

40 Spider Route 1   15m   Severe
About 4m right of Pinch two hairline cracks, one metre apart, run up the crag. High up they are separated by a mottled rib. Start just to the right and climb up and left to finish up the rib.

41 Spider Route 2   12m   Severe
Climb smooth slabs and a small capping overhang obvious at the top.

42 Shuffle   12m   Very Difficult
Start just right of Spider Route 2 and climb diagonally right then back left to a niche. Continue up to a large ledge beside a broom bush.

43 Floggle-Toggle   7m   Very Difficult
Climb directly to a broom bush at the right-hand end of the crag.

44 Parabola   35m   Severe
This is a left to right girdle of Lammer Wall. Start by traversing the diagonal fault across Tiger Wall. Cross the Vertical Ladder and traverse open slabs above the Pinch overhang, descending slightly to the end of the crag.

45 Queue Corner   12m   Severe *
This is the fine right-facing corner starting from some bushes above the right-hand end of the crag.

46 Turf Trundle   25m   VS 4b
To the right of Queue Corner is an expanse of mossy slabs. Pick the cleanest line and climb it.

About 20m right of Lammer Wall is a large cracked slab bounded on the right by a series of overhangs arching up to the right.

47 Hexagon Wall   25m   Very Difficult *
Start just right of small pillar leaning against the face. Climb the slab by the line of least resistance.

48 Dangle   20m   HVS 5a
Start below the left end of the overhangs on a black and sometimes wet slab. Go up the slab and gain a clean-cut right-facing corner. Climb this and pull over its capping overlap to join Hexagon Wall.

49 Frodo   20m   Hard Severe   (2002)
Climbs the hanging slab up and right of Dangle. Climb the slab to an ivy bulge. Step right into a hanging groove above Beatle Crack. Climb this to another bulge and over this to belay.

50 Tipp   10m   E2 6a
Scramble up below the overhangs for about 12m to take a belay under two steep thin cracks. Climb the left-hand crack, with a runner in the right-hand one.

51 Beatle Crack   10m   E1 5c *
Pull into the right-hand crack from the right and climb it, passing a peg runner, to easier ground.

52 Hanging Crack   10m   HVS 5a
Start up and right of Beatle Crack where a rib abuts the underside of the overhangs. Climb the right-hand side of the rib and pull over the overhang to finish up a groove.

53 Utang   8m   Very Difficult
Climb the obvious clean-cut corner 3m right of Hanging Crack.

54 Pip's Pillar   VS 4b
Below the band of overhangs there is an expanse of vegetated slabs. Right of centre are two huge flakes, one above the other. Climb the face of the lower flake, step across the gap and climb the face of the upper flake.

Diamond Wall

A small band of crags with a diamond-shaped wall lie near the top of the South-East Face. At the time of writing access was on bare soil due to the above mentioned fire and none of the routes has been checked.

Easy Ticket   6m   Severe   (2001)
An upside down diamond with a route up the left hand corner.

The Fox   7m   E3 6a   (1999)
Start on the left of the diamond-shaped wall and make hard thin moves up the centre of the wall on small sloping holds, passing a poor Quadcam 0, to reach better holds and some RPs at the top. Avoid the corner on the left. Side-runners reduce the grade.

Black Diamond   6m   VS   (2001)
The right-hand arete of the upside down diamond.

Diamond Back   8m   E1 5a   (2001)
Further round to the right of the diamond is an obvious overhang. Go up a ramp to the bottom of the overhang, climbed going from right to left on good holds. Strenuous and reachy.

TRAPRAIN LAW QUARRY

The quarry contains some impressive bits of rock, mixed with vast areas of very unstable rockface. Consequently, the routes are more serious than those on the sunny south side. Helmets should be worn. The crag should be avoided at nesting times from March to August.

Approach: Leave the A1 at the Haddington turn off and enter the town. Take the first main left turning and cross over the River Tyne. Continue until the hill becomes visible on the right. Park in the furthest layby on the left, climb over the gate and enter the quarry.

Descent: Via the path through woodland on the quarry's left side.

Main Wall - Left Side

Towards the left-hand side of the massive back wall of the quarry lie a series of tiered red walls. These form diagonal right to left corner-lines and slabs, cut at mid height by a large terrace with a small tree at its left end.

The routes finish up areas of loose stones at the top and it is recommended that a fixed rope is left hanging down this section to allow safe passage. Large blocks at the top of the cliff offer secure belays.

Stairway to Hell   50m   HVS *   *(1997)*
The lower red wall has a prominent right to left crack and is flanked by a stairway of blocks on its right-hand side. Scramble to the base of the wall.
1. 20m 4c Move up the obvious stairway of blocks and either go left to ascend a steep wall to the large ledge, or continue right until forced out onto the steep exposed wall and make a committing move up to the ledge and peg belay in the corner.
2. 30m 4c Climb either the centre or slightly more committing the left side of the slab each move is as easy as the last but the runner is at the top.

Mordor Crack   50m   HVS *   *(1997)*
Climbs the slanting corner-crack right of the slab taken by Stairway to Hell on the upper tier.
1. 20m 4c As for Stairway to Hell.
2. 30m 4c Climb the impressive curving crack which takes all sizes of cams getting smaller to the top.

The Doomsday Prophecies   55m   E2 *   *(1997)*
This route starts up the arete right of Mordor Crack on the upper tier, then the wall to the right.
1. 20m 4c As for Stairway to Hell.
2. 35m 5b From the ledge move up and right to a short hand-traverse. Turn the corner round to the right (poor peg) and climb the arete until a hard move up and right forces you out onto the open face. Continue to the top with no runners for comfort.

Top Tier - Left Side

Ascend via the descent path on the quarry's left side. Where the path levels out cross over the fence and these short walls are ahead, above the large blocks at the top of the Main Wall.

The Long Reach   5m   Very Difficult   *(1997)*
Climbs the left side of the first slab with a steep pull to finish.

A Wee Peach   5m   Severe   *(1998)*
Climb the middle of the slab trend left then right with awkward moves to get to the break.

A Loud Screech   5m   Severe   *(2001)*
The right side of the slab is climbed easily at first then more awkwardly to the top.

EAST LOTHIAN

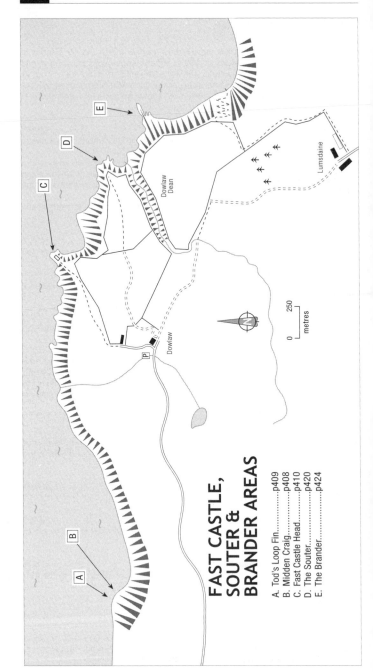

FAST CASTLE, SOUTER & BRANDER AREAS

BERWICKSHIRE COAST

This section describes the sea-cliffs between Burnmouth and Cockburnspath. The best area lies south from Fast Castle, and includes the fine sea-stack of The Souter. Much of the climbing is on upturned beds of greywacke, projecting into the sea at right-angles to the coast. These fins provide shelter and make climbing possible on sunny winter days on the south faces. However, the nature of the greywacke and its associated vegetation and lichen means that some dubious rock will be encountered. Many of the sea-cliffs are affected during the nesting season. There are no official restrictions. Any dates in the text are there to help climbers gauge the level of noise, smell and guano. It should be noted that the intentional disturbance of nesting birds such as razorbill, guillemot, puffin, fulmar, kittiwake and cormorant is a criminal offence. If in doubt contact the MCofS (see Environment p29).

COVE AREA

(NT 789718) Map p388

The obvious sea-stack on the west side of the bay is Hollow Rock. Long Rock is the prominent grey pinnacle on the east side of the bay.

Approach: Park in the Cove visitors car park. For Long Rock, follow the cliff-top path east for 1km. Descend an easy grassy ridge to a col connecting the pinnacle to the mainland. Hollow Rock can be accessed at low tide from the bay.

HOLLOW ROCK

Stegosaurus Ridge   15m   Difficult   *(2004)*
After tricky start, the landward ridge of the sea-stack gives straightforward scrambling to the summit. Simultaneous abseil descent.

LONG ROCK

Descend from the top by making an exposed scramble starting down the face overlooking the bay to a ledge, then trend round to an easy ramp leading down to the grassy col. The first routes start on the grassy platform below the short seaward face well above the sea.

Left-Hand Crack   7m   HVS 5b *   *(2001)*
Gain the niche then follow the short left-hand crack.

Ramalina Subfarinacea   9m   E1 5c   *(2001)*
Gain the niche then follow the thin right-hand crack.

These lie on the face looking into the bay and start at sea-level. There is some loose and friable rock. The shorter, steeper face to the left is unclimbed. Further left at the seaward end several routes have been soloed at Very Difficult – the rock requires care.

Grammarian's Delight   20m   Hard Severe 4b   *(2001)*
Climb the right side of the face and finish up the arete.

Were it not for Foot and Mouth   20m   VS 4c *   *(2001)*
Start 6m left of the previous route. Take a direct line to a hanging corner in the upper half of the face. From the corner move left and climb the arete to the top.

FAST CASTLE AREA

Maps p388, 406

Midden Crag lies 2.5km west along the coast from Fast Castle and is reached from the access road before Dowlaw Farm. The remaining cliffs lie below the ruins of Fast Castle and are accessed from the farm.

MIDDEN CRAIG

(NT 838 702)   Non-tidal   Map p406

This crag is characterised by a band of jagged overhangs at one-quarter height which gives most of the routes a strenuous start. At the seaward end is a small sea-stack, Midden Stack.

Approach: Leave the A1107 at NT 828 688 for a minor road signposted Dowlaw. Follow this for almost 1km and park on the right at a small quarry. Cross the road and go into the field. Head north-north-east into another field, aiming for a concrete post in the corner nearest the sea. Cross the fence, then turn right (east) and descend steep bracken to the bay. The crag is at the bottom of the slope on the left.

The first routes start from the scree slope at the left end of the crag.

Constant Hunger   25m   E4 6a *   (1993)
This sustained route starts between the left end of the crag and a right-slanting crack. Climb the wall, pull right over the bulge, then go up and left through the overhangs to gain a left-slanting crack. Move left and up to reach a thin resting ledge below the overlap. Move up to the overlap via a plaque, then pull through and follow a right-slanting crack. Near the end of the crack, move left and climb the wall to finish.

Welcome to the Midden   25m   E3 5c   (1993)
Start 6m right of Constant Hunger, on the wall right of the crack. Climb the wall to the break below the overhang, then pull up and right through the break to gain a right-sloping ledge. Climb the wall moving slightly right, then go up and slightly left to the niche. Finish up and right.

Inferno   25m   E3 5c   (1993)
An airy climb up the cracked wall between the two wide chossy grooves. Climb loose ledges to below the overhangs, then pull right through them to gain a wide right-slanting crack. Stand in the crack, then move up and left to reach another right-slanting crack. Where this crack divides, follow the feint left branch which forms a short slim groove (crux). Finish up and right.

The next routes are on the right section of crag. The most striking feature of the wall is a large inverted V-shaped overhanging alcove. (There are belay stakes somewhere on the slope back from the cliff edge.)

Curve of the Earth   20m   E2 5c   (1992)
This follows the slim clean-cut groove right of the large chossy groove. Climb the wall rightwards to the left side of the alcove. Move left through the overhangs to a crack, then follow the groove to the top.

Brucellosis   20m   E4 6b   (1993)
Climb the alcove to a very hard move to exit. Finish up the left slanting crack above.

Enigma   20m   E2 5b/c *   (1993)
Start right of the alcove at a small bay. Climb the wall to a smaller alcove. Pull over the overhang using large pinch-grips, then move right and up to a left-slanting crack. Follow this for a short distance, then climb the wall above and a small overlap near the top.

Mea Culpa   15m   E3 6a *   (1993)
Start right of Enigma. Climb up and left to a spike below a wide crack. Gain the

crack above (crux) and follow it for a short distance, then traverse right to a thin crack and follow this to the top.

Midden Stack

Non-tidal

The next routes lie on the small stack past the seaward end of the wall. In the middle of the south-east face there is a distinctive square-cut groove, capped by an overhang. The climbs are described from the right side of this face, moving left (clockwise) around the stack.

Descent: Abseil from blocks and in-situ pegs.

Starboard Bow   15m   E2 5c   *(1993)*
Start right of the square-cut groove. Climb the wall to the break below the overhang to the right of the start of the groove. Pull straight over the overhang onto the wall, then move up and right to the right edge of the wall. Finish up the arete.

Turning in-tide-out   20m   E2 5c *   *(1993)*
This takes the corner formed by the left side of the square-cut groove. Near the top, move out left to a ledge, then step up and right to climb a thin crack on the right to finish.

Lunar Pull   20m   E3 5c *   *(1993)*
A good route up the pillar forming the left side of the square-cut groove. Climb the double overhangs left of the corner, then go up the wall to the ledge and finish direct.

Port Bow   20m   E1 5b   *(1993)*
The left arete. Pull over the bulge (crux) to reach a jammed flake in the V-shaped groove. Climb the groove to the overhang, then move round the edge to finish up a wide crack.

Unnamed   20m   E1 5a   *(1990s)*
A serious route up the green slabby wall on the south-west face. Climb a groove near the left corner of the face. Move left to a ledge on the left arete, then move right onto the upper slab and climb to the top.

The north-west face of the stack is generally scrappy, but the short cracks on the summit block have been climbed at E1. It is possible to reach the summit by a bold scramble on the north side. Starting on the right, go up and traverse left to a blocky groove near the left edge, Very Difficult.

Tod's Loup Fin

(NT 837 702)   Tidal   Map p406

About 100m west of Midden Craig and its stack is another fin or stack with a fine north face. This consists of two slabs separated by an obvious corner.

Descent: Scramble down the chossy south face, or abseil.

Tidal Race   20m   20m   Moderate   *(1993)*
The green corner line on the left side of the face.

Ranald's Rant   20m   Very Difficult   *(1993)*
The arete just right of Tidal Race, finishing direct up a crack.

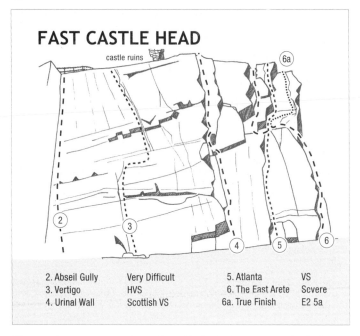

FAST CASTLE HEAD

castle ruins

2. Abseil Gully	Very Difficult	5. Atlanta	VS
3. Vertigo	HVS	6. The East Arete	Severe
4. Urinal Wall	Scottish VS	6a. True Finish	E2 5a

The next three routes start from a large block which is submerged at high tide.

Whitebait Can't Jump   15m   Very Difficult   *(1993)*
Climb cracks up the centre of the main slab. The direct start is 5a.

Flounder Member   15m   Severe   *(1993)*
Climb the big left-facing corner.

Pirrett's Progress   20m   VS 4c   *(1993)*
Climb the previous route for 3m, then traverse right to the arete using the obvious handholds. Continue the traverse to a clean-cut crack which splits the slab above, and climb this to finish.

Further west still, a slab and a small buttress provide pleasant routes from Very Difficult to VS.

FAST CASTLE HEAD

(NT 862 711)   Tidal   Map p406   Diagram p410
The following routes lie on the cliffs surrounding the ruins of Fast Castle and were some of the earliest done in the area. Much of the rock should be treated with caution and the climbs have not proved popular; some have probably never been repeated. (Having said that, there is some reasonable rock amongst the rubble). The abseil approach means that all routes are climbable at high tide although the base of the crag is tidal.

Approach: Leave the A1107 at NT 828 688 for a minor road signposted Dowlaw. Follow this for 2km and park on the left before the entrance to Dowlaw Farm. From the parking place cross the cattle grid at the entrance and turn left down a track, passing the end of a row of cottages. Go through two gates then turn right and follow a path to the headland and the remains of the castle. To the south-east the top of a sea-stack is visible, this is The Souter. Iron railings protect the bad step across to the headland and the gully dropping from here to the right is Abseil Gully.

To reach the foot of the cliffs there are several possibilities; 1) abseil from the railings down a gully (Abseil Gully), 2) abseil from a huge block at the top edge of the cliff near a big hollow in the ruins – the line of Atlanta, 3) scramble down steep grassy slopes to the south-east. Routes 8, 9 and 10 are reached by abseiling from the outermost tip of land beyond the ruins.

Routes are described from left to right facing the cliff.

1 Cyclops   100m   Scottish VS/A2   *(1974)*
An horrific-looking route. It lies on the high east-facing wall, well left of the main slab mass and Abseil Gully. Start at the right-hand side of a large cave, below a diagonal overhanging crack.
1. 15m Climb the crack using pegs, pull into a shallow groove and free climb to a stance and in-situ peg belay.
2. 15m Continue up the corner to an overhang (peg runner), go over this using a peg for aid, and climb the corner above moving out right to the arete. Use two pegs to move up to a big stance on the left.
3. 30m Climb the black corner above, then follow the arete breaking left to the foot of a big grassy groove. Follow the shaley slab to the right until it steepens. Stance and peg belay.
4. 15m Traverse left towards a steep solid wall and climb this to a stance and block belay on the right side of a right-slanting grassy rake.
5. 25m Climb steep loose rocks above the belay, trending left until overhangs force a traverse to the right. Climb straight up to finish and belay to the fence.

2 Abseil Gully   60m   Very Difficult   *(1965)*
A chossy route, but a viable escape option! Climb the wall to the right of the chimney for 10m, then continue up the right-angled groove, using many bridging moves, all the way to the railings at the top.

3 Vertigo   60m   HVS   *(1965)*
An interesting climb which would benefit from an increase in traffic as it is loose in places. It takes the middle of the slab right of Abseil Gully and below the castle ruins, following the obvious line of weakness.
1. 20m 4c Climb the slab to the foot of a crack. Climb the crack and continue to a small ledge.
2. 40m 4b Continue directly up over three slight bulges to the top. An enjoyable pitch.

4 Urinal Wall   55m   Scottish VS   *(1965)*
A fine line, but overgrown and loose. Start at the very foot of the corner bounding the slab mass on the right.
1. 40m Climb the wall and groove to a ledge and peg belay.
2. 15m Continue up the corner for 10m, then go left onto loose blocks on the arete, and so to the top.

5 Atlanta   45m   VS   *(1965)*
A continuously interesting route. Start 5m from the right end of the face, on a block strewn ledge at the foot of an apparently holdless corner.
1. 30m 4c Climb the corner (poor peg runner) to a ledge and thread belay.
2. 15m 4a Continue up the corner for 6m, then go left onto the arete (loose) and finish up a thin crack.
Variation: **Direct Finish   Hard Severe 4b**   *(1992)*
Climb the upper corner directly. Not as good as the original route.

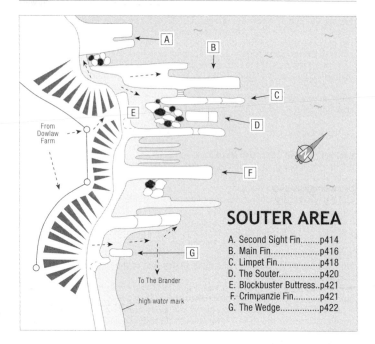

A. Second Sight Fin........p414
B. Main Fin....................p416
C. Limpet Fin.................p418
D. The Souter.................p420
E. Blockbuster Buttress..p421
F. Crimpanzie Fin...........p421
G. The Wedge................p422

SOUTER AREA

6 The East Arete   45m   Severe   *(1965)*

Another good line, but it is loose in places.

1. 30m Climb the slab and arete at the east end of the crag for 20m, then trend left to a ledge and thread belay in the Atlanta corner.

2. 15m Move left round the arete and into a corner. Follow this to finish up a wide broken crack on the right.

Variation: **True Finish   E2 5a**   *(1991)*

From the thread belay, move up and right onto the edge of the slab and follow a slim groove to a steepening finish. This can also be used as an alternative finish to Atlanta.

7 Gannet Groove   75m   Scottish VS   *(1966)*

Too appalling to contemplate! This route follows the obvious crack up the bands on the east face of the crag. As soon as the route is started one is over the sea.

1. 15m Step from the pinnacle at the left-hand corner into a groove. Move slightly down and to the right. Cross the wall, then move up to a pointed stance in the groove. Climb the groove (crux) with the right leg hanging over the wall and the left jammed in the groove. Continue up the wall above into another groove which leads to a stance and peg belay.

2. 25m Continue up the groove and go round the overhang at the top to a large stance.

3. 35m Traverse round a corner on the left and continue up a small gangway for 10m. Traverse right onto more solid rock and then go straight up to the top.

The next three routes are found to the right, behind the main slab mass, beyond a cave and a 12m strip of water. Abseil in from the outermost tip of land.

8 Rapunzel   40m   E1 5a   *(1992)*

Start 3m left of Castle Wall and climb straight up the unprotected slab to join that route at half-height.

9 Castle Wall   40m   VS 4b   *(1966)*
After a good start, this climb becomes a bit loose near the top. Climb the crack
in the right side of the face, then traverse left towards a groove. Finish by an
upward traverse to the right.

10 The Folly   35m   VS 4b   *(1991)*
Traverse right from the bottom of Castle Wall, just above sea-level, until the
second right leaning groove from the left is reached (or abseil in directly).
Rounded spike belay.
1. 10m Climb the groove and traverse left to belay on a shelf.
2. 25m Continue left around the edge and follow the right edge of the face to
the top. Poorly protected.

SOUTER AREA

(NT 869 709)   Maps p388, 412

This area lies about 1.5km east along the coast from Fast Castle. The centre of
attraction is the impressive 25m sea-stack of The Souter. It is surrounded by a
complex series of rock fins jutting out into the sea which give the best climbing
in the area. The cliffs are affected by nesting seabirds from mid April to early
August.

Approach: Leave the A1107 at NT 828 688 for a minor road signposted Dowlaw.
Follow this for 2km and park on the left before the entrance to Dowlaw Farm. From
the parking place walk right around the farm, then follow a track towards the
sea, passing through two gates. When it fades, trend left and go through a
drystone wall. Now head seawards down fields to the coast opposite The Souter.
Away to the right a big slabby promontory can be seen, The Brander.

Descend steep grassy slopes to the left to face The Souter. On the right is the
boulder-filled inlet containing the sea-stack. Facing the stack on the left is the
large Main Fin and smaller Limpet Fin. To the left (west) is a small inlet, beyond
which is the Second Sight Fin with a prominent crack running up its seaward
prow. Beyond this to the north-west is another fin; The Doll Fin.

THE DOLL FIN

Tidal   North-West & South-East facing

This is the small fin opposite the north-west face of Second Sight Fin. It is
recognisable by its cracked south-east face.

Approach: From The Souter at sea-level at very low tide, or descend grassy slopes
at the landward end of the Second Sight Fin.

North-West Face

This face forms a line of bulges which are unfortunately loose and dirty. In the
centre of the face there is an obvious cave which forms a hole through the fin.
Routes are described from right to left – lanward to seaward.

Carolyn   10m   HVS 5b   *(1997)*
Climb into the cave and exit with difficulty, moving left near the top.

Geronimo's Cadillac   12m   E3 5c   *(1997)*
Start 2m left of the cave below right slanting cracks in the bulging wall. Pull over
the bulge and climb the steep cracked wall to the half way ledge. Strenuous and
serious. Traverse left to a thin crack and climb this to the top.

South-East Face

The first two routes finish at the obvious terrace which is followed leftwards to descend. Routes are described from left to right – landward to seaward.

Flume   8m   Very Difficult   *(1996)*
The left-hand crack.

Plume   8m   Very Difficult   *(1996)*
The next crack to the right.

Spume   11m   Very Difficult   *(1996)*
Climb the left-slanting crack in the middle of the slab. Step right at the terrace and climb the chimney/crack to the top. Reverse to the terrace to descend.

Sea Spray   11m   Very Difficult   *(1996)*
Climb the next crack to the right. Move left at the terrace and climb a wide crack to the top. Reverse to the terrace to descend.

The walls between the cracks have been soloed in the 4a to 4b range, but the rock is friable, so care should be taken. The seaward nose has been climbed at VS 4b and is especially exciting during an incoming tide.

SECOND SIGHT FIN

Tidal   North-West & South-East facing   Map p412   Diagram p415

North-West Face

The first two routes are based on the cracks at the right-hand, landward end of the wall and are accessible at all but the highest tides. Routes are described from right to left – landward to seaward.

11 Severance   12m   HVS 5b *   *(1996)*
Start 1m left of the arete. A hard move up a crack gains a ledge. Move right to the arete and follow this to gain the right branch of the main crack in the headwall. Finish up this. It is also possible to gain and climb the right arete direct (harder).

12 Splice the Mainbrace   12m   HVS 5a *   *(1996)*
Start 4m left of the arete. Climb to first ledge. Follow the crack above finishing up the left crack, with a tricky move to gain the easy slab above.

The next obvious features are a chimney in the centre of the face and a large protruding block near the top of the crag further left.

13 Incision   10m   Difficult   *(1997)*
Climb the chimney in the centre of the face.

14 The Pig Thing   10m   Severe   *(1996)*
Climb the crack left of the chimney starting up a wider crack.

15 Potbellied Sheep   10m   VS 4b   *(1996)*
Climb the next crack to left starting at a small corner.

16 Daytrippers   10m   VS 4b *   *(1996)*
Climb twin cracks to finish up a corner on the right side of a large protruding block.

SECOND SIGHT FIN - North-west Face

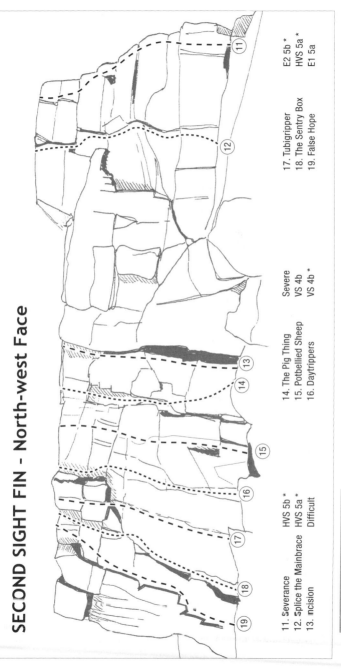

11. Severance   HVS 5b *
12. Splice the Mainbrace   HVS 5a *
13. Incision   Difficult

14. The Pig Thing   Severe
15. Potbellied Sheep   VS 4b
16. Daytrippers   VS 4b *

17. Tubigripper   E2 5b *
18. The Sentry Box   HVS 5a *
19. False Hope   E1 5a

17 Tubigripper   12m   E2 5b *   *(1996)*
Start directly below the large protruding block. Climb to the block. Gain and climb directly up the hanging groove in the front of the block. Sustained and bold.

18 The Sentry Box   11m   HVS 5a *   *(1996)*
Climb the right slanting crack to the left. Exit with difficulty from the wide section, to mantelshelf onto a good ledge. Finish up the crack behind the large protruding block.

19 False Hope   11m   E1 5a   *(1997)*
The thin flake line left of the wide crack at the left end of the crag.

South-East Face

Routes are described from left to right – landward to seaward.

Gull Talk   10m   Very Difficult
Climb the corner and slab at the back left-hand (landward) end of the fin. Walk right to descend a chimney.

The Fish Business   10m   E2 5c   *(1982)*
To the right of Gull Talk are three short corners. Climb a thin crack, just to the right of the corners, to gain an easy slab.

A Drop In the Ocean   12m   E2 5b *   *(1982)*
The left arete of the prow. Start below the wide crack of Second Sight. Move left to the arete and climb the wall just right of the arete on good holds. Swing round left into a small niche, pull out and continue more easily to the top.
Variation: **Direct Start   E1 5b**
When the tide is out, climb a line of cracks just left of the arete to join the original route.

Second Sight   12m   HVS 5b **   *(1982)*
The prominent crack running up the prow of the fin gives an excellent climb.

Bloodbath   10m   HVS 5a   *(1982)*
The short arete just right of Second Sight.

Something Fishy   20m   VS 5a *   *(1993)*
Climbs the prow right of the descent chimney.
Climb a shallow chimney to a large ledge. Climb the steep crack and overhang pulling out right to finish.

MAIN FIN

Non-tidal   South-East & North-West facing   Map p412   Diagram p419

This large fin runs out into the sea from the bottom of the steep grassy approach slope facing The Souter.

North-West Face

A rather sombre face, but with good rock. Do not be put off by the nest-strewn ledge – it does not affect the climbing. Routes are described from right to left.

Mordor Crack, HVS, Traprain Law Quarry. Climbers Scott & Fiona Galbraith.
(photo Adrian Plumb)

Approach: Descend a steep gully beside the face.

The first two climbs lie on the north-west face of the smaller subsidiary fin to the left, looking out, of the access gully for the main north-west face routes.

Fluorescent Flake   10m   E1 5b * (1996)
A short, sharp problem up the thin, luminous green flake.

Stiff Bunnies   10m   E1 5b (1982)
The thin crack up the prow of the fin.

The following routes are on the main face on the right, while descending the access gully.

Shades of Yellow   14m   VS 4b (1996)
The crack and arete right of Souterrain.

Souterrain   20m   E3 5c * (1982)
Climb the deep chimney near the right-hand side of the face and exit right to a ledge. Move up with difficulty to a recess and pull out left to the top.
Variation: **Direct Start   E3 6a** (1982)
Climb the crack to the right of the chimney.

Fast Bleeder   20m   E3 6a ** (1982)
The obvious central crack provides one of the better routes in the area. It is high in the grade. Climb into and up a narrow sentry box. Thrutch out right to good holds on the halfway ledge, then climb the crack above, pulling over a bulge (crux) to finish.

South-East Face

These routes face The Souter and are some of the most popular and best climbs in the area. Routes are described from left to right – landward to seaward.

20 Walli   4m   VS 5a (1982)
The short crack at the left-hand end of the face.

21 Wallow   6m   E3 6a * (1982)
Just right of Walli are two fierce thin cracks that converge near the top. Follow the left-hand crack. Desperate!

22 Wallette   8m   E2 6a ** (1982)
The right-hand crack, gained from the right is not quite as hard.

23 Zigzag   12m   E1 5b * (1979)
Start below a thin crack 6m left of an obvious diagonal fault. Climb the crack, then hand-traverse right to gain the fault. Finish up this.
Variation: **Direct Start   E2 5c *****
Start midway between the thin crack and the diagonal fault. Fingery moves lead to a jug and a hard move to gain the traverse line.
Variation: **Direct Finish   E2 5c**
From the start of the traverse, move up and left to climb a thin crack.

24 Mingy Metro   10m   E3 6a * (1982)
Immediately right of the diagonal fault is an undercut bulge. Surmount the

The Souter. Climbers unknown
(photo Tom Prentice)

bulge to gain an undercling below a block and thin crack. A long reach (crux) gains a wider crack and a resting place below the easier final wall.

25 Fraud Escort   10m   E3 5c * (1982)
From the undercling on the previous route, continue undercutting right on down-pointing flakes to a stopping place right of a crack. Move up into the crack, then follow it to the top.

26 Fated Panda   10m   E4 5c (1990)
Start 2m right of Fraud Escort. Climb over an obvious block and follow a thin crack to the top.

27 J.P.S.   8m   HVS 5a (1982)
Climb the slim corner above the col between the Main Fin and Limpets Fin.

28 Plain Sailing   15m   E1 5b *** (1982)
Start at the bottom of the deep cleft at the seaward end of the fin. Climb the superb crack-line which starts at the right-hand side of a large block. The crux is at the top.

29 Drunk and Disorderly   15m   E3 5c (1983)
Worthwhile variations on Wallnut. Climb parallel cracks to reach and pull over the overlap as for Wallnut. Step left and finish up a thin crack.

30 Wallnut   15m   E3 5c *** (1982)
Excellent wall climbing. Start midway between Plain Sailing and the end of the fin. Climb a thin crack into the middle of the wall. Move right and up to the overlap, then go left through the overlap at a good sidepull. Continue up the wall above to the top.

31 Porker's Wall   15m   E4 5c (1982)
A serious route. Start up the wall right of Wallnut then go up and right, passing a large pocket, to the arete. Move up and left to cross a bulge and continue to ledges and the top.

32 Coming up Roses   15m   HVS 4c (1992)
At the end of the Main Fin is a long green slab bounded by aretes on either side. The left-hand arete gives a good but serious climb.

33 Merlin and Wendy's Day Out   15m   VS 5a (1992)
Climb the right-hand arete; one hard move leads to pleasant easier climbing up cracks.

34 Return to Sender   50m   E3 (1982)
The girdle traverse of the Main Fin is an exciting excursion, especially at high tide with a stormy sea. Start below J.P.S.
1. 25m 5a Follow the obvious traverse line across the wall and round the arete to belay on a ledge at the start of the north-west face.
2. 25m 5c The return trip. Traverse the ledge to Souterrain, move up to the recess, then finish up a groove on the right.

LIMPET FIN

Non-tidal   South facing   Map p412   Diagram p419

Between the Main Fin and The Souter is a small narrow fin. All the routes are on the south-east side facing the stack, except the first one, Orgasmatron. Routes are described from left to right.

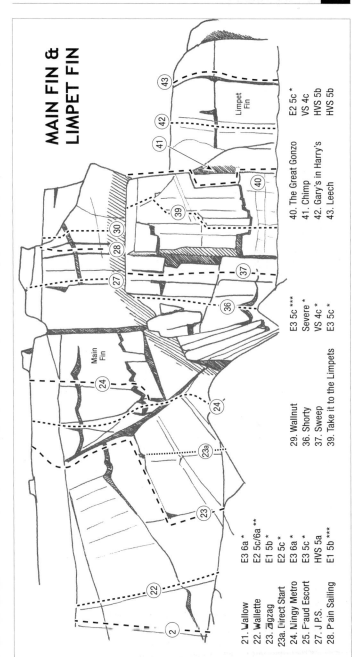

MAIN FIN &
LIMPET FIN

Main
Fin

Limpet
Fin

21. Wallow	E3 6a *
22. Wallette	E2 5c/6a **
23. Zigzag	E1 5b *
23a. Direct Start	E2 5c *
24. Ningy Metro	E3 6a *
25. Fraud Escort	E3 5c *
27. J.P.S.	HVS 5a
28. Pain Sailing	E1 5b ***

29. Wallnut	E3 5c ***
36. Shorty	Severe *
37. Sweep	VS 4c *
39. Take it to the Limpets	E3 5c *

40. The Great Gonzo	E2 5c *
41. Chimp	VS 4c
42. Gary's in Harry's	HVS 5b
43. Leech	HVS 5b

35 Orgasmatron   8m   E2 5c *   *(1982)*
Directly opposite Plain Sailing are twin thin cracks. Gain them from the right and
follow them with a tricky move near the top.

36 Shorty   8m   Severe *   *(1982)*
Climb the crack and arete at the left end of the south-east face.

37 Sweep   8m   VS 4c *   *(1982)*
Climb the cracks right of Shorty.

38 Sooty   8m   VS 5a *   *(1982)*
Follow the obvious short chimney and crack.

39 Take it to the Limpets   10m   E3 5c *   *(1983)*
A good bold face climb up the grey wall opposite the stack. Climb the left-hand
of two cracks to a jug in the centre of the wall. Move up and right to follow a
vague crack line to the top.
Variation: **E2 5c**
From the jug, go left to the arete. Move up and right under a small roof before
pulling onto the slab.

40 The Great Gonzo   10m   E2 5c *   *(1982)*
This route takes the crack in the arete to the right of the previous climb, gained
from the chimney on the right.

41 Chimp   10m   VS 4c   *(1982)*
Continue up the chimney from the start of The Great Gonzo.

42 Gary's in Harry's   7m   HVS 5b   *(1991)*
Climb the left-hand (wrinkled) of two short cracks right of Chimp.

43 Leech   6m   HVS 5b   *(1982)*
Climb the right-hand of two short cracks to the right of Chimp.

THE SOUTER

Various aspects   Tidal   Maps p406, 412

The next four routes tackle the sea-stack. While not one of Scotland's classic sea-
stacks, the thick vertical bed of greywacke forming The Souter (The Cobbler),
makes for an exciting and unusual adventure on reasonable rock.

Descent: Abseil down the landward face from in-situ pegs and slings. These
should be treated with great caution and replaced if necessary.

Landward Side   25m   Scottish VS   *(1965)*
The original route is ridden with nests and guano and cannot be recommended.
Start in the middle of the face. Climb to a ledge at 7m and traverse 3m right on
to the south-east face. Move up to a ledge, then traverse left to gain the top
slab. Climb this to the top turning an overhang on the right.
Variation: **Direct   Scottish VS**   *(1970)*
From the ledge at 7m, climb a smooth corner for 3m, break right and climb an
overhanging wall to a ledge left of a small wall. Cross the wall and climb a sharp
crack to join the original route at the top slab. It is also possible to finish over
the overhang. A nut and peg were used for aid on the first ascent.

Squid Vicious   25m   E5 6a ***   *(1983)*
The impressive crack-line on the north-west face gives a classic hard route. Climb
the crack to a small roof at 8m. Traverse right and climb to two obvious pockets

in the wall (peg runner up and right). Return to the crack and climb to the roof. Pull over on the right and climb to another roof. Go over this on the left and climb up and right across a wall to reach a V-groove; block belay on the left.

Ordinary Route   25m   HVS 5a ** (1970)
This takes the seaward, east, face starting from a raised platform. At high tide gain the platform by making an awkward traverse across the base of the south-east face. Climb the groove above the platform with difficulty to a ledge. Move up and right (peg runner) to a V-groove. Go left up this, then climb a diagonal crack and the wall above to the top.
Variation: **Scottish VS** (1970)
Traverse left from the ledge above the initial groove, then go round the arete and traverse a narrow ledge to join the landward route.

Seal of Approval   25m   HVS 5a (1990)
This is on the south-east face of The Souter. Start above the bad step at the south arete, next to a rusty peg.
1. 15m 5a Step up to a sloping ledge and climb an obvious crack over a bulge and small ledge to a continuation crack leading to the left side of a large ledge.
2. 10m 5a Pull over a bulge and continue up the crack on sharp holds to join the Landward Side near the top.

BLOCKBUSTER BUTTRESS
Non-tidal   East facing   Map p412
Opposite the landward face of The Souter is an impressive undercut buttress. A spare rope is recommended for setting up a fence post belay at the top. The first route takes the zigzag crack on the right wall, left of an impressive unclimbed groove.

Lightning Crack   15m   HVS 5a (1982)
Climb the crack right of the undercut arete to the break. Traverse left to the edge and follow a ramp to the top.

Moving Like a Slug   15m   E2 5b (1982)
From below Lightning Crack, follow a traverse line left to the arete. Climb boldly up the arete and finish up the ramp above.

Blockbuster   20m   E1 5b (1982)
Round on the seaward face is a break in the roof. Climb through this using a block of dubious stability, then continue up the crack and loose wall above.

Pigeon Shit   6m   E3 6a (1982)
Down and left of Blockbuster is a deep cave. Start just left of the entrance and climb the fierce crack up the wall.

Graddled   6m   E5 6a (1983)
Boldly climb the wall immediately left of Pigeon Shit.

CRIMPANZIE FIN
Tidal   South-East facing   Map p412
This is the second fin to the south-east of The Souter. The climbs are concentrated at the seaward end of the south east face and are only accessible at low tide. The face is broken by a guano splattered ledge at half-height where the climbs end. Below this is a short but steep wall offering superb climbing on compact grey rock. Routes are described from left to right – landward to seaward.

Approach: Go through an obvious gap in the fin opposite The Souter, or descend grassy slopes to the south and work back northwards crossing two minor fins.

There are in-situ pegs at the top of the fin for belaying and abseiling. Beware of quickly rising tides.

Kylie   6m   E1 5b   *(1990)*
The first crack-line left of the central groove.

Crimpanzie   8m   E5 6b *   *(1990)*
Blind, bold and fingery climbing up the wall left of the central groove line. Climb to an undercut flake. Move up and right past a hammered nut, then move right to a good hold under the roof. Move left and finish up the open groove.

Not the HVS   8m   E3 5c *   **(***1990)*
The central groove line.

First of Four   8m   E4 5c *   *(1990)*
The weakness right of the central groove. Climb the wall to an undercut flake. Move left and follow the scoop to the roof (good nut). Continue straight up to finish.

The Undercut Kid   8m   E4 6a   *(1990)*
An eliminate straight up the shield right of the previous route to reach the juggy spike on Tied up at Work.

Tied up at Work   8m   E3 6a *   *(1990)*
Climb to the first of two undercut flakes near the right end of the face. Break diagonally left up the wall to a juggy spike, then pull easily over the roof to finish.

Psittacosis   20m   E5 6b   *(1990)*
This is a left to right girdle which follows the weakness under the roof all the way to Tied up at Work. Stork-like manoeuvres are optional.

THE WEDGE

Tidal   South-East facing   Map p412

Where the series of fins end and a wide pebble bay starts there is an isolated, thin triangular pinnacle. The north-west face provides an excellent boulder problem traverse.

Edge of the Wedge   15m   E2 5a   *(1992)*
Climb the seaward edge through several bulges.

Fuzzy Stone   15m   E3 5b   *(1992)*
The south-east face of The Wedge. Pull through the overhang in the centre and traverse right along a narrow ramp. Climb the wall above, using holds on the right arete.

Skelpit Erse   10m   VS 4b   *(1997)*
Start left of Fuzzy Stone on the right side of the obvious arch. Climb the steep crack-line.

The next routes are on the small fin halfway towards The Brander from The Wedge, between the waterfall flowing out of Dowlaw Dean and the sea. The south-east face has two very short cracks.

Praying for Snow   8m   HVS 5a   *(1997)*
The left-hand crack with an awkward move near the top past a horizontal slot.

Don't Blink!   5m   VS 5b   *(1997)*
The right-hand crack. Short and sharp.

Between the Dowlaw Dean waterfall and The Brander lies a short stack with an easy seaward ridge and a cracked landward face. Opposite the landward face on the mainland is a wall below the bracken slopes. The next route climbs the centre of the wall.

Hale – Bopp   12m   E3 6a *   *(1997)*
Start below the crack splitting the bulge. Hard moves gain the left slanting break. Climb the crack-line to a move right to a thin horizontal break. Continue up the wall trending left to finish. Belay on stakes somewhere in the bracken above!

The next routes are centred on the west arete of the stack, which is the left arete of the landward face. Descent is an easy scramble down the seaward ridge then down the south-east face.

Banana Groove   10m   Hard Severe 4a   *(1997)*
Climbs the right side of the landward face up the wide broken groove right of the twin cracks. A hard start leads to a loose and bold finish.

Dried Peach Crack   10m   VS 5a *   *(1997)*
A good route. Start just just right of the arete. Climb the twin cracks over a bulge. Finish up the easier chimney trending right to belay on a ledge on the south-east face.

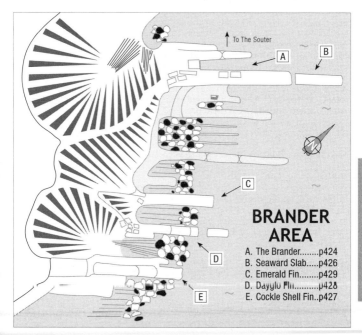

To The Souter

A

B

C

D

E

BRANDER AREA

A. The Brander........p424
B. Seaward Slab.....p426
C. Emerald Fin........p429
D. Dayglo Fin..........p428
E. Cockle Shell Fin..p427

Captain Ahab   12m   E1 5b *(1997)*
From the twin cracks, gain the arete on the left at a large pocket. Follow the arete (bold) to gain a ledge on the right. Step left round the arete and climb the left side moving left near the top.

Felo de Se   12m   E3 6a * *(1997)*
Good technical climbing in the lower section. Left of the arete is an obvious thin crack-line. Climb this to a thin horizontal break above some overlaps. Move right to gain the ledge just left of the arete. Follow Captain Ahab to finish.

BRANDER AREA

(NT 873 706)   Map p423

This area can be divided into two sections. The Brander is the long green slabby promontory running out into the sea, while East Brander Bay encompasses the shorter fins between The Brander and the big pebble bay to the south.

THE BRANDER

Non-tidal   North-West facing   Maps p406, 423   Diagram p425

The climbing is located on the north-west face, to the left of a small low promontory in front of the main slab.

Approach: Access has to be made from above. 1) From the field opposite The Souter descend a wide grassy bowl to the south to a pinnacle (The Wedge), and cross the pebble bay. The small low promontory has a ledge running out to its tip from here. A steep grass and scree gully leads up to a narrow col connecting The Brander promontory to the mainland. From the col traverse the narrow ridge down to ledges and large blocks overlooking a cave at the landward end of the slabs. It is possible to continue descending the whole promontory to the sea, doubling back along the base of the slabs, but many parties abseil from the blocks (near the top of Spring Shower) to a ledge above sea-level at the mouth of the cave. In rough seas some massive waves can swamp the cave, and spray has been known to reach the roof – beware!

2) From Dowlaw Farm, head east on a track along the edge of a field to a burn. This is at the head of a gorge called Dowlaw Dean. Cross the burn and follow the fence on the south side of the gorge, which turns right and rises steeply at the sea. A faint path goes diagonally left up the slope. When it relents, trend left and cross the fence. Find a steep grassy ridge running down to the col at the top of The Brander promontory, then continue as described in the first approach above.

The routes are described from right to left – landward to seaward.

44 Up-helly-aa   35m   E3 5c * *(1991)*
This route gains and climbs the right bounding corner of the slab at the mouth of the cave; an impressive line with some serious climbing. Start on the ledge directly below the crack of Bouma Sequence. Follow a line of holds up and right to a niche in a thin crack. Step out right, then go straight up (crux) to a ledge. Enter the corner and at its top move up and left to finish as for Bouma Sequence.

45 Bouma Sequence   35m   E1 5a * *(1991)*
A superb bold climb up the crack left of Up-helly-aa. Gain the crack directly up the slab (crux), moving right through the small overlap, then go back left.

46 The Ancient Mariner   35m   E2 5b * *(1991)*
Start midway between the cracks of Bouma Sequence and Spring Shower. Climb

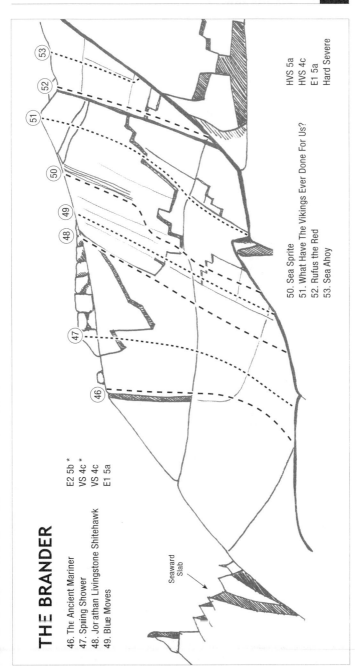

THE BRANDER

46. The Ancient Mariner — E2 5b *
47. Spring Shower — VS 4c *
48. Jor athan Livingstone Shitehawk — VS 4c
49. Blue Moves — E1 5a

50. Sea Sprite — HVS 5a
51. What Have The Vikings Ever Done For Us? — HVS 4c
52. Rufus the Red — E1 5a
53. Sea Ahoy — Hard Severe

Seaward Slab

direct to the right end of a ledge. Traverse this left and go up towards a crack in the overlap. Climb through this and follow a diagonal crack right to another ledge. Moves up and left lead to a crack and a loose finish.

47 Spring Shower   35m   VS 4c * (1981)
This is the obvious continuous crack right of the centre of the slab, started from the lower ledge. A traditional classic in an exciting position, low in its grade.

48 Jonathan Livingstone Shitehawk   35m   VS 4c (1981)
Start on the lower ledge about 6m left of Spring Shower. Climb up directly into the right bounding corner of a huge shield of rock. Surmount an overlap then move diagonally left to reach a thin crack-line which leads to the top.

49 Blue Moves   40m   E1 5a (1981)
At low tide, start from a hanging stance under the sea-level bulge directly below the centre of the huge shield in the middle of the slab. Make bold moves up and diagonally right to reach the lower ledge. Move up a shallow overlapped groove to reach the middle ledge. Climb through the overlap at the apex and go up the shield, passing some shallow pockets. Poorly protected.

50 Sea Sprite   40m   HVS 5a (1981)
Good climbing up the thin disjointed crack-line in the left side of the shield. Start as for Blue Moves and climb directly up the lower slab to the halfway ledge. Climb through the overlap and continue up cracks to the top.

51 What Have The Vikings Ever Done For Us?   40m   HVS 4c (1981)
Start just left of Blue Moves directly below the left bounding corner of the shield. Move up the slab to the corner and climb this to pull out right at the top.

52 Rufus the Red   35m   E1 5a (1981)
Start at the base of a ramp and follow cracks to the halfway ledge, then move up into the apex of the overlap near the top. Unprotected.

53 Sea Ahoy   35m   Hard Severe (1981)
Climb the crack-line left of Rufus the Red, bearing left at the top.

Seaward Slab

Tidal   North facing

This is the fine slab out at the tip of The Brander. The lower half is overlaid by a shield of good rough rock on the upper half. There are about five routes on 'go anywhere' rock with grades varying between 4a and 4c.

EAST BRANDER BAY

Map p423

Immediately south of The Brander are a series of fins at the northern end of a big pebble bay.

Approach: There are three access routes: 1) Approximately 80m above the col connecting The Brander to the mainland, a steep, grassy, rocky slope leads down into a gully between Lucky Day Wall and Dayglo Fin; 2) It is possible to scramble down the rubble slope immediately south-east of the Spring Shower abseil point. Work south with some interesting route finding to arrive at Lucky Day Wall, the smooth overhanging north face of Emerald Fin. Care should be taken in this area to avoid being cut off by the tide; 3) A more obscure but pleasant approach is to walk in from Lumsdaine Farm (NT 873 690), approached from the A1107 via the minor road at NT 892 666. Walk north-east from the farm on a track past some ruined cottages to a gate. Turn left and follow the fence to the far end of a wood. Turn right and go to the top of a wide overgrown gully dropping to the sea. An old smugglers' path winds down the wide slope just north of the gully to the shore. Head north to reach Cockle Shell Fin.

The fins are described south to north. The first route lies immediately left of Cockle Shell Fin.

The Skate   90m   Severe   (1970)
Climb a vegetated ramp until broken ground is reached. Follow this and trend right to the upper tier of rock. Finish up a chimney.

Cockle Shell Fin

North & South facing   Map p423
This is the main fin, which has a distinctive nest-infested forked crack in its south face (Cockle Shell Cracks). The rock is much poorer in this area and some of the routes described are probably best avoided. A few routes have good climbing and would benefit from more traffic.

Descent: By a grassy gully to the north of the fin.

South Face

The Bat Crack   25m   Severe *   (1989)
Well up and left of Cockle Shell Cracks is a short wall with a left-slanting crack in its left side and a narrower parallel crack to the right. Scramble up grass and loose rock to the base of the wall. Climb the wide left-slanting crack.

The Buoy Wonder   25m   E1 5b *   (1989)
The thin crack 3m right of the Bat Crack can be reached via a short wall and a right-facing corner.

Carapus   60m   E1 4c   (1970)
A horror show! Climb the obvious chimney line right of the Skate; wellies and a gas mask might help. A variation climbs the crack left of Carapus until progress is barred by an overhang. Move right and continue up the Carapus chimney.

Guano Corner   60m   E1 4c   (1981)
A wet suit might be useful for this one. Climb the slimy corner at the left end of the main wall. Avoid during periods of seismic activity.

The best descent from the next three routes is to traverse an exciting narrow ledge on the north face to the grassy gully.

The Twilight Hour   40m   E5 6a   (1989)
The impressive wall between Guano Corner and Cockle Shell Cracks gives some good climbing but is poorly protected and on dubious rock. Start from the boulder at the foot of Guano Corner. Climb straight up to a peg runner, move right and up to a large porthole, then go up to another peg and a couple of small but good wire placements. Go up and left through the bulge, then move up and diagonally left for 5m to a large flat hold. Continue up, keeping just left of loose cracks, to a 'thank God' ledge. Move right to finish up easier ground.

Cockle Shell Cracks   40m   Scottish VS   (1970)
Start in the middle of the wall and follow the crack system to where it splits. Take the left branch and climb past loose blocks to a ledge and easier ground.

BERWICKSHIRE COAST

Squid   50m   HVS 5a *   *(1970)*

A good route up the obvious corner on the seaward edge of the fin. Climb straight up the corner passing a large bulge (peg runner, crux) and ascend a chimney to reach the top.

Lucky Day Wall

The north face of Cockle Shell Fin is an impending black wall, split with crack-lines and a long right-trending ramp. The climbs traverse off rightwards along the ledge that splits the face starting at two-thirds height and petering out at the grassy gully.

Sperm   20m   Severe   *(1970)*

Another slime monster. Climb the chimney at the left end of the north face, if you must!

Seize the Day   20m   E1 5b *   *(1992)*

The first crack-line on the wall right of Sperm. Climb blocky cracks, taking the shorter left-hand finish to a ledge on the left. Finish up Sperm.

Lucky Day   30m   E3 5b   *(1981)*

A very serious route taking the right-trending diagonal ramp. Climb the ramp (poor peg runner) and pull onto an obvious block with difficulty. Traverse right on an overhung ledge, then climb a short ramp to a niche and the ledge above. Traverse off.

Drop the Pilot   20m   E4 6a *   *(1992)*

Start up the slope from Lucky Day, below a large boulder. Climb the thin crack-line to an overlap. Move over this (crux) to the upper crack, then go left onto the short ramp of Lucky Day and finish up this.

Dayglo Fin

North & South facing   Map p423

This is the small fin north of Cockle Shell Fin.

South Face

Dayglo   20m   HVS 5b *   *(1970)*

Climb the superb long crack running diagonally leftwards up the face. A short traverse left at mid-height leads to another crack and a groove leading to the top.

The Left-Hand Crack   15m   HVS 5a

Climb the cleaned crack right of Dayglo, finishing up the crest of the fin.

The Right-Hand Crack   15m   HVS 5a

Climb the shorter crack just to the right, to gain the crest.

North Face

Quasi's Back   12m   E3 6a *   *(1983)*

Climb the zigzag crack in the middle of the face to a ledge. Follow the crest to the top.

Emerald Fin

South facing   Map p423

The next fin to the north has a green and chossy south face and an impressively blank overhanging north face.

Purve   50m   Scottish VS *(1970)*
Take a confident partner, an ice axe and some valium then set off up the thin seaward arete of the fin. If you reach the top, belay to a block at the end of the crest or go up the slope to a peg and flake on the right.

The Voyage of the Mad Manxman   45m   E2 5c * *(1992)*
This takes a thin crack-line up the blank wall at the left end of the south face. Start 2m right of the left-bounding corner. Climb up to a left-slanting break. Move left and up to a thin left-trending crack, then go left and follow the main crack-line up the wall. At two-thirds height, make moves left to the crack branching left. Follow this to good flake holds, then move left to a short thin crack leading past a small niche to the top.

BURNMOUTH AREA

Map p330

Two sandstone sea-stacks have been climbed in the vicinity of the small harbour of Burnmouth.

Approach: From the A1 follow the steep road down to Burmouth harbour and a parking area at the seafront.

BREECHES ROCK

(NT 957 622)   Non-tidal

From the parking area, continue north past cottages and follow the coastline for 1km to reach this impressive 50m high stack.

Gunsight Arete   HVS *(2004)*
1. 45m 4a Climb the landward arete to reach a ramp. Up this to a prominent notch on the arete. Belay here (Friends 3.5 & 4).
2. 15m 4c Turn the step above on its left, before moving right below the final headwall into a hidden corner which is followed to the summit.

MAIDEN'S STONE

(NT 966 603)   Tidal

From the parking place follow the coast for 1km, southwards along the base of the cliffs and round Ross Point to reach this well known landmark.

Landward Side   20m   Very Difficult *(1994)*
Start up the west facing landward side. A series of three increasingly difficult mantelshelves leads to the north ridge which is followed to the top. The seaward face has been top-roped at 4c.

BERWICKSHIRE COAST

Space has precluded listing first ascents of the numerable boulder problems detailed in this guide. However, this data has been recorded and the SMC's intention that it will be published in the forthcoming guide to bouldering in Scotland, or on the website – www.smc.org.uk

The Trossachs & Loch Lomond
Rosneath & Clynder Quarries
All routes roped solo or solo by G.Szuca, 2001-2004.

Ben An

1896	May 21	Left-Hand Gully	G.Thomson, H.C.Boyd, Rev A.Boyd
1898	Jan 1	Right-Hand Gully	W.Naismith, W.Douglas, J.Maclay
1898	Jan 22	Oblique Crack	H.Raeburn, J.Napier
1930		Ash Wall	W.White
1930		The Last Eighty	J.B.Nimlin
1934		The Rent	J.B.Nimlin
1937		Birch Wall	J.B.Nimlin
1970	May 10	Coriander	K.V.Crocket, K.Simpson
1985	Jul 31	Tricky Vicky	G.Szuca, J.Parker

Achray Wall

1983	25 Jun	The Bow	G.Little
1983	14 Aug	The Arrow	G.Little, P Linning

Creagan an Amair Ghlais

1991	Jun	Sarsaparilla	G.Dudley
1992	May	Root Beer	G.Dudley, C.Dudley

Stronachlachar

1997	Sep 21	My Own Private Scotland	C.Miln
1997	Sep 22	Highland Cling	I.Watson
1997	Sep 27	Rakshasha	C.Miln
1998	May 16	Lady of the Loch	I.Watson
2000	May 7	El Mundo Fanatico	C.Miln
2000	May 13	Rhumba al Sol	I.Watson
2000	May 14	Venga Boys	G.Ridge
2001	Aug 18	Hideous Kinky	C.Miln, I.Watson
2004	Mar 7	High and Mighty	D.Macleod
2004	Sep 15	Live-in Skin	D.MacLeod, R.Waterton

Crag One, Wild Swans Buttress, Crystal Crag

1997	Oct 23	Wild Swans	I.Watson
1997	Oct 25	Hobble	C.Miln
1997	Nov 2	Dark Skies	C.Miln
1998	Mar 15	Rebel Without Applause	C.Miln
1998	Aug 22	Roadkill Recipies	G.Ridge
1998	Aug 22	Age of Aquarius	C.Miln
1998	Oct 3	Fear and Self Loathing	C.Miln
1998	Oct 31	The Ridge	C.Miln
1998	Nov 15	Moonlight Sonata	I.Watson
1999	May 2	Purgatory	C.Miln
1999	May 2	Far From the Malham Crowds	I.Watson
2000	Mar 18	Ruby Slippers	J.Horrocks
2004	Mar 7	Wild Goats	D.Macleod
2004	Nov 2	Been Caught Stealin'	D.MacLeod

Creagan Tom Dubh

1986	Oct 4	Athena	S.Yates, F.Mains, D.Gardner
1986	Oct 4	Perfect Strangers	S.Yates
1986	Oct 4	Crazy Cow	S.Yates, F.Mains
1989	Apr 30	Sequestrator	S.M.Richardson, R.Reid
1989	May 7	Mahabharata	R.Reid, S.M.Richardson

Carn na Muice

1987	Jul 22	Sallochy Slab	K.Black, N.Milton

| 1987 Jul 22 | Sunset Ridge | N.Milton, K.Black |
| 1987 Sep 2 | Twilight Slab | N.Milton, S.M.Richardson. |

Top section K.Black & N.Milton, 22 Jul 1987

1987 Sep 2	The Bat Flake	S.M.Richardson, N.Milton
1990 Mar	The Drag	J.Taylor
1991 Jun 1	Bite The Dust	J.Taylor
1991 Jun 7	Brimbles	A.Coon, J.Taylor

Ross Point

1986 May	Crystal Junction	J.Christie, A.Kirk
1987 May	One Way Trip	J.Christie, A.Leary
1987 May	Slug Death	J.Christie, A.Leary
1989 Jul	Forked Lightning	S.Robinson, K.Lawson
1991 May 16	Son of Cog	I.Taylor, J.Nairn
1991	Pullover	J.Taylor, A.Coon
1991	Legover	J.Taylor, A.Benson, P.Benson

Glasgow Area
The Whangie

The first ascent details of most routes have not been recorded

| 1985 Jul 30 | Sudden Death | S.M.Richardson, M.Fowler |

A free ascent of Slim Crack.

Slackdhu

1930	Black Craig	A.Sanders, A.N.O
1930s	Pinnacle Arete, Jenny's Lum Arete	Unknown
1992	Tendons, Blocker, Moss Kills,	
	Classic Crack	A.Coon, D.Adams

Probably climbed previously.

Dunglas

1975 May 6	Skirmish	J.Mackenzie, B.Clarke
1975 May 11	Downfall	J.Mackenzie, C.Garthwaite
1975 May 11	Dunglas Corner	J.Mackenzie, C.Garthwaite
1975 May 11	Joker's Groove	C.Garthwaite, J.Mackenzie
1975 May 15	Curioser and Curioser	J.Mackenzie, C.Garthwaite
1975 Jun 7	The Ramp	J.Mackenzie
1975 Jul 13	The Cross	J.Mackenzie, M.Astbury, G.Rooney

Top-roped and cleaned some weeks before.

1975 Sep 14	Little Gripper	J.Mackenzie
1976 Apr 15	Pullover	J.Mackenzie, D.Nicholson
1976 Apr 24	The Gentle Touch	J.Mackenzie, B.Clarke
1976 May 3	A Dream of Brown Trousers	J.Kerry, J.Mackenzie (both solo)
1976 May 3	Last Grasp	J.Mackenzie (solo)
1976 Summer	North-East Arete	J Mackenzie

Top-roped in 1975 before being lead.

1976 Jun 7	Moss Flop	J.Mackenzie
1976 Jul 3	The Nightmare	J.Mackenzie (roped solo)
1976 Jul 12	A Feet of Arms	J.Mackenzie, N.Tennent
1977 Jul 13	Wall of Horrors	J.Mackenzie, C.Garthwaite

Top-roped three days before being led.

1977 Aug 6	Ribbish	J.Mackenzie (solo)
1977 Aug 6	Rubbish	J.Mackenzie (solo)
1982 Jan 21	Overlord	G.Little, A.Savage (1PA)

FFA P.Linning, G.Little, 7 Jul 1983

1987 Aug 10	Deviant	S.M.Richardson, T.Prentice
1987 Aug 10	Bite them Bequerels	T.Prentice, S.M.Richardson
1989 Jul 2	The Beef Monster	B.Kerr, G.McIntyre
1991 Jun	Steel Finger	G.Dudley
1992 Aug	Negotiations with Isaac	A.Gallagher
1992 Aug	Political Legacy	A.Gallagher
1992 Aug	Airhead	C.Phair
1998	Unnamed	M.Conner (solo)

1998 Jul 25	Don't Wake Up Now	D.MacLeod (solo)
1999 Aug	Dream Delirious	D.MacLeod (solo)
2000 Jul 17	Drink Up For Tomorrow We Die	D.MacLeod

Dumbarton Rock

1963	Boulevard	N.MacNiven
1963	Frendo	B.Shields
1963	Stonefall Crack	N.MacNiven
1963	Stonefall Crack Direct	N.MacNiven, B.Shields
1963	Monsoon Gully	B.Shields, M.Connolly
1964	The Big Zipper	B.Shields, A.Baillie (aid)
FFA M.Hamilton. FFA Direct Start G.Latter, 1983		
1964	The Neilweg	B.Shields, M.Connolly
1964	Angel's Pavement	N.MacNiven
1964	Chemin de Fer	N.MacNiven, B.Shields (aid)
FFA D.Cuthbertson, 1980		
1964	Ganglion Grooves	K.Haggerty, B.Shields
1964	Grey Slab	B.Shields, M.Connolly
1964 Feb 2	Longbow	B.Shields, J.R.Houston (some aid)
FFA S.Belk, J.Dalrymple		
1964	Nameless Crack	N.MacNiven
1964	Poison Ivy	B.Shields
1964 Feb 19	Windjammer Crack	B.Shields, J.R.Houston
1965	Old Socks	B.Shields
1965	Requiem	B.Shields, M.Connolly (aid)
FFA D.Cuthbertson, climbed over several weeks in summer 1983		
1965	West Face Gully	B.Shields and others
1965	Route Three	B.Shields, K.Haggerty
1960s	Alleyway	N.MacNiven
	Hailstone Climb	M.Connolly
	Left Edge Route	I.Nicholson
	Plunge	L.Mitchell
	West Face Girdle	B.Shields, M.Connolly
1974 Mar	Cyclops	B.Shields, K.Haggerty (aid)
FFA D.Cuthbertson, 1981		
1970s	Banana Rib	I.Fulton
	Banana Groove	I.Nicolson, R.McFarlane
	Left Edge Route	I.Nicholson
	Bobtail	S.Belk, J.Dalrymple
	Rag	I.Nicholson
	Sunset Groove	I.Fulton, I.Nicolson
	Tag	I.Nicolson, R.McFarlane
	Desperado	B.Shields
	Ciamar A Tha Sibh	A.Kelso
	Snowwhite	A.Kelso (some aid).
FFA W.Todd		
	Fever Pitch	N.Colton
	Rough Sea	K.Johnstone
	Gaucho	W.Todd
	Slainte	K.Johnstone
	Drizzle	K.Johnstone
	Antigrav	K.Johnstone (2PA)
FFA W.Todd		
1980	Woops	D.Cuthbertson
1980	Datura	R.Kerr
1981	Big Ears	G.Latter, T.Prentice
1983 Mar 1	Requiem Direct Start	B.Masterton, A.Wren
1983 Mar 20	Rock of Ages	G.Latter
1983	Grey Wall	G.Latter
1984	Rising Power	G.Latter
1984	Samora	G.Latter
1988 May	Supple as a Brick	T.Prentice, R.Everett, S.M.Richardson
1993	Omerta	A.Gallagher
1993	Appliance of Violence	B.McLaughlan
1993	Bad Attitude	A.Gallagher

1993	Half Breed	C.Phair
1993	Unforgiven	A.Gallagher
1993	Stonefall Wall	A.Gallagher
1993	Eliminator	A.Gallagher
1993	Benny's Route (right)	J. Dunne
1993	Sufferance	A.Gallagher
1993	Tarrier	M.McGowan
1994	Benny's Route (left)	G. Sutcliffe
1995	Dum Dum Boys	A. Gallagher
1996	Natural Born Drillers	C.Phair
1996	Payback Time!	A.Gallagher
1997	Persistance Of Vision	A.Gallagher
1997	Casanostra	A.Gallagher
1998	Still Going	P.McGowan, D.MacLeod
1998 Feb 2	Friends In High Places	D.MacLeod
1998 Jun 3	Fatso	D.MacLeod
1998	Knees And Toes	D.MacLeod, R.Ewan
1999	Easter Rib	A.Gallagher
1999 May	Dumb And Dumber	D.MacLeod
2001 Oct 9	Achemine	D.MacLeod

11 long falls taken from the headwall before the successful first ascent.

2003 Sep	Calm Before the Storm	D.MacLeod, S.Richardson
2003 Oct 4	Blackout	D.MacLeod, S.Richardson
2003 Oct 5	Eh Gringo	D.MacLeod, R.McGhee
2003 Oct 19	Tolerance	D.MacLeod
2004 Jun 1	Abstract Art	D.MacLeod

Dumbuck

1992	Awaken	A.Gallagher
1992	Gentle Mass	A.Gallagher
1992	If Six Was Nine	C.Phair
1994	Flesh For Fantasy	C.Phair
1995	Parallel	A.Gallagher
1996	Voodoo Magic	A.Gallagher

Re-climbed in 2000 by D.MacLeod after loss of crucial holds.

1996	House of Pain	A.Gallagher
1997	Twister	D.Stevenson
1997	Tragically Hip	J.Jones
1998	Breathe the Pressure	D.Stevenson
1998	Filth Infatuated	R.Conaly
1999	Second Sights	D.Redpath
2000	So Be It	D.MacLeod
2000	Call of the Wild	R.McGhee, D.MacLeod
2001	Dirty Sanchez	M.Rudden
2004	Happiness in Slavery	D.MacLeod
2004 Oct 27	Devastation Generation	D.MacLeod

The hardest route in the guide and Scotland's first 8c.

Bowling

2000	Yogi's Wobble	J.Watson
2000	Booboo's Knob	J. Watson
2000	Astroboy	J.Watson
2000	Yosemite Crack	J.Watson
2000	Eiger Suction	J.Watson
2001	The Thin White Line	I.Beveridge, M.Casey
2001	The Pastor's Dirty Daughter	I.Beveridge
2002	The Fold	D.MacLeod

Auchinstarry Quarry

1975	Mascarade	K.Johnstone, D.Denn
1975 Nov	Gold Rush	J.Kerry, S.N.Smith
1976 Jun	Promontory Direct	J.Kerry, H.Reader
1976 Sep	Spirogyra	J.Kerry, D.McCallum
1976 Oc	Whiplash	J.Kerry, H.Reader, P.Greenwell

1976 Oct	Kelvin Way	H.Reader, J.Kerry, P.Greenwell
1976 Oct	Short Reach	P.Greenwell, H.Reader
1976 Oct	Fool's Gold	J.Kerry, D.McCallum, P.Greenwell
1976 Nov	Urea	H.Reader, J.Kerry
1976	Tar	C.Ogilvie, H.Reader
1976	Maypole	K.Johnsone, D.Benn

Direct: R.Kerr, 1978

1976	Christmas Corner	K.Johnstone, B.Swan
1977 Feb	Lion	J.Kerry, H.Reader

Re-climbed after partial demolition, by R.Everett, D.Gaffney 25 Sep 1993.

1977 Mar	Talisman	J.Kerry, H.Reader
1977 Mar	Lion Cub	D.Sanderson
1977 Mar	Pigeon Hole	J.Kerry, R.Kerr
1977 Apr	Separated Edge	J.Kerry, C.Macadam
1977 Jul	White Slab	K.McKluskie
1977 Jul	Trundle	K.Johnstone, B.Swan
1977 Sep	Red Lead	J.Kerry, F.Yeoman
1977 Sep	Cracked Arete	J.Kerry, P.Greenwell
1977 Oct	Scream	R.Kerr, A.Campbell
1977 Oct	Discord	J.Kerry, R.Kerr
1977 Oct	Knock Back	J.Kerry, N.Macfadyen
1977 Oc	After the Gold Rush	W.Todd
1977 Nov	Caftan, Bazaar	J.Kerry, H.Reader
1977	Slinky Lizard	D. Benn, D. McCallum
1978 Jun	Newcastle Brown	J.F. Kerry, R. Kerr
1978	Soft Machine	R. Kerr
1979 Sep	Power Play	R.Kerr, A.Colville
1980	Green Onion, Mr. Men	R.Kerr
1980	I Spy	N. Morrison, A.Kay
1980	Walk on the Wild Side	R.Kerr
1980	Midas Touch	M.Putnam
1981 Aug	BC's Return	S.Taylor, R.Kerr
1981	Southern Man	R.Kerr, S.Taylor
1982	Nijinski	D.Cuthbertson

Climbed previously with side runners by W.Todd.

1983 Feb	Dream Machine	J.Handren, J.Melrose
1980s	Blade Runner	J.Handren
1980s	Death is the Hunter	J.Handren, D.McCallum

Led without the siderunner by N.Tarmey, in 2000.

1980s	Carouselambra	G.Latter
1980s	Surface Tension	D.McCallum

The top part was straightened out by C.Gilchrist in 1986.

1980s	High Dive	C.Dale
1986 May	Shot in the Dark	T.Prentice, J.Christie
1986 May	Band Aid	T.Prentice, P.McAra
1986 May	Race Against Time	J.Christie, T.Prentice
1986 Jun	Both Toes Burning	T.Prentice, R.Everett
1986 Jun	The Color Purple	T.Prentice, P.McAra
1986 Jul	Red Snapper	J.Christie, T.Prentice
1988 Sep 26	The Gold Bug	I.Taylor, J.Nairn
1989 Apr 1	Promontory Runner	R.Anderson, K.Spence
1990 May 24	Harry Goes West	G.MacIntyre, T.Gould, J.Sime
1990 May 27	Hopelessly Treading Water	G.MacIntyre
1990 Jul 31	Spanking the Rustbucket	G.MacIntyre
1992 May	The Surf Shack	A.Gallagher
1992 May 28	The Seven Year Plan	I.Taylor, S.Munro
1992 Jun	Twilight Zone	A.Gallagher
1992 Jul	Three Cheers For Yer Uncle Bob, CP1, CP2	A.Wallace (solo)
1993 May	In Through the Out Door	G. Harrison, J. Thompson
1993 Sep 25	Glass	R.Everett, D.Gaffney

Probably climbed before.

1999	Team Ascent	M.Conner, N.McNair, D.MacLeod
1999	Shiny Happy People,The Javelin	D.MacLeod, S.Paterson
1999	Glasgow No More,	D.MacLeod, S.Paterson, R.Fraser

2000	Teardrops	A.Wallace
2003	Auch!	A.Wallace, R.Wallace
2003 Jun	Think of Scotland	D.MacLeod, S.Richardson

Both soloed after practice. The fall from the crux into the rocks/pool was taken without injury just prior to S.Richardson's ascent.

2003 Jul 23	Orange Flash	A.Wallace, C.McDaid

The line was previously taken by Fourth Wave before its destruction.

2003 Jul 27	Mister, Ye Can Walk Up Roon The Back	A.Wallace, C.Newlands
2003 Jul 27	Mister, You're On Fire Mister	A.Wallace, C.Newlands
2003 Oct 11	Cruiser's Creek, Golddigger	A.Wallace, R.Wallace
2003 Oct 11	Danger! U.S.R.	R.Wallace, A.Wallace
2003 Oct 12	Bouldermouse, The Return of the King	R.Wallace, A.Wallace
2003 Oct 16	Bruddaz Gonna Work It Out	D.MacLeod
2004 Feb 8	Cubigoruasry	A.Wallace, W.Upson
2004 Mar 31	Kein Trink Wasser	A.Wallace, R.Wallace
2004 May 11	No Stone Unturned	A.Wallace, R.Wallace
2004 Jun 19	Just Stand Up	A.Wallace, R.Wallace
2004 Jun 22	Solstice Slot	A.Wallace, R.Wallace
2004 Jun 22	Dwr Budr	A.Wallace, R.Wallace
2004 Jun 22	C.K.D.C.F.U	A.Wallace, R.Wallace, I.Halstead

Carron Glen - Kamikaze Squirrel Crag

All routes by A.Wallace & R.Wallace, May 2003. Wee Chimney, A.Wallace, 1995.

Neilston

1998 Sep 19	Hyperreality	D.Crawford, S.Burns
1998 Sep	Whitehorse Rib	D.Crawford
2004 May 17	Twisted	A.McDonald, P.McDonald
2004 May 22	Strawberry Direct	A.McDonald, K.Shields

Ayrshire
Loudoun Hill

1930s	Pulpit Arete, Left Crack	R.Anderson, D.Scott

Pulpit Arete showed signs of previous ascent.

1930s	Jackdaw Chimney	R.Anderson, D.Scott
1930s	Foxglove Chimney	R.Anderson, D.Scott
1930s	Dusk Route	R.Anderson, D.Scott
1960s	Pulpit Chimney	J.R.Jackson, D.W.Young
1960s	Lunge, Cling	J.R.Jackson
1960s	Amphitheatre Arete	J.R.Jackson
1960s	Mantleshelf Wall	J.R.Jackson
1960s	Conclusion Wall	J.R.Jackson, J.Clelland
1960s	Shattered Corner	J.R.Jackson, D.W.Young
1960s	Epitaph	D.W.Young
1960s	Epitaph Variation	J.R.Jackson, D.W.Young (aid)

FFA: R.Sandilands, D.Pratt, 1974

1960s	Slings	J.R.Jackson (some aid)

FFA: K.McClusky, R.Sandilands, 1978

1960s	Coffin Chimney, Ring	J.R.Jackson
1960s	Trench Direct	D.W.Young
1960s	Contortion Groove	J.R.Jackson
1960s	Sadist's Groove	J.R.Jackson, B.Dale
1960s	Tottering Layback	J.R.Jackson
1960s	Dee's Crack	J.R.Jackson, K.Bryan
1960s	Strife	J.R.Jackson, D.W.Young
1960s	Evening Groove	J.R.Jackson, B.Dale
1960s	Slab and Groove	J.R.Jackson, B.Dale
1960s	Cave Crack	J.R.Jackson, D.W.Young
1960s	Automation	J.R.Jackson, D.Brownlea (aid)
1978	Senile Slab	K.McClusky, R.Sandilands
1981	Chalkster	A.Taylor, K.McClusky
1993 May 19	Quick Skive	T.Prentice

1993	May 24	Busman's Holiday	T.Prentice
1993	Dec	Planet X	P.Brown, S.McFarlane
1995		The Vein	P.Brown

Direct Finish: S.Wright, E.Rice October 4, 2003

1995	Apr 12	Messiah	P.Brown (roped solo)
1995	Apr 12	Hobbit Crack	P.Brown (roped solo)
1995	Apr 25	Painless	P.Brown (roped solo)
1995	Apr 26	Boulder Suicide	P.Brown (roped solo)
1995	May 3	Leftover Crack	P.Brown (roped solo)
1995	May 11	Lambchops	P.Brown, J.McCulloch

A route, August Sensation, HVS 5a, was climbed in this vicinity by B.Duff & R.Sandlands, 1970s.

1998	May 10	The Cat	C.Pettigrew, T.Burley, H.Bruce
2003	Aug 14	Mur	S.Johnson, G.Johnson

Mauchline

1979/80		The Chimney	A.Watson, J.Wilson
1986		Purism Personified	S.Lampard (solo)
1986		Bowman's Corner	S.Lampard (solo)
1986		Gardener's Corner	S.Lampard, J.Lampard
1986		Dredge Boy	S.Lampard (solo)
1986		Monsterously Horrible	S.Lampard, J.Freeman, I.Rooney
1986		Corner Root	S.Lampard (solo)
1986		The Arete	S.Lampard (solo)
1987		Board Walk	S.Lampard (solo)
1987		Y Bother	S.Lampard (solo)
1987		Bye Eck	S.Lampard (solo)
1987		Green Machine	S.Lampard (solo)
1988		Bridge Over Troubled Water	S.Lampard
1988	Jun	Ayrheid	T.Prentice, P.McAra
1988	Jun	Games of Chance & Sandacing	T.Prentice, R.Everett
1989		Bushwhacker	S.Lampard, C.Stenhouse
1989		Lightning Crack	S.Lampard, M.Reed

Glen Afton

1977		Grass Roots	G.Little

Direct start: S.Lampard (solo), 1990.

1977		Rehabilitation Route	G.Little
1978		Two Plus Two	G.Little
1978		Deception Slab	G.Little
1978		Raven Slab	G.Little
1991	31 Jul	The Crack of Doon	S.Lampard, A.Fraser
1992	24 Jun	Midnight Express	R.McAllister, A.Fraser, D.McGimpsey
1992	7 Jul	Stone Circle	R.McAllister, D.McGimpsey
1992	10 Jul	Hyacinth House	R.McAllister, D.McGimpsey
1992	19 Jul	Magic Carpet	A.Fraser, R.McAllister
1992	21 Jul	Sweet Liberty	R.McAllister
1992	24 Aug	Delirium	R.McAllister, D.McGimpsey

One poor nut placed on abseil and removed after the ascent.
Direct Start: R.McAllister, 17 Sep 1992.

Galloway Hills

The routes on Gaw Glen Crag were put up by D.Sproat in the 1970s.

The Merrick

1920s		Black Gutter	G.Girdwood

Legend has it that this was first climbed in Victorian times by the farmer from Shalloch on Minnoch while rescuing a sheep. The ascent was accomplished at night in a thunderstorm with the added complications of rockfall and the unwanted attentions of an aggressive eagle!

First winter ascent not known. The earliest ascents traced to date are: via the right-branch D.Sproat, A.Kelso, 1970s, via the left branch, E.Christison, J.Wilson, C.George, A.Watson, M.Atkinson, 1985.

In the '70s and '80s various routes between grade II and IV were climbed, but not fully recorded by D.Sproat and Kyle MC members E.Christison, J.Wilson, A.Watson, A.Dowers, C.George, M.Pashke, M.Atkinson, and C.Murray. These included Left Rib o' the Gutter, D.Sproat and A.N.O.

W	1987		Right Rib o' the Gutter	D.McGimpsey, D.Sproat
W	1987		The Kyle Gully	E.Christison, M.Atkinson
W	1993	Dec 31	Interstellar Overdraft	R.McAllister, S.Mearns
W	1996	Feb	North-East Couloir	R.Gibson, T.Black
W	1996	Mar 17	Kenny's Folly	C.Hossack, J.Biggar, A.N.O
W	1996	Mar 17	Chippy's Downfall	C.Hossack, J.Biggar, A.N.O
W	2003	Feb 5	The Lang Scots Miles	A.Fraser, I.Magill (AL)

Mullwharchar

	ca1909		The Couloir	J.McBain (solo)
W	ca1970		The Couloir	G.Little (solo)

G.Little and J.Dykes did several unrecorded routes on the Giant's Staircase in the 1970s.

	1992	Mar 4	The Gullet	D.McGimpsey, S.Ravey
	1992	Jun 14	The Raiders	A.Fraser, D.McGimpsey

Dry Variations: C.King, S.Reid (AL), 10 Sep 2001

	1992	Jun 17	Bugle	D.McGimpsey, W.Cartner
	1992	Jun 17	Switchback	D.McGimpsey, W.Cartner

Variation Finish: S.Reid, J.Reid, 10 Aug 2001

	1992	Jun 21	Solstice	S.Lampard, G.Scott

Originally graded HVS!

	1992	Jun 21	The Dungeonmaster	A.Fraser, J.Dickson
	1992	Jun 21	Behind the Mask	R.McAllister, D.McGimpsey
	1992	Jun 21	Kids' Stuff	J.Dickson, A.Fraser
	1992	Jun 21	The Nose	S.Lampard (solo)
	1994	May 10	Concave Slab	R.McAllister, A.Fraser
	1994	May 10	Tiers for Fears	R.McAllister, A.Fraser
	1994	May 10	Where Beagles Dare	A.Fraser, R.McAllister
	1995	May 4	Brigadoon	A.Fraser, R.McAllister

Attempted by G.Little in the '70s – a peg adorned his high point for many years.

	1995	May	Yucatan	P.Brown (roped solo)
	1995	May	The Pagan	P.Brown (roped solo)
	1995	May	The Throne	P.Brown (roped solo)
	1995	Jun	Phoebus Mask	P.Brown (roped solo)
	2001	Sep 10	Tiers Before Bedtime	C.King, S.Reid (AL)
	2002	Sep 4	Dragonslayer	C.King, S.Reid
	2002	Sep 4	Smaug	C.King, S.Reid

Dungeon of Buchan - Dungeon Hill

	c1909		Lion's Head Gully	J.McBain (solo)
	1955	Sep	Cooran Buttress	J.Simpson, Miss J.Ractcliffe, A.Waldie, Miss M.Shields

Roraima was climbed by A.Fraser, W.Todd, D.Walker, M.Burgess in May 1978 – they were unaware of the line of the earlier route. Pitch 4 was recorded by S.Reid, R.Thomas 2001. The line taken by the original finishes of both routes is uncertain.

	1968	Apr 12	The Highway Man	G.Little, J.Dykes

The route was climbed but unrecorded and unnamed. Named by J.Fotheringham and P.Whillance on the second ascent in 1982. Little subsequently almost fell off while soloing, when a large flake broke. Other shorter routes in the area were done by G.Little and J.Dykes but not recorded.

	1976	Apr 12	Cooran Gully	A.Fraser, D.Gibson, W.Todd

Andrew Fraser's first of many new routes in the area – the youthful team's equipment consisted of 20m of hemp rope, 3 pegs and a hammer.

	1982	Jul	Cyclopath	J.Fotheringham, P.Whillance (AL)
	1982	Jul	Saddle Tramp	J.Fotheringham, P.Whillance (AL)
	1984	Jun 10	Traitor's Gait	A.Fraser (solo)

A bold ascent. Fraser fell off while soloing Cooran Buttress the same day, but fortunately grabbed the heather ledge he landed on.

	1991	Apr 24	Galloway Grooves	S.Reid, J.Grinbergs
	1991	Apr 24	Carrick Corner	S.Reid, J.Grinbergs
	1991	Apr 24	Scots Wha' Hae	S.Reid, J.Grinbergs
	1991	Apr 24	Battle Axe	J.Grinbergs, S.Reid
	1991	May 5	The Colonel's Corner	S.Reid, J.Grinbergs (AL)
	1991	May 12	Bruce's Stone	S.Reid, J.Grinbergs
	1991	May 12	Comyn Corner	J.Grinbergs, S.Reid
	1991	Jul 17	Heir Apparent	S.Reid, J.Grinbergs (AL)

Direct Finish: S.Reid, J.Grinbergs, same day (top-roped before leading)

	1991 Aug 20	Incy WincySpider	S.Reid, J.Grinbergs

Early attempts involved interesting ropework.

	1991 Aug 20	Bannockburn	J.Grinbergs, S.Reid

The English leader took some falls.

	1991 Aug 20	Hammer of the Scots	S.Reid, J.Grinbergs
	1991 Aug 29	Monkey Puzzle	D.Wilson, S.Reid (AL)
	1991 Sep 3	English Gold	S.Reid, D.Wilson (AL), W.O'Connor
	1991 Sep 3	Parcel of Rogues	D.Wilson, W.O'Connor, S.Reid
	1991 Sep 10	Free Land	S.Reid, W.Freeland (AL)
	1993 Jun 9	Cooran Chimney	S.Reid, D.Scott (AL)
	1994 Jul 17	Parcel of Rogues Direct	A.Shand, R.Everett
	1994	Red Otter Day	S.Reid, J.Campbell
W	2001 Jan 21	Hell Freezes Over	A.Fraser, I.Magill
	2001 Aug 22	Cooran Buttress Direct	S.Reid, J.Biggar (VL), J.Reid, M.Thompson
	2001 Aug 26	The Wee Slanter	J.Biggar, L.Biggar
	2002 Apr 6	The Lion's Mane	A.Gillies, S.Reid (AL)
	2002 Apr 6	Aslan	A.Fraser, I.Magill (AL)
	2002 Apr 6	Buchan Arete	S.Reid, A.Gillies
	2002 Apr 6	Horns of a Dilemma	I.Magill, A.Fraser (AL)

A bold on-sight ascent in encroaching dusk.

	2002 Apr 6	Jaw Jaw	S.Reid, A.Gillies
	2002 Apr 11	War War	C.King, S.Reid
	2002 May 5	Castles in the Air	S.Reid, M.Cundy

Via the easier variation on Pitch 1. Climbed direct S.Reid, C.King, 13 Sep 2002.

	2002 Sep 1	Snakes and Ladders	S.Reid, C.King (AL)
	2002 Sep 26	The Big Smirr	J.Biggar, S.Reid, C.King
	2002 Oct 2	The Scrieve	J.Biggar, S.Reid, C.King
	2002 Oct 10	Aughty Star	S.Reid, C.King (AL)

Originally climbed via the Direct Finish. The finish described was added by C.King, S.Reid, 17 Oct 2002, though they had climbed much of it earlier.

	2002 Oct 17	Sprauchler's Groove	J. Biggar, L.Biggar
	2002 Oct 17	Pembroke Mist	L.Biggar, J.Biggar

New start added by K.Livingston, N.Stapleton, 20 Jun 2004. The route originally started via Stairway to Heather.

	2002 Oct 17	Brishie Buttress	S.Reid, C.King
	2002 Dec 10	Bickerdike's Buttress	S.Reid, C.King (AL)
	2004 Jun 20	Stairway to Heather	J.Biggar, I.Livingston

Craignaw

	1950s	Two Difficults, Snibe Hill	A.Waldie
	1981 Jun 6	Drainpipe Gully	A.Fraser, W.Todd, A.Sloan
	1987	The Arete, Snibe Hill	A.Plumb, S.Aird
W	1991 Feb 2	Dow Spout	M.Gennaro, C.MacNee (AL)

A route, probably incompletely formed, was soloed in this area by E.Christison in 1987. Summer ascent, A.Fraser (solo), 23 Nov 2003.

W	1994 Jan 16	Silver Flow	S.Lampard, J.Thompson

Direct Finish: S.Reid, J.Fotheringham, 4 Jan 2002

W	2002 Jan 2	Drainpipe Gully	A.Fraser, I.Magill, S.Reid (AL)
W	2003 Jan 5	The Sleigh Team	I.Magill, A.Fraser
W	2003 Jan 5	Full Metal Jacket	A.Fraser, I.Magill
W	2003 Jan 8	Shot Cleugh Left-Hand Start	A. Hinkes, S.Reid
W	2003 Jan 8	Hidden Chimney	S.Reid, A. Hinkes
W	2003 Jan 10	Goat Track Gully, and Direct Finish	J.Biggar, S.Reid
W	2003 Jan 10	Broad Gully	S.Reid, J.Biggar
W	2003 Jan 10	Shot Cleugh Right-Hand Start	S.Reid (solo)
W	2003 Jan 10	Silver Sliver	A.Hinkes, S.Prior

Craiglee

	1994	Hoo-Haa	K.Livingston, I.Livingston
	2003 Oct 2	Sheuch o' the Clint, Pauchler's Wa', Keep yer Heid,	

	Neb o' the Clint	J.Biggar, S.Reid
2003 Oct 2	Caw Canny, Pecher's Redemption, Skelf Wa', Pernicketie Wa'	S.Reid, J.Biggar
2003 Oct 2	Heeliegalerie and Direct, Tak a Brek	S.Reid

Rhinns of Kells

W	1970s	North Gairy Top Routes	G.Little
W	1996	Millfire Icefalls	R.Gibson, T.Black
W	1990s	Milldown Neuter	R.Gibson
W	2004 Mar 11	Biggar Gully, Better Gully	J.Biggar, L.Biggar (solo)

Mulldonoch & Lamachan Hill

| W | 2003 Jan 11 | Tack it Easy | K.Mackay, A.McFadzean, G.Anderson |
| W | 2003 Jan 11 | Bit o' Fun | K.Mackay, A.McFadzean, G.Anderson |

Routes by members of the Tackety Bits Hill Walking Club.

Craigencallie

A.Waldie and others climbed various easy routes at Craigencallie in the 1950s but none were recorded.

1977 Aug 9	Cranium Edge	G.Little (unseconded)
1977 Sep 9	Deviator	G.Little, R Little
1977 Sep 18	Eliminator	G.Little, R Little
1984 Aug	The Cry	A.Plumb
1984 Aug	The Shout	A.Plumb, S.Aird
1984 Aug	The Scream	A.Plumb, S.Aird

The exact line of the first pitch is uncertain. It may have started more easily to the right, and it may have finished up Alligator. A Direct Start to Alligator was recorded by D.McGimpsey, G.Gerrard 8 Aug 1992, and may or may not have been new. It has been incorporated into this route.

1984 Aug	Secret Garden	A.Plumb, S.Aird
1985 Mar	Talk to the Wind	S.Aird, A.Plumb
1985 Mar	Walkabout	A.Plumb, S.Aird
1985 Mar	Raven Seek thy Brother	A.Plumb, S.Aird
1991 Apr 16	Alligator	A.Fraser, R.McAllister
1991 Apr 16	Decaffenator	R.McAllister (solo)
1992 Oct 18	Across the Barricades	A.Fraser, D.McGimpsey, R.McAllister
1993 Apr	Thumbs Up	A.Scougall, A.Plumb
1993 Jun 8	Tree Sanctuary	M.Reed, A.Fraser, J.Freeman, R.McAllister
1993 Jun 8	The Grey Man	A.Fraser, D.Gibson, R.McAllister

Left-Hand Finish: C.King, S.Reid, 17 Jul 2002

| 1993 Jun 8 | Delta of Venus | D.Gibson, R.McAllister, M.Reed, A.Fraser |
| 1994 Jun 23 | The Empty Quarter | A.Fraser, S.Mearns |

Direct Start: C.King, A.Mawer, S.Reid, 28 Jul 2001

1994 Jul 6	Corbie Steps	A.Fraser, K.Douglas.
1994 Oct 14	Heinous Venus	R.McAllister, A.Fraser, W.Todd
1994 Oct 14	Old Mortality	A.Fraser R.McAllister, W.Todd
1995 Jun 22	The Heretic	P.Brown (roped solo)
1998 Aug 19	The Whirling Dervishes	A.Fraser, A.Murdoch.

The local midge population bays for blood.

Craigdews

| c1959 | Central Route | G.Fraser |

Originally graded Severe with the Original (5a) Finish!
Alternative Pitch 3: S.Reid, J.Reid, 18 Sep 2001.

| 1984 Jul 26 | Cemetery Goats | J.Grove, K.Livingstone, I.Livingstone |

For many years the crag lay in a goat park and climbing was banned. This team were escorted from the crag by the local constabulary and the route unrecorded. Other climbers are known to have climbed on the crag, met similar resistance and not recorded their routes.
As described and named: A.Fraser, I.Magill, 26 Jul 2000

| 2000 Jun 6 | Das Goat | A.Fraser (solo) |

2000 Jun 28	Goats of Delirium	A.Fraser, I.Magill

Upper Crack Variation, Pitch 2: C.King, S.Reid, 20 Sep 2001. Pitch 3 was originally climbed as part of Central Route by G.Fraser, 1959.

2000 Jul 26	Capricorn Relish	I.Magill, A.Fraser
2000 Aug 30	Vorsprung Goat Technique	A.Murdoch, A.Fraser

Right-Hand Start: S.Reid, C.King, 20 Sep 2001

2001 Sep 16	Amazing Technicolour Dreamgoat	A.Fraser, I.Magill
2001 Sep 16	Dirty Old Raingoat	I.Magill, A.Fraser
2001 Sep 16	Goathouse of Fleet	I.Magill, A.Fraser
2001 Sep 16	Astrogoat	A.Fraser, I.Magill
2001 Sep 18	Three Men in a Goat	S.Reid, J.Reid
2001 Sep 18	One Man, One Goat	S.Reid (solo)
2002 Oct 31	Up Perisgoat!	S.Reid, J.Biggar
2004 Oct 8	The Dark Side	C.King, S.Reid (AL)
2004 Oct 8	Nanny State	C.King, S.Reid
2004 Oct 8	Just Kidding	S.Reid (solo)

Corwar

1998 May 13	Bigger Than Tigger	J.Biggar, A.Owen
1998 May 20	Pinus Worship	C.Hossack, J.Biggar (AL)
1998 Jun 2	The Prune	J.Biggar, L.Biggar, L.Cannon
1999 Oct 17	The Peach	J.Biggar, C.Hossack.

FRCC Finish: S.Reid, R.Kenyon, D.Staton, 30 Apr 2000

1999 Oct 20	Ruta Aurelio	S.Reid, J.Biggar, D.Aurelio
1999 Oct 20	Alpamayo no More	J.Biggar, S.Reid, D.Aurelio

Direct Start: S.Reid, J.Biggar, 3 May 2000

1999 Nov 10	Plum Line	S.Reid, J.Biggar
1999 Nov 10	Corwar Wall	S.Reid, J.Blggar
2000 May 3	Tutti Frutti	S.Reid, J.Biggar
2000 May 3	The Midge	J.Biggar, S.Reid
2000 May 3	Nutcase	S.Reid, J.Biggar
2000 Sep 9	The Harvesters	D.Armstrong, M.Hetherington

Craignelder

1978 Apr 22	The Original Route	A.Fraser, M.Burgess, W.Todd
c1982/3	Eilte Pinnacle Rib	I.Livingston, K.Livingston
1984 Jun 18	Gloom	A.Fraser, D.Walker

Direct Finish: S.Reid, J.Campbell, A.Moore 19 May 1992
Super Direct Finish: A.Moore, S.Reid, J.Campbell 19 May 1992

1984 Jun 18	Pale Face	A.Fraser, D.Walker
1990	Rock Lobster	K.Livingstone, I.Livingstone
1991 Sep	Kerb Crawler	J.Biggar, L.Biggar

Misdescribed as a variation of Eilte Pinnacle Rib in the last guide.
Direct Start: A.Faulk, M.Harvey, April 1997

1992 May 14	The Flesh Market	S.Reid, J.Campbell
1992 May 14	Guledig	S.Reid, J.Campbell
1992 May 14	Gwry Y Goggledd	S.Reid, J.Campbell
1992 May 14	No Hawkers of Campbells	S.Reid, J.Campbell
1997 Apr	Diagonal Route	M.Harvey, A.Faulk
2000 May 11	Adder Country	J.Biggar, S.Reid
2000 May 11	Y Geifr	S.Reid, J.Biggar
2000 May 30	Coel Fain	S.Reid, W.Phipps, M.Nunwick

Direct as described: C.King, S.Reid, 30 Aug 2002

2002 Aug 17	Minas Tirith	S.Reid, C.Bonington
2002 Aug 17	Minas Morgul	C.Bonington, S.Reid
2002 Aug 30	Snozzle	S.Reid, C.King
2002 Aug 30	Slab-u-like	C.King, S.Reid
2002 Aug 30	Slabadabadoo	S.Reid, C.King
2002 Aug 30	In the Hall of the Mountain King	S.Reid, C.King
W 2003 Jan 10	Dream of Grey Mares	J.Biggar, S.Prior, A.Swann
W 2003 Jan 10	Hinkes's Downfal	A.Hinkes, S.Reid
W 2003 Jan 10	Gorm	A.Fraser, I.Magill
W 2003 Jan 10	Flowers of the Forest	A.Fraser, I.Magill
W 2003 Jan 11	Talnotry Trickle	J.Biggar, L.Biggar, C.Biggar

Cairnsmore of Fleet

	1992 May 19	Spout of the Clints	S.Reid, A.Moore (AL), J.Campbell

Originally named Lost Pilots' Gully after the aircraft debris littering the climb.

W	1997 Jan 5	Spout of the Clints	S.Reid, C.Bonington (AL)
W	1997 Jan 7	Smear Test	S.Reid, D.Scott (AL)

Clints of Dromore

1978 May 7	Far Right Rib	A.Fraser, A.Carmichael, K.Donaldson
1978 May 7	Left Slab	A.Fraser, A.Carmichael, K.Donaldson
1978 May 7	Central Buttress	A.Fraser, K.Donaldson, A.Carmichael.

Alternative Finish: A.Fraser, A.Carmichael, K.Donaldson, the same day.

1978 May 7	Spare Rib	A.Fraser, A.Carmichael, K.Donaldson.

Direct Start: J.Biggar, L.Biggar, August 1991

1981 Aug 27	White Slab	A.Fraser (solo)
1981 Aug 27	Left of Centre	A.Fraser (solo)
1981 Aug 27	Black Streaker	A.Fraser (solo)

Several other routes were soloed by Fraser on this slab, 2 Sep 1982, including Flake Climb and Left Rib.

1991 Aug 25	The Spanish Inquisition	A.Fraser, R.McAllister

So called because "Nobody expects the...". Fraser and McAllister had made the first ascent of Ancient Mariner at Meikle Ross that morning!

Direct Finish: C.King, S.Reid, 12 Dec 2001

2001 Feb 14	Left Edge	S.Reid (solo)
2001 Feb 14	Cupid's Bow	S.Reid, A.Hewison

Right-Hand Finish C.King, S.Reid, 9 Nov 2001

2001 Feb 14	Cupid's Arrow	A.Hewison, S.Reid
2001 Nov 2	Stupid Cupid	S.Reid, C.King, J.Biggar
2001 Nov 2	Sheer Cupidity	J.Biggar, C.King, S.Reid
2001 Nov 2	Make My Day!	C.King, S.Reid
2001 Nov 2	White Scoop	S.Reid, J.Biggar, C.King
2001 Nov 2	Do You Feel Lucky?	C.King, S.Reid
2001 Nov 2	Sweet Heart	S.Reid, C.King, J.Biggar
2001 Nov 9	White Arete	S.Reid, C.King
2001 Nov 9	The Climb with No Name	C.King, S.Reid
2001 Nov 9	Honeysuckle Groove	S.Reid, C.King
2001 Nov 9	The Notch	S.Reid, C.King
2001 Nov 14	The Comfy Chair	S.Reid, J.Biggar

Direct Start: S.Reid, C.King, 12 Dec 2001

2001 Dec 12	Just Left of Centre	S.Reid (solo)

The upper groove had been climbed by J.Biggar, 14 Nov 2001.

2001 Dec 12	Quoth the Raven	S.Reid, C.King
2002 Feb 15	Diagonal Line & others	S.Reid, J.Reid

Loch Grannoch & Minor Outcrops

Many of the Lodge Slab routes had obviously been climbed before, mainly by J and L Biggar.

1981 Apr	Left Rib, Shortie, Captain Madman, Goat Grooves, Goat Slab, Kid's Stuff, M1, M6, Bypass	D.Gibson, A.Fraser (VL)
2002 Sep 19	Spike Slab, Wall Left, Right & Centre, Centre Crack, Diagonals 1, 2, 2.5, & 3, Kids R Us, Kid You Not, M62, Detour., Stemline, Black Ball, Left Rib	C.King, S.Reid (VL)
2002 Nov 7	Dam It	S.Reid (solo)

The Borders & Dumfries
Glenwhargen Craig & Craighoar

1950s	Glenwhargen Craig	A.Waldie & others

The climbs are described diagrammatically in the 1950 SMC Journal. The finding of a boot nail indicated previous climbers.

1977 Apr 10	Gibson's Route	D.Gibson
1977 Apr 10	Fraser's First Climb	A.Fraser, D.Gibson, D.Walker
1979 Jul 8	Fraser's Second Climb	A.Fraser, M.Burgess, A.Carmichael

2002	Mar 17	Silence of the Ram	I.Scobie, J.Smith
2002	Mar 17	Crooked Brae	I.Scobie, A.Carruthers
2002	Apr 10	Scobie-Doo	I.Scobie, J.Smith
2002	Apr 10	Hoar Crack	A.Carruthers, J.Smith
2002	Apr 10	Hoar Cleft	J.Smith, I.Scobie

Swatte Fell, White Coomb & Moffat Dale

There has been no history of recording first ascents in the Moffat Hills and the dates given are only the first known. Most of these routes, with the probable exception of the Grey Mare's Tail, were undoubtedly climbed much earlier.

| W | 1969 Feb 18 | Grey Mare's Tail | G.Anderson, W.Anderson, D.Bathgate, I.MacEacheran |

The team took advantage of a severe cold spell. Both flanks were climbed.

| W | 1979 Feb 24 | Black Crag Gully | A.Fraser (solo) |
| W | 1979 Feb 24 | Central Gully | A.Fraser, D.Gibson, D.Snell |

The easy Swatte Fell gullies and buttresses were climbed by D.Kingswood, A.Fraser, 19 Dec 1976.

W	1987 Jan 11	Dob's Linn Left Hand	A.Fraser (solo)
W	1990	Loch Skeen Gullies	I.Scobie
W	1995 Dec 26	Dob's Linn	R.Jackson, I.Scobie
W	1996	Raven Craig Fall	G.Kellet, P.Messer
W	2000 Dec 31	Shortfall Gully	G.Little (solo)
W	2000 Dec 31	Firthope Falls	G.Little (solo)
W	2000 Dec	Broken Cleugh	G.Kellet, A.Reid
W	2002 Jan 2	Witch Linn	S.Mortlock, J.Lawrence, C.Barr
W	2003 Jan 11	Blackout Gully	M.Holland, J.Blackford
W	2003 Jan 11	Paok!	M.Holland, J.Blackford

Fatlips Crag

| 1993 Jul 7 | Who Youse Callin' Fatlips? | S.Reid, J.Campbell |
| 1993 Jul 7 | Fatlips Corner | J.Campbell, S.Reid |

There were signs that the crag had been climbed on previously.

1996	Top Lip	A.Reid, C.Young
1997 Jun	Whin Some, Lose Some	M.Lyons, C.Scott, R.Clark
1997 Jun	Hotlips	C.Scott, M.Lyons, R.Clark

Originally finished up Fatlips Corner.
As described: S.Reid, C.King, 19 Jun 2002

| 1997 Jun | Big Fella | R.Clark, M.Lyons, C.Scott |
| 2000 May | Crest of a Knave | M.Lyons, C.Scott |

After top-rope practice, but still an impressive lead.

| 2002 May 12 | Fatlips Rib | G.Little |
| 2002 June 19 | Minto | S.Reid, C.King |

Dumfries Crags

| 1976 Mar | Maidenbower Chimneys | D.Gibson, W.Todd, D.Walker, A.Fraser |
| 1980 | Geronimo | C.Macadam, D.Austin, D.Todd |

Clifton

Between 1950 and 1960 some 16 routes up to VS were climbed by A.Waldie, M.Slesser, I.Cumming & J.Simpson. Between 1976 and 1978 all the existing routes were repeated and named and all other climbs without first ascent details below were added by C.Macadam, and G.Macadam.

| 1975 Dec 13 | Hollowstones Chimney | D. Gibson, A.Fraser |
| 1976 May 22 | Novice Crack | C.Macadam, D.Gibson, A.Fraser |

Tiger Finish: C.King, S.Reid, 24 Apr 2002

1977	Jugular Vein	C.Macadam, G.Macadam
1977	Wall Street	C.Macadam, G.Macadam
1978	The Arete	C.Macadam
1979	Lemur	C.Macadam
1979	Fingerlust	C.Macadam
1980s	Gramercy	M.Jacob & party by the Direct Finish

Right-Hand Finish: J.Biggar & K.Livingstone, 1996

| 1984 | Beyond the Terminator | D.Austin |
| 1984 | Loneliness of the Long Distance Runner | D.Austin |

1984		Toddamundo	C.Macadam
1991		Muckle Knob	J.Biggar, L.Biggar
1995	May 26	Monkey Business	S.Reid, J.Grinbergs
1995	May 26	The Pinnacles	J.Grinbergs, S.Reid
1995	May 26	Essence of Giraffe	S.Reid, J.Grinbergs
1995	Jun 2	Pegasus Direct Start	S.Reid, W.Phipps
1995	Jun 2	Bullet	S.Reid, W.Phipps
1997	Jun 26	Infill	S.Reid, S.Stout

Direct Start: C.King, S.Reid, 22 Oct 1997

1997	Jun 26	Stiff Upper Lip	S.Reid, C.King
1998	Apr 24	Lip Service Direct	S.Reid, D.Bodecott
2000	Apr 23	Clifton Pinnacle	S.Reid, C.Read
2000	Apr 29	Bright Eyes	I.Scobie, J.Smith
2000	Jul 7	Long Ears	J. Smith, I. Scobie
2000	Aug 3	Le Tour	I.Scobie, J.Smith
2000	Aug 3	Le Coin	J.Smith, I.Scobie
2001	Jan 13	Easy Street	I.Scobie, J.Smith
2002	Jul 10	Sideshow	S.Reid, C.King
2003	Feb 13	Dolce Cour	S.Reid, W.Hurford

Much had already been climbed by S.Reid and C.King.

Lion's Head

Four climbs whose descriptions have been lost were made by A.Waldie, M.Slesser (and possibly R.Smith) in the 1950s and 1960s.

1976-78	Snout Direct, Catspaw, Twinkletoe Wall, Sheer Can, Claustrophobia	C.Macadam, G.Macadam

Direct Start to Claustrophobia: C.King, S.Reid, 18 Apr 2002

Galloway Sea-cliffs
Powillimont - The Thirlstane

The outer routes are probably quite old, with the exception of those undernoted.

1981	Jul	Goodnight Irene	C.Macadam (solo)
1984/5		Overhanging Crack	D.Gibson
1990		Thank You Irene	D.Gibson (solo)

Lot's Wife, The Lookout, Needle's Eye, Sandyhills

1975	Dec 6	Southwick Needle's Eye Routes	D.Gibson, A.Fraser, A.Carmichael, K.Donaldson
1978		Amethyst Crack	J.Fotheringham, I.Tattersall
1979	Jun 28	Lot's Wife Slab	A.Fraser, W.Todd
1980	Oct 2	Lookout Slab	W.Todd, A.Fraser
1980	Oct 2	The Watchtower	A.Fraser, W.Todd
1982	Aug 30	The Tombstone	A.Fraser, R.Duff
1990		Sandyhills Needle's Eye	D.Gibson, D.Austin

Balcary Bay

1979	Dec 1	The Cave Traverse	A.Fraser, D.Walker
1990s		Lot's Wife	W.Birkett, J.White, P.Cheung

Meikle Ross

1972	Apr 22	Rift Route	W.Cheverst, R.Scoltock, C.Dickinson

The cliffs were discovered by a Lancashire team, but the death of Bill Cheverst in the Alps that summer stopped development.

1972	Apr 22	Limehouse Blues	W.Cheverst, C.Dickinson
1972	Apr 22	Access Ridge	W.Cheverst, R.Scoltock, C.Dickinson
1972	Apr 23	Yellow Dog	C.Dickinson, W.Cheverst (AL)
1972	Apr 23	Dogwalk	C.Dickinson, R.Scoltock
1972	May 28	K9	W.Cheverst, J.Cottingham, C.Dickinson

One peg for aid.

1975	Clockwork Orange, Crack and Corner, Curving Arete, Exit Groove, Orange Chimney,	

	Pigeon Chimney, Promontory Wall	J.Kerry (probably).
1975 Mar 31	Mellow Yellow, Salty Dog	J.Kerry, F.Craddock
1975 Mar 31	Stepped Corner	F.Craddock, J.Kerry
1975 Apr 6	Amnesia, Left Corner	B.Shields, G.Hamilton, J.Kerr
1975 Apr 26	Galloway Corner	J.Kerry, J.Mackenzie
1975 Sep 26	Crack Track	J.Kerry, K.Johnstone
1975 Dec 6	Side Track	J.Kerry, G.Todd
1975 Dec 7	Headcase	J.Kerry, G.Todd
1975/77	White Out, Groovey	J.Kerry (probably)
1976	Sorcerer's Apprentice	K.Johnstone, D.Benn
1976 Jan	Bloody Crack, Green Wall, Right Corner	J.Kerry, G.Todd
1976 Jan 17	Ken's Groove	K.Johnstone, D.Benn
1976 Jan 31	Tinman	D.Mullen, H.Reader
1976 Feb	Blue Finger	K.Johnstone, D.McCallum

Originally included what is now the first pitch of Maple Leaf Rag, climbed by J.Kerry and C.Macadam in Sept 1977.

1976 Feb 1	Dolphin Groove, Coffin Crack	J.Kerry, G.Todd
1977	The Battle of Osfrontalis	C.Macadam, G.Macadam.

A death route climbed on sight by the inexperienced, but quick-learning, father and son team.

1977	Pinking Sheer, Dogleg	C.Macadam, G.Macadam.

Originally mis-named Orangutang in the Glasgow Outcrops guide, allegedly to insult Craig Macadam's natural ability and follicle challenge.

1977	Seadog	J.Kerry, H.Reader
1977 May 17	Back Track	J.Kerry, H.Reader
1977 Sep	Rhythm and Blues	J.Kerry, C.Macadam (alt leads)
1978	Grand Central Couloir.	Bottom unknown, top W.Todd, C.Macadam 1983/84
1978 Sep	Route One	W.Todd, G.Macadam
1978 Oct	Maple Leaf Rag	C.Macadam, N.MacFadyen (pitch 2)
1978 Oct	Finesse	C.Macadam, R.Souter, N.Cockburn
1978 Dec 17	Accutrac	C.Macadam, E.Todd
1978-80	Akela	C.Macadam
1978-80	Argus	C.Macadam
1979 Aug	Steve's Route	S.Bartlett (solo)
1979 Aug	A Walk on the Wild Side	C.Macadam, S.Bartlett
1979 Aug	Dolce Vita	C.Macadam, D.Lampard
1979 Aug	Scared to Dance	C.Macadam, S.Bartlett
1979	Cairn's Cream	C.Macadam, J.Gerrard
1979 Sep 30	Mental Block	C.Macadam, A.Fraser, W.Todd
1979 Sep 30	Fil d' Or	C.Macadam (seconds declined)

The hardest Galloway route of the '70s.

1980 Sep 6	Compulsion	C.Macadam, A.Fraser
1981 Mar 29	Zugsfang	C.Macadam, D.Austin
1981 Jun 23	Bad Medicine Waltz	C.Macadam, A.Fraser, E.Kellar
1981 Sep 6	A Sop for Cerberus, Eminence Grise	C.Macadam, G.Macadam
1981 Sep 6	Route Three	A.Fraser, W.Todd
1981 Sep 6	Avernal Buttress	C.Macadam (solo)
1982 Apr 6	Blistering Barnacles	A.Fraser, E.Kellar, D.Gibson
1982 Apr 11	Marie Celeste	A.Fraser, G.Macadam
1982 May 20	Titan's Corner	A.Fraser, M.Whitford.

Poetic justice – Gibson had inadequately gardened the route, a fact Fraser was unaware of when he stole it. As a result, the gear consisted of micro wires pressed into mud, a thoroughly gripping experience.

1982 Jun 20	Poison Ivy	A.Fraser, W.Todd (solo)
1982 Jun 20	Barnacle Bill	A.Fraser, W.Todd
1982 Sep 15	Bumper Dumper	D.Austin, A.Fraser, D.Gibson, W.Todd.

Austin had a 'dump' at the top of the crag, did the route and promptly stepped in it.

1982 Sep 18	The Moosetrap	A.Fraser, R.Webb
1983-84	Route Two	C.Macadam (solo)
1983-84	Demolition Tango	C.Macadam, W.Todd
1984	Corridor of Power	D.Austin, C.Macadam.

1984	Sunshine Superman	C.Macadam
1984-5	Alligator Crawl, Fats Waller,	
	Shark's Tooth	C.Macadam, S.Steer, D.Gibson
1987 Apr 11	Pinko-Subversive	A.Fraser, G.Robb
1987 Sep 27	Grapeshot	A.Wilson, S.Jackson
1988 Apr 4	Meikle Gorbachov	A.Fraser, G.Robb
1990 Apr 1	Old Zawn, Evens	A.Caren, I.Taylor
1991 Aug 21	Manic Nirvana	R.McAllister, A.Fraser
1991 Aug 25	Ancient Mariner	R.McAllister, A.Fraser
1995 Sep	Spectacular Bid	R.McAllister, S.Mearns, E.Brunskill

An old Macadam project.

1996 Aug	Rez Route	M.Thomson
1999 Aug 11	Born to Boogie	M.Whitaker, I.Weir
1999 Sep 20	Meikle Ross Traverse	J.Biggar, C.Hossack
2000 May 29	Shake,Rattle and Roll	M.Whitaker, I.Weir
2000 Jul 24	A Wee Cracker, The Slips	M.Whitaker, P.Cocks
2000 Jul 24	Mid-Wicket, Silly Mid Off,	
	Silly Mid On, Nursery End	M.Whitaker, J.Bolton, P.Cocks
2002 Mar 23	Chairman's Crack,	
	Glenfinnan Hotel, Dinner Meat	N.Crookston, C.Prowse
2002 May 31	Whale Meat Again	A.Fraser, I.Magill

Burrow Head

1980 Jan	Conquistador, Bright Eyes	C.Macadam, D.Lampard
1980	The Cut	C.Macadam, G.Macadam
1980 Jul 26	Watership Down	C.Macadam, A.Fraser

Climbed in a thundersorm, water pouring in waves down the crag.

1980 Aug 15	Flensing Knife	C.Macadam, A.Fraser
1980 Aug 16	Naked Fun, Yellow Crack,	
	Prometheus (on his crag)	C.Macadam, A.Fraser
1980 Aug 17	Guardian Angel	C.Macadam, A.Fraser

A dislodged block, aiming straight for Fraser's unhelmeted head, fragmented in mid air.

1980 Aug 23	Run Rabbit Run, Devil's	
	Daughter, Mephistopheles	C.Macadam, A.Fraser.

A weekend visit, the crags tame in comparison to the surreal and twilight world of the Burrow Head Campsite disco. Bottom feeders only.

1980 Sep 24	The Fin	C.Macadam, A.Fraser
1980 Sep 24	The Cutter	C.Macadam, A.Fraser

A sharp edge at the top of the crag sawed through Macadam's rope while gardening and only one strand of the core was left by the time he reached the bottom.

1981 Apr 5	Lemming's Wall	C.Macadam, D.Austin, G.Macadam,
		W.Todd, D.Todd, D.Gibson, A.Fraser

A rogues gallery of the Dumfries team.

1981 Apr 5	Boozer's Chimney,	
	The Python	A.Fraser, G.Macadam
1981 Apr 5	The Newt	W.Todd
1981 Aug 7	The Beastie	C.Macadam, A.Fraser
1981 Aug 7	Waiting for Godot	C.Macadam, A.Fraser.

Five hours were spent gardening the route. Steps were carefully carved up the high angled guano at the top.

1981	Mirror, Mirror	I.Duckworth, C.Macadam.

Led on sight – a very bold undertaking.

1981	The Changeling	C.Macadam (solo)

This all too obvious sandbag Severe awaits a repeat.

1981	Wild Horses	C.Macadam
1982 Jun 21	Adventures in	
	the Skin Trade	C.Macadam, A.Fraser
1983	The Shootist	C.Macadam, S.Steer
1991 Aug 14	Gublin's Eyer	A.Fraser, R.McAllister
1991 Aug 14	Killer on the Loose	R.McAllister, A.Fraser

Monreith

1987 May 15	Do Barnacles Bite	F.Stevenson, A.Long
1987 May 15	Soup Dragon,	
	Stingray, Hack Crack	F.Stevenson (solo)

1987	May 16	Fireball XL 1.5, Mobile-Kack	F.Stevenson (solo)
1987	Aug 7	Jelly Fish	F.Stevenson (solo)
1987	Aug 9	Mobile-Bat,	
		Iron Age Crack	F.Stevenson (solo)
1987	Aug 18	Jelly Fish	F.Stevenson (solo)
1987	Aug 30	Satori	F.Stevenson
1987	Sep 5	The Big Dig	S.Smith, F.Stevenson (alts)
1987	Sep 14	St Ninians Crack	F.Stevenson (solo)

Garheugh Port

1985	Two Tyred	A.Greig

The first holds reached from two tyres washed up on the beach.

1985	Deathwish	A.Greig

Various other routes and boulder problems were climbed around this time but unrecorded by Andy Greig, Pete Botterill and other Carlisle and Lakes based climbers.

1985	Secrets of the Coast	A.Plumb, S.Aird
1985/6	Jackdaw Crack	A.Plumb, S.Aird
1985/6	Wee Pig, Nay Sweat	S.Aird, A.Plumb
1985/6	Gorilla, Fine Line	A.Plumb (solo)
1987 Apr	Battle of the Bulge	D.Gibson
1987 Aug 1	Snailey-Whaley	F.Stevenson, A.Smith, B.Davison, J.Vlasto
1987 Aug 1	Flubb	A.Smith, J.Vlasto, F.Stevenson
1987 Aug 10	The E-6 Process	F.Stevenson
1987 Sep 3	Landmark, Smuggler's Grill, Cash 'n' Carry	F.Stevenson (solo)
1993 May	T Bone	A.Scougall, A.Plumb
1995 May 28	Ranti-Crack, Catapult Suzie	T.Rankin (solo)
1995 Oct 14	Trainspotter's Traverse, Pause for Thought	T.Rankin (solo)

The fourth crack proved harder than it looked and Rankin received several stitches after a ground fall.

1999	Buba Luba	N.Taylor
2001 Apr 4	Bombin the L', Dr Hemlock and Mr. Damocles, Foot in Mouth	A.Fraser, A.Gillies
2001 Apr 4	Too EC	A.Gillies, A.Fraser
2001 May 29	The Fat Lady Sings	A.Fraser, I.Magill, A.Gillies

Another night-time affair, with headtorches required to second.

2001 Jun 5	An Idea of Excellence	I.Magill, A.Magill, A.Gillies, A.Fraser
2001 Jun 5	Full Moon Fever	A.Fraser, I.Magill
2001 Jun 5	Cock Inn Cap'n Birdseye	A.Gillies, A.Magill
2001 Jun 28	My Bonny Lies Over the Ocean, Stone Crop	S.Reid, T.Mosedale
2001 Jun 28	Gooseberry in a Lift	T. Mosedale, S.Reid
2004 Apr 10	Too Cold to Chew	B.Davison, F.Smith

Finnarts Point

1995 Mar 29	Bustin' Surfboards	R.McAllister, A.Fraser

McAllister had spotted the crag from the Irish ferry.

1995 Sep 18	I Should Coco	R.McAllister, D.McGimpsey, S.Mearns
1995 Sep 18	Baywatch Babes	S.Mearns, R.McAllister, D.McGimpsey
1995 Sep	Rhythm Nation	R.McAllister, S.Christie
1996 Aug 15	Smuggler's Ridge	A.Fraser (solo)
1996 Aug 22	Electric Brae	A.Fraser, R.McAllister
1996 Aug 22	Edge of the Abyss	R.McAllister, A.Fraser
1996 Aug 28	Lloyd Quinan is a Weatherman	D.McGimpsey, R.McAllister, S.Mearns
1996 Aug 28	Red Hot and Blue	R.McAllister, D.McGimpsey, S.Mearns
1997 Aug 14	Full Speed Ahead	R.McAllister, A.Fraser, D.McGimpsey
1997 Aug 14	Last Night at the Prawns	A.Fraser, R.McAllister, D.McGimpsey
1997 Sep 28	Camp Boss, Can't Cook, Won't Cook	D.McGimpsey, R.McAllister, S.Mearns.

The last Galloway route by this team before they moved north. The name apparently stems from McGimpsey's experiences as a mudlogger in Angola.

Portobello

| 1987 | Apr | Thunderbolt, | |
| | | Crawford's Crackers | C.Rice, T.Prentice, R.Webb. |

Prentice explored the west coast of the peninsula, discovering Portobello, Laggantalluch and Kiln o' the Fuffock in the process. Like Fraser he walked straight past Crammag Head!

1987	Apr	Happy Man	R.Webb, C.Rice
1987	Apr	The Man from Del Monte	T.Prentice
1987	Apr	Only Monsters	R.Webb, T.Prentice, C.Rice
1987	Jul	Floating Voter	S.M.Richardson, T.Prentice
1987	Jul	Blockhead	S.M.Richardson (solo)
1989	Dec 9	Surfin' Safari,, Puffin Nuffin,	
		Riverboat Gambler	A.Fraser, J.Thomson
1989	Dec 9	Warsteiner	J.Thomson, A.Fraser
1989	Dec 9	Sanity Claus	A.Fraser, J.Thomson

The first route on the face, climbed in pitch darkness, to discover that it was not the top of the crag and another pitch lay beyond.

| 1990 | Mar 18 | Basking up the Wrong Tree | J.Dickson, A.Fraser |

Dickson was supposed to be on Speed Limpets, but a moment's inattention allowed him to escape.

| 1990 | Mar 18 | Cutty Shark | A.Fraser, J.Dickson |
| 1991 | Apr 4 | Speed Limpets | A.Fraser, J.Thomson. |

Named after a speeding ticket and Lampard's broken ankle, the latter which necessitated a limp across the fields.

1990	Apr 4	Dead Sea Strolls	A.Fraser, J.Thomson
1991	Jul 17	Feeling the Pinch	R.McAllister, A.Fraser
1990	Jul 17	The Zombie	A.Fraser, R.McAllister
1990	Jul 31	Aqua Vitae, Cockle Sucker	R.McAllister, A.Fraser
1990	Jul 31	Mussel Bound, Shellfish Bastard	A.Fraser, R.McAllister
1990	Oct 21	Parallel Lines, Count Duckula	A.Fraser, S.Lampard
1990	Oct 21	Return of the Limpet,	
		Hanging Duck	S.Lampard, A.Fraser
1991	Jul 3	The Water Margin	A.Fraser, R.McAllister
1991	Jul 17	The Cruel Seaside	R.McAllister
1991	Aug 7	The Ducking Stool	A.Fraser, J.Thomson
1992	Mar 29	Soul Kitchen	R.McAllister, A.Fraser
1992	May 10	Bootless	S.Lampard, J.Blyth.

Blyth, now a Chamonix guide, was drawn to the greater ranges by his sea-cliff experiences, (although his lack of rock boots hardly helped here).

1992	May 13	Basic Instinct, Winklepicker	M.Reed, A.Fraser, D.McGimpsey
1992	May 13	Silence of the Clams	A.Fraser, M.Reed, D.McGimpsey
1992	Jun 26	Acid Test	R.McAllister
1992	Jul 2	Pushed to the Limit	R.McAllister, A.Fraser, D.McGimpsey
1992	Jul 9	St Elmo's Fire	A.Fraser, R.McAllister, D.McGimpsey

Right-hand start: R.McAllister, D.McGimpsey, A.Fraser, Mar 10, 1996

1992	Jul 9	Ramplet	D.McGimpsey, A.Fraser, R.McAllister
1992	Jul 9	Critical Mass	R.McAllister, A.Fraser, D.McGimpsey
1992	Oct 1	Figgitt's Rest	D.McGimpsey, S.Figgitt, R.McAllister
1993	Apr 26	Water Dance	R.McAllister, M.Reed
1993	May 8	Betty Blue	K.McClusky, R.McAllister
1993	May 9	Sweaty Trembler	R.McAllister
1993	May 20	Underling	M.Reed, A.Fraser
1993	May 20	The Crayfish Twins	A.Fraser, M.Reed
1993		Changeling	R.McAllister, M.Reed, K.McCluskey.

Without the pegs: R.McAllister, D.McGimpsey, June 1997

| 1993 | Jul 14 | Lost at Sea, Horse Latitudes | R.McAllister, A.Fraser |
| 1993 | Aug | The Waster | M.Reed. |

First lead without pre-placed runners: R.McAllister, S.Mearns 4 Sep 1993.

1993	Dec 5	Another One Bites The Dust	M.McConnell, R.McAllister
1995	Apr	Grim Reefer	R.McAllister, S.Christie
1995	Apr	Brain Dead Fred	R.McAllister, S.Christie, D.McGimpsey
1996	Mar 10	A Close Shave	A.Fraser, C.French, D.McGimpsey,
			T.Prentice, R.McAllister.

In 1991 Stuart Lampard had nearly topped-out on this route when he pulled off a massive block, narrowly missing his second but breaking his ankle in the process.

| 1996 | Aug | Unhappy, NRG, | |
| | | Slime Based Organism, | |

		They're Watching Me, Tactical Anti-Jellyfish Weaponry,	
		Jellyfish Szechuan Style	M.Thomson (solo)
1997	Mar 6	Carrycots of Fire	A.Fraser, R.McAllister, R.Rankin

The Portobello farmer finally gets his name in the FA list.

1997	Jun	Screamadelica	R.McAllister
1997	Jun	Monsieur Dubois	R.McAllister, S,Mearns
1997	Jun	Buckets of Doom	D.McGimpsey, R.McAllister, M.Reed
1998	Aug 5	Walking the Plank	A.Fraser, I.Magill, A.Taylor, A.Murdoch
2000	May 19	The Prawnbroker	A.Fraser, I.Magill
2000	May 27	Lurchin'with the Urchins	M.Whitaker, P.Cocks
2000	May 27	Flaked Halibut, Herring Aid	M.Whitaker, P.Cocks
2000	May 30	Mussels from Brussels	A.Fraser, I.Magill
2000	Aug 15	One Green Bottle, A Dream of White Helmets	M.Whitaker, P.Cocks, I.Weir
2000	Aug 27	Doon the Watter	A.Fraser, I.Magill, R.Rankin, R.McAllister.

The team returned from the crag in darkness but style – held high in the bucket of Roger's tractor.

2001	May 11	Bottom Feeders	A.Fraser, I.Magill
2001	May 11	Fanny Haddock	I.Magill, A.Fraser
2001	Jun 13	The Dogs Pollacks	A.Fraser, I.Magill, A.Gillies
2001	Jun 20	The Elle Factor	A.Gillies, A.Fraser
2001	Jul 22	Tales of the Rubblebank, Jack the Kipper	A.Fraser, A.Gillies, I.Magill
2001	Oct 28	Traverse of the Cods, Like it or Limpet	S.Reid, R.Kenyon
2001	Oct 28	Limpetstiltskin	R.Kenyon,S.Reid
2002	Sep 11	Portobello Belle	A.Fraser,I.Magill
2002	Sep 18	Yon Kipper (Fish of Atonement)	A.Fraser,I.Magill,A.Gillies
2003	May 27	Haddock's Left Fin, The Snail Trail, Whiting For Godot, Johnny Dory, Ann Chovy, Mullet Of Cocktail, Sick Squid	M.Whitaker, P.Cocks

Juniper Rock & the Fish Kettle

1993	May 5	The Beauty of Flight	M.Reed, R.McAllister
1993	May 5	Bridg it	M.Reed
2003	Aug 12	One Hand Clapping	A.Fraser, I.Magill
2003	Aug 12	Absent Friends	I.Magill, A.Fraser
2003	Aug 16	Midshipman Hornblower	I.Magill, A.Fraser
		Rust Never Sleeps	A.Fraser, I.Magill
		Gullslinger Slab	A.Fraser, I.Magill
2003	Sep 5	Hanging from the Yardarm	I.Magill, A.Fraser
2003	Sep 19	Singing Kettle	A.Fraser, I.Magill, R.Rankin
2003	Sep 19	The Jolly Roger	I.Magill, A.Fraser, R.Rankin
2003	Sep 19	Trouble with the Mizen Mast	I.Magill, A.Fraser, A.Gillies, P.Michal, R.Rankin
2003	Oct 3	Tilting at Windmills	A.Fraser, A.Gilllies, I.Magill
2003	Oct 3	Magillas in the Mist	A.Gillies, A.Fraser, I.Magill.

Magill stoically belayed, invisible in the spray of monstrous waves breaking onto his head.

Kiln o' the Fuffock

1993	Feb 18	Rock Lobster	R.McAllister, M.Reed, A.Fraser, D.McGimpsey
1993	Feb 18	Penguin Parade	A.Fraser, D.McGimpsey
1993	Oct 16	Saturation Point	R.McAllister, G.Borland.

Development starts in earnest, McAllister's ropes being stored above the crag for the next fortnight

1993	Oct 17	Body Swerve	S.Mearns, R.McAllister
1993	Oct 18	Burning the Boats	R.McAllister, A.Fraser
1993	Oct 18	The Pincer	S.Mearns, R.McAllister, A.Fraser
1993	Oct 18	Sea Fowl	A.Fraser (solo)
1993	Oct 21	Echo Beach	R.McAllister, S.Mearns

1993 Oct 26	Total Immersion	R.McAllister, S.Muir
1993 Oct 28	Arc of a Diver	A.Fraser, R.McAllister
1993 Oct 28	Abide With Me	R.McAllister, A.Fraser, S.Muir
1993 Oct 28	Point Break	S.Muir, R.McAllister, A.Fraser
1993 Oct 28	Seaside Buddies	S.Muir, S.Mearns
1993 Oct 28	Water Wings	S.Mearns, S.Muir
1993 Oct 31	Breakaway	G.Borland, D.McGimpsey, A.Fraser
1993 Oct 31	Spirit Level	A.Fraser, G.Borland, D.McGimpsey
1993 Oct 31	The Bends, The Bends	R.McAllister, M.Reed, D.McGimpsey, A.Fraser, G.Borland
1994 Jun 26	The Niche	M.Reed, R.McAllister
1994 Sep	Suggestive Digestive	M.Reed, R.McAllister
1996 Sep	Ocean Colour Scene, Spinning Wheel	R.McAllister, D.McGimpsey, S.Mearns
1996 Sep 19	Stonehead	M.Reed, R.McAllister (both solo)
1996 Sep 19	Hate thy Neighbour	M.Reed, R.McAllister, J.Hagan
1996 Sep 19	Medicine Man	J.Hagan, M.Reed, R.McAllister

Climbed the same day as Reed's solo of Ocean Colour Scene (E4) and Reed and McAllister's solo of Total Immersion (E4), Rock Lobster and Spirit Level. Reed recalls: 'absolutely buzzing when I got to work that night'.

2000 Aug 20	Fuffocking Contortions	M.Whitaker, P.Cocks
2000 Aug 20	Zari's Slant	M.Whitaker, I.Weir, P.Cocks
2001 Aug 18	Rubbledance	A.Fraser, I.Magill

Larbrax

1994 Nov 19	Ace is Low	G.Brookes, M.Dale
1995 Jul 1	Haste Ye Back	M.Dale, G.Brookes
1995 Jul 1	O'er the Dyke	G.Brookes, L.Walker, J.Nelson, M.Dale
1995 Jul 3	Soor Ploom	M.Dale, G.Brookes
1995 Jul 3	Mealy Puddding	G.Brookes, M.Dale
1995 Jul 3	Cranberry Jam	M.Dale

The crag and the routes remained secret from the locals for a further three years.

1998 Jun 3	Ceud Mille a Failte	R.McAllister, A.Fraser
1999 Jul 23	The Lotus Eaters	A.Fraser, I.Magill
1999 Sep 1	Caledonia Dreaming	A.Fraser, I.Magill
2000 Sep 19	Elegance	J.Lines, D.McGimpsey.

Julian Lines, a Cairngorms slab expert, was lured south for this last great problem.

2000 Sep 22	Reach or Beach	J.Lines (solo)
2001 Aug 18	Trapdoor Fandango	A.Fraser, A.Gillies, I.Magill
2001	Summit or Plummet	S.Lampard (solo)
2001	Ship's Prow, The Fin	S.Lampard, P.Roy
2001	Mont Vin	V.Lampard, S.Lampard

Portpatrick

| 1899 Jun 25 | The Witch Rock, E & W Faces | E.C.M.Heath (solo). |

The first recorded route on the Galloway Sea-cliffs. An article on the first ascent appears in the Climbers' Club Journal for that year, adjacent to a report on the Dent Blanche accident in which Owen Glynne Jones died. Portpatrick Quarry routes by A.Plumb, S.Aird 1984-6.

Money Head

1992 Apr 22	Ecu Wall	A.Fraser, R.McAllister
1992 Apr 22	Slot Machine	R.McAllister, A.Fraser
1992 Apr 22	Pay Day	R.McAllister (solo)
1992 May 1	Filthy Lucre, Pot of Gold	R.McAllister, A.Fraser
1992 May 1	Insider Dealing, Rainbow's End	A.Fraser, R.McAllister
1992 Jun 11	The Liquidator	A.Fraser, K.Douglas
1992 Jun 14	The Root of All Evil	R.McAllister, A.Fraser
1992 Jun 14	Bolivars	J.Thompson, D.McGimpsey
1992 Jun 14	Free Enterprise, Cash Flow	R.McAllister, D.McGimpsey
1992 Jun 14	Tumbling Dice, Tax Evasion	A.Fraser, K.Douglas, J.Thomson
1994 Jun 3	Jug Jive	R.D.Everett, D.Gaffney
1994 Aug	Cash Flow Crisis	R.McAllister, D.McGimpsey

| 2000 May 26 | High Finance | M.Whitaker, P.Cocks |
| 2000 Jul 26 | Martin's Bank, Loan Shark | M.Whitaker, J.Bolton, P.Cocks |

Laggantalluch

| 1987 | Stingray | S.M.Richardson, T.Prentice |

The geological map showed granite so they went to look for it. Laggantalluch and Portobello indicated the amount of rock still unclimbed. and led to a decade of furious activity on the coast.

1987	Dublin Packet	T.Prentice, S.M.Richardson
1987	Laggantalluch Corner	S.M.Richardson, T.Prentice
1987	First Touch	S.M.Richardson, T.Prentice
1987	Seal Song	T.Prentice, S.M.Richardson
1987	Pillar	S.M.Richardson, T.Prentice
1987	Freewheeling	T.Prentice, R.Everett
1987	Irish Mist	R.Everett, T.Prentice
1987	Ape Escape	T.Prentice, R.Everett
1987	Sciatic Nerve	R.Everett (solo)
1987	Seventh Wave	S.M.Richardson, R.Reid
1987	Arete	R.Reid, S.M.Richardson
1987	Tormentil	R.Reid, S.M.Richardson
1987	Wave Goodbye	R.Reid, S.M.Richardson
1987	Rogered	R.Everett (solo)

Direct: R.McAllister, D.McAllister 20 Sept 1991

1987	Refusnik	T.Prentice, R.Everett
1987	Back Burner	T.Prentice
1991 Sep 1	Fish Tales, Little Feat, The Fish Ladder	A.Fraser, C.Stenhouse
1991 Sep 1	Good Morning Ladies, Skating	C.Stenhouse, A.Fraser
1991 Sep 8	Bouillabaisse, Darwin's Waiting Room	A.Fraser, R.McAllister
1991 Sep 8	Waiting for the Sun	R.McAllister (solo)
1991 Sep 8	Stepped Corner	R.McAllister, A.Fraser
1991 Sep 8	Heart of Darkness	R.McAllister, A.Fraser.

The route was climbed in gathering gloom and rapidly rising tide, while stones rolling in the sea cave produced an unearthly roaring sound. Three shags landed ominously on a ledge 3m above McAllister and silently watched him climb. The end of the world was obviously nigh.

| 1991 Sep 20 | Mourning Rib | D.McGimpsey (solo) |
| 1991 Sep 20 | Spongonema | J.Blyth, R.McAllister, C.Stenhouse, A.Fraser |

As Blyth attempted to layback the overhanging left arete of the chimney, onlookers speculated on how high his second would go when he peeled.

1991 Sep 20	Desert Island Discs, The Origin of Species	A.Fraser, C.Stenhouse
1991 Sep 20	The Blind Man	C.Stenhouse, A.Fraser
1991 Sep 20	The Oyster Thief, The Clam Catcher, The Shadow Line	J.Blyth, D.McGimpsey
1991 Oct 9	A Plaice by the Sea	S.Lampard, M.Reed
1991 Oct 9	Bright Side of Life	M.Reed, S.Lampard
1991 Oct 9	Unnamed	S.Lampard, M.Reed
1991 Oct 12	Aqualung	D.McGimpsey A.Fraser, R.McAllister
1991 Oct 12	Fish Fingers	R.McAllister, A.Fraser
1991 Oct 12	White Sauce	D.McGimpsey (solo)
1991 Oct 12	Tunes of Glory	A.Fraser, R.McAllister, D.McGimpsey
1992 May	Quick Seal	G.Dudley

Snatched from the jaws of the locals.

1992 Jun 17	Micro Niche	R.McAllister, M.Reed
1992 Jul 29	Obliteration	R.McAllister, D.McGimpsey
1992 Sep 19	Davy Jones's Locker	A.Fraser, R.McAllister
1993 Oct 6	Truncheon Muncher, PC Plummet, The Holy Grail	R.McAllister, A.Fraser, D.McGimpsey

The previous year a policeman had fallen from the top of Truncheon Muncher, hitting the ground on rope stretch, and injuring his ankles.

| 1995 Sep 17 | Stolen Moments | M.Reed, R.McAllister |

Nicked from Lampard after three years of waiting.

| 1997 Jun 29 | Higher than the Sun | R.McAllister, A.Fraser |
| 1997 Jun 29 | The Auld Ship | A.Fraser, R.McAllister |

| 1997 Jul 9 | Optical Illusions | A.Fraser, R.McAllister |
| 1997 Aug 10 | Zero Tolerance | R.McAllister, D.McGimpsey. |

Repeated and long falls taken onto RPs before success gained.

1997 Aug 11	Toxygene	R.McAllister, D.McGimpsey
1997 Aug 17	Sam I Am	D.McGimpsey, S.Mearns, R.McAllister
1997 Aug	Green Eggs and Ham	S.Mearns, R.McAllister
1997 Aug	Read the Small Print	R.McAllister, S.Mearns

Reed, the ultimate technician, had failed to read the route, allowing McAllister to step in.

1999 May 2	Sea Monkey	N.Taylor
2000 Apr 27	Jellyfish Jive	M.Whitaker, P.Cocks
2004 Jun 18	The Brothers Grim	I.Magill, A.Fraser

Point of the Cleugh

1992 Aug 28	The Chancer	D.McGimpsey (solo)
1992 Aug 28	Cleuch Clamber	D.McGimpsey, S.Ravey
1992 Aug 28	Just Friends	S.Ravey, D.McGimpsey
1992 Aug 28	The Slot	S.Ravey (solo)
1992 Aug 28	Comatose	D.McGimpsey, R.McAllister
2003 Mar 21	Corkie the Catfish	A.Fraser,A.Gillies

Crammag Head

| 1992 Aug 8 | Molotov Cocktail | A.Fraser, D.McGimpsey. |

Discovery of the crag was third time lucky – Fraser had walked over the crag on two previous occasions during the last 10 years.

1992 Aug 8	Kalashnikov	C.Stenhouse, R.McAllister
1992 Aug 8	Freedom Fighter	R.McAllister (unseconded)
1992 Aug 8	Gorilla Warfare	D.McGimpsey, A.Fraser
1992 Aug 8	Skol's Out	R.McAllister, A.Fraser, C.Stenhouse, D.McGimpsey (all solo)
1992 Aug 16	The Soft Parade	R.McAllister, J.Freeman, D.McGimpsey
1992 Aug 16	Fallen Star	D.McGimpsey, C.Stenhouse
1992 Aug 16	Lighthouse Wall	R.McAllister, C.Stenhouse
1992 Aug 16	Hourglass Slab	C.Stenhouse, R.McAllister
1992 Aug 16	Hagar The Horrible	C.Stenhouse, D.McGimpsey, J.Freeman
1992 Aug 16	Dormouse	J.Freeman, D.McGimpsey (solo)
1992 Aug 18	Enfant Terrible, The Ships Cat	A.Fraser, D.McGimpsey, R.McAllister
1992 Aug 18	Yosemite Sam, Funeral Pyre	R.McAllister, D.McGimpsey, A.Fraser
1992 Aug 18	Mog	D.McGimpsey, A.Fraser, R.McAllister

Stuart Lampard phoned at the unheard of hour of 7.30am to discover that the team had left for 'secret crag x', leaving him none the wiser.

1992 Aug 23	Accomodations of Desire	R.McAllister, D.McGimpsey, T.Allan
1992 Aug 23	Shining Path	T.Allan, R.McAllister
1992 Aug 23	Poisoned Ocean	R.McAllister, T.Allan
1992 Aug 23	Fragile Edge	R.McAllister, D.McGimpsey
1992 Aug 23	Orabidoo	D.McGimpsey, G.Gerrard
1992 Aug 27	Pillage	D.McGimpsey, S.Ravey
1992 Aug 29	The White Rabbit	A.Fraser, R.McAllister, D.McGimpsey
1992 Aug 29	Ragnarok	A.Fraser, D.McGimpsey
1993 Apr 11	Fresh Air	R.Everett, D.Gaffney
1993 Apr 29	Anvil Chorus, Down Under	R.McAllister, M.Sayers
1993 Sep 24	Sid Stingray	D.McGimpsey, S.Meffen-Main
1993 Sep 24	Bully Beef	D.McGimpsey, S.Meffen-Main (solo)
1993 Nov 6	The Four Bees	D.McGimpsey, R.McAllister
1993 Nov 6	The Seven Seas	R.McAllister, D.McGimpsey
1994 Apr	Krapton Factor	M.Reed (solo)
1994 May 23	Ultima Thule	A.Fraser, R.McAllister
1994 Jul 3	Firefly	R.D.Everett, D.Gaffney
1994 Jul 24	Razamatazz	R.Smith, A.Munro
1994 Jul 28	Rocky Relations	S.Mearns, R.McAllister
1994 Aug 7	Matador	R.McAllister, D.McGimpsey
1994 Sep	Violently Happy	R.McAllister, S.Mearns
1995 May 1	Beers, Smeers and Queers	R.McAllister, D.McGimpsey

1999 Aug 12	Little Flasher	M.Whitaker,I.Weir
2000 Apr 15	Up Helly Aa	A.Fraser, I.Magill
2000 Sep 20	Twenty, Anniversary Outing	S.Reid, J.Reid
2002 Dec 20	Santa's Little Helper,	
	The Pantomime Horse	A.Fraser (solo)
2003 Mar 21	Bjorn Again	A.Fraser, A.Gillies

Crammag Head South

| 1992 Aug 8 | The Barricades of Heaven | R.McAllister, C.Stenhouse |

Climbed minutes before Crammag was discovered and overlooked in the subsequent gold rush.

2000 Aug 2	Custer, Eldora, Old Ted,	
	Big Sandy, Wi-Ped Biped	M.Whitaker, P.Cocks
2000 Aug 18	Firearms Certificate, Baked Potato	I.Weir, P.Cocks, M.Whitaker
2000 Aug 18	Fried, Boiling, Done to a Turn	M.Whitaker, I.Weir
2000 Aug 18	Char Grilled	I.Weir, M.Whitaker
2003 Mar 21	Axis of Weasels	A.Fraser.

A.Gillies was unable to second in dark and the usual night-time debacle followed.

| 2003 Jun 15 | Holy Mackerel | A.Fraser, I.Magill |
| 2003 Jun 15 | The Ba'ath Party | I.Magill, A.Fraser |

Fortress Slab

| 2002 Aug 25 | Fortress Slab | A.Fraser, IMagill |

Mull of Galloway

It is known that Fred Harper climbed and bouldered around these cliffs in the 1950s.

1971 Aug 3	Vomit	W.Renshaw, R.Kenyon
1991 Sep 1	Bible Class	C.Stenhouse, A.Fraser
1991 Sep 1	Sundae School	A.Fraser, C.Stenhouse

Stenhouse and Fraser moved to Laggantalluch the same day, thus overlooking the crag's potential.

| 1997 | The Traverse | S. Lampard, D.McGimpsey |

An epic outing recorded over four days – 6 Apr and three days in Jun and Jul.

| 1997 Apr 6 | Carrick-kee, Hare Ridge | S.Lampard, D.McGimpsey |

These two routes were climbed as part of the traverse. Lampard swore McGimpsey to secrecy but a confession was extracted within 10 days.

| 1997 Apr 16 | Porpoise and the Hare | A.Fraser, R. McAllister, D.McGimpsey |

A monstrous, bloated hare floated past the crag.

1997 Apr 16	Catch the Sun	R.McAllister, A.Fraser, D.McGimpsey
1997 Apr 16	Smartypants	D.McGimpsey, A.Fraser, R.McAllister
1997 Apr 16	Ridgeard Corie	A.Fraser (solo)
1997 Aug	Wrecker's Wall	S.Lampard, D.McGimpsey
1997 Aug	Anchor Chimney	S.Lampard, J.Thomson
1997 Aug	Playtime	S.Lampard
1997 Aug	Release the Pressure	D.McGimpsey, R.McAllister
1997 Sep	Unscathed	R.McAllister, S.Mearns
2000 May 28	Ruddy'ard Kipperling, Friends on	
	the Right, Enemas on the Left	M.Whitaker, P.Cocks
2000 May 30	Not a Fiend in the World	J.Bolton, P.Cocks, M.Whitaker
2000 May 30	Hula in a Brass Skirt	J.Bolton, P.Cocks
2000 May 30	Happy as a Sand Martin	M.Whitaker(solo)
2000 May 30	Oook	M.Whitaker
2000 May 30	Gun Slot Wounds,	
	An Arm and a Leg	M.Whitaker, I.Weir
2000 May 30	Anemone Action	M.Whitaker, J.Bolton,P.Cocks
2000 May 30	Cod Moves in Mysterious Waves	M.Whitaker, I.Weir, P.Cocks
2000 May 30	Old Whippersnappers	M.Whitaker, I.Weir, J.Bolton, P.Cocks

The team had a combined age of 207!

2000 Jun 2	Weigh Out, Awkward Bustard	M.Whitaker, P.Cocks
2001 Jun 2	No Tern Unstoned, Still Waiting	
	for a Bolt Hole, A Pint and a Fag	M Whitaker
2000 Jul 29	Outer Limpets, A Load of Pollacks,	
	The Hissing of Summer Prawns,	
	A Plaice in the Sun, On Porpoise,	
	Flounders of the Baskervilles	M.Whitaker, P.Cocks

2000 Aug 1	Astrofest, I'm Sorry, I haven't a Cleugh, Any Corona Left, Coroner Wright, Absolute Crab	M.Whitaker, P.Cocks
2000 Aug 16	Slartibartfast, Zaphod Beeblebrox, Marvin, Costellation Prize, Hyperspatial Bypass	M.Whitaker, I.Weir, P.Cocks
2000 Aug 21	Enema Territory	M.Whitaker, I.Weir. P.Cocks
2000 Aug 21	A Different Kettle of Fish, Castor Oil and Pollacks	M.Whitaker, P.Cocks
2002 Sep 29	Anticlimax Arete, Fighting Fat, Survival of the Fattest, Fit for Nutting	M.Whitaker, P.Cocks
2002 Sep 30	His Flounders to Perform, Katinka, Neptune's Bell-cord, Rhythm of the Reign, Everest, Sagarmatha, Chomolungma	M.Whitaker, P.Cocks
2004 May 29	Friends in High Plaices, Your Plaice or Mine?	D.Pendlebury, L.McLeish
2004 May 29	Mullet Over, Carrickcorie Corner	M.Whitaker, P.Cocks.

Stirling Area
Thorntons Quarry - Cambusbarron

1983	Big Country Dreams	A.Kay, R.Cowells
Pre 1984	Three Step Corner	Unknown
1984	Visions of Monaco	C.Macadam
1984	The Purr-Blind Doomster	C.Macadam
1984	Quasi Pulls Through	K.Spence
1984	Formica Crack, Murray's Groove	M.Hamilton
1984	Fuel for Thought	R.Anderson
1984 May	Both Ends Burning	D.McCallum
1984 May	Quantum Grunt	G.Pedley
1984	Power of Endurance	G.Latter
1984	Spanking the Monkey	G.Livingstone
1985 May 13	Economy Drive	R.Anderson, J.McKenzie
1985 May 19	Adulterer's Repentence	D.McCallum, D.Simmonds
1985 Jun 14	The Crowd	D.McCallum
1986 Jun 8	Trail Blazer	R.Anderson, A.Russell
1986 Sep 7	Pathfinder	R.Anderson, N.Elstone, G.Nicoll
1988 Jul 31	Thug of War	R.Anderson
1994 May	Pig Route	M. Worsley, C. Pettigrew.

Accidentally missed from previous edition.

1994 Jun	Blockbuster	C. Adam, S. Baker
1995 Jun 12	Cumacoma	G.Lennox, C.Adam
1998 Jun	The Bustup	D. MacLeod, S.Patterson
1998 Jun	In Hiding D.MacLeod	
1996 May 14	Bo's Groove, Bo's Arete	C.Adam, C.Lennox
1996 May 14	Bo's Arete Direct	C.Adam solo
1998 Sep 26	Auto Giro	G. Lennox, C.Adam
1996 Aug 30	Contortionism	G.Lennox, D.Parr
1996 May 14	Anabolic Steroids	G.Lennox, C.Adam
2001 May	Tarzan	M.Tweedley, L.Byrnes

Bolts for protection and a bolted lower-off at the large ledge. All were later removed and the route led to the top by C.Adam 1st Nov 2003 who offered the name Cheeta.

2001 May	Moving Shadow	M.Tweedley, L.Byrnes

Originally led with a peg for protection.

2002 Sep 24	Grangemouth High Grooves	N.Tait, S.Tait
2003 Aug 17	Dr. Dre's Orgazmatron	R.Wallace, A.Wallace
2003 Sep 28	Phantom Power	A.Wallace, R.Wallace
2003 Oct 26	Bobbin Robin	R.Wallace, A.Wallace
2004 Feb 26	Sexed Up	S.Munro

Controversially bolted against the wishes of many local activists. Just how long the bolts will stay in place before an ascent in the style of the other routes in the quarry remains to be seen.

2004 Mar	Jerkin' the Gherkin	S.Munro
2004 Mar 28	Nandralone	G.Lennox

Cambusbarron breaks into the eighth grade. The first ascent was redpointed with the gear in-situ.

2004 Apr 24	Ground Force	A.Wallace, W.Upson
2004 Apr 25	Ballroom Blitz	R.Wallace, A.Wallace
2004 May 15	Gun Fury	A.Wallace, R.Wallace
2004 Jun 19	Anger Management	C.Adam

Forth Quarry - Cambusbarron

1980s	Another One Bites The Dust	G.Harrison, P.Laughlan
1980s	Malky the Alky	G.Harrison, P.Laughlan
1980s	Not Easy Contract	G.Harrison, P.Laughlan
1985 May 1	Easy Contract	C.Hewitt, N.Shepherd, K.Clark

Numerous variations to this route have been claimed over the years.

1990 Jul 17	Gobi Roof	M.Garthwaite, G.Szuca, G.Campbell
1991 May 21	Wind Up, Force 8	M.Garthwaite, G.Szuca
1991 Jul 14	Scaresville	G.Szuca, P.Hyde
2001	Scaresville Variation	A. Pert, S. Burge

Replaces an earlier variation to Scaresville which fell down.

1991 Jul 17	Brat Attack	M.Garthwaite, G.Szuca
1991 May 23	Slot Shot	M.Garthwaite, G.Szuca
1991 May 22	The Doobie Brothers	M.Garthwaite, G.Szuca
1993 Jun	Cross in Oz	R. Wallace, A. Wallace

Missed in the previous guide, four other FA claims to this route and its neighbour Cross-town Traffic!

1993 Jun	Cross-town Traffic	R. Wallace, A. Wallace

Missed in the previous guide.

1993 Jun	Pipistrelle	R. Wallace, A. Wallace.

Missed in the previous guide.

1993 Jun	Ramplin'	R. Wallace, A. Wallace

Despite later claims, this cherry had already been popped.

1993 Jun	Yoshimi	R. Wallace, A. Wallace

Missed in the previous guide.

1993 Jul	The Ubiquitous Chip	M.Worsley, G.Urquhart
1993 Summer	Cha	G.Szuca, D.Gregg
1993 Summer	Chisel	D.Gregg, G.Szuca
1993 Oct 25	Ninety-Five	G.Szuca (roped solo)
1993 Apr 27	Production Line	A. Wren

Climbed without the pegs for protection by Gordon Lennox, April 1997.

1994 Aug 8	Crack Attack	G.Lennox, S.Baker
1995 Apr 8	Frustration	G.Lennox, C.Adam
1995 Apr 9	Decidedly Dodgy	G.Lennox, C.Adam
1995 Apr 7	Bo's Girdle	C.Adam, G.Lennox
1996 Aug	Confessions of a Speed Freak	M.Worsley, T.Wood
1996 Aug	The Rock of Crack	M.Worsley, T.Wood
1996 Jul	Bird's Nest Crack	M.Worsley, T.Wood

Climbed to the ledge in June 1993 by Raymond Wallace, but unfinished due to loose rock.

1999 Aug	Arse on Stumps	M.Somerville, A.Morris
1999 May	Looney Tunes	M.Tweedly, M.Somerville
1999 Aug	Somnambulism	M.Somerville
2000 Jan	Scales of Injustice	M.Somerville
2000 Jan	Miss Po	M.Somerville, L.Byrnes
2001	Thank God for Friends	A. Pert, M.Hindmarsh, P.McAllister
2001 Aug	Public Spirited Individual	R.Welch, A.Marr, M.Tweedly
2001	Buttons	A.Pert, S.Mcguire
2002 Jun 1	The Cutter	A.Wallace

As loose as it looks – a second was not forthcoming.

2003 Aug 17	Here Come The Mini-monks	A.Wallace, R.Wallace

Almost certainly climbed earlier.

2003 Aug 2	The Consolation Prize	A.Wallace, R.Wallace
2003 Aug 16	Smack My Birch Up	A.Wallace, R.Wallace
2003 Aug 16	Furrowed Prow	A.Wallace, R.Wallace
2002 Sept 25	Toddle	A.Wallace, C.McDaid
2003 Aug	Scrubbers	T.Brady, T.Stone
2004 May 16	One for the Buzzards	A.Wallace, R.Wallace
2004 May 30	Le Bal des Oiseaux Fantomes	A.Wallace, R.Wallace

Climbed without using the gear placement chipped by a different party on an earlier attempt.

| 2004 Jun 19 | Chime | A.Wallace, R.Wallace |
| 2004 Jul 28 | Climn on you Crazy Diamond | T.Higgins, S.Hawkins |

North Third

1982	The Flying Dragon	R.Cowels
1982	Jezebel	R.Cowels
1982	Red Shift	R.Cowels, A.Kay (some aid)

FFA: G.Latter 1984. Start as described: K.Spence

Wolfcrag Quarry

1970s	The Arétc	D.Powers, N.Morrison
1970s	Leonardo	I.Duckworth
1980s	Ian's Wa	I.Duckworth
1980s	Up on the Catwalk	A.Kay
1980s	Experiments in Incest	A.Kay
1980s	Tribal Look	A.Kay
1980s	Waterfront	C.Macadam
1980s	The Outsider	C.Macadam
1980s	Lock-it	R.Cowels
1980s	Thirty Frames a Second	R.Cowels
1990s	Unnamed	R.Fielding
1992	Kalahari	Unknown

D.Powers and N.Morrison climbed a similar line in 1979.

1995 Apr 22	Snakebite	C.Adam, G.Lennox, D.Parr
1995 Apr 30	Hair of the Dog	G.Lennox, C.Adam
1995 Apr 20	Seriously Silly	G.Lennox, C.Adam

Other Crags

Craig Rossie, all routes by R.Cowells, 1984. Dollar Quarry, all routes by J.Main, 1980s

Fife
North Queensferry Quarry

1985	Scharnhorst	R.Baker, R.Howard
1985	The Boat	R.Baker, R.Howard
1986 Mar 15	Dive Dive Dive	R.Baker, R.Howard
1987 Mar 3	Edge of Time	R.Campbell, P.Morozzo

Original route now variation. As described S.Jenkins, E.Cameron, 14 Apr 1987.

| 1989 Oct 8 | Bismark | A.Perkins, M.Duff |
| 1989 Oct 14 | Fleet Air Arm | A.Perkins, I.Tattersall, M.Duff |

Perkins broke an arm during the ascent.

| 1991 Apr | Nearly an Angel | G.MacIntyre, T.Gould |

MacIntyre went one better, breaking an arm and a leg.

| 1991 May 24 | The Vital Spark | A.Matthewson, J.Andrew, D.Kirk |

Rosyth Quarry

1972	Gold Foil, Route to Root, Wireworm	R.Baker
1972	Chemical Warfare	P.De Mengle
1972	Smith's Dilemma, Sickle	M.Smith
1972	Jack's Route, Broken Pillar	J.Rice
1972	Legover Groove	R.Baker
1972	Heathy, Cathy	I.Conway
1973	Iconoclast	First aided ascent unknown.

FFA: W.Jeffrey, M.Plant 1975

| 1973 | Grenville | I.Conway |
| 1973 | The Stinking Swordsman | I.Conway (6PA) |

Originally called Matinee Cracks.

FFA: I.Cropley 1986

1974	Andy's Route	A.McCord
1974	Drizzle, C.N.D	I.Conway
1974	Phillistine	R.Baker (6PA)
1974	Pogo Groove	R.Baker
1974	Fat Sam	A.McCord
1974	Serendipity	P.De Mengle

1975	Hands Off, Ram Jam Corner, Gift Horse	A.McCord
1975	Late Night Final	R.Baker
1975 Aug 10	Grot Corner	W.Jeffrey, M.Martin
1975 Aug 16	The Beast	W.Jeffrey, A.Davidson
1975 Aug 16	Tiger Pad	W.Jeffrey
1975 Aug 25	Inspiration	W.Jeffrey, M.Plant
1975 Aug 31	The Waullie	W.Jeffrey, C.Craggs
1975 Aug 31	Corpuscle	M.Plant, L.Linaker, M.Martin (10PA)
1975 Aug 31	The Grinder	W.Jeffrey, C.Craggs
1975 Sep 5	Changeling	M.Plant, M.Martin, R.Columbo (5PA)
1975 Sep 10	Flakeoff	M.Plant (6PA)
1976	The Beauty, The Flying Bink	C.Craggs, C.Binks
1977	If Pigs Could Fly	M.Hamilton
1985 Oct 28	Jagdhond	R.Howard, R.Baker
1986 May	Plod	D.Moffat
1990 May	Skinny Lizzie	S.Brown, D.Moffat
1992 Jun 10	The Rust Bucket	I.Taylor
2000 Jul 13	Master Fwap	S.Templeman
2004 Apr 24	Suspect Device	C.McSais, A.Pert

Limekilns

1981	Humbug	M.Bennett
1983 Jun	Hunter and the Hunted	A.Kay
1983 Jun	Dingley Dell	D.Claxton, N.Morrison, A.Kay
1983 Jun	Marley's Ghost	R.Cowels, A.Kay
1983 Jun 25	Cruel Summer	N.Morrison, D.Claxton
1983 Jun 27	Methods of Dance	A.Kay, N.Morrison
1983 Jun 27	New Gold Dream	N.Morrison, A.Kay, D.Claxton
1983 Jun 27	Colours Fly	N.Morrison
1984	Elgin's Crack	A.Pettit, R.Cowels
1984 Mar	The Iron Fist	J.McKenzie
1984 Mar	Velvet Glove	K.Spence, J.McKenzie, D.McCallum
The Satin Finish: R.Anderson, 5 Oct 1984		
1984 Apr 28	The Struggler	N.Morrison, C.McLean, A.Ross
1985	Neutral Gear	D.Moffat
1985	Forbidden Colours	A.Borthwick, M.Russell
1985 Apr 16	D-Day	D.Moffat, R.Baker
1985 Apr 21	White Ensign	R.Baker, A.McCord, D.Moffat
1985 Apr 21	Red Flag	A.McCord, R.Baker
1985 Apr 23	DT's	D.Moffat, K.Todd
1985 Apr 24	Sunsetter	A.Borthwick, M.Russell
1985 May	Link Rib	A.Borthwick, D.Forsyth
1985 May	One Ringer	A.Borthwick, D.Forsyth
1985 May	Two Ringer	A.Borthwick, D.Forsyth
1985 May	Edge of Fear	A.Borthwick
1985 May	Protectless	A.Borthwick
1985 May	The Ivy League, Yuppie	D.McCallum
1985 May 3	VE Day	D.Moffat, R.Baker
1985 May 31	Grasp the Nettle	R.Howard, R.Baker
1985 Jun 3	The Sting	D.Moffat, I.Todd
1985 Jun 5	Dead Ringer	D.Moffat, R.Baker
1985 Jul 20	The Charleston	M.Hamilton, R.Anderson
1985 Aug 10	Rock Around the Block	R.Anderson, A.Russell
1985 Sep 15	Slots	R.Anderson
1985 Oct 13	Through the Motions	R.Anderson, K.Spence
1986 Aug 3	On the Blocks	R.Anderson, K.Spence, G.Cohen

The Hawkcraig

1965	Fish Head Arete, Pain Pillar	N.Macniven
1965	Saki, Brutus	N.Macniven
1965	Torment, Eureka	N.Macniven
1965	Fish Head Wall, Ugh	J.Knight
1965	The Lilly, Escalator	J.Knight

1965	Tink, Shadow Corner	J.Knight
1965	Termination, The Low Girdle	J.Knight
1965	Sacrilege, Squirrel Slab	D.Bathgate
1965	Gismo, Gaucho, Diptera	D.Bathgate
1965	Urmi, The High Girdle	D.Bathgate
1965	Eech, Cranium Crack, Gaucho	I.MacEacheran
1965	Rebel's Groove, Chimney Arete	I.MacEacheran
1965	Gunga Din, Saracen, Toerag's Wall	I.MacEacheran
1965	Halleluja Wall, The Whang	I.MacEacheran
1965	Flake and Wall, Destiny Groove	I.MacEacheran
1965	Maureen	J.MacEacheran
1965	Conquistador Crack	B.Robertson
1965	Stomach-Ache, Crusader	A.McKeith
1965	The High Girdle	A.McKeith
1965	Guano	J.Brumfitt
Variation: D.Cuthbertson, R.Anderson, 1975		
1965	Ganja, The Chimney	J.Renny
1970 May 24	Sublimation	D.Edwards, A.Ford
1975	The Arete	D.Cuthbertson, R.Anderson
1975	Weasel Wall	M.Hamilton
1983	Serendipity	S.Murdoch, J.Murdoch
1990 Jul 31	Where Were You?	S.Brown, J.Armour
1990 Oct 13	Psylocibie	A.Connolly, G.Szuca
1998 Aug 5	Hip Replacement	J.Dyble, J.Shanks
1998 Aug 5	Rib and Groove	J.Dyble, J.Shanks
1999 Apr 28	Garlic Bread	T.Muirhead, P.Hague
1999 Apr 28	Pizza	P.Hague, T.Muirhead
2000 Apr 21	The Dreeping Beak	J.Dyble (unsec)
2001 Mar 3	Guillemot Head Mush	J.Dyble, I.Simpson
2004 May 31	Aaron's Way	M.Hunt, J.Dyble

Benarty Hill

1982	Cubism	K.Spence
1983	A Fist Job	J.McKenzie, K.Spence
1983	Dolly Parton	K.Spence, J.McKenzie
1983	Ram	J.McKenzie, K.Spence
1991 Jul 22	Treasure Seeker	A.Matthewson
1991 Jul 22	Demerara, Goblin, Oat Flake	A.Matthewson
1991 Jul 31	Hot Potato	N.Armstrong, J.Andrew, A.Matthewson
1996 Jun 13	Pamela Anderson	J.Andrew
1996 Jun 13	Wizard	A.Matthewson, A.Hume, C.Pasteur

Edinburgh Area
Dalmahoy Hill

Many of the climbs were first done by the 'Currie Boys' in the late '50s and early '60s. Unfortunately, no details are available and the cliff was neglected until the late '70s, when members of the Edinburgh JMCS re-cleaned, climbed and named most of the routes. A further burst of activity is detailed below.

1987	Scree Surfing	A.Plumb, R.Ferguson
1991 Aug 14	Elation	J.Inglis, G.Jones, C.Eilbeck
1991 Aug 22	Midgey Gem	J.Inglis, A.McCleish, C.Eilbeck
1991 Aug 31	Cleaned Sweep	J.Inglis, C.Eilbeck
1992 May 20	The Lemming	J.Inglis, D.Buchanan, C.Eilbeck

Ratho Quarry

1975	Godzilla	W.Jeffrey, C.Craggs
1975	Terminal Street	C.Craggs, W.Jeffrey
1975	Terminal Case	W Jeffrey, C.Craggs
1976	Shear Fear	W.Jeffrey
1976	Ouroborus	W.Jeffrey, C.Craggs
1976	Beanpud	M Pettifer, W.Jeffrey
1976	Scotty Arete	J.Hutchison
1976	Spiny Norman	J.Hutchison

| 1976 | Shoskred | W.Jeffrey, C.Craggs |
| 1980 | Doomed Oasis | P.Hunter, K.Spence |

Originally E2, but harder since the loss of a flake.

1980	Diverticulitis	P.Hunter, W.Jeffrey
1980	Pettifer's Wall	P.Hunter, W.Jeffrey
1981	Pete's Wall	P.Hunter
1981	Ouroborus Eliminate	P.Hunter, K.Spence
1981	Pete's Wall	P.Hunter, C.Lees
1981	Up the Creek	P.Hunter, K.Spence
1981	Sedge Warbler	P.Hunter
1981	Sahara	P.Hunter

Originally E3 but harder since the loss of the flake. Re-climbed by J.Andrew, 1992.

1982	Gruel Brittania	K.Spence
1982	Slow Strain	R.Anderson
1983	Wally 1	K.Spence
1983	Wally 2	K.Spence
1983	Wally 3	K.Spence
1983	Rebel Without Claws	R.Anderson
1983	The Lone Groover	G.Handren
1983	Artho	K.Spence
1983	This Septic Heil	K.Spence
1983	Welcome to the Cruise	R.Anderson

Formerly called In Memoriam.

1983	Time's Last Gift	J.Melrose
1983	Ane Ledge	R.Anderson
1985 May 3	The Blob	D.McCallum, G.Pedley
1985 Jul 1	Right Under	R.Anderson, A.Russell
1985 Jul 7	Left Over	R.Anderson, R.Milne, A.Russell
1988 Apr 24	Lone Groover alternative	R.Anderson, A.Williams
1989	So It Goes	G.McIntyre
1990 Jul 4	Pull the Other One	G.Nicoll, K.Noble, A.Chamings
1991 Nov 20	5000 Christmas Trees	J.Andrew, N.Armstrong

Probably climbed previously in mistake for Beanpud.

1991 Nov 25	Danger No Entry	J.Andrew
1991 Nov 28	Business as Usual	J.Andrew, N.Armstrong
1992 Mar 24	In a Prickle	J.Andrew, N.Armstrong
1992 Mar 24	Thorn in my Side	N.Armstrong, J.Andrew
1992 Mar 26	Chalk and Cheese	J.Andrew, N.Armstrong
1992 Mar 26	Strongarm	J.Andrew, N.Armstrong
1992 Mar 26	Election Sickness	N.Armstrong, J.Andrew
1993 Apr	Alopecia	I.Taylor, I.Pitcairn
1993 Apr 28	Fledge	J.Inglis, J.Ritchie
1994 Jul 19	Wounded Knee	I.Taylor, S.Munro
1998 Jun	The Grapes of Ratho	I.Taylor

Holyrood Park

| 1897 | Eastern Buttress Face Route | H.Raeburn |

Later called Hackenback.

1897	Fallen Column Climb	H.Raeburn
1900 Jul 11	Cat Nick Buttress	H.Raeburn, W.Inglis Clark
1902 Jul 25	Great Buttress	W.Morrison, W.Newbigging, L.Briquet

Formerly called Eastern Buttress.

1933 Sep 4	Hewit's Groove	J.Hewit, W.Nisbet
1935 Aug 4	Sentry Box	J.Hewit, J.Donaldson
1936 Jul 5	Initial Route	J.Hewit
1937 Oct 2	Wall Route	J.Hewit, W.Nisbet
1944 Apr 23	Pinnacle Corner	A.Hendry
1944 May 14	Hyphen Route	A.Hendry
1945	Archie's Slab	A.Hendry
1945	Harrison's Climb	A.Harrison
1945	Horne's Slab	A.Horne
1945	Red Buttress	A.Graham
1945	Question Mark Crack	J.Berkeley
1945 Apr 22	The Lift Arete	G.Scott

1945 Oct 7	Athlete's Arete	G.Scott, D.Haworth
1945 Oct 26	Overhanging Route No.1	D.Haworth
Later called Evening Pillar.		
1946	Barbed Wire Route	D.Haworth, A.Myerscough, A.Dick
1946	Stomach Layback	J.Berkeley
1946	Steeplejack's Staircase	D.Haworth
1946	Hanging Slab	P.Myerscough
1946 Apr 20	Overhanging Route No.2	D.Haworth
Later called Evening Crack.		
1946 Apr 23	Pinnacle Face	D.Haworth, P.Myerscough
1946 Apr 23	The Conflict with Temptation	D.Haworth
1946 May 1	Hanging Over Gladys, Gladys' Rib, No Love Rib	M.Slesser
1946 May 12	Rib and Mantleshelf	D.Haworth, A.Dick
1946 May 15	Wicked Lady	D.Haworth
1946 May 25	Eureka	D.Haworth
1946 May 25	Bacchus' Buttress Route	D.Haworth
1946 Jun 16	Waverley Crack	G.Parish, D.Duff
1946 Oct 25	Tournez	D.Haworth, A.Myrescough
1946 Oct 25	Toujours	D.Haworth, A.Dick
1946 Nov 2	Moonlight Traverse	D.Haworth, I.McPhail, A.Dick
1946 Nov 13	Great Electrocardiogram Traverse	D.Haworth, I.McPhail
1946 Nov 24	Graham's Route	D.Haworth
Later called Smoker's Slab Route.		
1946 Dec 2	Cracked Slab	A.Wright
1946 Dec 6	Cracked Slab Crack	A.Liver
1947 Jan 19	Editor's Crack	G.Dutton, M.Slesser, Miss Bainton
1947 Jan 22	Doubledecker	D.Haworth, G.Parish
1947 Feb 22	Wee Chokestone Crack	D.Haworth
1947 May 29	Grand Finale Route	D.Haworth, G.Ritchie
1952	Doubledecker variation	A.More, D.Mill
1956	Left Ribs	R.Smith
1960	Scuttle	R.Smith
1960	Black Corner	Unknown
FFA J.Andrew 1991		
1982	Ginger Nympho's Lust	J.Handren, J.Melrose
1982 Dec 8	Straight Satan	J.Handren, B.Kerr
1983	The Blackdance	J.Handren, J.Melrose
1983	After the Axe	J.Handren, B.Kerr
1983	Walking on Sunshine	J.Handren, J.Melrose
1983	Transatlantic Trip	J.Handren, D.McCallum
1987 Mar	Vague Arete	A.Matthewson
1987 Jun 10	Election Special	R.Anderson, G.Taylor, D.Bond, A.Williams, K.Spence
1991 Aug 14	Second Offence	J.Andrew, J.Tout
1991 Dec 2	Walk On By	J.Andrew
1991 Dec 13	The Ragged Rascals	J.Andrew, J.Tout
1992 Jun 3	Idle Gossip	J.Andrew
1992 Jun 24	Ped Xing	J.Andrew, J.Tout, A.Matthewson, A.Tibbs
1996 Feb 8/9	Excalibur	Unknown
The SMCJ attributed the route to 'essence of' H.Raeburn, W.Naismith.		
2001 Mar 1	Red Chimney	D.Rubens, C.Smith

Blackford Hill

Quarry Pinnacle was climbed by H.Raeburn in 1896 and the routes dated 1950s were done by members of the EUMC. The other routes were climbed by J.Andrew (with A.Matthewson on Running Bush) but these and possibly others may well have been climbed before.

Roslin Glen

1976	Centre Line	W.Jeffrey, C.Craggs, P.Buckley
1980	Beyond Trapraln	P.Hunter, W.Jeffrey
1980	Gaping Gab	P.Hunter
1980	Ham Jam	W.Jeffrey

1985	Jun	Red Face	K.Spence, J.Rooney
1985	Jun	The Forty-Twa	K.Spence, J.Rooney
1985	Jun	Day of the Jockal	K.Spence
1985	Jun	The Climbist	K.Spence
1985	Jun	The Wrinklies	K.Spence, J.Rooney
1985	Jun	The Thin Crack	J.Rooney, K.Spence
1985	Jun 30	Pinky and Perky	K.Spence, J.Rooney
1985	Jul 3	Cave Crack	J.Rooney, K.Spence
1985	Jul 3	Rampo	K.Spence, J.Rooney
1985	Jul 7	Gruesome Gamboge	K.Spence, J.Rooney
1985	Jul 7	Faustus Entor	K.Spence, J.Rooney
1985	Jul 9	Rufus	K.Spence
1985	Jul 14	Rock All Over Me	K.Spence, J.Rooney
1985	Jul 14	The Slater's Revenge	J.Rooney, K.Spence
1985	Jul 15	Plunging Neckline	K.Spence, J.Rooney
1985	Jul 19	Hanging Rock	K.Spence, J.Rooney
1985	Jul 21	Panama Red	J.Rooney, K.Spence
1985	Aug 3	Brown Sugar	K.Spence
1985	Aug 5	Dusty Road	K.Spence, J.MacKenzie
1985	Aug 11	Red Wedge	K.Spence, J.Rooney
1985	Oct 6	The Cue	K.Spence, J.MacKenzie, R.Anderson
1985	Oct 6	Enzyme	R.Anderson
1985	Oct 12	No Picnic	R.Anderson, K.Spence
1985	Oct 26	Edge of Darkness	R.Anderson, K.Spence
1985	Oct 26	Piano Player	K.Spence, R.Anderson
1985	Oct 27	Ruff Stuff	R.Anderson, K.Spence
1985	Nov 2	Mein Sumph	K.Spence, R.Anderson
1985	Nov 3	Red Ringer	R.Anderson, K.Spence, J.Rooney
1985	Nov 10	Old Red Eye	J.Rooney, K.Spence, R.Anderson
1985	Dec 14	Harry Dodder's Crack	R.Anderson, K.Spence
1985	Dec 15	Robert the Moose	R.Anderson, K.Spence
1985	Dec 22	Scots Wha Hae	K.Spence, J.MacKenzie
1986	Mar 29	Two Tier Crack	J.Rooney, K.Spence
1986	Mar 29	Ruggosities	K.Spence, J.Rooney
1986	May 24	Praying Mantle	R.Anderson, J.Rooney, K.Spence
1986	May 24	Last Slap	K.Spence, J.Rooney, R.Anderson
1986	Jun 7	Duncrankin	K.Spence, R.Anderson
1986	Jun 8	Shinbones Field	J.Rooney, K.Spence
1986	Jun 14	Belly Bulger	R.Anderson, R.Milne, A.Russell
1986	Jul 7	Under Pressure	R.Anderson, K.Spence
1987	Mar 3	Voice in the Dark	R.Campbell, P.Morozzo
1988	Apr 9	Eddie the Eejit	R.Campbell, N.Craig
1988	Oct 1	Deep in Diana	R.Campbell, D.Simmonds
1988	Oct 10	Bum Fun	O.Hayward
1988	Oct 10	Monodoigtism	R.Campbell
1988	Nov	Life in the Bus Lane	R.Campbell, O.Hayward
1988	Nov	Roslin Roulette	O.Hayward

Top-roped prior to leading.

1988	Dec 24	Dangleberries	O.Hayward
1989	Apr 27	Hezbollah	R.Campbell

Top-roped prior to leading.

1989	Jun 16	Harry Dodder's Variation	J.Andrew
1990	Dec	The Shouting Man	P.Thorburn, R.Campbell
1991		Incarnadine	G.Cohen, D.Rubens
1991	Apr	Claymore Crack	G.Nicoll, W.Jeffrey
1991	May	Basil Brush	A.Matthewson
1991	Jul 29	Rock Lobster	A.Matthewson, J.Andrew
1991	Aug 13	Syzygy	J.Andrew
1991	Aug 13	The Flying Start	J.Andrew
1991	Aug 13	Aficionado	J.Andrew
1991	Oct	Absentee Landlord	A.Matthewson, N.Armstrong, S.Elworthy
1991	Dec 4	Hoppy's Least Favorite	J.Andrew
1991	Dec 14	Strange Apparatus	G.Nicoll
1991	Dec 15	The Golden Apple	

| | | of Eternal Desire | R.Campbell, G.Latter |
| 1992 | Jan | Give 'em enough rope | P.Thorburn, R.Campbell |

Top-roped prior to leading.

| 1992 | Feb | Survival of the Fattest | R.Campbell |
| 1992 | Mar 26 | Walk On By | P.Thorburn |

Top-roped prior to leading.

| 1992 | Apr 3 | Jumbo's Proctoscopy | J.Andrew |

Medical advice, Dr G.Irvine. Top-roped prior to leading.

| 1992 | Apr 3 | Turn the Other Cheek | J.Andrew, N.Armstrong |

Top-roped prior to leading.

1992	May 7	Scotch Corner	J.Andrew, A.Matthewson
1992	May 7	Gadaffi's Ear	J.Andrew
1992	Jun 18	Always the Sun	J.Andrew

Top-roped prior to leading.

| 1993 | Nov 11 | The Chocolate Orgasm | J.Andrew, G.Watt |

East Lothian
Yellow Craigs

2003	Jul	Introductory Slapping	A.Plumb, O.Plumb
2003	Jul	Slippers and Sloppers	A.Plumb, O.Plumb
2003	Jul	Prickly Heat	A.Plumb, O.Plumb
2003	Aug	Attack of the Gorse Fairies	A.Plumb, O.Plumb
2003	Aug	Spikes Downfall	A.Plumb, O.Plumb

Craigy Hill

2002		Lucky Dip	A.Plumb, N.Ramsey
2002		Lucky for Some	A.Plumb, N.Ramsey
2002		Lucky B	N.Ramsey, A.Plumb
2002		Lucky Break	A.Plumb, N.Ramsey
2002		Do You Feel Lucky	A.Plumb, N.Ramsey
2002		Scum Bag 1	I.Taylor
2002		Scum Bag 2	I.Taylor
2002		Lothian Crack	A.Plumb, W.Rooney

Variation: A.Plumb W.Rooney, 2002

2002		Lothian Arete	A.Plumb
2003		The Tomb Stone	T.Lilig
2003		Lucky Star	A.Plumb
2003		Lucky I Only Tore My Ligaments	A.Plumb, O.Plumb
2003		Nay Luck	A.Plumb, O.Plumb
2003		Lucky Ticket	A.Plumb, O.Plumb
2003		Un Lucky Arete	O.Plumb, A.Plumb
2003		Un Lucky 13	A.Plumb, O.Plumb
2003		Lucky The Cat	A.Plumb, O.Plumb
2003		Lucky Traverse	A.Plumb, O.Plumb
2004	May 16	Little Black Roof	F.Sheridan
2004	May 16	Easy Rider	F.Sheridan, A.Plumb

North Berwick Law

1989	Apr 9	Old Lawbreaker	R.Anderson, C.Greaves, K.Spence
1989	Apr 29	Jaws of the Law	R.Anderson, C.Anderson
1989	May 5	Law of Gravity	R.Anderson
1989	Sep 9	Necktie	B.Kerr, R.Young

Originally climbed without bolts, then retrobolted with permission.

1989	Sep 9	Fogtown	B.Kerr, R.Young
1989	Sep 18	Law of the Flies	R.Anderson
1989	Sep 25	Law and Disorder	R.Anderson, C.Anderson
1992		Eliminate Law	I.Pitcairn
1993	Apr 21	Igneous Intruder	N.Ashton
1996	Apr 25	Mr Slappy	A.Plumb, M.Balharry
1996	Apr 30	Neck it or Deck It	A.Plumb, M.Balharry
1996	Apr 30	The Grim Rurper	A Scougall, M.Ballhary, A.Plumb
1996	May 3	Bored Stupid	M.Balharry, A.Plumb
1996	May 3	Sod's Law	A.Plumb, M.Balharry
1996	May 3	The Menhir	A.Plumb, M.Balharry

1996 May 3	Jennifer	M.Balharry, A.Plumb
1996 May 3	Grasp the Nettle	A.Plumb, M.Balharry
1996 May 3	Peglust	A.Plumb, M.Balharry
1996 May 5	Diarrhoea 1	M.Balharry, A.Plumb
1996 May 5	Diarrhoea 2	M.Balharry, A.Plumb
1996 May 5	Up the Spout and Out	M.Balharry, A.Plumb
1996 May 5	Obelix Goes North	A.Plumb, M.Balharry
1996 May 5	Needs Gear	M.Balharry, A.Plumb
1996 May 5	Sarah	A.Plumb, M.Balharry
1996 May 6	Slab and Tickle	A.Plumb, M.Balharry
1996 May 6	Vital Statistics	A.Plumb, M.Balharry
1996 May 6	Statistical Variations	A.Plumb, M.Balharry
1996 May 6	Aldeberan	M.Balharry, A.Plumb
1996 May 14	Finis Horribilis	A.Plumb, M.Balharry
1996 May 16	Leftovers	C.McDermot.A.Plumb
1996 May 16	Eejit's Wall	A.Plumb, M.Balharry
1996 May 17	Anarchic Law	M.Balharry, A.Plumb
1996 May 21	Cresent Moon Rising	A.Plumb, M.Balharry
1996 May 21	A Gauling Crack	A.Plumb, M.Balharry
1996 May 21	Getafix	A.Plumb, M.Balharry
1996 May 21	Hadrian's Wall	A.Plumb, M.Balharry
1996 May 21	Caesar's Nose	A.Plumb, M.Balharry
1996 Jun 2	Technical Ecstasy	A.Plumb, M.Balharry
1996 Jun 2	Traverse of the Sods	A.Plumb, M.Balharry
1997	Skyline Arete	A.Plumb, M.Balharry
1997	The Advocate	M.Ballhary, A.Plumb
1997	Seiesmic Activity	A.Plumb, M.Balharry
1997	A Right Crack	A.Plumb, M.Balharry
1998	Short	A.Scougall, M.Ballhary, A.Plumb
1998	Sharp	A.Scougall, M.Ballhary, A.Plumb
2000	Red Wall	A.Plumb, B.Mayo
2000	Right Red Wall	A.Plumb, B.Mayo
2000	Brutus Minimus	B.Mayo, A.Plumb.
2002	Solitary Soul	C.Mayland
2003	Darkness Falling	C.Mayland, T.Muirhead
2003 Jul	Wild Iris	C.Mayland, T.Muirhead

Dunbar

1991	Celebration Day	G.Latter
2001 Sep 9	Flown Back From Boston	C.Mayland, B.Ridder
2001 Oct	Aching Arms and Dragging Heels	C.Mayland
2001 Oct	Reaching for the Pilot	C.Mayland, B.Ridder
2002 May	Hoochie Coochie Man	C.Mayland, D.MacDonnell

Traprain Law

No first ascent records have been kept for the South Face crags, however it is known that those mentioned below have played a part in their development. G.Anderson, M.Anderson, J.Andrew (FFA Tipp), A.Barclay, D.Bathgate, RN.Campbell, D.Cuthbertson, G.Dutton, G.Elliot, A.Ewing, M.Fleming, J.Hall, M.Hamilton (FFA Beatle Crack), D.Haston, R.Holt, B.MacDonald, N.MacNiven, A.McKeith, J.Marshall (Wobble, Piglet), R.Marshall, J.Moriarty, G.Murray, R.Phillips, G.Ritchie, B.Robertson, R.Smith (Burp, Chute), J.Stenhouse, R.Swanson, A.Taylor, G.Tiso.

1997	Mordor Crack	A.Plumb, M.Balharry
1997	The Doomsday Prophecies	M.Balharry, A.Plumb
1997	Stairway to Hell	A.Plumb, M.Balharry
1997	The Long Reach	A.Plumb, M.Balharry
1998	A Wee Peach	M.Balharry, A.Plumb
1999 Feb	The Fox	M.Somerville, J.Barker
2001	A Loud Screech	A.Plumb
2001 Aug	Easy Ticket, Black Diamond, Diamond Back	D.Hunter, M.Greenwood
2002 Feb 17	Frodo	D.Brown, G.Bannister

Berwickshire Coast

1965	The Souter, Landward Side	D.Bathgate, RN.Campbell

Direct Variant: S.Black, D.Smith, 1970

1965 Jul	Abseil Gully, Vertigo	G.Davidson, J.Binns
1965	Urinal Wall, Atlanta	G.Davidson, J.Binns
1965	The East Arete	G.Davidson, J.Binns
1966 Sep	Gannet Groove, Castle Wall	G.Davidson, P.Lockey
1970	The Souter, Ordinary Route	I.Clough, J.Cleare

Direct Variant: D.Bathgate, R.Sharp, 1970

1970	The Skate	I.Rowe, D.Godfrey
1970	Carapus	J.Wells, P.Brian
1970	Cockle Shell Cracks	B.McDonald, R.Sharp
1970	Squid	D.Bathgate, M.Watson
1970	Sperm	D.Bathgate, I.Rowe
1970	Dayglo	S.Black, J.Porteous
1970	Purve	S.Black, T.Blenkinsop
1974 Aug 24	Cyclops	G.Davidson, M.Moran
1979 Feb	Zigzag	B.Kerr, F.Hughes
1981 Mar	Guano Corner	J.Griffiths, A.Moist
1981 Mar	Lucky Day	K.Howett
1981 Apr	Spring Shower	J.Griffiths, K.Howett
1981 Apr	Jonathan Livingstone Shitehawk	K.Howett, J.Griffiths
1981 Apr	Blue Moves, Sea Sprite	P.Clarke, A.Hinks
1981 Apr	What have the Vikings...	P.Clarke, A.Hinks
1981 Apr	Rufus the Red, Sea Ahoy	P.Clarke, A.Hinks
1982 Feb	A Drop in the Ocean	J.Handren
1982 Feb	The Fish Business	J.Handren
1982 Feb	Second Sight, Fast Bleeder	J.McKenzie, R.Duncan
1982 Feb	J.P.S.	R.Anderson, K.Spence
1982 Feb	Plain Sailing	K.Spence, R.Anderson
1982 Feb	Shorty, Sweep	A.Taylor, K.Spence, R.Anderson
1982 Feb	Sooty	A.Taylor, K.Spence, R.Anderson
1982 Feb	Chimp, Walli	A.Taylor
1982 Feb	The Great Gonzo	R.Duncan, J.Handren
1982 Feb	Moving Like a Slug	J.McKenzie, R.Duncan
1982 Mar	Bloodbath	J.Melrose
1982 Mar	Stiff Bunnies	R.Anderson, K.Spence
1982 Mar	Fraud Escort	K.Spence, R.Anderson
1982 Mar	Walnut	J.McKenzie, R.Anderson
1982 Mar	Orgasmatron	J.Handren, R.Duncan
1982 Mar	Lightning Crack	R.Young, B.Kerr
1982 Mar	Blockbuster	R.Anderson, J.McKenzie
1982 Apr	Mingy Metro	M.Hamilton, R.Anderson, R.Duncan
1982 Apr	Souterrain	K.Spence, J.McKenzie
1982 Apr	Leech	M.Hamilton
1982 May	Souterrain Direct Start	P.Hunter, K.Spence
1982 May	Pigeon Shit	M.Hamilton, R.Anderson
1982 Jun	Wallow, Wallette	K.Spence, D.Jamieson
1982 Jul	Porker's Wall	M.Hamilton, R.Anderson
1982 Sep	Return to Sender	R.Anderson, K.Spence
1983 Apr	Take it to the Limpets	K.Spence, R.Anderson
1983 Jul	Squid Vicious	K.Spence, D.McCallum
1983 Oct	Graddled, Drunk and Disorderly	J.McKenzie
1983 Oct	Quasi's Back	K.Spence, J.McKenzie
1989 Nov 4	The Twilight Hour	B.Kerr, G.McIntyre
1989 Nov	The Bat Crack	G.Nicoll, K.Noble, N.McNeill
1989 Nov	The Buoy Wonder	G.Nicoll, K.Noble, N.McNeill
1990 Mar 24	Fated Panda	M.Smith, R.Campbell
1990 Apr 1	Seal of Approval	R.Campbell
1990	Kylie	P.Thorburn, R.Campbell
1990	Crimpanzie	M.Smith
1990	Not the HVS	P.Thorburn, I.Dawson
1990	First of Four	R.Campbell, I.Dawson
1990	The Undercut Kid	M.Smith, R.Campbell
1990	Tied up at Work	R.Campbell
1990	Psittacosis	P.Thorburn
1991	Gary's in Harry's	G.McIntyre, G.Nicoll

1991 Apr	Bouma Sequence	A.Matthewson, D.Kirk
1991 Jul 18	The Ancient Mariner	J.Andrew, A.Matthewson
1991 Jul 28	Up-helly-aa	A.Matthewson, J.MacLaurin
1991 Nov 3	The East Arete True Finish	J.Andrew, J.Tout, A.Matthewson
1991 Nov 23	The Folly	A.Matthewson, A.Tibbs
1992 Jan 11	Rapunzel, Atlanta Direct Finish	A.Matthewson
1992 Mar 17	Coming Up Roses	J.Andrew
1992 Mar 17	Merlin and Wendy's Day Out	N.Armstrong, J.Andrew
1992 Apr 3	Seize the Day	B.Kerr, G.McIntyre
1992 Apr 3	Drop the Pilot	G.McIntyre, B.Kerr
1992 Apr 28	Edge of the Wedge	J.Andrew
1992 Apr 28	Fuzzy Stone	J.Andrew, N.Armstrong
1992 Apr 4	The Voyage of the Mad Manxman	B.Kerr, J.Reeves
1992 Oct	Curve of the Earth	G.MacIntyre, M.Davies
1993 Mar 13	Starboard Bow	G.MacIntyre, C.McKee, B.Kerr
1993 Mar 13	Turning in-tide-out	G.MacIntyre, C.McKee, B.Kerr
1993 Mar 14	Mea Culpa, Enigma	B.Kerr, R.Robertson
1993 Mar 21	Constant Hunger	G.MacIntyre, B.Kerr
1993 Mar 21	Inferno	B.Kerr, G.MacIntyre
1993 Apr 4	Welcome to the Midden	B.Kerr, G.MacIntyre
1993 Apr 4	Lunar Pull	G.MacIntyre, B.Kerr, D.Leckie
1993 Apr 4	Port Bow	G.MacIntyre, B.Kerr
1993 Aug	Brucellosis	R.Campbell
1993 Sep 12	Something Fishy	A. Mathewson, A. Hume
1993 Sep 18	Tidal Race, Ranald's Rant	A.Matthewson, G.Watt, A.Hume
1993 Sep 18	Whitebait Can't Jump	A.Matthewson, G.Watt, A.Hume
1993 Sep 18	Flounder Member	A.Matthewson, G.Watt, A.Hume
1993 Sep 18	Pirrett's Progress	A.Matthewson, G.Watt, A.Hume
1994 Apr 17	The Maiden's Stone	M.Shaw (solo)
1996 Mar 3	Shades of Yellow	M.Robson, T.Ward
1996 Mar 3	Fluorescent Flake	M.Robson, T.Ward
1996 Mar 10	The Sentry Box	M.Robson, T.Ward
1996 Mar 10	Daytrippers	B.Ottewell, J.Vince
1996 Mar 10	Pot Bellied Sheep	B.Ottewell, J.Vince
1996 Mar 10	The Pig Thing	J.Vince, B.Ottewell
1996 Mar 10	Splice the Mainbrace	M.Robson, T.Ward
1996 Mar 10	Severance	M.Robson, T.Ward
1996 Mar 10	Flume	B.Ottewell, J.Vince
1996 Mar 10	Plume	J.Vince, B.Ottewell
1996 Mar 10	Spume	M.Robson, T.Ward
1996 Mar 23	Sea Spray	M.Robson, T.Ward
1996 May 20	Tubigripper	C.Pasteur, A.Mathewson, J.Andrew
1997 Feb 1	Dried Peach Crack	B.Kerr, A.Taylor
1997 Feb 1	Don't Blink	B.Kerr, A.Taylor
1997 Feb 14	Captain Ahab	B.Kerr, G.Stein
1997 Feb 14	Praying for Snow	G.Stein, B.Kerr
1997 Mar 3	Felo De Se	B.Kerr, A.Taylor
1997 Mar 3	Skelpit Erse	A.Taylor, A.Callum
1997 Mar 23	Hale-Bopp	B.Kerr, M.Davies, G.McIntyre
1997 May 25	Banana Groove	J.Sanders, C.MacIntyre
1997 Aug 23	Geronimo's Cadillac	B.Kerr, J.Sanders
1997 Aug 30	False Hope	A.Taylor, A.Smith, B.Crawford
1997 Sep 4	Incision	J.Glen, B.Kerr
1997 Sep 9	Carolyn	J.Sanders, C.MacIntyre
2001 May 27	Left-Hand Crack	T.Pitcairn, A.Smith
2001 May 27	Ramalina Subfarinacea	A.Smith, T.Pitcairn
2001 Jun 3	Were it not for Foot and Mouth	A.Smith, T.Pitcairn
2001 Jun 3	Grammarian's Delight	T.Pitcairn, A.Smith
2004 Oct 31	Stegosaurus Ridge	M.Robson, S.M.Richardson
2004 Oct 31	Gunsight Arete	S.M.Richardson, M.Robson

SCOTTISH MOUNTAINEERING CLUB
SCOTTISH MOUNTAINEERING TRUST

Prices were correct at time of publication, but are subject to change

CLIMBERS' GUIDES

Glen Coe	£18.50
Ben Nevis	£19.95
Arran, Arrochar and Southern Highlands	£14.95
The Cairngorms Vol. 1	£10.95
The Cairngorms Vol. 2	£11.95
North-east Outcrops	£18.50
Highland Outcrops	£16.50
Northern Highlands North	£20.00
Northern Highlands Vol. 1	£12.95
Skye and the Hebrides (2 Vols)	£19.95
Scottish Winter Climbs	£17.95
Scottish Rock Climbs	In preparation

HILLWALKERS' GUIDES

The Munros	£20.00
The Munros CD-ROM	£40.00
Munros GPS data disk – from SMC website	£10.48
The Corbetts & Other Scottish Hills	£18.00
The Corbetts & Other Scottish Hills CD-ROM	£30.00
The Cairngorms	£17.95
Central Highlands	£17.95
Islands of Scotland Including Skye	£19.95
North-west Highlands	£22.00
Southern Highlands	£16.95
Southern Uplands	£16.95

SCRAMBLERS' GUIDES

Skye Scrambles	£14.50

OTHER PUBLICATIONS

Munro's Tables	£15.95
A Chance in a Million? Avalanches in Scotland	£14.95
The Munroist's Companion	£16.00
Scottish Hill and Mountain Names	£9.95
Ben Nevis – Britain's Highest Mountain	£14.95
Ski Mountaineering in Scotland	£12.95

Visit our website for more details and to purchase on line.
www.smc.org.uk

Distributed by:
Cordee Ltd, 3a De Montfort Street, Leicester LE1 7HD
(t) 0116 254 3579 (f) 0116 247 1176
www.cordee.co.uk

*These publications are available from bookshops and mountain
equipment suppliers.*

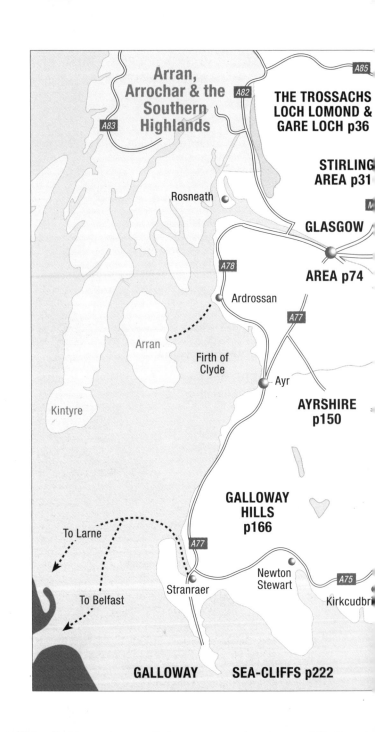

Arran,
Arrochar & the
Southern
Highlands

A83
A82
A85

**THE TROSSACHS
LOCH LOMOND &
GARE LOCH p36**

**STIRLING
AREA p31**

Rosneath

GLASGOW

A78

AREA p74

Ardrossan

A77

Arran

Firth of
Clyde

Ayr

Kintyre

**AYRSHIRE
p150**

**GALLOWAY
HILLS
p166**

To Larne

A77

Newton
Stewart

A75

Stranraer

Kirkcudbr

To Belfast

GALLOWAY   **SEA-CLIFFS p222**